An Introduction to Programming Using
Visual Basic® 2010

with Microsoft® Visual Studio® 2010 Express Editions DVD

Eighth Edition

AN INTRODUCTION TO PROGRAMMING USING

VISUAL BASIC® 2010

with Microsoft® Visual Studio® 2010 Express Editions DVD

EIGHTH EDITION

David I. Schneider

University of Maryland

Upper Saddle River   Boston   Columbus   San Francisco   New York   Indianapolis
London   Toronto   Sydney   Singapore   Tokyo   Montreal   Dubai   Madrid   Hong Kong
Mexico City   Munich   Paris   Amsterdam   Cape Town

Vice President and Editorial Director, ECS: Marcia J. Horton
Executive Editor: Tracy Dunkelberger
Assistant Editor: Melinda Haggerty
Editoiral Assistant: Allison Michael
Vice President, Production: Vince O'Brien
Senior Managing Editor: Scott Disanno
Production Liaison: Irwin Zucker
Senior Operations Specialist: Alan Fischer
Art Director: Kenny Beck
Cover Designer: Jodi Notowitz
Art Editor: Greg Dulles
Media Editor: Daniel Sandin
Composition/Full-Service Project Management: Laserwords, Inc.

Visual Basic is a registered trademark of Microsoft Corporation.

10 9 8 7 6 5 4 3 2 1

ISBN-13: 978-0-13-800334-0
ISBN-10:   0-13-800334-3

Guide to VideoNotes

www.pearsonhighered.com/Schneiderinternational

Guide to Application Topics

Business and Economics

Admission fee, 171, 579, 581
Airline reservations, 369, 476
Amount of stock purchase, 90
Analyze a Loan case study, 356
Analyze fuel economy, 372
Analyze sales data, 351
Annuity, 91, 198, 253, 265
APY, 152
Automated directory assistance, 371
Automobile depreciation, 264
Bank account, 560
Bond rates, 573
Break-even analysis, 90, 165
Business travel expenses, 125
Calculate a tip, 121, 150, 212, 576, 577
Calculate weekly pay, 188, 530, 584
Car loan, 253, 265
Cash award, 166
Cash register, 530, 540, 558
Change from a sale, 151
Checking account transactions, 459, 560
Compare interest rates, 152
Compare two salary options, 267
Compound interest, 91, 121, 152, 179, 189, 198, 246, 252, 253, 265, 459
Computers in the workplace, 351
Consumer price index, 253
Cost of a computer system, 175, 583
Cost of benefits plan, 172, 173, 571
Cost of purchases, 191
Credit card account, 224, 460
Crop production, 91, 266
Currency exchange rates, 499
Depreciation, 264, 277
Discount price, 90, 106
Discount rate, 573
Display economic data in a bar chart, 467, 468, 471
Display economic data in a pie chart, 464, 471, 473
Display sales data, 266
Dividend yield, 574
Doubling time of an investment, 119, 252
Employee paycheck receipt, 541
Enrollment in a pension plan, 181
Estate tax, 120
FICA tax, 142, 230, 531
Fixed cost, 165
Future value, 189

Gather billing information, 460
Generate an order form, 239
Gross pay, 151, 230
Growth of pizza chains, 593, 594
Health club fees, 583
Income tax, 152, 179
Inventory control, 355, 475, 558
ISBN numbers, 370
Itemized bill, 124, 178, 238
Lifetime earnings, 265
Loan analysis, 459
Mail-order company, 511
Maintain a membership list, 475
Manage telephone directories, 422
Marginal cost and revenue, 165
Membership fee, 177
Minimum wage, 471
Monetary units of countries, 494, 498
Mortgage, 179, 224, 253
Pay raise, 224
Payroll, 230, 455, 558
Percentage increase in cost, 121
Percentage profit, 91
Postage costs, 198
Price-to-earnings ratio, 107
Profit, 90, 107, 140, 198
Recording Checks and Deposits case study, 412
Restaurant order, 180, 541
Revenue, 165, 593, 594
Rule of "96", 276
Sales commission, 108
Sales tax, 119, 436, 573
Savings account, 151, 198
Savings plan, 253
Simple interest, 265
Simulate a lottery, 435
Subscriber data, 388
Supply and demand, 266
Tabulate sales amounts, 351, 405
Tax return, 177
Total cost, 150
Total income, 451
Total salaries paid, 353
Universal Product Code, 423
Weekly pay, 455
Weekly Payroll case study, 230
Withholding tax, 231, 541

7

General Interest

Mathematics

Sports and Games

CONTENTS

Chapter 4 Decisions 127

Chapter 5 General Procedures 183

Chapter 6 Repetition 241

Chapter 7 Arrays 281

Chapter 8 Text Files   373

Chapter 9 Additional Controls and Objects   425

Chapter 10 Databases   481

PREFACE

Since its introduction in 1991, Visual Basic has become one of the world's most widely used programming languages. The latest incarnation, Visual Basic 2010, further refines the language and extends features such as Language Integrated Query. Visual Basic programmers are enthusiastically embracing VB 2010's powerful capabilities. Likewise, students learning their first programming language will find VB 2010 the ideal tool for understanding the development of computer programs.

My objectives in writing this text are as follows:

1. *To develop focused chapters.* Rather than covering many topics superficially, I concentrate on important ones and cover them thoroughly.

2. *To use examples and exercises that students can relate to, appreciate, and feel comfortable with.* I frequently use real data. Examples do not have so many embellishments that they distract students from the programming techniques illustrated.

3. *To produce compactly written text that students will find both readable and informative.* The main points of each topic are discussed first, and then peripheral details are presented as comments.

4. *To teach good programming practices that are in step with modern programming methodology.* Problem-solving techniques and structured programming are discussed early and used throughout the book. The style follows object-oriented programming principles.

5. *To provide insights into the major applications of computers.*

Unique and Distinguishing Features

Microsoft® Visual Studio® 2010 Express editions DVD. The textbook comes with a Visual Studio 2010 Express Edition DVD. It contains several Microsoft products including Visual Basic 2010, SQL Server 2010, and Visual Web Developer.

VideoNotes. VideoNotes are step-by-step video tutorials specifically designed to enhance the programming concepts presented in the eighth edition. Students can view the entire problem-solving process outside the classroom, when they need help the most. A VideoNote icon in the margin of the textbook alerts the reader that a topic is discussed in a video. Also, a Guide to VideoNotes in the front of the book summarizes the different videos found in the text. Nearly 50 VideoNotes for this edition are available at www.pearsonhighered.com/schneiderinternational. See the Student Resources section later in the Preface for information on how to access VideoNotes.

Exercises for Most Sections. Each section that teaches programming has an exercise set. The exercises reinforce the understanding of the key ideas of the section, and they challenge the student to explore applications. Most of the exercise sets require the student to trace programs, find errors, and write programs. The answers to all the odd-numbered exercises in Chapters 2 through 8 and selected odd-numbered exercises from Chapters 9, 10, 11, and 12 are given at the end of the text. Screen captures accompany most programming answers.

Practice Problems. Practice Problems are carefully selected exercises located at the end of a section, just before the exercise set. Complete solutions are given following the exercise set. The practice problems often focus on points that are potentially confusing or are best appreciated after the student has worked on them. Readers should seriously attempt the practice problems and study their solutions before moving on to the exercises.

Programming Projects. Beginning with Chapter 3, every chapter contains programming projects. These projects reflect the variety of ways that computers are used in the business community, and they also present some games and general-interest topics. The large number and range of difficulty of the programming projects provide flexibility to adapt the course to the students' interests and abilities. Some programming projects in later chapters can be assigned as end-of-the-semester projects.

Comments. To avoid breaking the flow of the presentation, extensions and fine points of new topics are deferred to the "Comments" portion at the end of each section.

Case Studies. Each of the three case studies focuses on an important programming application. The problems are analyzed and the programs are developed with top-down charts and pseudocode. The programs can be downloaded from the companion website at http://www.pearsonhighered.com/schneiderinternational.

Chapter Summaries. At the end of each of Chapters 2 through 12, the key concepts are stated and the important terms summarized`.

"How To" Appendix. Appendix B provides a compact, step-by-step reference on how to carry out standard tasks in the Visual Basic environment.

Appendix on Debugging. The discussion of Visual Basic's sophisticated debugger is located in Appendix D, allowing the instructor flexibility in deciding when to cover this topic.

How to Access Instructor and Student Resource Materials

Pearson offers many different products around the world to facilitate learning. In countries outside the United States, some products and services related to this textbook may not be available due to copyright and/or permissions restrictions. If you have questions, you can contact your local office by visiting www.pearsonhighered.com/international

Instructor Resources

The following protected instructor resource materials are available on the publisher's website at www.pearsonhighered.com/schneiderinternational. For username and password information, please contact your local Pearson Representative.

- Computerized Test Generator
- PowerPoint Lecture Slides
- Instructor Solutions Manual: A complete solutions manual is available in pdf format. The manual contains the code for every programming exercise along with screen captures of the output.
- All the programs in the book
- Links to online premium content
  - VideoNotes
  - Student Solutions Manual

Student Resources

Access to the Premium Website and VideoNotes tutorials is located at www.pearsonhighered .com/schneiderinternational. Students must use the access card located in the front of the book to register and access the online material. If no access card is provided, students can purchase access by going to www.pearsonhighered.com/schneiderinternational and selecting "purchase access to premium content." Instructors must register on the site to access the material.

The following content is available through the Premium Web site:

- VideoNotes: Pearson's new visual tool designed for teaching key programming concepts
- Student Solutions Manual: All the answers to the odd-numbered exercises (along with screen captures) will be available for download in a solutions manual in pdf format.
- All programs in the book and all text files and databases needed for the exercises.

Notice: This book contains many screen captures. When you run one of the programs downloaded from the website, what you see on your monitor might not look exactly like the screen capture shown in the book. To make them appear the same, you must check that your monitor is set to display 96 DPI (Dots Per Inch). To determine and/or change the DPI setting for your monitor, see the first item under "Configuring the Windows Environment" in Appendix B on pages 608–9. Also, there may be slight differences due to the version of Windows being used. See page 27.

What's New in the Eighth Edition

New Sections

1. A section on using radio buttons, check boxes, and list boxes for selection has been added to Chapter 4. (Much of this material was previously in Chapter 9. Now it appears alongside If and Select Case blocks.)

2. A section on using loops with list boxes has been added to Chapter 6. (This section presents many operations on lists, such as searching, summing, and finding maximum values.)

3. A section on XML has been added to Chapter 8. (LINQ techniques developed earlier are applied to XML files.)

4. A chapter on Web applications has been added. (The three sections in this chapter cover the use of Visual Web Developer to create Web programs. Topics include tables, hyperlinks, postbacks, validation controls, and databases. Data extracted from databases are displayed in both grids and the new-to-VB2010 Chart controls.)

New Concepts

1. Chapter 3: Implicit line continuation. (The underscore line-continuation character is rarely needed in VB 2010.)

2. Chapter 3: Date data type. (This data type enables us to create some interesting programs, such as a program that tells users whether they are eligible to run for president in 2012. See Exercise 20 on page 176.)

3. Chapter 3: Sending output to the printer. (This optional material demonstrates how to produce a major type of output with Visual Basic.)

4. Chapter 7: The ReadAllLines method for filling an array with the contents of a text file. (This powerful method allows us to place the contents of a text file in an array without having to use repeated ReDim Preserve statements.)

5. Chapter 7: Language Integrated Query. (This recent addition to Visual Basic and other .NET languages provides a standardized way to specify queries for a variety of data sources. In this textbook, LINQ is used to sort, search, and filter information from arrays, text files, XML files, and databases. This approach enables students to write concise, higher-level code focused more on problem solving than on data-structure manipulation. Instructors wishing to teach a more elementary or traditional course can omit or reduce the use of LINQ. The textbook presents most of the standard operations on arrays and sequential files with and without LINQ.)

6. Chapter 8: The Set operators Concat, Union, Intersect, and Except are used to manage data from text files. (These operators allow us to perform tasks that previously required complicated algorithms.)

7. Chapter 9: ToolTip control. (This control gives us a capability possessed by nearly every commercial Windows application.)

8. Chapter 11: Auto-Implemented properties. (This new-to-VB-2010 concept simplifies the creation of classes.)

Other Changes

1. The version of Visual Basic has been upgraded from Visual Basic 2008 to Visual Basic 2010, and relevant new features of Visual Basic 2010 have been added.

2. The real-life data in the examples and exercises have been updated and revised.

3. Some new large collections of data have been added. For instance, data on every Supreme Court justice (past and present) are contained in both a text file and a database.

4. Named constants are introduced earlier (Chapter 3).

5. The use of input validation has been increased (Chapter 4 on).

6. Function procedures are presented before Sub procedures (Chapter 5). With this change, students begin learning about general procedures with a familiar and essential construct. Also, the instructor has the option of omitting the concept of passing by reference.

7. The use of text files for input has been postponed until Chapter 7.

8. Tables are displayed in DataGridView controls rather than in list boxes (Chapter 7 on).

9. Many new business applications have been added. See the Guide to Application Topics on page 7.

10. The OpenFileDialog control is discussed earlier (Chapter 8, Text Files).

11. The discussion of multiple-form programs in Chapter 9 has been expanded to an entire section.

12. Databases are connected to programs with the Visual Basic wizard rather than with code (Chapter 10).

New Materials for Instructors

1. Guide to Application Topics. (This section provides an index of programs that deal with various topics including Business, Mathematics, and Sports.)

2. A complete solution manual in pdf format. (The manual will contain the code for every programming exercise along with a screen capture of the output.)

New Materials for Students

1. Screen captures have been added to the programs in the answer section of the book.

2. All the answers to the odd-numbered exercises (along with screen captures) will be available for download in a solutions manual in pdf format.

3. Nearly 50 VideoNotes are available at www.pearsonhighered.com/schneiderinternational. VideoNotes are Pearson's new visual tool designed for teaching key programming concepts and techniques. A VideoNote icon in the margin of the textbook alerts the reader when a topic is discussed in a video. See the Student Resources section earlier in this Preface for information on how to access VideoNotes.

ACKNOWLEDGMENTS

Many talented instructors and programmers provided helpful comments and constructive suggestions during the various editions of this text, and I am most grateful for their contributions. The current edition benefited greatly from the valuable comments of the following reviewers:

G.W. Willis, Baylor University
Jaygarl Hojun, Iowa State University
Teresa Peterman, Grand Valley State University
Joel Weinstein, Northeastern University
Daniel E. Turk, Colorado State University
Paul Norrod, Lorain County Community College
Cynthia Brown, Portland State University
Karen Arlien, Bismarck State College
Ron Conway, Bowling Green State University
Phil Larschan, Tulsa Community College
Carol Roberts, University of Maine at Orono
Markita Price, University of Missouri - Columbia
Josh Pauli, Dakota State University

Many people are involved in the successful publication of a book. I wish to thank the dedicated team at Pearson whose support and diligence made this textbook possible, especially Melinda Haggerty, Assistant Editor of Computer Science, and Scott Disanno, Senior Managing Editor.

I also express my thanks to John Tarcza, a talented programmer, who helped with the development of the book and provided valuable insights and careful proofreading. I would like to thank Jeremy Schneider and Rob Teagarden for their helpful proofreading. Production editor Irwin Zucker did a fantastic job producing the book and keeping it on schedule. I am grateful to John Russo of the Wentworth Institute of Technology for producing the VideoNotes that accompany the book. The skill and graciousness of the team at Laserwords made for a pleasant production process. Copyeditor Bob Lentz contributed many suggestions for improving the book's quality.

I extend special thanks to my editor Tracy Dunkelberger. Her ideas and enthusiasm helped immensely with the preparation of the book.

David I. Schneider
dis@math.umd.edu

Using This Book For A Short or Condensed Course

This book provides more than enough material for a full-semester course. For a shorter course, it will be necessary to bypass some sections. The following syllabus provides one possible way to present an abbreviated introduction to programming.

---

[1]Passing by reference can be omitted or just mentioned briefly. In Chapters 6 through 12, ByRef is used only in Example 6 of Section 7.3 (Arrays of Structures) and in the Chapter 7 case study. In both of those programs it is used to obtain input.

[2]Sections 8.1 and 8.2 are independent of each other.

AN INTRODUCTION TO PROGRAMMING USING

VISUAL BASIC® 2010

with Microsoft® Visual Studio® 2010 Express Editions DVD

EIGHTH EDITION

1

An Introduction to Computers and Problem Solving

1.1 An Introduction to Computers

An Introduction to Programming Using Visual Basic 2010 is a book about problem solving using computers. The programming language used is Visual Basic 2010 (hereafter shortened to Visual Basic), but the principles taught apply to many modern programming languages. The examples and exercises present a sampling of the ways that computers are used in the real world. Here are some questions that you might have about computers and programming.

Question: *How do we communicate with the computer?*

Answer: Many languages are used to communicate with the computer. At the lowest level, there is *machine language*, which is understood directly by the microprocessor but is awkward for humans. Visual Basic is an example of a *higher-level language*. It consists of instructions to which people can relate, such as Click, If, and Do.

Question: What is a compiler?

Answer: A compiler is a program that translates a high-level language such as Visual Basic into machine language. The Visual Basic compiler detects (and points out) certain types of errors during the translation process.

Question: What is a GUI?

Answer: GUI (pronounced GOO-ee) stands for "graphical user interface." Both Windows and Visual Basic use a graphical user interface; that is, they employ graphic objects such as buttons and menus to interact with the user. Non-GUI text-based programs were common before 1990 but are now quite rare.

Question: *How do we get computers to perform complicated tasks?*

Answer: Tasks are broken down into a sequence of instructions that can be expressed in a computer language. (This text uses the language Visual Basic.) This sequence of instructions is called a *program*. Programs can range in size from two or three instructions to millions of instructions. Instructions are typed on the keyboard or read in from a file on a disk and are stored in the computer's memory. The process of executing the instructions is called *running* the program.

Question: *Are there certain features that all programs have in common?*

Answer: Most programs do three things: take in data, manipulate them, and give desired information. These operations are referred to as *input*, *processing*, and *output*. The input data might be held in a portion of the program, reside on a disk drive, or be provided by the computer user in response to requests made by the computer while the program is running. The processing of the input data occurs inside the computer and can take from a fraction of a second to many hours. The output data are either displayed on the monitor, printed on the printer, or recorded on a disk. As a simple example, consider a program that computes sales tax. An item of input data is the cost of the thing purchased. The processing consists of multiplying the cost by a certain percentage. An item of output data is the resulting product, the amount of sales tax to be paid.

Question: *What are the meanings of the terms "hardware" and "software"?*

Answer: *Hardware* refers to the physical components of the computer, including all peripherals, the central processing unit, disk drives, and all mechanical and electrical devices. Programs are referred to as *software*.

Question: *What are the meanings of the terms "programmer" and "user"?*

Answer: A *programmer* is a person who solves problems by writing programs on a computer. After analyzing the problem and developing a plan for solving it, he or she writes and tests the program that instructs the computer how to carry out the plan. The program might be run many times, either by the programmer or by others. A *user* is any person who uses a program. While working through this text, you will function both as a programmer and as a user.

Question: *What is meant by problem solving?*

Answer: Problems are solved by carefully reading them to determine what data are given and what outputs are requested. Then a step-by-step procedure is devised to process the given data and produce the requested output. This procedure is called an *algorithm*.

Question: *How did Visual Basic 2010 evolve?*

Answer: In the early 1960s, two mathematics professors at Dartmouth College developed BASIC to provide their students with an easily learned language that could tackle complicated programming projects. As the popularity of BASIC grew, refinements were introduced that permitted structured programming, which increased the reliability of programs. Visual Basic 1.0 is a version of BASIC developed in 1991 by the Microsoft Corporation to allow easy, visual-oriented development of Windows applications. Visual Basic 2010 is a language similar to the original Visual Basic, but more powerful.

Question: *Are there any prerequisites to learning Visual Basic 2010?*

Answer: Since Visual Basic is used to write Windows applications, you should be familiar with Windows and understand how folders and files are managed with Windows. The key concepts are presented succinctly in Section 1.2 and discussed in detail in Appendix C.

Question: *Will it matter whether I use Windows XP, Windows Vista, or Windows 7 as the operating system?*

Answer: Visual Basic runs fine with all three versions of Windows. However, the windows will vary in appearance. Figures 1.1(a) and 1.1(b) show the appearance of a typical window produced in Visual Basic with Windows XP and Windows Vista. With Windows 7, the appearance of windows depends on the Windows 7 product edition (such as Starter, Home Basic, Home Premium, etc.), the hardware on your system, and your own personal preferences. If you are using Windows 7 Starter or Windows 7 Home Basic, most likely your windows will look like the one in Fig. 1.1(c). With higher-end versions of Window 7 and recent hardware, your windows most likely will have an appearance similar to Fig. 1.1(b), known as *Aero*. In this book, all windows have the Aero appearance. No matter which operating system and appearance is used, the size and placement of the items inside the window should be the same.

(a) Windows XP

(b) Windows Vista

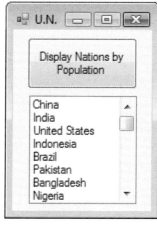
(c) Windows 7

FIGURE 1.1 A Visual Basic window.

1.2 Windows, Folders, and Files

This preliminary section presents some terms used in this book.

▨ Windows and Its Little Windows

Windows gets its name from the way it organizes the screen into rectangular regions. When you run a program, the program runs inside a bordered rectangular box. Unfortunately Windows jargon calls these *windows*, so there's only a lowercase "w" to distinguish them from the operating system called Windows. Figure 1.2 shows the window that results from running one of the programs in this book. In Visual Basic terminology, such a window is also called a **form**.

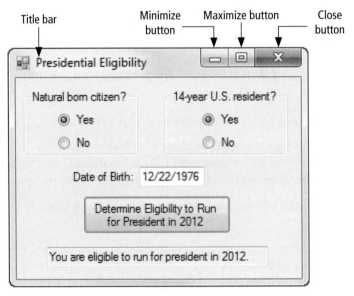

FIGURE 1.2   **A Visual Basic window.**

▨ Mouse Actions

Hover: Linger the mouse at a particular place and wait for a message (such as a tooltip) to appear.

Drag an object: Move the mouse pointer until it is at the object, press the left mouse button and hold it down, move the mouse pointer until the object moves to where you want it to be, and finally, release the mouse button. (Sometimes this whole activity is called *drag-and-drop*.)

Right-click: Press and release the right mouse button once.

Click: Press and release the left mouse button once. (sometimes referred to as *single-click* or *left-click*)

Double-click: Click the left mouse button twice in quick succession.

Note: An important Windows convention is that clicking selects an object so you can give Windows further directions about it, but double-clicking tells it to perform a default operation. For example, double-clicking on a folder will open that folder.

▨ Files and Folders

(A detailed discussion of files and folders can be found in Appendix C.)

Disk: A hard disk, a diskette, a USB flash drive, a CD, or a DVD. Each disk drive is identified by a letter followed by a colon.

File: Either a program file or a data file. Its name typically consists of letters, digits, and spaces. The name of the file is also called the *base name*.

Extension of a file name: One or more letters, preceded by a period, that identify the type of file. For example, files created with Word have the extension *doc* or *docx*.

Filename: The combination of the base name, the period, and the extension. The only characters that cannot be used in filenames are \, /, :, *, ?, <, >, ", and |. Filenames are not case sensitive.

Folder: A container holding files and other folders. Folders also are known as *directories*.

Subfolder: A folder contained inside another folder.

Path: A sequence of folders, separated by backslashes (\), where each folder is a subfolder of the folder preceding it. Paths are used to identify the locations of folders and files. An example is:

`Programs\Ch07\Text_Files_for_Exercises`

Filespec: An abbreviation of *file specification*, it is the combination of a drive letter followed by a colon, a path, and a filename. An example is:

`C:\Programs\Ch07\Text_Files_for_Exercises\USPres.txt`

In practice, you rarely have to type a filespec, since both Windows and Visual Basic provide Browse facilities that locate files and folders for you.

Root folder (also known as the **base folder**): The highest folder on a disk. It contains all the other folders on the disk and can also contain files. The filespec of the root folder of your hard drive is most likely C:\.

Windows Explorer: A program used to view, organize, and manage the folders and files on your disks. The details are presented in Appendix B in the section *Manage Files and Folders with Windows Explorer*. To invoke Windows Explorer, right-click the Windows Start button and click on *Explore* or *Open Windows Explorer* in the context menu that appears.

Displaying File Extensions: By default, Windows shows only the base names of files. The following steps configure Windows to also display the extensions. (In this book we assume that extensions are always shown).

Windows Vista and Windows 7

1. Click on the Start button.
2. **Windows Vista:** Type "Folder Options" into the "Start Search" box and press the Enter key. (A Folders Options dialog box will appear.)

   Windows 7: Type "Folder Options" into the "Search programs and files" box. (A Control Panel box will appear.) Click on *Folder Options*. (A Folders Options dialog box will appear.)
3. Click on the View tab in the Folder Options dialog box. (With Windows 7, the dialog box in Fig. 1.3 will appear. A similar dialog box will appear with Windows Vista.)
4. If there is a check mark in the box next to "Hide extensions for known file types," click on the box to remove the check mark.
5. Click on the *OK* button to close the Folder Options dialog box.

Windows XP

1. From Windows Explorer, click on *Options* in the *Tools* menu to display the Folder Options dialog box.

FIGURE 1.3   **Folder Options dialog box.**

2. Click on the View tab in the dialog box. (A dialog box similar to the one in Fig. 1.3 will appear.)

3. If there is a check mark in the box next to "Hide extensions for known file types," click on the box to remove the check mark.

4. Click on the OK button to close the Folder Options dialog box.

1.3   Program Development Cycle

We learned in Section 1.1 that hardware refers to the machinery in a computer system (such as the monitor, keyboard, and CPU) and software refers to a collection of instructions, called a **program**, that directs the hardware. Programs are written to solve problems or perform tasks on a computer. Programmers translate the solutions or tasks into a language the computer can understand. As we write programs, we must keep in mind that the computer will do only what we instruct it to do. Because of this, we must be very careful and thorough with our instructions. **Note:** A program is also known as a **project, application,** or **solution**.

■ Performing a Task on the Computer

The first step in writing instructions to carry out a task is to determine what the **output** should be—that is, exactly what the task should produce. The second step is to identify the data, or

input, necessary to obtain the output. The last step is to determine how to **process** the input to obtain the desired output—that is, to determine what formulas or ways of doing things can be used to obtain the output.

This problem-solving approach is the same as that used to solve word problems in an algebra class. For example, consider the following algebra problem:

How fast is a car moving if it travels 50 miles in 2 hours?

The first step is to determine the type of answer requested. The answer should be a number giving the speed in miles per hour (the output). (*Speed* is also called *velocity*.) The information needed to obtain the answer is the distance and time the car has traveled (the input). The formula

$$\text{speed} = \text{distance/time}$$

is used to process the distance traveled and the time elapsed in order to determine the speed. That is,

$$\text{speed} = 50 \text{ miles/2 hours}$$
$$= 25 \text{ miles/hour}$$

A pictorial representation of this problem-solving process is

We determine what we want as output, get the needed input, and process the input to produce the desired output.

In the chapters that follow we discuss how to write programs to carry out the preceding operations. But first we look at the general process of writing programs.

▮ Program Planning

A baking recipe provides a good example of a plan. The ingredients and the amounts are determined by what is to be baked. That is, the *output* determines the *input* and the *processing*. The recipe, or plan, reduces the number of mistakes you might make if you tried to bake with no plan at all. Although it's difficult to imagine an architect building a bridge or a factory without a detailed plan, many programmers (particularly students in their first programming course) try to write programs without first making a careful plan. The more complicated the problem, the more complex the plan may be. You will spend much less time working on a program if you devise a carefully thought out step-by-step plan and test it before actually writing the program.

Many programmers plan their programs using a sequence of steps, referred to as the **program development cycle**. The following step-by-step process will enable you to use your time efficiently and help you design error-free programs that produce the desired output.

1. ***Analyze:*** Define the problem.

   Be sure you understand what the program should do—that is, what the output should be. Have a clear idea of what data (or input) are given and the relationship between the input and the desired output.

2. ***Design:*** Plan the solution to the problem.

   Find a logical sequence of precise steps that solve the problem. Such a sequence of steps is called an **algorithm**. Every detail, including obvious steps, should appear in the algorithm. In the next section, we discuss three popular methods used to develop the logic plan: flowcharts, pseudocode, and top-down charts. These tools help the programmer break a problem into a sequence of small tasks the computer can perform to solve the problem. Planning also involves using representative data to test the logic of the algorithm by hand to ensure that it is correct.

3. ***Design the interface:*** Select the objects (text boxes, buttons, etc.).

   Determine how the input will be obtained and how the output will be displayed. Then create objects to receive the input and display the output. Also, create appropriate buttons and menus to allow the user to control the program.

4. ***Code:*** Translate the algorithm into a programming language.

   Coding is the technical word for writing the program. During this stage, the program is written in Visual Basic and entered into the computer. The programmer uses the algorithm devised in Step 2 along with a knowledge of Visual Basic.

5. ***Test and debug:*** Locate and remove any errors in the program.

   Testing is the process of finding errors in a program, and **debugging** is the process of correcting errors that are found. (An error in a program is called a **bug**.) As the program is typed, Visual Basic points out certain kinds of program errors. Other kinds of errors will be detected by Visual Basic when the program is executed; however, many errors due to typing mistakes, flaws in the algorithm, or incorrect use of the Visual Basic language rules can be uncovered and corrected only by careful detective work. An example of such an error would be using addition when multiplication was the proper operation.

6. ***Complete the documentation:*** Organize all the material that describes the program.

   Documentation is intended to allow another person, or the programmer at a later date, to understand the program. Internal documentation (comments) consists of statements in the program that are not executed but point out the purposes of various parts of the program. Documentation might also consist of a detailed description of what the program does and how to use it (for instance, what type of input is expected). For commercial programs, documentation includes an instruction manual and on-line help. Other types of documentation are the flowchart, pseudocode, and hierarchy chart that were used to construct the program. Although documentation is listed as the last step in the program development cycle, it should take place as the program is being coded.

1.4 Programming Tools

This section discusses some specific algorithms and describes three tools used to convert algorithms into computer programs: flowcharts, pseudocode, and hierarchy charts.

You use algorithms every day to make decisions and perform tasks. For instance, whenever you mail a letter, you must decide how much postage to put on the envelope. One rule of thumb is to use one stamp for every five sheets of paper or fraction thereof. Suppose a friend asks you to determine the number of stamps to place on an envelope. The following algorithm will accomplish the task.

1. Request the number of sheets of paper; call it Sheets.   (*input*)
2. Divide Sheets by 5.   (*processing*)
3. Round the quotient up to the next highest whole number; call it Stamps.   (*processing*)
4. Reply with the number Stamps.   (*output*)

The preceding algorithm takes the number of sheets (Sheets) as input, processes the data, and produces the number of stamps needed (Stamps) as output. We can test the algorithm for a letter with 16 sheets of paper.

1. Request the number of sheets of paper; Sheets = 16.

2. Dividing 5 into 16 gives 3.2.

3. Rounding 3.2 up to 4 gives Stamps = 4.

4. Reply with the answer, 4 stamps.

This problem-solving example can be pictured by

Of the program design tools available, three popular ones are the following:

Flowcharts: Graphically depict the logical steps to carry out a task and show how the steps relate to each other.

Pseudocode: Uses English-like phrases with some Visual Basic terms to outline the task.

Hierarchy charts: Show how the different parts of a program relate to each other.

■ Flowcharts

A flowchart consists of special geometric symbols connected by arrows. Within each symbol is a phrase presenting the activity at that step. The shape of the symbol indicates the type of operation that is to occur. For instance, the parallelogram denotes input or output. The arrows connecting the symbols, called **flowlines**, show the progression in which the steps take place. Flowcharts should "flow" from the top of the page to the bottom. Although the symbols used in flowcharts are standardized, no standards exist for the amount of detail required within each symbol.

Symbol	Name	Meaning
⟶	*Flowline*	Used to connect symbols and indicate the flow of logic.
⬭	*Terminal*	Used to represent the beginning (Start) or the end (End) of a task.
▱	*Input/Output*	Used for input and output operations, such as reading and displaying. The data to be read or displayed are described inside.
▭	*Processing*	Used for arithmetic and data-manipulation operations. The instructions are listed inside the symbol.
◇	*Decision*	Used for any logic or comparison operations. Unlike the input/output and processing symbols, which have one entry and one exit flowline, the decision symbol has one entry and two exit paths. The path chosen depends on whether the answer to a question is "yes" or "no."
◯	*Connector*	Used to join different flowlines.
- - -▭	*Annotation*	Used to provide additional information about another flowchart symbol.

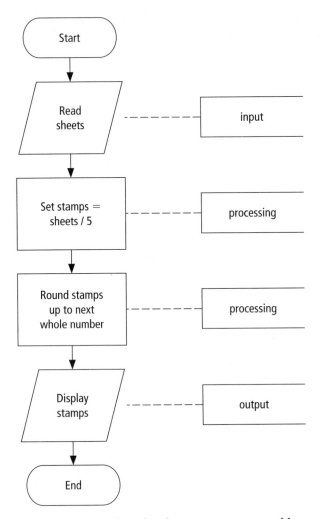

FIGURE 1.4 **Flowchart for the postage-stamp problem.**

The table of the flowchart symbols shown on the previous page has been adopted by the American National Standards Institute (ANSI). Figure 1.4 shows the flowchart for the postage-stamp problem.

The main advantage of using a flowchart to plan a task is that it provides a pictorial representation of the task, which makes the logic easier to follow. We can clearly see every step and how each is connected to the next. The major disadvantage is that when a program is very large, the flowcharts may continue for many pages, making them difficult to follow and modify.

■ Pseudocode

Pseudocode is an abbreviated plain English version of actual computer code (hence, *pseudocode*). The geometric symbols used in flowcharts are replaced by English-like statements that outline the process. As a result, pseudocode looks more like computer code than does a flowchart. Pseudocode allows the programmer to focus on the steps required to solve a problem rather than on how to use the computer language. The programmer can describe the algorithm in Visual Basic-like form without being restricted by the rules of Visual Basic. When the pseudocode is completed, it can be easily translated into the Visual Basic language.

The following is pseudocode for the postage-stamp problem:

Program: Determine the proper number of stamps for a letter
Read Sheets   *(input)*
Set the number of stamps to Sheets / 5   *(processing)*
Round the number of stamps up to the next whole number   *(processing)*
Display the number of stamps   *(output)*

Pseudocode has several advantages. It is compact and probably will not extend for many pages as flowcharts commonly do. Also, the plan looks like the code to be written and so is preferred by many programmers.

■ Hierarchy Chart

The last programming tool we'll discuss is the **hierarchy chart**, which shows the overall program structure. Hierarchy charts are also called structure charts, HIPO (Hierarchy plus Input-Process-Output) charts, top-down charts, or VTOC (Visual Table of Contents) charts. All these names refer to planning diagrams that are similar to a company's organization chart.

Hierarchy charts depict the organization of a program but omit the specific processing logic. They describe what each part, or **module**, of the program does and they show how the modules relate to each other. The details on how the modules work, however, are omitted. The chart is read from top to bottom and from left to right. Each module may be subdivided into a succession of submodules that branch out under it. Typically, after the activities in the succession of submodules are carried out, the module to the right of the original module is considered. A quick glance at the hierarchy chart reveals each task performed in the program and where it is performed. Figure 1.5 shows a hierarchy chart for the postage-stamp problem.

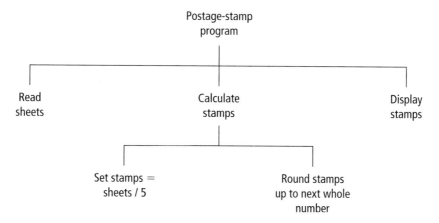

FIGURE 1.5   **Hierarchy chart for the postage-stamp problem.**

The main benefit of hierarchy charts is in the initial planning of a program. We break down the major parts of a program so we can see what must be done in general. From this point, we can then refine each module into more detailed plans using flowcharts or pseudocode. This process is called the **divide-and-conquer** method.

■ Decision Structure

The postage-stamp problem was solved by a series of instructions to read data, perform calculations, and display results. Each step was in a sequence; that is, we moved from one line to the next without skipping over any lines. This kind of structure is called a **sequence structure**. Many problems, however, require a decision to determine whether a series of instructions should be executed. If the answer to a question is "yes," then one group of instructions is

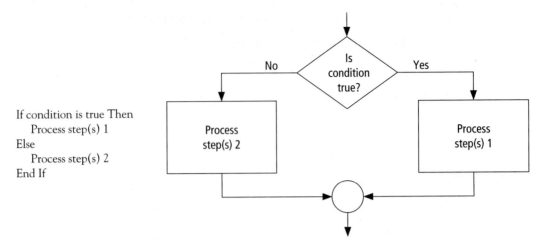

If condition is true Then
    Process step(s) 1
Else
    Process step(s) 2
End If

FIGURE 1.6 **Pseudocode and flowchart for a decision structure.**

executed. If the answer is "no," then another is executed. This structure is called a **decision structure**. Figure 1.6 contains the pseudocode and flowchart for a decision structure.

Sequence and decision structures are both used to solve the following problem.

■ Direction of Numbered NYC Streets Algorithm

Problem: Given a street number of a one-way street in New York, decide the direction of the street, either eastbound or westbound.

Discussion: There is a simple rule to tell the direction of a one-way street in New York: Even-numbered streets run eastbound.

Input: Street number.

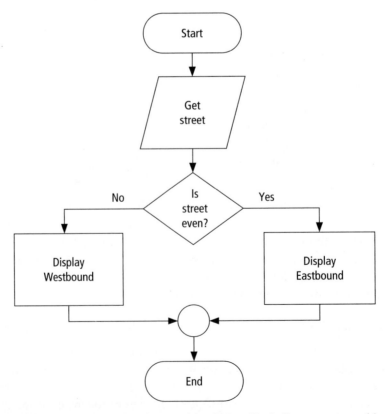

FIGURE 1.7 **Flowchart for the numbered New York City streets problem.**

Program: Determine the direction of a numbered NYC street.
Get street
If street is even Then
    Display Eastbound
Else
    Display Westbound
End If

FIGURE 1.8   Pseudocode for the numbered New York City streets problem.

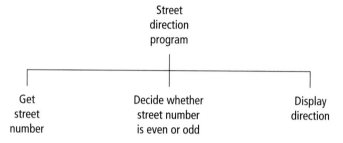

FIGURE 1.9   Hierarchy chart for the numbered New York City streets problem.

Processing: Decide if the street number is divisible by 2.

Output: "Eastbound" or "Westbound".

Figures 1.7 through 1.9 show the flowchart, pseudocode, and hierarchy chart for the numbered New York City streets problem.

■ Repetition Structure

A programming structure that executes instructions many times is called a **repetition structure** or a **loop structure**. Loop structures need a test (or condition) to tell when the loop should end. Without an exit condition, the loop would repeat endlessly (an infinite loop). One way to control the number of times a loop repeats (often referred to as the number of passes or iterations) is to check a condition before each pass through the loop and continue executing the loop as long as the condition is true. See Fig. 1.10. The solution of the next problem requires a repetition structure.

Do While condition is true
    Process step(s)
Loop

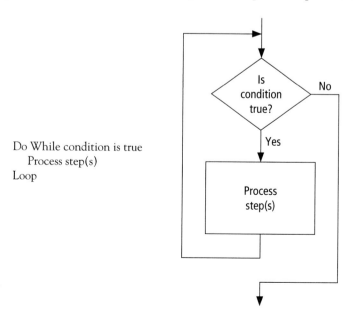

FIGURE 1.10   Pseudocode and flowchart for a loop.

■ Class Average Algorithm

Problem: Calculate and report the average grade for a class.

Discussion: The average grade equals the sum of all grades divided by the number of students. We need a loop to read and then add (accumulate) the grades for each student in the class. Inside the loop, we also need to total (count) the number of students in the class. See Figs. 1.11 to 1.13.

Input: Student grades.

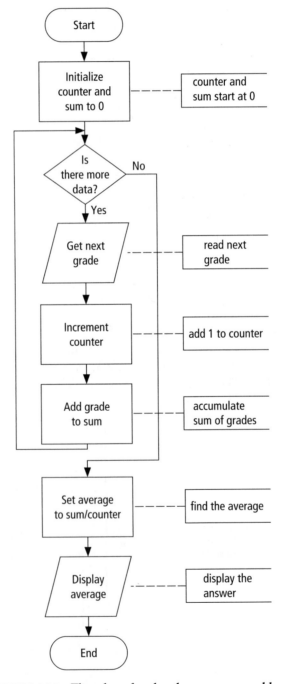

FIGURE 1.11 Flowchart for the class average problem.

Program: Calculate and report the average grade of a class.
Initialize Counter and Sum to 0
Do While there is more data
    Get the next Grade
    Increment the Counter
    Add the Grade to the Sum
Loop
Compute Average = Sum/Counter
Display Average

FIGURE 1.12 Pseudocode for the class average problem.

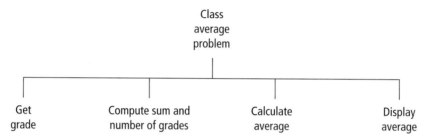

FIGURE 1.13 Hierarchy chart for the class average problem.

Processing: Find the sum of the grades; count the number of students; calculate average grade = sum of grades / number of students.

Output: Average grade.

■ Comments

1. Tracing a flowchart is like playing a board game. We begin at the Start symbol and proceed from symbol to symbol until we reach the End symbol. At any time, we will be at just one symbol. In a board game, the path taken depends on the result of spinning a spinner or rolling a pair of dice. The path taken through a flowchart depends on the input.

2. The algorithm should be tested at the flowchart stage before being coded into a program. Different data should be used as input, and the output checked. This process is known as **desk checking**. The test data should include nonstandard data as well as typical data.

3. Flowcharts, pseudocode, and hierarchy charts are universal problem-solving tools. They can be used to construct programs in any computer language, not just Visual Basic.

4. Flowcharts are used throughout this text to provide a visualization of the flow of certain programming tasks and Visual Basic control structures. Major examples of pseudocode and hierarchy charts appear in the case studies.

5. Flowcharts are time consuming to write and difficult to update. For this reason, professional programmers are more likely to favor pseudocode and hierarchy charts. Because flowcharts so clearly illustrate the logical flow of programming techniques, however, they are a valuable tool in the education of programmers.

6. There are many styles of pseudocode. Some programmers use an outline form, whereas others use a form that looks almost like a programming language. The pseudocode appearing in the case studies of this text focuses on the primary tasks to be performed by the program and leaves many of the routine details to be completed during the coding process. Several Visual Basic keywords, such as If, Else, Do, and While, are used extensively in the pseudocode appearing in this text.

2

Visual Basic, Controls, and Events

2.1　An Introduction to Visual Basic 2010

Visual Basic 2010 is the latest generation of Visual Basic, a language used by many software developers. Visual Basic was designed to make user-friendly programs easier to develop. Prior to the creation of Visual Basic, developing a friendly user interface usually required a programmer to use a language such as C or C++, often requiring hundreds of lines of code just to get a window to appear on the screen. Now the same program can be created in much less time with fewer instructions.

■ Why Windows and Why Visual Basic?

What people call **graphical user interfaces**, or GUIs (pronounced "gooies"), have revolutionized the computer industry. Instead of the confusing textual prompts that earlier users once saw, today's users are presented with such devices as icons, buttons, and drop-down lists that respond to mouse clicks. Accompanying the revolution in how programs look was a revolution in how they feel. Consider a program that requests information for a database. Figure 2.1 shows how a program written before the advent of GUIs got its information. The program requests the six pieces of data one at a time, with no opportunity to go back and alter previously entered information. Then the screen clears and the six inputs are again requested one at a time.

> **Enter name (Enter EOD to terminate):** <u>Mr. President</u>
> **Enter Address:** <u>1600 Pennsylvania Avenue</u>
> **Enter City:** <u>Washington</u>
> **Enter State:** <u>DC</u>
> **Enter Zip code:** <u>20500</u>
> **Enter Phone Number:** <u>202-456-1414</u>

FIGURE 2.1　Input screen of a pre-Visual Basic program to fill a database.

Figure 2.2 shows how an equivalent Visual Basic program gets its information. The boxes may be filled in any order. When the user clicks on a box with the mouse, the cursor moves to that box. The user can either type in new information or edit the existing information. When satisfied that all the information is correct, the user clicks on the *Write to Database* button. The boxes will clear, and the data for another person can be entered. After all names

FIGURE 2.2　Input screen of a Visual Basic program to fill a database.

have been entered, the user clicks on the Exit button. In Fig. 2.1, the program is in control; in Fig. 2.2, the user is in control!

How You Develop a Visual Basic Program

A key element of planning a Visual Basic program is deciding what the user sees—in other words, designing the user interface. What data will he or she be entering? How large a window should the program use? Where will you place the buttons the user clicks on to activate actions in the program? Will the program have places to enter text (text boxes) and places to display output? What kind of warning boxes (message boxes) should the program use? In Visual Basic, the responsive objects a program designer places on windows are called *controls*. Two features make Visual Basic different from traditional programming tools:

1. You literally draw the user interface, much like using a paint program.

2. Perhaps more important, when you're done drawing the interface, the buttons, text boxes, and other objects that you have placed in a blank window will automatically recognize user actions such as mouse movements and button clicks. That is, the sequence of procedures executed in your program is controlled by "events" that the user initiates rather than by a predetermined sequence of procedures in your program.

In any case, only after you design the interface does anything like traditional programming occur. Objects in Visual Basic recognize events like mouse clicks; how the objects respond to them depends on the instructions you write. You always need to write instructions in order to make controls respond to events. This makes Visual Basic programming fundamentally different from traditional programming. Programs in traditional programming languages ran from the top down. For these programming languages, execution started from the first line and moved with the flow of the program to different parts as needed. A Visual Basic program works differently. Its core is a set of independent groups of instructions that are activated by the events they have been told to recognize. This event-driven methodology is a fundamental shift. The user decides the order in which things happen, not the programmer.

Most of the programming instructions in Visual Basic that tell your program how to respond to events like mouse clicks occur in what Visual Basic calls *event procedures*. Essentially, anything executable in a Visual Basic program either is in an event procedure or is used by an event procedure to help the procedure carry out its job. In fact, to stress that Visual Basic is fundamentally different from traditional programming languages, Microsoft uses the term *project* or *application*, rather than *program*, to refer to the combination of programming instructions and user interface that makes a Visual Basic program possible. Here is a summary of the steps you take to design a Visual Basic program:

1. Design the appearance of the window that the user sees.

2. Determine the events that the controls on the window should respond to.

3. Write the event procedures for those events.

Now here is what happens when the program is running:

1. Visual Basic monitors the controls in the window to detect any event that a control can recognize (mouse movements, clicks, keystrokes, and so on).

2. When Visual Basic detects an event, it examines the program to see if you've written an event procedure for that event.

3. If you have written an event procedure, Visual Basic executes the instructions that make up that event procedure and goes back to Step 1.

4. If you have not written an event procedure, Visual Basic ignores the event and goes back to Step 1.

These steps cycle continuously until the program ends. Usually, an event must happen before Visual Basic will do anything. Event-driven programs are reactive more than active—and that makes them more user friendly.

■ The Different Versions of Visual Basic

Visual Basic 1.0 first appeared in 1991. It was followed by version 2.0 in 1992, version 3.0 in 1993, version 4.0 in 1995, version 5.0 in 1997, and version 6.0 in 1998. VB.NET, initially released in February 2002, was not backward compatible with the earlier versions of Visual Basic. It incorporated many features requested by software developers, such as true inheritance. Visual Basic 2005, released in November 2005, Visual Basic 2008, released in November 2007, and Visual Basic 2010, released in April 2010 are significantly improved versions of VB.NET.

2.2   Visual Basic Controls

Visual Basic programs display a Windows-style screen (called a **form**) with boxes into which users type (and in which users edit) information and buttons that they click to initiate actions. The boxes and buttons are referred to as **controls**. In this section, we examine forms and four of the most useful Visual Basic controls.

■ Starting a New Visual Basic Program

Each program is saved (as several files and subfolders) in its own folder. Before writing your first program, you should use Windows Explorer to create a folder to hold your programs.

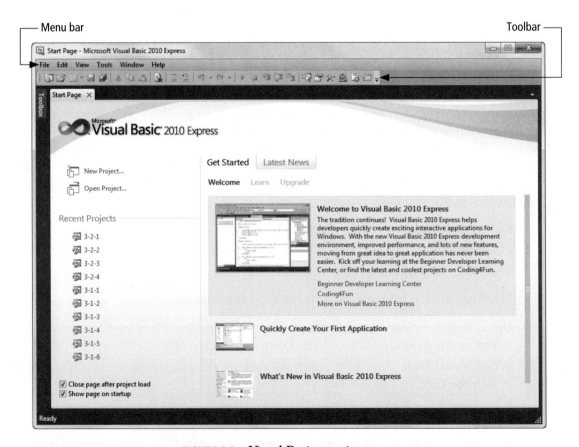

FIGURE 2.3   Visual Basic opening screen.

The process for invoking Visual Basic varies slightly with the edition of Visual Basic installed on the computer. To invoke Visual Basic from a computer that has Visual Basic Express installed, click the Windows Start button, hover over All Programs, and then click on Microsoft Visual Basic 2010 Express. With the other editions of Visual Basic, hover over All Programs, hover over Microsoft Visual Studio 2010, and then click on Microsoft Visual Studio 2010 in the short list that is revealed.

Figure 2.3 shows the top half of the screen after Visual Basic is invoked. A Menu bar and a Toolbar are at the very top of the screen. These two bars, with minor variations, are always present while you are working with Visual Basic. The remainder of the screen is called the **Start Page**. Some tasks can be initiated from the Menu bar, the Toolbar, and the Start Page. We will usually initiate them from the Menu bar or the Toolbar.

The first item on the Menu bar is *File*. Click on *File*, and then click on *New Project* to produce a New Project dialog box. Figure 2.4 shows the New Project dialog box produced by Visual Basic Express.

The Windows Forms Application item should be selected in the center list. If this is not the case, click on *Windows Forms Application* to select it. **Note:** The number of items in the list will vary depending on the edition of Visual Basic you are using.

The name of the program, initially set to WindowsApplication1, can be specified at this time. Since we will have a chance to change it later, let's just use the name WindowsApplication1 for now. Click on the *OK* button to invoke the Visual Basic programming environment. See Fig. 2.5. The Visual Basic programming environment is referred to as the **Integrated Development Environment** or **IDE**.

Very likely, your screen will look different than Fig. 2.5. The IDE is extremely configurable. Each window in Fig. 2.5 can have its location and size altered. New windows can be displayed in the IDE, and any window can be closed or hidden behind a tab. For instance, in Fig. 2.5 the Toolbox window is hidden behind a tab. The *View* menu is used to add additional windows to the IDE. If you would like your screen to look exactly like Fig. 2.5, click on *Reset Windows Layout* in the *Windows* menu, and then click on *Yes*.

FIGURE 2.4   The Visual Basic New Project dialog box.

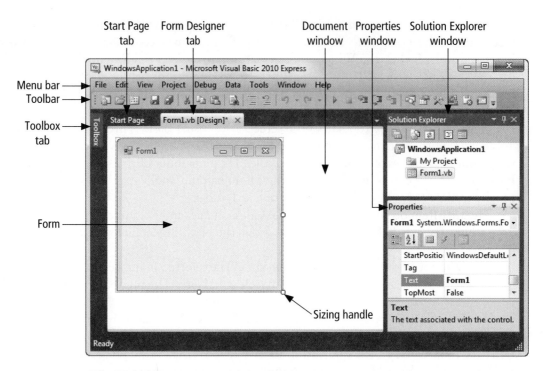

FIGURE 2.5   **The Visual Basic integrated development environment in Form Designer mode.**

The **Menu bar** of the IDE displays the menus of commands you use to work with Visual Basic. Some of the menus, like *File*, *Edit*, *View*, and *Window*, are common to most Windows applications. Others, such as *Project*, *Data*, and *Debug*, provide commands specific to programming in Visual Basic.

The **Toolbar** holds a collection of buttons that carry out standard operations when clicked. For example, you use the fifth button, which looks like a stack of three diskettes, to save the files associated with the current program. To reveal the purpose of a Toolbar button, hover the mouse pointer over it. The little information rectangle that pops up is called a **tooltip**.

The **Document window** currently holds the rectangular **Form window**, or **form** for short. The form becomes a Windows window when a program is executed. Most information displayed by the program appears on the form. The information usually is displayed in controls that the programmer has placed on the form. You can change the size of the form by dragging one of its sizing handles.

The **Properties window** is used to change how objects look and react.

The **Solution Explorer** window displays the files associated with the program and provides access to the commands that pertain to them. (**Note:** If the Solution Explorer or the Properties window is not visible, click on it in the *View/Other Windows* menu.)

The **Toolbox** holds icons representing objects (called controls) that can be placed on the form. If your screen does not show the Toolbox, hover the mouse over the Toolbox tab at the left side of the screen. The Toolbox will slide into view. Then click on the pushpin icon in the title bar at the top of the Toolbox to keep the Toolbox permanently displayed in the IDE. (**Note:** If there is no tab marked Toolbox, click on *Toolbox* in the *View/Other Windows* menu.)

The controls in the Toolbox are grouped into categories such as *All Windows Forms* and *Common Controls*. Figure 2.6 shows the Toolbox after the *Common Controls* group has been expanded. Most of the controls discussed in this text can be found in the list of common controls. (You can obtain a description of a control by hovering the mouse over the control.) The four controls discussed in this chapter are text boxes, labels, buttons, and list boxes. In order to see all the group names, collapse each of the groups.

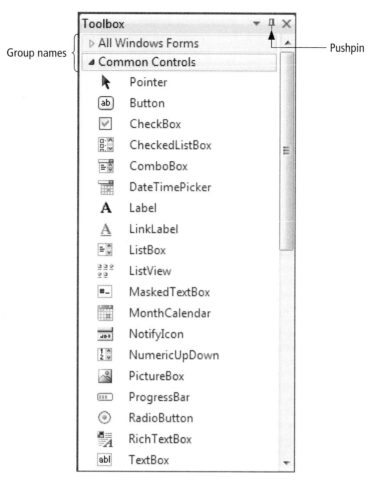

FIGURE 2.6 The Toolbox's common controls.

Text boxes: You use a text box to get information from the user, referred to as **input**, or to display information produced by the program, referred to as **output**.

Labels: You place a label near a text box to tell the user what type of information is displayed in the text box.

Buttons: The user clicks a button to initiate an action.

List boxes: In the first part of the book, we use list boxes to display output. Later, we use list boxes to make selections.

VideoNote
Visual Basic
controls

A Text Box Walkthrough

1. Double-click on the text box icon in the *Common Controls* group of the Toolbox. A rectangle with two small squares, called **sizing handles**, appears at the upper left corner of the form. (You can alter the width of the text box by dragging one of its sizing handles.) Move the mouse arrow to any point of the text box other than a sizing handle, hold down the left mouse button, and drag the text box to the center of the form. See Fig. 2.7. (**Note:** Tasks buttons are used to set certain properties of controls.)

FIGURE 2.7 A text box with sizing handles.

2. Click anywhere on the form outside the rectangle to deselect the text box.

3. Click on the rectangle to restore the handles. An object showing its handles is said to be **selected**. A selected text box can have its width altered, location changed, and other properties modified.

4. Move the mouse arrow to the handle in the center of the right side of the text box. The cursor should change to a double arrow (↔). Hold down the left mouse button, and move the mouse to the right. The text box is stretched to the right. Similarly, grabbing the text box on the left side and moving the mouse to the left stretches the text box to the left. You also can use the handles to make the text box smaller. Steps 1 and 4 allow you to place a text box of any width anywhere on the form. **Note:** The text box should now be selected; that is, its sizing handles should be showing. If not, click anywhere inside the text box to select it.

5. Press the delete key, DEL, to remove the text box from the form. Step 6 gives an alternative way to place a text box of any width at any location on the form.

6. Click on the text box icon in the Toolbox. Then move the mouse pointer to any place on the form. (When over the form, the mouse pointer becomes a pair of crossed thin lines.) Hold down the left mouse button, and drag the mouse on a diagonal to generate a rectangle. Release the mouse button to obtain a selected text box. You can now alter the width and location as before. **Note:** The text box should now be selected. If not, click anywhere inside the text box to select it.

7. Press F4 to activate the Properties window. [You also can activate the Properties window by clicking on it, clicking on the *Properties Window* button (🖼) on the Toolbar, selecting *Properties Window* from the *View* menu, or clicking on the text box with the right mouse button and selecting *Properties*.] See Fig. 2.8. The first line of the Properties window (called the **Object box**) reads "TextBox1 etc." TextBox1 is the current name of the text box. The first two buttons below the Object box permit you to view the list of properties either grouped into categories or alphabetically. Use the up- and down-arrow keys (or the up- and

Categorized view   Alphabetic view

FIGURE 2.8   **Text box Properties window.**

down-scroll arrows) to move through the list. The left column gives the property names, and the right column gives the current settings of the properties. We discuss four properties in this walkthrough.

Note 1: The third and fourth buttons below the Object box, the Properties button and the Events button, determine whether properties or events are displayed in the Properties window. Normally the Properties button is highlighted. If not, click on it.

Note 2: If the Description pane is not visible, right-click on the Properties window, then click on *Description*. The Description pane describes the currently highlighted property.

8. Move to the Text property with the up- and down-arrow keys. (Alternatively, scroll until the property is visible, and click on the property.) The Text property, which determines the words displayed in the text box, is now highlighted. Currently, there is no text displayed in the **Settings box** on the right.

9. Type your first name. Then press the Enter key, or click on another property. Your name now appears in both the Settings box and the text box. See Fig. 2.9.

FIGURE 2.9   **Setting the Text property to David.**

10. Click at the beginning of your name in the Text Settings box, and add your title, such as Mr., Ms., or The Honorable. (If you mistyped your name, you can easily correct it now.) Then, press Enter.

11. Use the up-arrow key or the mouse to move to the ForeColor property. This property determines the color of the information displayed in the text box.

12. Click on the down arrow in the right part of the Settings box, and then click on the Custom tab to display a selection of colors. See Fig. 2.10. Click on one of the colors, such as *blue* or *red*. Notice the change in the color of your name. (**Note:** The sixteen white boxes at the bottom of the grid are used to create custom colors. See item L under "Manage Visual Basic Controls" in Appendix B for details.)

13. Select the Font property with a single click of the mouse. The current font is named Microsoft Sans Serif.

14. Click on the ellipsis (...) box in the right part of the Settings box to display a dialog box. See Fig. 2.11. The three lists give the current name (Microsoft Sans Serif), current style

FIGURE 2.10 **Setting the ForeColor property.**

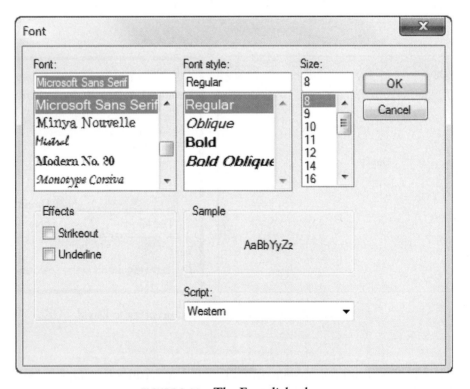

FIGURE 2.11 **The Font dialog box.**

(Regular), and current size (8) of the font. You can change any of these attributes by clicking on an item in its list or by typing into the box at the top of the list. Click on Bold in the style list, and click on 12 in the size list. Now click on the *OK* button to see your name displayed in a larger bold font. The text box will be longer so that it can accommodate the larger font.

15. Click on the text box and resize it to be about 3 inches wide.

Visual Basic programs consist of three parts: interface, values of properties, and code. Our interface consists of a form with a single object, a text box. We have set a few properties for the text box—the text (namely, your name), the foreground color, the font style, and the font size. In Section 2.3, we discuss how to place code into a program. Visual Basic endows certain capabilities to programs that are independent of any code we will write. We will now run the existing program without adding any code in order to experience these capabilities.

16. Click on the *Start Debugging* button (▶) on the Toolbar to run the program. [Alternatively, you can press F5 to run the program or can click on *Start Debugging* in the *Debug* menu.] After a brief delay, a copy of the form appears that has neither the form nor the text box selected.

17. Your name is highlighted. Press the End key to move the cursor to the end of your name. Now type in your last name, and then keep typing. Eventually, the words will scroll to the left.

18. Press Home to return to the beginning of the text. You have a miniature word processor at your disposal. You can place the cursor anywhere you like in order to add or delete text. You can drag the cursor across text to select a block, place a copy of the block in the Clipboard with Ctrl+C, and then duplicate it elsewhere with Ctrl+V.

19. Click on the *Stop Debugging* button (■) on the Toolbar to end the program. [Alternatively, you can end the program by clicking on the form's *Close* button (X) or pressing Alt + F4.]

20. Select the text box, activate the Properties window, select the ReadOnly property, click on the down-arrow button, and finally click on True. Notice that the background color is now gray.

21. Run the program, and try typing into the text box. You can't. Such a text box is used for output. Only code can display information in the text box.

    (**Note:** In this textbook, whenever a text box will be used only for the purpose of displaying output, we will always set the ReadOnly property to True.)

22. End the program.

23. Let's now save the program on a disk. Click on the Toolbar's *Save All* button (▦) to save the work done so far. (Alternatively, you can click on *Save All* in the *File* menu.) You will be prompted for the name of the program and the path to the folder where you want the program to be saved. Type a name, such as "VBdemo". You can either type a path or use Browse to locate a folder. (This folder will automatically be used the next time you click on the *Save All* button.) The files for the program will be saved in a subfolder of the selected folder.

    Important: If the "Create directory for solution" check box is checked, then click on the check box to uncheck it. Finally, click on the *Save* button.

24. Create a new program as before by clicking on *New Project* in the *File* menu. [Alternatively, you can click on the *New Project* button (▤), the first button on the Toolbar, or you can click on *New Project* in the Start Page.] A New Project dialog box will appear.

25. Give a name to the project, such as MyProgram, and then click on the *OK* button.

26. Place three text boxes on the form. (If you use the double-click technique, move the text boxes so that they do not overlap.) Notice that they have the names TextBox1, TextBox2, and TextBox3.

27. Run the program. Notice that the cursor is in TextBox1. We say that TextBox1 has the **focus**. (This means that TextBox1 is the currently selected object and any keyboard actions will be sent directly to this object.) Any text typed will display in that text box.

28. Press Tab once. Now, TextBox2 has the focus. When you type, the characters appear in TextBox2.

29. Press Tab several times, and then press Shift+Tab a few times. With Tab, the focus cycles through the objects on the form in the order they were created. With Shift+Tab, the focus cycles in the reverse order.

30. End the program you created.

31. We would now like to return to the first program. Click on *Open Project* from the *File* menu. An Open Project dialog box will appear stating that "You must choose to either save or discard changes in the current project before opening a project." There is no need to save this program, so click on the *Discard* button. Then a second Open Project dialog box will appear.

32. Navigate to the folder corresponding to the program you saved earlier, double-click on the folder, and double-click on the file with extension *sln*. You have now reloaded the first program.

    Note: As an alternative to using the Open Project dialog box in Steps 31 and 32 to return to the first program, click on the Start Page tab at the top of the Document window, and click on the program in the Recent Projects part of the Start Page.

33. If you do not see the Form Designer for the program, double-click on Form1.vb in the Solution Explorer.

34. Click on *Close Project* in the *File* menu to close the program.

■ A Button Walkthrough

1. Click on the *New Project* button to start a new program. (Give a name, such as ButtonProg, to the program, and click on the OK button.)

2. Double-click on the Button icon in the Toolbox to place a button on the form. (The Button icon is the second icon in the Common Controls group of the Toolbox.)

3. Move the button to the center of the form.

4. Activate the Properties window, highlight the Text property, type "Please Push Me", and press Enter. See Fig. 2.12. The button is too small.

FIGURE 2.12 **Setting the Text property.**

5. Click on the button to select it, and then widen it to accommodate the phrase "Please Push Me" on one line.

6. Run the program, and click on the button. The button appears to move in and then out. In Section 2.3, we will write code that is executed when a button is clicked on.

7. End the program and select the button.

8. From the Properties window, edit the Text setting by inserting an ampersand (&) before the first letter, P. Press the Enter key, and notice that the first letter P on the button is now underlined. See Fig. 2.13. Pressing Alt+P while the program is running causes the same event to occur as does clicking the button. However, the button will not appear to move in and out. Here, P is referred to as the **access key** for the button. (The access key is always specified as the character following the ampersand.)

9. Click on *Close Project* in the *File* menu to close the program.

FIGURE 2.13   **Designating P as an access key.**

■ A Label Walkthrough

1. Click on the *New Project* button to begin a new program. Feel free to keep the default name, such as WindowsApplication1.

2. Double-click on the label icon to place a label on the form. (The label icon is a large letter A.) Move the label to the center of the form.

3. Activate the Properties window, highlight the Text property, type "Enter Your Phone Number:", and press Enter. (Such a label is placed next to a text box into which the user will type a phone number.) Notice that the label widened to accommodate the text. This happened because the AutoSize property of the label is set to True by default.

4. Change the AutoSize property to False. Press Enter. Notice that the label now has eight sizing handles when selected.

5. Make the label narrower and longer until the words occupy two lines.

6. Activate the Properties window, and click on the down arrow to the right of the setting for the TextAlign property. Experiment by clicking on the various rectangles and observing their effects. The combination of sizing and alignment permits you to design a label easily.

7. Run the program. Nothing happens, even if you click on the label. Labels just sit there. The user cannot change what a label displays unless you write code to make the change.

8. End the program.

9. Click on *Close Project* in the *File* menu to close the program.

■ A List Box Walkthrough

1. Click on the New Project button to begin a new program. Feel free to keep the default name, such as WindowsApplication1.

2. Place a list box on the form. (The list box icon is the ninth icon in the *Common Controls* group of the Toolbox.)

3. Press F4 to activate the Properties window and notice that the list box does not have a Text property. The word ListBox1 is actually the setting for the Name property.

4. Also place a text box, a button, and a label on the form.

5. Click on the Object box just below the title bar of the Properties window. The name of the form and the names of the four controls are displayed. If you click on one of the names, that object will become selected and its properties displayed in the Properties window.

6. Run the program. Notice that the word ListBox1 has disappeared, but the words Button1 and Label1 are still visible. The list box is completely blank. In subsequent sections, we will write code to place information into the list box.

7. End the program and then click on *Close Project* in the *File* menu.

■ The Name Property

The form and each control on it has a Name property. By default, the form is given the name Form1 and controls are given names such as TextBox1 and TextBox2. These names can (and should) be changed to descriptive ones that reflect the purpose of the form or control. Also, it is good programming practice to have each name begin with a three-letter prefix that identifies the type of the object. See Table 2.1.

TABLE 2.1	Some three-letter prefixes.		
	Object	Prefix	Example
	form	frm	frmPayroll
	button	btn	btnComputeTotal
	label	lbl	lblAddress
	list box	lst	lstOutput
	text box	txt	txtCity

To change the name of the form, change the base name of the file Form1.vb appearing in the Solution Explorer. To make the change, right-click on Form1.vb in the Solution Explorer window, click on *Rename* in the context menu that appears, type in a new name (such as frm-Payroll.vb), and press the Enter key. **Important:** Make sure that the new filename keeps the extension "vb".

The name of a control is changed from the control's Properties window. (The Name property is always the third property in the alphabetized list of properties.) Names of controls and forms must begin with a letter and can include numbers and underscore (_) characters but cannot include punctuation marks or spaces.

The Name and Text properties of a button are both initially set to something like Button1. However, changing one of these properties does not affect the setting of the other property, and similarly for the Name and Text properties of forms, text boxes, and labels. The Text property of a form specifies the words appearing in the form's title bar.

■ Fonts

The default font for controls is Microsoft Sans Serif. Two other useful fonts are Courier New and Wingdings.

Courier New is a fixed-width font; that is, each character has the same width. With such a font, the letter i occupies the same space as the letter m. Fixed-width fonts are used with tables when information is to be aligned in columns.

The Wingdings font consists of assorted small pictures and symbols, each corresponding to a character on the keyboard. For instance if one of the characters %, (, 1, or J is typed into the Text setting of a control whose Font is Wingdings, the control will display a bell, phone, open folder, or smiling face, respectively.

To view the character set for a Windows font, click on the Windows Start button in the Windows task bar and successively click on All Programs, Accessories, System Tools, and Character Map. A rectangular array of characters will appear. After selecting the font, click on any item to enlarge it. You can insert the keyboard character for the item into the Clipboard by pressing the *Select* button and then the *Copy* button. To place the character into the Text property of a control having that font, just move the cursor to the Settings box for the Text property for that control and press Ctrl+V.

■ Auto Hide

The Auto Hide feature allows you to make more room for the Document window of the screen by hiding windows (such as the Toolbox, Solution Explorer, or Properties window). Let's illustrate the feature with a walkthrough using the Toolbox window. We start by discussing the situation where the feature is *disabled*.

1. If the Toolbox window is currently visible and the pushpin icon in the window title is vertical, then the Auto Hide feature is disabled. (If the Toolbox window is not visible, click on *Toolbox* in the menu bar's *View* menu. If the pushpin icon is horizontal, then click on the icon to make it vertical.) When the Auto Hide feature is disabled, the Toolbox window stays fixed and is always ready for use.

2. Click the mouse cursor somewhere outside the Toolbox window and note that the Toolbox window stays fixed.

3. Click on the pushpin icon to make it horizontal. The Auto Hide feature is now *enabled*.

4. Move the mouse cursor somewhere outside the Toolbox window and note that the window slides into a tab on the left side of the screen. The name and icon of the Toolbox window appear on the tab.

5. Hover the mouse cursor over the tab. The window slides into view and is ready for use.

   Note: We recommend that you keep the Toolbox, Solution Explorer, and Properties windows displayed unless you are creating a program with a very large form and need extra space.

■ Positioning and Aligning Controls

VideoNote

Positioning and aligning controls

Visual Basic provides several tools for positioning and aligning controls on a form. **Proximity lines** are short line segments that help you place controls a comfortable distance from each other and from the sides of the form. **Snap lines** are horizontal and vertical line segments that help you align controls. The **Format** menu is used to align controls, center controls horizontally and vertically in a form, and make a group of selected controls the same size.

A Positioning and Aligning Walkthrough

1. Begin a new program.
2. Place a button near the center of the form.

3. Drag the button toward the upper-right corner of the form until two short line segments appear. See Fig. 2.14(a). The button is now a comfortable distance from the two sides of the form.

4. Place a second button below the first button and drag it upward until a proximity line appears between the two buttons. The buttons are now a comfortable distance apart.

5. Resize and position the two buttons as shown in Fig. 2.14(b).

6. Drag Button2 upward until a blue line appears along the bottoms of the two buttons. See Fig. 2.14(c). This blue line is called a **snap line**. The bottoms of the two buttons are now aligned.

7. Continue dragging Button2 upward until a purple snap line appears just underneath the words Button1 and Button2. See Fig. 2.14(d). The middles of the two buttons are now aligned. If we were to continue dragging Button2 upward, a blue snap line would tell us when the tops were aligned. Step 10 shows another way to align the controls.

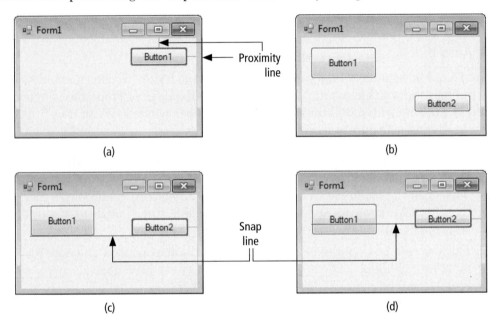

FIGURE 2.14   Positioning controls.

8. Click on Button1 and then hold down the Ctrl key and click on Button2. After the mouse button is released, both buttons will be selected.

Note: This process (called **selection of multiple controls**) can be repeated to select a group of any number of controls.

9. With the two buttons still selected, press F4 to open the Properties window. Then set the ForeColor property to Blue. Notice that the ForeColor property has been altered for both buttons at the same time. Actually, any property that is common to every control in selected multiple controls can be set simultaneously for the entire group.

10. With the two buttons still selected, open the *Format* menu in the Menu bar, hover over *Align*, and click on *Tops*. The tops of the two buttons are now aligned. Precisely, Button1 (the first button selected) will stay fixed, and Button2 will move up so that its top is aligned with the top of Button1.

The most common uses of the submenus of the *Format* menu are as follows:

Align: Align middles or corresponding sides of a group of selected controls.

Make Same Size: Make the width and/or height of a group of selected controls the same.

Horizontal Spacing: Equalize the horizontal spacing between a group of three or more selected controls arranged in a row.

Vertical Spacing: Equalize the vertical spacing between a group of three or more selected controls arranged in a column.

Center in Form: Center a selected control either horizontally or vertically in a form.

When multiple controls are selected with the Ctrl key, the first control selected (called the **primary control** of the group) will have white sizing handles, while the other controls will have black sizing handles. All alignment and sizing statements initiated from the *Format* menu will keep the primary control fixed and will align (or size) the other controls with respect to the primary control.

After multiple controls have been selected, they can be dragged as a group and deleted as a group. Exercises 35 and 36 show how the arrow keys can be used to move and size a control. The arrow keys also can be used to move and size multiple controls as a group.

A group of controls also can be selected by clicking the mouse outside the controls, dragging it across the controls, and releasing it. The *Select All* command from the *Edit* menu (or the key combination Ctrl + A) causes all the controls on the form to be selected. Although these methods are easy to apply, they do not allow the programmer to designate the primary control.

■ Setting Tab Order

Each time the Tab key is pressed while a program is running, the focus moves from one control to another. The tab order for the controls is determined by the settings of their TabIndex properties. Initially, controls receive the focus in the order they were placed on the form. The first control placed on the form has a TabIndex setting of 0, the second control has a setting of 1, and so on. The tab order can be changed by renumbering the controls' TabIndex settings.

Whether or not a control can receive the focus by tabbing is determined by the setting of its TabStop property. By default, this setting is True for buttons, text boxes, and list boxes, and False for labels. In this book we always use these default settings. **Note:** Even though labels do not receive the focus while tabbing, they are still assigned a tab index.

■ Comments

1. While you are working on a program, the program resides in memory. Removing a program from memory is referred to as **closing** the program. A program is automatically closed when you begin a new program. Also, it can be closed directly with the *Close Project* command from the *File* menu.

2. Three useful properties that have not been discussed are the following:

   (a) BackColor: This property specifies the background color for the form or a control.

   (b) Visible: Setting the Visible property to False causes an object to disappear when the program is run. The object can be made to reappear with code.

   (c) Enabled: Setting the Enabled property of a control to False restricts its use. It appears grayed and cannot receive the focus. Controls sometimes are disabled temporarily if they do not apply to the current state of the program.

3. Most properties can be set or altered with code as the program is running instead of being preset from the Properties window. For instance, a button can be made to disappear with a line such as **Button1.Visible = False**. The details are presented in Section 2.3.

4. If you inadvertently double-click on a form, a window containing text will appear. (The first line is Public Class Form1.) This is the Code Editor, which is discussed in the next

section. Press Ctrl+Z to undo the addition of this new code. To return to the Form Designer, click on the tab at the top of the Document window labeled "Form1.vb [Design]."

5. We have seen two ways to place a control onto a form. Another way is to just click on the control in the Toolbox and then click on the location in the form where you would like to place the control. Alternatively, you can just drag the control from the Toolbox to the location in the form.

6. Figure 2.9 shows a small down-arrow button on the right side of the Text property setting box. When you click on that button, a rectangular box appears. The setting for the Text property can be typed into this box instead of into the Settings box. This method of specifying the setting is especially useful when you want the button to have a multiline caption.

Practice Problems 2.2

1. What is the difference between the Text and the Name properties of a button?
2. The first two group names in the Toolbox are *All Windows Forms* and *Common Controls*. How many groups are there?

EXERCISES 2.2

1. Create a form with two buttons, run the program, and click on each button. Do you notice anything different about a button after it has been clicked?
2. While a program is running, a control is said to lose focus when the focus moves from that control to another control. Give three ways the user can cause a control to lose focus.

In Exercises 3 through 24, carry out the task.

3. Place "CHECKING ACCOUNT" in the title bar of a form.
4. Create a text box containing the words "PLAY IT, SAM" in blue letters.
5. Create a text box with a yellow background.
6. Create a text box named txtGreeting and containing the word "Welcome to my world!" in large italic letters.
7. Create a label containing the sentence "After all is said and done, more is said than done." The sentence should occupy three lines, and each line should be centered horizontally in the label.
8. Create a read-only text box containing the words "Visual Basic" in bold white letters on a dark blue background.
9. Create a text box named txtLanguage and containing the words "Visual Basic 2010" in Courier New font.
10. Create a yellow button named btnPush and containing the word "PUSH".
11. Create a white button containing the word "PUSH" in large italic letters.
12. Create a button containing the word "PUSH" in bold letters with the letter P underlined.
13. Create a button containing the word "PUSH" with the letter H as the access key.
14. Create a label containing the word "ALIAS" in white on a blue background.
15. Create a label named lblAKA and containing the centered italicized word "ALIAS".
16. Place "BALANCE SHEET" in the title bar of a form having a yellow background.
17. Create a label containing "VISUAL" on the first line and "BASIC" on the second line. Each word should be right-justified.

18. Create a form named frmHello whose title bar reads "Hello World".

19. Create a label containing a picture of a diskette. (**Hint:** Use the Wingdings character <.) Make the diskette as large as possible.

20. Create a label containing the bold word "ALIAS" in the Courier New font.

21. Create a list box with a yellow background.

22. Create a list box that will be invisible when the program is run.

23. Create a form named frmYellow with a yellow background.

24. Create a button containing a picture of a red bell. (**Hint:** Use the Wingdings character %.) Make the bell as large as possible.

In Exercises 25 through 30, create the interface shown in that figure. (These exercises give you practice creating controls and assigning properties. The interfaces do not necessarily correspond to actual programs.)

31. Create a replica of your bank check on a form. Words common to all checks, such as "PAY TO THE ORDER OF", should be contained in labels. Items specific to your checks, such as your name at the top left, should be contained in text boxes. Make the check on the screen resemble your personal check as much as possible. **Note:** Omit the account number.

32. Create a replica of your campus ID on a form. Words that are on all student IDs, such as the name of the college, should be contained in labels. Information specific to your ID, such as

your name and student ID number, should be contained in text boxes. Simulate your picture with a text box containing a smiling face—a size 24 Wingdings J.

33. Consider the form shown in Exercise 25. Assume the *Batman* button was added to the form before the *Robin* button. What is the tab index of the *Robin* button?

34. Consider the form shown in Exercise 26. Assume the first control added to the form was the button. What is the tab index of the button?

The following hands-on exercises develop additional techniques for manipulating and accessing controls placed on a form.

VideoNote

Moving a textbox
(Homework)

35. Place a text box on a form and select the text box. What is the effect of pressing the various arrow keys?

36. Place a text box on a form and select the text box. What is the effect of pressing the various arrow keys while holding down the Shift key?

37. Repeat Exercise 36 for selected multiple controls.

38. Repeat Exercise 35 for selected multiple controls.

39. Place a label and a list box on a form and change their font sizes to 12 at the same time.

40. Place a button in the center of a form and select it. Hold down the Ctrl key and press an arrow key. Repeat this process for each of the other arrow keys. Describe what happens.

41. Place a label and a text box on a form with the label to the left of and above the text box. Select the label. Hold down the Ctrl key and press the down-arrow key twice. With the Ctrl key still pressed, press the right-arrow key. Describe what happens.

42. Place two buttons on a form with one button to the right of and below the other button. Select the lower button, hold down the Ctrl key, and press the left-arrow key. With the Ctrl key still pressed, press the up-arrow key. Describe the effect of pressing the two arrow keys.

43. Experiment with the *Align* command on the *Format* menu to determine the difference between the *center* and the *middle* of a control.

44. Place four large buttons vertically on a form. Use the *Format* menu to make them the same size and to make the spacing between them uniform.

45. Place a label and a text box on a form as in Exercise 26, and then lower the label slightly and lower the text box until it is about one inch lower than the label. Use the mouse to slowly raise the text box to the top of the form. Three snap lines will appear along the way: a blue snap line, a purple snap line, and finally another blue snap line. What is the significance of each snap line?

46. Place a text box on a form, select the text box, and open its Properties window. Double-click on the name (not the Settings box) of the ReadOnly property. Double-click again. What is the effect of double-clicking on a property whose possible settings are True and False?

47. Place a button on a form, select the button, and open its Properties window. Double-click on the name (not the Settings box) of the ForeColor property. Double-click repeatedly. Describe what is happening.

Solutions to Practice Problems 2.2

1. The text is the words appearing on the button, whereas the name is the designation used to refer to the button in code. Initially, they have the same value, such as Button1. However, each can be changed independently of the other.

2. The Toolbox in the Express Edition of Visual Basic contains 11 groups. Figure 2.15 shows the Toolbox after each group has been collapsed. **Note:** In the other editions of Visual Basic the Toolbox contains 12 groups.

FIGURE 2.15 Toolbox group names.

2.3 Visual Basic Events

When a Visual Basic program runs, the form and its controls appear on the screen. Normally, nothing happens until the user takes an action, such as clicking a control or pressing a key. We call such an action an **event**. The programmer writes code that reacts to an event by performing some functionality. VideoNote

Event procedures

The three steps in creating a Visual Basic program are as follows:

1. Create the interface; that is, generate, position, and size the objects.
2. Set properties; that is, configure the appearance of the objects.
3. Write the code that executes when events occur.

Section 2.2 covered Steps 1 and 2; this section is devoted to Step 3. Code consists of statements that carry out tasks. Writing code in Visual Basic is assisted by an autocompletion system called **IntelliSense** that reduces the amount of memorization needed and helps prevent errors. In this section, we limit ourselves to statements that change properties of a control or the form while a program is running.

Properties of controls are changed in code with statements of the form

```
controlName.property = setting
```

where *controlName* is the name of the control, *property* is one of the properties of the control, and *setting* is a valid setting for that property. Such statements are called **assignment statements**. They assign values to properties. Here are three examples of assignment statements:

1. The statement

```
txtBox.Text = "Hello"
```

displays the word *Hello* in the text box.

2. The statement

```
btnButton.Visible = True
```

makes the button visible.

3. The statement

```
txtBox.ForeColor = Color.Red
```

sets the color of the characters in the text box named txtBox to red.

Most events are associated with controls. The event "click on btnButton" is different from the event "click on lstBox". These two events are specified btnButton.Click and lstBox.Click. The statements to be executed when an event occurs are written in a block of code called an **event procedure** or **event handler**. The first line of an event procedure (called the **header**) has the form

```
Private Sub objectName_event(ByVal sender As System.Object,
        ByVal e As System.EventArgs) Handles objectName.event
```

Since we do not make any use of the lengthy text inside the parentheses in this book, for the sake of readability we replace it with an ellipsis. However, it will automatically appear in our programs each time Visual Basic creates the header for an event procedure. The structure of an event procedure is

```
Private Sub objectName_event(...) Handles objectName.event
  statements
End Sub
```

where the three dots (that is, the ellipsis) represent

```
ByVal sender As System.Object, ByVal e As System.EventArgs
```

Words such as "Private," "ByVal," "As," "Sub," "Handles," and "End" have special meanings in Visual Basic and are referred to as **keywords** or **reserved words**. The Code Editor automatically capitalizes the first letter of a keyword and displays the word in blue. The word "Sub" in the first line signals the beginning of the procedure, and the first line identifies the object and the event occurring to that object. The last line signals the termination of the event procedure. The statements to be executed appear between these two lines. These statements are referred to as the **body** of the event procedure. (**Note:** The word "Private" indicates that the event procedure cannot be invoked by another form. This will not concern us until much later in the book. The expression following Handles identifies the object and the event happening to that object. The expression `"objectName_event"` is the default name of the procedure and can be changed if desired. In this book, we always use the default name. The word "Sub" is an abbreviation of *Subroutine*.) For instance, the event procedure

```
Private Sub btnButton_Click(...) Handles btnButton.Click
  txtBox.ForeColor = Color.Red
End Sub
```

changes the color of the words in the text box to red when the button is clicked. The clicking of the button is said to **raise** the event, and the event procedure is said to **handle** the event.

■ An Event Procedure Walkthrough

The form in Fig. 2.16, which contains two text boxes and a button, will be used to demonstrate what event procedures are and how they are created. Three event procedures will be used to alter the appearance of a phrase appearing in a text box. The event procedures are named txtFirst_TextChanged, btnRed_Click, and txtFirst_Leave.

OBJECT	PROPERTY	SETTING
frmDemo	Text	Demonstration
txtFirst		
txtSecond		
btnRed	Text	Change Color to Red

FIGURE 2.16 The interface for the event procedure walkthrough.

1. Create the interface in Fig. 2.16 in the Form Designer. The Name properties of the form, text boxes, and button should be set as shown in the Object column. The Text property of the form should be set to Demonstration, and the Text property of the button should be set to Change Color to Red. No properties need be set for the text boxes.

2. Click the right mouse button anywhere on the Form Designer, and click on *View Code*. The Form Designer IDE is replaced by the **Code Editor IDE** (also known as the *Code view* or the *Code window*). See Fig. 2.17.

FIGURE 2.17 The Visual Basic IDE in Code Editor mode.

The tab labeled frmDemo.vb corresponds to the Code Editor. Click on the tab labeled frmDemo.vb [Design], when you want to return to the Form Designer. We will place our program code between the two lines shown. Let's refer to this region as the **program region**.

Figure 2.17 shows that the Code Editor IDE has a Toolbox, Solution Explorer, and Properties window that support Auto Hide. The Solution Explorer window for the Code Editor functions exactly like the one for the Form Designer. The Code Editor's Toolbox has just one group, General, that is used to store code fragments which can be copied into a program when needed. The Code Editor's Properties window will not be used in this textbook.

3. Click on the tab labeled "frmDemo.vb [Design]" to return to the Form Designer. (You also can invoke the Form Designer by clicking *Designer* in the *View* menu, or by right-clicking the Code Editor and clicking *View Designer*.)

4. Double-click on the button. The Code Editor reappears, but now the following two lines of code have been added to the program region and the cursor is located on the blank line between them.

```
Private Sub btnRed_Click(...) Handles btnRed.Click

End Sub
```

The first line is the header for the event procedure named btnRed_Click. This procedure is invoked by the event btnRed.Click. That is, whenever the button is clicked, the code between the two lines just shown will be executed.

5. Type the line

```
txtFirst.ForeColor = Color.Red
```

at the cursor location.

This statement begins with the name of a control, txtFirst. Each time you type a letter of the name, IntelliSense drops down a list containing possible completions for the name.[1] As you continue typing, the list is shortened to match the letters that you have typed. Figure 2.18 shows the list after the letters *tx* have been typed. At this point, you have the following three options on how to continue:

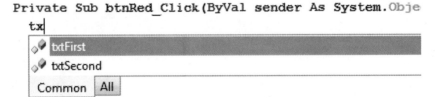

FIGURE 2.18   Drop-down list produced by IntelliSense.

  i. Double-click on txtFirst in the list.

 ii. Keep the cursor on txtFirst, and then press the Tab key or the Enter key.

iii. Directly type in the remaining six letters of txtFirst.

After you type the dot (.) following txtFirst, IntelliSense drops down a list containing properties of text boxes. See Fig. 2.19(a). Each property is preceded by a properties icon (🖬). [The list also contains items called *methods*, which we will discuss later. Methods are preceded by a method icon (🔹).] At this point, you can scroll up the list and double-click on ForeColor to automatically enter that property. See Fig. 2.19(b). Or, you can keep typing. After you have typed "For", the list shortens to the single word ForeColor. At that point, you can press the Tab key or the Enter key, or keep typing to obtain the word ForeColor.

After you type in the equal sign, IntelliSense drops down the list of colors shown in Fig. 2.20. You have the option of scrolling to Color.Red and double-clicking on it, or typing Color.Red into the statement.

---

[1]This feature of IntelliSense is referred to as **Complete Word**.

(a)   (b)

FIGURE 2.19   Drop-down list produced by IntelliSense.

```
Private Sub btnRed_Click(ByVal sender As System.Object
    txtFirst.ForeColor =
```

```
Color.AliceBlue
Color.AntiqueWhite
Color.Aqua
Color.Aquamarine
Color.Azure
Color.Beige
Color.Bisque
Color.Black
Color.BlanchedAlmond
Color.Blue
Color.BlueViolet
Color.Brown
Color.BurlyWood
Color.CadetBlue
```

FIGURE 2.20   Drop-down list of colors produced by IntelliSense.

6. Return to the Form Designer and double-click on the first text box. The Code Editor reappears, and the first and last lines of the event procedure txtFirst_TextChanged appear in the program region. This procedure is raised by the event txtFirst.TextChanged—that is, whenever there is a change in the text displayed in the text box txtFirst. Type the line that sets the ForeColor property of txtFirst to Blue. The event procedure will now appear as follows:

```
Private Sub txtFirst_TextChanged(...) Handles txtFirst.TextChanged
    txtFirst.ForeColor = Color.Blue
End Sub
```

7. Return to the Form Designer and select txtFirst.

8. Click on the *Events* button ( ) in the toolbar at the top of the Properties window. The 63 events associated with text boxes are displayed, and the Description pane describes the currently selected event. (Don't be alarmed by the large number of events. Only a few events are used in this book.) Scroll to the Leave event. See Fig. 2.21.

FIGURE 2.21 Events displayed in the Properties window.

9. Double-click on the Leave event. (The event txtFirst.Leave is raised when the focus is moved away from the text box.) The header and last line of the event procedure txtFirst_Leave will be displayed. In this procedure, type the line that sets the ForeColor property of txtFirst to Black. The Code Editor will now look as follows:

```
Public Class frmDemo
  Private Sub btnRed_Click(...) Handles btnRed.Click
    txtFirst.ForeColor = Color.Red
  End Sub

  Private Sub txtFirst_Leave(...) Handles txtFirst.Leave
    txtFirst.ForeColor = Color.Black
  End Sub

  Private Sub txtFirst_TextChanged(...) Handles txtFirst.TextChanged
    txtFirst.ForeColor = Color.Blue
  End Sub
End Class
```

10. Hover the cursor over the word "ForeColor". Visual Basic now displays information about the foreground color property. This illustrates another help feature of Visual Basic.

11. Run the program by pressing F5.

12. Type something into the first text box. In Fig. 2.22, the blue word "Hello" has been typed. (Recall that a text box has the focus whenever it is ready to accept typing—that is, whenever it contains a blinking cursor.)

13. Click on the second text box. The contents of the first text box will become black. When the second text box was clicked, the first text box lost the focus; that is, the event Leave

FIGURE 2.22 **Text box containing input.**

happened to txtFirst. Thus, the event procedure txtFirst_Leave was invoked, and the code inside the procedure was executed.

14. Click on the button. This invokes the event procedure btnRed_Click, which changes the color of the words in txtFirst to Red.

15. Click on the first text box, and type the word "Friend" after the word "Hello". As soon as typing begins, the text in the text box is changed and the TextChanged event is raised. This event causes the color of the contents of the text box to become blue.

16. You can repeat Steps 12 through 15 as many times as you like. When you are finished, end the program by clicking on the *Stop Debugging* button on the Toolbar, clicking on the form's Close button, or pressing Alt + F4.

Note: After viewing events in the Properties window, click on the *Properties* button ⎛ ⎡▦⎤ ⎞ to the left of the *Events* button to return to displaying properties in the Properties window.

▨ Properties and Event Procedures of the Form

You can assign properties to the form itself in code. However, a statement such as

```
frmDemo.Text = "Demonstration"
```

will not work. The form is referred to by the keyword *Me*. Therefore, the proper statement is

```
Me.Text = "Demonstration"
```

To display a list of all the events associated with frmDemo, select the form in the Form Designer and click on the Events button in the Properties window's toolbar.

▨ The Header of an Event Procedure

As mentioned earlier, in the header for an event procedure such as

```
Private Sub btnOne_Click(...) Handles btnOne.Click
```

btnOne_Click is the name of the event procedure, and btnOne.Click identifies the event that invokes the procedure. The name can be changed at will. For instance, the header can be changed to

```
Private Sub ButtonPushed(...) Handles btnOne.Click
```

Also, an event procedure can handle more than one event. For instance, if the previous line is changed to

```
Private Sub ButtonPushed(...) Handles btnOne.Click, btnTwo.Click
```

the event procedure will be invoked if either btnOne or btnTwo is clicked.

We have been using ellipses (. . .) as place holders for the phrase

```
ByVal sender As System.Object, ByVal e As System.EventArgs
```

In Chapter 5, we will gain a better understanding of this type of phrase. Essentially, the word "sender" carries a reference to the object that raised the event, and the letter "e" carries some additional information that the sending object wants to communicate. We will not make use of either "sender" or "e".

▓ Opening a Program

Beginning with the next chapter, each example contains a program. These programs can be downloaded from the Pearson website for this book. See the discussion on pages 14–15 of the Preface for details. The process of loading a program stored on a disk into the Visual Basic environment is referred to as **opening** the program. Let's open the downloaded program 7-2-3 from Chapter 7. That program allows you to enter a first name, and then displays U.S. Presidents having that first name.

1. From Visual Basic, click on *Open Project* in the *File* menu. (A dialog box will appear.)
2. Display the contents of the Ch07 subfolder downloaded from the website.
3. Double-click on 7-2-3.
4. Double-click on 7-2-3.sln.
5. If the Solution Explorer window is not visible, click on *Solution Explorer* in the *View/Other Windows* menu.
6. In the Solution Explorer window, click on frmPresident.vb. (Five buttons will appear at the top of the Solution Explorer. See Fig. 2.23.) At any time you can click on the *View Code* button to invoke the Code Editor, or you can click on the *View Designer* button to invoke the Form Designer. The *Show All Files* and *Refresh* buttons, which allow you to view all the files in a program's folder and to update certain files, will be used extensively beginning with Chapter 7. The first button will not be used in this textbook.

FIGURE 2.23   Solution Explorer window.

7. Press F5 to run the program.
8. Type in a name (such as James or William), and press the *Display Presidents* button. (See Fig. 2.24.) You can repeat this process as many times as desired.
9. End the program.

FIGURE 2.24 Output for program 7-2-3.

The program just executed uses a text file named USPres.txt. To view the text file, open the folder *bin*, open the subfolder *Debug*, and click on USPres.txt. (If the *bin* folder is not visible, click on the *Show All Files* button. If USPres.txt is not listed in the *Debug* subfolder, click the *Refresh* button and reopen the folders. After reading Chapter 7, you will understand why text files are placed in the *Debug* subfolder of the *bin* folder.) The first line of the file gives the name of the first president; the second line gives the name of the second president, and so on. To close the text file, click on the close button (✖) on the USPres.txt tab.

■ Comments

1. The Visual Basic editor automatically indents the statements inside procedures. In this book, we indent by two spaces. To instruct your editor to indent by two spaces, select *Options* from the *Tools* menu, and uncheck the "Show all settings" box in the Options window that appears. Expand "Text Editor Basic" or "Text Editor", click on "Editor", enter 2 into the "Indent size:" box, and click on OK.

2. The event *controlName*.Leave is raised when the specified control loses the focus. Its counterpart is the event *controlName*.Enter which is raised when the specified control gets the focus. A related statement is

    ```
    controlName.Focus()
    ```

    which moves the focus to the specified control.

3. We have ended our programs by clicking the Stop Debugging button or pressing Alt + F4. A more elegant technique is to create a button, call it btnQuit, with caption Quit and the following event procedure:

    ```
    Private Sub btnQuit_Click(...) Handles btnQuit.Click
      Me.Close()
    End Sub
    ```

4. For statements of the form

    ```
    object.Text = setting
    ```

    the expression for *setting* must be surrounded by quotation marks. (For instance, lblName. Text = "Name".) For properties where the proper setting is one of the words True or False, these words should *not* be surrounded by quotation marks.

5. Names of existing event procedures associated with an object are not automatically changed when you rename the object. You must change them yourself. However, the event

that invokes the procedure (and all other references to the control) will change automatically. For example, suppose an event procedure is

```
Private Sub btnOne_Click(...) Handles btnOne.Click
  btnOne.Text = "Press Me"
End Sub
```

and, in the Form Designer, you change the name of btnOne to btnTwo. Then, when you return to the Code Editor, the procedure will be

```
Private Sub btnOne_Click(...) Handles btnTwo.Click
  btnTwo.Text = "Press Me"
End Sub
```

6. The Code Editor has many features of a word processor. For instance, the operations cut, copy, paste, and find can be carried out with the sixth through ninth buttons on the Toolbar. These operations, and several others, also can be executed from the *Edit* menu.

7. The Code Editor can detect certain types of errors. For instance, if you type

```
txtFirst.Text = hello
```

and then move away from the line, the automatic syntax checker will underline the word "hello" with a blue squiggle to indicate that something is wrong. When the mouse cursor is hovered over the underlined expression, the editor will display a message explaining what is wrong. If you try to run the program without correcting the error, the dialog box in Figure 2.25 will appear.

FIGURE 2.25 **Error dialog box.**

8. Each control has a favored event, called the **default event**, whose event procedure template can be generated from the Form Designer by double-clicking on the control. Table 2.2 shows some controls and their default events. The most common event appearing in this book is the Click event for a button. The TextChanged event for a text box was used in this section. The SelectedIndexChanged event for a list box is introduced in Section 4.4, and the Load event for a form is introduced in Section 7.1. The Click event for a label is never used in this book.

TABLE 2.2 **Some default events.**

Control	Default Event
form	Load
button	Click
label	Click
list box	SelectedIndexChanged
text box	TextChanged

9. Font properties, such as the name, style, and size, are usually specified at design time. The setting of the properties can be displayed in code with statements such as

```
lstBox.Items.Add(txtBox.Font.Name)
lstBox.Items.Add(txtBox.Font.Bold)
lstBox.Items.Add(txtBox.Font.Size)
```

However, a font's name, style, and size properties cannot be altered in code with statements of the form

```
txtBox.Font.Name = "Courier New"
txtBox.Font.Bold = True
txtBox.Font.Size = 16
```

10. When you make changes to a program, asterisks appear as superscripts on the tabs labeled "frmName.vb [design]" and "frmName.vb" to indicate that some part of the program has not been saved. The asterisks disappear when the program is saved or run.

   Note: If the program has been saved to disk, all files for the program will be automatically updated on the disk whenever the program is saved or run.

11. You can easily change the size of the font used in the current program's Code Editor. Just hold down the Ctrl key and move the mouse's scroll wheel.

12. Notes on IntelliSense:

   (a) Whenever an item in an IntelliSense drop-down list is selected, a tooltip describing the item appears to the right of the item.

   (b) From the situation in Fig. 2.18, we can display txtFirst by double-clicking on the highlighted item, pressing the Tab key, or pressing the Enter key. Another option is to press the period key. In this case, both the name txtFirst and the dot following it will be displayed. **Note:** The period key option works only if the selected item is always followed by a dot in code.

   (c) IntelliSense drop-down lists have tabs labeled *Common* and *All*. When the *All* tab is selected, every possible continuation choice appears in the list. When the *Common* tab is selected, only the most frequently used continuation choices appear.

   (d) Occasionally, the IntelliSense drop-down list will cover some of your program. If you hold down the Ctrl key, the drop-down list will become transparent and allow you to see the covered-up code.

Practice Problems 2.3

1. Describe the event that invokes the following event procedure.

```
Private Sub btnCompute_Click() Handles txtBox.Leave
  txtBox.Text = "Hello world"
End Sub
```

2. Give a statement that will prevent the user from typing into txtBox.

EXERCISES 2.3

In Exercises 1 through 6, describe the contents of the text box after the button is clicked.

1.
```
Private Sub btnOutput_Click(...) Handles btnOutput.Click
  txtBox.Text = "Hello"
End Sub
```

2.
```
Private Sub btnOutput_Click(...) Handles btnOutput.Click
    txtBox.ForeColor = Color.Blue
    txtBox.Text = "Hello"
End Sub
```

3.
```
Private Sub btnOutput_Click(...) Handles btnOutput.Click
    txtBox.BackColor = Color.Orange
    txtBox.Text = "Hello"
End Sub
```

4.
```
Private Sub btnOutput_Click(...) Handles btnOutput.Click
    txtBox.Text = "Goodbye"
    txtBox.Text = "Hello"
End Sub
```

5.
```
Private Sub btnOutput_Click(...) Handles btnOutput.Click
    txtBox.Text = "Hello"
    txtBox.Visible = False
End Sub
```

6.
```
Private Sub btnOutput_Click(...) Handles btnOutput.Click
    txtBox.BackColor = Color.Yellow
    txtBox.Text = "Hello"
End Sub
```

In Exercises 7 through 10, assume that the three objects on the form were created in the order txtFirst, txtSecond, and lblOne. Determine the output displayed in lblOne when the program is run and the Tab key is pressed. *Note:* Initially, txtFirst has the focus.

7.
```
Private Sub txtFirst_Leave(...) Handles txtFirst.Leave
    lblOne.ForeColor = Color.Green
    lblOne.Text = "Hello"
End Sub
```

8.
```
Private Sub txtFirst_Leave(...) Handles txtFirst.Leave
    lblOne.BackColor = Color.White
    lblOne.Text = "Hello"
End Sub
```

9.
```
Private Sub txtSecond_Enter(...) Handles txtSecond.Enter
    lblOne.BackColor = Color.Gold
    lblOne.Text = "Hello"
End Sub
```

10.
```
Private Sub txtSecond_Enter(...) Handles txtSecond.Enter
    lblOne.Visible = False
    lblOne.Text = "Hello"
End Sub
```

In Exercises 11 through 16, determine the errors.

11.
```
Private Sub btnOutput_Click(...) Handles btnOutput.Click
    Form1.Text = "Hello"
End Sub
```

12.
```
Private Sub btnOutput_Click(...) Handles btnOutput.Click
    txtBox.Text = Hello
End Sub
```

13.
```
Private Sub btnOutput_Click(...) Handles btnOutput.Click
    txtFirst.ForeColor = Blue
End Sub
```

14.
```
Private Sub btnOutput_Click(...) Handles btnOutput.Click
    txtBox = "Hello"
End Sub
```

15.
```
Private Sub btnOutput_Click(...) Handles btnOutput.Click
    txtBox.Font.Size = 20
End Sub
```

16.
```
Private Sub btnOutput_Click(...) Handles btn1.Click, btn2.Click
    Me.Color = Color.Yellow
End Sub
```

In Exercises 17 through 28, write a line (or lines) of code to carry out the task.

17. Display "E.T. phone home." in lblTwo.

18. Display "Play it, Sam." in lblTwo.

19. Display "The stuff that dreams are made of." in red letters in txtBox.

20. Display "Life is like a box of chocolates." in txtBox with blue letters on a gold background.

21. Disable txtBox.

22. Change the words in the form's title bar to "Hello World."

23. Make lblTwo disappear.

24. Change the color of the letters in lblName to red.

25. Enable the disabled button btnOutcome.

26. Give the focus to btnCalculate.

27. Give the focus to txtBoxTwo.

28. Change the background color of the form to White.

29. Describe the Enter event in your own words.

30. Describe the Leave event in your own words.

31. The label control has an event called DoubleClick that is raised by double-clicking the left mouse button. Write a simple program to test this event. Determine whether you can raise the DoubleClick event without also raising the Click event.

32. Write a simple program to demonstrate that a button's Click event is raised when you press the Enter key while the button has the focus.

In Exercises 33 through 38, the interface and initial properties are specified. Write the program to carry out the stated task.

33. When one of the three buttons is pressed, the words on the button are displayed in the text box with the stated alignment. *Note:* Rely on IntelliSense to provide you with the proper settings for the TextAlign property.

OBJECT	PROPERTY	SETTING
frmAlign	Text	Text Alignment
txtBox	ReadOnly	True
btnLeft	Text	Left Justify
btnCenter	Text	Center
btnRight	Text	Right Justify

34. When one of the buttons is pressed, the face changes to a smiling face (Wingdings character "J") or a frowning face (Wingdings character "L").

OBJECT	PROPERTY	SETTING
frmFace	Text	Face
lblFace	Font Name	Wingdings
	Font Size	24
	Text	K
btnSmile	Text	Smile
btnFrown	Text	Frown

35. Pressing the buttons alters the background and foreground colors in the text box.

OBJECT	PROPERTY	SETTING
frmColors	Text	Colorful Text
lblBack	Text	Background
btnGold	Text	Gold
btnBlue	Text	Blue
txtBox	Text	It's a Beautiful Day
	TextAlign	Center
lblFore	Text	Foreground
btnWhite	Text	White
btnYellow	Text	Yellow

36. When one of the three text boxes receives the focus, its text becomes red. When it loses the focus, the text returns to black. The buttons set the alignment in the text boxes to Left or Right. **Note:** Rely on IntelliSense to provide you with the proper settings for the TextAlign property.

OBJECT	PROPERTY	SETTING
frm123	Text	One, Two, Three
txtOne	Text	One
txtTwo	Text	Two
txtThree	Text	Three
btnLeft	Text	Left
btnRight	Text	Right

37. When the user moves the focus to one of the three small text boxes at the bottom of the form, an appropriate saying is displayed in the large text box. Use the sayings "I like life, it's something to do."; "The future isn't what it used to be."; and "Tell the truth and run."

OBJECT	PROPERTY	SETTING
frmQuote	Text	Sayings
txtQuote	ReadOnly	True
txtLife	Text	Life
txtFuture	Text	Future
txtTruth	Text	Truth

38. The user can disable or enable the text box by clicking on the appropriate button. After the user clicks the Enable button, the text box should receive the focus.

OBJECT	PROPERTY	SETTING
frmTextBox	Text	Text Box
txtBox		
btnDisable	Text	Disable Text Box
btnEnable	Text	Enable Text Box

In Exercises 39 through 44, write a program to carry out the task.

39. The form contains four square buttons arranged in a rectangular array. Each button has the caption "Push Me". When the user clicks on a button, the button disappears and the other three become or remain visible. See Fig. 2.26.

FIGURE 2.26   Form for Exercise 39.

FIGURE 2.27   Form for Exercise 40.

40. Simulate a traffic light with three small square text boxes placed vertically on a form. See Fig. 2.27. Initially, the bottom text box is solid green and the other text boxes are dark gray. When the Tab key is pressed, the middle text box turns yellow and the bottom text box turns dark gray. The next time Tab is pressed, the top text box turns red and the middle text box turns dark gray. Subsequent pressing of the Tab key cycles through the three colors. **Hint:** First place the bottom text box on the form, then the middle text box, and finally the top text box.

41. Use the same form and properties as in Exercise 34, with the captions for the buttons replaced with Vanish and Reappear. Clicking a button should produce the stated result.

42. A form contains two text boxes and one large label between them with no preset caption. When the first text box receives the focus, the label reads "Enter your full name." When the second text box receives the focus, the label reads "Enter your phone number, including area code."

43. The form contains a single read-only text box and two buttons. When the user clicks on one of the buttons, the sentence "You just clicked on a button." is displayed in the text box. The program should consist of a single event procedure.

44. The form contains two text boxes into which the user types information. When the user clicks on one of the text boxes, it becomes blank and its contents are displayed in the other text box. *Note:* A text box can be cleared with the statement `txtBox.Clear()` or the statement `txtBox.Text = ""`.

Solutions to Practice Problem 2.3

1. The event is raised when txtBox loses the focus since txtBox.Leave is the event following the keyword Handles. The name of the event procedure, btnCompute_Click, can be anything; it plays no role in determining the action that raises the event.

2. Three possibilities are

```
txtBox.Enabled = False
txtBox.ReadOnly = True
txtBox.Visible = False
```

CHAPTER 2   SUMMARY

1. The Visual Basic Form Designer displays a *form* that can hold a collection of *controls* for which various properties can be set. Some examples of controls are text boxes, labels, buttons, and list boxes. Some useful properties are Text (sets the text displayed in a control), Name (used to give a meaningful name to a control), Font.Name (selects the name of the font used), Font.Size (sets the size of the text displayed), Font.Bold (displays boldface text), Font.Italic (displays italics text), BackColor (sets the background color), ForeColor (sets the color of the text), ReadOnly (determines whether text can be typed into a text box when the program is running), TextAlign (sets the type of alignment for the text in a control), Enabled (determines whether a control can respond to user interaction), and Visible (determines whether an object can be seen or is hidden).

2. An *event procedure* is invoked when something happens to a specified object. Some events are *object*.Click (*object* is clicked), *object*.TextChanged (a change occurred in the value of the object's Text property), *object*.Leave (*object* loses the focus), and *object*.Enter (*object* receives the focus). **Note:** The statement *object*.Focus() moves the focus to the specified object.

3. *IntelliSense* provides a host of features that help you write code.

4. *Tab order*, the order in which the user moves the focus from one control to another by pressing the Tab key while the program is running, can be set from the Properties window.

3

Variables, Input,
and Output

3.1 Numbers

Much of the data processed by computers consists of numbers. In computerese, numbers are called **numeric literals**. This section discusses the operations that are performed with numbers and the ways numbers are displayed.

■ Arithmetic Operations

The five standard arithmetic operations in Visual Basic are addition, subtraction, multiplication, division, and exponentiation. Addition, subtraction, and division are denoted in Visual Basic by the standard symbols +, −, and /, respectively. However, the notations for multiplication and exponentiation differ from the customary mathematical notations as follows:

Mathematical Notation	Visual Basic Notation
$a \cdot b$ or $a \times b$	$a*b$
a^r	$a{\char`\^}r$

(The asterisk [*] is the upper character of the 8 key. The caret [^] is the upper character of the 6 key.)

One way to show a number on the screen is to display it in a list box. If n is a number, then the instruction

```
lstBox.Items.Add(n)
```

displays the number n as the last item in the list box. *Add* is called a **method**. (Generally, a method is a process that performs a task for a particular object.) If the parentheses contain a combination of numbers and arithmetic operations, the *Add* method carries out the operations and displays the result. Another important method is *Clear*. The statement

```
lstBox.Items.Clear()
```

removes all the items displayed in the list box lstBox.

 Example 1 The following program applies each of the five arithmetic operations. Preceding the program are the form design and a table showing the names of the objects on the form and the settings, if any, for properties of these objects. This form design is also used in the discussion and examples in the remainder of this section.

The word "Run" in the phrasing [Run . . .] indicates that the *Start Debugging* button or F5 should be pressed to execute the program. Notice that in the output 3 / 2 is displayed in decimal form. Visual Basic never displays numbers as fractions. In the evaluation of $2*(3+4)$, the operation inside the parentheses is calculated first.

Note: All programs appearing in examples and case studies are provided on the companion website for this book. See the discussion on page 15 for details.

OBJECT	PROPERTY	SETTING
frmArithmetic	Text	3-1-1
lstResults		
btnCompute	Text	Compute

```
Private Sub btnCompute_Click(...) Handles btnCompute.Click
  lstResults.Items.Clear()
  lstResults.Items.Add(3 + 2)
  lstResults.Items.Add(3 — 2)
  lstResults.Items.Add(3 * 2)
  lstResults.Items.Add(3 / 2)
  lstResults.Items.Add(3 ^ 2)
  lstResults.Items.Add(2 * (3 + 4))
End Sub
```

[Run, and then click on the button.]

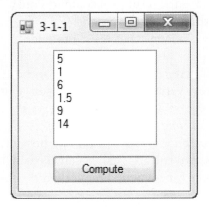

■ Variables

In applied mathematics problems, quantities are referred to by names. For instance, consider the following high school algebra problem: "If a car travels at 50 miles per hour, how far will it travel in 14 hours? Also, how many hours are required to travel 410 miles?" The solution to this problem uses the well-known formula

$$\text{distance} = \text{speed} \times \text{time elapsed}$$

Here's how this problem would be solved with a computer program:

```
Private Sub btnCompute_Click(...) Handles btnCompute.Click
  Dim speed As Double
```

```
Dim timeElapsed As Double
Dim distance As Double
lstResults.Items.Clear()
speed = 50
timeElapsed = 14
distance = speed * timeElapsed
lstResults.Items.Add(distance)
distance = 410
timeElapsed = distance / speed
lstResults.Items.Add(timeElapsed)
End Sub
```

[Run, and then click on the button. The following is displayed in the list box.]

```
700
8.2
```

Skip the second, third, and fourth lines of the event procedure for now. We will return to them soon. The sixth line sets the speed to 50, and the seventh line sets the time elapsed to 14. The eighth line multiplies the value for the speed by the value for the time elapsed and sets the distance to this product. The next line displays the answer to the distance-traveled question. The three lines before the End Sub statement answer the time-required question in a similar manner.

The names *speed, timeElapsed,* and *distance*, which hold values, are referred to as **variables**. Consider the variable *timeElapsed*. In the seventh line, its value was set to 14. In the eleventh line, its value was changed as the result of a computation. On the other hand, the variable *speed* had the same value, 50, throughout the program.

VideoNote

Numbers

In general, a variable is a name that is used to refer to an item of data. The value assigned to the variable may change during the execution of the program. In Visual Basic, variable names must begin with a letter or an underscore, and can consist only of letters, digits, and underscores. (The shortest variable names consist of a single letter.) Visual Basic does not distinguish between uppercase and lowercase letters used in variable names. Some examples of variable names are *total, numberOfCars, taxRate_2010,* and *n.* As a convention, we write variable names in lowercase letters except for the first letters of each additional word (as in *gradeOnFirstExam*). This convention is called **camel casing**.

If *var* is a variable and *n* is a numeric literal, then the statement

```
var = n
```

assigns the number *n* to the variable *var.* Such a statement is another example of an **assignment statement**.

A variable is declared to be of a certain type depending on the sort of data that can be assigned to it. The most versatile type for holding numbers is called **Double**. A variable of type Double can hold whole, fractional, or mixed numbers between about $-1.8 \cdot 10^{308}$ and $1.8 \cdot 10^{308}$. Dim statements (also called **declaration statements**) declare the names and types of the variables to be used in the program. The second, third, and fourth lines of this event procedure declare three variables of type Double and give them the names *speed, timeElapsed,* and *distance.* Variables must be declared before values can be assigned to them.

In general, a statement of the form

```
Dim varName As Double
```

declares a variable named *varName* to be of type Double. Actually, the Dim statement causes the computer to set aside a location in memory referenced by *varName.* Since *varName* is a numeric variable, the Dim statement initially places the number zero in that memory location. (We say that zero is the **initial value** or **default value** of the variable.) Each subsequent assignment statement having *varName* to the left of the equal sign will change the value of the number.

The initial value can be set to a value other than zero. To specify a nonzero initial value, follow the declaration statement with an equal sign followed by the initial value. The statement

```
Dim varName As Double = 50
```

declares the specified variable as a variable of type Double and gives it the initial value 50.

The statement

```
lstBox.Items.Add(varName)
```

looks into this memory location for the current value of the variable and displays that value in the list box.

IntelliSense provides assistance with both declaration and assignment statements. Consider the pair of statements

```
Dim interestRate As Double
interestRate = 0.05
```

In the first statement, IntelliSense will suggest the word "As" after you type "Dim interestRate", and will suggest the word "Double" after you type "Dou". In the second statement, IntelliSense will suggest the word "interestRate" after you type "inte".

A combination of literals, variables, and arithmetic operations that can be evaluated to yield a number is called a **numeric expression**. Expressions are evaluated by replacing each variable by its value and carrying out the arithmetic. Some examples of expressions are $2 * distance + 7$, $n + 1$, and $(a + b)/3$.

  Example 2 The following program displays the default value of a variable and the value of an expression:

```
Private Sub btnCompute_Click(...) Handles btnCompute.Click
  Dim a As Double
  Dim b As Double = 3
  lstResults.Items.Clear()
  lstResults.Items.Add(a)
  lstResults.Items.Add(b)
  a = 5
  lstResults.Items.Add(a * (2 + b))
End Sub
```

[Run, and then click on the button. The following is displayed in the list box.]

```
0
3
25
```

If *var* is a variable, then the assignment statement

```
var = expression
```

first evaluates the expression on the right and *then* assigns its value to the variable on the left. For instance, the event procedure in Example 2 can be written as

```
Private Sub btnCompute_Click(...) Handles btnCompute.Click
  Dim a As Double
  Dim b As Double = 3
  Dim c As Double
  lstResults.Items.Clear()
  lstResults.Items.Add(a)
  lstResults.Items.Add(b)
  a = 5
  c = a * (2 + b)
  lstResults.Items.Add(c)
End Sub
```

The expression a*(2 + b) is evaluated to 25, and then this value is assigned to the variable *c*.

Incrementing the Value of a Variable

Because the expression on the right side of an assignment statement is evaluated *before* an assignment is made, a statement such as

```
var = var + 1
```

is meaningful. It first evaluates the expression on the right (that is, it adds 1 to the value of the variable *var*) and then assigns this sum to the variable *var*. The effect is to increase the value of the variable *var* by 1. In terms of memory locations, the statement retrieves the value of *var* from *var*'s memory location, uses it to compute *var* + 1, and then places the sum back into *var*'s memory location. This type of calculation is so common that Visual Basic provides a special operator to carry it out. The statement **var = var + 1** can be replaced with the statement

```
var += 1
```

In general, if *n* has a numeric value, then the statement

```
var += n
```

adds *n* to the value of *var*.

Built-In Functions: Math.Sqrt, Int, Math.Round

There are several common operations that we often perform on numbers other than the standard arithmetic operations. For instance, we may take the square root of a number or round a number. These operations are performed by built-in functions. Functions associate with one or more values, called the *input*, a single value called the *output*. The function is said to **return** the output value. The three functions considered here have numeric input and output.

The function Math.Sqrt calculates the square root of a number. The function Int finds the greatest integer less than or equal to a number. Therefore, Int discards the decimal part of positive numbers. The value of Math.Round(*n*, *r*) is the number *n* rounded to *r* decimal places. The parameter *r* can be omitted. If so, *n* is rounded to a whole number. Some examples follow:

Math.Sqrt(9) is 3.	Int(2.7) is 2.	Math.Round(2.7) is 3.
Math.Sqrt(0) is 0.	Int(3) is 3.	Math.Round(2.317, 2) is 2.32.
Math.Sqrt(6.25) is 2.5.	Int(−2.7) is −3.	Math.Round(2.317, 1) is 2.3.

The terms inside the parentheses can be numbers (as shown), numeric variables, or numeric expressions. Expressions are first evaluated to produce the input.

 Example 3   The following program evaluates each of the functions for a specific input given by the value of the variable *n*:

```
Private Sub btnCompute_Click(...) Handles btnCompute.Click
   Dim n As Double
   Dim root As Double
   n = 6.76
   root = Math.Sqrt(n)
   lstResults.Items.Clear()
   lstResults.Items.Add(root)
   lstResults.Items.Add(Int(n))
   lstResults.Items.Add(Math.Round(n, 1))
End Sub
```

[Run, and then click on the *Compute* button. The following is displayed in the list box.]

```
2.6
6
6.8
```

 Example 4   The following program evaluates each of the preceding functions within an expression:

```
Private Sub btnCompute_Click(...) Handles btnCompute.Click
   Dim a As Double
   Dim b As Double
   a = 2
   b = 3
   lstResults.Items.Clear()
   lstResults.Items.Add(Math.Sqrt((5 * b) + 1))
   lstResults.Items.Add(Int((a ^ b) + 0.8))
   lstResults.Items.Add(Math.Round(a / b, 3))
End Sub
```

[Run, and then click on the button. The following is displayed in the list box.]

```
4
8
0.667
```

▓ The Integer Data Type

In this text, we sometimes need to use variables of type Integer. An integer variable is declared with a statement of the form

```
Dim varName As Integer
```

and can be assigned only whole numbers from about −2 billion to 2 billion. Integer variables are commonly used for counting.

▧ Multiple Declarations

Several variables of the same type can be declared with a single Dim statement. For instance, the two Dim statements in Example 2 can be replaced by the single statement

```
Dim a, b As Double
```

Two other types of multiple-declaration statement are

```
Dim a As Double, b As Integer
Dim c As Double = 2, b As Integer = 5
```

▧ Two Integer-Valued Operators

In addition to the five arithmetic operators discussed at the beginning of this section, the **Mod operator** and the **integer division operator (\)** are also useful operators. Let m and n be positive whole numbers. When you use long division to divide m by n, you obtain an integer quotient and an integer remainder. In Visual Basic, $m \setminus n$ is the integer quotient and m Mod n is the integer remainder. For instance,

$14 \setminus 3$ is 4   and   14 Mod 3 is 2
$19 \setminus 5$ is 3   and   19 Mod 5 is 4
$10 \setminus 2$ is 5   and   10 Mod 2 is 0.

Example 5   The following program converts 41 inches to 3 feet and 5 inches.

```
Private Sub btnCompute_Click(...) Handles btnCompute.Click
  Dim totalInches, feet, inches As Integer
  totalInches = 41
  feet = totalInches \ 12
  inches = totalInches Mod 12
  lstResults.Items.Add(feet)
  lstResults.Items.Add(inches)
End Sub
```

[Run, and then click on the button. The following is displayed in the list box.]

```
3
5
```

▧ Parentheses

Parentheses should be used when needed to clarify the meaning of an expression. When there are no parentheses, the arithmetic operations are performed in the order exponentiation, multiplication and ordinary division, integer division, Mod, and addition and subtraction. In the event of a tie, the leftmost operation is carried out first. See Table 3.1. **Note:** If you use parentheses liberally,

TABLE 3.1   **Level of precedence for arithmetic operations.**

()	Inner to outer, left to right
^	Left to right in expression
* /	Left to right in expression
\	Left to right in expression
Mod	Left to right in expression
+ −	Left to right in expression

you will not have to rely on the precedence table for arithmetic operations. For instance, write $(2*3) + 4$ instead of $2*3 + 4$. Write $(2^\wedge 3) + 4$ instead of $2^\wedge 3 + 4$.

Parentheses cannot be used to indicate multiplication, as is commonly done in algebra. For instance, the expression $x(y + z)$ is not valid. It must be written as $x*(y + z)$.

■ Three Types of Errors

Grammatical errors, such as misspellings, omissions, or incorrect punctuations, are called **syntax errors**. Most syntax errors are spotted by the Code Editor when they are entered. The editor underlines the syntax error with a blue squiggly line and displays a description of the error when the mouse cursor is hovered over the squiggly line. Some incorrect statements and their errors are as follows:

Statement	*Reason for Error*
lstBox.Itms.Add(3)	The word Items is misspelled.
lstBox.Items.Add(2+)	The number following the plus sign is missing.
Dim m; n As Integer	The semicolon should be a comma.

Errors that occur while a program is running are called **runtime errors** or **exceptions**. They usually occur because something outside the program, such as a user, database, or hard disk, does not behave as expected. For instance, if the file Data.txt is not in the root folder of the C drive, then a statement that refers to the file by the filespec "C:\Data.txt" will cause the program to stop executing and produce a message box with the title

```
FileNotFoundException was unhandled.
```

Also, a yellow arrow will appear at the left side of the line of code that caused the error. At that point, you should end the program.

A third type of error is called a **logic error**. Such an error occurs when a program does not perform the way it was intended. For instance, the line

```
average = firstNum + secondNum / 2
```

is syntactically correct. However, an incorrect value will be generated, since the correct way to calculate the average is

```
average = (firstNum + second Num) / 2
```

Logic errors are the most difficult type to find. Appendix D discusses debugging tools that can be used to detect and correct logic errors.

■ The Error List Window

Syntax errors are not only indicated in the Code Editor, but also are listed in the Error List window. **Note:** If the window is not visible, click on *Error List* in the *View/Other Windows* menu.

Example 6   The following program contains three errors. **Note:** Line 1 contains the Public Class statement and line 2 is a blank line. Therefore, the Private Sub statement is in line 3 and the Dim statement is in line 4.

```
Private Sub btnCompute_Click(...) Handles btnCompute.Click
    Dim m; n As Double
    lstResults.Items.Add(5
    lstResults.Items.Add(a)
End Sub
```

[Run, click on the button, and click on the *No* button in the error dialog box that appears.]

■ Comments

1. Declaring variables at the beginning of each event procedure is regarded as good programming practice, because it makes programs easier to read and helps prevent certain types of errors.

2. Keywords (reserved words) cannot be used as names of variables. For instance, the statements `Dim private as Double` and `Dim sub As Double` are not valid.

3. Names given to variables are sometimes referred to as *identifiers*.

4. In math courses, *literals* are referred to as *constants*. However, the word "constant" has a special meaning in programming languages.

5. Numeric literals used in expressions or assigned to variables must not contain commas, dollar signs, or percent signs. Also, mixed numbers, such as 8 1/2, are not allowed.

6. Although requesting the square root of a negative number does not terminate the execution of the program, it can produce unexpected results. For instance, the statement

```
lstBox.Items.Add(Math.Sqrt(-1))
```

displays **NaN**. **Note:** NaN is an abbreviation for "Not a Number."

7. If the value of *numVar* is 0 and *numVar* has type Double, then the statements

```
numVarInv = 1 / numVar
lstBox.Items.Add(numVarInv)
lstBox.Items.Add(1 / numVarInv)
```

cause the following items to be displayed in the list box:

```
Infinity
0
```

8. When *n* is halfway between two successive whole numbers (such as 1.5, 2.5, 3.5, and 4.5), then it rounds to the nearest even number. For instance, Math.Round (2.5) is 2 and Math.Round (3.5) is 4.

9. In scientific notation, numbers are written in the form $b \cdot 10^r$, where b is a number of magnitude from 1 up to (but not including) 10, and r is an integer. Visual Basic displays very large numbers in **scientific notation**, where $b \cdot 10^r$ is written as *b*E*r*. (The letter E is an abbreviation for *exponent*.) For instance, when the statement `lstBox.Items.Add(123 * 10 ^ 15)` is executed, 1.23E+17 is displayed in the list box.

10. If the total number of items added to a list box exceeds the number of items that can be displayed, a vertical scroll bar is automatically added to the list box.

11. When you first enter a statement such as `Dim n As Double`, a green squiggle will appear under the variable name and the Error List window will record a warning. The squiggle

merely indicates that the variable has not yet been assigned a value. If the squiggle is still present after the entire event procedure has been entered, this will tell you that the variable was never used and that the declaration statement should be removed.

Practice Problems 3.1

1. Evaluate 2 + 3 * 4.

2. Explain the difference between the assignment statement

   ```
   var1 = var2
   ```

   and the assignment statement

   ```
   var2 = var1
   ```

3. Complete the table by filling in the value of each variable after each line is executed.

	a	b	c
`Private Sub btnEvaluate_Click(...) Handles btnEvaluate.Click`			
`    Dim a, b, c As Double`	0	0	0
`    a = 3`	3	0	0
`    b = 4`	3	4	0
`    c = a + b`			
`    a = c * a`			
`    lstResults.Items.Add(a − b)`			
`    b = b * b`			
`End Sub`			

4. Write a statement that increases the value of the numeric variable *var* by 5%.

EXERCISES 3.1

In Exercises 1 through 6, evaluate the numeric expression without the computer, and then use Visual Basic to check your answer.

1. 3 * 4   2. 7^2

3. $1/(2^3)$ 4. 3 + (4 * 5)

5. (5 − 3) * 4   6. $3 * ((−4)^2)$

In Exercises 7 through 10, evaluate the expression.

7. 7 \ 3   8. 14 Mod 4

9. 7 Mod 3   10. 14 \ 4

In Exercises 11 through 16, determine whether the name is a valid variable name.

11. sales.2008   12. room&Board

13. fOrM_1040   14. 1099MISC

15. expenses?   16. INCOME 2008

In Exercises 17 through 22, evaluate the numeric expression where a = 2, b = 3, and c = 4.

17. (a * b) + c   18. a * (b + c)

19. (1 + b) * c   20. a^c

21. $b^{(c − a)}$ 22. $(a − c)^b$

In Exercises 23 through 28, write an event procedure to calculate and display the value of the expression.

23. $7 \cdot 8 + 5$

24. $(1 + 2 \cdot 9)^3$

25. 5.5% of 20

26. $12 - 4(3 + 5^3)$

27. $17(3 + 162)$

28. $4\ 1/2 - 3\ 5/8$

In Exercises 29 and 30, complete the table by filling in the value of each variable after each line is executed.

29.

	x	y
`Private Sub btnEvaluate Click(...) Handles btnEvaluate.Click`		
`    Dim x, y As Double`		
`    x = 2`		
`    y = 3 * x`		
`    x = y + 5`		
`    lstResults.Items.Clear()`		
`    lstResults.Items.Add(x + 4)`		
`    y = y + 1`		
`End Sub`		

30.

	bal	inter	withDr
`Private Sub btnEvaluate_Click(...) Handles btnEvaluate.Click`			
`    Dim bal, inter, withDr As Double`			
`    bal = 100`			
`    inter = 0.05`			
`    withDr = 25`			
`    bal += inter * bal`			
`    bal = bal - withDr`			
`End Sub`			

In Exercises 31 through 38, determine the output displayed in the list box by the lines of code.

31.
```
Dim amount As Double
amount = 10
lstOutput.Items.Add(amount - 4)
```

32.
```
Dim a, b As Integer
a = 4
b = 5 * a
lstOutput.Items.Add(a + b)
```

33.
```
Dim n As Integer = 8
n += 1
lstOutput.Items.Add(1)
lstOutput.Items.Add(n)
lstOutput.Items.Add(n * 2)
```

34.
```
Dim num As Integer = 5
num = 2 * num
lstOutput.Items.Add(num)
```

35.
```
Dim a, b As Integer
lstOutput.Items.Add(a + 1)
a = 4
b = a * a
lstOutput.Items.Add(a * b)
```

36.
```
Dim tax As Double
tax = 200
tax = 25 + tax
lstOutput.Items.Add(tax)
```

37.
```
Dim totalMinutes, hours, minutes As Integer
totalMinutes = 135
hours = totalMinutes \ 60
minutes = totalMinutes Mod 60
lstResults.Items.Add(hours)
lstResults.Items.Add(minutes)
```

38.
```
Dim totalOunces, pounds, ounces As Integer
totalOunces = 90
pounds = totalOunces \ 16
ounces = totalOunces Mod 16
lstResults.Items.Add(pounds)
lstResults.Items.Add(ounces)
```

In Exercises 39 through 44, identify the errors.

39.
```
Dim a, b, c As Double
a = 2
b = 3
a + b = c
lstOutput.Items.Add(c)
```

40.
```
Dim a, b, c, d As Double
a = 2
b = 3
c = d = 4
lstOutput.Items.Add(5((a + b) / (c + d))
```

41.
```
Dim balance, deposit As Double
balance = 1,234
deposit = $100
lstOutput.Items.Add(balance + deposit)
```

42.
```
Dim interest, balance As Double
0.05 = interest
balance = 800
lstOutput.Items.Add(interest * balance)
```

43.
```
Dim 6X As Double
6X = 2(9W)
lstOutput.Items.Add(9W)
```

44.
```
Dim n As Double = 1.2345
lstOutput.Items.Add(Round(n, 2))
```

In Exercises 45 and 46, rewrite the code using one line.

45. `Dim quantity As Integer`
    `quantity = 12`

46. `Dim m As Integer`
    `Dim n As Double`
    `m = 2`
    `n = 3`

In Exercises 47 through 52, find the value of the given function.

47. Int(10.75)   48. Int(9 − 2)   49. Math.Sqrt(3*12)

50. Math.Sqrt(64)   51. Math.Round(3.1279, 3) 52. Math.Round(−2.6)

In Exercises 53 through 58, find the value of the given function where *a* and *b* are numeric variables of type Double, *a* = 5 and *b* = 3.

53. Int(−a/2)   54. Math.Round(a / b)   55. Math.Sqrt(a − 5)

56. Math.Sqrt(4 + a)   57. Math.Round(a + .5)   58. Int(b*0.5)

In Exercises 59 through 66, write an event procedure with the header `Private Sub btnCompute_Click(...) Handles btnCompute.Click`**, and having one line for each step. Lines that display data should use the given variable names.**

59. The following steps calculate a company's profit:

   (a) Declare all variables as type Double.
   (b) Assign the value 98456 to the variable *revenue*.
   (c) Assign the value 45000 to the variable *costs*.
   (d) Assign the difference between the variables *revenue* and *costs* to the variable *profit*.
   (e) Display the value of the variable *profit* in a list box.

60. The following steps calculate the amount of a stock purchase:

   (a) Declare all variables as type Double.
   (b) Assign the value 25.625 to the variable *costPerShare*.
   (c) Assign the value 400 to the variable *numberOfShares*.
   (d) Assign the product of *costPerShare* and *numberOfShares* to the variable *amount*.
   (e) Display the value of the variable *amount* in a list box.

61. The following steps calculate the price of an item after a 30% reduction:

   (a) Declare all variables as type Double.
   (b) Assign the value 19.95 to the variable *price*.
   (c) Assign the value 30 to the variable *discountPercent*.
   (d) Assign the value of (*discountPercent* divided by 100) times *price* to the variable *markdown*.
   (e) Decrease *price* by *markdown*.
   (f) Display the value of *price* (rounded to two decimal places) in a list box.

62. The following steps calculate a company's break-even point, the number of units of goods the company must manufacture and sell in order to break even:

   (a) Declare all variables as type Double.
   (b) Assign the value 5000 to the variable *fixedCosts*.
   (c) Assign the value 8 to the variable *pricePerUnit*.
   (d) Assign the value 6 to the variable *costPerUnit*.

(e) Assign the value *fixedCosts* divided by (the difference of *pricePerUnit* and *costPerUnit*) to the variable *breakEvenPoint*.

(f) Display the value of the variable *breakEvenPoint* in a list box.

63. The following steps calculate the balance after three years when $100 is deposited in a savings account at 5% interest compounded annually:

(a) Declare all variables as type Double.
(b) Assign the value 100 to the variable *balance*.
(c) Increase the variable *balance* by 5% of its value.
(d) Increase the variable *balance* by 5% of its value.
(e) Increase the variable *balance* by 5% of its value.
(f) Display the value of *balance* (rounded to two decimal places) in a list box.

64. The following steps calculate the balance at the end of three years when $100 is deposited at the beginning of each year in a savings account at 5% interest compounded annually:

(a) Declare all variables as type Double.
(b) Assign the value 100 to the variable *balance*.
(c) Increase the variable *balance* by 5% of its value, and add 100.
(d) Increase the variable *balance* by 5% of its value, and add 100.
(e) Increase the variable *balance* by 5% of its value.
(f) Display the value of *balance* (rounded to two decimal places) in a list box.

65. The following steps calculate the balance after 10 years when $100 is deposited in a savings account at 5% interest compounded annually:

(a) Declare all variables as type Double.
(b) Assign the value 100 to the variable *balance*.
(c) Multiply the variable *balance* by 1.05 raised to the 10th power.
(d) Display the value of *balance* (rounded to two decimal places) in a list box.

66. The following steps calculate the percentage profit from the sale of a stock:

(a) Declare all variables as type Double.
(b) Assign the value 10 to the variable *purchasePrice*.
(c) Assign the value 15 to the variable *sellingPrice*.
(d) Assign, to the variable *percentProfit*, 100 times the value of the difference between *sellingPrice* and *purchasePrice* divided by *purchasePrice*.
(e) Display the value of the variable *percentProfit* in a list box.

In Exercises 67 through 72, write a program to solve the problem and display the answer in a list box. The program should use variables for each of the quantities.

67. Suppose each acre of farmland produces 18 tons of corn. How many tons of corn can be produced on a 30-acre farm?

68. Suppose a ball is thrown straight up in the air with an initial velocity of 50 feet per second and an initial height of 5 feet. How high will the ball be after 3 seconds?

   Note: The height after t seconds is given by the expression $-16t^2 + v_0t + h_0$, where v_0 is the initial velocity and h_0 is the initial height.

69. If a car left Washington, D.C., at 2 o'clock and arrived in New York at 7 o'clock, what was its average speed? **Note:** New York is 233 miles from Washington.

70. A motorist wants to determine her gas mileage. At 23,352 miles (on the odometer) the tank is filled. At 23,695 miles the tank is filled again with 14 gallons. How many miles per gallon did the car average between the two fillings?

71. A U.S. geological survey showed that Americans use an average of 1600 gallons of water per person per day, including industrial use. How many gallons of water are used each year in the United States? **Note:** The current population of the United States is about 315 million people.

72. According to FHA specifications, each room in a house should have a window area equal to at least 10% of the floor area of the room. What is the minimum window area for a 18-ft by 20-ft room?

Solutions to Practice Problem 3.1

1. 14. Multiplications are performed before additions. If the intent is for the addition to be performed first, the expression should be written (2 + 3)*4.

2. The first assignment statement assigns the value of the variable *var2* to the variable *var1*, whereas the second assignment statement assigns *var1*'s value to *var2*.

3.

	a	b	c
`Private Sub btnEvaluate_Click(...) Handles` `    btnEvaluate.Click`			
`  Dim a, b, c As Double`	0	0	0
`  a = 3`	3	0	0
`  b = 4`	3	4	0
`  c = a + b`	3	4	7
`  a = c * a`	21	4	7
`  lstResults.Items.Add(a − b)`	21	4	7
`  b = b * b`	21	16	7
`End Sub`			

Each time an assignment statement is executed, only one variable (the variable to the left of the equal sign) has its value changed.

4. Each of the three following statements increases the value of *var* by 5%.

```
var = var + (0.05 * var)
var = 1.05 * var
var += 0.05 * var
```

3.2   Strings

The most common types of data processed by Visual Basic are numbers and strings. Sentences, phrases, words, letters of the alphabet, names, telephone numbers, addresses, and social security numbers are all examples of strings. Formally, a **string literal** is a sequence of characters that is treated as a single item. String literals can be assigned to variables, displayed in text boxes and list boxes, and combined by an operation called concatenation (denoted by &).

▪ Variables and Strings

VideoNote

Strings

A **string variable** is a name used to refer to a string. The allowable names of string variables are the same as those of numeric variables. The value of a string variable is assigned or altered with assignment statements and displayed in a list box like the value of a numeric variable. String variables are declared with statements of the form

```
Dim varName As String
```

Example 1   The following program shows how assignment statements and the Add method are used with strings. The string variable *president* is assigned a value by the third line, and this value is displayed by the sixth line. The quotation marks surrounding each string literal are not part of the literal and are not displayed by the Add method. (The form for this example contains a button and a list box.) **Note:** The Code Editor colors string literals red.

```
Private Sub btnDisplay_Click(...) Handles btnDisplay.Click
  Dim president As String
  president = "George Washington"
  lstOutput.Items.Clear()
  lstOutput.Items.Add("president")
  lstOutput.Items.Add(president)
End Sub
```

[Run, and then click on the button. The following is displayed in the list box.]

```
president
George Washington
```

If $x, y, \ldots, z$ are characters and *strVar* is a string variable, then the statement

```
strVar = "xy...z"
```

assigns the string literal $xy \ldots z$ to the variable and the statement

```
lstBox.Items.Add("xy...z")
```

or

```
lstBox.Items.Add(strVar)
```

displays the string $xy \ldots z$ in a list box. If *strVar2* is another string variable, then the statement

```
strVar2 = strVar
```

assigns the value of the variable *strVar* to the variable *strVar2*. (The value of *strVar* will remain the same.) String literals used in assignment or lstBox.Items.Add statements must be surrounded by quotation marks, but string variables are never surrounded by quotation marks.

■ Option Explicit and Option Strict

Option Explicit and **Option Strict** both affect programming. Throughout this book, we assume that both options are in effect. Having them enabled is considered good programming practice. Option Explicit requires that all variables be declared with Dim statements. The disabling of this option can lead to errors resulting from the misspelling of names of variables. Option Strict requires explicit conversions in most cases where a value or variable of one type is assigned to a variable of another type. The absence of this option can lead to data loss.

Visual Basic provides a way to enforce Option Explicit and Option Strict for all programs you create. Click on *Options* in the menu bar's *Tools* menu to open the Options dialog box. In the left pane, click on the symbol (⊞ or ▷) to the left of Projects and Solutions to expand that entry. Then click on the subentry VB Defaults. Four default project settings will appear on the right. (See Fig. 3.1.) If the settings for Option Explicit and Object Strict are not already set to On, change them to On. **Note:** Option Infer is discussed in Chapter 6.

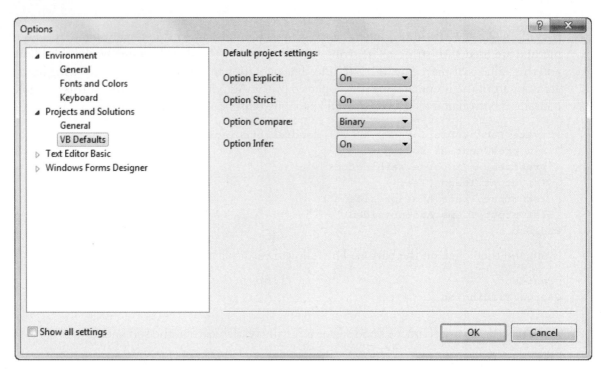

FIGURE 3.1   **Option default project settings.**

▥ Using Text Boxes for Input and Output

The content of a text box is always a string. Therefore, statements such as

```
strVar = txtBox.Text
```

and

```
txtBox.Text = strVar
```

can be used to assign the contents of the text box to the string variable *strVar* and vice versa.

Numbers typed into text boxes are stored as strings. With Option Strict set to On, such strings must be explicitly converted to numeric values before they can be assigned to numeric variables or used in numeric expressions. The functions CDbl and CInt convert strings representing numbers into numbers of type Double and Integer, respectively. Going in the other direction, the function CStr converts a number into a string representation of the number. Therefore, statements such as

```
dblVar = CDbl(txtBox.Text)
```

and

```
txtBox.Text = CStr(dblVar)
```

can be used to assign the contents of a text box to the double variable *dblVar* and vice versa. CDbl, CInt, and CStr, which stand for "convert to Double," "convert to Integer," and "convert to String," are referred to as **data conversion** or **typecasting functions**.

Example 2 The following program adds two numbers supplied by the user.

OBJECT	PROPERTY	SETTING
frmAdd	Text	Addition
lblFirstNum	AutoSize	False
	Text	First number:
txtFirstNum		
lblSecondNum	AutoSize	False
	Text	Second number:
txtSecondNum		
btnCompute	Text	Compute Sum
lblSum	Text	Sum:
txtSum	ReadOnly	True

```
Private Sub btnCompute_Click(...) Handles btnCompute.Click
  Dim num1, num2, sum As Double
  num1 = CDbl(txtFirstNum.Text)
  num2 = CDbl(txtSecondNum.Text)
  sum = num1 + num2
  txtSum.Text = CStr(sum)
End Sub
```

[Run, type 45 into the first text box, type 55 into the second text box, and click on the button.]

■ Auto Correction

The **Auto Correction** feature of IntelliSense suggests corrections when errors occur and allows you to select a correction to be applied to the code. When an invalid statement is entered, a blue squiggly error line appears under the incorrect part of the statement. If the squiggly line has a short red line segment at its right end, the Auto Correction feature is available for the error. When you hover the cursor over the squiggly line, a small Error Correction Options box (🛈 ▾) appears. Clicking on the small box produces an Auto Correction helper box that describes the error and makes a suggestion for fixing it. Figure 3.2 shows a typical Auto Correction helper box for a data-type-conversion error. If you click on the line beginning "Replace," the change will be made for you.

FIGURE 3.2 **An Auto Correction helper box.**

▓ Concatenation

Two strings can be combined to form a new string consisting of the strings joined together. The joining operation is called **concatenation** and is represented by an ampersand (&). For instance, "good" & "bye" is "goodbye". A combination of strings and ampersands that can be evaluated to form a string is called a **string expression**. The assignment statement and the Add method evaluate expressions before assigning them or displaying them.

 Example 3 The following program illustrates concatenation. (The form for this example contains a button and a text box.) Notice the space at the end of the string assigned to *quote1*. If that space weren't present, then the statement that assigns a value to *quote* would have to be `quote = quote1 & " " & quote2`.

```
Private Sub btnDisplay_Click(...) Handles btnDisplay.Click
  Dim quote1, quote2, quote As String
  quote1 = "The ballgame isn't over, "
  quote2 = "until it's over."
  quote = quote1 & quote2
  txtOutput.Text = quote & "   Yogi Berra"
End Sub
```

[Run, and then click on the button. The following is displayed in the text box.]

```
The ball game isn't over, until it's over.   Yogi Berra
```

Visual Basic also allows strings to be concatenated with numbers and allows numbers to be concatenated with numbers. In each case, the result is a string.

 Example 4 The following program concatenates a string with a number. Notice that a space was inserted after the word "has" and before the word "keys." (The form for this example contains a button and a text box.)

```
Private Sub btnDisplay_Click(...) Handles btnDisplay.Click
  Dim str As String, numOfKeys As Integer
  str = "The piano keyboard has "
  numOfKeys = 88
  txtOutput.Text = str & numOfKeys & " keys."
End Sub
```

[Run, and then click on the button. The following is displayed in the text box.]

```
The piano keyboard has 88 keys.
```

The statement

```
strVar = strVar & strVar2
```

will append the value of *strVar2* to the end of the current value of *strVar*. The same result can be accomplished with the statement

```
strVar &= strVar2
```

▨ String Properties and Methods: Length Property and ToUpper, ToLower, Trim, IndexOf, and Substring Methods

We have seen that controls, such as text and list boxes, have properties and methods. A control placed on a form is an example of an object. A string is also an object, and, like a control, has both properties and methods that are specified by following the string with a period and the name of the property or method. The Length property gives the number of characters in a string. The ToUpper and ToLower methods convert a string to uppercase and lowercase characters. The Trim method deletes all leading and trailing spaces from a string. The Substring method extracts a sequence of consecutive characters from a string. The IndexOf method searches for the first occurrence of one string in another and gives the position at which the first occurrence is found.

If *str* is a string, then

```
str.Length
```

is the number of characters in the string,

```
str.ToUpper
```

is the string with all its letters capitalized,

```
str.ToLower
```

is the string with all its letters in lowercase, and

```
str.Trim
```

is the string with all spaces removed from the front and back of the string. For instance,

```
"Visual".Length is 6.             "Visual".ToUpper is VISUAL.
"123 Hike".Length is 8.           "123 Hike".ToLower is 123 hike.
"a" & "  bcd  ".Trim & "efg" is abcdefg.
```

In Visual Basic, the **position** of a character in a string is identified with one of the numbers 0, 1, 2, 3, ... (In this textbook we will see several instances of enumeration beginning with 0 instead of 1.) A **substring** of a string is a sequence of consecutive characters from the string. For instance, consider the string "Just a moment". The substrings "Jus", "mom", and "nt" begin at positions 0, 7, and 11, respectively.

If *str* is a string, then

```
str.Substring(m, n)
```

is the substring of *str* consisting of *n* characters beginning with the character in position *m* of *str*. If the comma and the number *n* are omitted, then the substring starts at position *m* and continues until the end of *str*. The value of

```
str.IndexOf(str2)
```

is −1 if *str2* is not a substring of *str*; otherwise it is the beginning position of the first occurrence of *str2* in *str*. Some examples using these two methods are as follows:

```
"fanatic".Substring(0, 3) is "fan".        "fanatic".IndexOf("ati") is 3.
"fanatic".Substring(4, 2) is "ti".         "fanatic".IndexOf("a") is 1.
"fanatic".Substring(4) is "tic".           "fanatic".IndexOf("nt") is −1.
```

The IndexOf method has a useful extension. The value of `str.IndexOf(str2,n)`, where *n* is an integer, is the position of the first occurrence of *str2* in *str* in position *n* or greater. For instance, the value of `"Mississippi".IndexOf("ss",3)` is 5.

Like the numeric functions discussed before, string properties and methods also can be applied to variables and expressions.

 Example 5　The following program uses variables and expressions with the property and methods just discussed.

```
Private Sub btnEvaluate_Click(...) Handles btnEvaluate.Click
  Dim str1, str2, str3 As String
  str1 = "Quick as "
  str2 = "a wink"
  lstResults.Items.Clear()
  lstResults.Items.Add(str1.Substring(0, 7))
  lstResults.Items.Add(str1.IndexOf("c"))
  lstResults.Items.Add(str1.Substring(0, 3))
  lstResults.Items.Add((str1 & str2).Substring(6, 6))
  lstResults.Items.Add((str1 & str2).ToUpper)
  lstResults.Items.Add(str1.Trim & str2)
  str3 = str2.Substring(str2.Length − 4)
  lstResults.Items.Add("The average " & str3 & " lasts .1 second.")
End Sub
```

[Run, and then click on the button. The following is displayed in the list box.]

```
Quick a
3
Qui
as a w
QUICK AS A WINK
Quick asa wink
The average wink lasts .1 second.
```

Note: In Example 5, *c* is in the third position of *str1*, and there are three characters of *str1* to the left of *c*. In general, there are *n* characters to the left of the character in position *n*. This fact is used in Example 6.

 Example 6　The following program parses a name. The fifth line locates the position, call it *n*, of the space separating the two names. The first name will contain *n* characters, and the last name will consist of all characters to the right of the *n*th character.

```
Private Sub btnAnalyze_Click(...) Handles btnAnalyze.Click
  Dim fullName, firstName, lastName As String
  Dim m, n As Integer
  fullName = txtName.Text
```

```
    n = fullName.IndexOf(" ")
    firstName = fullName.Substring(0, n)
    lastName = fullName.Substring(n + 1)
    m = lastName.Length
    lstResults.Items.Clear()
    lstResults.Items.Add("First name: " & firstName)
    lstResults.Items.Add("Your last name has " & m & " letters.")
End Sub
```

[Run, type "John Doe" into the text box, and then click on the button.]

The Empty String

The string **""**, which contains no characters, is called the **empty string** or the **zero-length string**. It is different from **" "**, the string consisting of a single space.

The statement **lstBox.Items.Add("")** inserts a blank line into the list box. The contents of a text box can be cleared with either the statement

```
txtBox.Clear()
```

or the statement

```
txtBox.Text = ""
```

Initial Value of a String

When a string variable is declared with a Dim statement, it has the keyword Nothing as its default value. To specify a different initial value, follow the declaration statement with an equal sign followed by the initial value. For instance, the statement

```
Dim pres As String = "Adams"
```

declares the variable *pres* to be of type String and assigns it the initial value "Adams".

An error occurs whenever an attempt is made to access a property or method for a string variable having the value Nothing or to display it in a list box. Therefore, unless a string variable is guaranteed to be assigned a value before being used, you should initialize it—even if you just assign the empty string to it.

Widening and Narrowing

The assignment of a value or variable of type Double to a variable of type Integer is called **narrowing** because the possible values of an Integer variable are a subset of the possible values of a Double variable. For the same reason, assigning in the reverse direction is called **widening**. Option Strict requires the use of a conversion function when narrowing, but allows widening without a conversion function. Specifically, a widening statement of the form

VideoNote
Widening
and
narrowing,
scope

```
dblVar = intVar
```

is valid. However, a narrowing statement of the form

```
intVar = dblVar
```

is not valid. It must be replaced with

```
intVar = CInt(dblVar)
```

Great care must be taken when computing with Integer variables. For instance, the value of an expression involving division or exponentiation has type Double and therefore cannot be assigned to an Integer variable without explicit conversion even if the value is a whole number. For instance, Option Strict makes each of the following two assignment statements invalid.

```
Dim m As Integer
m = 2 ^ 3
m = 6 / 2
```

In order to avoid such errors, we primarily use variables of type Integer for counting or identifying positions.

■ Internal Documentation

Program documentation is the inclusion of **comments** that specify the intent of the program, the purpose of the variables, and the tasks performed by individual portions of the program. To create a comment statement, begin the line with an apostrophe. Such a statement appears green on the screen and is completely ignored when the program is executed. Comments are sometimes called **remarks**. A line of code can be documented by adding an apostrophe, followed by the desired information, after the end of the line. The *Comment Out* button (▤) and the *Uncomment* button (⤺) on the Toolbar can be used to comment and uncomment selected blocks of code.

 Example 7 The following rewrite of Example 6 uses internal documentation. The first comment describes the entire program, the comment in line 5 gives the meaning of the variable, and the final comment describes the purpose of the three lines that follow it.

```
Private Sub btnAnalyze_Click(...) Handles btnAnalyze.Click
  'Determine a person's first name and the length of the second name
  Dim fullName, firstName, lastName As String
  Dim m As Integer
  Dim n As Integer    'location of the space separating the two names
  fullName = txtName.Text
  n = fullName.IndexOf(" ")
  firstName = fullName.Substring(0, n)
  lastName = fullName.Substring(n + 1)
  m = lastName.Length
  'Display the desired information in a list box
  lstResults.Items.Clear()
  lstResults.Items.Add("First name: " & firstName)
  lstResults.Items.Add("Your last name has " & m & " letters.")
End Sub
```

Some of the benefits of documentation are as follows:

1. Other people can easily understand the program.

2. You can understand the program when you read it later.

3. Long programs are easier to read because the purposes of individual pieces can be determined at a glance.

Good programming practice dictates that programmers document their code at the same time that they are writing it. In fact, many software companies require a certain level of documentation before they release a version, and some judge a programmer's performance on how well their code is documented.

■ Line Continuation

Thousands of characters can be typed in a line of code. If you use a statement with more characters than can fit in the window, Visual Basic scrolls the Code Editor toward the right as needed. However, most programmers prefer having lines that are no longer than the width of the Code Editor. A long statement can be split across two or more lines by ending each line (except the last) with an underscore character (_) preceded by a space. For instance, the line

```
Dim quotation As String = "Good code is its own best documentation."
```

can be written as

```
Dim quotation As String = "Good code is its own " & _
                "best documentation."
```

A new-to-VB2010 feature called **implicit line continuation** allows underscore characters to be omitted from the end of a line that obviously has a continuation—for instance, a line that ends with an ampersand, an arithmetic operator, or a comma. We use this feature throughout this textbook. For example, the line above will be written

```
Dim quotation As String = "Good code is its own " &
                "best documentation."
```

Line continuation, with or without an underscore character, cannot be used inside a pair of quotation marks. Whenever you want to display a literal string on two lines of the screen, you must first break it into two shorter strings joined with an ampersand. IntelliSense is extremely dependable in letting you know if you have broken a line improperly.

Line continuation, with or without an underscore character, does not work with comment statements. Therefore, each line of a comment statement must begin with its own apostrophe.

■ Scope of a Variable

When a variable is declared in an event procedure with a Dim statement, a portion of memory is set aside to hold the value of the variable. As soon as the End Sub statement for the procedure is reached, the memory location is freed up; that is, the variable ceases to exist. The variable is said to be **local** to the procedure or to have **local scope**. In general, the **scope** of a variable is the portion of the program that can refer to it.

When variables of the same name are declared with Dim statements in two different event procedures, Visual Basic gives them separate memory locations and treats them as two different variables. A value assigned to a variable in one procedure will not affect the value of the identically named variable in the other procedure.

Visual Basic provides a way to make a variable recognized by every procedure in a form's code. Such a variable is called a **class-level variable** and is said to have **class-level scope**. The

Dim statement for a class-level variable can be placed anywhere between the statements `Public Class formName` and `End Class`, provided that the Dim statement is not inside an event procedure. Normally, we place the `Dim` statement just after the `Public Class formName` statement. (We refer to this region as the **Declarations section** of the Code Editor.) When a class-level variable has its value changed by a procedure, the value persists even after the procedure has finished executing. If an event procedure declares a local variable with the same name as a class-level variable, then the name refers to the local variable for code inside the procedure.

 Example 8   The following program uses a class-level variable to keep track of the number of times a button has been clicked.

```
Public Class frmCount
  Dim numTimes As Integer = 0     'Class-level variable
  Private Sub btnPushMe_Click(...) Handles btnPushMe.Click
    numTimes += 1
    txtOutput.Text = "The button has been clicked " &
                      numTimes & " times."
  End Sub
End Class
```

[Run, and click on the button three times.]

■ Comments

1. From the Code Editor, you can determine the type of a variable by letting the mouse pointer hover over the variable name until a tooltip giving the type appears. This feature of IntelliSense is called **Quick Info**.

2. Variable names should describe the role of the variable. Also, some programmers use a prefix, such as *dbl* or *str*, to identify the type of a variable. For example, they would use names like *dblInterestRate* and *strFirstName*. This naming convention is not needed in Visual Basic for the reason mentioned in Comment 1, and is no longer recommended by Microsoft.

3. The functions CInt and CDbl are user friendly. If the user types a number into a text box and precedes it with a dollar sign or inserts commas as separators, the values of CInt(txtBox.Text) and CDbl(txtBox.Text) will be the number with the dollar sign and/or commas removed.

4. The Trim method is useful when reading data from a text box. Sometimes users type spaces at the end of the input. Unless the spaces are removed, they can cause havoc elsewhere in the program.

5. There are several alternatives to CStr for casting a value to a string value. For instance, the statement

```
strVar = CStr(dblVar)
```

can be replaced with any of the following statements:

```
strVar = CType(dblVar, String)
strVar = Convert.ToString(dblVar)
strVar = dblVar.ToString
```

Some alternatives to the use of CInt and CDbl are

```
dblVar = CType(strVar, Double)
intVar = CType(strVar, Integer)
intVar = CType(dblVar, Integer)
intVar = Integer.Parse(strVar)
dblVar = Double.Parse(strVar)
dblVar = Convert.ToDouble(strVar)
intVar = Convert.ToInt32(strVar)
intVar = Convert.ToInt32(dblVar)
```

These alternatives are common to all the Visual Studio languages and therefore are preferred by advanced programmers. We have decided to use CStr, CDbl, and CInt for the following two reasons:

(a) These functions make statements less cluttered, and therefore easier for beginning programmers to read.

(b) When an incorrect conversion is detected by the Code Editor, the Auto Correction helper box recommends and implements the use of the CStr, CDbl, and CInt functions.

Practice Problems 3.2

1. What is the value of "Computer".IndexOf("E")?

2. What is the difference in the output produced by the following two statements? Why is CStr used in the first statement, but not in the second?

```
txtBox.Text = CStr(8 + 8)
txtBox.Text = 8 & 8
```

3. Give an example of a prohibited statement that invokes an Auto Correction helper box with the heading "Option Strict On disallows implicit conversion from 'String' to 'Double'." Also, give the suggestion for fixing the error.

EXERCISES 3.2

In Exercises 1 through 26, determine the output displayed in the text box or list box by the lines of code.

1. ```
txtBox.Text = "Visual Basic"
```

2. ```
lstBox.Items.Add("Hello")
```

3. ```
Dim var As String
var = "Ernie"
lstBox.Items.Add(var)
```

4. ```
Dim var As String
var = "Bert"
txtBox.Text = var
```

5. ```
txtBox.Text = "f" & "lute"
```

6. ```
lstBox.Items.Add("a" & "cute")
```

7. ```
Dim var As Double
var = 123
txtBox.Text = CStr(var)
```

8. ```
Dim var As Double
var = 5
txtBox.Text = CStr(var + 6)
```

9. ```
txtBox.Text = "Your age is " & 21 & "."
```

10. ```
txtBox.Text = "Fred has " & 2 & " children."
```

11. ```
Dim r, b As String
r = "A ROSE"
b = " IS "
txtBox.Text = r & b & r & b & r
```

12. ```
Dim s As String, n As Integer
s = "trombones"
n = 76
txtBox.Text = n & " " & s
```

13. ```
Dim num As Double
txtBox.Text = "5"
num = 0.5 + CDbl(txtBox.Text)
txtBox.Text = CStr(num)
```

14. ```
Dim num As Integer = 2
txtBox.Text = CStr(num)
txtBox.Text = CStr(1 + CInt(txtBox.Text))
```

15. ```
txtBox.Text = "good"
txtBox.Text &= "bye"
```

16. ```
Dim var As String = "eight"
var &= "h"
txtBox.Text = var
```

17. ```
Dim var1 As String = "WALLA"
Dim var2 As String = "BINGBANG"
var1 &= var1
txtBox.Text = var & var2
```

18. ```
txtBox.Text = "mur"
txtBox.Text &= txtBox.Text
```

19. ```
lstBox.Items.Add("aBc".ToUpper)
lstBox.Items.Add("Wallless".IndexOf("lll"))
lstBox.Items.Add("five".Length)
lstBox.Items.Add(" 55 ".Trim & " mph")
lstBox.Items.Add("UNDERSTUDY".Substring(5, 3))
```

20. ```
lstBox.Items.Add("8 Ball".ToLower)
lstBox.Items.Add("colonel".IndexOf("k"))
lstBox.Items.Add("23.45".Length)
lstBox.Items.Add("revolutionary".Substring(1))
lstBox.Items.Add("whippersnapper".IndexOf("pp", 5))
```

21. ```
Dim a As Integer = 4
Dim b As Integer = 2
Dim c As String = "Municipality"
```
```

```
    Dim d As String = "pal"
    lstBox.Items.Add(c.Length)
    lstBox.Items.Add(c.ToUpper)
    lstBox.Items.Add(c.Substring(a, b) & c.Substring(5 * b))
    lstBox.Items.Add(c.IndexOf(d))
```

22. ```
    Dim m As Integer = 4
    Dim n As Integer = 3
    Dim s As String = "Microsoft"
    Dim t As String = "soft"
    lstOutput.Items.Add(s.Length)
    lstOutput.Items.Add(s.ToLower)
    lstOutput.Items.Add(s.Substring(m, n − 1))
    lstOutput.Items.Add(s.IndexOf(t))
    ```

23. How many positions does a string of eight characters have?

24. What is the highest numbered position for a string of nine characters?

25. (True or False) If *n* is the length of *str*, then `str.Substring(n − 1)` is the string consisting of the last character of *str*.

26. (True or False) If *n* is the length of *str*, then `str.Substring(n − 2)` is the string consisting of the last two characters of *str*.

In Exercises 27 through 32, identify any errors.

27. ```
    Dim phoneNumber As Double
    phoneNumber = "234-5678"
    txtBox.Text = "My phone number is " & phoneNumber
    ```

28. ```
    Dim quote As String
    quote = I came to Casablanca for the waters.
    txtBox.Text = quote & ": " & "Bogart"
    ```

29. ```
    Dim end As String
    end = "happily ever after."
    txtBox.Text = "They lived " & end
    ```

30. ```
    Dim hiyo As String
    hiyo = "Silver"
    txtBox = "Hi-Yo " & hiYo
    ```

31. ```
    Dim num As Double = 1492
    txtBox.Text = CStr(num.IndexOf("2"))
    ```

32. ```
    Dim num As Integer = 45
    txtBox.Text = CStr(num.Length)
    ```

In Exercises 33 through 36, write an event procedure with the header `Private Sub btnCompute_Click(...) Handles btnCompute.Click`, and having one line for each step. Display each result by assigning it to the txtOutput.Text property. Lines that display data should use the given variable names.

33. The following steps give the name and birth year of a famous inventor:
    (a) Declare all variables used in steps (b)–(e).
    (b) Assign "Thomas" to the variable *firstName*.
    (c) Assign "Alva" to the variable *middleName*.
    (d) Assign "Edison" to the variable *lastName*.
    (e) Assign 1847 to the variable *yearOfBirth*.
    (f) Display the inventor's full name followed by a comma and his year of birth.
    ```

34. The following steps compute the price of ketchup:

    (a) Declare all variables used in steps (b)–(d).
    (b) Assign "ketchup" to the variable *item*.
    (c) Assign 2.29 to the variable *regularPrice*.
    (d) Assign .23 to the variable *discount*.
    (e) Display the phrase "2.06 is the sale price of ketchup."

35. The following steps display a copyright statement:

    (a) Declare the variable used in step (b).
    (b) Assign "Prentice Hall, Inc." to the variable *publisher*.
    (c) Display the phrase "(c) Prentice Hall, Inc."

36. The following steps give advice:

    (a) Declare the variable used in step (b).
    (b) Assign "Fore" to the variable *prefix*.
    (c) Display the phrase "Forewarned is Forearmed."

In Exercises 37 and 38, write a line of code to carry out the task. Specify where in the program the line of code should be placed.

37. Declare the variable *str* as a string variable visible to all parts of the program.

38. Declare the variable *strItem* as a string variable visible only to the btnCalculate_Click event procedure.

In Exercises 39 through 42, the interface is specified. Write a program to carry out the stated task.

39. If *n* is the number of seconds between lightning and thunder, the storm is *n*/5 miles away. Write a program that reads the number of seconds between lightning and thunder and reports the distance of the storm. A sample run is shown in Fig. 3.3.

FIGURE 3.3   Sample output of Exercise 39.   FIGURE 3.4   Sample output of Exercise 40.

40. The American College of Sports Medicine recommends that you maintain your *training heart rate* during an aerobic workout. Your training heart rate is computed as .7*(220 − a) + .3*r, where *a is* your age and *r is* your resting heart rate (your pulse when you first awaken). Write a program to read a person's age and resting heart rate and display the training heart rate. (Determine *your* training heart rate.) A sample run is shown in Fig. 3.4.

41. The number of calories burned per hour by cycling, running, and swimming are 200, 475, and 275, respectively. A person loses 1 pound of weight for each 3500 calories burned.

Write code to read the number of hours spent at each activity and then display the number of pounds worked off. A sample run is shown in Fig. 3.5.

FIGURE 3.5 Sample output of Exercise 41.

FIGURE 3.6 Sample output of Exercise 42.

42. Write code to read the name of a baseball team, the number of games won, and the number of games lost, and display the name of the team and the percentage of games won. A sample run is shown in Fig. 3.6.

In Exercises 43 through 48, write a program to carry out the task. The program should use variables for each of the quantities and display the outcome in a text box with a label as in Example 2.

43. Request a company's annual revenue and expenses as input, and display the company's net income (revenue minus expenses). (Test the program with the amounts $550,000 and $410,000.)

44. Request a company's earnings-per-share for the year and the price of one share of stock as input, and then display the company's price-to-earnings ratio (that is, price/earnings). (Test the program with the amounts $5.25 and $68.25.)

45. Calculate the amount of a waiter's tip, given the amount of the bill and the percentage tip as input. (Test the program with $20 and 15 percent.)

46. Convert a percentage to a decimal. For instance, if the user enters 125% into a text box, then the output should be 1.25.

47. Write a program that contains a button and a read-only text box on the form, with the text box initially containing 100. Each time the button is clicked on, the number in the text box should decrease by 1.

48. Write a program that requests a (complete) phone number in a text box and then displays the area code in another text box when a button is clicked on.

49. Write a program that requests a sentence, a word in the sentence, and another word and then displays the sentence with the first word replaced by the second. For example, if the user responds by typing "What you don't know won't hurt you." into the first text box and *know* and *owe* into the second and third text boxes, then the message "What you don't owe won't hurt you." is displayed.

50. Write a program that requests a letter, converts it to uppercase, and gives its first position in the sentence "THE QUICK BROWN FOX JUMPS OVER A LAZY DOG." For example, if the user responds by typing *b* into the text box, then the message "B first occurs in position 10." is displayed.

51. The formula $s = \sqrt{24d}$ gives an estimate of the speed in miles per hour of a car that skidded d feet on dry concrete when the brakes were applied. Write a program that requests the

distance skidded and then displays the estimated speed of the car. (Try the program for a car that skids 54 feet.)

52. Write a program that requests a positive number containing a decimal point as input and then displays the number of digits to the left of the decimal point and the number of digits to the right of the decimal point.

53. Write a program that allows scores to be input one at a time, and then displays the average of the scores upon request. (See Fig. 3.7.) The user should type a score into the top text box and then click on the *Record* button. This process can be repeated as many times as desired. At any time the user should be able to click on the *Calculate* button to display the average of all the scores that were entered so far. **Note:** This program requires two class-level variables.

FIGURE 3.7 **Sample output of Exercise 53.**

FIGURE 3.8 **Sample output of Exercise 54.**

54. Write a program that allows furniture sales (item and price) to be displayed in a list box one at a time, and then shows the total commission of the sales (6%) upon request. (See Fig. 3.8.) The user should type each item and price into the text boxes and then click on the *Display* button. This process can be repeated as many times as desired. At any time the user should be able to press the *Show* button to display the total commission of all the sales that were entered. **Note:** This program requires a class-level variable.

55. Add an event procedure to Example 2 so that txtSum will be cleared whenever either the first number or the second number is changed.

Solutions to Practice Problems 3.2

1. −1. There is no uppercase letter E in the string "Computer". IndexOf distinguishes between uppercase and lowercase.

2. The first statement displays 16 in the text box, whereas the second statement displays 88. With Option Strict in effect, the first statement would not be valid if CStr were missing, since 8 + 8 is a number and txtBox.Text is a string. Visual Basic treats the second statement as if it were

```
txtBox.Text = CStr(8) & CStr(8)
```

3. Some possibilities are

PROHIBITED STATEMENT	SUGGESTION FOR FIXING
`Dim x As Double = "23"`	Replace '"23"' with 'CDbl("23")'.
`dblVar = txtBox.Text`	Replace 'txtBox.Text' with 'CDbl(txtBox.Text)'.
`dblVar = 2 & 3`	Replace '2 & 3' with 'CDbl(2 & 3)'.

3.3 Input and Output

Formatting Output with Format Functions

VideoNote

Formatting output

The Format functions are used to display numbers in familiar forms. Here are some examples of how numbers are converted to strings with Format functions:

FUNCTION	STRING VALUE
`FormatNumber(12345.628, 1)`	`12,345.6`
`FormatCurrency(12345.628, 2)`	`$12,345.63`
`FormatPercent(0.185, 2)`	`18.50%`

The value of FormatNumber(n, r) is the string containing the number n rounded to r decimal places and displayed with commas as thousands separators. The value of FormatCurrency(n, r) is the string consisting of a dollar sign followed by the value of FormatNumber(n, r). FormatCurrency uses the accountant's convention of denoting negative amounts with surrounding parentheses. The value of FormatPercent(n, r) is the string consisting of the number n displayed as a percent and rounded to r decimal places. With all three functions, r can be omitted. If so, the number is rounded to two decimal places. Strings corresponding to numbers less than one in magnitude have a zero to the left of the decimal point. Also, n can be a number, a numeric expression, or even a string corresponding to a number.

FUNCTION	STRING VALUE
`FormatNumber(1 + Math.Sqrt(2), 3)`	`2.414`
`FormatCurrency(-1000)`	`($1,000.00)`
`FormatPercent(".05")`	`5.00%`

Using a Masked Text Box for Input

Problems can arise when the wrong type of data is entered as input into a text box. For instance, if the user replies to the request for an age by entering "twenty-one" into a text box, the program can easily crash. Sometimes this type of predicament can be avoided by using a masked text box for input. (In later chapters, we will consider other ways of insuring the integrity of input.)

In the Toolbox, the icon for the MaskedTextBox control consists of a rectangle containing the two characters # and _. The most important property of a masked text box is the Mask property that can be used to restrict the characters entered into the box. Also, the Mask property can be used to show certain characters in the control—to give users a visual cue that they should be entering a phone number or a social security number, for example. Some possible settings for the Mask property are shown in Table 3.2. The first four settings can be selected from a list of specified options. The last three settings generalize to any number of digits, letters, or ampersands. If the Mask property is left blank, then the MaskedTextBox control is nearly identical to the TextBox control.

TABLE 3.2 Some settings for the Mask property.

Setting	Effect
000-00-0000	The user can enter a social security number.
000-0000	The user can enter a phone number (without an area code).
(000)000-0000	The user can enter a phone number (with an area code).
00/00/0000	The user can enter a date.
0000000	The user can enter a positive integer consisting of up to 7 digits.
LLLLL	The user can enter a string consisting of up to 5 letters.
&&&&&&&&	The user can enter a string consisting of up to 8 characters.

Suppose a form contains a masked text box whose Mask property has the setting 000-00-0000. When the program is run, the string "___-__-____" will appear in the masked text box. The user will be allowed to type a digit in place of each of the nine underscore characters. The hyphens cannot be altered, and no characters can be typed anywhere else in the masked text box.

At run time, the characters 0, L, and & in the setting for a Mask property are replaced by underscore characters that are place holders for digits, letters, and characters, respectively. (Spaces are also allowed. However, trailing spaces are dropped.) When the characters "-", "(", ")", or "/" appear in a setting for a Mask property, they appear as themselves in the masked text box and cannot be altered. There are some other mask settings, but these seven will suffice for our purposes.

Figure 3.9(a) shows a masked text box during design time. It looks like an ordinary text box. However, the Tasks button for the masked text box is used to set the Mask property rather than the Multiline property. Figure 3.9(b) shows the result of clicking on the Tasks button. Then, clicking on "Set Mask . . ." brings up the Input Mask dialog box shown in Figure 3.10. (This input dialog box is the same input dialog box that is invoked when you click on the

(a)   (b)

FIGURE 3.9   The Masked TextBox control.

FIGURE 3.10   Input dialog box used to set the Mask property of a masked text box.

ellipses in the Mask property's Settings box.) You can use this input dialog box to select a commonly used value for the Mask property, or create your own customized mask in the Mask text box. To produce the settings 00/00/0000 and 000-00-0000, click on "Short date" and "Social security number", respectively. We use the prefix *mtb* for the names of masked text boxes.

■ Dates as Input and Output

So far, all input and output has been either numbers or strings. However, applications sometimes require dates as input and output. Visual Basic has a Date data type and a Date literal.

A variable of type Date is declared with a statement of the form

```
Dim varName As Date
```

Just as string literals are written surrounded by quotation marks, date literals are written surrounded by number signs. For instance, the statement

```
Dim dayOfIndependence As Date = #7/4/1776#
```

declares a date variable and assigns a value to it.

The function CDate converts a string to a date. For instance, the statement

```
Dim d As Date = CDate(txtBox.Text)
```

assigns the contents of a text box to a variable of type Date.

Dates can be formatted with the FormatDateTime function. If *dateVar* is a variable of type Date, then the value of

```
FormatDateTime(dateVar, DateFormat.LongDate)
```

is a string consisting of the date specified by *dateVar* with the day of the week and the month spelled out. For instance, the two lines of code

```
Dim dayOfIndependence As Date = #7/4/1776#
txtBox.Text = FormatDateTime(dayOfIndependence, DateFormat.LongDate)
```

display Thursday, July 04, 1776 in the text box. **Note:** If **DateFormat.LongDate** is replaced with **DateFormat.ShortDate**, 7/4/1776 will be displayed in the text box.

There are many functions involving dates. Two very useful ones are Today and DateDiff. The value of

```
Today
```

is the current date as determined by the computer system's clock. The value of

```
DateDiff(DateInterval.Day, d1, d2)
```

is the number of days between the two dates.

AddYears is a useful method for working with dates. If *d* is a variable of type Date, and *n* is an integer, then the value of

```
d.AddYears(n)
```

is the value of *d* advanced by *n* years. Two similar methods are AddDays and AddMonths.

OBJECT	PROPERTY	SETTING
frmAge	Text	Birth Data
lblDayOfBirth	Text	Date of birth:
mtbDayOfBirth	Mask	00/00/0000
btnCompute	Text	Compute Data
lblFullDate	Text	Full birth date:
txtFullDate	ReadOnly	True
lblToday	Text	Today's date:
txtToday	ReadOnly	True
lblAgeInDays	Text	Age in days:
txtAgeInDays	ReadOnly	True

Example 1 The following program gives information pertaining to a date input by the user. The mask for the masked text box can be set by clicking on *Short date* in the Input Mask dialog box.

```
Private Sub btnCompute_Click(...) Handles btnCompute.Click
  Dim d As Date = CDate(mtbDayOfBirth.Text)
  txtFullDate.Text = FormatDateTime(d, DateFormat.LongDate)
  txtToday.Text = FormatDateTime(Today, DateFormat.LongDate)
  txtAgeInDays.Text = FormatNumber(DateDiff(DateInterval.Day, d, Today), 0)
End Sub
```

[Run, enter your birthday, and click on the button. One possible outcome is the following.]

■ Getting Input from an Input Dialog Box

Normally, a text box is used to obtain input, where the type of information requested is specified in a label adjacent to the text box. Sometimes, we want just one piece of input and would rather not have a text box and label stay on the form permanently. The problem can be solved with an **input dialog box**. When a statement of the form

```
stringVar = InputBox(prompt, title)
```

is executed, an input dialog box similar to the one shown in Fig. 3.11 pops up on the screen. After the user types a response into the text box at the bottom of the dialog box and presses Enter (or clicks OK), the response is assigned to the string variable. The *title* argument is optional and provides the text that appears in the Title bar. The *prompt* argument is a string that tells the user what information to type into the text box.

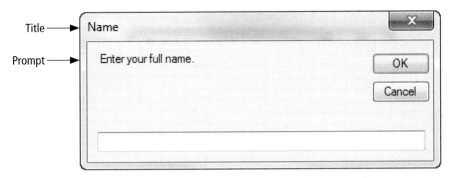

FIGURE 3.11   Sample input dialog box.

When you type the opening parenthesis following the word InputBox, the Code Editor displays a line containing the general form of the InputBox statement. See Fig. 3.12. This feature of IntelliSense is called **Parameter Info**. Optional parameters are surrounded by square brackets. All the parameters in the general form of the InputBox statement are optional except for *prompt*.

```
Dim prompt, title, fullName, firstName As String
Dim dayOfBirth As Date
prompt = "Enter your full name."
title = "Name"
fullName = Inputbox(|
```

InputBox(**Prompt As String,** [Title As String = ""], [DefaultResponse As String = ""], [XPos As Integer = −1], [YPos As Integer = −1]) As String

Displays a prompt in a dialog box, waits for the user to input text or click a button, and then returns a string

Prompt: *Required String expression displayed as the message in the dialog box. The maximum length of Prompt is approximately 1024 characters, depending on the width of the characters used. If Prompt consists of more than one line, you can separate the lines using a carriage return character (Chr(13)), a line feed character (Chr(10)), or a carriage return/line feed combination (Chr(13) & Chr(10)) between each line.*

FIGURE 3.12   Parameter Info feature of IntelliSense.

 Example 2   The following program uses two InputBox functions. Whenever an Input-Box function is encountered in a program, an input dialog box appears, and execution stops until the user responds to the request. The function returns the value entered into the input dialog box.

```
Private Sub btnDisplay_Click(...) Handles btnDisplay.Click
  Dim prompt, title, fullName, firstName As String
  Dim dateOfBirth As Date
  prompt = "Enter your full name."
  title = "Name"
  fullName = InputBox(prompt, title)
  firstName = fullName.Substring(0, fullName.IndexOf(" "))
  prompt = "Enter your date of birth."
  title = "Birthday"
  dateOfBirth = CDate(InputBox(prompt, title))
  txtOutput.Text = firstName & ", you are " &
          DateDiff(DateInterval.Day, dateOfBirth, Today) & " days old."
End Sub
```

[Run, click on the button, enter *Emma Smith* into the first input dialog box, and enter *4/6/1992* into the second input dialog box.]

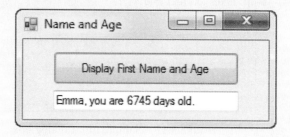

The response typed into an input dialog box is treated as a single string value, no matter what is typed. (Quotation marks are not needed and, if included, are considered as part of the string.) Numeric data typed into an input dialog box should be converted to a number with CDbl or CInt before being assigned to a numeric variable or used in a calculation. Just as with a text box, the typed data must be a literal. It cannot be a variable or an expression. For instance, *num*, 1/2, and 2 + 3 are not acceptable.

Using a Message Dialog Box for Output

Sometimes you want to grab the user's attention with a brief message such as "Correct" or "Nice try, but no cigar." You want this message to appear on the screen only until the user has read it. This task is easily accomplished with a **message dialog box** such as the one shown in Fig. 3.13.

FIGURE 3.13 Sample message dialog box.

When a statement of the form

```
MessageBox.Show(prompt, title)
```

is executed, where *prompt* and *title* are strings, a message dialog box appears with *prompt* displayed and the Title bar caption *title*, and stays on the screen until the user presses Enter, clicks on the *Close* button in the upper-right corner, or clicks OK. For instance, the statement

```
MessageBox.Show("Nice try, but no cigar.", "Consolation")
```

produces Fig. 3.13. You can omit the value for the argument *title* and just execute `MessageBox.Show(prompt)`. If you do, the Title bar will be blank and the rest of the message dialog box will appear as before.

Named Constants

Often a program uses a special constant whose value does not change during program execution. Some examples might be the minimum wage, the sales tax rate, and the name of a master file. Programs are often made easier to understand and maintain if such a constant is given a name. Visual Basic has an object, called a **named constant**, that serves this purpose. A named constant is declared and used in a manner similar to a variable. The two main differences are that in the declaration of a named constant, Dim is replaced with Const, and the value of the named constant cannot be changed elsewhere in the program. Named constants can be thought of as read-only variables.

A named constant is declared and assigned a value with a statement of the form

```
Const CONSTANT_NAME As DataType = value
```

The standard convention is that the names be written in uppercase letters with words separated by underscore characters. Like a Dim statement, a Const statement can be placed in the Declaration sections of a program (for class-level scope) or in a procedure (for local scope). Named constant declarations in procedures usually are placed near the beginning of the procedure. Some examples of named constant declarations are

```
Const INTEREST_RATE As Double = 0.04
Const MINIMUM_VOTING_AGE As Integer = 18
Const BOOK_TITLE As String = "Programming with VB2010"
```

Examples of statements using these named constants are

```
interestEarned = INTEREST_RATE * CDbl(txtAmount.Text)

If (age >= MINIMUM_VOTING_AGE) Then
  MessageBox.Show("You are eligible to vote.")
End If

MessageBox.Show(BOOK_TITLE, "Title of Book")
```

Although the value of a named constant such as **INTEREST_RATE** will not change during the execution of a program, the value may need to be changed at a later time. The programmer can adjust to this change by altering just one line of code instead of searching through the entire program for each occurrence of the old interest rate.

▨ Sending Output to the Printer (optional)

The following five steps send output to the printer.

1. Double-click on the PrintDocument control in the *All Windows Forms* or *Printing* group of the Toolbox. (The control will appear with the default name PrintDocument1 in a separate pane called the **component tray**, at the bottom of the Form Designer.)

2. Double-click on PrintDocument1 to invoke its PrintPage event procedure. (The code for printing text will be placed in this event procedure.)

3. Place the statement

```
Dim gr As Graphics = e.Graphics
```

in the event procedure. (This statement declares *gr* as a graphics object capable of printing both text and graphics.)

4. Enter a statement of the form

```
gr.DrawString(str, font, Brushes.color, x, y)
```

for each line of text to be printed. Here *str* is a string, *font* specifies the font name, size, and style, *color* specifies the color of the text, and *x* and *y* are integers giving the location on the page of the beginning of the string. (The values of *x* and *y* are specified in **points**, where 100 points are about one inch.) Visual Basic indents all text by about 25 points from the left side of the page. The beginning of the string will be printed *x* + 25 points from the left side and *y* points from the top side of the page. Two different ways of specifying the font will be given in the example that follows.

5. Place the statement

```
PrintDocument1.Print()
```

in another event procedure, such as a button's Click event procedure. (This statement will cause all of the text specified in step 4 to be printed.)

Some examples of DrawString statements are as follows. The statement

```
gr.DrawString("HELLO WORLD", Me.Font, Brushes.DarkBlue, 100, 150)
```

prints the words HELLO WORLD using the form's font in dark blue letters 1.25 inches from the left side of the page and 1.5 inches from the top of the page. The pair of statements

```
Dim font As New Font("Courier New", 12, FontStyle.Bold)
gr.DrawString("HELLO WORLD", font, Brushes.DarkBlue, 100, 150)
```

produce the same output using a 12-point bold Courier New font.

Visual Basic provides a control, called the **PrintPreviewDialog control**, which allows you to see how output will look before you send it to the printer. Just follow two steps:

1. Double-click on the PrintPreviewDialog control in the *All Windows Forms* or *Printing* group of the Toolbox. (The control will appear with the default name PrintPreviewDialog1 in the component tray at the bottom of the Form Designer.)

2. Place the pair of statements

```
PrintPreviewDialog1.Document = PrintDocument1
PrintPreviewDialog1.ShowDialog()
```

in another event procedure, such as a button's Click event procedure. These statements cause the text specified in the PrintDocument1_PrintPage event procedure to be displayed in a "Print preview" window when the event procedure is invoked. The preview window's toolbar contains a magnifying-glass button ( ) that allows you to zoom in on the text.

✓ **Example 3** The following program produces a two-column table of the top three all-time home-run hitters. Notice that the font is changed after the table's header is printed.

OBJECT	PROPERTY	SETTING
frmHR	Text	Sluggers
btnPrint	Text	Print Table
btnPreview	Text	Preview Table
PrintDocument1		
PrintPreviewDialog1		

```
Const ONE_INCH As Integer = 100      'number of points in an inch
Const LINE_HEIGHT As Integer = 25    'one-quarter of an inch

Private Sub btnPrint_Click(...) Handles btnPrint.Click
  PrintDocument1.Print()
End Sub
```

```
Private Sub btnPreview_Click(...) Handles btnPreview.Click
  PrintPreviewDialog1.Document = PrintDocument1
  PrintPreviewDialog1.ShowDialog()
End Sub

Private Sub PrintDocument1_PrintPage(...) Handles PrintDocument1.PrintPage
  Dim gr As Graphics = e.Graphics
  Dim x1 As Integer = ONE_INCH          'use one inch beyond left margin
  Dim x2 As Integer = 3 * ONE_INCH      'offset for second column
  Dim y As Integer = ONE_INCH           'use one inch top margin
  Dim font As New Font("Courier New", 10, FontStyle.Bold)
  gr.DrawString("PLAYER", font, Brushes.Blue, x1, y)
  gr.DrawString("HR", font, Brushes.Blue, x2, y)
  font = New Font("Courier New", 10, FontStyle.Regular)
  y += LINE_HEIGHT                       'move down one=quarter inch
  gr.DrawString("Barry Bonds", font, Brushes.Black, x1, y)
  gr.DrawString("762", font, Brushes.Black, x2, y)
  y += LINE_HEIGHT
  gr.DrawString("Hank Aaron", font, Brushes.Black, x1, y)
  gr.DrawString("755", font, Brushes.Black, x2, y)
  y += LINE_HEIGHT
  gr.DrawString("Babe Ruth", font, Brushes.Black, x1, y)
  gr.DrawString("714", font, Brushes.Black, x2, y)
End Sub
```

[Run, click on the *Preview Table* button, click the Zoom down-arrow to the right of the magnifying glass, and select 100%. The following text appears in the preview window.]

PLAYER	HR
Barry Bonds	762
Hank Aaron	755
Babe Ruth	714

▓ Comments

1. A variation of the DateDiff function discussed earlier is `DateDiff(DateInterval.Year, d1, d2)` which gives the number of years (sort of) between the two dates. It is of limited value, since it only uses the year parts of the two dates in its computation.

2. The section "Use the Printer" in Appendix B shows how to print a program and a form.

Practice Problems 3.3

1. Is the statement

   ```
   txtOutput.Text = FormatNumber(12345.628, 1)
   ```

   correct, or should it be written as follows?

   ```
   txtOutput.Text = CStr(FormatNumber(12345.628, 1))
   ```

2. What is the difference in the outcomes of the following two sets of code?

   ```
   strVar = InputBox("How old are you?", "Age")
   numVar = CDbl(strVar)
   txtOutput.Text = numVar
   ```

   ```
   numVar = CDbl(InputBox("How old are you?", "Age"))
   txtOutput.Text = numVar
   ```

In Exercises 1 through 48, determine the output produced by the lines of code.

1. `txtOutput.Text = FormatNumber(1234.56, 0)`

2. `txtOutput.Text = FormatNumber(-12.3456, 3)`

3. `txtOutput.Text = FormatNumber(1234, 1)`

4. `txtOutput.Text = FormatNumber(12345.88)`

5. `txtOutput.Text = FormatNumber(0.012, 1)`

6. `txtOutput.Text = FormatNumber(5 * (10 ^ -2), 1)`

7. `txtOutput.Text = FormatNumber(-2 / 3)`

8. `Dim numVar As Double = Math.Round(1.2345, 1)`
   `txtOutput.Text = FormatNumber(numVar)`

9. `Dim numVar As Double = Math.Round(12345.9)`
   `txtOutput.Text = FormatNumber(numVar, 3)`

10. `Dim numVar As Double = Math.Round(12.5)`
    `txtOutput.Text = FormatNumber(numVar, 0)`

11. `Dim numVar As Double = Math.Round(11.5)`
    `txtOutput.Text = FormatNumber(numVar, 0)`

12. `txtOutput.Text = FormatCurrency(1234.5)`

13. `txtOutput.Text = FormatCurrency(23456.67, 0)`

14. `txtOutput.Text = FormatCurrency(-1234567)`

15. `txtOutput.Text = FormatCurrency(-0.225)`

16. `txtOutput.Text = FormatCurrency(32 * (10 ^ 2))`

17. `txtOutput.Text = FormatCurrency(4 / 5)`

18. `txtOutput.Text = FormatPercent(0.04, 0)`

19. `txtOutput.Text = FormatPercent(0.075)`

20. `txtOutput.Text = FormatPercent(-.05, 3)`

21. `txtOutput.Text = FormatPercent(1)`

22. `txtOutput.Text = FormatPercent(0.01)`

23. `txtOutput.Text = FormatPercent(2 / 3)`

24. `txtOutput.Text = FormatPercent(3 / 4, 2)`

25. `txtOutput.Text = "Pay to France " & FormatCurrency(27267622)`

26. `txtOutput.Text = "Manhattan was purchased for " & FormatCurrency(24)`

27. `Dim popUSover24 As Double = 177.6        'Million`
    `Dim collegeGrads As Double = 45.5        'Million`
    `'                                45.5/177.6 = 0.2561937`
    `txtOutput.Text = FormatPercent(collegeGrads / popUSover24, 1) &`
    `  " of the U.S. population 25+ years old are college graduates."`

28. `Dim degrees As String = FormatNumber(1711500, 0)`
    `txtOutput.Text = degrees & " degrees were conferred."`

29. `txtOutput.Text = "The likelihood of Heads is " &`
    `                 FormatPercent(1 / 2, 0)`

30. `txtOutput.Text = "Pi = " & FormatNumber(3.1415926536, 4)`

31. `txtOutput.Text = CStr(#10/23/2010#)`

32. ```
Dim d As Date = #6/19/2011#   'Father's Day
txtOutput.Text = FormatDateTime(d, DateFormat.LongDate)
```

33. ```
Dim d As Date = #11/25/2010#    'Thanksgiving Day
txtOutput.Text = FormatDateTime(d, DateFormat.LongDate)
```

34. ```
Dim d As Date = #1/1/2000#
txtOutput.Text = CStr(d.AddYears(11))
```

35. ```
Dim d As Date = #9/29/2011#
txtOutput.Text = CStr(d.AddDays(3))
```

36. ```
Dim d As Date = #10/9/2010#
txtOutput.Text = CStr(d.AddMonths(4))
```

37. ```
Dim d As Date = #4/5/2011#
txtOutput.Text = CStr(d.AddYears(2))
```

38. ```
Dim d As Date = #10/1/2010#
txtOutput.Text = CStr(d.AddDays(32))
```

39. ```
Dim d1 As Date = #2/1/2012#    '2012 is a leap year
Dim d2 As Date = d1.AddMonths(1)
txtOutput.Text = CStr(DateDiff(DateInterval.Day, d1, d2))
```

40. ```
Dim d1 As Date = #1/1/2012#   '2012 is a leap year
Dim d2 As Date = #1/1/2013#
txtOutput.Text = CStr(DateDiff(DateInterval.Day, d1, d2))
```

41. ```
Dim bet As Double    'Amount bet at roulette
bet = CDbl(InputBox("How much do you want to bet?", "Wager"))
txtOutput.Text = "You might win " & 36 * bet & " dollars."
```

    (Assume that the response is *10*.)

42. ```
Dim word As String
word = InputBox("Word to negate:", "Negatives")
txtOutput.Text = "un" & word
```

    (Assume that the response is *tied*.)

43. ```
Dim lastName, message, firstName As String
lastName = "Jones"
message = "What is your first name Mr. " & lastName & "?"
firstName = InputBox(message, "Name")
txtOutput.Text = "Hello " & firstName & " " & lastName
```

    (Assume that the response is *John*.)

44. ```
Dim intRate, doublingTime As Double 'interest rate, time to double
intRate = CDbl(InputBox("Current interest rate?", "Interest"))
doublingTime = 72 / intRate
lstOutput.Items.Add("At the current interest rate, money will")
lstOutput.Items.Add("double in " & doublingTime & " years.")
```

    (Assume that the response is *4*.)

45. ```
Const SALES_TAX_RATE As Double = 0.06
Dim price As Double = 100
Dim cost = (1 + SALES_TAX_RATE) * price
txtOutput.Text = FormatCurrency(cost)
```

46.
```
Const ESTATE_TAX_EXEMPTION As Double = 1000000
Const TAX_RATE = 0.45
Dim valueOfEstate As Double = 3000000
Dim tax As Double = TAX_RATE * (valueOfEstate - ESTATE_TAX_EXEMPTION)
txtOutput.Text = "You owe " & FormatCurrency(tax) & " in estate taxes."
```

47.
```
Dim gr As Graphics = e.Graphics
Dim font As New Font("Courier New", 10, FontStyle.Bold)
gr.DrawString("Hello World", font, Brushes.Blue, 175, 200)
```

48.
```
Dim gr As Graphics = e.Graphics
Dim font As New Font("Times New Roman", 12, FontStyle.Italic)
gr.DrawString("Hello", font, Brushes.Blue, 75, 100)
gr.DrawString("World", font, Brushes.Blue, 75, 125)
```

In Exercises 49 through 56, identify any errors.

49.
```
Const n As Integer = 5
n = n*2
txtOutput.Text = CStr(n)
```

50.
```
Const n As String = "FBI"
n = n.ToLower
txtOutput.Text = n
```

51.
```
Dim num As Double
num = InputBox("Pick a number from 1 to 10.")
txtOutput.Text = "Your number is " & num
```

52.
```
info = InputBox()
```

53.
```
Dim num As Double = FormatNumber(123456)
lstOutput.Items.Add(num)
```

54.
```
txtOutput.Text = FormatCurrency($1234)
```

55.
```
MessageBox("Olive Kitteridge", "Pulitzer Prize for Fiction")
```

56.
```
MessageBox.Show(1776, "Year of Independence")
```

In Exercises 57 through 62, give a setting for the Mask property of a masked text box used to input the stated information.

57. A number from 0 to 999.

58. A word of at most ten letters.

59. A Maryland license plate consisting of three letters followed by three digits. (*Example*: BHC365)

60. A California license plate consisting of a digit followed by three letters and then three digits. (*Example*: 7BHC365)

61. An ISBN number. [Every book is identified by a ten-character International Standard Book Number (ISBN). The first nine characters are digits and the last character is either a digit or the letter X.] (*Example*: 0-32-108599-X)

62. A two-letter state abbreviation. (*Example*: CA)

In Exercises 63 and 64, write a statement to carry out the task.

63. Pop up a message dialog box with "Good Advice" in the title bar and the message "First check the weather. Then decide whether to wear shorts and sandals."

64. Pop up a message dialog box with "Taking Risks Proverb" in the title bar and the message "You can't steal second base and keep one foot on first."

In Exercises 65 and 66, write an event procedure with the header `Private Sub btnCompute_Click(...) Handles btnCompute.Click`, and having one, two, or three lines for each step. Lines that display data should use the given variable names.

65. The following steps calculate the percent increase in the cost of a typical grocery basket of goods:
   (a) Declare all variables used in the steps that follow.
   (b) Assign 200 to the variable *begOfYearCost*.
   (c) Request the cost at the end of the year with an input dialog box, and assign it to the variable *endOfYearCost*.
   (d) Assign (*endOfYearCost* – *begOfYearCost*) / *begOfYearCost* to the variable *percentIncrease*.
   (e) Display a sentence giving the percent increase for the year.

   (Test the program with a $215 end-of-year cost.)

66. The following steps calculate the amount of money earned in a walk-a-thon:
   (a) Declare all variables used in the steps that follow.
   (b) Request the amount pledged per mile from an input dialog box, and assign it to the variable *pledge*.
   (c) Request the number of miles walked from an input dialog box, and assign it to the variable *miles*.
   (d) Display a sentence giving the amount to be paid.

   (Test the program with a pledge of $2.00 per mile and a 15-mile walk.)

67. Write a program that requests a year in a masked text box and then displays the number of days in the year. **Hint:** Use the AddYears method and the DateDiff function.

68. Write a program that calculates the number of days since the Declaration of Independence was ratified (7/4/1776).

69. Write a program that requests a date in a masked text box, and then displays the day of the week (such as Sunday, Monday, …) for that date.

70. Write a program that requests a date as input and then displays the day of the week (such as Sunday, Monday, …) for that date ten years hence.

71. Write a program that requests a month and a year as input and then displays the number of days in that month. **Hint:** Use the AddMonths method.

72. Write a program that requests the user's date of birth and then displays the day of the week (such as Sunday, Monday, …) on which they will have (or had) their 21st birthday.

73. Design a form with two text boxes labeled "Name" and "Phone number". Then write an event procedure that shows a message dialog box stating "Be sure to include the area code!" when the second text box receives the focus.

74. Write a program to calculate the amount of savings when purchasing an item that is marked down with a discount percentage. Obtain the item's original price and the discount percentage via input dialog boxes. The output should be a complete sentence that reiterates the inputs and gives the final price of the item, as shown in Fig. 3.14.

VideoNote
Mortgage
calculator
(Homework)

75. When P dollars are deposited in a savings account at interest rate r compounded annually, the balance after n years is $P(1 + r)^n$. Write a program to request the principal P and the interest rate r as input, and compute the balance after 10 years, as shown in Fig. 3.15 on the next page.

FIGURE 3.14   Sample output of
              Exercise 74.

FIGURE 3.15   Sample output of
              Exercise 75.

76. Write a program to print the list of Internet lingo in Fig. 3.16.

```
PLS        Please                                    % of
TAFN       That's all for now      Rank    Country   WW Users
HHOK       Ha, ha - only kidding   1       USA        16.0%
FWIW       For what its worth      2       China      11.9%
IMO        In my opinion           3       Japan      6.5%
```

FIGURE 3.16   Output of Exercise 76.

FIGURE 3.17   Output of Exercise 77.

77. Write a program to print the top three ranking counties by the percentage of worldwide Internet users they contain as shown in Fig. 3.17.

Solutions to Practice Problems 3.3

1. The first statement is correct, since FormatNumber evaluates to a string. Although the second statement is not incorrect, the use of CStr is redundant.

2. The outcomes are identical. In this text, we primarily use the second style.

CHAPTER 3 SUMMARY

1. Three types of *literals* that can be stored and processed by Visual Basic are numbers, strings, and dates.

2. Many Visual Basic tasks are carried out by methods such as Clear (erases the contents of a text box or list box), Add (places an item into a list box), ToUpper (converts a string to uppercase), ToLower (converts a string to lowercase), Trim (removes leading and trailing spaces from a string), IndexOf (searches for a specified substring in a string and gives its position if found), and Substring (produces a sequence of consecutive characters from a string).

3. The *arithmetic operations* are $+$, $-$, $*$, $/$, $\wedge$, $\backslash$, and Mod. The only string operation is &, concatenation. An *expression* is a combination of literals, variables, functions, and operations that can be evaluated.

4. A *variable* is a name used to refer to data. Variable names must begin with a letter or an underscore and may contain letters, digits, and underscores. Dim statements declare variables,

specify the data types of the variables, and assign initial values to the variables. In this book, most variables have data types Double, Integer, String, or Date.

5. Values are assigned to variables by *assignment statements*. The values appearing in assignment statements can be literals, variables, or expressions. String literals used in assignment statements must be surrounded by quotation marks. Date literals used in assignment statements must be surrounded by number signs.

6. *Comment statements* are used to explain formulas, state the purposes of variables, and articulate the purposes of various parts of a program.

7. *Option Explicit* requires that all variables be declared with Dim statements. *Option Strict* requires the use of conversion functions in certain situations.

8. The *Error List window* displays, and helps you find, errors in the code. The *Auto Correction* feature of IntelliSense suggests corrections when errors occur.

9. Line continuation is used to extend a Visual Basic statement over two or more lines.

10. The *scope* of a variable is the portion of the program in which the variable is visible and can be used. A variable declared inside an event procedure is said to have *local* scope and is visible only inside the procedure. A variable declared in the Declarations section of a program is said to have *class-level* scope and is visible throughout the entire program.

11. *Masked text boxes* help obtain correct input with a Mask property that specifies the kind of data that can be typed into the text box.

12. The *Date* data type facilitates computations involving dates.

13. An *input dialog box* is a window that pops up and displays a message for the user to respond to in a text box. The response is assigned to a variable.

14. A *message dialog box* is a window that pops up to display a message to the user.

15. *Named constants* store values that cannot change during the execution of a program. They are declared with Const statements.

16. The *PrintDocument control* is used to send output to the printer, and the *PrintPreviewDialog control* is used to preview the output.

17. The following *functions* accept numbers, strings, or dates as input and return numbers or strings as output.

FUNCTION	INPUT	OUTPUT
CDbl	string or number	number
CInt	string or number	number
CStr	string or number	string
FormatCurrency	number	string
FormatNumber	number	string
FormatPercent	number	string
FormatDateTime	date	string
DateDiff	date, date	number
InputBox	string, string	string
Int	number	number
Math.Round	number, number	number
Math.Sqrt	number	number

CHAPTER 3   PROGRAMMING PROJECTS

1. Write a program that allows the user to specify two numbers and then adds, subtracts, or multiplies them when the user clicks on the appropriate button. The output should give the type of arithmetic performed and the result. See Fig. 3.18. **Note:** If one of the numbers in an input text box is changed, the output text box should be cleared.

FIGURE 3.18   Possible outcome of Programming Project 1.

FIGURE 3.19   Possible outcome of Programming Project 2.

2. Suppose automobile repair customers are billed at the rate of $55 per hour for labor. Also, a waste disposal fee is added, and costs for parts and supplies are subject to a 5% sales tax. Write a program to display a simplified bill. The customer's name, the number of hours of labor, the cost of parts and supplies, and the disposal fee should be entered into the program via text boxes. When a button is clicked, the customer's name and the four costs should be displayed in a list box, as shown in the sample run in Fig. 3.19.

3. Write a program to make change for an amount of money from 0 through 99 cents input by the user. The output of the program should show the number of coins from each denomination used to make change. See Fig. 3.20.

FIGURE 3.20   Possible outcome of Programming Project 3.

FIGURE 3.21   Possible outcome of Programming Project 4.

4. Write a program to convert a U.S. Customary System length in miles, yards, feet, and inches to a Metric System length in kilometers, meters, and centimeters. A sample run is shown in Fig. 3.21. After the numbers of miles, yards, feet, and inches are read from the text boxes, the length should be converted entirely to inches and then divided by 39.37 to obtain the value in meters. The Int function should be used to break the total number of

meters into a whole number of kilometers and meters. The number of centimeters should be displayed to one decimal place. The needed formulas are as follows:

$$\text{total inches} = 63360 * \text{miles} + 36 * \text{yards} + 12 * \text{feet} + \text{inches}$$

$$\text{total meters} = \text{total inches}/39.37$$

$$\text{kilometers} = \text{Int}(\text{meters}/1000)$$

5. Write a program to print a business travel expenses attachment for an income tax return. The program should request as input the name of the organization visited, the dates and location of the visit, and the expenses for meals and entertainment, airplane fare, lodging, and taxi fares. (Only 50% of the expenses for meals and entertainment are deductible.) A possible form layout and run are shown in Figs. 3.22 and 3.23, respectively.

FIGURE 3.22   **Form with sample data for Programming Project 5.**

Business Travel Expenses

Trip to attend meeting of
SIGCSE 2010
March 10–13 in Milwaukee, WI

Meals and entertainment:	$190.10
Airplane fare:	$250.15
Lodging:	$675.35
Taxi fares:	$45.00

Total other than meals and entertainment: $970.50
50% of meals and entertainment: $95.05

TOTAL DEDUCTIBLE EXPENSES: $1,065.55

FIGURE 3.23   **Output for sample run of Programming Project 5.**

4

Decisions

4.1 Relational and Logical Operators

In Chapter 1, we discussed the two logical programming constructs *decision* and *loop*. In order to make a decision or control a loop, you need to specify a condition that determines the course of action.

A **condition** is an expression involving relational operators (such as $<$ and $=$) that is either true or false. Conditions also may incorporate logical operators (such as And, Or, and Not). ANSI values determine the order used to compare strings with the relational operators. Boolean variables and literals can assume the values True or False.

▨ ANSI Values

Each of the 47 different keys in the center typewriter portion of the keyboard can produce two characters, for a total of 94 characters. Adding 1 for the character produced by the space bar makes 95 characters. Associated with these characters are numbers ranging from 32 to 126. These values, called the ANSI (or ASCII) values of the characters, are given in Appendix A. Table 4.1 shows a few of them.

TABLE 4.1 **A few ANSI values.**

32 (space)	48 0	66 B	122 z
33 !	49 1	90 Z	123 {
34 "	57 9	97 a	125 }
35 #	65 A	98 b	126 ~

Most of the best-known fonts, such as Courier New, Microsoft San Serif, and Times New Roman, adhere to the ANSI standard, which assigns characters to the numbers from 0 to 255. Table 4.2 shows a few of the higher ANSI values.

TABLE 4.2 **A few higher ANSI values.**

162 ¢	177 $\pm$	181 μ	190 $\frac{3}{4}$
169 ©	178 ^{2}	188 $\frac{1}{4}$	247 $\div$
176 °	179 ^{3}	189 $\frac{1}{2}$	248 ϕ

If n is a number between 0 and 255, then

```
Chr(n)
```

is the string consisting of the character with ANSI value n. If *str* is any string, then

```
Asc(str)
```

is the ANSI value of the first character of *str*. For instance, the statement

```
txtBox.Text = Chr(65)
```

displays the letter A in the text box, and the statement

```
lstBox.Items.Add(Asc("Apple"))
```

displays the number 65 in the list box.

Concatenation can be used with Chr to obtain strings using the higher ANSI characters. For instance, with one of the fonts that conforms to the ANSI standard, the statement

```
txtBox.Text = 32 & Chr(176) & " Fahrenheit"
```

displays 32° Fahrenheit in the text box.

The quotation-mark character (") can be placed into a string by using Chr(34). For example, after the statement

```
txtBox.Text = "George " & Chr(34) & "Babe" & Chr(34) & " Ruth"
```

is executed, the text box contains

```
George "Babe" Ruth
```

■ Relational Operators

The relational operator *less than* (<) can be applied to numbers, strings, and dates. The number a is said to be less than the number b if a lies to the left of b on the number line. For instance, $2 < 5$, $-5 < -2$, and $0 < 3.5$.

The string a is said to be less than the string b if a precedes b alphabetically when using the ANSI table to alphabetize their values. For instance, "cat" < "dog", "cart" < "cat", and "cat" < "catalog". Digits precede uppercase letters, which precede lowercase letters. Two strings are compared working from left to right, character by character, to determine which one should precede the other. Therefore, "9W" < "bat", "Dog" < "cat", and "Sales-99" < "Sales-retail".

The date $d1$ is said to be less than the date $d2$ if $d1$ precedes $d2$ chronologically. For instance, #12/7/1941# < #6/6/1944#.

Table 4.3 shows the different relational operators and their meanings.

VideoNote
Relational and logical operators

TABLE 4.3 Relational operators.

Visual Basic Notation	Numeric Meaning	String Meaning	Date Meaning
=	equal to	identical to	same as
<>	not equal to	different from	different than
<	less than	precedes alphabetically	precedes chronologically
>	greater than	follows alphabetically	follows chronologically
<=	less than or equal to	precedes alphabetically or is identical to	precedes chronologically or is the same as
>=	greater than or equal to	follows alphabetically or is identical to	follows chronologically or is the same as

 Example 1 Determine whether each of the following conditions is true or false.

(a) 1 <= 1

(b) 1 < 1

(c) "car" < "cat"

(d) "Dog" < "dog"

(e) Today < Today.AddDays(1)

SOLUTION

(a) True. The notation <= means "less than *or* equal to." That is, the condition is true provided either of the two circumstances holds. The second one (equal to) holds.

(b) False. The notation < means "strictly less than" and no number can be strictly less than itself.

(c) True. The characters of the strings are compared one at a time working from left to right. Because the first two match, the third character decides the order.

(d) True. Because uppercase letters precede lowercase letters in the ANSI table, the first character of "Dog" precedes the first character of "dog".

(e) True. Today precedes tomorrow chronologically.

Conditions also can involve variables, numeric operators, and functions. To determine whether a condition is true or false, first evaluate the numeric or string expressions and then decide if the resulting assertion is true or false.

Example 2   Suppose the numeric variables *a* and *b* have values 4 and 3, and the string variables *c* and *d* have values "hello" and "bye". Are the following conditions true or false?

(a) (a + b) < 2*a

(b) (c.Length − b) = (a/2)

(c) c < ("good" & d)

SOLUTION

(a) The value of a + b is 7 and the value of 2*a is 8. Because 7 < 8, the condition is true.

(b) True, because the value of c.Length − b is 2, the same as (a / 2).

(c) The condition "hello" < "goodbye" is false, because "h" follows "g" in the ANSI table.

■ Logical Operators

Programming situations often require more complex conditions than those considered so far. For instance, suppose we would like to state that the value of a numeric variable, *n*, is strictly between 2 and 5. The proper Visual Basic condition is

$$(2 < n) \text{ And } (n < 5)$$

The condition (2 < n) And (n < 5) is a combination of the two conditions 2 < n and n < 5 with the logical operator And.

The three main logical operators are And, Or, and Not. If *cond1* and *cond2* are conditions, then the condition

`cond1 And cond2`

is true if both *cond1* and *cond2* are true. Otherwise, it is false. The condition

`cond1 Or cond2`

is true if either *cond1* or *cond2* (or both) is true. Otherwise, it is false. The condition

`Not cond1`

is true if *cond1* is false, and is false if *cond1* is true.

Example 3   Suppose the numeric variable *n* has value 4 and the string variable *answ* has value "Y". Determine whether each of the following conditions is true or false.

(a) $(2 < n)$ And $(n < 6)$

(b) $(2 < n)$ Or $(n = 6)$

(c) Not $(n < 6)$

(d) $(answ = "Y")$ Or $(answ = "y")$

(e) $(answ = "Y")$ And $(answ = "y")$

(f) Not $(answ = "y")$

(g) $((2 < n)$ And $(n = 5 + 1))$ Or $(answ = "No")$

(h) $((n = 2)$ And $(n = 7))$ Or $(answ = "Y")$

(i) $(n = 2)$ And $((n = 7)$ Or $(answ = "Y"))$

SOLUTION

(a) True, because the conditions $(2 < 4)$ and $(4 < 6)$ are both true.

(b) True, because the condition $(2 < 4)$ is true. The fact that the condition $(4 = 6)$ is false does not affect the conclusion. The only requirement is that at least one of the two conditions be true.

(c) False, because $(4 < 6)$ is true.

(d) True, because the first condition becomes $("Y" = "Y")$ when the value of *answ* is substituted for *answ*.

(e) False, because the second condition is false. Actually, this compound condition is false for every value of *answ*.

(f) True, because $("Y" = "y")$ is false.

(g) False. In this logical expression, the compound condition $((2 < n)$ And $(n = 5 + 1))$ and the simple condition $(answ = "No")$ are joined by the logical operator Or. Because both these conditions are false, the total condition is false.

(h) True, because the second Or clause is true.

(i) False. Comparing (h) and (i) shows the necessity of using parentheses to specify the intended grouping.

■ Boolean Data Type

A statement of the form

```
txtBox.Text = CStr(condition)
```

will display either True or False in the text box, depending on the condition. Any variable or expression that evaluates to either True or False is said to have a **Boolean data type**. The following lines of code display False in the text box.

```
Dim x As Integer = 5
txtBox.Text = CStr((3 + x) < 7)
```

A variable is declared to be of type Boolean with a statement of the form

```
Dim varName As Boolean
```

The following lines of code will display True in the text box.

```
Dim boolVar As Boolean
Dim x As Integer = 2
Dim y As Integer = 3
boolVar = x < y
txtBox.Text = CStr(boolVar)
```

The answer to part (i) of Example 3 can be confirmed to be False by executing the following lines of code.

```
Dim n as Integer = 4
Dim answ as String = "Y"
txtBox.Text = CStr((n = 2) And ((n = 7) Or (answ = "Y")))
```

■ Two Boolean-Valued Methods

If *strVar* is a string variable, then the expression

```
strVar.Substring(strVar.length − 3) = "ing"
```

is true if and only if the value of *strVar* ends with *ing*. To generalize, if *strVar2* is another string variable, then the expression

```
strVar.SubString(strVar.length - strVar2.Length) = strVar2                    (1)
```

is true if and only if the value of *strVar* ends with the value of *strVar2*.

The EndsWith method provides an alternate way to test for the end of a string. The value of

```
strVar.EndsWith(strVar2)                                                       (2)
```

is True if and only if the value of *strVar* ends with the value of *strVar2*.

Condition (2) is preferable to condition (1) since it is more concise and readable. Code such as condition (2) is called **declarative code** (or **self-evident code**), since it clearly declares *what* you want to accomplish. Expression (1) shows *how* to accomplish the task but requires some deciphering in order to figure out what is being achieved. One of our guiding programming principles will be to write declarative code whenever possible. We prefer *what* to *how*.

The counterpart of the EndsWith method is the StartsWith method. The value of

```
strVar.StartsWith(strVar2)
```

is True if and only if the value of *strVar* begins with the value of *strVar2*.

■ A Boolean-Valued Function

The IsNumeric function is used to determine if a value input by the user, say in a text box or input dialog box, can be used in numeric computations. The value of

```
IsNumeric(strVar)
```

is True if *strVar* can be converted to a number with CInt or CDbl, and is False otherwise. For instance, `IsNumeric(strVar)` will be True when the value of *strVar* is "2345", "$123", or "5,677,890". The function value will be False when the value of *strVar* is "five" or "4 − 2".

▨ Comments

1. A condition involving numeric variables is different from an algebraic truth. The assertion $(a + b) < 2*a$, considered in Example 2, is not a valid algebraic truth because it isn't true for all values of a and b. When encountered in a Visual Basic program, however, it will be considered true if it is correct for the current values of the variables.

2. Conditions evaluate to either True or False. These two values often are called the possible **truth values** of the condition.

3. A condition such as $2 < n < 5$ should never be used, because Visual Basic will not evaluate it as intended. The correct condition is $(2 < n)$ And $(n < 5)$.

4. A common error is to replace the condition Not $(n < m)$ by the condition $(n > m)$. The correct replacement is $(n >= m)$.

Practice Problems 4.1

1. Is the condition `"Hello " = "Hello"` true or false?
2. Explain why $(27 > 9)$ is true, whereas $("27" > "9")$ is false.
3. Complete Table 4.4.

TABLE 4.4 Truth values of logical operators.

cond1	cond2	cond1 And cond2	cond1 Or cond2	Not cond2
True	True	True		
True	False		True	
False	True			False
False	False			

EXERCISES 4.1

In Exercises 1 through 6, determine the output displayed in the text box.

1. ```
txtBox.Text = Chr(104) & Chr(105)
```

2. ```
txtBox.Text = "C" & Chr(35)
```

3. ```
txtBox.Text = "The letter after G is " & Chr(Asc("G") + 1)
```

4. ```
txtBox.Text = Chr(Asc("B"))  'The ANSI value of B is 66
```

5. ```
Dim quote, person, qMark As String
quote = "We're all in this alone."
person = "Lily Tomlin"
qMark = Chr(34)
txtBox.Text = qMark & quote & qMark & " - " & person
```

6. ```
Dim letter As String
letter = "D"
txtBox.Text = letter & " is the " & (Asc(letter) - Asc("A") + 1) &
              "th letter of the alphabet."
```

In Exercises 7 through 18, determine whether the condition is true or false. Assume a = 2 and b = 3.

7. $3*a = 2*b$

8. $(5 - b)*a < 7$

9. $b <= 3$

10. $a^b = b^a$

11. $a^(5 - 2) > 7$

12. $3E-02 < .01*a$

13. $(a < b)$ Or $(b < a)$

14. $(a*a < b)$ Or Not $(a*a < a)$

15. Not $((a < b)$ And $(a < (b + a)))$

16. Not $(a < b)$ Or Not $(a < (b + a))$

17. $((a = b)$ And $(a*a < b*b))$ Or $((b < a)$ And $(2*a < b))$

18. $((a = b)$ Or Not $(b < a))$ And $((a < b)$ Or $(b = a + 1))$

In Exercises 19 through 30, determine whether the condition is true or false.

19. "9W" <> "9w"

20. "Inspector" < "gadget"

21. "Car" < "Train"

22. "J" >= "J"

23. "99" > "ninety-nine"

24. "B" < "?"

25. ("Duck" < "pig") And ("pig" < "big")

26. "Duck" < "Duck" & "Duck"

27. Not (("B" = "b") Or ("Big" < "big"))

28. #7/4/1776# >= #7/4/1776#

29. #6/17/1775# <= #7/4/1776#

30. (7 < 34) And ("7" > "34")

In Exercises 31 through 40, determine whether or not the two conditions are equivalent—that is, whether they will be true or false for exactly the same values of the variables appearing in them.

31. $a <= b$; $(a < b)$ Or $(a = b)$

32. Not $(a < b)$; $a > b$

33. $(a = b)$ And $(a < b)$; $a <> b$

34. Not $((a = b)$ Or $(a = c))$; $(a <> b)$ And $(a <> c)$

35. $(a < b)$ And $((a > d)$ Or $(a > e))$; $((a < b)$ And $(a > d))$ Or $((a < b)$ And $(a > e))$

36. Not $((a = b + c)$ Or $(a = b))$; $(a <> b)$ Or $(a <> b + c)$

37. $(a < b + c)$ Or $(a = b + c)$; Not $((a > b)$ Or $(a > c))$

38. Not $(a >= b)$; $(a <= b)$ Or Not $(a = b)$

39. Not $(a >= b)$; $(a <= b)$ And Not $(a = b)$

40. $(a = b)$ And $((b = c)$ Or $(a = c))$; $(a = b)$ Or $((b = c)$ And $(a = c))$

In Exercises 41 through 45, write a condition equivalent to the negation of the given condition. (For example, a <> b is equivalent to the negation of a = b).

41. a < b

42. (a = b) Or (a = d)

43. (a < b) And (c <> d)

44. Not ((a = b) Or (a > b))

45. (a <> "") And (a < b) And (a.Length < 5)

46. Rework Exercise 20 by evaluating the Boolean expression in a program.

47. Rework Exercise 21 by evaluating the Boolean expression in a program.

48. Rework Exercise 22 by evaluating the Boolean expression in a program.

49. Rework Exercise 23 by evaluating the Boolean expression in a program.

In Exercises 50 through 59, determine whether True or False is displayed in the text box.

50.
```
Dim str As String = "target"
txtBox.Text = CStr(str.StartsWith("t") And str.EndsWith("t"))
```

51.
```
Dim str As String = "ticket"
txtBox.Text = CStr(str.StartsWith("T") Or str.EndsWith("T"))
```

52.
```
Dim str1 As String = "target"
Dim str2 As String = "get"
txtBox.Text = CStr(str1.EndsWith(str2))
```

53.
```
Dim str1 As String = "Teapot"
Dim str2 As String = "Tea"
txtBox.Text = CStr(str1.EndsWith(str2))
```

54.
```
Dim str As String = "$1,234.56"
txtBox.Text = CStr(IsNumeric(str))
```

55.
```
Dim str As String = "10,000,000"
txtBox.Text = CStr(IsNumeric(str))
```

56.
```
Dim str As String = "10 million"
txtBox.Text = CStr(IsNumeric(str))
```

57.
```
Dim str As String = "2 + 3"
txtBox.Text = CStr(IsNumeric(str))
```

58.
```
Dim str As String = "10E+06"
txtBox.Text = CStr(IsNumeric(str))
```

59.
```
Dim str As String = "5E-12"
txtBox.Text = CStr(IsNumeric(str))
```

Solutions to Practice Problems 4.1

1. False. The first string has six characters, whereas the second has five. Two strings must be 100% identical to be called equal.

2. When 27 and 9 are compared as strings, their first characters, *2* and *9*, determine their order. Since *2* precedes *9* in the ANSI table, "27" < "9".

3.

cond1	cond2	cond1 And cond2	cond1 Or cond2	Not cond2
True	True	True	True	False
True	False	False	True	True
False	True	False	True	False
False	False	False	False	True

4.2   If Blocks

An **If block** allows a program to decide on a course of action based on whether a certain condition is true or false.

■ If Block

A block of the form:

```
If condition Then
    action 1
Else
    action 2
End If
```

causes the program to take *action 1* if *condition* is true and *action 2* if *condition* is false. Each action consists of one or more Visual Basic statements. After an action is taken, execution continues with the line after the If block. Figure 4.1 contains the pseudocode and flowchart for an If block.

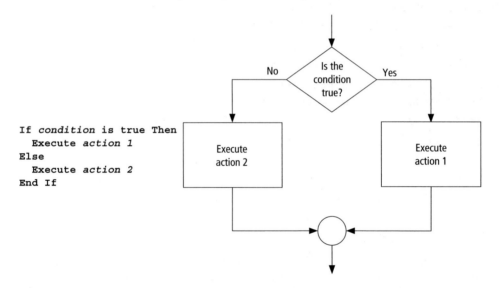

```
If condition is true Then
    Execute action 1
Else
    Execute action 2
End If
```

FIGURE 4.1   Pseudocode and flowchart for an If block.

 Example 1   The following program finds the larger of two numbers input by the user. The condition is

```
num1 > num2
```

and each action consists of a single assignment statement. With the inputs 3 and 7, the condition is false, and so the second action is taken.

OBJECT	PROPERTY	SETTING
frmMaximum	Text	Maximum
lblFirstNum	Text	First number:
txtFirstNum		
lblSecondNum	Text	Second number:
txtSecondNum		
btnFindLarger	Text	Find Larger Number
txtResult	ReadOnly	True

```
Private Sub btnFindLarger_Click(...) Handles btnFindLarger.Click
  Dim num1, num2, largerNum As Double
  num1 = CDbl(txtFirstNum.Text)
  num2 = CDbl(txtSecondNum.Text)
  If num1 > num2 Then
    largerNum = num1
  Else
    largerNum = num2
  End If
  txtResult.Text = "The larger number is " & largerNum & "."
End Sub
```

[Run, type 3 and 7 into the text boxes, and click on the button.]

 Example 2   The If block in the following program has a logical operator in its condition.

OBJECT	PROPERTY	SETTING
frmQuiz	Text	A Quiz
lblQuestion	AutoSize	False
	Text	How many gallons does a ten-gallon hat hold?
txtAnswer		
btnEvaluate	Text	Evaluate Answer
txtSolution	ReadOnly	True

```
Private Sub btnEvaluate_Click(...) Handles btnEvaluate.Click
  'Evaluate answer
  Dim answer As Double
  answer = CDbl(txtAnswer.Text)
  If (answer >= 0.5) And (answer <= 1) Then
    txtSolution.Text = "Good, "
  Else
    txtSolution.Text = "No, "
  End If
  txtSolution.Text &= "it holds about 3/4 of a gallon."
End Sub
```

[Run, type 10 into the text box, and click on the button.]

The Else part of an If block can be omitted. This important type of If block appears in the next example.

 Example 3   The following program offers assistance to the user before presenting a quotation.

OBJECT	PROPERTY	SETTING
frmQuotation	Text	Quotation
lblQuestion	Text	Do you know what the game of skittles is (Y/N)?
mtbAnswer	Mask	L
btnDisplay	Text	Display Quotation
txtQuote	ReadOnly	True

```
Private Sub btnDisplay_Click(...) Handles btnDisplay.Click
  Dim message As String
  message = "Skittles is an old form of bowling in which a wooden " &
            "disk is used to knock down nine pins arranged in a square."
  If mtbAnswer.Text.ToUpper = "N" Then
     MessageBox.Show(message, "Definition")
  End If
  txtQuote.Text = "Life ain't all beer and skittles." &
               " - Du Maurier (1894)"
End Sub
```

[Run, type "N" into the masked text box, and click on the button.]

[Press OK.]

[Rerun the program, type "Y" into the masked text box, click on the button, and observe that the description of the game is skipped.]

Note: Logic errors are the most difficult errors to find. A common type of logic error is the omission of the ToUpper method in Example 3.

Nested If Blocks

An action part of an If block can consist of another If block. In this situation the If blocks are said to be **nested**. Examples 4 and 5 employ nested If blocks.

Example 4   The color of the beacon light atop Boston's old John Hancock building forecasts the weather according to the following rhyme:

Steady blue, clear view.
Flashing blue, clouds due.
Steady red, rain ahead.
Flashing red, snow instead.

The following program requests a color (Blue or Red) and a mode (Steady or Flashing) as input and displays the weather forecast. Both actions associated with the main If block consist of If blocks.

OBJECT	PROPERTY	SETTING
frmWeather	Text	Weather Beacon
lblColor	Text	Color of the light (B or R):
mtbColor	Mask	L
lblMode	Text	Mode (S or F):
mtbMode	Mask	L
btnInterpret	Text	Interpret Beacon
txtForecast	ReadOnly	True

```
Private Sub btnInterpret_Click(...) Handles btnInterpret.Click
  'Interpret a weather beacon
  Dim color, mode As String
  color = mtbColor.Text
  mode = mtbMode.Text
  If mode = "S" Then
    If color = "B" Then
      txtForecast.Text = "CLEAR VIEW"
    Else      'color = "R"
      txtForecast.Text = "RAIN AHEAD"
    End If
  Else        'mode = "F"
    If color = "B" Then
      txtForecast.Text = "CLOUDS DUE"
    Else      'color = "R"
      txtForecast.Text = "SNOW AHEAD"
    End If
  End If
End Sub
```

[Run, type *R* and *S* into the masked text boxes, and click on the button.]

Example 5   The following program requests the costs and revenue for a company and displays the message "Break even" if the costs and revenue are equal; otherwise, it displays the profit or loss. The action following Else is another If block.

OBJECT	PROPERTY	SETTING
frmStatus	Text	Profit/Loss
lblCosts	Text	Costs:
txtCosts		
lblRev	Text	Revenue:
txtRev		
btnShow	Text	Show Financial Status
txtResult	ReadOnly	True

```
Private Sub btnShow_Click(...) Handles btnShow.Click
  Dim costs, revenue, profit, loss As Double
  costs = CDbl(txtCosts.Text)
```

```
  revenue = CDbl(txtRev.Text)
  If costs = revenue Then
    txtResult.Text = "Break even"
  Else
    If costs < revenue Then
      profit = revenue — costs
      txtResult.Text = "Profit is " & FormatCurrency(profit) & "."
    Else
      loss = costs — revenue
      txtResult.Text = "Loss is " & FormatCurrency(loss) & "."
    End If
  End If
End Sub
```

[Run, type 9500 and 8000 into the text boxes, and click on the button.]

▥ ElseIf Clauses

An extension of the If block allows for more than two possible alternatives with the inclusion of ElseIf clauses. A typical block of this type is

```
If condition 1 Then
  action 1
ElseIf condition 2 Then
  action 2
ElseIf condition 3 Then
  action 3
Else
  action 4
End If
```

Visual Basic searches for the first true condition, carries out its action, and then skips to the statement following End If. If none of the conditions are true, then Else's action is carried out. Execution then continues with the statement following the block. In general, an If block can contain any number of ElseIf clauses. As before, the Else clause is optional.

 Example 6 The following program redoes Example 1 so that the program reports if the two numbers are equal.

```
Private Sub btnFindLarger_Click(...) Handles btnFindLarger.Click
  Dim num1, num2 As Double
  num1 = CDbl(txtFirstNum.Text)
  num2 = CDbl(txtSecondNum.Text)
```

```
    If (num1 > num2) Then
        txtResult.Text = "The larger number is " & num1
    ElseIf (num2 > num1) Then
        txtResult.Text = "The larger number is " & num2
    Else
        txtResult.Text = "The two numbers are equal."
    End If
End Sub
```

[Run, type 7 into both text boxes, and press the button.]

The If block in Example 7 allows us to calculate values that are not determined by a simple formula.

 Example 7   The Social Security or FICA tax has two components—the Social Security benefits tax, which in 2009 is 6.2% on the first $106,800 of earnings for the year, and the Medicare tax, which is 1.45% of earnings. The following program calculates an employee's FICA tax for the current pay period.

OBJECT	PROPERTY	SETTING
frmFICA	Text	FICA Taxes
lblToDate	AutoSize	False
	Text	Total earnings for this year prior to the current pay period:
txtToDate		
lblCurrent	Text	Earnings for the current pay period:
txtCurrent		
btnCalculate	Text	Calculate FICA Taxes
lblTax	Text	FICA taxes for the current pay period:
txtTax	ReadOnly	True

```
Private Sub btnCalculate_Click(...) Handles btnCalculate.Click
    'Calculate social security benefits tax and Medicare tax
    'for a single pay period in 2009
    Const WAGE_BASE As Double = 106800    'There is no social security benefits
    '                                      tax on income above this level.
    Dim ytdEarnings, curEarnings As Double
```

```
   Dim socialSecurityBenTax, medicareTax, ficaTaxes As Double
   ytdEarnings = CDbl(txtToDate.Text)
   curEarnings = CDbl(txtCurrent.Text)
   If (ytdEarnings + curEarnings) <= WAGE_BASE Then
     socialSecurityBenTax = 0.062 * curEarnings
   ElseIf ytdEarnings < WAGE_BASE Then
     socialSecurityBenTax = 0.062 * (WAGE_BASE − ytdEarnings)
   End If
   medicareTax = 0.0145 * curEarnings
   ficaTaxes = socialSecurityBenTax + medicareTax
   txtTax.Text = FormatCurrency(ficaTaxes)
End Sub
```

[Run, type 12345.67 and 543.21 into the top two text boxes and click on the button.]

The following example illustrates the fact that when an If block contains ElseIf clauses, Visual Basic executes the action corresponding to the first condition that is satisfied and ignores all subsequent clauses—even if they also satisfy the condition.

 Example 8 The following program assumes that the user will graduate (that is, has a GPA of 2 or more) and determines if the user will graduate with honors.

```
Private Sub btnDetermine_Click(...) Handles btnDetermine.Click
  Dim gpa As Double = CDbl(txtGPA.Text)
  Dim honors As String
  If gpa >= 3.9 Then
    honors = " summa cum laude."
  ElseIf gpa >= 3.6 Then
    honors = " magna cum laude."
  ElseIf gpa >= 3.3 Then
    honors = " cum laude."
  ElseIf gpa >= 2 Then
    honors = "."
  End If
  txtOutput.Text = "You graduated" & honors
End Sub
```

[Run, enter a grade point average between 2 and 4, and click on the button.]

■ Input Validation with If Blocks

Suppose a program calls for the user to enter a number into a text box, and then the program uses the number in a computation. If the user leaves the text box empty or enters an inappropriate number, the program will crash. The Boolean-valued function IsNumeric can be used to prevent this from happening.

Note: When *boolVal* is a Boolean value, a statement of the form

```
If boolVal = True Then
```

can be shortened to

```
If boolVal Then
```

Similarly, a statement of the form

```
If boolVal = False Then
```

can be shortened to

```
If Not boolVal Then
```

Example 9 The following program uses the function IsNumeric to guard against improper input.

OBJECT	PROPERTY	SETTING
frmAddition	Text	Addition
lblFirstNum	Text	First number:
txtFirstNum		
lblSecondNum	Text	Second number:
txtSecondNum		
btnAdd	Text	Add Numbers
lblSum	Text	Sum:
txtSum	ReadOnly	True

```
Private Sub btnAdd_Click(...) Handles btnAdd.Click
  If IsNumeric(txtFirstNum.Text) And IsNumeric(txtSecondNum.Text) Then
    txtSum.Text = CStr(CDbl(txtFirstNum.Text) + CDbl(txtSecondNum.Text))
  ElseIf Not IsNumeric(txtFirstNum.Text) Then
    If Not IsNumeric(txtSecondNum.Text) Then
      MessageBox.Show("Each text box is empty or has an improper entry.")
```

```
    Else
      MessageBox.Show("The first text box is empty or has an improper entry.")
    End If
  Else
    MessageBox.Show("The second text box is empty or has an improper entry.")
  End If
End Sub
```

[Run, leave the first text box empty, enter "two" into the second text box, and click on the button.]

If blocks also can be used to guarantee that a number input by the user is in the proper range. For instance, when the user is asked to input an exam grade, a statement such as

```
If (grade >= 0) And (grade <= 100) Then
```

can be used to guarantee that the number input is between 0 and 100.

■ Comments

1. Care should be taken to make If blocks easy to understand. For instance, in Fig. 4.2, the block on the left is difficult to follow and should be replaced by the clearer block on the right.

```
If cond1 Then                 If cond1 And cond2 Then
  If cond2 Then                  action
    action                     End If
  End If
End If
```

FIGURE 4.2   A confusing If block and an improvement.

2. In Appendix D, the section "Stepping through Programs Containing Decision Structures: Chapter 4" uses the Visual Basic debugging tools to trace the flow through an If block.

1. Suppose the user is asked to input a number into txtNumber for which the square root is to be taken. Fill in the If block so that the lines of code that follow will display either the message "Number can't be negative." or the square root of the number.

```
Private Sub btnSqrt_Click(...) Handles btnSqrt.Click
  'Check reasonableness of data
  Dim num As Double
  num = CDbl(txtNumber.Text)
  If

  End If
End Sub
```

2. Improve the block

```
If a < b Then
  If c < 5 Then
    txtBox.Text = "hello"
  End If
End If
```

In Exercises 1 through 12, determine the output displayed in the text box when the button is clicked.

1.
```
Private Sub btnDisplay_Click(...) Handles btnDisplay.Click
  Dim num As Double = 4
  If num <= 9 Then
    txtOutput.Text = "Less than ten."
  Else
    If num = 4 Then
      txtOutput.Text = "Equal to four."
    End If
  End If
End Sub
```

2.
```
Private Sub btnDisplay_Click(...) Handles btnDisplay.Click
  Dim gpa As Double = 3.74
  txtOutput.Clear()
  If gpa >= 3.75 Then
    txtOutput.Text = "Dean's List "
  End If
  txtOutput.Text &= "Student"
End Sub
```

3.
```
Private Sub btnDisplay_Click(...) Handles btnDisplay.Click
  Dim a As Double = 4
  txtOutput.Clear()
  If (3 * a - 4) < 9 Then
    txtOutput.Text = "Remember, "
  End If
  txtOutput.Text &= "tomorrow is another day."
End Sub
```

4.
```
Private Sub btnDisplay_Click(...) Handles btnDisplay.Click
    Dim change As Double = 356      'Amount of change in cents
    If change >= 100 Then
        txtOutput.Text = "Your change contains " &
                        Int(change / 100) & " dollars."
    Else
        txtOutput.Text = "Your change contains no dollars."
    End If
End Sub
```

5.
```
Private Sub btnDisplay_Click(...) Handles btnDisplay.Click
    Dim a as Double = 2
    Dim b As Double = 3
    Dim c As Double = 5
    If a * b < c Then
        b = 7
    Else
        b = c * a
    End If
    txtOutput.Text = CStr(b)
End Sub
```

6.
```
Private Sub btnDisplay_Click(...) Handles btnDisplay.Click
    'Cost of phone call from New York to London
    Dim length, cost As Double
    'Request the length of a phone call
    length = CDbl(InputBox("Duration of the call in minutes?"))
    'Calculate cost of phone call
    If length < 1 Then
        cost = 0.46
    Else
        cost = 0.46 + (length − 1) * 0.36
    End If
    'Display the cost of the call
    txtBox.Text = "Cost of call: " & FormatCurrency(cost)
End Sub
```
(Assume the response is *31*.)

7.
```
Private Sub btnDisplay_Click(...) Handles btnDisplay.Click
    Dim letter As String
    letter = InputBox("Enter A, B, or C.")
    letter = letter.ToUpper
    If letter = "A" Then
        txtOutput.Text = "A, my name is Alice."
    ElseIf letter = "B" Then
        txtOutput.Text = "To be, or not to be."
    ElseIf letter = "C" Then
        txtOutput.Text = "Oh, say, can you see."
    Else
        txtOutput.Text = "Not a valid letter."
    End If
End Sub
```
(Assume the response is *B*.)

8.
```
Private Sub btnDisplay_Click(...) Handles btnDisplay.Click
    Dim vowel As Boolean = False
    Dim ltr As String
    ltr = InputBox("Enter a letter.")
    ltr = ltr.ToUpper
    If (ltr = "A") Or (ltr = "E") Or (ltr = "I") Or
      (ltr = "O") Or (ltr = "U") Then
      vowel = True
    End If
    If vowel Then
      txtOutput.Text = ltr & " is a vowel."
    Else
      txtOutput.Text = ltr & " is not a vowel."
    End If
End Sub
```
(Assume the response is *a*.)

9.
```
Private Sub btnDisplay_Click(...) Handles btnDisplay.Click
    Dim a As Double = 8
    If (a > 2) And ((a = 3) Or (a < 7)) Then
      txtOutput.Text = "Hi"
    End If
End Sub
```

10.
```
Private Sub btnDisplay_Click(...) Handles btnDisplay.Click
    Dim num As Double = 5
    If num < 0 Then
      txtOutput.Text = "neg"
    Else
      If num = 0 Then
        txtOutput.Text = "zero"
      Else
        txtOutput.Text = "positive"
      End If
    End If
End Sub
```

11.
```
Private Sub btnCompute_Click(...) Handles btnCompute.Click
    Dim msg As String = "You are old enough to vote"
    Dim dateOfBirth As Date = CDate(InputBox("Enter your date of birth."))
    If dateOfBirth.AddYears(18) <= Today Then
      txtOutput.Text = msg & "."
    Else
      txtOutput.Text = msg & " in " &
          DateDiff(DateInterval.Day, Today, dateOfBirth.AddYears(18)) &
          " days."
    End If
End Sub
```
(Assume that your 18th birthday is one week away.)

12.
```
Private Sub btnCompute_Click(...) Handles btnCompute.Click
    Dim dateOfBirth As Date = CDate(InputBox("Enter your date of birth."))
```

```
Dim nicksDateOfBirth As Date = #9/16/1992#
If dateOfBirth < nicksDateOfBirth Then
  txtOutput.Text = "You are older than Nick."
ElseIf dateOfBirth = nicksDateOfBirth Then
  txtOutput.Text = "You are the exact same age as Nick."
Else
  txtOutput.Text = "You are younger than Nick."
End If
End Sub
```

(Assume that the response is *10/25/1992.*)

In Exercises 13 through 16, identify the errors, state the type of each error (syntax, run-time, or logic), and correct the block of code.

13.
```
Private Sub btnDisplay_Click(...) Handles btnDisplay.Click
  Dim num As Double = 0.5
  If (1 < num < 3) Then
    txtOutput.Text = "Number is between 1 and 3."
  End If
End Sub
```

14.
```
Private Sub btnDisplay_Click(...) Handles btnDisplay.Click
  Dim num As Double = 6
  If num > 5 And < 9 Then
    txtOutput.Text = "Yes"
  Else
    txtOutput.Text = "No"
  End If
End Sub
```

15.
```
Private Sub btnDisplay_Click(...) Handles btnDisplay.Click
  Dim major As String
  major = "Computer Science"
  If major = "Business" Or "Computer Science" Then
    txtOutput.Text = "Yes"
  End If
End Sub
```

16.
```
Private Sub btnDisplay_Click(...) Handles btnDisplay.Click
  'Toggle switch from on to off and from off to on
  Dim switchOn As Boolean
  switchOn = CBool(InputBox("Enter True of False.", "The switch is on."))
  If switchOn Then
    switchOn = False
  End If
  If Not switchOn Then
    switchOn = True
  End If
  txtOutput.Text = CStr(switchOn)
End Sub
```

In Exercises 17 through 20, simplify the code.

17.
```
If (a = 2) Then
  a = 3 + a
Else
```

```
      a = 5
   End If
```

18.
```
If (j = 7) Then
   b = 1
Else
   If (j <> 7) Then
      b = 2
   End If
End If
```

19.
```
message = "Is Alaska bigger than Texas and California combined?"
answer = InputBox(message)
If (answer.Substring(0, 1) = "Y") Then
   answer = "YES"
End If
If (answer.Substring(0, 1) = "y") Then
   answer = "YES"
End If
If (answer = "YES") Then
   txtOutput.Text = "Correct"
Else
   txtOutput.Text = "Wrong"
End If
```

20.
```
message = "How tall (in feet) is the Statue of Liberty?"
feet = CDbl(InputBox(message))
If (feet <= 141) Then
   lstOutput.Items.Add("Nope")
End If
If (feet > 141) Then
   If (feet < 161) Then
     lstOutput.Items.Add("Close")
   Else
     lstOutput.Items.Add("Nope")
   End If
End If
lstOutput.Items.Add("The statue is 151 feet from base to torch.")
```

21. Write a program to determine how much to tip the server in a restaurant. The tip should be 15% of the check, with a minimum of $1.

22. A bagel shop charges 75 cents per bagel for orders of less than a half-dozen bagels and 60 cents per bagel for orders of a half-dozen or more. Write a program that requests the number of bagels ordered and displays the total cost. (Test the program for orders of four bagels and a dozen bagels.)

23. A store sells widgets at 50 cents each for small orders or at 45 cents each for orders of 150 or more. Write a program that requests the number of widgets ordered and displays the total cost. (Test the program for purchases of 10 and 200 widgets.)

24. A copy center charges 5 cents per copy for the first 100 copies and 3 cents per copy for each additional copy. Write a program that requests the number of copies as input and displays the total cost. (Test the program with the quantities 25 and 125.)

25. Write a quiz program to ask "Who was the first Ronald McDonald?" The program should display "Correct." if the answer is "Willard Scott" and "Nice try." for any other answer.

26. Suppose a program has a button with the caption "Quit". Suppose also that the Name property of this button is btnQuit. Write a btnQuit_Click event procedure that gives the user a second chance before ending the program. The procedure should use an input box to request that the user confirm that the program should be terminated, and then end the program only if the user responds in the affirmative.

27. Write a program that requests three scores as input and displays the average of the two highest scores.

28. Write a program to handle a savings-account withdrawal. The program should request the current balance and the amount of the withdrawal as input and then display the new balance. If the withdrawal is greater than the original balance, the program should display "Withdrawal denied." If the new balance is less than $150, the message "Balance below $150." also should be displayed.

29. A supermarket sells apples for $1.70 per pound. Write a cashier's program that requests the number of pounds and the amount of cash tendered as input and displays the change from the transaction. If the cash is not enough, the message "I need $x.xx more." should be displayed, where $x.xx is the difference between the total cost and the cash. (Test the program with six pounds and $20, and four pounds and $10.)

30. Write a program that requests a word (with lowercase letters) as input and translates the word into pig latin. The rules for translating a word into pig latin are as follows:

    (a) If the word begins with a group of consonants, move them to the end of the word and add *ay*. For instance, *chip* becomes *ipchay*.
    (b) If the word begins with a vowel, add *way* to the end of the word. For instance, *else* becomes *elseway*.

31. Federal law requires that hourly employees be paid "time-and-a-half" for work in excess of 40 hours in a week. For example, if a person's hourly wage is $8 and he works 60 hours in a week, his gross pay should be

$$(40 \times 8) + (1.5 \times 8 \times (60 - 40)) = \$560$$

Write a program that requests as input the number of hours a person works in a given week and his hourly wage, and then displays his gross pay.

32. The current calendar, called the Gregorian calendar, was introduced in 1582. Every year divisible by four was declared to be a leap year, with the exception of the years ending in 00 (that is, those divisible by 100) and not divisible by 400. For instance, the years 1600 and 2000 are leap years, but 1700, 1800, and 1900 are not. Write a program that requests a year as input and states whether it is a leap year. The program should not use any variables of type Date. (Test the program on the years 2008, 2009, 1900, and 2000.)

33. Create a form with a text box and two buttons captioned Bogart and Raines. When Bogart is first pressed, the sentence "I came to Casablanca for the waters." is displayed in the text box. The next time Bogart is pressed, the sentence "I was misinformed." is displayed. When Raines is pressed, the sentence "But we're in the middle of the desert." is displayed. Run the program and then press Bogart, Raines, and Bogart to obtain a dialogue.

34. Write a program that allows the user to use a button to toggle the color of the text in a text box between black and red.

35. Write a program that allows the user ten tries to answer the question, "Which U.S. President was born on July 4?" After three incorrect guesses, the program should display the hint, "He once said, 'If you don't say anything, you won't be called upon to repeat it.'" in a message box. After seven incorrect guesses, the program should give the hint, "His nickname was 'Silent Cal.'" The number of guesses should be displayed in a text box. (See Fig. 4.3.) **Note:** Calvin Coolidge was born on July 4, 1872.

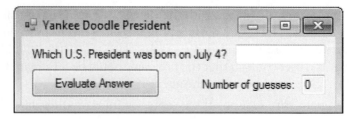

FIGURE 4.3   Form for Exercise 35.

36. Write a program that reads a test score from a text box each time a button is clicked and then displays the two highest scores whenever a second button is clicked. Use two class-level variables to track the two highest scores.

37. Write a program to play "Hide and Seek" with the name of our programming language. When the button is clicked on, the name should disappear and the caption on the button should change to "Show Name of Language." The next time the button is pressed, the name should reappear and the caption should revert to "Hide Name of Language," and so on.

OBJECT	PROPERTY	SETTING
frmHideSeek	Text	Hide and Seek
lblLanguage	Text	VB 2010
	Font.Size	26
btnDisplay	Text	Hide Name of Language

38. The flowchart in Fig. 4.5 (on the next page) calculates a person's state income tax. Write a program corresponding to the flowchart. (Test the program with taxable incomes of $15,000, $30,000, and $60,000.)

39. Rework Exercise 32 using a variable of type Date and the DateDiff function.

40. Write a program that requests your date of birth as input and tells you whether or not you are 25 years old or older. If not, the program should tell you the number of days until you will have your 25th birthday.

41. Write a program that requests your date of birth as input and tells your age. **Hint:** Use the Date-Diff function with the DateInterval.Year option, and then use an If block to modify the result.

42. Savings accounts state an interest rate and a compounding period. If the amount deposited is P, the stated interest rate is r, and interest is compounded m times per year, then the balance in the account after one year is $P \cdot \left(1 + \dfrac{r}{m}\right)^m$. For instance, if $1000 is deposited at 3% interest compounded quarterly (that is, 4 times per year), then the balance after one year is

$$1000 \cdot \left(1 + \frac{.03}{4}\right)^4 = 1000 \cdot 1.0075^4 = \$1,030.34.$$

Interest rates with different compounding periods cannot be compared directly. The concept of APY (annual percentage yield) must be used to make the comparison. The APY for a stated interest rate r compounded m times per year is defined by

$$\text{APY} = \left(1 + \frac{r}{m}\right)^m - 1.$$

(The APY is the simple interest rate that yields the same amount of interest after one year as the compounded annual rate of interest.) Write a program to compare interest rates offered by two different banks and determine the most favorable interest rate. See Fig. 4.4.

FIGURE 4.4   Possible outcome of Exercise 42.

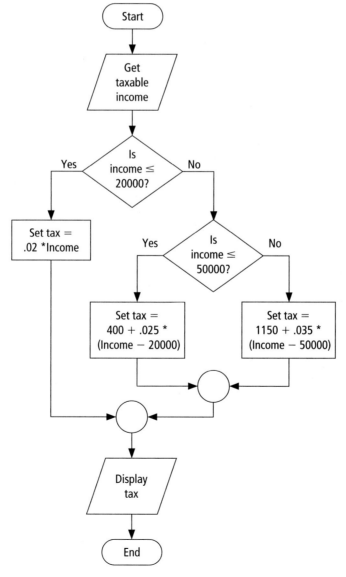

FIGURE 4.5   Flowchart for Exercise 38.

43. Rewrite the program in Example 8 without using ElseIf clauses. That is, the task should be carried out with a sequence of simple If blocks.

44. Rewrite the program in Example 8 so that the GPA is validated to be between 2 and 4 before the If block is executed.

Solutions to Practice Problems 4.2

1.
```
If (num < 0) Then
   MessageBox.Show("Number can't be negative.", "Input Error")
   txtNumber.Clear()
   txtNumber.Focus()
Else
   txtSquareRoot.Text = CStr(Math.Sqrt(num))
End If
```

2. The word "hello" will be displayed when (a < b) is true and (c < 5) is also true. That is, it will be displayed when both of these two conditions are true. The clearest way to write the block is

```
If (a < b) And (c < 5) Then
   txtBox.Text = "hello"
End If
```

4.3 Select Case Blocks

A Select Case block is an efficient decision-making structure that simplifies choosing among several actions. It avoids complex If constructs. If blocks make decisions based on the truth value of a condition; Select Case choices are determined by the value of an expression called a **selector**. Each possible action is preceded by a clause of the form

```
Case valueList
```

where *valueList* itemizes the values of the selector for which the action should be taken.

 Example 1 The following program converts the finishing position in a horse race into a descriptive phrase. After the variable *position* is assigned a value from txtPosition, Visual Basic searches for the first Case clause whose value list contains that value and executes the succeeding statement. If the value of *position* is greater than 5, then the statement following Case Else is executed.

OBJECT	PROPERTY	SETTING
frmRace	Text	Horse Race
lblPosition	AutoSize	False
	Text	Finishing position (1, 2, 3, ...):
txtPosition		
btnEvaluate	Text	Evaluate Position
txtOutcome	ReadOnly	True

```
Private Sub btnEvaluate_Click(...) Handles btnEvaluate.Click
   Dim position As Integer       'selector
   position = CInt(txtPosition.Text)
```

```
   Select Case position
     Case 1
       txtOutcome.Text = "Win"
     Case 2
       txtOutcome.Text = "Place"
     Case 3
       txtOutcome.Text = "Show"
     Case 4, 5
       txtOutcome.Text = "You almost placed in the money."
     Case Else
       txtOutcome.Text = "Out of the money."
   End Select
End Sub
```

[Run, type 2 into the text box, and click on the button.]

 Example 2   In the following variation of Example 1, the value lists specify ranges of values. The first value list provides another way to stipulate the numbers 1, 2, and 3. The second value list covers all numbers from 4 on.

```
Private Sub btnEvaluate_Click(...) Handles btnEvaluate.Click
  'Describe finishing positions in a horse race
  Dim position As Integer
  position = CInt(txtPosition.Text)
  Select Case position
    Case 1 To 3
      txtOutcome.Text = "In the money. Congratulations."
    Case Is >= 4
      txtOutcome.Text = "Not in the money."
  End Select
End Sub
```

[Run, type 2 into the text box, and click on the button.]

■ General Form of a Select Case Block

A typical form of the Select Case block is

```
Select Case selector
  Case valueList 1
     action 1
  Case valueList 2
     action 2
  Case Else
     action of last resort
End Select
```

where Case Else (and its action) is optional, and each value list contains one or more of the following types of items:

1. a literal;
2. a variable;
3. an expression;
4. an inequality sign preceded by Is and followed by a literal, variable, or expression;
5. a range expressed in the form **a To b**, where *a* and *b* are literals, variables, or expressions.

Two or more items appearing in the same list must be separated by commas. Each action consists of one or more statements. After the selector is evaluated, Visual Basic looks for the first value-list item including the value of the selector and carries out its associated action. (If the value of the selector appears in two different value lists, only the action associated with the first value list will be carried out.) If the value of the selector does not appear in any of the value lists and there is no Case Else clause, execution of the program will continue with the statement following the Select Case block.

Figure 4.6 contains the flowchart for a Select Case block. The pseudocode for a Select Case block is the same as for the equivalent If block.

 Example 3 The following program requests a month and a year, and then displays the number of days in that month. The program uses an If block nested inside a Select Case block. The If block determines whether the year is a leap year. (A year is a leap year if there are 366 days from January 1 of that year to January 1 of the next year.) The value lists come from the rhyme "Thirty days hath September."

OBJECT	PROPERTY	SETTING
frmDays	Text	Count Days
lblMonth:	Text	Month (1–12):
mtbMonth	Mask	00
lblYear	Text	Year:
mtbYear	Mask	0000
btnDetermine	Text	Determine Number of Days in Month
txtOutput	ReadOnly	True

```
Private Sub btnDetermine_Click(...) Handles btnDetermine.Click
  Dim month As Integer = CInt(mtbMonth.Text)
  Dim yr As Integer = CInt(mtbYear.Text)
```

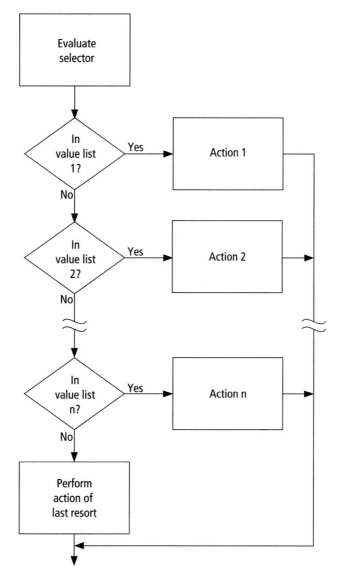

FIGURE 4.6   Flowchart for a select case block.

```
Dim d1, d2 As Date
Dim numberOfDays As Integer
Select Case month
  Case 9, 4, 6, 11    'September, April, June, and November
    numberOfDays = 30
  Case 2      'February
    d1 = CDate("1/1/" & yr)
    d2 = d1.AddYears(1)
    If DateDiff(DateInterval.Day, d1, d2) = 366 Then
      numberOfDays = 29
    Else
      numberOfDays = 28
    End If
  Case Else    'all the rest
    numberOfDays = 31
End Select
```

```
    txtOutput.Text = month & "/" & yr & "  has " &
        numberOfDays & " days."
End Sub
```

[Run, enter 2 and 2012 into the text boxes, and click on the button to find the number of days in February, 2012.]

In the three preceding examples, the selector was a numeric variable; however, the selector also can be a string variable, a date variable, or an expression.

 Example 4 The following program has the string variable *firstName* as a selector.

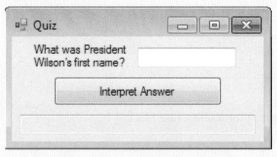

OBJECT	PROPERTY	SETTING
frmQuiz	Text	Quiz
lblQuestion	AutoSize	False
	Text	What was President Wilson's first name?
txtName		
btnInterpret	Text	Interpret Answer
txtReply	ReadOnly	True

```
Private Sub btnInterpret_Click(...) Handles btnInterpret.Click
    'Quiz
    Dim firstName As String
    firstName = txtName.Text.ToUpper
    Select Case firstName
        Case "THOMAS"
            txtReply.Text = "Correct."
        Case "WOODROW"
            txtReply.Text = "Sorry, his full name was " &
                            "Thomas Woodrow Wilson."
        Case "PRESIDENT"
            txtReply.Text = "Are you for real?"
        Case Else
            txtReply.Text = "Nice try, but no cigar."
    End Select
End Sub
```

[Run, type "Woodrow" into the text box, and click on the button.]

 Example 5   The following program has the string selector *anyString.Substring (0, 1)*. In the sample run, only the first action was carried out, even though the value of the selector was in both of the first two value lists. Visual Basic stops looking as soon as it finds the value of the selector.

OBJECT	PROPERTY	SETTING
frmAnalyze	Text	Analyze First Character
lblEnter	Text	Enter a string:
txtString		
btnAnalyze	Text	Analyze
txtResult	ReadOnly	True

```
Private Sub btnAnalyze_Click(...) Handles btnAnalyze.Click
   'Analyze the first character of a string
   Dim anyString As String
   anyString = txtString.Text.ToUpper
   Select Case anyString.Substring(0, 1)
     Case "S", "Z"
       txtResult.Text = "The string begins with a sibilant."
     Case "A" To "Z"
       txtResult.Text = "The string begins with a nonsibilant."
     Case "0" To "9"
       txtResult.Text = "The string begins with a digit."
     Case Is < "0"
       txtResult.Text = "The string begins with a character of " &
                        "ANSI value less than 48."
     Case Else
       txtResult.Text = "The string begins with : ; < = > " &
                        " ? @ [ \ ] ^ _ or ` . "
   End Select
End Sub
```

[Run, type "Sunday" into the text box, and click on the button.]

■ Comments

1. In a Case clause of the form `Case b To c`, the value of *b* should be less than or equal to the value of *c*. Otherwise, the clause is meaningless.

2. If the word `Is`, which should precede an inequality sign in a value list, is accidentally omitted, the editor will automatically insert it when checking the line.

3. The items in the value list must evaluate to a literal of the same type as the selector. For instance, if the selector evaluated to a string value, as in

```
Dim firstName As String
firstName = txtBox.Text
Select Case firstName
```

then the clause

```
Case firstName.Length
```

would be meaningless.

4. Any variable declared inside an If or Select Case block has **block-level scope**; that is, the variable cannot be referred to by code outside the block.

5. In Appendix D, the section "Stepping through Programs Containing Selection Structures: Chapter 4" uses the Visual Basic debugging tools to trace the flow through a Select Case block.

Practice Problems 4.3

1. Suppose the selector of a Select Case block is the numeric variable *num*. Determine whether each of the following Case clauses is valid.

    (a) `Case 1, 4, Is < 10`
    (b) `Case Is < 5, Is >= 5`
    (c) `Case num = 2` (where the selector *num* is of type Double)

2. Do the following two programs always produce the same output for a whole-number grade from 0 to 100?

```
grade = CInt(txtBox.Text)          grade = CInt(txtBox.Text)
Select Case grade                  Select Case grade
  Case Is >= 90                      Case Is >= 90
    txtOutput.Text = "A"               txtOutput.Text = "A"
  Case Is >= 60                      Case 60 To 89
    txtOutput.Text = "Pass"            txtOutput.Text = "Pass"
  Case Else                          Case 0 To 59
    txtOutput.Text = "Fail"            txtOutput.Text = "Fail"
End Select                         End Select
```

EXERCISES 4.3

In Exercises 1 through 6, for each of the responses shown in the parentheses, determine the output displayed in the text box when the button is clicked on.

```
1. Private Sub btnDisplay_Click(...) Handles btnDisplay.Click
     Dim age, price As Double
     age = CDbl(InputBox("What is your age?"))
     Select Case age
```

```
      Case Is < 13
        price = 4.25
      Case 13 To 19
        price = 6.75
      Case Is >= 19
        price = 8.00
    End Select
    txtOutput.Text = "The price is " & FormatCurrency(price)
  End Sub
```

   (14.5, 20)

2.
```
Private Sub btnDisplay_Click(...) Handles btnDisplay.Click
  Dim num As Double
  num = CDbl(InputBox("Enter a number from 5 to 12"))
  Select Case num
    Case 5
      txtOutput.Text = "case 1"
    Case 5 To 7
      txtOutput.Text = "case 2"
    Case 7 To 12
      txtOutput.Text = "case 3"
  End Select
End Sub
```

   (7, 5, 11.2)

3.
```
Private Sub btnDisplay_Click(...) Handles btnDisplay.Click
  Dim age As Integer
  age = CInt(InputBox("Enter age (in millions of years)"))
  Select Case age
    Case Is < 70
      txtOutput.Text = "Cenozoic Era"
    Case Is < 225
      txtOutput.Text = "Mesozoic Era"
    Case Is <= 600
      txtOutput.Text = "Paleozoic Era"
    Case Else
      txtOutput.Text = "?"
  End Select
End Sub
```

   (100, 600, 700)

4.
```
Private Sub btnDisplay_Click(...) Handles btnDisplay.Click
  Dim pres As String
  pres = InputBox("Who was the youngest U.S. president?")
  Select Case pres.ToUpper
    Case "THEODORE ROOSEVELT", "TEDDY ROOSEVELT"
      txtOutput.Text = "Correct. He became president at age 42 " & _
                        "when President McKinley was assassinated."
    Case "JFK", "JOHN KENNEDY", "JOHN F. KENNEDY"
      txtOutput.Text = "Incorrect. At age 43, he was the youngest " & _
                        "person elected president."
```

```
      Case Else
        txtOutput.Text = "Nope"
    End Select
  End Sub
```

(JFK, Teddy Roosevelt)

5.
```
Private Sub btnDisplay_Click(...) Handles btnDisplay.Click
  Dim message As String, a, b, c As Double
  message = "Analyzing solutions to the quadratic equation " &
            "AX^2 + BX + C = 0.  Enter the value for "
  a = CDbl(InputBox(message & "A"))
  b = CDbl(InputBox(message & "B"))
  c = CDbl(InputBox(message & "C"))
  Select Case (b ^ 2) - (4 * a * c)
    Case Is < 0
      txtOutput.Text = "The equation has no real solutions."
    Case 0
      txtOutput.Text = "The equation has exactly one solution."
    Case Is > 0
      txtOutput.Text = "The equation has two solutions."
  End Select
End Sub
```

$(1,2,3; 1,5,1; 1,2,1)$

6.
```
Private Sub btnDisplay_Click(...) Handles btnDisplay.Click
  Dim whatever As Double
  whatever = CDbl(InputBox("Enter a number:"))
  Select Case whatever
    Case Else
      txtOutput.Text = "Hi"
  End Select
End Sub
```

$(7, -1)$

In Exercises 7 through 12, identify the errors.

7.
```
Private Sub btnDisplay_Click(...) Handles btnDisplay.Click
  Dim num As Double = 2
  Select Case num
    txtOutput.Text = "Two"
  End Select
End Sub
```

8.
```
Private Sub btnDisplay_Click(...) Handles btnDisplay.Click
  Dim num1 As Double = 5
  Dim num2 As Double = 2
  Select Case num1
    Case 3 <= num1 <= 10
      txtOutput.Text = "between 3 and 10."
    Case num2 To 5; 4
      txtOutput.Text = "near 5."
  End Select
End Sub
```

9. ```
Private Sub btnDisplay_Click(...) Handles btnDisplay.Click
    Dim nom As String
    nom = InputBox("What is your name?")
    Select Case nom
      Case nom = "Bob"
        txtOutput.Text = "Hi, Bob."
      Case Else
    End Select
End Sub
```

10. ```
Private Sub btnDisplay_Click(...) Handles btnDisplay.Click
    Dim word As String = "hello"
    Select Case word.Substring(0,1)
      Case h
        txtOutput.Text = "begins with h."
    End Select
End Sub
```

11. ```
Private Sub btnDisplay_Click(...) Handles btnDisplay.Click
    Dim fruit As String = "Peach"
    Select Case fruit.ToUpper
      Case Is >= "Peach"
        txtOutput.Text = "Georgia"
      Case "ORANGE To PEACH"
        txtOutput.Text = "Ok"
    End Select
End Sub
```

12. ```
Private Sub btnDisplay_Click(...) Handles btnDisplay.Click
    Dim purchase As Double
    purchase = CDbl(InputBox("Quantity purchased?"))
    Select Case purchase
      Case purchase < 10000
        txtOutput.Text = "Five dollars per item."
      Case Is 10000 To 30000
        txtOutput.Text = "Four dollars per item."
      Case Is > 30000
        txtOutput.Text = "Three dollars per item."
    End Select
End Sub
```

In Exercises 13 through 18, suppose the selector of a Select Case block, *word*, evaluates to a String value. Determine whether the Case clause is valid.

13. `Case "un" & "til"`

14. `Case "hello"`

15. `Case 0 To 9`

16. `Case word <> "No"`

17. `Case "abc".Substring(0, 1)`

18. `Case Is <> "No"`

In Exercises 19 through 22, rewrite the code using a Select Case block.

19.
```
If a = 1 Then
    txtOutput.Text = "one"
Else
  If a > 5 Then
    txtOutput.Text = "two"
  End If
End If
```

20.
```
If a = 1 Then
    lstOutput.Items.Add("lambs")
End If
If ((a <= 3) And (a < 4)) Then
  lstOutput.Items.Add("eat")
End If
If ((a = 5) Or (a > 7)) Then
  lstOutput.Items.Add("ivy")
End If
```

21.
```
If a > 5 Then
  If a = 7 Then
    txtOutput.Text = "yes"
  Else
    txtOutput.Text = "no"
  End If
Else
  If a = 2 Then
   txtOutput.Text = "maybe"
  End If
End If
```

22.
```
If a = 3 Then
  a = 1
End If
If a = 2 Then
  a = 3
End If
If a = 1 Then
  a = 2
End If
```

23. Table 4.5 gives the terms used by the National Weather Service to describe the degree of cloudiness. Write a program that requests the percentage of cloud cover as input and then displays the appropriate descriptor.

TABLE 4.5   **Cloudiness descriptors.**

Percentage of Cloud Cover	Descriptor
0–30	clear
31–70	partly cloudy
71–99	cloudy
100	overcast

24. Table 4.6 shows the location of books in the library stacks according to their call numbers. Write a program that requests the call number of a book as input and displays the location of the book.

TABLE 4.6   Location of library books.

100 to 199	basement
200 to 500 and over 900	main floor
501 to 900 except 700 to 750	upper floor
700 to 750	archives

25. Figure 4.7 shows some geometric shapes and formulas for their areas. Write a program that requests the user to select one of the shapes, requests the appropriate lengths, and then gives the area of the figure.

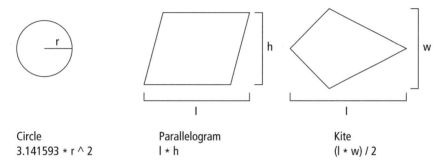

Circle	Parallelogram	Kite
3.141593 * r ^ 2	l * h	(l * w) / 2

FIGURE 4.7   Areas of geometric shapes.

26. *Break-Even Analysis.* Suppose a certain product sells for a dollars per unit. Then the revenue from selling x units of the product is ax dollars. If the cost of producing each unit of the product is b dollars and the company has overhead costs of c dollars, then the total cost of producing x units of the product is $bx + c$ dollars. (**Note: Revenue** is the amount of money received from the sale of the product. The values of a, b, and c are called the **marginal revenue, marginal cost,** and **fixed cost** respectively. The break-even point is the value of x for which the revenue equals the total cost.) Write a program that requests the marginal revenue, marginal cost, fixed cost, and number of units of the product produced and sold (x) and then displays one of the following three outputs: PROFIT, LOSS, or BREAK EVEN.

27. Write a program that requests an exam score and assigns a letter grade with the scale 90–100 (A), 80–89 (B), 70–79 (C), 60–69 (D), 0–59 (F). (Test the program with the grades 84, 100, and 57.)

VideoNote

Grading
system
(Homework)

28. Table 4.7 contains information on several states. Write a program that requests a state and category (flower, motto, and nickname) as input and displays the requested information. If the state or category requested is not in the table, the program should so inform the user.

TABLE 4.7   State flowers, nicknames, and mottoes.

State	Flower	Nickname	Motto
California	Golden Poppy	Golden State	Eureka
Indiana	Peony	Hoosier State	Crossroads of America
Mississippi	Magnolia	Magnolia State	By valor and arms
New York	Rose	Empire State	Ever upward

29. IRS informants are paid cash awards based on the value of the money recovered. If the information was specific enough to lead to a recovery, the informant receives 10 percent of the first $75,000, 5 percent of the next $25,000, and 1 percent of the remainder, up to a maximum award of $50,000. Write a program that requests the amount of the recovery as input and displays the award. (Test the program on the amounts $10,000, $125,000, and $10,000,000.) **Note:** The source of this formula is *The Book of Inside Information*, Boardroom Books, 1993.

30. Table 4.8 contains the meanings of some abbreviations doctors often use for prescriptions. Write a program that requests an abbreviation and gives its meaning. The user should be informed if the meaning is not in the table.

TABLE 4.8   **Physicians' abbreviations.**

Abbreviation	Meaning
ac	before meals
ad lib	freely as needed
bid	twice daily
gtt	a drop
hs	at bedtime
qid	four times a day

31. Write a program that, given the last name of one of the six recent presidents beginning with Carter, displays his state and a colorful fact about him. (**Hint:** The program might need to request further information.) (**Note:** Carter: Georgia; The only soft drink served in the Carter White House was Coca-Cola. Reagan: California; His Secret Service code name was Rawhide. George H. W. Bush: Texas; He celebrated his 85th birthday by parachuting out of an airplane. Clinton: Arkansas; In college he did a good imitation of Elvis Presley. George W. Bush: Texas; He once owned the Texas Rangers baseball team. Obama: Illinois; He was the eighth left-handed president.)

32. Write a programs in which the user enters a number into a masked text box and then clicks on the appropriate button to have either one of three pieces of humor or one of three insults displayed in a text box below the buttons. If the number entered is not between 1 and 3, the masked text box should be cleared. (**Note:** Some possible bits of humor are "I can resist everything except temptation," "I just heard from Bill Bailey. He's not coming home," and "Adding people to a late software project makes it later." Some possible insults are "How much would you charge to haunt a house?" "I bet you have no more friends than an alarm clock," and "When your IQ rises to 30, sell.")

OBJECT	PROPERTY	SETTING
frmExercise32	Text	4.3 Exercise 32
lblNumber	Text	Number (1–3):
mtbNumber	Mask	0
btnHumor	Text	&Humor
btnInsult	Text	&Insult
txtSentence	ReadOnly	True

Solutions to Practice Problems 4.3

1. (a) Valid. These items are redundant because 1 and 4 are just special cases of **Is < 10**. However, this makes no difference in Visual Basic.

   (b) Valid. These items are contradictory. However, Visual Basic looks at them one at a time until it finds an item containing the value of the selector. The action following this Case clause will always be carried out.

   (c) Not valid. It should be **Case 2**.

2. Yes. However, the program on the right is clearer and therefore preferable.

4.4 Input via User Selections

Programs frequently ask the user to make selections from lists of options. In the questionnaire in Fig. 4.8, students can select their major from a list box, their year from a set of radio buttons, and their computer languages studied from a set of check boxes. After the selections have been made, the user clicks on the *Record Data* button to process the information. The set of radio buttons and set of check boxes are each contained in a group box control. The titles sunk into the tops of the group boxes are *Year* and *Languages Studied.* After selections are made from the three sets of choices, decision structures can be used to process the information. Let's consider the four types of controls in Fig. 4.8 one at a time.

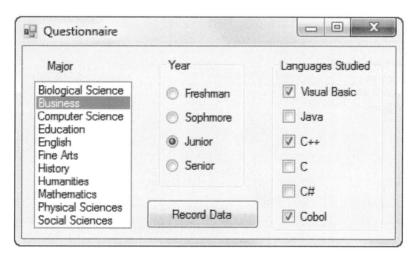

FIGURE 4.8 Selection controls.

▨ Using a List Box for Input

The easiest way to populate a list box with items is to place the items into the list box's String Collection Editor at design time. When you click on the list box's *Tasks* button and then click on *Edit Items* (Fig. 4.9), the String Collection Editor appears. Figure 4.10 shows the String Collection Editor filled with the items from Fig. 4.8. Three ways to fill the String Collection Editor are as follows:

1. Type the items directly into the String Collection Editor.

2. Copy a list of items from any text editor (such as Notepad or Word) with Ctrl + C and paste the list into the String Collection Editor with Ctrl + V.

3. Copy a column of data from a spreadsheet program (such as Excel) and paste it into the String Collection Editor.

When the user clicks on an item at run time, that item is highlighted, and the value of lstBox.Text is that item represented as a string.

FIGURE 4.9 Click on *Edit Items* to invoke the String Collection Editor.

FIGURE 4.10 String Collection Editor.

 Example 1 The following program uses a list of months. The months can be typed directly into the String Collection Editor. An alternate way to obtain the list of months is to generate it with Excel. To do so, type January into a cell of an Excel spreadsheet [see Fig. 4.11(a)], click on the cell, drag its fill handle down to create the other months [see Fig. 4.11(b)], and press Ctrl + C. Then the list of twelve months can be pasted into the String Collection Editor with Ctrl + V.

```
Private Sub btnDetermine_Click(...) Handles btnDetermine.Click
  Dim daysInMonth As String
  Select Case lstMonths.Text
    Case "September", "April", "June", "November"
      daysInMonth = "30"
    Case "February"
      daysInMonth = "28 or 29"
```

```
      Case Else
        daysInMonth = "31"
    End Select
    txtDays.Text = daysInMonth
  End Sub
```

[Run, click on a month, and then click on the button.]

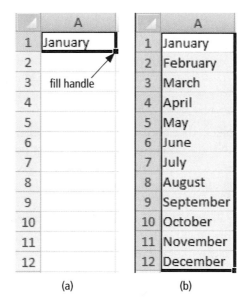

FIGURE 4.11   **Creating a list of months with Excel.**

✓ **Example 2**   The following program presents a list of famous movie lines spoken by leading male actors. After the user makes a selection and clicks on the button, the actor is identified. The numbering of the lines allows the Select Case block to be simplified.

```
Private Sub btnDetermine_Click(...) Handles btnDetermine.Click
  Dim actor As String = ""
  Select Case lstLines.Text.Substring(0, 1)
    Case "1", "2"
      actor = "Marlon Brando"
    Case "3", "4"
```

```
            actor = "Humphrey Bogart"
        Case "5", "6"
            actor = "Harrison Ford"
        Case "7"
            actor = "Leonardo DiCaprio"
        Case "8"
            actor = "Roy Scheider"
    End Select
    txtActor.Text = actor
End Sub
```

[Run, click on one of the lines in the list box, and then click on the button.]

When no item in a list box is highlighted, the value of lstBox.SelectedItem is *Nothing*. Also, the statement `lstBox.SelectedItem = Nothing` deselects any item that has been selected. By default, only one item at a time can be selected in a list box.

■ Group Box Control

Group boxes are passive objects that contain related sets of controls. In Fig. 4.7, the group box titled *Year* contains four radio button controls and the group box titled *Languages Studied* contains six check boxes. Clusters of radio buttons are almost always contained in group boxes. Actually, any set of controls can be placed into a group box for visual effect.

You rarely write event procedures for group boxes. When you move a group box, the controls inside it follow as a unit. Therefore, the controls are said to be **attached** to the group box. If you hide a group box, the attached controls will be hidden as well. To attach a control to a group box, just create the control any way you like and drag it inside the group box. The standard prefix for the name of a group box is *grp*. The title sunk into the top of a group box's border is set with the Text property.

■ Using Radio Buttons for Input

Radio buttons allow the user to make a single choice from among several options. The name "radio button" comes from a reference to the first car radios, which had buttons that pressed in. Pressing one button would move the dial to a preset station and would raise any other button that was depressed.

Normally, a collection of several radio buttons is attached to a group box. Each button consists of a small circle accompanied by a caption that is set with the Text property. (As with ordinary buttons, an ampersand can be used to create an access key for a radio button.) When a circle or its accompanying caption is clicked, a solid dot appears in the circle and the button is said to be on. At most one radio button in a group can be on at any one time. Therefore, if one button is on and another button in the group is clicked, the first button will be turned off. The standard prefix for the name of a radio button is *rad*. A single form can have several groups of radio buttons.

The Checked property of a radio button tells if the button is on or off. The condition

`radButton.Checked`

is true when radButton is on and false when radButton is off. The statement

`radButton.Checked = True`

turns on radButton and turns off all other buttons in its group. The statement

`radButton.Checked = False`

turns off radButton and has no effect on the other buttons in its group.

 Example 3   The following program displays the admission fee to an event. After the user clicks on a radio button and clicks on the *Determine Fee* button, the fee is displayed in a text box. The Else clause in the If block handles the case where no selection was made.

OBJECT	PROPERTY	SETTING
frmFee	Text	Admission Fee
grpAge	Text	Age
radChild	Text	child (< 6)
radMinor	Text	minor (6-17)
radAdult	Text	adult (18-64)
radSenior	Text	senior (65+)
btnDetermine	Text	Determine Fee
lblFee	Text	Fee:
txtFee	ReadOnly	True

```
Private Sub btnDetermine_Click(...) Handles btnDetermine.Click
  If radChild.Checked Then
    txtFee.Text = FormatCurrency(0)
  ElseIf radMinor.Checked Then
    txtFee.Text = FormatCurrency(5)
  ElseIf radAdult.Checked Then
    txtFee.Text = FormatCurrency(10)
  ElseIf radSenior.Checked Then
    txtFee.Text = FormatCurrency(7.5)
  Else
    MessageBox.Show("You must make a selection.")
  End If
End Sub
```

[Run, click on a radio button, and click on the *Determine Fee* button]

■ Using Check Boxes for Input

A **check box**, which consists of a small square and a caption (set with the Text property), presents the user with a yes/no choice. The form in Fig. 4.7 contains six check box controls. The Checked property of a check box has the value False when the square is empty and True when the square is checked. At run time, the user clicks on the square (or its accompanying caption) to toggle between the unchecked and checked states.

 Example 4 The following program calculates the monthly cost of a company health plan. The user checks the desired plans, and then clicks on the button to calculate the total cost.

OBJECT	PROPERTY	SETTING
frmMenu	Text	Benefits Menu
chkDrug	Text	Prescription Drug Plan ($39.15)
chkDental	Text	Dental Plan ($10.81)
chkVision	Text	Vision Plan ($2.25)
chkMedical	Text	Medical Plan ($55.52)
btnDetermine	Text	Determine Total Monthly Cost
lblTotal	Text	Total monthly cost:
txtTotal	ReadOnly	True

```
Private Sub btnDetermine_Click(...) Handles btnDetermine.Click
  Dim sum As Double = 0
  If chkDrug.Checked Then
    sum += 39.15
  End If
  If chkDental.Checked Then
    sum += 10.81
  End If
  If chkVision.Checked Then
    sum += 2.25
  End If
  If chkMedical.Checked Then
    sum += 55.52
  End If
  txtTotal.Text = FormatCurrency(sum)
End Sub
```

[Run, select plans, and then click on the button.]

When a check box has the focus, the spacebar can be used to check (or uncheck) the box. In addition, the state of a check box can be toggled from the keyboard without first setting the focus to the check box if you create an access key for the check box by including an ampersand in the Text property. (At run time, access keys appear underlined after the Alt key is pressed.) For instance, if the Text property for the Dental Plan in Example 4 is set as "&Dental Plan", then the user can check (or uncheck) the box by pressing Alt + D.

■ Events Raised by Selections

In most real-life programs, the user is asked to make selections from several different controls and then click on a button in order to process the information. Such is the case with the Visual Basic Font selection window shown in Fig. 4.12, where the OK button is clicked after the selections have been made. Sometimes however, you would like to process information as soon as an item in a list box, a radio button, or a check box is clicked. Visual Basic provides event procedures for immediate processing.

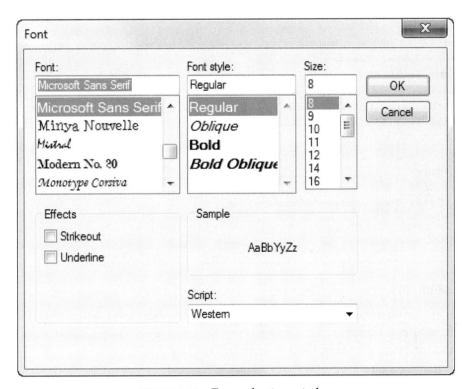

FIGURE 4.12   Font selection window.

When you click on an item in a list box, the **SelectedIndexChanged event** is raised. When you click on a radio button or a check box, the **CheckedChanged event** is raised. These events are the default events for their controls.

   Example 5   The following variation of Example 4 keeps a running total of the monthly cost of the benefits. The amount in the text box is increased each time a check box becomes checked and is decreased each time a check box becomes unchecked. To create the header for the event procedure we double-clicked on the first check box, changed the name of the event procedure from chkDrug_CheckedChanged to checkBox_CheckedChanged, and added three additional events following the keyword Handles.

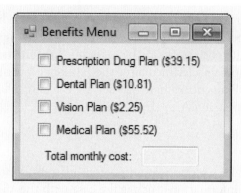

OBJECT	PROPERTY	SETTING
frmMenu	Text	Benefits Menu
chkDrug	Text	Prescription Drug Plan ($39.15)
chkDental	Text	Dental Plan ($10.81)
chkVision	Text	Vision Plan ($2.25)
chkMedical	Text	Medical Plan ($55.52)
lblTotal	Text	Total monthly cost:
txtTotal	ReadOnly	True

```
Private Sub checkBox_CheckedChanged(...) Handles _
                    chkDrug.CheckedChanged, chkDental.CheckedChanged,
                    chkVision.CheckedChanged, chkMedical.CheckedChanged
    Dim sum As Double
    If chkDrug.Checked Then
       sum += 39.15
    End If
    If chkDental.Checked Then
       sum += 10.81
    End If
    If chkVision.Checked Then
       sum += 2.25
    End If
    If chkMedical.Checked Then
       sum += 55.52
    End If
    txtTotal.Text = FormatCurrency(sum)
End Sub
```

■ Comments

1. Both list boxes and radio buttons can be used to select a single item from a list of options. As a rule of thumb, radio buttons should be used with short lists (at most seven options) and list boxes should be used with long lists.

2. When the user clicks on a checked check box, it becomes unchecked. Such is not the case with a radio button. A radio button can only be unchecked with code or by clicking on another radio button.

Practice Problems 4.4

1. What is the difference between a set of check boxes attached to a group box and a set of radio buttons attached to a group box?

2. Suppose a form contains two sets of radio buttons. Why is it essential for the sets to be contained in separate group boxes? Do the same concerns apply to sets of check boxes?

3. Suppose a group box contains a set of radio buttons. Give two ways to guarantee that the user will select one of the radio buttons.

In Exercises 1 through 8, determine the effect of setting the property to the value shown.

1. `GroupBox1.Text = "Income"`

2. `CheckBox1.Checked = True`

3. `CheckBox1.Checked = False`

4. `CheckBox1.Text = "&Vanilla"`

5. `RadioButton1.Checked = False`

6. `txtOutput.Text = lstBox.Text`

7. `RadioButton1.Text = "Clear &All"`

8. `RadioButton1.Checked = True`

In Exercises 9 through 12, write one or more lines of code to carry out the task.

9. Set the caption for RadioButton1 to "Yes".

10. Clear the small rectangular box of CheckBox1.

11. Guarantee that CheckBox1 is checked.

12. Turn off RadioButton2.

In Exercises 13 and 14, determine the state of the two radio buttons after Button1 is clicked.

13.
```
Private Sub Button1_Click(...) Handles Button1.Click
    RadioButton1.Checked = True
    RadioButton2.Checked = True
End Sub
```

14.
```
Private Sub Button1_Click(...) Handles Button1.Click
    RadioButton1.Checked = False
    RadioButton2.Checked = False
End Sub
```

15. Suppose that a group box has two radio buttons attached to it. If the statement

    `GroupBox1.Visible = False`

    is executed, will the radio buttons also vanish? Test your answer.

16. Create a form with two group boxes, each having two radio buttons attached to it. Run the program and confirm that the two pairs of radio buttons operate independently of each other.

17. A computer dealer offers two basic computers, the Deluxe ($1000) and the Super ($1500). The customer can order any of the following additional options: upgraded video card ($200), internal modem plus Wi-Fi ($30), or 1 GB of added memory ($120). Write a program that computes the cost of the computer system selected. See Fig. 4.13.

18. Write a program to book an airline flight. See Fig. 4.14 on the next page. If the same airport is selected from the two list boxes, the user should be informed immediately that the departure and arrival airports must be different. If no airport has been selected from one or both of the list boxes when the button is clicked, then the user should be told what information must be supplied. Use message boxes to inform the user of problems.

FIGURE 4.13   **Possible outcome of Exercise 17.**   FIGURE 4.14   **Possible outcome of Exercise 18.**

19. Write a program that allows you to vote for one of two presidential candidates. See Fig. 4.15. When the *Cast Vote* button is clicked on, the text box should display your vote. In the event that neither radio button is on, the sentence "You voted for neither." should appear in the text box.

FIGURE 4.15   **Possible output for Exercise 19.**   FIGURE 4.16   **Possible output for Exercise 20.**

20. Article II, Section 1, Clause 5 of the Constitution of the United States, states that "No Person except a natural born Citizen, or a Citizen of the United States at the time of the Adoption of this Constitution, shall be eligible to the Office of President; neither shall any Person be eligible to that Office who shall not have attained to the Age of thirty five Years, and been fourteen Years a Resident within the United States." Write a program that determines if a person is eligible to run for President of the United States in 2012. (**Note:** A natural born citizen is a person who is born within the jurisdiction of the U.S. government. A 2012 candidate for president must achieve age 35 by Inauguration Day, 1/21/2013.) See Fig. 4.16. **Hint:** Use the AddYears method.

21. Write a program that uses the form in Fig. 4.8 at the beginning of the section. When the button is clicked, the program should first determine if a selection has been made from both the list box and the group of radio buttons. If not, a message box should appear telling the user which types of selections have not been made. If both selections have been made, the message "Information Processed" should be displayed.

22. Write a program that uses the form in Fig. 4.8 at the beginning of the section. When the button is clicked, the program should print the names of the computer languages studied. If no check boxes have been checked, the sentence "No languages studied." should be printed.

23. Figure 4.17 shows an item from the 2008 U.S. Individual Income Tax Return. Write a program whose form resembles item 39a. The program should look at the four check boxes and display in the large text box at the right of the item the number of boxes checked.

39a Check ⎰ ☐ **You** were born before January 2, 1944, ☐ Blind. ⎱ **Total boxes**
     if: ⎱ ☐ **Spouse** was born before January 2, 1944, ☐ Blind. ⎰ **checked ▶ 39a** ☐

FIGURE 4.17   **Item 39a from Form 1040 of the 2008 U.S. Individual Income Tax Return.**

24. Write a program to specify the foreground and background colors for a label containing the words VISUAL BASIC. See Fig. 4.18. If the same color is selected from the two group boxes, the user should be informed immediately that the two colors must be different. If no color has been selected from one or both of the group boxes when the button is clicked, then the user should be told what information must be supplied. Use message boxes to inform the user of problems.

FIGURE 4.18   **Possible outcome for Exercise 24.**

FIGURE 4.19   **Possible outcome of Exercise 25.**

25. The basic monthly cost of a membership in a sport and health club is $100 for adults and $75 for seniors. Available extras cost $25 each per month. Write a program that uses the form in Fig. 4.19 to calculate a member's monthly fee. Before calculating the fee, make sure that a membership category has been selected.

Solutions to Practice Problems 4.4

1. With radio buttons, at most one button can be on at any given time, whereas several check boxes can be checked simultaneously.

2. With two sets of radio buttons, you would like to make two selections. However if the two sets are in the same group box, then at most one radio button can be on at any time.

   Since several check boxes can be checked at any time, you needn't have this concern with check boxes. However, the two sets of check boxes are usually placed in separate group boxes to improve the visual effect.

3. Method 1: Make one of the radio buttons the default radio button; that is, set its Checked property to True at design time.

   Method 2: Place the code that refers to the radio buttons in an If block that displays a message when no radio button in the group box has been checked.

CHAPTER 4 SUMMARY

1. The function *Chr* associates a character with each number from 0 through 255 as determined by the ANSI table. The function *Asc* is the inverse of the Chr function.

2. The *relational operators* are <, >, =, <>, <=, and >=.

3. The principal *logical operators* are And, Or, and Not.

4. A *condition* is an expression involving literals, variables, functions, and operators (arithmetic, relational, or logical) that can be evaluated as either True or False.

5. The value of a variable or expression of *Boolean data type* is either True or False.

6. An *If block* decides what action to take depending on the truth values of one or more conditions. To allow several courses of action, the If, ElseIf, and Else parts of an If statement can contain other If statements.

7. A *Select Case block* selects from one of several actions depending on the value of an expression, called the *selector*. The entries in the *value lists* should have the same type as the selector.

8. *List boxes, radio buttons,* and *check boxes* provide an efficient way for a program to select among a set of possible options.

CHAPTER 4 PROGRAMMING PROJECTS

1. Table 4.9 gives the price schedule for Eddie's Equipment Rental. Full-day rentals cost one-and-a-half times half-day rentals. Write a program that displays Table 4.9 in a list box when an appropriate button is clicked on and displays a bill in another list box based on the item number and time period chosen by a customer. The bill should include a $30.00 deposit. A sample output is shown in Fig. 4.20.

TABLE 4.9 Price schedule for Eddie's Equipment Rental.

Piece of Equipment	Half-Day	Full-Day
1. Rug cleaner	$16.00	$24.00
2. Lawn mower	$12.00	$18.00
3. Paint sprayer	$20.00	$30.00

FIGURE 4.20 Form layout and sample output for Programming Project 1.

2. The American Heart Association suggests that at most 30% of the calories in our diet come from fat, and 10% from saturated fat. Although food labels give the number of calories and amount of fat per serving, they often do not give the percentage of calories from fat or saturated fat. The percentage of calories from fat (or saturated fat) can be calculated by multiplying the number of grams of fat (or saturated fat) in one serving by 9, dividing that number by the total number of calories per serving, and multiplying the result by 100. Write a program that requests the name, number of calories per serving, the grams of fat per serving, and the grams of saturated fat per serving as input, and tells us whether the food meets the American Heart Association recommendations. A sample run is as in Fig. 4.21.

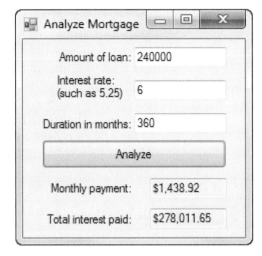

FIGURE 4.21   **Possible output for Practice Problem 2.**

FIGURE 4.22   **Possible output for Practice Problem 3.**

3. Write a program to analyze a mortgage. See Fig. 4.22. The user should enter the amount of the loan, the annual percentage rate of interest, and the duration of the loan in months. When the user clicks on the button, the information that was entered should be checked to make sure it is reasonable. If bad data have been supplied, the user should be so advised. Otherwise, the monthly payment and the total amount of interest paid should be displayed. The formula for the monthly payment is

$$\text{payment} = p*r/(1 - (1 + r)^{\wedge}(-n)),$$

where p is the amount of the loan, r is the monthly interest rate (annual rate divided by 12) given as a number between 0 (for 0 percent) and 1 (for 100 percent), and n is the duration of the loan in months. The formula for the total interest paid is

$$\text{total interest} = n*\text{payment} - p.$$

4. Table 4.10 gives the 2010 federal income tax rate schedule for single taxpayers. Write a program that requests taxable income and calculates the federal income tax.

TABLE 4.10   **2010 federal income tax rates for single taxpayers.**

Taxable Income Over	But Not Over	The Tax Is	Of Amount Over
$0	$8,375	10%	$0
$8,375	$34,000	$837.50 + 15%	$8,375
$34,000	$82,400	$4,681.25 + 25%	$34,000
$82,400	$171,850	$16,781.25 + 28%	$82,400
$171,850	$373,650	$41,827.25 + 33%	$171,850
$373,650		$108,421.25 + 35%	$373,650

5. Write a program to determine the real roots of the quadratic equation $ax^2 + bx + c = 0$ (where $a \neq 0$) after requesting the values of a, b, and c. Before finding the roots, ensure that a is nonzero. [**Note:** The equation has 2, 1, or 0 solutions depending on whether the value of $b^2 - 4*a*c$ is positive, zero, or negative. In the first two cases, the solutions are given by the quadratic formula $(-b \pm \text{Math.Sqrt}(b^2 - 4*a*c))/(2*a)$.] Test the program with the following sets of coefficients:

$a = 1$	$b = -11$	$c = 28$	Solutions are 4 and 7
$a = 1$	$b = -6$	$c = 9$	Solution is 3
$a = 1$	$b = 4$	$c = 5$	No solution

6. Write a program to place an order from the restaurant menu in Table 4.11. Use the form in Fig. 4.23, and write the program so that each group box is invisible and becomes visible only when its corresponding check box is checked. After the button is clicked, the cost of the meal should be calculated. (**Note:** The Checked property of the first radio button in each group box should be set to True in its Properties window. This guarantees that a selection is made in each visible group box. Of course, when the cost of the meal is calculated, only the visible group boxes should be considered.) See Fig. 4.24.

TABLE 4.11	Menu of Oceanside Burgers & Fries.		
	Burgers	Fries	Drinks
	Regular (4.19)	Small (2.39)	Soda (1.69)
	w/ cheese (4.79)	Medium (3.09)	Bottled Water (1.49)
	w/ bacon (4.79)	Large (4.99)	
	w/ bacon and cheese (5.39)		

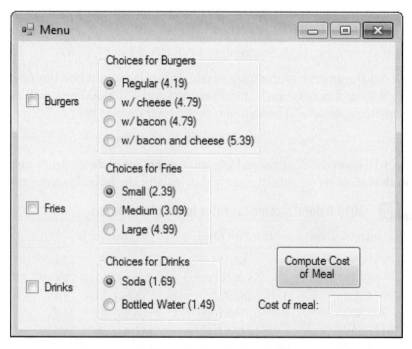

FIGURE 4.23 **Form for Programming Project 6.**

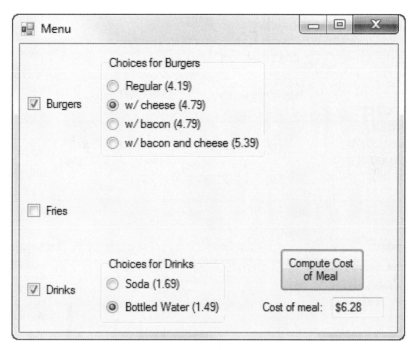

FIGURE 4.24 Possible outcome of Programming Project 6.

7. *College Admissions.* The admissions offices of colleges often rely on a point system. A point system similar to the one in Fig. 4.25 on the next page is used by a large state university. Write a program that allows an admissions officer to determine whether an applicant should be admitted. The numbers in brackets give the point count for each response. The GPA score entered into the text box at the top of the form should be from 2.0 to 4.0. The point value in the brackets to the right of the text box is 20 times the GPA and should appear automatically after the focus leaves the text box. A total of at most 40 points can be earned for the responses below the line. The program should calculate the total score and then admit an applicant whose score is at least 100.

8. Many employers offer their employees a retirement pension plan [known as a 401(k) plan]. Retirement pension plans are usually beneficial to an employee, since they force the employee to save. In addition, employers often match part of the employee's contribution; therefore the employee receives free money.

   (a) Write a program that uses the form in Fig. 4.26(a) on the next page to ask an employee whether or not they would like to participate. When the program starts, the check box should be unchecked and the text box should be empty. If the employee clicks on the button without checking the check box, the statement "You have opted out of the retirement plan." should appear in the text box.

   (b) Write a program that uses the form in Fig. 4.26(b) to ask an employee whether or not they would like to participate. When the program starts, both radio buttons should be unchecked and the text box should be empty. If the employee clicks on the button without checking a radio button, the message "You must make a selection." should be displayed in a message box. Otherwise, one of the two statements appearing in the text boxes in Fig. 4.26(a) and (b) should appear in the text box.

   Note: In part (a), opting out is the default option. A study[1] has shown that employees are more likely to opt-in for the retirement plan when the question is posed as in part (b).

---

[1]Gabriel D. Carroll, James J. Choi, David Laibson, Brigitte Madrian, and Andrew Metrick, *Optimal Defaults and Active Decisions*, NBER Working Paper no. 11074, 2005.

FIGURE 4.25   **Sample run of Programming Project 7.**

(a)   (b)

FIGURE 4.26   **Possible outputs for parts (a) and (b) of Programming Project 8.**

5

General Procedures

5.1 Function Procedures

Visual Basic has two devices, **Function procedures** and **Sub procedures**, that are used to break complex problems into small problems to be solved one at a time. To distinguish them from event procedures, Function and Sub procedures are referred to as **general procedures**. General procedures allow us to write and read a program in such a way that we first focus on the tasks and later on how to accomplish each task. They also eliminate repetitive code and can be reused in other programs.

In this section we show how Function procedures are defined and used. Sub procedures are presented in Sections 5.2 and 5.3.

Visual Basic has many built-in functions. In one respect, functions are like miniature programs. They receive input, they process the input, and they have output. Some functions we encountered earlier are listed in Table 5.1.

TABLE 5.1 Some Visual Basic built-in functions.

Function	Example	Input	Output
Int	Int(2.6) is 2	number	number
Chr	Chr(65) is "A"	number	string
Asc	Asc("Apple") is 65	string	number
FormatNumber	FormatNumber(12345.628, 1) is 12,345.6	number, number	string

Although the input can consist of several values, the output is always a single value. A function is said to **return** its output. For instance, in the first example of Table 5.1, we say that the Int function returns the value 2. The items inside the parentheses are called **arguments**. The first three functions in Table 5.1 have one argument and the fourth function has two arguments. Arguments can be literals (as in Table 5.1), variables, or expressions. Variables are the most common types of arguments. The following lines of code illustrate the use of variables and expressions as arguments for the Int function.

```
Dim num1 As Double = 2.6
Dim num2 As Double = Int(num1)      'variable as an argument

Dim num1 As Double = 1.3
Dim num2 As Double = Int(2 * num1)  'expression as an argument
```

The second line of code above is said to **call** the Int function and to **pass** the value of *num1* to the function.

In addition to using built-in functions, we can define functions of our own. These new functions, called **Function procedures** or **user-defined functions**, are used in the same way as built-in functions. Like built-in functions, Function procedures have a single output that can be of any data type. Function procedures are used in exactly the same way as built-in functions. Function procedures are defined by function blocks of the form

VideoNote

Function procedures

```
Function FunctionName(ByVal var1 As Type1,
                ByVal var2 As Type2, ...) As ReturnDataType
    statement(s)
    Return expression
End Function
```

The variables appearing in the header are called **parameters**. If the word ByVal is omitted when you type in the header, ByVal will be inserted automatically by the Code Editor when you move the cursor away from the header. For now, think of ByVal as a keyword analogous to Dim; that is, it declares a parameter to be of a certain type and sets aside a portion of memory to hold its value. The scope of each parameter is limited to its function block, as is any variable declared inside the Function procedure.

Function names should be suggestive of the role performed and must conform to the rules for naming variables. By convention, function names begin with an uppercase letter. *ReturnDataType*, which specifies the type of the output, will be one of String, Integer, Double, Date, Boolean, and so on. In the preceding general code, the Return statement specifies the output, which must be of type *ReturnDataType*. Function procedures can contain several Return statements, and must contain at least one.

Function procedures are typed directly into the Code Editor outside any other procedure. After you type the header and then press the Enter key, the editor automatically inserts the line "End Function" and a blank line separating the two lines of code. Also, the smart indenting feature of the Code Editor automatically indents all lines in the block of code between the header and "End Function" statements.

■ User-Defined Functions Having One Parameter

The following two Function procedures have just one parameter. (Figure 5.1 identifies the different parts of the first function's header.)

```
Function FtoC(ByVal t As Double) As Double
  'Convert Fahrenheit temperature to Celsius
  Return (5 / 9) * (t - 32)
End Function

Function FirstName(ByVal fullName As String) As String
  'Extract the first name from a full name
  Dim firstSpace As Integer
  firstSpace = fullName.IndexOf(" ")
  Return fullName.Substring(0, firstSpace)
End Function
```

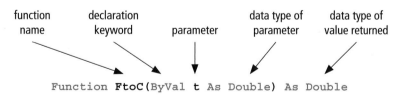

FIGURE 5.1 **Header of the FtoC Function procedure.**

 Example 1 The following program uses the Function procedure FtoC. The fourth line of the btnConvert_Click event procedure, `celsiusTemp = FtoC(fahrenheitTemp)`, calls the function FtoC. The value of the argument *fahrenheitTemp* is assigned to the parameter *t* in the Function procedure header. (We say that the value of *fahrenheitTemp* is passed to the parameter *t*.) After the Function procedure does a calculation using the parameter *t*,

the calculated value is the output of the function FtoC and is assigned to the variable *celsiusTemp*.

OBJECT	PROPERTY	SETTING
frmConvert	Text	Convert Fahrenheit to Celsius
lblTempF	Text	Temperature (Fahrenheit)
txtTempF		
btnConvert	Text	Convert to Celsius
lblTempC	Text	Temperature (Celsius)
txtTempC	ReadOnly	True

```
Private Sub btnConvert_Click(...) Handles btnConvert.Click
  Dim fahrenheitTemp, celsiusTemp As Double
  fahrenheitTemp = CDbl(txtTempF.Text)
  celsiusTemp = FtoC(fahrenheitTemp)
  txtTempC.Text = CStr(celsiusTemp)
  'Note: The above four lines can be replaced with the single line
  'txtTempC.Text = CStr(FtoC(CDbl(txtTempF.Text)))
End Sub

Function FtoC(ByVal t As Double) As Double
  'Convert Fahrenheit temperature to Celsius
  Return (5 / 9) * (t − 32)
End Function
```

[Run, type 212 into the text box, and then click on the button.]

Example 2   The following program uses the Function procedure FirstName. The fifth line of the btnDetermine_Click event procedure, **txtFirstName.Text = FirstName(fullName)**, passes the value of the argument *fullName* to the parameter *fullName* in the Function procedure. Although the parameter in the Function procedure has the same name as the argument passed to

it, they are different variables. This is analogous to the situation in which variables in two different event procedures have the same name, but separate identities.

OBJECT	PROPERTY	SETTING
frmFirstName	Text	Extract First Name
lblName	Text	Full name:
txtFullName		
btnDetermine	Text	Determine First Name
lblFirstName	Text	First Name:
txtFirstName	ReadOnly	True

```
Private Sub btnDetermine_Click(...) Handles btnDetermine.Click
  'Determine a person's first name
  Dim fullName As String
  fullName = txtFullName.Text
  txtFirstName.Text = FirstName(fullName)
End Sub

Function FirstName(ByVal fullName As String) As String
  'Extract the first name from a full name
  Dim firstSpace As Integer
  firstSpace = fullName.IndexOf(" ")
  Return fullName.Substring(0, firstSpace)
End Function
```

[Run, type Franklin Delano Roosevelt into the text box, and then click on the button.]

In general, consider a calling statement of the form

```
Dim var1 as Type1 = FunctionName(arg)
```

where the Function procedure header has the form

```
Function FunctionName(ByVal par As parameterType) As ReturnDataType
```

The variables *arg* and *par* must have the same data type, and *Type1* must be the same as *ReturnDataType*. In many cases, code is easier to read when the same name is used for the argument and the parameter it is passed to. Although they needn't have the same name, they must have the same data type.[1]

---

[1] There are exceptions to this rule. For instance, if *Type1* is a numeric data type, then *parameterType* can have any numeric data type that is wider than *Type1*. In this book, the two data types will always be the same. Similar considerations apply to *ReturnDataType* and *Type1*

■ User-Defined Functions Having Several Parameters

The following two Function procedures have more than one parameter. In the second function, one-letter names have been used for the parameters so that the mathematical formulas will look familiar and be easy to read. Because the names are not descriptive, the meanings of these parameters are spelled out in comment statements.

```
Function Pay(ByVal wage As Double, ByVal hrs As Double) As Double
  'Calculate weekly pay with time-and-a-half for overtime
  Dim amount As Double
  Select Case hrs
    Case Is <= 40
      amount = wage * hrs
    Case Is > 40
      amount = (wage * 40) + ((1.5) * wage * (hrs - 40))
  End Select
  Return amount
End Function

Function FutureValue(ByVal p As Double, ByVal r As Double,
                     ByVal c As Integer, ByVal n As Integer) As Double
  'Find the future value of a bank savings account
  'p  principal, the amount deposited
  'r  annual rate of interest in decimal form
  'c  number of times interest is compounded per year
  'n  number of years
  Dim i As Double      'interest rate per period
  Dim m As Integer     'total number of times interest is compounded
  i = r / c
  m = c * n
  Return p * ((1 + i) ^ m)
End Function
```

When a function with several parameters is called, there must be the same number of arguments as parameters in the function. Also, the data types of the arguments must be the same (and in the same order) as the data types of the parameters. For instance, in a statement of the form

```
numVar = FutureValue(arg1, arg2, arg3, arg4)
```

arg1 and *arg2* must be of type Double, and *arg3* and *arg4* must be of type Integer.

 Example 3   The following program uses the Function procedure Pay. Here the arguments have different names than the corresponding parameters. As required, however, they have the same data types.

OBJECT	PROPERTY	SETTING
frmPay	Text	Weekly Pay
lblWage	Text	Hourly wage:
txtWage		
lblHours	Text	Hours worked:
txtHours		
btnCalculate	Text	Calculate Earnings for the Week
lblEarnings	Text	Earnings:
txtEarnings	ReadOnly	True

```
Private Sub btnCalculate_Click(...) Handles btnCalculate.Click
  'Calculate a person's weekly pay
  Dim hourlyWage, hoursWorked As Double
  hourlyWage = CDbl(txtWage.Text)
  hoursWorked = CDbl(txtHours.Text)
  txtEarnings.Text = FormatCurrency(Pay(hourlyWage, hoursWorked))
End Sub

Function Pay(ByVal wage As Double, ByVal hrs As Double) As Double
  'Calculate weekly pay with time-and-a-half for overtime
  Dim amount As Double
  Select Case hrs
    Case Is <= 40
      amount = wage * hrs
    Case Is > 40
      amount = (wage * 40) + ((1.5) * wage * (hrs − 40))
  End Select
  Return amount
End Function
```

[Run, enter values into the top two text boxes, and click on the button.]

Example 4

The following program uses the Function procedure FutureValue. With the responses shown when the program is run, the program computes the balance in a savings account when $100 is deposited for five years at 4% interest compounded quarterly. Interest is earned four times per year at the rate of 1% per interest period. There will be 5·4, or 20, interest periods.

OBJECT	PROPERTY	SETTING
frmBank	Text	Bank Deposit
lblAmount	Text	Amount of bank deposit:
txtAmount		
lblRate	Text	Annual rate of interest:
txtRate		
lblNumComp	AutoSize	False
	Text	Number of times interest is compounded per year:
txtNumComp		
lblNumYrs	Text	Number of years:
txtNumYrs		
btnCompute	Text	Compute Balance
lblBalance	Text	Balance:
txtBalance	ReadOnly	True

```
Private Sub btnCompute_Click(...) Handles btnCompute.Click
  'Find the future value of a bank deposit
  Dim p As Double = CDbl(txtAmount.Text)
  Dim r As Double = CDbl(txtRate.Text)
  Dim c As Integer = CInt(txtNumComp.Text)
  Dim n As Integer = CInt(txtNumYrs.Text)
  Dim balance As Double = FutureValue(p, r, c, n)
  txtBalance.Text = FormatCurrency(balance)
End Sub

Function FutureValue(ByVal p As Double, ByVal r As Double,
                     ByVal c As Integer, ByVal n As Integer) As Double
  'Find the future value of a bank savings account
  'p  principal, the amount deposited
  'r  annual rate of interest in decimal form
  'c  number of times interest is compounded per year
  'n  number of years
  Dim i As Double      'interest rate per period
  Dim m As Integer     'total number of times interest is compounded
  i = r / c
  m = c * n
  Return p * ((1 + i) ^ m)
End Function
```

[Run, type 100, .04, 4, and 5 into the text boxes, and then click on the button.]

▨ User-Defined Functions Having No Parameters

A Function procedure needn't have any parameters.

 Example 5   The following program allows a person to determine the total cost of several purchases. The user enters the data for a purchase in the top two text boxes and then clicks on the *Purchase This Item* button. The user can continue to enter data for further purchases. After

all purchases have been made, the user clicks on the *Calculate Total Cost* button to display the sum of the costs of the purchases plus the sales tax.

OBJECT	PROPERTY	SETTING
frmCost	Text	Total Cost
lblPrice	Text	Price of item:
txtPrice		
lblQuantity	Text	Quantity purchased:
txtQuantity		
btnPurchase	Text	Purchase This Item
btnCalculate	Text	Calculate Total Cost
lblTotal	Text	Total cost:
txtTotal	ReadOnly	True

```
Dim subTotal As Double
Const SALES_TAX = 0.05

Private Sub btnPurchase_Click(...) Handles btnPurchase.Click
  subTotal += CostOfItem()
  txtPrice.Clear()
  txtQuantity.Clear()
  txtPrice.Focus()
End Sub

Private Sub btnCalculate_Click(...) Handles btnCalculate.Click
  Dim totalCost As Double = subTotal + (SALES_TAX * subTotal)
  txtTotal.Text = FormatCurrency(totalCost)
End Sub

Function CostOfItem() As Double
  Dim price As Double = CDbl(txtPrice.Text)
  Dim quantity As Integer = CInt(txtQuantity.Text)
  Dim cost = price * quantity
  Return cost
End Function
```

[Run, enter 5 and 2, click on the *Purchase* button, enter 6 and 1, click on the *Purchase* button, and click on the *Calculate* button.]

$16.80 is displayed in the "Total cost" text box.

■ User-Defined Boolean-Valued Functions

So far, the values returned by Function procedures have been numbers or strings. However, a Function procedure can also return a Boolean value—that is, True or False. The following program uses a Boolean-valued function and demonstrates an important feature of Function procedures: namely, a Function procedure can contain more than one Return statement. When the first Return statement is encountered, it determines the function value, and the execution of code in the function block terminates.

Example 6 The following program uses a Boolean-valued function to determine whether a word input by the user is a vowel word—that is, contains every vowel. Some examples of vowel words are "sequoia", "facetious", and "dialogue". The Function procedure IsVowelWord examines the word for vowels one at a time and terminates when a vowel is found to be missing.

```
Private Sub btnDetermine_Click(...) Handles btnDetermine.Click
  Dim word As String
  word = txtWord.Text.ToUpper
  If IsVowelWord(word) Then
    txtOutput.Text = word & " contains every vowel."
  Else
    txtOutput.Text = word & " does not contain every vowel."
  End If
End Sub

Function IsVowelWord(ByVal word As String) As Boolean
  If word.IndexOf("A") = -1 Then
    Return False
  End If
  If word.IndexOf("E") = -1 Then
    Return False
  End If
  If word.IndexOf("I") = -1 Then
    Return False
  End If
  If word.IndexOf("O") = -1 Then
    Return False
  End If
  If word.IndexOf("U") = -1 Then
    Return False
  End If
  Return True        'All vowels are present.
End Function
```

[Run, type a word into the top text box, and click on the button.]

■ Comments

1. After a Function procedure has been defined, IntelliSense helps you call the function. Word Completion helps type the function's name, and Parameter Info displays the function's parameters. As soon as you type in the left parenthesis preceding the arguments, a Parameter Info banner appears giving information about the number, names, and types of

the parameters required by the function. See Fig. 5.2. A syntax error occurs if the number of arguments in the calling statement is different from the number of parameters in the called Function procedure. Also, having an argument of a data type that cannot be assigned to the corresponding parameter is a syntax error. Parameter Info helps you prevent both of these kinds of syntax errors.

```
Private Sub btnSalary_Click(...) Handles btnSalary.Click
  Dim wage As Double = 15.75
  Dim hrs As Double = 45
  txtSalary.Text = FormatCurrency(Pay(|
```
Pay(**wage As Double**, hrs As Double) As Double

FIGURE 5.2   **The Parameter Info help feature.**

2. In this text, Function procedure names begin with uppercase letters in order to distinguish them from variable names. Like variable names, however, they can be written with any combination of uppercase and lowercase letters.

Practice Problems 5.1

1. Suppose a program contains the lines

```
Dim n As Double, x As String
lstOutput.Items.Add(Arc(n, x))
```

What types of inputs (numeric or string) and output does the function Arc have?

2. Determine the error in the following program.

```
Private Sub btnOutput_Click(...) Handles btnOutput.Click
  Dim num As Integer = 3
  Dim word As String = "Visual"
  MessageBox.Show("The third letter of the word is " &
                  FindLetter(word, num) & ".")
End Sub


Function FindLetter(ByVal num As Integer, ByVal word As String) As String
  Return word.Substring(num - 1, 1)
End Function
```

EXERCISES 5.1

In Exercises 1 through 10, determine the output displayed when the button is clicked.

```
1. Private Sub btnConvert_Click(...) Handles btnConvert.Click
     'Convert Celsius to Fahrenheit
     Dim temp As Double = 95
     txtOutput.Text = CStr(CtoF(temp))
   End Sub
```

```
Function CtoF(ByVal t As Double) As Double
  Return ((9 / 5) * t) + 32
End Function
```

2.
```
Private Sub btnDisplay_Click(...) Handles btnDisplay.Click
  Dim acres As Double 'Number of acres in a parking lot
  acres = 3
  txtOutput.Text = "You can park about " & Cars(acres) & " cars."
End Sub

Function Cars(ByVal x As Double) As Double
  'Number of cars that can be parked
  Return 125 * x
End Function
```

3.
```
Private Sub btnDisplay_Click(...) Handles btnDisplay.Click
  'Rule of 72
  Dim p As Double
  p = CDbl(txtPopGr.Text) 'Population growth as a percent
  txtOutput.Text = "The population will double in " &
                    DoublingTime(p) & " years."
End Sub

Function DoublingTime(ByVal x As Double) As Double
  'Estimate time required for a population to double
  'at a growth rate of x percent
  Return 72 / x
End Function
```

(Assume the text box txtPopGr contains the number 3.)

4.
```
Private Sub btnDetermine_Click(...) Handles btnDetermine.Click
  Dim numOne, numTwo, numThree, numLowest As Double
  numOne = CDbl(txtOne.Text)
  numTwo = CDbl(txtTwo.Text)
  numThree = CDbl(txtThree.Text)
  numLowest = FindLowest(numOne, numTwo, numThree)
  txtLowest.Text = CStr(numLowest)
End Sub

Function FindLowest(ByVal x As Double, ByVal y As Double,
                    ByVal z As Double) As Double
  'Find the lowest of three numbers denoted by x, y, and z
  Dim lowest As Double
  lowest = x
  If y < lowest Then
    lowest = y
  End If
  If z < lowest Then
    lowest = z
  End If
  Return lowest
End Function
```

(Assume the first three text boxes contain the numbers 7, 4, and 3.)

5.
```
Private Sub btnOutput_Click(...) Handles btnOutput.Click
    Dim num As Integer = 27
    If IsEven(num) Then
      MessageBox.Show(num & " is an even number.")
    Else
      MessageBox.Show(num & " is an odd number.")
    End If
End Sub


Function IsEven(ByVal n As Integer) As Boolean
    If n Mod 2 = 0 Then
      Return True
    Else
      Return False
    End If
End Function
```

6.
```
Private Sub btnDisplay_Click(...) Handles btnDisplay.Click
    Dim d As Date = #12/4/2011#
    txtOutput.Text = MonthAbbr(d)
End Sub


Function MonthAbbr(ByVal d As Date) As String
    Dim str As String = FormatDateTime(d, DateFormat.LongDate)
    Dim n As Integer = str.IndexOf(" ")
    Return str.Substring(n + 1, 3)
End Function
```

7.
```
Private Sub btnOutput_Click(...) Handles btnOutput.Click
    Dim taxableIncome As Double = 15000
    MessageBox.Show("Your state income tax is " & _
    FormatCurrency(StateTax(taxableIncome)) & ".")
End Sub


Function StateTax(ByVal income As Double) As Double
    'Calculate state tax for a single resident of Connecticut
    Select Case income
      Case Is <= 10000
        Return 0.03 * income
      Case Else
        Return 500 + (0.05 * (income - 10000))
    End Select
End Function
```

8.
```
Private Sub btnDisplay_Click(...) Handles btnDisplay.Click
    'Triple a number
    Dim num As Double = 5
    lstOutput.Items.Add(Triple(num))
    lstOutput.Items.Add(num)
End Sub
```

```
Function Triple(ByVal x As Double) As Double
  Dim num As Double = 3
  Return num * x
End Function
```

9.
```
Private Sub btnOutput_Click(...) Handles btnOutput.Click
  Dim word1 As String = "beauty"
  Dim word2 As String = "age"
  MessageBox.Show(First(word1, word2) & " before " & Last(word1, word2))
End Sub

Function First(ByVal w1 As String, ByVal w2 As String) As String
  If w1 < w2 Then
    Return w1
  Else
    Return w2
  End If
End Function

Function Last(ByVal w1 As String, ByVal w2 As String) As String
  If w1 > w2 Then
    Return w1
  Else
    Return w2
  End If
End Function
```

10.
```
Private Sub btnOutput_Click(...) Handles btnOutput.Click
  Dim num1 As Integer = 84
  Dim num2 As Integer = 96
  If IsAnA(num1, num2) Then
    MessageBox.Show("A average")
  Else
    MessageBox.Show("not an A average")
  End If
End Sub

Function IsAnA(ByVal n1 As Integer, ByVal n2 As Integer) As Boolean
  If ((n1 + n2) / 2) >= 89.5 Then
    Return True
  Else
    Return False
  End If
End Function
```

In Exercises 11 and 12, identify the errors.

11.
```
Private Sub btnDisplay_Click(...) Handles btnDisplay.Click
  'Select a greeting
  Dim answer As Integer
  answer = CInt(InputBox("Enter 1 or 2."))
  txtOutput.Text = CStr(Greeting(answer))
End Sub
```

```
Function Greeting(ByVal x As Integer) As Integer
  Return "hellohi ya".Substring(5 * (x - 1), 5)
End Function
```

12.
```
Private Sub btnDisplay_Click(...) Handles btnDisplay.Click
  Dim word As String
  word = InputBox("What is your favorite word?")
  txtOutput.Text = "When the word is written twice, " &
  Twice(word) & " letters are used."
End Sub


Function Twice(ByVal w As String) As Integer
  'Compute twice the length of a string
  Dim len As Integer
  len = 2 * w.Length
End Function
```

In Exercises 13 through 23, construct user-defined functions to carry out the primary task(s) of the program.

13. To determine the number of square centimeters of tin needed to make a tin can, add the square of the radius of the can to the product of the radius and height of the can, and then multiply this sum by 6.283. Write a program that requests the radius and height of a tin can in centimeters as input and displays the number of square centimeters of tin required to make the can.

14. Table 5.2 gives the Saffir-Simpson scale for categorizing hurricanes. Write a program that requests a wind speed in miles/hour and displays the category of the storm.

TABLE 5.2   Rating of hurricanes.

Wind Speed (in mph)	Rating
74 to 95	Category One
96 to 110	Category Two
111 to 130	Category Three
131 to 155	Category Four
Over 155	Category Five

15. The federal government developed the body mass index (BMI) to determine ideal weights. Body mass index is calculated as 703 times the weight in pounds, divided by the square of the height in inches, and then rounded to the nearest whole number. Write a program that accepts a person's weight and height as input and gives the person's body mass index. **Note:** A BMI of 19 to 25 corresponds to a healthy weight.

16. In order for exercise to be beneficial to the cardiovascular system, the heart rate (number of heart beats per minute) must exceed a value called the *training heart rate*, THR. A person's THR can be calculated from their age and resting heart rate (pulse rate when first awakening) as follows:

   (a) Calculate the maximum heart rate as 220 − age.
   (b) Subtract the resting heart rate from the maximum heart rate.
   (c) Multiply the result in step (b) by 60%, and then add the resting heart rate.

   Write a program to request a person's age and resting heart rate as input and display their THR. (Test the program with an age of 20 and a resting heart rate of 70, and then determine *your* training heart rate.)

17. The three components for a serving of popcorn at a movie theater are popcorn, butter substitute, and a bucket. Write a program that requests the cost of these three items and the price of the serving as input and then displays the profit. (Test the program where popcorn costs 5 cents, butter substitute costs 2 cents, the bucket costs 25 cents, and the selling price is $5.)

18. Write a program that requests the numeric grades on a midterm and a final exam and then uses a Function procedure to assign a semester grade (A, B, C, D, or F). The final exam should count twice as much as the midterm exam, the semester average should be rounded up to the nearest whole number, and the semester grade should be assigned by the following criteria: 90–100 (A), 80–89 (B), ... Use a function called Ceil that rounds noninteger numbers up to the next integer. The function Ceil can be defined by $Ceil(x) = -Int(-x)$.

19. The original cost of airmail letters was 5 cents for the first ounce and 10 cents for each additional ounce. Write a program to compute the cost of a letter whose weight is given by the user in a text box. Use a function called Ceil that rounds noninteger numbers up to the next integer. The function Ceil can be defined by $Ceil(x) = -Int(-x)$. (Test the program with the weights 4, 1, 2.5, and .5 ounces.)

20. Suppose a fixed amount of money is deposited at the beginning of each month into a savings account paying 6% interest compounded monthly. After each deposit is made, [new balance] = 1.005 * [previous balance one month ago] + [fixed amount]. Write a program that requests the fixed amount of the deposits as input and displays the balance after each of the first four deposits. Shown below is the outcome when 1000 is typed into the text box for the amount deposited each month.

```
Month 1:   $1,000.00
Month 2:   $2,005.00
Month 3:   $3,015.03
Month 4:   $4,030.10
```

21. Write a program to request the name of a United States senator as input and display the address and salutation for a letter to the senator. Assume the name has two parts, and use a function to determine the senator's last name. The outcome when Robert Smith is typed into the input dialog box requesting the senator's name follows.

```
The Honorable Robert Smith
United States Senate
Washington, DC 20001

Dear Senator Smith,
```

22. Write a program that requests a date as input and then gives the spelled-out day of the week for that date as output. The program should use a function with the following header.

```
Function DayOfWeek(ByVal d As Date) As String
```

23. Write a program that requests a year as input and then tells whether or not the year is a leap year. The program should use a Boolean-value function named IsLeapYear. **Hint:** Use the DateDiff function.

Solutions to Practice Problems 5.1

1. The first argument, n takes a value of type Double and the second argument, x, takes a String value; therefore, the input consists of a number and a string. From the two lines shown here, there is no way to determine the type of the output. This can be determined only by looking at the definition of the function.

2. The two arguments in **FindLetter(word, num)** are in the wrong order. Since the two parameters in the header for the Function procedure have types Integer and String, in that order, the arguments must have the same types and order when the Function procedure is called. The function call should be **FindLetter(num, word)**. Visual Basic matches arguments to parameters based on their positions, not on their names.

5.2 Sub Procedures, Part I

Sub procedures share several features with Function procedures.

- Both are written as a separate block of code that can be called to perform a specific task.
- Both are used to break complex problems into small problems.
- Both are used to eliminate repetitive code.
- Both can be reused in other programs.
- Both make a program easier to read by separating it into logical units.
- Both have parameters that are declared in a header.

Sub procedures, however, do not return a value associated with their name. The most common uses of Sub procedures are to receive input, process input, or display output.

▨ Defining and Calling Sub Procedures

Sub procedures are defined by blocks of the form

VideoNote
Sub
procedures

```
Sub ProcedureName(ByVal par1 As Type1,
                  ByVal par2 As Type2,
                        ⋮
                  ByVal parN As TypeN)
  statement(s)
End Sub
```

In the block above, one or more of the ByVals can be replaced with the keyword ByRef. (The use of ByRef will be discussed in the next section.)

Like Function procedure names, the names of Sub procedures must conform to the rules for naming variables. By convention, Sub procedure names begin with an uppercase letter and describe its purpose. In this section all parameters will be preceded by the keyword ByVal. The primary difference will be that Sub procedures will perform some task (such as displaying output) rather than return a value.

Sub procedures are called by statements of the form

```
ProcedureName(arg1, arg2, ..., argN)
```

When a Sub procedure is called, the value of each argument is assigned to the corresponding parameter, the statement(s) inside the procedure block are carried out, and execution continues with the statement following the calling statement.

Here is an example of a Sub procedure.

```
Sub DisplaySum(ByVal num1 As Double, ByVal num2 As Double)
  Dim z As Double
  z = num1 + num2
  lstOutput.Items.Add(z)
End Sub
```

When a statement such as

```
DisplaySum(3, 4)
```

is executed in an event procedure, the number 3 is assigned to the parameter *num1*, the number 4 is assigned to the parameter *num2*, and the three statements inside the Sub procedure block are carried out. As a result, the number 7 is displayed in the list box. We say that the numbers 3 and 4 are **passed** to the Sub procedure. See Fig. 5.3.

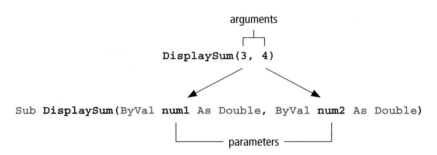

FIGURE 5.3 **Passing arguments to a procedure.**

■ Variables and Expressions as Arguments

Just as with function calls, the arguments in Sub procedure calls can be literals (as in Fig. 5.3), variables, or expressions.

  Example 1 The following program calls an expanded version of the Sub procedure DisplaySum three times. The first time the arguments are literals, the second time the arguments are variables, and the third time the arguments are expressions. In the second call of DisplaySum, the values of the variables are passed to the Sub procedure. In the third call, the expressions are evaluated and the resulting numbers are passed to the Sub procedure.

```
Private Sub btnAddNumbers_Click(...) Handles btnAddNumbers.Click
  DisplaySum(1, 2)
  Dim x As Double = 3
  Dim y As Double = 4
  DisplaySum(x, y)
  DisplaySum(2 * x, y + 5)
End Sub

Sub DisplaySum(ByVal num1 As Double, ByVal num2 As Double)
  Dim z As Double
  z = num1 + num2
  lstOutput.Items.Add("The sum of " & num1 & " and " & num2 &
                  " is " & z & ".")
End Sub
```

[Run, and click on the button.]

Example 2   The following program passes a string and two numbers to a Sub procedure. When the Sub procedure is first called, the string parameter *state* is assigned the value "Hawaii", and the numeric parameters *pop* and *area* are assigned the values 1275194 and 6471, respectively. The Sub procedure then uses these parameters to carry out the task of calculating the population density of Hawaii. The second calling statement assigns different values to the parameters.

OBJECT	PROPERTY	SETTING
frmDensities	Text	Densities
btnDisplay	Text	Display Demographics
lstDensity		

```
Private Sub btnDisplay_Click(...) Handles btnDisplay.Click
    'Calculate the population densities of states
    lstDensity.Items.Clear()
    Dim state As String, pop As Double, area As Double
    state = "Hawaii"
    pop = 1275194
    area = 6471
    CalculateDensity(state, pop, area)
    lstDensity.Items.Add("")
    state = "Alaska"
    pop = 663661
    area = 591000
    CalculateDensity(state, pop, area)
End Sub

Sub CalculateDensity(ByVal state As String,
                     ByVal pop As Double, ByVal area As Double)
    'The density (number of people per square mile)
    'will be displayed rounded to one decimal place.
    Dim density As Double
    density = pop / area
    lstDensity.Items.Add("The density of " & state & " is")
    lstDensity.Items.Add(FormatNumber(density, 1) & " people per square mile.")
End Sub
```

[Run, and then click on the button.]

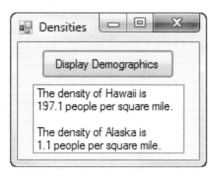

Notice that in the calling statement

```
CalculateDensity(state, pop, area)
```

the variable types have the order String, Double, and Double; the same types and order as in the Sub procedure header. This order is essential. For instance, the calling statement cannot be written as

```
CalculateDensity(pop, area, state)
```

In Example 2 the arguments and parameters have the same name. Using same names sometimes makes a program easier to read. However, arguments and their corresponding parameters often have different names. What matters is that the *order*, *number*, and *types* of the arguments and parameters match. For instance, the following code is a valid revision of the btnDisplay_Click event procedure in Example 2. (Figure 5.4 shows how arguments are passed to parameters with this code.)

```
Private Sub btnDisplay_Click(...) Handles btnDisplay.Click
    'Calculate the population densities of states.
    lstDensity.Items.Clear()
    Dim s As String, p As Double, a As Double
    s = "Hawaii"
    p = 1275194
    a = 6471
    CalculateDensity(s, p, a)
    lstDensity.Items.Add("")
    s = "Alaska"
    p = 663661
    a = 591000
    CalculateDensity(s, p, a)
End Sub
```

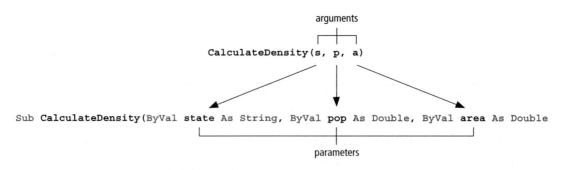

FIGURE 5.4   **Passing arguments to a procedure.**

▓ Sub Procedures Having No Parameters

Sub procedures, like Function procedures, are not required to have any parameters. A parameterless Sub procedure can be used to give instructions or provide a description of a program.

Example 3 The following variation of Example 2 gives the population density of a single state. The parameterless Sub procedure DescribeTask gives an explanation of the program.

```
Private Sub btnDisplay_Click(...) Handles btnDisplay.Click
  DescribeTask()
  CalculateDensity("Hawaii", 1275194, 6471)
End Sub

Sub DescribeTask()
  lstOutput.Items.Clear()
  lstOutput.Items.Add("This program displays the")
  lstOutput.Items.Add("population density of the last state")
  lstOutput.Items.Add("to become part of the United States.")
End Sub

Sub CalculateDensity(ByVal state As String,
                     ByVal pop As Double, ByVal area As Double)
  Dim density As Double
  density = pop / area
  lstDensity.Items.Add("")
  lstDensity.Items.Add("The density of " & state & " is")
  lstDensity.Items.Add(FormatNumber(density, 1) & " people per square mile.")
End Sub
```

[Run, and then click on the button.]

■ Sub Procedures Calling Other Sub Procedures

A Sub procedure can call another Sub procedure. If so, after the End Sub statement at the end of the called Sub procedure is reached, execution continues with the line in the calling Sub procedure following the calling statement.

 Example 4 In the following program, the Sub procedure FirstPart calls the Sub procedure SecondPart. After the statements in SecondPart are executed, execution continues with the remaining statements in the Sub procedure FirstPart before returning to the event procedure. The form contains a button and a list box.

```
Private Sub btnDisplay_Click(...) Handles btnDisplay.Click
  'Demonstrate Sub procedure calling other Sub procedures
  FirstPart()
```

```
    lstOutput.Items.Add(4 & " from event procedure")
End Sub

Sub FirstPart()
  lstOutput.Items.Add(1 & " from FirstPart")
  SecondPart()
  lstOutput.Items.Add(3 & " from FirstPart")
End Sub

Sub SecondPart()
  lstOutput.Items.Add(2 & " from SecondPart")
End Sub
```

[Run, and click on the button. The following is displayed in the list box.]

```
1 from FirstPart
2 from SecondPart
3 from FirstPart
4 from event procedure
```

■ Comments

1. Sub procedures allow programmers to focus on the main flow of a complex task and defer the details of implementation. Modern programs use them liberally. This method of program construction is known as **modular** or **top-down** design. As a rule, a Sub procedure should perform only one task, or several closely related tasks, and should be kept relatively small.

2. The first line inside a Sub procedure is often a comment statement describing the task performed by the Sub procedure. If necessary, several comment statements are devoted to this purpose. Conventional programming practice also recommends that all variables used by the Sub procedure be listed in comment statements with their meanings. In this text, we give several examples of this practice, but adhere to it only when the variables are especially numerous or lack descriptive names.

3. In Section 5.1, we saw that Word Completion and Parameter Info help us write a function call. These IntelliSense features provide the same assistance for Sub procedure calls. (Of course, Word Completion and Parameter Info work only when the Sub procedure has already been created.) See Fig. 5.5.

```
Private  Sub btnAddNumbers_Click(ByVal sender As System.Object,
    DisplaySum(1, 2)
    Dim x As Double = 3
    Dim y As Double = 4
    DisplaySum(|
    DisplaySum (num1 As Double, num2 As Double)
```

FIGURE 5.5 **The Parameter Info help feature.**

4. In early versions of Basic, statements that called Sub procedures had to be written in the form

```
Call ProcedureName(arg1, arg2, ... , argN)
```

Therefore, statements that call Sub procedures are often referred to as **Call statements**.

1. What is the difference between an event procedure and a Sub procedure?

2. What is wrong with the following code?

```
Private Sub btnDisplay_Click(...) Handles btnDisplay.Click
  Dim phone As String
  phone = mtbPhoneNum.Text
  AreaCode(phone)
End Sub


Sub AreaCode()
  txtOutput.Text = "Your area code is " & phone.Substring(0, 3)
End Sub
```

In Exercises 1 through 20, determine the output displayed when the button is clicked.

1.
```
Private Sub btnDisplay_Click(...) Handles btnDisplay.Click
  Piano(88)
End Sub


Sub Piano(ByVal num As Integer)
  txtOutput.Text = num & " keys on a piano"
End Sub
```

2.
```
Private Sub btnDisplay_Click(...) Handles btnDisplay.Click
  'Opening line of Moby Dick
  FirstLine("Ishmael")
End Sub


Sub FirstLine(ByVal name As String)
  'Display first line
  txtOutput.Text = "Call me " & name & "."
End Sub
```

3.
```
Private Sub btnDisplay_Click(...) Handles btnDisplay.Click
  Dim color As String
  color = InputBox("What is your favorite color?")
  Flattery(color)
End Sub


Sub Flattery(ByVal color As String)
  txtOutput.Text = "You look dashing in " & color & "."
End Sub
```

(Assume the response is *blue*.)

4.
```
Private Sub btnDisplay_Click(...) Handles btnDisplay.Click
  Dim num As Double = 144
  Gross(num)
End Sub
```

```
Sub Gross(ByVal amount As Double)
  txtOutput.Text = amount & " items in a gross"
End Sub
```

5.
```
Private Sub btnDisplay_Click(...) Handles btnDisplay.Click
  Dim hours As Double
  hours = 24
  Minutes(60 * hours)
End Sub


Sub Minutes(ByVal num As Double)
  txtOutput.Text = num & " minutes in a day"
End Sub
```

6.
```
Private Sub btnDisplay_Click(...) Handles btnDisplay.Click
  Dim states, senators As Double
  states = 50
  senators = 2
  Senate(states * senators)
End Sub


Sub Senate(ByVal num As Double)
  txtBox.Text = "The number of U.S. Senators is " & num
End Sub
```

7.
```
Private Sub btnDisplay_Click(...) Handles btnDisplay.Click
  Question()
  Answer()
End Sub


Sub Answer()
  lstOutput.Items.Add("Because they were invented in the northern")
  lstOutput.Items.Add("hemisphere where sundials go clockwise.")
End Sub


Sub Question()
  lstOutput.Items.Add("Why do clocks run clockwise?")
  lstOutput.Items.Add("")
End Sub
```

8.
```
Private Sub btnDisplay_Click(...) Handles btnDisplay.Click
  Answer()
  Question()
End Sub


Sub Answer()
  lstOutput.Items.Add("The answer is 9W.")
  lstOutput.Items.Add("What is the question?")
End Sub


Sub Question()
  'Note: "Wagner" is pronounced "Vagner"
```

```
      lstOutput.Items.Add("Do you spell your name with a V,")
      lstOutput.Items.Add("Mr. Wagner?")
   End Sub

9. Private Sub btnDisplay_Click(...) Handles btnDisplay.Click
      'Beginning of Tale of Two Cities
      Times("best")
      Times("worst")
   End Sub

   Sub Times(ByVal word As String)
     'Display sentence
     lstOutput.Items.Add("It was the " & word & " of times.")
   End Sub

10. Private Sub btnDisplay_Click(...) Handles btnDisplay.Click
      'Sentence using number, thing, and place
      Sentence(168, "hour", "a week")
      Sentence(76, "trombone", "the big parade")
   End Sub

   Sub Sentence(ByVal num As Double, ByVal thing As String,
              ByVal where As String)
      lstOutput.Items.Add(num & " " & thing & "s in " & where)
   End Sub

11. Private Sub btnDisplay_Click(...) Handles btnDisplay.Click
      'The fates of Henry the Eighth's six wives
      CommonFates()
      lstOutput.Items.Add("died")
      CommonFates()
      lstOutput.Items.Add("survived")
   End Sub

   Sub CommonFates()
     'The most common fates
     lstOutput.Items.Add("divorced")
     lstOutput.Items.Add("beheaded")
   End Sub

12. Private Sub btndisplay_Click(...) Handles btndisplay.Click
      Dim pres, college As String
      pres = "Bush"
      college = "Yale"
      PresAlmaMater(pres, college)
      pres = "Obama"
      college = "Columbia"
      PresAlmaMater(pres, college)
   End Sub

   Sub PresAlmaMater(ByVal pres As String, ByVal college As String)
      lstOutput.Items.Add("President " & pres & " is a graduate of " &
                      college & ".")
   End Sub
```

13.
```
Private Sub btnDisplay_Click(...) Handles btnDisplay.Click
    HowMany(24)
    lstOutput.Items.Add("a pie.")
End Sub

Sub HowMany(ByVal num As Integer)
    What(num)
    lstOutput.Items.Add("baked in")
End Sub

Sub What(ByVal num As Integer)
    lstOutput.Items.Add(num & " blackbirds")
End Sub
```

14.
```
Private Sub btnDisplay_Click(...) Handles btnDisplay.Click
    'Good advice to follow
    Advice()
End Sub

Sub Advice()
    Source()
    lstOutput.Items.Add("Keep cool, but don't freeze.")
End Sub

Sub Source()
    lstOutput.Items.Add("Source: A dozen eggs.")
End Sub
```

15.
```
Private Sub btnDisplay_Click(...) Handles btnDisplay.Click
    Dim word As String, num As Integer
    word = "Visual Basic"
    num = 6
    FirstPart(word, num)
End Sub

Sub FirstPart(ByVal term As String, ByVal digit As Integer)
    txtOutput.Text = "The first " & digit & " letters are " &
                     term.Substring(0, digit) & "."
End Sub
```

16.
```
Private Sub btnDisplay_Click(...) Handles btnDisplay.Click
    Dim d As Date = Today
    DisplayTypeOfDay(d)
End Sub

Sub DisplayTypeOfDay(ByVal d As Date)
    If IsWeekendDay(d) Then
        txtOutput.Text = "Today is a weekend day."
    Else
        txtOutput.Text = "Today is a weekday."
    End If
End Sub
```

```vb
Function IsWeekendDay(ByVal d As Date) As Boolean
    Dim when As String = FormatDateTime(d, DateFormat.LongDate)
    If when.StartsWith("Saturday") Or when.StartsWith("Sunday") Then
        Return True
    Else
        Return False
    End If
End Function
```

17.
```vb
Private Sub btnDisplay_Click() Handles btnDisplay.Click
    Dim cost As Double = 550
    DisplayBill(cost, ShippingCost(cost))
End Sub


Function ShippingCost(ByVal costOfGoods As Double) As Double
    Select Case costOfGoods
        Case Is < 100
            Return 10
        Case Is < 500
            Return 15
        Case Else
            Return 20
    End Select
End Function


Sub DisplayBill(ByVal cost As Double, ByVal addedCost As Double)
    lstOutput.Items.Add("Cost: " & FormatCurrency(cost))
    lstOutput.Items.Add("Shipping cost: " & FormatCurrency(addedCost))
    lstOutput.Items.Add("Total cost: " & FormatCurrency(cost + addedCost))
End Sub
```

18.
```vb
Private Sub btnDisplay_Click() Handles btnDisplay.Click
    Dim language As String = "Visual Basic"
    ShowWord(language)
End Sub


Sub ShowWord(ByVal word As String)
    If word.Length < 5 Then
        txtOutput.ForeColor = Color.Red
    Else
        txtOutput.ForeColor = Color.Blue
    End If
    txtOutput.Text = word
End Sub
```

19.
```vb
Private Sub btnDisplay_Click() Handles btnDisplay.Click
    Dim grade = CDbl(InputBox("What is your numeric grade?", "Grade"))
    ShowResult(grade)
End Sub


Sub ShowResult(ByVal grade As Double)
    If PassedExam(grade) Then
        txtOutput.Text = "You passed with a grade of " & grade & "."
```

```
      Else
        txtOutput.Text = "You failed the exam."
      End If
    End Sub


    Function PassedExam (ByVal grade As Double) As Boolean
      Select Case grade
        Case Is >= 60
          Return True
        Case Else
          Return False
      End Select
    End Function
```

(Assume the response is 92.)

20.
```
Private Sub btnDisplay_Click() Handles btnDisplay.Click
  Dim anyDate As Date
  anyDate = CDate(InputBox("Input a date. (mm/dd/yyyy)"))
  ShowCentury(anyDate)
End Sub


Sub ShowCentury(ByVal anyDate As Date)
  Select Case anyDate
    Case Is >= #1/1/2000#
      txtOutput.Text = "twenty-first century"
    Case Is >= #1/1/1900#
      txtOutput.Text = "twentieth century"
    Case Else
      txtOutput.Text = "prior to the twentieth century"
  End Select
End Sub
```

(Assume the response is 6/5/1955.)

In Exercises 21 through 24, find the errors.

21.
```
Private Sub btnDisplay_Click(...) Handles btnDisplay.Click
  Dim n As Integer = 5
  Alphabet()
End Sub


Sub Alphabet(ByVal n As Integer)
  txtOutput.Text = "abcdefghijklmnopqrstuvwxyz".Substring(0, n)
End Sub
```

22.
```
Private Sub btnDisplay_Click(...) Handles btnDisplay.Click
  Dim word As String, number As Double
  word = "seven"
  number = 7
  Display(word, number)
End Sub
```

```
    Sub Display(ByVal num As Double, ByVal term As String)
      txtOutput.Text = num & " " & term
    End Sub
```

23.
```
    Private Sub btnDisplay_Click(...) Handles btnDisplay.Click
      Dim name As String
      name = InputBox("Name")
      Handles(name)
    End Sub


    Sub Handles(ByVal moniker As String)
      txtOutput.Text = "Your name is " & moniker
    End Sub
```

24.
```
    Private Sub btnDisplay_Click(...) Handles btnDisplay.Click
      Dim num As Integer = 2
      txtOutput.Text = Tea(num)
    End Sub


    Function Tea() As Integer
      Return num
    End Sub
```

In Exercises 25 through 28, rewrite the program with the output performed by a call to a Sub procedure.

25.
```
    Private Sub btnDisplay_Click(...) Handles btnDisplay.Click
      'Display a lucky number
      Dim num As Integer = 7
      txtOutput.Text = num & " is a lucky number."
    End Sub
```

26.
```
    Private Sub btnDisplay_Click(...) Handles btnDisplay.Click
      'Greet your cousin
      Dim name As String = "Jack"
      txtOutput.Text = "Hi, Cousin " & name
    End Sub
```

27.
```
    Private Sub btnDisplay_Click(...) Handles btnDisplay.Click
      'Information about trees
      Dim tree As String, ht As Double
      tree = "redwood"
      ht = 362
      lstBox.Items.Add("The tallest " & tree &
                       " tree in the U.S. is " & ht & " feet.")
      tree = "pine"
      ht = 223
      lstBox.Items.Add("The tallest " & tree &
                       " tree in the U.S. is " & ht & " feet.")
    End Sub
```

28.
```
    Private Sub btnDisplay_Click(...) Handles btnDisplay.Click
      Dim city As String, salary As Double
      lstOutput.Items.Clear()
      city = "San Jose"
```

```
    salary = 83089
    lstOutput.Items.Add("In 2008, the average salary for " & city &
                        " residents was " & FormatCurrency(salary, 0) & ".")
    city = "Hartford"
    salary = 46000
    lstOutput.Items.Add("In 2008, the average salary for " & city &
                        " residents was " & FormatCurrency(salary, 0) & ".")
End Sub
```

In Exercises 29 through 32, write a program that displays the output shown in a list box. The last two lines of the output should be displayed by one or more Sub procedures using data passed by variables from an event procedure.

29. (Assume that the following is displayed.)

```
According to a 2008 survey of college freshmen taken by the Higher
Education Research Institute:
16.7 percent said they intend to major in business.
1 percent said they intend to major in computer science.
```

30. (Assume that the current date is 12/31/2010, the label for txtBox reads "What is your date of birth?", and the user enters 2/3/1984 into txtBox before btnDisplay is clicked.)

```
You are now 26 years old.
You have lived for 9824 days.
```

31. (Assume that the label for txtBox reads "What is your favorite number?", and the user types 7 into txtBox before btnDisplay is clicked.)

```
The sum of your favorite number with itself is 14.
The product of your favorite number with itself is 49.
```

32. (Assume that the following is displayed.)

```
In a recent year,
823 thousand college students took a course in Spanish
206 thousand college students took a course in French
```

33. Write a program to display three verses of "Old McDonald Had a Farm." The primary verse, with variables substituted for the animals and sounds, should be contained in a Sub procedure. The program should pass the following animal and sound pairs to the Sub procedure: lamb, baa; duck, quack; firefly, blink. The first verse of the output should be

```
Old McDonald had a farm. Eyi eyi oh.
And on his farm he had a lamb. Eyi eyi oh.
With a baa baa here, and a baa baa there.
Here a baa, there a baa, everywhere a baa baa.
Old McDonald had a farm. Eyi eyi oh.
```

34. Write a program to compute tips for services rendered. The program should request the person's occupation, the amount of the bill, and the percentage tip as input and pass this information to a Sub procedure to display the person and the tip. A sample run is shown in Fig. 5.6.

35. Write a program that requests three grades as input and then passes the three grades to a Sub procedure that determines and displays the highest two grades. See Fig. 5.7.

36. Write a program that requests a student's first name, last name and the numeric grades on three exams, and then uses a Sub procedure to display the student's name and semester

FIGURE 5.6   **Sample run of Exercise 34.**

FIGURE 5.7   **Sample run of Exercise 35.**

grade (A, B, C, D, or F). A Function procedure (called by the Sub procedure) should be used to calculate the semester grade. The lowest grade should be dropped, the semester average should be rounded to the nearest whole number, and the semester grade should be assigned using the following criteria: 90–100 (A), 80–89 (B), ... See Fig. 5.8.

FIGURE 5.8   **Sample run of Exercise 36.**

FIGURE 5.9   **Sample run of Exercise 37.**

37. Write a program that requests two words as input and then passes the words to a Sub procedure that displays the words in alphabetical order. See Fig. 5.9.

38. Write a program that asks a quiz show contestant to select one of the numbers 1, 2, or 3 and then calls a Sub procedure that asks the question having that number and requests the answer. The Sub procedure should then call another Sub procedure to tell the contestant if the answer is correct. Use the following three questions:

   1. Who was the only living artist to have his work displayed in the Grand Gallery of the Louvre?

   2. Who said, "Computers are useless. They can only give you answers."?

   3. By what name is Pablo Blasio better known?

   Note: These questions have the same answer, Pablo Picasso.

Solutions to Practice Problems 5.2

1. The header of an event procedure has parameters (such as e and sender) that are provided automatically by Visual Basic, and the procedure is invoked when an event is raised. On the other hand, a Sub procedure is invoked by a line of code containing the name of the Sub procedure.

2. The statement **Sub AreaCode()** must be replaced by **Sub AreaCode(ByVal phone As String)**. Whenever a value is passed to a Sub procedure, the Sub statement must provide a parameter to receive the value.

5.3　Sub Procedures, Part II

In the previous section values were passed to Sub procedures. In this section we show how to pass values back from Sub procedures.

▓ Passing by Value

In Section 5.2, all parameters appearing in Sub procedures were preceded by the word ByVal, which stands for "By Value." When a variable is passed to such a parameter, we say that the variable is "passed by value." A variable that is passed by value will retain its original value after the Sub procedure terminates—regardless of what changes are made to the value of the corresponding parameter inside the Sub procedure. Example 1 illustrates this feature.

Example 1　The following program illustrates the fact that changes to the value of a parameter passed by value have no effect on the value of the argument in the calling statement.

```
Private Sub btnDisplay_Click(...) Handles btnDisplay.Click
  'Illustrate that a change in value of parameter
  'does not alter the value of the argument
  Dim amt As Double = 2
  lstResults.Items.Add(amt & " from event procedure")
  Triple(amt)
  lstResults.Items.Add(amt & " from event procedure")
End Sub

Sub Triple(ByVal num As Double)
  'Triple a number
  lstResults.Items.Add(num & " from Sub procedure")
  num = 3 * num
  lstResults.Items.Add(num & " from Sub procedure")
End Sub
```

[Run, and then click the button. The following is displayed in the list box.]

```
2 from event procedure
2 from Sub procedure
6 from Sub procedure
2 from event procedure
```

When a variable is passed by value, two memory locations are involved. Figure 5.10 shows the status of the memory locations as the program in Example 1 executes. At the time the Sub procedure is called, a temporary second memory location for the parameter is set aside for the Sub procedure's use and the value of the argument is copied into that location. After the completion of the Sub procedure, the temporary memory location is released, and the value in it is lost.

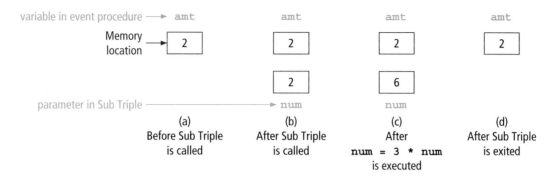

FIGURE 5.10   **Passing a variable by value to a Sub procedure.**

■ Passing by Reference

Another way to pass a variable to a Sub procedure is "By Reference." In this case the parameter is preceded by the keyword ByRef. Suppose a variable, call it *arg*, appears as an argument in a procedure call, and its corresponding parameter in the Sub procedure's header, call it *par*, is preceded by ByRef. After the Sub procedure has been executed, *arg* will have whatever value *par* had in the Sub procedure.

In Example 1, if the header of the Sub procedure is changed to

```
Sub Triple(ByRef num As Double)
```

then the last number of the output will be 6. Although this feature may be surprising at first glance, it provides a vehicle for passing values from a Sub procedure back to the place from which the Sub procedure was called. Different names may be used for an argument and its corresponding parameter, but only one memory location is involved. Initially, the btnDisplay_Click() event procedure allocates a memory location to hold the value of *amt* (Fig. 5.11(a)). When the Sub procedure is called, the parameter *num* becomes the Sub procedure's name for this memory location (Figure 5.11(b)). When the value of *num* is tripled, the value in the memory location becomes 6 (Figure 5.11(c)). After the completion of the Sub procedure, the parameter name *num* is forgotten; however, its value lives on in *amt* (Figure 5.11(d)). The variable *amt* is said to be **passed by reference**.

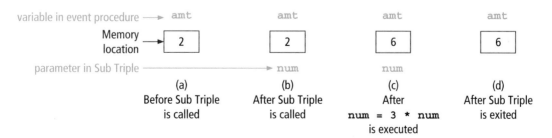

FIGURE 5.11   **Passing a variable by reference to a Sub procedure.**

Note: The Sub procedure Triple discussed above is solely for illustrative purposes and is not representative of the way Sub procedures are used in practice. Examples 2 and 3 show typical uses of Sub procedures.

Example 2 The following program uses a Sub procedure to acquire the input. The variables *x* and *y* are not assigned values prior to the execution of the first procedure call. Therefore, before the procedure call is executed, they have the value 0. After the procedure call is executed, however, they have the values entered into the text boxes. These values then are passed by the second procedure call to the Sub procedure DisplaySum.

OBJECT	PROPERTY	SETTING
frmAdd	Text	Add Two Numbers
lblFirstNum	Text	First number:
txtFirstNum		
lblSecondNum	Text	Second number:
txtSecondNum		
btnCompute	Text	Compute Sum
txtResult	ReadOnly	True

```
Private Sub btnCompute_Click(...) Handles btnCompute.Click
  'This program requests two numbers and
  'displays the two numbers and their sum.
  Dim x, y As Double
  GetNumbers(x, y)
  DisplaySum(x, y)
End Sub

Sub GetNumbers(ByRef x As Double, ByRef y As Double)
  'Record the two numbers in the text boxes
  x = CDbl(txtFirstNum.Text)
  y = CDbl(txtSecondNum.Text)
End Sub

Sub DisplaySum(ByVal num1 As Double, ByVal num2 As Double)
  'Display two numbers and their sum
  Dim sum As Double
  sum = num1 + num2
  txtResult.Text = "The sum of " & num1 & " and " &
                   num2 & " is " & sum & "."
End Sub
```

[Run, type 2 and 3 into the text boxes, and then click on the button.]

Example 3   The following program alphabetizes two words.

OBJECT	PROPERTY	SETTING
frmWords	Text	Alphabetize
lblFirst	Text	First word:
txtFirst		
lblSecond	Text	Second word:
txtSecond		
btnSort	Text	Sort and Display Words
txtOutput	ReadOnly	True

```
Private Sub btnSort_Click(...) Handles btnSort.Click
  Dim word1 As String = txtFirst.Text
  Dim word2 As String = txtSecond.Text
  If (word2 < word1) Then
    SwapWords(word1, word2)
  End If
  txtOutput.Text = word1 & " before " & word2
End Sub

Sub SwapWords(ByRef word1 As String, ByRef word2 As String)
  Dim temp As String
  temp = word1
  word1 = word2
  word2 = temp
End Sub
```

[Run, enter words in the top two text boxes, and click on the button.]

■ Sub Procedures that Return a Single Value

A Sub procedure having the ByRef keyword in its list of parameters can be thought of as return-ing values to the calling statement. In Examples 2 and 3, the Sub procedures returned two val-ues to the event procedure. Sub procedures also can be used to return just a single value. However, good programming practice dictates that unless the Sub procedure does more that just return a single value, it should be replaced with a Function procedure. For instance, con-sider the following procedure call and Sub procedure combination where the Sub procedure returns a single value, namely the sum of two numbers.

```
CalculateSum(x, y, s)

Sub CalculateSum(ByVal num1 As Double, ByVal num2 As Double,
                 ByRef sum As Double)
  'Add the values of num1 and num2
  sum = num1 + num2
End Sub
```

It should be replaced with the combination

```
s = CalculateSum(x, y)

Function CalculateSum(ByVal num1 As Double, ByVal num2 As Double) As Double
  Dim sum As Double
  sum = num1 + num2
  Return sum
End Function
```

■ Lifetime and Scope of Variables and Constants

When a variable or constant is declared inside a Function, Sub, or event procedure with a Dim statement, a portion of memory is set aside to hold the value of the variable. That portion of memory is released when the procedure's End Function or End Sub statement is reached. The **lifetime** of a variable or constant is the period during which it remains in memory. (A variable's value can change over its lifetime, but it always holds some value.) The **scope** of a variable or constant is the portion of the program that can refer to it. A variable or constant declared in a procedure with a Dim, Const, ByVal, or ByRef keyword is a **local variable** or a **local constant** and is said to have **local scope**. (It cannot be accessed outside the procedure.) When variables or constants declared in two different procedures have the same name, Visual Basic treats them as two different objects.

A variable or constant declared outside of a procedure has **class-level scope** and can be referred to by any procedure. A variable or constant declared inside an If or a Select Case block has **block-level scope** and cannot be accessed outside the block. Good programming practice dictates that the scope of a variable or constant be as small as possible. For a variable, this reduces the number of places in which its value can be modified incorrectly or accidentally.

 Example 4 The following program illustrates the fact that variables are local to the part of the program in which they reside. The variable *x* in the event procedure and the variable *x* in the Sub procedure are treated as different variables. Visual Basic handles them as if their names were separate, such as xbtnDisplay_Click and xTrivial. Also, each time the Sub procedure is called, the value of variable *x* inside the Sub procedure is reset to 0.

```
Private Sub btnDisplay_Click(...) Handles btnDisplay.Click
  'Demonstrate the local nature of variables
  Dim x As Double = 2
  lstResults.Items.Add(x & " : event procedure")
  Trivial()
  lstResults.Items.Add(x & " : event procedure")
  Trivial()
  lstResults.Items.Add(x & " : event procedure")
End Sub

Sub Trivial()
  Dim x As Double
  lstResults.Items.Add(x & " : Sub procedure")
```

```
    x = 3
    lstResults.Items.Add(x & " : Sub procedure")
End Sub
```

[Run, and then click on the button.]

Debugging

VideoNote

Debugging procedures

Programs with Sub procedures are easier to debug. Each Sub procedure can be checked individually before being placed into the program.

    In Appendix D, the section "Stepping through a Program Containing a General Procedure: Chapter 5" uses the Visual Basic debugger to trace the flow through a program and observe the interplay between arguments and parameters.

Comments

1. In this textbook, passing by reference is used primarily to acquire input.
2. When an argument that is a literal or an expression is passed to a procedure, there is no difference between passing it by reference and passing it by value. Only a variable argument can possibly have its value changed by a Sub procedure.

Practice Problems 5.3

1. In Example 3, change the header of the Sub procedure to

   ```
   Sub SwapWords(ByRef word1 As String, ByVal word2 As String)
   ```

   and determine the output when the input is *beauty* and *age*.

2. When the following program in entered, Visual Basic will display a green wavy line under the argument *state* in the fourth line. However, there is no wavy line under the argument *pop*. What do you think the reason is for Visual Basic's concern?

   ```
   Private Sub btnDisplay_Click(...) Handles btnDisplay.Click
     Dim state As String
     Dim pop As Double
     InputData(state, pop)
     txtOutput.Text = state & " has population " & FormatNumber(pop, 0)
   End Sub
   ```

```
Sub InputData(ByRef state As String, ByRef pop As Double)
  state = "California"
  pop = 34888000
End Sub
```

EXERCISES 5.3

In Exercises 1 through 10, determine the output displayed when the button is clicked on.

1. ```
Private Sub btnDisplay_Click(...) Handles btnDisplay.Click
   Dim name As String = ""
   Dim yob As Integer
   GetVita(name, yob)
   txtOutput.Text = name & " was born in the year " & yob & "."
End Sub

Sub GetVita(ByRef name As String, ByRef yob As Integer)
  name = "Gabriel"
  yob = 1980   'Year of birth
End Sub
```

2. ```
Private Sub btnDisplay_Click(...) Handles btnDisplay.Click
   Dim country As String = ""
   Dim pop As Double
   GetFacts(country, pop)
   txtOutput.Text = "The population of " & country & " is about " &
                    FormatNumber(pop, 0) & "."
End Sub


Sub GetFacts(ByRef country As String, ByRef pop As Double)
  country = "the United States"
  pop = 313000000     'population
End Sub
```

3. ```
Private Sub btnDisplay_Click(...) Handles btnDisplay.Click
   Dim state As String = ""
   Dim flower As String = ""
   GetFacts(state, flower)
   txtOutput.Text = "The state flower of " & state & _
                    " is the " & flower & "."
End Sub

Sub GetFacts(ByRef place As String, ByRef plant As String)
  place = "Florida"
  plant = "Orange Blossom"
End Sub
```

4. ```
Private Sub btnDisplay_Click(...) Handles btnDisplay.Click
   Dim film As String = ""
   Dim year As Integer
   GetFacts(film, year)
   txtOutput.Text = film & " won the award in " & year & "."
End Sub
```

```
Sub GetFacts(ByRef movie As String, ByRef yr As Integer)
  movie = "Slumdog Millionaire"
  yr = 2009
End Sub
```

5.
```
Private Sub btnDisplay_Click(...) Handles btnDisplay.Click
   Dim word As String = ""
   Dim num As Integer
   GetFacts(word, num)
   txtOutput.Text = "The first " & num & " letters of " & word &
                    " are " & BegOfWord(word, num) & "."
End Sub


Sub GetFacts(ByRef w As String, ByRef n As Integer)
  w = InputBox("Enter a word:")
  n = CInt(InputBox("Enter a number less than the length of the word:"))
End Sub


Function BegOfWord(ByVal word As String, ByVal num As Integer) As String
   Return word.Substring(0, num)
End Function
```

(Assume the two responses are *EDUCATION* and *3*.)

6.
```
Private Sub btnDisplay_Click(...) Handles btnDisplay.Click
   Dim price, markdown, salesTax, finalCost As Double
   InputData(price, markdown, salesTax)
   finalCost = CostOfItem(price, markdown, salesTax)
   DisplayOutput(price, finalCost)
End Sub


Sub InputData(ByRef price As Double, ByRef markdown As Double,
             ByRef salesTax As Double)
  price = CDbl(InputBox("Price of item:"))
  markdown = CDbl(InputBox("Percentage discount:"))
  salesTax = CDbl(InputBox("Percentage state sales tax:"))
End Sub


Function CostOfItem(ByVal pr As Double, ByVal md As Double,
                   ByVal st As Double) As Double
  Dim reducedPrice, cost As Double
  reducedPrice = pr − ((md / 100) * pr)
  cost = reducedPrice + ((st / 100) * reducedPrice)
  Return cost
End Function


Sub DisplayOutput(ByVal amount, ByVal customerCost)
   lstOutput.Items.Add("Original Price: " & FormatCurrency(amount))
   lstOutput.Items.Add("Cost: " & FormatCurrency(customerCost))
End Sub
```

(Assume the three responses are *125*, *20*, and *6*.)

7.
```
Dim inventory As Integer = 5

Private Sub btnDisplay_Click(...) Handles btnDisplay.Click
  Dim numPurchased, newInventory As Integer
  numPurchased = CInt(InputBox("Enter number of items to be purchased:"))
  UpdateInventory(newInventory, numPurchased)
  inventory = newInventory
  txtOutput.Text = "Current inventory: " & inventory
End Sub

Sub UpdateInventory(ByRef newInventory As Integer,
                    ByVal numPurchased As Integer)
  Select Case numPurchased
    Case Is <= inventory
      newInventory = inventory — numPurchased
      If newInventory = 0 Then
        MessageBox.Show("No items remaining.")
      End If
    Case Is > inventory
      MessageBox.Show("Insufficient inventory, purchase cancelled.")
      newInventory = inventory
  End Select
End Sub
```

(Assume btnDisplay is pressed twice with the response 3 given each time.)

8.
```
Dim balance As Double = 100

Private Sub btnDisplay_Click(...) Handles btnDisplay.Click
  Dim deposit, withdrawal, newBalance As Double
  deposit = CDbl(InputBox("Amount of deposit:"))
  withdrawal = CDbl(InputBox("Amount of withdrawal:"))
  UpdateBalance(deposit, withdrawal, newBalance)
  balance = newBalance
  txtOutput.Text = CStr(balance)
End Sub

Sub UpdateBalance(ByVal deposit As Double, ByVal withdrawal As Double,
                  ByRef newBalance As Double)
  Select Case withdrawal
    Case Is = balance + deposit
      MessageBox.Show("Account depleted.")
      newBalance = 0
    Case Is > balance + deposit
      MessageBox.Show("Account overdrawn. Withdrawal denied.")
      newBalance = balance + deposit
    Case Else
      newBalance = balance + deposit — withdrawal
  End Select
End Sub
```

(Assume the responses are 90 and 200.)

9.
```
Private Sub btnDisplay_Click(...) Handles btnDisplay.Click
   Dim a, b, s, d As Integer
   InputData(a, b)
   Combine(a, b, s, d)
   DisplayResults(s, d)
End Sub


Sub InputData(ByRef num1 As Integer, ByRef num2 As Integer)
   num1 = 3
   num2 = 1
End Sub


Sub Combine(ByVal x As Integer, ByVal y As Integer,
            ByRef sum As Integer, ByRef difference As Integer)
   sum = x + y
   difference = x — y
End Sub


Sub DisplayResults(ByVal s As Integer, ByVal d As Integer)
   lstOutput.Items.Add("sum = " & s)
   lstOutput.Items.Add("difference = " & d)
End Sub
```

10.
```
Private Sub btnCalculate_Click(...) Handles btnCalculate.Click
   Dim wholesaleCost, salePrice, percentCommission,
       salesTax, profit As Double
   InputData(wholesaleCost, salePrice, percentCommission)
   CalculateSomeValues(wholesaleCost, salePrice, percentCommission,
                       salesTax, profit)
   DisplayData(salesTax, profit)
End Sub


Sub InputData(ByRef wholesaleCost As Double, ByRef salePrice As Double,
              ByRef percentCommission As Double)
   wholesaleCost = 100
   salePrice = 300
   percentCommission = 5
End Sub


Sub CalculateSomeValues(ByVal wholesaleCost As Double,
         ByVal salePrice As Double, ByVal percentCommission As Double,
         ByRef salesTax As Double, ByRef profit As Double)
   salesTax = 0.06 * salePrice
   profit = salePrice — wholesaleCost —
            salePrice * (percentCommission / 100)
End Sub


Sub DisplayData(ByVal salesTax As Double, ByVal profit As Double)
   lstOutput.Items.Add("sales tax: " & FormatCurrency(salesTax))
   lstOutput.Items.Add("profit: " & FormatCurrency(profit))
End Sub
```

11. Write a pay-raise program that requests a person's first name, last name, and current annual salary, and then displays their salary for next year. People earning less than $40,000 will receive a 5% raise, and those earning $40,000 or more will receive a raise of $2,000 plus 2% of the amount over $40,000. Use Sub procedures for input and output, and a Function procedure to calculate the new salary. See Fig. 5.12.

FIGURE 5.12   **Possible output for Exercise 11.**

FIGURE 5.13   **Possible output for Exercise 12.**

12. Write a program to calculate the balance and minimum payment for a credit card statement. See Fig. 5.13. The program should use the event procedure shown in Fig. 5.14. The finance charge is 1.5% of the old balance. If the new balance is $20 or less, the minimum payment should be the entire new balance. Otherwise, the minimum payment should be $20 plus 10% of the amount of the new balance above $20.

```
Private Sub btnCalculate_Click(...) Handles btnCalculate.Click
    Dim oldBalance, charges, credits, newBalance, minPayment As Double
    InputData(oldBalance, charges, credits)
    CalculateNewValues(oldBalance, charges, credits, newBalance, minPayment)
    DisplayData(newBalance, minPayment)
End Sub
```

FIGURE 5.14   **Event procedure for Exercise 12.**

13. Write a program to calculate the monthly values associated with a mortgage. See Fig. 5.15. The program should use the event procedure shown in Fig. 5.16. The interest paid each

FIGURE 5.15   **Sample output for Exercise 13.**

```
Private Sub btnCalculate_Click(...) Handles btnCalculate.Click
   Dim annualRateOfInterest, monthlyPayment, begBalance As Double
   Dim intForMonth, redOfPrincipal, endBalance As Double
    InputData(annualRateOfInterest, monthlyPayment, begBalance)
    Calculate(annualRateOfInterest, monthlyPayment, begBalance,
            intForMonth, redOfPrincipal, endBalance)
   DisplayData(intForMonth, redOfPrincipal, endBalance)
  End Sub
```

FIGURE 5.16   Event procedure for Exercise 13.

month is the monthly rate of interest applied to the balance at the beginning of the month. Each month the reduction of principal equals the monthly payment minus the interest paid. At any time, the balance of the mortgage is the amount still owed; that is, the amount required to pay off the mortgage. The end of month balance is calculated as [beginning of month balance] − [reduction of principal].

14. Write a program to determine a person's weekly pay, where they receive time-and-a-half for overtime work beyond forty hours. See Fig. 5.17. The program should use the event procedure shown in Fig. 5.18.

FIGURE 5.17   Sample output for Exercise 14.

```
Private Sub btnCalculate_Click(...) Handles btnCalculate.Click
   Dim hours, payPerHour, overtimeHours, pay As Double
    InputData(hours, payPerHour)
    CalculateValues(hours, payPerHour, overtimeHours, pay)
    DisplayData(overtimeHours, pay)
  End Sub
```

FIGURE 5.18   Event procedure for Exercise 14.

Solutions to Practice Problems 5.3

1. `age before age`

2. Since *state* is a string variable, its default value is the keyword *Nothing*. The assignment of *Nothing* to an argument makes Visual Basic nervous. Therefore, to keep Visual Basic happy, we will assign the empty string to String variables that are passed to procedures. That is, we will change the first line inside the event procedure to `Dim state As String = ""`.

   Since the default value of the numeric variable *pop* is 0, Visual Basic has no issue with passing that value to a Sub procedure.

5.4　Modular Design

�no Top-Down Design

Full-featured software usually requires large programs. Writing the code for an event procedure in such a Visual Basic program might pose a complicated problem. One method programmers use to make a complicated problem more understandable is to divide it into smaller, less complex subproblems. Repeatedly using a "divide-and-conquer" approach to break up a large problem into smaller subproblems is called **stepwise refinement**. Stepwise refinement is part of a larger methodology of writing programs known as **top-down design**, in which the more general tasks occur near the top of the design and tasks representing their refinement occur below. Top-down design and structured programming emerged as techniques to enhance programming productivity. Their use leads to programs that are easier to read and maintain. They also produce programs containing fewer initial errors, with these errors being easier to find and correct. When such programs are later modified, there is a much smaller likelihood of introducing new errors.

The goal of top-down design is to break a problem into individual tasks, or **modules**, that can easily be transcribed into pseudocode, flowcharts, or a program. First, a problem is restated as several simpler problems depicted as modules. Any modules that remain too complex are broken down further. The process of refining modules continues until the smallest modules can be coded directly. Each stage of refinement adds a more complete specification of what tasks must be performed. The main idea in top-down design is to go from the general to the specific. This process of dividing and organizing a problem into tasks can be pictured using a hierarchy chart. When using top-down design, certain criteria should be met:

1. The design should be easily readable and emphasize small module size.
2. Modules proceed from general to specific as you read down the chart.
3. The modules, as much as possible, should be single minded. That is, they should perform only a single well-defined task.
4. Modules should be independent of each other as much as possible, and any relationships among modules should be specified.

The following example illustrates this process.

 Example 1　Figure 5.19 is the beginning of a hierarchy chart for a program that gives information about a car loan. The inputs are the amount of the loan, the duration (in years), and the interest rate. The output consists of the monthly payment and the amount of interest paid for the first month. In the broadest sense, the program calls for obtaining the input, making calculations, and displaying the output. Figure 5.19 shows these tasks as the first row of a hierarchy chart.

FIGURE 5.19　**Beginning of a hierarchy chart for the car loan program.**

Each task can be refined into more specific subtasks. (See Fig. 5.20 for the final hierarchy chart.) Most of the subtasks in the third row are straightforward and do not require further refinement. For instance, the first month's interest is computed by multiplying the amount of the loan by one-twelfth of the annual rate of interest. The most complicated subtask, the computation of the monthly payment, has been broken down further. This task is carried out by applying a standard formula found in finance books; however, the formula requires the number of payments.

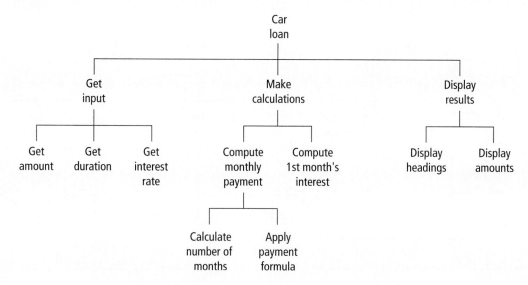

FIGURE 5.20 **Hierarchy chart for the car loan program.**

It is clear from the hierarchy chart that the top modules manipulate the modules beneath them. While the higher-level modules control the flow of the program, the lower-level modules do the actual work. By designing the top modules first, we can delay specific processing decisions.

▨ Structured Programming

A program is said to be **structured** if it meets modern standards of program design. Although there is no formal definition of the term **structured program**, computer scientists agree that such programs should have modular design and use only the three types of logical structures discussed in Chapter 1: sequences, decisions, and loops.

Sequences: Statements are executed one after another.

Decisions: One of several blocks of program code is executed based on a test for some condition.

Loops (iteration): One or more statements are executed repeatedly as long as a specified condition is true.

One major shortcoming of the earliest programming languages was their reliance on the GoTo statement. This statement was used to branch (that is, jump) from one line of a program to another. It was common for a program to be composed of a convoluted tangle of jumps and branches that produced confusing code referred to as **spaghetti code**. At the heart of structured programming is the assertion of E. W. Dijkstra that GoTo statements should be eliminated entirely because they lead to complex and confusing programs. Two Italians, C. Bohm and G. Jacopini, were able to prove that GoTo statements are not needed and that any program can be written using only the three types of logic structures discussed before.

Structured programming requires that all programs be written using sequences, decisions, and loops. Nesting of such statements is allowed. All other logical constructs, such as GoTos, are not allowed. The logic of a structured program can be pictured using a flowchart that flows smoothly from top to bottom without unstructured branching (GoTos). The portion of a flowchart shown in Fig. 5.21(a) contains the equivalent of a GoTo statement and, therefore, is not structured. A correctly structured version of the flowchart in which the logic flows from the top to the bottom appears in Fig. 5.21(b).

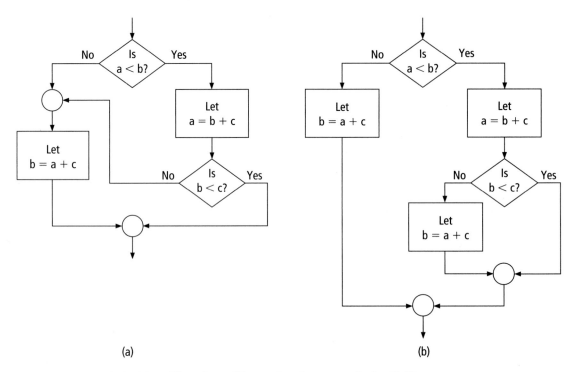

(a)   (b)

FIGURE 5.21 **Flowcharts illustrating the removal of a GoTo statement.**

■ Advantages of Structured Programming

The goal of structured programming is to create correct programs that are easy to write, debug, understand, and change. Let us now take a closer look at the way modular design, along with a limited number of logical structures, contributes to attaining these goals.

1. *Easy to write.*

   Modular design increases the programmer's productivity by allowing him or her to look at the big picture first and focus on the details later. During the actual coding, the programmer works with a manageable chunk of the program and does not have to think about an entire complex program.

   Several programmers can work on a single large program, each taking responsibility for a specific module.

   Studies have shown that structured programs require significantly less time to write than standard programs.

   Often, procedures written for one program can be reused in other programs requiring the same task. Not only is time saved in writing a program, but reliability is enhanced, because reused procedures will already be tested and debugged. A procedure that can be used in many programs is said to be **reusable**.

2. *Easy to debug.*

Because each procedure is specialized to perform just one task or several related tasks, a procedure can be checked individually to determine its reliability. A dummy program, called a **driver**, is set up to test the procedure. The driver contains the minimum definitions needed to call the procedure to be tested. For instance, if the procedure to be tested is a function, the driver program assigns diverse values to the arguments and then examines the corresponding function return values. The arguments should contain both typical and special-case values.

The program can be tested and debugged as it is being designed with a technique known as **stub programming**. In this technique, the key event procedures and perhaps some of the smaller procedures are coded first. Dummy procedures, or stubs, are written for the remaining procedures. Initially, a stub procedure might consist of a message box to indicate that the procedure has been called, and thereby confirm that the procedure was called at the right time. Later, a stub might simply display values passed to it in order to confirm not only that the procedure was called, but also that it received the correct values from the calling procedure. A stub also can assign new values to one or more of its parameters to simulate either input or computation. This provides greater control of the conditions being tested. The stub procedure is always simpler than the actual procedure it represents. Although the stub program is only a skeleton of the final program, the program's structure can still be debugged and tested. (The stub program consists of some coded procedures and the stub procedures.)

Old-fashioned unstructured programs consist of a sequence of instructions that are not grouped for specific tasks. The logic of such a program is cluttered with details and therefore difficult to follow. Needed tasks are easily left out and crucial details easily neglected. Tricky parts of the program cannot be isolated and examined. Bugs are difficult to locate because they might be present in any part of the program.

3. *Easy to understand.*

The interconnections of the procedures reveal the modular design of the program.

The meaningful procedure names, along with relevant comments, identify the tasks performed by the modules.

The meaningful variable names help the programmer to recall the purpose of each variable.

4. *Easy to change.*

Because a structured program is self-documenting, it can easily be deciphered by another programmer.

Modifying a structured program often amounts to inserting or altering a few procedures rather than revising an entire complex program. The programmer does not even have to look at most of the program. This is in sharp contrast to the situation with unstructured programs, where one must understand the entire logic of the program before any changes can be made with confidence.

■ Object-Oriented Programming

An object is an encapsulation of data and code that operates on the data. Like controls, objects have properties, respond to methods, and raise events. The most effective type of programming for complex problems is called **object-oriented** design. An object-oriented program can be viewed as a collection of cooperating objects. Many modern programmers use a blend of traditional structured programming along with object-oriented design.

Visual Basic.NET was the first version of Visual Basic that was truly object oriented; in fact, every element such as a control or a string is actually an object. This book illustrates the building blocks of Visual Basic in the early chapters and then puts them together using object-oriented techniques in Chapter 11. Throughout the book, an object-oriented approach is taken whenever feasible.

■ A Relevant Quote

We end this section with a few paragraphs from *Dirk Gently's Holistic Detective Agency*, by Douglas Adams, Simon & Schuster, 1987:

> "What really is the point of trying to teach anything to anybody?"
> This question seemed to provoke a murmur of sympathetic approval from up and down the table.
> Richard continued, "What I mean is that if you really want to understand something, the best way is to try and explain it to someone else. That forces you to sort it out in your own mind. And the more slow and dim-witted your pupil, the more you have to break things down into more and more simple ideas. And that's really the essence of programming. By the time you've sorted out a complicated idea into little steps that even a stupid machine can deal with, you've certainly learned something about it yourself. The teacher usually learns more than the pupil. Isn't that true?"

5.5   A Case Study: Weekly Payroll

This case study processes a weekly payroll using the 2009 Employer's Tax Guide. Table 5.3 shows typical data used by a company's payroll office. (**Note:** A withholding allowance is sometimes referred to as an *exemption*.) These data are processed to produce the information in Table 5.4 that is supplied to each employee along with his or her paycheck. The program should request the data from Table 5.3 for an individual as input and produce output similar to that in Table 5.4.

TABLE 5.3   Employee data.

Name	Hourly Wage	Hours Worked	Withholding Allowances	Marital Status	Previous Year-to-Date Earnings
Al Clark	$45.50	38	4	Married	$88,600.00
Ann Miller	$44.00	35	3	Married	$68,200.00
John Smith	$17.95	50	1	Single	$30,604.75
Sue Taylor	$25.50	43	2	Single	$36,295.50

TABLE 5.4   Payroll information.

Name	Current Earnings	Yr. to Date Earnings	FICA Tax	Income Tax Wh.	Check Amount
Al Clark	$1,729.00	$90,329.00	$132.27	$163.44	$1,433.29

The items in Table 5.4 should be calculated as follows:

Current Earnings: hourly wage times hours worked (with time-and-a-half after 40 hours)

Year-to-Date Earnings: previous year-to-date earnings plus current earnings

FICA Tax: sum of 6.2% of earnings if part of the first $106,800 of earnings (social security benefits tax) and 1.45% of earnings (Medicare tax)

Federal Income Tax Withheld: subtract $70.19 from the current earnings for each withholding allowance and use Table 5.5 or Table 5.6, depending on marital status

Check Amount: [current earnings] − [FICA taxes] − [income tax withheld]

TABLE 5.5 2009 Federal income tax withheld for a single person paid weekly.

Adjusted Weekly Income	Income Tax Withheld
$0 to $138	$0
Over $138 to $200	10% of amount over $138
Over $200 to $696	$6.20 + 15% of amount over $200
Over $696 to $1,279	$80.60 + 25% of amount over $696
Over $1,279 to $3,338	$226.35 + 28% of amount over $1,279
Over $3,338 to $7,212	$802.87 + 33% of amount over $3,338
Over $7,212	$2,081.29 + 35% of amount over $7,212

TABLE 5.6 2009 Federal income tax withheld for a married person paid weekly.

Adjusted Weekly Income	Income Tax Withheld
$0 to $303	$0
Over $303 to $470	10% of amount over $303
Over $470 to $1,455	$16.70 + 15% of amount over $470
Over $1,455 to $2,272	$164.45 + 25% of amount over $1,455
Over $2,272 to $4,165	$368.70 + 28% of amount over $2,272
Over $4,165 to $7,321	$898.74 + 33% of amount over $4,165
Over $7,321	$1,940.22 + 35% of amount over $7,321

▨ Designing the Weekly Payroll Program

After the data for an employee from Table 5.3 have been input, the program must compute the five amounts appearing in Table 5.4 and then display the payroll information. These five computations form the basic tasks of the program:

1. Compute current earnings.
2. Compute year-to-date earnings.
3. Compute FICA tax.
4. Compute federal income tax withheld.
5. Compute paycheck amount (that is, take-home pay).

Tasks 1, 2, 3, and 5 are fairly simple. Each involves applying a formula to given data. (For instance, if hours worked are at most 40, then [Current Earnings] = [Hourly Wage] times [Hours Worked].) Thus, we won't break down these tasks any further. Task 4 is more complicated, so we continue to divide it into smaller subtasks.

4. *Compute federal income tax withheld.* First, the employee's pay is adjusted for withholding allowances, and then the amount of income tax to be withheld is computed. The computation of the income tax withheld differs for married and single individuals. Task 4 is, therefore, divided into the following subtasks:

4.1 Compute pay adjusted by withholding allowances.

4.3 Compute income tax withheld for single employee.

4.3   Compute income tax withheld for married employee.

The hierarchy chart in Fig. 5.22 shows the stepwise refinement of the problem.

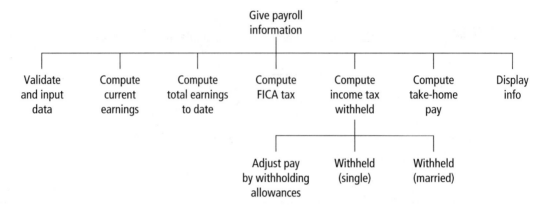

FIGURE 5.22   **Hierarchy chart for the weekly payroll program.**

▓ Pseudocode for the Display Payroll Event Procedure

VALIDATE data (Function DataOK)
INPUT employee data (Sub procedure InputData)
COMPUTE CURRENT GROSS PAY (Function Gross_Pay)
COMPUTE TOTAL EARNINGS TO DATE (Function Total_Pay)
COMPUTE FICA TAX (Function FICA_Tax)
COMPUTE INCOME TAX WITHHELD (Function Fed_Tax)
    Adjust pay for withholding allowances
    If employee is single Then
      COMPUTE INCOME TAX WITHHELD (Function TaxSingle)
    Else
      COMPUTE INCOME TAX WITHHELD (Function TaxMarried)
    End If
COMPUTE PAYCHECK AMOUNT (Function Net_Check)
DISPLAY PAYROLL INFORMATION (Sub procedure ShowPayroll)

▓ Writing the Weekly Payroll Program

The btnDisplay_Click event procedure calls a sequence of seven procedures. Table 5.7 shows the tasks and the procedures that perform the tasks.

TABLE 5.7   **Tasks and their procedures.**

Task	Procedure
0. Validate and input employee data	DataOK, InputData
1. Compute current earnings.	Gross_Pay
2. Compute year-to-date earnings.	Total_Pay
3. Compute FICA tax.	FICA_Tax
4. Compute federal income tax withheld.	Fed_Tax
4.1 Compute adjusted pay.	Fed_Tax
4.2 Compute amount withheld for single employee.	TaxSingle
4.3 Compute amount withheld for married employee.	TaxMarried
5. Compute paycheck amount.	Net_Check
6. Display payroll information.	ShowPayroll

The Program and the User Interface

Figure 5.23 and Table 5.8 define the user interface for the Weekly Payroll Program. Figure 5.24 shows a sample output.

FIGURE 5.23   **Form for weekly payroll program.**

TABLE 5.8	Objects and initial properties for the weekly payroll program.		
	Object	Property	Setting
	frmPayroll	Text	Weekly Payroll
	lblName	Text	Employee name:
	txtName		
	lblWage	Text	Hourly wage:
	txtWage		
	lblHours	Text	Number of hours worked:
	txtHours		
	lblAllowances	AutoSize	False
		Text	Number of withholding allowances:
	txtAllowances		
	lblPriorPay	Text	Total pay prior to this week:
	txtPriorPay		
	grpMarital	Text	Marital Status:
	radSingle	Text	Single
	radMarried	Text	Married
	btnDisplay	Text	Display Payroll
	btnNext	Text	Next Employee
	btnQuit	Text	Quit
	lstResults	Font	Courier New

FIGURE 5.24   Sample output of weekly payroll problem.

```
Private Sub btnDisplay_Click(...) Handles btnDisplay.Click
  Dim empName As String = ""    'Name of employee
  Dim hrWage As Double          'Hourly wage
  Dim hrsWorked As Double       'Hours worked this week
  Dim allowances As Integer     'Number of withholding allowances
    '                              for employee
  Dim prevPay As Double         'Total pay for year excluding this week
  Dim mStatus As String = ""    'Marital status: S for Single; M for Married
  Dim pay As Double             'This week's pay before taxes
  Dim totalPay As Double        'Total pay for year including this week
  Dim ficaTax As Double         'FICA tax for this week
  Dim fedTax As Double          'Federal income tax withheld this week
  Dim check As Double           'Paycheck this week (take-home pay)
  'Verify and obtain data, compute payroll, display results
  If Not DataOK() Then
    Dim msg As String = "At least one piece of requested data is missing" & _
                   " or is provided improperly."
    MessageBox.Show(msg)
  Else
    InputData(empName, hrWage, hrsWorked, allowances, prevPay, mStatus)  'Task 0
    pay = Gross_Pay(hrWage, hrsWorked)                                   'Task 1
    totalPay = Total_Pay(prevPay, pay)                                   'Task 2
    ficaTax = FICA_Tax(pay, prevPay, totalPay)                           'Task 3
    fedTax = Fed_Tax(pay, allowances, mStatus)                           'Task 4
    check = Net_Check(pay, ficaTax, fedTax)                              'Task 5
    ShowPayroll(empName, pay, totalPay, ficaTax, fedTax, check)          'Task 6
  End If
End Sub

Private Sub btnNext_Click(...) Handles btnNext.Click
  'Clear all text boxes and radio buttons for next employee's data
  txtName.Clear()
  txtWage.Clear()
  txtHours.Clear()
```

```vb
    txtAllowances.Clear()
    txtPriorPay.Clear()
    radSingle.Checked = False
    radMarried.Checked = False
    lstResults.Items.Clear()
    txtName.Focus()
End Sub

Private Sub btnQuit_Click(...) Handles btnQuit.Click
    Me.Close()
End Sub

Function DataOK() As Boolean
    'Task 0: Validate data
    If (txtName.Text = "") Or (Not IsNumeric(txtWage.Text)) Or
      (Not IsNumeric(txtHours.Text)) Or (Not IsNumeric(txtAllowances.Text)) Or
      (Not IsNumeric(txtPriorPay.Text)) Or
      ((Not radSingle.Checked) And (Not radMarried.Checked)) Then
        Return False
    Else
        Return True
    End If
End Function

Sub InputData(ByRef empName As String, ByRef hrWage As Double,
              ByRef hrsWorked As Double, ByRef allowances As Integer,
              ByRef prevPay As Double, ByRef mStatus As String)
    'Task 0: Input data
    empName = txtName.Text
    hrWage = CDbl(txtWage.Text)
    hrsWorked = CDbl(txtHours.Text)
    allowances = CInt(txtAllowances.Text)
    prevPay = CDbl(txtPriorPay.Text)
    If radMarried.Checked Then
        mStatus = "M"
    Else
        mStatus = "S"
    End If
End Sub

Function Gross_Pay(ByVal hrWage As Double,
                   ByVal hrsWorked As Double) As Double
    'Task 1: Compute weekly pay before taxes
    If hrsWorked <= 40 Then
        Return hrsWorked * hrWage
    Else
        Return 40 * hrWage + (hrsWorked - 40) * 1.5 * hrWage
    End If
End Function

Function Total_Pay(ByVal prevPay As Double, ByVal pay As Double) As Double
    'Task 2: Compute total pay before taxes
    Return prevPay + pay
End Function
```

```vb
Function FICA_Tax(ByVal pay As Double, ByVal prevPay As Double,
                  ByVal totalPay As Double) As Double
  'Task 3: Compute social security and Medicare tax
  Dim socialSecurity As Double       'Social security tax for this week
  Dim medicare As Double             'Medicare tax for this week
  Dim sum As Double                  'Sum of above two taxes
  Const WAGE_BASE As Double = 106800
  If totalPay <= WAGE_BASE Then
    socialSecurity = 0.062 * pay
  ElseIf prevPay < WAGE_BASE Then
    socialSecurity = 0.062 * (WAGE_BASE - prevPay)
  End If
  medicare = 0.0145 * pay
  sum = socialSecurity + medicare
  Return Math.Round(sum, 2)          'Round to nearest cent
End Function


Function Fed_Tax(ByVal pay As Double, ByVal allowances As Integer,
                 ByVal mStatus As String) As Double
  'Task 4: Compute federal income tax withheld rounded to 2 decimal places.
  Dim adjPay As Double
  Dim tax As Double               'Unrounded federal tax withheld
  adjPay = pay - (70.19 * allowances)      'Task 4.1
  If adjPay < 0 Then
    adjPay = 0
  End If
  If mStatus = "S" Then
    tax = TaxSingle(adjPay)     'Task 4.2
  Else
    tax = TaxMarried(adjPay)    'Task 4.3
  End If
  Return Math.Round(tax, 2)     'Round to nearest cent
End Function

Function TaxSingle(ByVal adjPay As Double) As Double
  'Task 4.2: Compute federal tax withheld for single person.
  Select Case adjPay
    Case 0 To 138
      Return 0
    Case 138 To 200
      Return (0.1 * (adjPay — 138))
    Case 200 To 696
      Return 6.2 + 0.15 * (adjPay — 200)
    Case 696 To 1279
      Return 80.6 + 0.25 * (adjPay — 696)
    Case 1279 To 3338
      Return 226.35 + 0.28 * (adjPay — 1279)
    Case 3338 To 7212
      Return 802.87 + 0.33 * (adjPay — 3338)
    Case Is > 7212
      Return 2081.29 + 0.35 * (adjPay — 7212)
  End Select
End Function
```

```
Function TaxMarried(ByVal adjPay As Double) As Double
  'Task 4.3: Compute federal tax withheld for married person.
  Select Case adjPay
    Case 0 To 303
      Return 0
    Case 303 To 470
      Return 0.1 * (adjPay — 303)
    Case 470 To 1455
      Return 16.7 + 0.15 * (adjPay — 470)
    Case 1455 To 2272
      Return 164.45 + 0.25 * (adjPay — 1455)
    Case 2272 To 4165
      Return 368.7 + 0.28 * (adjPay — 2272)
    Case 4165 To 7321
      Return 898.74 + 0.33 * (adjPay — 4165)
    Case Is > 7321
      Return 1940.22 + 0.35 * (adjPay — 7321)
  End Select
End Function


Function Net_Check(ByVal pay As Double, ByVal ficaTax As Double,
                  ByVal fedTax As Double) As Double
  'Task 5: Compute amount of money paid to employee.
  Dim checkAmount As Double = pay — ficaTax — fedTax
  Return checkAmount
End Function


Sub ShowPayroll(ByVal empName As String, ByVal pay As Double,
                ByVal totalPay As Double, ByVal ficaTax As Double,
                ByVal fedTax As Double, ByVal check As Double)
  'Task 6: Display results of payroll computations
  lstResults.Items.Clear()
  lstResults.Items.Add("Payroll results for " & empName)
  lstResults.Items.Add("")
  lstResults.Items.Add("Gross pay this period:" & "   " &
                    FormatCurrency(pay))
  lstResults.Items.Add("")
  lstResults.Items.Add("Year-to-date earnings:" & "   " &
                    FormatCurrency(totalPay))
  lstResults.Items.Add("")
  lstResults.Items.Add("FICA tax this period:" & "   " &
                    FormatCurrency(ficaTax))
  lstResults.Items.Add("")
  lstResults.Items.Add("Income tax withheld:" & "    " &
                    FormatCurrency(fedTax))
  lstResults.Items.Add("")
  lstResults.Items.Add("Net pay (check amount):" & "  " &
                    FormatCurrency(check))
End Sub
```

▨ Comments

1. In the function FICA_Tax, care has been taken to avoid computing social security benefits tax on income in excess of $106,800 per year. The logic of the program makes sure an employee whose income for the year crosses the $106,800 threshold during a given week is taxed only on the difference between $106,800 and their previous year-to-date earnings.

2. The two functions TaxMarried and TaxSingle use Select Case blocks to incorporate the tax brackets given in Tables 5.5 and 5.6 for the amount of federal income tax withheld. The upper limit of each Case clause is the same as the lower limit of the next Case clause. This ensures that fractional values for *adjPay*, such as 138.50 in the TaxSingle function, will be properly treated as part of the higher salary range.

CHAPTER 5   SUMMARY

1. A *general procedure* is a portion of a program that is accessed by event procedures or other general procedures. The two types of general procedures are *Function procedures* and *Sub procedures*.

2. *Function procedures* are defined in blocks beginning with Function headers and ending with End Function statements. A function is executed by a reference in an expression and returns a value.

3. *Sub procedures* are defined in blocks beginning with Sub headers and ending with End Sub statements. A Sub procedure is accessed (called) by a statement consisting of the name of the procedure.

4. In any procedure, the *arguments* appearing in the calling statement must match the *parameters* of the Sub or Function statement in number, type, and order. They need not have the same names.

5. The *lifetime* of a variable or constant is the period during which it remains in memory. (The value of the variable might change over its lifetime, but it always holds some value.)

6. The *scope* of a variable or constant is the portion of the program that can refer to it. A variable or constant declared inside a Function, Sub, or event procedure has *local* scope and is visible only inside the procedure.

7. *Structured programming* uses modular design to refine large problems into smaller subproblems. Programs are coded using the three logical structures of sequences, decisions, and loops.

CHAPTER 5   PROGRAMMING PROJECTS

1. Write a program to determine a student's GPA. See Fig. 5.25. The user should enter the grade (A, B, C, D, or F) and the number of credit hours for a course, and then click on the *Record This Course* button. The user should then repeat this process for all his or her courses. After all the courses have been recorded, the user should click on the *Calculate GPA* button. A Function procedure should be used to calculate the quality points for a course. **Hint:** This program is similar to Example 5 in Section 5.1.

2. A fast-food vendor sells pizza slices ($1.75), fries ($2.00), soft drinks ($1.25), and cookies ($1.50). Write a program to compute a customer's bill. The program should request the quantity of each item ordered in a Sub procedure, calculate the total cost with a Function procedure, and use a Sub procedure to display an itemized bill. A sample output is shown in Fig. 5.26.

FIGURE 5.25 Form design for Programming Project 1.

FIGURE 5.26 Sample output for Programming Project 2.

3. An office furniture manufacturer makes two types of furniture—office chairs and desks. The cost per chair is $320, the cost per desk is $950, and the sales tax rate is 7%. Write a program to create an invoice form for an order. See Fig. 5.27. After the data on the left side of Fig. 5.27 are entered, the user can display an invoice in a list box by pressing the *Process Order* button. The user can click on the *Clear Order Form* button to clear all text boxes and the list box, and can click on the *Quit* button to exit the program. The invoice number consists of the capitalized first two letters of the customer's last name, followed by the last four digits of the zip code. The customer name is input with the last name first, followed by a comma, a space, and the first name. However, the name is displayed in the invoice in the proper order. The generation of the invoice number and the reordering of the first and last names should be carried out by Function procedures.

VideoNote
Hardware store (Homework)

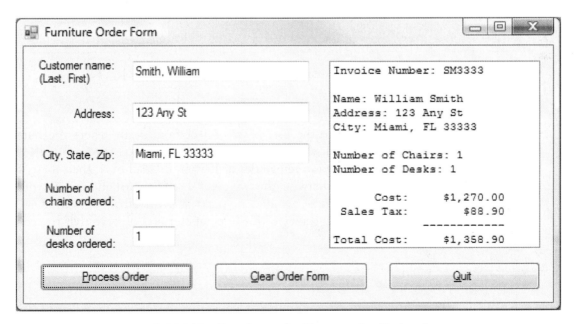

FIGURE 5.27 Sample run for Programming Project 3.

4. Table 5.9 contains seven proverbs and their truth values. Write a program that presents these proverbs one at a time and asks the user to evaluate them as true or false. The program should then tell the user how many questions were answered correctly and display one

TABLE 5.9	Seven proverbs.

Proverb	Truth Value
The squeaky wheel gets the grease.	True
Cry and you cry alone.	True
Opposites attract.	False
Spare the rod and spoil the child.	False
Actions speak louder than words.	True
Familiarity breeds contempt.	False
Marry in haste, repent at leisure.	True

Source: "You Know What They Say ...," by Alfie Kohn, *Psychology Today*, April 1988.

of the following evaluations: Perfect (all correct), Excellent (5 or 6 correct), You might consider taking Psychology 101 (less than 5 correct).

5. *Five, Six, Pick up Sticks.* Write a program that allows the user to challenge the computer to a game of Pick-up-Sticks. Here is how the game is played. The user chooses the number of matchsticks (from 5 to 50) to place in a pile. Then, the computer chooses who will go first. At each turn, the contestant can remove one, two, or three matchsticks from the pile. The contestant who removes the last matchstick loses. See Fig. 5.28.

FIGURE 5.28   **A possible outcome of Programming Project 5.**

The computer should make the user always select from a pile where the number of matchsticks has a remainder of 1 when divided by 4. For instance, if the user initially chooses a number of matchsticks that has a remainder of 1 when divided by 4, then the computer should have the user go first. Otherwise, the computer should go first and remove the proper number of matchsticks. [**Note:** The remainder when *n* is divided by 4 is (*n* Mod 4).] After writing the program, play a few games with the computer and observe that the computer always wins.

6

Repetition

6.1 Do Loops

A **loop**, one of the most important structures in programming, is used to repeat a sequence of statements a number of times. At each repetition, or **pass**, the statements act upon variables whose values are changing.

The **Do loop** repeats a sequence of statements either as long as or until a certain condition is true. A Do statement precedes the sequence of statements, and a Loop statement follows the sequence of statements. The condition, preceded by either the word "While" or the word "Until", follows the word "Do" or the word "Loop".

■ Pretest Form of a Do Loop

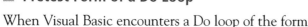

VideoNote
Do loops

When Visual Basic encounters a Do loop of the form

```
Do While condition
    statement(s)
Loop
```

it first checks the truth value of *condition*. If *condition* is false, then the statements inside the loop are not executed, and the program continues with the line after the statement Loop. If *condition* is true, then the statements inside the loop are executed. When the statement Loop is encountered, the entire process is repeated, beginning with the testing of *condition* in the Do While statement. In other words, the statements inside the loop are repeatedly executed as long as (that is, while) the condition is true. Figure 6.1 contains the pseudocode and flowchart for this loop.

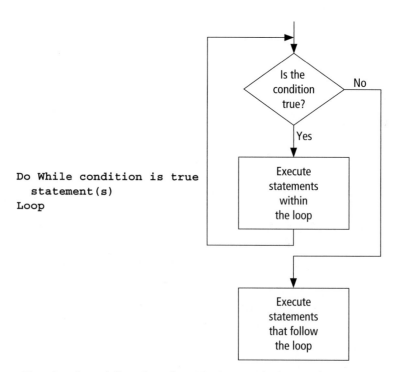

```
Do While condition is true
    statement(s)
Loop
```

FIGURE 6.1 Pseudocode and flowchart for a Do loop with the condition tested at the top.

Example 1   The following program, in which the condition in the Do loop is "num <= 7", displays the numbers from 1 through 7. (After the Do loop terminates, the value of *num* will be 8.)

```
Private Sub btnDisplay_Click(...) Handles btnDisplay.Click
  'Display the numbers from 1 to 7
  Dim num As Integer = 1
  Do While num <= 7
    lstNumbers.Items.Add(num)
    num += 1     'Add 1 to the value of num
  Loop
End Sub
```

[Run, and click on the button. The following is displayed in the list box.]

```
1
2
3
4
5
6
7
```

Do loops can be used to ensure that a proper response is received from the InputBox function.

 Example 2   The following program requires the user to enter a number from 1 through 3. The Do loop repeats the request until the user gives a proper response.

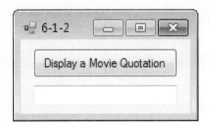

OBJECT	PROPERTY	SETTING
frmMovie	Text	6-1-2
btnDisplay	Text	Display a Movie Quotation
txtQuotation	ReadOnly	True

```
Private Sub btnDisplay_Click(...) Handles btnDisplay.Click
  Dim response As Integer, quotation As String = ""
  response = CInt(InputBox("Enter a number from 1 to 3."))
  Do While (response < 1) Or (response > 3)
    response = CInt(InputBox("Enter a number from 1 to 3."))
  Loop
  Select Case response
    Case 1
      quotation = "Plastics."
    Case 2
      quotation = "Rosebud."
```

```
      Case 3
         quotation = "That's all folks."
      End Select
      txtQuotation.Text = quotation
End Sub
```

[Run, and click on the button.]

[Type 3 into the box and click on the *OK* button.]

Do loops often are used to process data input from a file or from the user.

 Example 3 The following program finds the average of a sequence of numbers entered by the user from input dialog boxes. The user should type in the number −1 to indicate the end of data entry. Since the first input dialog box appears before the loop is entered, there is the possibility that the entire loop will be skipped.

```
Private Sub btnCompute_Click(...) Handles btnCompute.Click
   Dim num As Double = 0
   Dim count As Integer = 0
   Dim sum As Double = 0
   Dim prompt As String = "Enter a nonnegative number. " &
                       "Enter −1 to terminate entering numbers."
   num = CDbl(InputBox(prompt))
   Do While num <> −1
      count += 1
      sum += num
      num = CDbl(InputBox(prompt))
```

```
Loop
If count > 0 Then
   MessageBox.Show("Average: " & sum / count)
Else
   MessageBox.Show("No numbers were entered.")
End If
End Sub
```

[Run, click on the button, and respond to the requests for input with 80, 90, and −1. The following is displayed in the message box.]

Average: 85

In Example 3, the variable *count* is called a **counter variable**, the variable *sum* is called an **accumulator variable**, the number −1 is called a **sentinel value**, and the loop is referred to as having **sentinel-controlled repetition**.

Posttest Form of a Do Loop

In Examples 1 and 2, the condition was checked at the top of the loop—that is, before the statements were executed. Alternatively, the condition can be checked at the bottom of the loop when the Loop statement is reached. When Visual Basic encounters a Do loop of the form

```
Do
   statement(s)
Loop Until condition
```

it executes the statements inside the loop and then checks the truth value of *condition*. If *condition* is true, then the program continues with the line after the Loop statement. If *condition* is false, then the entire process is repeated beginning with the Do statement. In other words, the statements inside the loop are executed once and then are repeatedly executed *until* the condition is true. Figure 6.2 shows the pseudocode and flowchart for this type of Do loop.

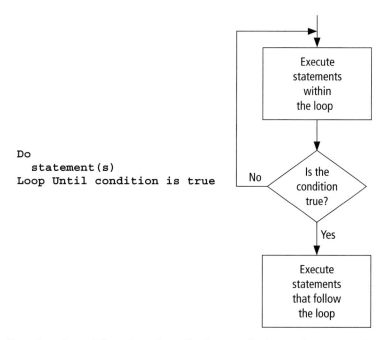

```
Do
   statement(s)
Loop Until condition is true
```

FIGURE 6.2   Pseudocode and flowchart for a Do loop with the condition tested at the bottom.

Example 4 The following program is equivalent to Example 2, except that the condition is tested at the bottom of the loop:

```
Private Sub btnDisplay_Click(...) Handles btnDisplay.Click
  Dim response As Integer, quotation As String = ""
  Do
    response = CInt(InputBox("Enter a number from 1 to 3."))
  Loop Until (response >= 1) And (response <= 3)
  Select Case response
    Case 1
      quotation = "Plastics."
    Case 2
      quotation = "Rosebud."
    Case 3
      quotation = "That's all folks."
  End Select
  txtQuotation.Text = quotation
End Sub
```

Do loops allow us to calculate useful quantities for which we might not know a simple formula.

 Example 5 Suppose you deposit money into a savings account and let it accumulate at 6% interest compounded annually. The following program determines when you will be a millionaire:

OBJECT	PROPERTY	SETTING
frmMillionaire	Text	6% Interest
lblAmount	Text	Amount deposited:
txtAmount		
btnCalculate	Text	Calculate Years to Become a Millionaire
txtWhen	ReadOnly	True

```
Private Sub btnCalculate_Click(...) Handles btnCalculate.Click
  'Compute years required to become a millionaire
  Dim balance As Double, numYears As Integer
  balance = CDbl(txtAmount.Text)
  Do While balance < 1000000
    balance += 0.06 * balance
    numYears += 1
  Loop
  txtWhen.Text = "In " & numYears &
                 " years you will have a million dollars."
End Sub
```

[Run, type 100000 into the text box, and click on the button.]

Comments

1. Be careful to avoid infinite loops—that is, loops that are never exited. The following loop is infinite, because the condition "balance < 1000" will always be true. This logic error can be avoided by initializing *intRate* with a value greater than 0.

```
Private Sub btnButton_Click(...) Handles btnButton.Click
  'An infinite loop
  Dim balance As Double = 100, intRate As Double
  Do While balance < 1000
    balance = (1 + intRate) * balance
  Loop
  txtBalance.Text = FormatCurrency(balance)
End Sub
```

Important: While an infinite loop is executing, the program can be terminated by clicking on the *Stop Debugging* button on the Toolbar.

2. Visual Basic provides a way to break out of a Do loop before the loop condition is met. When the statement **Exit Do** is encountered in the body of a loop, execution jumps immediately to the statement following the Loop statement.

3. A variable declared inside a Do loop has block-level scope; that is, the variable cannot be referred to by code outside of the loop.

4. Visual Basic allows the use of the words "While" and "Until" at either the top or bottom of a Do loop. For instance, the fourth line in the program in Example 1 can be replaced with

```
Do Until num > 7
```

and the fifth line of the program in Example 4 can be replaced with

```
Loop While (response < 1) Or (response > 3)
```

Practice Problem 6.1

1. How do you decide whether a condition should be checked at the top of a loop or at the bottom?

2. Change the following code segment so that the loop will execute at least once:

```
Do While continue = "Yes"
  answer = InputBox("Do you want to continue? (Y or N)")
```

```
      If answer.ToUpper = "Y" Then
        continue = "Yes"
      Else
        continue = "No"
      End If
    Loop
```

EXERCISES 6.1

In Exercises 1 through 6, determine the output displayed when the button is clicked on.

1. ```
Private Sub btnDisplay_Click(...) Handles btnDisplay.Click
  Dim num As Integer = 3
  Do While num < 15
    num += 5
  Loop
  txtOutput.Text = CStr(num)
End Sub
```

2. ```
Private Sub btnDisplay_Click(...) Handles btnDisplay.Click
  Dim num As Integer = 3
  Do
    num = 2 * num
  Loop Until num > 15
  txtOutput.Text = CStr(num)
End Sub
```

3. ```
Private Sub btnDisplay_Click(...) Handles btnDisplay.Click
  Dim total As Double = 0
  Dim num As Integer = 1
  Do Until num > 5
    total += num
    num += 1
  Loop
  txtOutput.Text = CStr(total)
End Sub
```

4. ```
Private Sub btnDisplay_Click(...) Handles btnDisplay.Click
  Dim total As Double = 0
  Dim num As Integer = 1
  Do
    total += num
    num += 1
  Loop Until num >= 5
  txtOutput.Text = CStr(total)
End Sub
```

5. ```
Private Sub btnCompute_Click(...) Handles btnCompute.Click
  Dim num As Double = 0
  Dim max As Double = −1
  Dim prompt As String = "Enter a nonnegative number. " &
                         "Enter −1 to terminate entering numbers."
```
```

```
        num = CDbl(InputBox(prompt))
        Do While num >= 0
          If num > max Then
            max = num
          End If
          num = CDbl(InputBox(prompt))
        Loop
        If max <> -1 Then
          MessageBox.Show("Maximum number: " & max)
        Else
          MessageBox.Show("No numbers were entered.")
        End If
      End Sub
```

(Assume that the responses are 4, 7, 3, and −1.)

6.
```
Private Sub btnDisplay_Click(...) Handles btnDisplay.Click
    Dim numTries As Integer
    Dim yr As Integer
    Dim msg As String = "In what year did the Beatles invade the U.S.?"
    Do
      numTries += 1
      yr = CInt(InputBox(msg, "Try #" & numTries))
      Select Case yr
        Case 1964
          MessageBox.Show("They appeared on the Ed Sullivan show in " &
                          "February 1964." & " You answered the question " &
                          "correctly in " & numTries & " tries.", "Correct")
        Case Is < 1964
          MessageBox.Show("Later than " & yr & ".")
        Case Is > 1964
          MessageBox.Show("Earlier than " & yr & ".")
      End Select
    Loop Until (yr = 1964) Or (numTries = 7)
    If yr <> 1964 Then
      MessageBox.Show("Your 7 tries are up, the answer is 1964.", "Sorry")
    End If
  End Sub
```

(Assume that the responses are 1950, 1970, and 1964.)

In Exercises 7 through 10, identify the errors.

7.
```
Private Sub btnDisplay_Click(...) Handles btnDisplay.Click
    Dim q As Double = 1
    Do While q > 0
      q = 3 * q - 1
      lstOutput.Items.Add("q")
    Loop
  End Sub
```

8.
```
Private Sub btnDisplay_Click(...) Handles btnDisplay.Click
    'Display the numbers from 1 to 5
    Dim num As Integer
```

```
      Do While num <> 6
        num = 1
        lstOutput.Items.Add(num)
        num += 1
      Loop
    End Sub
```

9. ```
   Private Sub btnDisplay_Click(...) Handles btnDisplay.Click
     'Repeat until a yes response is given
     Dim answer As String = "N"
     Loop
       answer = InputBox("Did you chop down the cherry tree (Y/N)?")
     Do Until (answer.ToUpper = "Y")
   End Sub
   ```

10. ```
    Private Sub btnDisplay_Click(...) Handles btnDisplay.Click
      'Repeat as long as desired
      Dim n As Integer, answer As String = ""
      Do
        n += 1
        lstOutput.Items.Add(n)
        answer = InputBox("Do you want to continue (Y/N)?")
      Until answer.ToUpper = "N"
    End Sub
    ```

In Exercises 11 through 20, replace each phrase containing "Until" with an equivalent phrase containing "While", and vice versa. For instance, the phrase (Until sum = 100) would be replaced by (While sum <> 100).

11. `Until num < 7`

12. `Until name = "Bob"`

13. `While response = "Y"`

14. `While total = 10`

15. `While name <> ""`

16. `While balance >= 100`

17. `While (a > 1) And (a < 3)`

18. `Until (ans = "") Or (n = 0)`

19. `Until Not (n = 0)`

20. `While (ans = "Y") And (n < 7)`

In Exercises 21 and 22, write simpler and clearer code that performs the same task as the given code.

21. ```
    Private Sub btnDisplay_Click(...) Handles btnDisplay.Click
      Dim name As String
      name = InputBox("Enter a number from 1 to 9:")
      lstOutput.Items.Add(name)
      name = InputBox("Enter a number from 1 to 9:")
      lstOutput.Items.Add(name)
      name = InputBox("Enter a number from 1 to 9:")
    ```
    ```

```
      lstOutput.Items.Add(name)
    End Sub
```

22.
```
Private Sub btnDisplay_Click(...) Handles btnDisplay.Click
  Dim loopNum As Integer, answer As String = ""
  Do
    If loopNum >= 1 Then
      answer = InputBox("Do you want to continue (Y/N)?")
      answer = answer.ToUpper
    Else
      answer = "Y"
    End If
    If (answer = "Y") Or (loopNum = 0) Then
      loopNum += 1
      txtOutput.Text = CStr(loopNum)
    End If
  Loop Until (answer <> "Y")
End Sub
```

23. Write a program that displays a Celsius-to-Fahrenheit conversion table in a list box. Entries in the table should range from 10 to 95 degrees Celsius in increments of 5 degrees. **Note:** The formula $f = (9/5 * c) + 32$ converts Celsius to Fahrenheit.

24. The *coefficient of restitution* of a ball, a number between 0 and 1, specifies how much energy is conserved when a ball hits a rigid surface. A coefficient of .9, for instance, means a bouncing ball will rise to 90% of its previous height after each bounce. Write a program to input a coefficient of restitution and an initial height in meters, and report how many times a ball bounces when dropped from its initial height before it rises to a height of less than 10 centimeters. Also report the total distance traveled by the ball before this point. The coefficients of restitution of a tennis ball, basketball, super ball, and softball are .7, .75, .9, and .3, respectively.

25. Write a program that requests a word containing the two letters *r* and *n* as input and determines which of these appears first. If the word does not contain both letters, the program should so advise the user. (Test the program with the words "colonel" and "merriment.")

26. Write a program that finds the smallest number in a sequence of nonnegative numbers entered by the user from input dialog boxes. The user should be told to type in the number −1 to indicate that the entire sequence has been entered.

27. Write a program that finds the range of a sequence of nonnegative numbers entered by the user from input dialog boxes. (The *range* is the difference between the largest and the smallest numbers in the sequence.) The user should be told to type in the number −1 to indicate that the entire sequence has been entered.

In Exercises 28 and 29, write a program corresponding to the flowchart.

28. The flowchart in Fig. 6.3 on the next page requests a whole number greater than 1 as input and factors it into a product of prime numbers. **Note:** A number is *prime* if its only factors are 1 and itself.

VideoNote

Sieve of Eratosthenes (Homework)

29. The flowchart in Fig. 6.4 on the next page finds the greatest common divisor (the largest integer that divides both) of two positive integers input by the user. Write a program that corresponds to the flowchart.

FIGURE 6.3 **Prime factors.**

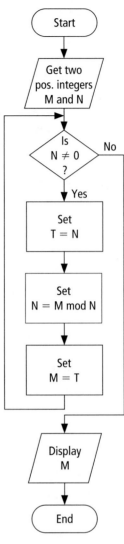

FIGURE 6.4 **Greatest common divisor.**

30. Illustrate the growth of money in a savings account. When the user presses the button, values for Amount and Interest Rate are obtained from text boxes and used to calculate the number of years until the money doubles. Use the form design shown below.

Note: The balance at the end of each year is $(1 + r)$ times the previous balance, where r is the annual rate of interest in decimal form.

OBJECT	PROPERTY	SETTING
frmInterest	Text	Compound Interest
lblAmount	Text	Amount:
txtAmount		
lblRate	AutoSize	False
	Text	Interest rate: [Annual]
txtRate		
btnDetermine	Text	Determine Years
lblDouble	AutoSize	False
	Text	Doubling time: [Years]
txtDouble	ReadOnly	True

In Exercises 31 through 38, write a program to answer the question.

31. A person born in 1980 can claim, "I will be x years old in the year x squared." What is the value of x?

32. The world population reached 6.83 billion people in January 2010 and was growing at the rate of 1.12% each year. Assuming that the population will continue to grow at the same rate, when will the population reach 10 billion?

33. Strontium-90, a radioactive element that is part of the fallout from nuclear explosions, has a half-life of 28 years. This means that a given quantity of strontium-90 will emit radioactive particles and decay to one-half its size every 28 years. How many years are required for 100 grams of strontium-90 to decay to less than 1 gram?

34. The *consumer price index* (CPI) indicates the average price of a fixed basket of goods and services. It is customarily taken as a measure of inflation and is frequently used to adjust pensions. The CPI was 9.9 in July 1913, was 100 in July 1983, and was 215.35 in July 2009. This means that $9.90 in July 1913 had the same purchasing power as $100.00 in July 1983, and the same purchasing power as $215.35 in July 2009. In 2009, the CPI fell for the first time since 1955. However, for most of the preceding 15 years it had grown at an average rate of 2.5% per year. Assuming that the CPI will rise at 2.5% per year in the future, in what year will the July CPI have at least doubled from its July 2009 level? **Note:** Each year, the CPI will be 1.025 times the CPI for the previous year.

35. When you borrow money to buy a house or a car, the loan is paid off with a sequence of equal monthly payments incorporating a stated annual interest rate compounded monthly. The amount borrowed is called the *principal*. If the annual interest rate is 6% (or .06), then the monthly interest rate is .06/12 = .005. At any time, the *balance* of the loan is the amount still owed. The balance at the end of each month is calculated as the balance at the end of the previous month, plus the interest due on that balance, and minus the monthly payment. For instance, with an annual interest rate of 6%,

$$[\text{new balance}] = [\text{previous balance}] + .005 \cdot [\text{previous balance}] - [\text{monthly payment}]$$
$$= 1.005 \cdot [\text{previous balance}] - [\text{monthly payment}].$$

Suppose you borrow $15,000 to buy a new car at 6% interest compounded monthly and your monthly payment is $290.00. After how many months will the car be half paid off? That is, after how many months will the balance be less than half the principal?

36. An *annuity* is a sequence of equal periodic payments. One type of annuity, called a *savings plan*, consists of monthly payments into a savings account in order to generate money for a future purchase. Suppose you decide to deposit $100 at the end of each month into a savings account paying 3% interest compounded monthly. The monthly interest rate will be .03/12 or .0025, and the balance in the account at the end of each month will be computed as

$$[\text{balance at end of month}] = (1.0025) \cdot [\text{balance at end of previous month}] + 100.$$

After how many months will there be more than $3000 in the account, and how much money will be in the account at that time?

37. An *annuity* is a sequence of equal periodic payments. For one type of annuity, a large amount of money is deposited into a bank account and then a fixed amount is withdrawn each month. Suppose you deposit $10,000 into such an account paying 3.6% interest compounded monthly, and then withdraw $600 at the end of each month. The monthly interest rate will be .036/12 or .003, and the balance in the account at the end of each month will be computed as

$$[\text{balance at end of month}] = (1.003) \cdot [\text{balance at end of previous month}] - 600.$$

After how many months will the account contain less than $600, and what will be the amount in the account at that time?

38. Redo Exercise 37 with the amount of money deposited being input by the user.

Solutions to Practice Problems 6.1

1. As a rule of thumb, the condition is checked at the bottom if the loop should be executed at least once.
2. Either precede the loop with the statement `continue = "Yes"`, or change the first line to **Do** and replace the Loop statement with `Loop Until continue <> "Yes"`.

6.2 For . . . Next Loops

When we know exactly how many times a loop should be executed, a special type of loop, called a For . . . Next loop, can be used. For . . . Next loops are easy to read and write and they have features that make them ideal for certain common tasks. The following code uses a For . . . Next loop to display a table:

```
Private Sub btnDisplayTable_Click(...) Handles btnDisplayTable.Click
  'Display a table of the first 5 numbers and their squares
  'Assume the font for lstTable is Courier New
  For i As Integer = 1 To 5
    lstTable.Items.Add(i & "   " & i ^ 2)
  Next
End Sub
```

[Run, and click on the button. The following is displayed in the list box.]

```
1   1
2   4
3   9
4   16
5   25
```

A similar program written with a Do loop is as follows.

```
Private Sub btnDisplayTable_Click(...) Handles btnDisplayTable.Click
  'Display a table of the first 5 numbers and their squares
  Dim i As Integer
  i = 1
  Do While i <= 5
    lstTable.Items.Add(i & "   " & i ^ 2)
    i += 1      'Add 1 to i
  Loop
End Sub
```

VideoNote

For . . . Next loops

■ General Form of a For . . . Next Loop

In general, a portion of a program of the form

constitutes a For . . . Next loop. The pair of statements For and Next cause the statements between them to be repeated a specified number of times. The For statement declares a numeric variable, called the **counter variable**, that is initialized and then automatically changes after each pass through the loop. Also, the For statement gives the range of values this variable will assume. The Next statement increments the counter variable. If $m \leq n$, then i is assigned the values $m, m + 1, \ldots, n$ in order, and the body is executed once for each of these values. If $m > n$, then the body is skipped and execution continues with the statement after the For... Next loop.

When program execution reaches a For...Next loop, such as the one shown previously, the For statement assigns to the counter variable i the **initial value** m and checks to see whether i is greater than the **terminating value** n. If so, then execution jumps to the line following the Next statement. If $i <= n$, the statements inside the loop are executed. Then, the Next statement increases the value of i by 1 and checks this new value to see if it exceeds n. If not, the entire process is repeated until the value of i exceeds n. When this happens, the program moves to the line following the loop. Figure 6.5 contains the pseudocode and flowchart of a For...Next loop.

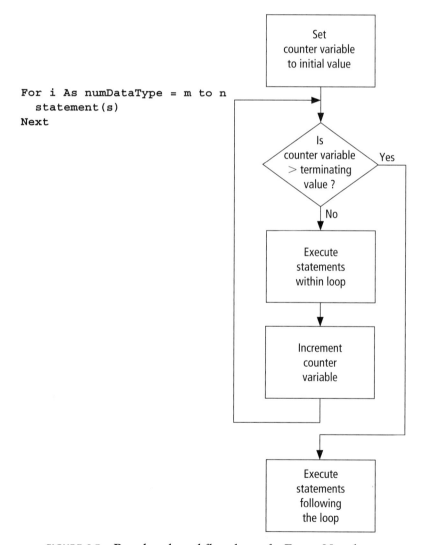

```
For i As numDataType = m to n
    statement(s)
Next
```

FIGURE 6.5   Pseudocode and flowchart of a For...Next loop.

The counter variable can be any numeric variable. The most common single-letter names are i, j, and k; however, if appropriate, the name should suggest the purpose of the counter variable.

The counter variable, and any variable declared inside a For...Next loop, has **block-level scope**; that is, the variable cannot be referred to by code outside of the loop.

A counter variable also can be declared with a Dim statement outside of the For...Next loop. For instance, the following program produces the same output as the program shown at the beginning of this section.

```
Private Sub btnDisplay_Click(...) Handles btnDisplay.Click
  'Display a table of the first 5 numbers and their squares
  'Assume the font for lstTable is Courier New
  Dim i As Integer
  For i = 1 To 5
    lstTable.Items.Add(i & "   " & i ^ 2)
  Next
End Sub
```

In this case, the variable *i* does not have block-level scope, and therefore it violates the principle that the scope of a variable should be as small as possible. In this book, we never declare a counter variable outside a For ... Next loop.

 Example 1 Suppose the population of a city is 300,000 in the year 2010 and is growing at the rate of 3% per year. The following program displays a table showing the population each year until 2014.

OBJECT	PROPERTY	SETTING
frmPopulation	Text	Population Growth
btnDisplay	Text	Display Population
lstTable	Font	Courier New

```
Private Sub btnDisplay_Click(...) Handles btnDisplay.Click
  'Display population from 2010 to 2014
  Dim pop As Double = 300000
  For yr As Integer = 2010 To 2014
    lstTable.Items.Add(yr & "     " & FormatNumber(pop, 0))
    pop += 0.03 * pop
  Next
End Sub
```

[Run, and click on the button.]

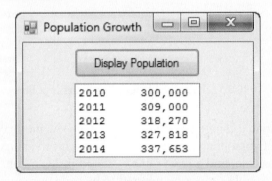

The initial and terminating values can be literals, variables, or expressions. For instance, the For statement in the preceding program can be replaced by

```
Dim firstYr As Integer = 2010
Dim lastYr As Integer = 2014
For yr As Integer = firstYr To lastYr
```

In Example 1, the counter variable was increased by 1 after each pass through the loop. A variation of the For statement allows any number to be used as the increment. The statement

```
For i As numDataType = m To n Step s
```

instructs the Next statement to add *s* to the counter variable instead of 1. The numbers *m*, *n*, and *s* do not have to be whole numbers. The number *s* is called the **step value** of the loop. **Note 1:** If the counter variable will assume values that are not whole numbers, then the variable must be of type Double. **Note 2:** The counter variable is also called the **index**.

 Example 2   The following program displays the values of the index of a For . . . Next loop before terminating and the step values input by the user:

OBJECT	PROPERTY	SETTING
frmIndex	Text	For index = 0 To n Step s
lblN	Text	n:
txtEnd		
lblS	Text	s:
txtStep		
btnDisplay	Text	Display Values of Index
lstValues		

```
Private Sub btnDisplay_Click(...) Handles btnDisplay.Click
  'Display values of index ranging from 0 to n Step s
  Dim n, s As Double
  n = CDbl(txtEnd.Text)
  s = CDbl(txtStep.Text)
  lstValues.Items.Clear()
  For index As Double = 0 To n Step s
    lstValues.Items.Add(index)
  Next
End Sub
```

[Run, type 3.2 and .5 into the text boxes, and click on the button.]

In the examples considered so far, the counter variable was successively increased until it reached the terminating value. However, if a negative step value is used and the initial value is greater than the terminating value, then the counter value is decreased until reaching the terminating value. In other words, the loop counts backward.

 Example 3   The following program accepts a word as input and displays it backwards:

OBJECT	PROPERTY	SETTING
frmBackwards	Text	Write Backwards
lblWord	Text	Enter word:
txtWord		
btnReverse	Text	Reverse Letters
txtBackwards	ReadOnly	True

```
Private Sub btnReverse_Click(...) Handles btnReverse.Click
  txtBackwards.Text = Reverse(txtWord.Text)
End Sub

Function Reverse(ByVal info As String) As String
  Dim m As Integer, temp As String = ""
  m = info.Length
  For j As Integer = m — 1 To 0 Step —1
    temp &= info.Substring(j, 1)
  Next
  Return temp
End Function
```

[Run, type "SUEZ" into the text box, and click on the button.]

Note: The initial and terminating values of a For . . . Next loop can be expressions. For instance, the third and fourth lines of the function in Example 3 can be consolidated to

```
For j As Integer = info.Length — 1 To 0 Step —1
```

■ Nested For . . . Next Loops

The body of a For . . . Next loop can contain any sequence of Visual Basic statements. In particular, it can contain another For . . . Next loop. However, the second loop must be completely contained inside the first loop and must have a different counter variable. Such a configuration is called **nested For . . . Next loops**.

✔ **Example 4**   The following program displays a multiplication table for the integers from 1 to 3. Here j denotes the left factors of the products, and k denotes the right factors. Each factor takes on a value from 1 to 3. The values are assigned to j in the outer loop (lines 4–11) and to k in the inner loop (lines 6–9). Initially, j is assigned the value 1, and then the inner loop is traversed three times to produce the first row of products. At the end of these three passes, the value of j will still be 1, and the first execution of the inner loop will be complete. Following this, the statement Next increments the value of j to 2. The statement beginning "For k" is then executed. It resets the value of k to 1. The second row of products is displayed during the next three executions of the inner loop, and so on.

OBJECT	PROPERTY	SETTING
frmTable	Text	Multiplication Table
btnDisplay	Text	Display Table
lstTable	Font	Courier New

```
Private Sub btnDisplay_Click(...) Handles btnDisplay.Click
  Dim row, entry As String
  lstTable.Items.Clear()
  For j As Integer = 1 To 3
    row = ""
    For k As Integer = 1 To 3
```

```
        entry = j & " x " & k & " = " & (j * k)
        row &= entry & "      "
    Next
    lstTable.Items.Add(row)
  Next
End Sub
```

[Run, and click on the button.]

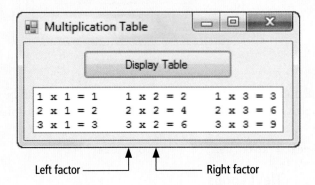

Left factor —————— —————— Right factor

■ Local Type Inference

Local type inference (also referred to as *implicit typing)* allows you to declare and initialize a local variable without explicitly stating its type with an As clause. Local type inference is enabled if Option Infer is set to On in the VB Defaults dialog box shown in Figure 3.1 of Section 3.2. (It is enabled by default.)

Some examples of the use of local type inference are as follows:

Standard Declaration	Local Type Inference Equivalent
For i As Integer = 1 To 3	For i = 1 To 3
For i As Double = 1 To 3 Step 0.5	For i = 1 To 3 Step 0.5
Dim count As Integer = 5	Dim count = 5
Dim rate as Double = 0.05	Dim rate = 0.05
Dim name As String = "Fred"	Dim name = "Fred"
Dim d as Date = #6/4/2010#	Dim d = #6/4/2010#

With local type inference, the type of a local variable is determined by the values following the equal sign. If the values are all whole numbers (written without a decimal point) and in the range of values for Integers, then the variable is declared to be of type Integer. If any of the values are numbers containing a decimal point or are outside the range of values for Integers, then the variable is declared to be of type Double. If the value is surrounded in quotes, then it is declared to be of type String. If the value is a date literal, then the variable is declared to be of type Date. **Note:** This feature *does not* apply to class-level variables.

The following walkthrough (which assumes that Option Infer is On) demonstrates how local type inference works in a For . . . Next loop.

1. Create a new program consisting of a form having a button (btnConfirm) and a list box (lstBox).

2. Enter the following code.

```
Private Sub btnConfirm_Click(...) Handles btnConfirm.Click
   For i = 1 To 5 Step 2
```

```
        lstBox.Items.Add(i)
    Next
  End Sub
```

3. In the Code Editor, hover the mouse pointer over the variable *i*. (The tooltip `Dim i As Integer` appears to confirm that the variable *i* has indeed been declared as type Integer.)

4. In the header of the For . . . Next loop, change the 5 to 5.0 and again hover the pointer over the letter *i*. (This time the tooltip reads `Dim i As Double`.)

Local type inference was added to Visual Basic because it is needed for LINQ (Language INtegrated Query), an innovative language feature that unifies the manipulation of diverse collections of data. LINQ is introduced in Chapter 7 of this book and is used extensively from then on. By necessity, we rely on local type inference when using LINQ. Although we do not use local type inference in the declaration of ordinary variables, you may feel free to do so if you prefer and your instructor permits.

Local type inference is also known as **duck typing**. This name comes from the well-known quote, "If it walks like a duck, and quacks like a duck, then it is a duck."

■ Comments

1. For and Next statements must be paired. If one is missing, the syntax checker will complain with a wavy underline and a message such as "A 'For' must be paired with a 'Next'."

2. Consider a loop beginning with For *i* = *m* To *n* Step *s*. The loop will be executed exactly once if *m* equals *n* no matter what value *s* has. The loop will not be executed at all if *m* is greater than *n* and *s* is positive, or if *m* is less than *n* and *s* is negative.

3. The value of the counter variable should not be altered within the body of the loop; doing so might cause the loop to repeat indefinitely or have an unpredictable number of repetitions.

4. Noninteger Step values in For . . . Next loops can result in unexpected outcomes. For instance, if you run Example 2 with *n* = 2 and *s* = .1, the last number displayed will not be 2 as intended. In general, the use of counter variables of type Double is poor programming practice and should be avoided. From now on, all counter variables appearing in this book will have type Integer.

5. Visual Basic provides a way to abort an iteration in a For . . . Next loop. When the statement `Continue For` is encountered in the body of the loop, execution immediately jumps to the Next statement. An analogous statement `Continue Do` is available for Do loops. Typically, Continue For and Continue Do statements appear inside conditional structures such as If blocks.

6. Visual Basic provides a way to back out of a For . . . Next loop. When the statement `Exit For` is encountered in the body of the loop, execution jumps immediately to the statement following the Next statement.

7. Counter variables and variables declared inside For . . . Next loops have block-level scope; that is, they cannot be referred to by code outside the loops.

8. Any type of loop can be nested inside another loop. For example, For . . . Next loops can be nested inside Do loops and vice versa. Also, Do loops can be nested inside other Do loops.

Practice Problem 6.2

1. Why won't the following lines of code work as intended?

```
For i As Integer = 15 To 1
  lstBox.Items.AddItem(i)
Next
```

2. When is a For . . . Next loop more appropriate than a Do loop?

In Exercises 1 through 10, determine the output displayed in the list box when the button is clicked.

1.
```
Private Sub btnDisplay_Click(...) Handles btnDisplay.Click
    For i As Integer = 1 To 4
      lstBox.Items.Add("Pass #" & i)
    Next
End Sub
```

2.
```
Private Sub btnDisplay_Click(...) Handles btnDisplay.Click
    For i As Integer = 4 To 7
      lstBox.Items.Add(2 * i)
    Next
End Sub
```

3.
```
Private Sub btnDisplay_Click(...) Handles btnDisplay.Click
    For j As Integer = 2 To 8 Step 2
      lstBox.Items.Add(j)
    Next
    lstBox.Items.Add("Who do we appreciate?")
End Sub
```

4.
```
Private Sub btnDisplay_Click(...) Handles btnDisplay.Click
    For countdown As Integer = 10 To 1 Step −1
      lstBox.Items.Add(countdown)
    Next
    lstBox.Items.Add("blastoff")
End Sub
```

5.
```
Private Sub btnDisplay_Click(...) Handles btnDisplay.Click
    Dim num As Integer = 5
    For i As Integer = num To (2 * num − 3)
      lstBox.Items.Add(i)
    Next
End Sub
```

6.
```
Private Sub btnDisplay_Click(...) Handles btnDisplay.Click
    For i As Integer = −9 To −1 Step 3
      lstBox.Items.Add(i)
    Next
End Sub
```

7.
```
Private Sub btnDisplay_Click(...) Handles btnDisplay.Click
    'Chr(149) is a large dot
    Dim stringOfDots As String = ""
    For i As Integer = 1 To 10
      stringOfDots &= Chr(149)
    Next
    txtBox.Text = stringOfDots
End Sub
```

8.
```
Private Sub btnDisplay_Click(...) Handles btnDisplay.Click
  Dim n As Integer = 3
  Dim total As Integer = 0
  For i As Integer = 1 To n
    total += i
  Next
  txtBox.Text = CStr(total)
End Sub
```

9.
```
Private Sub btnDisplay_Click(...) Handles btnDisplay.Click
  'Note: Chr(65) is A and Chr(90) is Z
  Dim sentence, letter As String
  Dim numCaps As Integer = 0
  sentence = "The United States of America"
  For i As Integer = 0 To sentence.Length - 1
    letter = sentence.Substring(i, 1)
    If (Asc(letter) >= 65) And (Asc(letter) <= 90) Then
      numCaps += 1
    End If
  Next
  txtBox.Text = CStr(numCaps)
End Sub
```

10.
```
Private Sub btnDisplay_Click(...) Handles btnDisplay.Click
  Dim word As String = "courage"
  Dim letter As String = ""
  Dim numVowels As Integer = 0
  For i As Integer = 0 To word.Length - 1
    letter = word.Substring(i, 1)
    If IsVowel(letter) Then
      numVowels += 1
    End If
  Next
  txtBox.Text = CStr(numVowels)
End Sub

Function IsVowel(ByVal letter As String) As Boolean
  letter = letter.ToUpper
  If (letter = "A") Or (letter = "E") Or (letter = "I") Or
     (letter = "O") Or (letter = "U") Then
    Return True
  Else
    Return False
  End If
End Function
```

In Exercises 11 through 14, identify the errors.

11.
```
Private Sub btnDisplay_Click(...) Handles btnDisplay.Click
  For j As Integer = 1 To 25 Step -1
    lstBox.Items.Add(j)
  Next
End Sub
```

12.
```
Private Sub btnDisplay_Click(...) Handles btnDisplay.Click
    For i As Integer = 3 To 0 Step -1
        lstBox.Items.Add(i & " " & 2 ^ i)
End Sub
```

13.
```
Private Sub btnDisplay_Click(...) Handles btnDisplay.Click
    'Display all numbers from 0 through 20 except for 13
    For i As Integer = 20 To 0
        If i = 13 Then
            i = 12
        End If
        lstBox.Items.Add(i)
    Next
End Sub
```

14.
```
Private Sub btnDisplay_Click(...) Handles btnDisplay.Click
    For j As Integer = 1 To 4 Step 0.5
        lstBox.Items.Add(j)
    Next
End Sub
```

In Exercises 15 and 16, rewrite the program using a For . . . Next loop.

15.
```
Private Sub btnDisplay_Click(...) Handles btnDisplay.Click
    Dim num As Integer = 1
    Do While num <= 9
        lstBox.Items.Add(num)
        num += 2      'Add 2 to value of num
    Loop
End Sub
```

16.
```
Private Sub btnDisplay_Click(...) Handles btnDisplay.Click
    lstBox.Items.Add("ding")
    lstBox.Items.Add("dong")
    lstBox.Items.Add("ding")
    lstBox.Items.Add("dong")
    lstBox.Items.Add("ding")
    lstBox.Items.Add("dong")
End Sub
```

In Exercises 17 through 37, write a program containing a For . . . Next loop to carry out the stated task.

17. Display the multiples of 5 from 5 through 100 in a list box.

18. Find the sum of the first one hundred positive integers.

19. Find the average of five numbers obtained from the user with input dialog boxes.

20. Find the largest of five numbers obtained from the user with input dialog boxes.

21. Find the value of $1 + 1/2 + 1/3 + 1/4 + \cdots + 1/100$.

22. Ask the user to input a positive integer (call it n) and then display a string of n large dots. **Note:** Chr(149) is a large dot. Strings of dots can be used to create histograms, as in Fig. 6.11 on page 266.

23. *Automobile Depreciation.* A rule of thumb states that cars in personal use depreciate by 15% each year. Suppose a new car is purchased for $20,000. Produce a table showing the value of the car at the end of each of the next five years.

24. Accept a word as input and determine if its letters are in alphabetical order. (Test the program with the words "almost", "imply", and "biopsy".)

25. Estimate how much a young worker will make before retiring at age 65. Request the worker's name, age, and starting salary as input. Assume the worker receives a 5% raise each year. For example, if the user enters Helen, 25, and 20000, then the text box should display the following:

```
Helen will earn about $2,415,995.
```

26. When $1000 is invested at 5% simple interest, the amount grows by $50 each year. When money is invested at 5% interest compounded annually, the amount at the end of each year is 1.05 times the amount at the beginning of that year. Display the amounts for 9 years for a $1000 investment at 5% simple and compound interest. See Fig. 6.6.

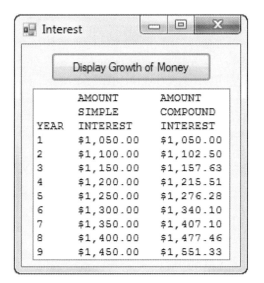

FIGURE 6.6   Output of Exercise 26.

FIGURE 6.7   Possible output for Exercise 27.

27. According to researchers at Stanford Medical School, the ideal weight for a woman is found by multiplying her height in inches by 3.5 and subtracting 108. The ideal weight for a man is found by multiplying his height in inches by 4 and subtracting 128. Request a lower and upper bound for heights and then produce a table giving the ideal weights for women and men in that height range. For example, when a lower bound of 62 and an upper bound of 71 are specified, Fig. 6.7 shows the output displayed in the list box.

28. Request a sentence, and then determine the number of sibilants (that is, letters S or Z) in the sentence. Carry out the counting with a Function procedure.

29. Refer to the annuity discussed in Exercise 36 of Section 6.1. Assume that the first deposit is made at the end of January 2010, and display the balances in the account at the end of each year from 2010 to 2019. See Fig. 6.8 on the next page.

30. Consider the car loan discussed in Exercise 35 of Section 6.1. The loan will be paid off after five years. Assume that the car was purchased at the beginning of January 2010, and display the balance at the end of each year for five years. See Fig. 6.9. **Note:** The last payment will be slightly less than the other payments, since otherwise the final balance would be a negative amount.

31. *Radioactive Decay.* Cobalt 60, a radioactive form of cobalt used in cancer therapy, decays over a period of time. Each year, 12% of the amount present at the beginning of the year will have decayed. If a container of cobalt 60 initially contains 10 grams, determine the amount remaining after five years.

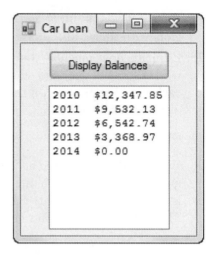

| FIGURE 6.8 Output of Exercise 29. | FIGURE 6.9 Output of Exercise 30. |

32. The keyboard in use on nearly all computers is known as the Qwerty keyboard, since the letters in the top letter line read QWERTYUIOP. A word is called a Qwerty word if all its letters appear on the top letter line of the keyboard. Some examples are *typewriter*, *repertoire*, and *treetop*. Accept a word as input and determine whether or not it is a Qwerty word. Use a Boolean-valued function named IsQwerty that accepts a word as input.

33. *Supply and Demand.* Each year's level of production and price (per bushel) for most agricultural products affects the level of production and price for the following year. Suppose the soybean crop in a country was 80 million bushels in 2010 and

[price each year] = 20 − .1 * [quantity that year]
[quantity each year] = 5 * ([price from the preceding year]) − 10,

where quantity is measured in units of millions of bushels. Generate a table to show the quantity and price from now until 2020. See Fig. 6.10.

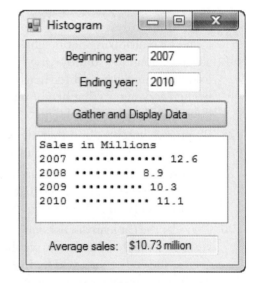

| FIGURE 6.10 Output of Exercise 33. | FIGURE 6.11 Possible output of Exercise 34. |

34. Display a company's sales figures for several years in a histogram and calculate the average yearly sales. See Fig. 6.11. When the user clicks on the button, the amount of sales for each year should be obtained from the user with input dialog boxes. **Note:** Chr(149) is a large dot.

35. You are offered two salary options for ten days of work. Option 1: $100 per day. Option 2: $1 the first day, $2 the second day, $4 the third day, and so on, with the amount doubling each day. Determine which option pays better.

Exercises 36 and 37 should use the following Function procedure.

```
Function DayOfWeek(ByVal d As Date) As String
  Dim str As String = FormatDateTime(d, DateFormat.LongDate)
  Dim n As Integer = str.IndexOf(",")
  Return str.Substring(0, n)
End Function
```

36. Request a year as input and then display the date of the first Tuesday of that year.

37. Request a year as input and then display the dates of the first Tuesdays of each month of that year.

Solutions to Practice Problem 6.2

1. The loop will never be entered because 15 is greater than 1. The intended first line might have been

```
For i As Integer = 15 To 1 Step −1
```
or
```
For i As Integer = 1 To 15
```

2. If the exact number of times the loop will be executed is known before entering the loop, then a For...Next loop should be used. Otherwise, a Do loop is more appropriate.

6.3   List Boxes and Loops

In previous sections we used list boxes to display output and to facilitate selection. In this section we explore some additional features of list boxes and use loops to analyze data in list boxes.

▦ Some Properties, Methods, and Events of List Boxes

During run time, the value of

VideoNote

List boxes
and loops

```
lstBox.Items.Count
```

is the number of items currently in the list box. Each item in lstBox is identified by an **index number** ranging from 0 through lstBox.Items.Count − 1. For instance, if the list box contains 10 items, then the first item has index 0, the second item has index 1, ..., and the last item has index 9. In general, the nth item in a list box has index $n − 1$.

During run time, the user can highlight an item in a list box by clicking on the item with the mouse or by moving to it with the up- and down-arrow keys when the list box has the focus. The SelectedIndexChanged event occurs each time an item of a list box is clicked on or each time an arrow key is used to change the highlighted item. It is the default event for list box controls.

The value of

```
lstBox.SelectedIndex
```

is the index number of the item currently highlighted in lstBox. If no item is highlighted, the value of SelectedIndex is −1. The statement

```
lstBox.SelectedIndex = −1
```

will unhighlight any highlighted item in the list. **Note:** This statement also raises the SelectedIndexChanged event.

The value of

```
lstBox.Items(n)
```

is the item of lstBox having index *n*. The elements of the list are of a data type called Object. A value of any type may be added to the list. However, type casting must take place whenever an element of the list is assigned to a numeric or string variable or is concatenated with another variable or literal. For instance, the statement

```
txtBox.Text = CStr(lstBox.Items(0))
```

displays the first item of lstBox in a text box.

The value of

```
lstBox.Text
```

is the currently highlighted item of lstBox converted to a string.

The Sorted property is perhaps the most interesting list box property. When it is set to True (at either design time or run time), items will automatically be displayed in alphabetical (i.e., ANSI) order. The default value of the Sorted property is False.

After the SelectedIndexChanged event, the two most important events for list boxes are the Click and DoubleClick events. However, if a program contains procedures for both of these events and the user double-clicks on the list box, only the Click event will be raised.

The items in a list box are usually all strings or all numbers. When the items are all strings, we use loops to search for items and to extract information. When the items are all numbers, we use loops to perform calculations.

■ List Boxes Populated with Strings

Example 1   The following program uses two list boxes, named lstStates and lstLastTen. We assume that the String Collection Editor of lstStates contains the names of the 50 U.S. states in the order they joined the union. The program displays the last 10 states to join the union beginning with the most recent. **Note:** If *n* is the number of items in lstStates, then the last item in lstStates has index $n - 1$.

```
Private Sub btnDisplay_Click(...) Handles btnDisplay.Click
  Dim n As Integer = lstStates.Items.Count
  For i As Integer = (n - 1) To (n - 10) Step -1
    lstLastTen.Items.Add(lstStates.Items(i))
  Next
End Sub
```

[Run, and click on the button.]

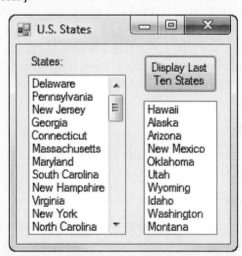

When a list is searched, we often use a Boolean variable called a **flag** to tell us whether or not the sought-after item has been found. The value of the flag is set to False initially and then is changed to True if and when the sought-after item is found.

 Example 2   The following program uses a list box named lstStates whose String Collection Editor contains the names of the 50 U.S. states in the order they joined the union. The program also uses a masked text box with Mask "LL". After the user enters two letters into the masked text box, the program uses a Do loop to search the list box for a state beginning with those letters. The Do loop terminates when the state is found or when the last item in the list box has been examined. If a state is found, the program reports its full name and the order in which it joined the union. If there is no state beginning with the pair of letters, the program so reports.

```
Private Sub btnSearch_Click(...) Handles btnSearch.Click
  Dim letters As String = mtbFirstTwoLetters.Text.ToUpper
  Dim foundFlag As Boolean = False   'indicates whether state has been found
  Dim i As Integer = -1    'index of the state currently considered
  Do Until (foundFlag) Or (i = lstStates.Items.Count - 1)
    i += 1
    If CStr(lstStates.Items(i)).ToUpper.StartsWith(letters) Then
      foundFlag = True
    End If
  Loop
  If foundFlag Then
    txtOutput.Text = CStr(lstStates.Items(i)) & " is state #" & (i + 1) & "."
  Else
    txtOutput.Text = "No state begins with " & mtbFirstTwo.Text & "."
  End If
End Sub
```

[Run, enter two letters into the masked text box, and click on the button.]

▓ List Boxes Populated with Numbers

 Example 3   The following program evaluates exam grades. The user inserts a grade into the list box by typing it into the txtGrade text box and then clicking on the *Record* button. After all the grades have been entered, the user clicks on the *Calculate* button to determine the average grade and the highest grade for the exam. The average grade is calculated as [sum of grades] / [number of grades]. The variable *sum* adds up the grades during a loop through the grades. The number of grades is just the number of items in the list box. The variable *maxGrade* starts out set to 0. It is then adjusted during each pass through the loop. **Note:** To prevent the program from crashing, the btnCalculate_Click event procedure checks that the list box contains some items.

OBJECT	PROPERTY	SETTING
frmGrades	Text	Analyze Grades
lblGrade	Text	Grade:
txtGrade		
btnRecord	Text	Record Grade
btnCalculate	Text	Calculate Average and Highest Grade
lblAverage	Text	Average grade:
txtAverage	ReadOnly	True
lblHighest	Text	Highest grade:
txtHighest	ReadOnly	True
lstGrades		

```
Private Sub btnRecord_Click(...) Handles btnRecord.Click
  lstGrades.Items.Add(txtGrade.Text)
  txtGrade.Clear()
  txtGrade.Focus()
End Sub


Private Sub btnCalculate_Click(...) Handles btnCalculate.Click
  Dim sum As Double = 0
  Dim maxGrade As Double = 0
  If lstGrades.Items.Count > 0 Then 'condition is true when list box is nonempty
    For i As Integer = 0 To lstGrades.Items.Count - 1
      sum += CDbl(lstGrades.Items(i))
      If CDbl(lstGrades.Items(i)) > maxGrade Then
        maxGrade = CDbl(lstGrades.Items(i))
      End If
    Next
    txtAverage.Text = FormatNumber(sum / lstGrades.Items.Count, 2)
    txtHighest.Text = CStr(maxGrade)
  Else
    MessageBox.Show("You must first enter some grades.")
  End If
End Sub
```

[Run, enter some grades, and then click on the *Calculate* button.]

Note: In Example 3, the average grade and the highest grade could have been calculated without the grades being stored in a list box. Some calculations, however, such as the standard deviation, do require the grades to be stored.

■ Searching an Ordered List

When the items in a list of strings are in alphabetical order, the search can be shortened. For instance, if you are searching an ordered list of words for one that begins with the letter *D*, you can certainly stop the search when you reach words beginning with *E*. Consider Example 2. Whenever the pair of letters entered into the masked text box were not the first two letters of a state, the entire list was searched. Such searches can be shortened considerably if the states are first ordered.

  Example 4   The following program has the same controls and settings as Example 2, except that the Sorted property of the list box is set to True. The program begins by looking at the items one at a time until it locates a state whose name exceeds the sought-after letters alphabetically. If that state doesn't begin with the sought-after letters, we can assume that no state in the list does.

```
Private Sub btnSearch_Click(...) Handles btnSearch.Click
  Dim letters As String = mtbFirstTwoLetters.Text.ToUpper
  Dim i As Integer = 0     'index of the state currently considered
  Do Until (CStr(lstStates.Items(i)).ToUpper > letters) Or
          (i = lstStates.Items.Count − 1)
    i += 1
  Loop
  If CStr(lstStates.Items(i)).ToUpper.StartsWith(letters) Then
    txtOutput.Text = CStr(lstStates.Items(i)) & " begins with " &
                   mtbFirstTwoLetters.Text & "."
  Else
    txtOutput.Text = "No state begins with " & mtbFirstTwoLetters.Text & "."
  End If
End Sub
```

■ Comments

1. A list box containing numbers might not be numerically in increasing order even when the Sorted property is set to True. For instance, since the ANSI table determines order, the number 88 will precede the number 9.

2. Example 4 presents one way to search a list of strings that are in alphabetical order. A more efficient technique, called a *binary search*, is discussed in Programming Project 8.

Practice Problems 6.3

1. Write a program that displays a message box telling you whether a SelectedIndexChanged event was caused by the pressing of an arrow key or was caused by clicking on an item.

2. Consider Example 3. Why couldn't the maximum grade be calculated with the following code?

```
lstGrades.Sorted = True
maxGrade = CDbl(lstGrades.Items(lstGrades.Items.Count − 1))
```

EXERCISES 6.3

In Exercises 1 through 6, assume that lstBox is as shown below. Determine the contents of the text box after the code is executed.

1. `txtOutput.Text = lstBox.Text`

2. `txtOutput.Text = CStr(lstBox.Items(3))`

3. `txtOutput.Text = CStr(lstBox.Items(lstBox.Items.Count − 1))`

4. `txtOutput.Text = CStr(lstBox.Items(lstBox.SelectedIndex))`

5. `txtOutput.Text = CStr(lstBox.SelectedIndex)`

6.
```
Dim total As Integer = 0
For n As Integer = 0 To lstBox.Items.Count − 1
  If CStr(lstBox.Items(n)).Length = 6 Then
    total += 1
  End If
Next
txtOutput.Text = CStr(total)
```

In Exercises 7 through 12, assume that lstBox is as shown below. Determine the contents of the text box after the code is executed.

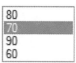

7. `txtOutput.Text = CStr(lstBox.Items(2))`

8. `txtOutput.Text = lstBox.Text`

9. `txtOutput.Text = CStr(lstBox.Items(lstBox.SelectedIndex − 1))`

10. `txtOutput.Text = CStr(lstBox.SelectedIndex)`

11.
```
Dim num As Integer = 0
For n As Integer = 0 To lstBox.Items.Count − 2
  num += CInt(lstBox.Items(n))
Next
txtOutput.Text = CStr(num)
```

12.
```
Dim min As Double = 100
For n As Integer = 0 To lstBox.Items.Count − 1
  If CDbl(lstBox.Items(n)) < min Then
    min = CDbl(lstBox.Items(n))
  End If
Next
txtOutput.Text = CStr(min)
```

In Exercises 13 through 18, fill the String Collection Editor of lstBox at design time with the winners of the nearly 100 Rose Bowl games that have been played.[1] The first three items in the list box will be Michigan, Washington State, and Oregon. Some colleges appear many times in the list. Write a program that performs the indicated task.

13. Count the number of times USC has won the Rose Bowl.

14. After the user clicks on the name of a college in lstBox, count the number of times the college has won the Rose Bowl.

15. Determine if a college input by the user in a text box has won the Rose Bowl. Assume that the Sorted property of lstBox is set to False. The procedure should terminate the search if and when the college is found.

16. Determine if a college input by the user in a text box has won the Rose Bowl. Assume that the Sorted property of lstBox is set to True. The procedure should terminate the search as soon as possible.

17. Fill lstBox2 with the entries of lstBox, but in reverse order.

18. Fill lstBox2 with the colleges (in alphabetical order) that have won the Rose Bowl, with each winner appearing just once.

Suppose lstBox has been filled with the 50 U.S. states in the order they joined the union.[2] In Exercises 19 through 34, write a program to perform the indicated task.

19. Display in lstBox2 the states in alphabetical order.

20. Display in lstBox2 the states in reverse alphabetical order.

21. Display in lstBox2 the states whose names (including spaces) are seven letters long.

22. Determine the first state in lstBox whose name is seven letters long. The program should terminate the search as soon as the state is found.

---

[1] The file Rosebowl.txt (found in the folder Programs\Ch06\Text_Files_for_Exercises) contains the names of the Rose Bowl winners in the order the games were played. Copy the contents of the text file and Paste them into the String Collection Editor of lstBox.

[2] The file States.txt (found in the folder Programs\Ch06\Text_Files_for_Exercises) contains the names of the states in the order they joined the union.

23. Determine the first state in lstBox whose name begins with "New". The program should terminate the search as soon as the state is found.

24. Display in lstBox2 the states whose names begin with "New".

25. Determine the length of the longest state name, and display in lstBox2 the states having that length.

26. Determine the length of the shortest state name, and display in lstBox2 the states having that length.

27. Display in lstBox2 the states whose names have four letters that are vowels. The program should call a Function procedure NumberOfVowels that counts the number of letters in a string that are vowels.

28. After the user clicks on a state, determine the number of letters in the state's name that are vowels.

29. Determine the maximum number of letters that are vowels for the names of the 50 states. The program should call a Function procedure NumberOfVowels that counts the number of letters in a string that are vowels.

30. Determine the number of states whose names consist of two words.

31. Display the name of the first state to join the union.

32. Display the name of the last state to join the union.

33. Display the name of the fifth state to join the union.

34. Display in lstBox2 the names of the original thirteen states.

35. Alter Example 3 so that the btnCalculate_Click event procedure calculates the lowest grade instead of the highest grade.

36. The **standard deviation** measures the spread or dispersal of a set of numbers about the mean. Formally, if $x_1, x_2, x_3, \ldots, x_n$ is a collection of n numbers with average value m, then

$$\text{standard deviation} = \sqrt{\frac{(x_1 - m)^2 + (x_2 - m)^2 + (x_3 - m)^2 + \cdots + (x_n - m)^2}{n}}.$$

Extend Example 3 so that the btnCalculate_Click event procedure also calculates the standard deviation of the grades.

37. The **range** of a set of numbers is the difference between the highest and the lowest numbers. Modify Example 3 so that the btnCalculate_Click procedure calculates the range of the grades instead of the highest grade.

38. Alter Example 3 so that the btnCalculate_Click event procedure calculates the number of above-average grades instead of the maximum grade.

39. Rewrite Example 4 so that the btnSearch_Click event procedure starts at the last item and searches backwards.

Solutions to Practice Problems 6.3

1.
```
Dim clickFlag As Boolean

Private Sub lstBox_Click(...) Handles lstBox.Click
   clickFlag = True
End Sub

Private Sub lstBox_SelectedIndexChanged(...) Handles _
                   lstBox.SelectedIndexChanged
   Dim msg As String = "The SelectedIndexChanged event was caused by "
```

```
   If clickFlag Then
      MessageBox.Show(msg & "clicking on an item of the list box.")
   Else
      MessageBox.Show(msg & "pressing an arrow key.")
   End If
   clickFlag = False
End Sub
```

2. The ordering in the list box is determined by the ANSI table (where the items are treated as strings), not the numerical value. Therefore the last item in the list box might not have the greatest numerical value.

CHAPTER 6   SUMMARY

1. A *Do loop* repeatedly executes a block of statements either as long as or until a certain condition is true. The condition can be checked either at the top of the loop or at the bottom.

2. A *For . . . Next loop* repeats a block of statements a fixed number of times. The *counter variable* assumes an initial value and increases it by one after each pass through the loop until it reaches the terminating value. Alternative increment values can be specified with the *Step* keyword.

3. Visual Basic uses *local type inference* to infer the data types of local variables declared without an As clause by looking at the data type of the initialization expression.

4. The items in a list box are assigned *index numbers* ranging from 0 to [number of items minus 1]. Loops can use the index numbers to extract information from list boxes.

5. A *flag* is a Boolean variable used to indicate whether a certain event has occurred or a certain situation exists.

CHAPTER 6   PROGRAMMING PROJECTS

1. *Caffeine Absorption.* After caffeine is absorbed into the body, 13% is eliminated from the body each hour. Assume a person drinks an 8-oz cup of brewed coffee containing 130 mg of caffeine, and the caffeine is absorbed immediately into the body. Write a program to compute the following values. See Fig. 6.12.

   (a) The number of hours required until 65 mg (one-half the original amount) remain in the body.

FIGURE 6.12   Output of Programming Project 1.   FIGURE 6.13   Output of Programming Project 2.

(b) The amount of caffeine in the body 24 hours after the person drinks the coffee.

(c) Suppose the person drinks a cup of coffee at 7 a.m. and then drinks a cup of coffee at the end of each hour until 7 a.m. the next day. How much caffeine will be in the body at the end of the 24 hours?

2. The *Rule of 72* is used to approximate the time required for prices to double due to inflation. If the inflation rate is r%, then the Rule of 72 estimates that prices will double in $72/r$ years. For instance, at an inflation rate of 6%, prices double in about 72/6 or 12 years. Write a program to test the accuracy of this rule. For each interest rate from 1% to 20%, the program should display the rounded value of $72/r$ and the actual number of years required for prices to double at an r% inflation rate. (Assume prices increase at the end of each year.) The program should also show the accuracy rate (percentage of correct values). See Fig. 6.13.

3. Write a program to provide information on the height of a ball thrown straight up into the air. The program should request as input the initial height, h feet, and the initial velocity, v feet per second. The height of the ball (in feet) after t seconds is given by the formula $h + vt - 16t^2$ feet. The five options to be provided by buttons are as follows:

(a) Determine the maximum height of the ball. **Note:** The ball will reach its maximum height after $v/32$ seconds.

(b) Determine approximately when the ball will hit the ground. **Hint:** Calculate the height after every .1 second and observe when the height is no longer a positive number.

(c) Determine approximately when the ball will begin to descend. **Hint:** Calculate the height after every .1 second and observe when the height is no longer greater than the previous height.

(d) Display a table showing the height of the ball every quarter second for five seconds or until it hits the ground. See Fig. 6.14.

(e) Quit.

FIGURE 6.14   Sample Output for Programming Project 3.

4. A *palindrome* is a word or phrase that reads the same forwards and backwards, character for character, disregarding punctuation, case, and spaces. Some examples are "racecar", "Madam, I'm Adam.", and "Was it a cat I saw?". Write a program that allows the user to input a word or phrase and then determines if it is a palindrome. The program should use a

Boolean-valued Function procedure named IsPalindrome that returns the value True when the word or phrase is a palindrome and the value False otherwise.

5. The following words have three consecutive letters that are also consecutive letters in the alphabet: THI**RST**Y, AF**GHI**ANISTAN, S**TU**DENT. Write a program that accepts a word as input and determines whether or not it has three consecutive letters that are consecutive letters in the alphabet. The program should use a Boolean-valued function named IsTripleConsecutive that accepts an entire word as input. **Hint:** Use the Asc function.

6. Write a program that uses a flag and does the following:

   (a) Ask the user to input a sentence containing parentheses. **Note:** The closing parenthesis should not directly precede the period.

   (b) Display the sentence with the parentheses and their contents removed. Test the program with the following sentence as input: BASIC (Beginner's All-purpose Symbolic Instruction Code) was once the world's most widely known computer language.

7. *Depreciation to a Salvage Value of 0.* For tax purposes an item may be depreciated over a period of several years, n. With the *straight-line* method of depreciation, each year the item depreciates by 1/nth of its original value. With the *double-declining-balance* method of depreciation, each year the item depreciates by 2/nths of its value at the beginning of that year. (In the final year it is depreciated by its value at the beginning of the year.) Write a program that performs the following tasks:

   (a) Request a description of the item, the year of purchase, the cost of the item, the number of years to be depreciated (estimated life), and the method of depreciation. The method of depreciation should be chosen by clicking on one of two buttons.

   (b) Display a year-by-year description of the depreciation. See Fig. 6.15.

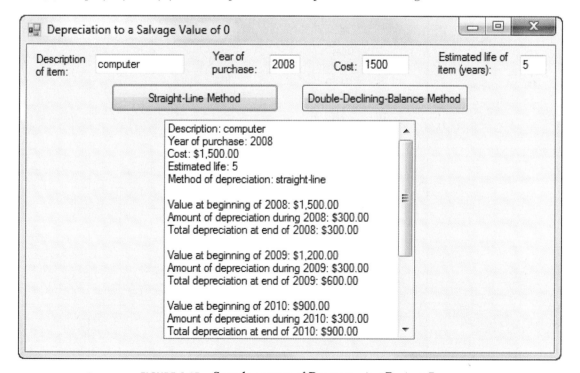

FIGURE 6.15   Sample output of Programming Project 7.

8. An especially efficient technique for searching an ordered list of items is called a **binary search**. A binary search looks for a value by first determining in which half of the list it resides. The other half of the list is then ignored, and the retained half is temporarily regarded as the entire list. The process is repeated until the item is found or the entire list

has been considered. Use the algorithm and flowchart for a binary search shown below to rewrite the btnSearch_Click event procedure from Example 4 of Section 6.3.

Figure 6.16 shows a partial flowchart for a binary search. (The sought-after value is denoted by *quarry*. The Boolean variable *flag* keeps track of whether or not *quarry* has been found.) The algorithm for a binary search of the items in an ordered list box is as follows:

(i) At each stage, denote the index of the first item in the retained list by *first* and the index of the last item by *last*. Initially, set the value of *first* to 0, set the value of *last* to one less than the number of items in the list, and set the value of *flag* to False.

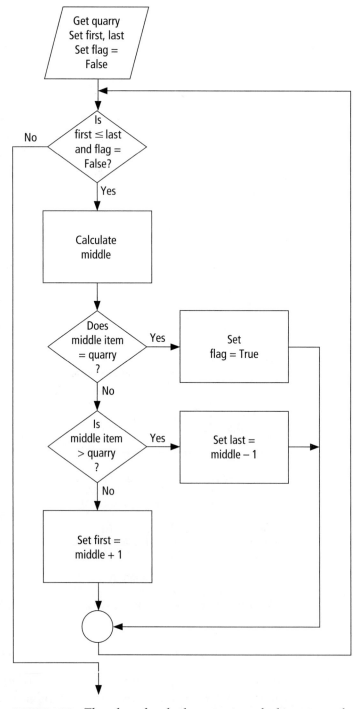

FIGURE 6.16 Flowchart for the loop portion of a binary search.

(ii) Look at the middle item of the current list—the item having index $middle = $ $\text{CInt}((first + last)/2)$.

(iii) If the middle item is *quarry*, then set *flag* to True and end the search.

(iv) If the middle item is greater than *quarry*, then *quarry* should be in the first half of the list. So the index of *quarry* must lie between *first* and *middle* − 1. Set *last* to *middle* − 1.

(v) If the middle item is less than *quarry*, then *quarry* should be in the second half of the list of possible items. So the index of *quarry* must lie between *middle* + 1 and *last*. Set *first* to *middle* + 1.

(vi) Repeat steps (ii) through (v) until *quarry* is found or until the halving process uses up the entire list. (When the entire list has been used up, *first* > *last*.) In the second case, *quarry* was not in the original list.

7

Arrays

7.1 Creating and Accessing Arrays

A variable (or simple variable) is a name to which Visual Basic can assign a single value. An **array variable** is an indexed list of simple variables of the same type, to and from which Visual Basic can efficiently assign and access a list of values.

Consider the following situation: Suppose you want to evaluate the exam grades for 30 students. Not only do you want to compute the average score, but you also want to display the names of the students whose grades are above average. You might run the program outlined below. *Note:* Visual Basic prefers zero-based numberings—that is, numberings beginning with 0 instead of 1. (We saw this preference in Chapter 3, where the numbering of the positions in a string began with 0.) Therefore we will number the 30 student names and grades from 0 through 29 instead of from 1 through 30.

```
Private Sub btnDisplay_Click(...) Handles btnDisplay.Click
  Dim student0 As String, grade0 As Double
  Dim student1 As String, grade1 As Double
    .
    .
    .
  Dim student29 As String, grade29 As Double
  'Analyze exam grades
  Dim promptName As String = "Enter name of student #"
  Dim promptGrade As String = "Enter grade for student #"
  student0 = InputBox(promptName & 0, "Name")
  grade0 = CDbl(InputBox(promptGrade & 0, "Grade"))
  student1 = InputBox(promptName & 1, "Name")
  grade1 = CDbl(InputBox(promptGrade & 1, "Grade"))
    .
    .
    .
  student29 = InputBox(promptName & 29, "Name")
  grade29 = CDbl(InputBox(promptGrade & 29, "Grade"))
  'Compute the average grade
    .
    .
    .
  'Display the names of students with above-average grades
    .
    .
    .
End Sub
```

This program is going to be uncomfortably long. What's most frustrating is that the 30 Dim statements and 30 pairs of statements obtaining input are very similar and look as if they should be condensed into a loop. A shorthand notation for the many related variables would be welcome. It would be nice if we could just write

```
For i As Integer = 0 To 29
  studenti = InputBox(promptName & i, "Name")
  gradei = CDbl(InputBox(promptGrade & i, "Grade"))
Next
```

Of course, this will not work. Visual Basic will treat *studenti* and *gradei* as two variables and keep reassigning new values to them. At the end of the loop, they will have the values of the thirtieth student.

Declaring an Array Variable

Visual Basic provides a data structure called an **array** that lets us do what we tried to accomplish in the loop above. The variable names, similar to those in the loop, will be

```
students(0), students(1), students(2), students(3), ..., students(29)
```

and

```
grades(0), grades(1), grades(2), grades(3), ..., grades(29)
```

We refer to these collections of variables as the array variables *students* and *grades*. The numbers inside the parentheses of the individual variables are called **subscripts** or **indexes**, and each individual variable is called a **subscripted variable** or **element**. For instance, *students*(3) is the fourth element of the array *students*, and *grades*(20) is the twenty-first element of the array *grades*. The elements of an array are located in successive memory locations. Figure 7.1 shows the memory locations for the array *grades*.

FIGURE 7.1   The array *grades*.

Names of array variables follow the same naming conventions as simple variables. If *arrayName* is the name of an array variable and *n* is a literal, variable, or expression of type Integer, then the declaration statement

```
Dim arrayName(n) As DataType
```

reserves space in memory to hold the values of the subscripted variables *arrayName*(0), *arrayName*(1), *arrayName*(2), ..., *arrayName*(n). The value of *n* is called the **upper bound** of the array. The number of elements in the array, $n + 1$, is called the **size** of the array. The subscripted variables will all have the same data type—namely, the type specified by *DataType*. For instance, they could all be variables of type String or all be variables of type Double. In particular, the statements

```
Dim students(29) As String
Dim grades(29) As Double
```

declare the 30-element arrays needed for the preceding program.

Values can be assigned to individual subscripted variables with assignment statements and displayed in text boxes and list boxes just like values of ordinary variables. The default initial value of each subscripted variable is the same as with an ordinary variable—that is, the keyword Nothing for String types and 0 for numeric types. The statement

```
Dim grades(29) As Double
```

sets aside a portion of memory for the array *grades* and assigns the default value 0 to each element.

The statements

```
grades(0) = 87
grades(1) = 92
```

assign values to the first two elements of the array.

	grades(0)	grades(1)	grades(2)		grades(29)
grades	87	92	0	. . .	0

The statements

```
For i As Integer = 0 To 2
  lstBox.Items.Add(grades(i))
Next
```

then produce the following output in the list box:

```
87
92
0
```

As with an ordinary variable, an array declared in the Declarations section of the Code Editor is class-level. That is, it will be visible to all procedures in the form, and any values assigned to it in a procedure will persist after the procedure terminates. Array variables declared inside a procedure are local to that procedure and cease to exist when the procedure is exited.

 Example 1   The following program creates a string array consisting of the names of the first four Super Bowl winners. Figure 7.2 shows the array created by the program.

	teamNames(0)	teamNames(1)	teamNames(2)	teamNames(3)
teamNames	Packers	Packers	Jets	Chiefs

FIGURE 7.2   **The array *teamNames* of Example 1.**

OBJECT	PROPERTY	SETTING
frmBowl	Text	Early Super Bowls
lblNumber	Text	Number from 1 to 4:
mtbNumber	Mask	0
btnWhoWon	Text	Who Won?
lblWinner	Text	Winning team:
txtWinner	ReadOnly	True

```
Private Sub btnWhoWon_Click(...) Handles btnWhoWon.Click
  Dim teamNames(3) As String
  Dim n As Integer
  'Place Super Bowl Winners into the array
```

```
   teamNames(0) = "Packers"
   teamNames(1) = "Packers"
   teamNames(2) = "Jets"
   teamNames(3) = "Chiefs"
   'Access array
   n = CInt(mtbNumber.Text)
   txtWinner.Text = teamNames(n — 1)
End Sub
```

[Run, type 2 into the masked text box, and click on the button.]

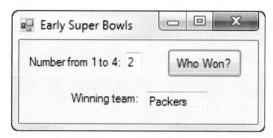

The Load Event Procedure

In Example 1, the array *teamNames* was assigned values in the btnWhoWon_Click event procedure. Every time the button is clicked, the values are reassigned to the array. This approach can be very inefficient, especially in programs with large arrays, where the task of the program (in Example 1, looking up a fact) may be repeated numerous times for different user input. When, as in Example 1, the data to be placed in an array are known at the time the program begins to run, a more efficient location for the statements that fill the array is in the form's Load event procedure. A form's Load event occurs just before the form is displayed to the user. It is the default event for the form. The header for the Load event procedure is

VideoNote
Filling arrays

```
Private Sub frmName_Load(...) Handles MyBase.Load
```

The keyword MyBase is similar to the Me keyword and refers to the form. Example 2 uses the frmBowl_Load procedure to improve Example 1.

 Example 2   The following variation of Example 1 makes *teamNames* a class-level array and assigns values to the elements of the array in the event procedure frmBowl_Load.

```
Dim teamNames(3) As String

Private Sub frmBowl_Load(...) Handles MyBase.Load
   'Place Super Bowl Winners into the array
   teamNames(0) = "Packers"
   teamNames(1) = "Packers"
   teamNames(2) = "Jets"
   teamNames(3) = "Chiefs"
End Sub

Private Sub btnWhoWon_Click(...) Handles btnWhoWon.Click
   Dim n As Integer
   n = CInt(mtbNumber.Text)
   txtWinner.Text = teamNames(n — 1)
End Sub
```

■ Implicit Array Sizing and Initialization

Like ordinary variables, array variables can be assigned initial values when they are declared. A statement of the form

```
Dim arrayName() As DataType = {value0, value1, value2, ..., valueN}
```

declares an array having upper bound N and assigns *value0* to *arrayName*(0), *value1* to *arrayName*(1), *value2* to *arrayName*(2), ..., and *valueN* to *arrayName*(N). For instance, in Example 2, the Dim statement and frmBowl_Load event procedure can be replaced by the single line

```
Dim teamNames() As String = {"Packers", "Packers", "Jets", "Chiefs"}
```

Note: You cannot use a list of values in braces to fill an array if an upper bound has been specified for the array. For instance, the following line of code is not valid:

```
Dim teamNames(3) As String = {"Packers", "Packers", "Jets", "Chiefs"}
```

■ Text Files

The two methods we have used to fill an array are fine for small arrays. However, in practice arrays can be quite large. One way to fill a large array is to use a simple data file known as a **text file**. Text files can be created, viewed, and modified with sophisticated word processors such as Word, or with elementary word processors such as the Windows accessories WordPad and Notepad. They differ from files normally created with Word in that they have no formatting (such as line spacing and font style). They are pure text and nothing else—hence the name *text file*. For instance, a text file that could be used to fill the array in Example 1 would look as follows:

```
Packers
Packers
Jets
Chiefs
```

The text files needed for exercises in this book have been created for you and are in the material you downloaded from the companion website. They are contained in a subfolder (named Text_Files_for_Exercises) of the appropriate chapter folder. Each text file ends with the extension ".txt".

The Visual Basic IDE provides simple ways to create and edit text files. The details can be found in Appendix B. Chapter 8 shows how to create text files programmatically.

A statement of the form

```
Dim strArrayName() As String = IO.File.ReadAllLines(filespec)
```

where *filespec* refers to a text file, declares a string array whose size equals the number of lines in the file, and fills it with the contents of the file. A numeric array can be filled with a text file by first filling a temporary string array with the file and then using a loop, along with CInt or CDbl, to transfer the numbers into the numeric array. (See Example 3.) **Note:** In Section 7.2, we present a way to fill a numeric array with the contents of a numeric text file without using a loop.

The Solution Explorer window has the name of the program as its first line. If only a few entries appear in the Solution Explorer, you can click on the *Show All Files* button ( ) at the top of the Solution Explorer window to display all the files and subfolders. One subfolder is named *bin*. The folder *bin* has a subfolder named *Debug*. If the *filespec* above consists only of a filename (that is, if no path is given), Visual Basic will look for the file in the *Debug* subfolder of the program's *bin* folder. **Throughout this book, we assume that every text file accessed by a program is located in the program's *bin\Debug* folder.** Every program downloaded from the companion website has this feature. When you write a program that uses one of the text files from a Text_Files_for_Exercises folder, you should use Windows Explorer to place a copy of the text file into the program's *bin\Debug* folder.

■ Array Methods

VideoNote
Array
methods

Both numeric and string arrays have the Count, Max, Min, First, and Last methods.[1] The value of *arrayName*.Count is the size of the array, *arrayName*.Max is the highest value (alphabetically or numerically), *arrayName*.Min is the lowest value, *arrayName*.First is the first element of the array, and *arrayName*.Last is the last element. **Note:** The upper bound of the array is *arrayName*.Count − 1. Table 7.1 shows some values with the array from Example 1.

TABLE 7.1	Some values from Example 1.	
	Expression	Value
	`teamNames.Count`	4
	`teamNames.Max`	Packers
	`teamNames.Min`	Chiefs
	`teamNames.First`	Packers
	`teamNames.Last`	Chiefs

When working with numeric arrays, we often also want to compute the average and total values for the elements. The average value is given by *arrayName*.Average and the total value by *arrayName*.Sum. The program that follows illustrates the use of array methods for a numeric array.

 Example 3   The file AgesAtInaugural.txt gives the ages at inauguration of the 44 U.S. presidents. The first four lines contain the data 57, 61, 57, 57—the ages of Washington, Adams, Jefferson, and Madison at their inaugurations. (To see the contents of the file in a text editor, locate the file in the *bin\Debug* folder of the Solution Explorer and double-click on the file. You can remove the text editor by clicking the × symbol on its tab.)

```
Private Sub btnDisplay_Click(...) Handles btnDisplay.Click
  Dim ages(43) As Integer
  Dim temp() As String = IO.File.ReadAllLines("AgesAtInaugural.txt")
  For i As Integer = 0 To 43
    ages(i) = CInt(temp(i))
  Next
  lstValues.Items.Add("Obama: " & ages(ages.Count − 1))
  lstValues.Items.Add("Washington: " & ages.First)
  lstValues.Items.Add("Obama: " & ages.Last)
  lstValues.Items.Add("Oldest age: " & ages.Max)
  lstValues.Items.Add("Youngest age: " & ages.Min)
  lstValues.Items.Add("Average age: " & FormatNumber(ages.Average))
```

---

[1]The property Length can be used instead of the Count method. We favor Count, since it also can be used with LINQ queries.

```
    lstValues.Items.Add("Average age: " & FormatNumber(ages.Sum / ages.Count))
End Sub
```

[Run, and click on the button.]

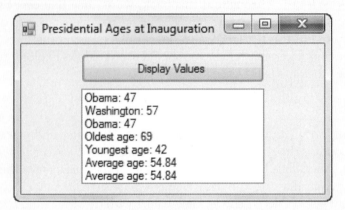

Calculating an Array Value with a Loop

Some of the values discussed above also can be calculated with loops. The following example shows how the value returned by the Max method can be calculated with a For...Next loop. Some other values returned by methods are calculated with loops in the exercise set.

Example 4   Consider the array consisting of the ages at inauguration of the last nine presidents. To find the maximum age, we temporarily take the age of the first of the nine presidents as the maximum and then adjust the maximum, if required, after looking at each successive age.

```
Private Sub btnCalculate_Click(...) Handles btnCalculate.Click
  'Calculate the maximum age at inauguration for the last 9 presidents
  Dim ages() As Integer = {55, 56, 61, 52, 69, 64, 46, 54, 47}
  Dim max As Integer = ages(0)
  For i As Integer = 1 To ages.Count − 1
    If ages(i) > max Then
      max = ages(i)
    End If
  Next
  txtOutput.Text = "The greatest age is " & max & "."
End Sub
```

[Run, and click on the button. The following is displayed in the text box.]

The greatest age is 69.

The ReDim Statement

After an array has been declared, its size (but not its type) can be changed with a statement of the form

ReDim *arrayName*(*m*)

where *arrayName* is the name of the already declared array and *m* is an Integer literal, variable, or expression. **Note:** Since the type cannot be changed, there is no need for an "As *DataType*" clause at the end of a ReDim statement.

Visual Basic allows you to declare an array without specifying an upper bound with a statement of the form

```
Dim arrayName() As DataType
```

Later, the size of the array can be specified with a ReDim statement. (No values can be assigned to the elements of the array until a size is specified.)

The ReDim statement has one shortcoming: It causes the array to lose its current contents. That is, it resets all string values to Nothing and resets all numeric values to 0. This situation can be remedied by following ReDim with the keyword Preserve. The general form of a ReDim Preserve statement is

```
ReDim Preserve arrayName(m)
```

Of course, if you make an array smaller than it was, data at the end of the array will be lost.

 Example 5 The following program reads the names of the winners of the first 44 Super Bowl games from a text file and places them into an array. The user can type a team's name into a text box and then display the numbers of the Super Bowl games won by that team. The user has the option of adding winners of subsequent games to the array of winners. The program uses the file SBWinners.txt, whose lines contain the names of the winners in order. That is, the first four lines of the file contain the names Packers, Packers, Jets, and Chiefs.

```vb
Dim teamNames() As String
Dim numGames As Integer

Private Sub frmBowl_Load(...) Handles MyBase.Load
  teamNames = IO.File.ReadAllLines("SBWinners.txt")
  numGames = teamNames.Count
  'Note: "Me" refers to the form
  Me.Text = "First " & numGames & " Super Bowls"
  'Specify the caption of the Add Winner button
  btnAddWinner.Text = "Add Winner of Game " & (numGames + 1)
End Sub


Private Sub btnDisplay_Click(...) Handles btnDisplay.Click
  'Display the numbers of the games won by the team in the text box
  Dim noWins As Boolean = True    'Flag to detect if any wins
  lstGamesWon.Items.Clear()
  For i As Integer = 0 To numGames - 1
    If teamNames(i).ToUpper = txtName.Text.ToUpper Then
      lstGamesWon.Items.Add(i + 1)
      noWins = False
    End If
  Next
  If noWins Then
    lstGamesWon.Items.Add("No Games Won")
  End If
End Sub


Private Sub btnAddWinner_Click(...) Handles btnAddWinner.Click
  'Add winner of next Super Bowl to the array
  Dim prompt As String
  'Add one more element to the array
```

```
    ReDim Preserve teamNames(numGames)
    numGames += 1
    'Request the name of the next winner
    prompt = "Enter winner of game #" & numGames & "."
    teamNames(numGames — 1) = InputBox(prompt, "Super Bowl")
    'Update the title bar of the form and the caption of the button
    Me.Text = "First" & numGames & "Super Bowls"
    btnAddWinner.Text = "Add Winner of Game " & (numGames + 1)
End Sub
```

[Run, type "Steelers" into the text box, and press the *Display* button. Then feel free to add subsequent winners. Your additions will be taken into account when you next press the *Display* button.]

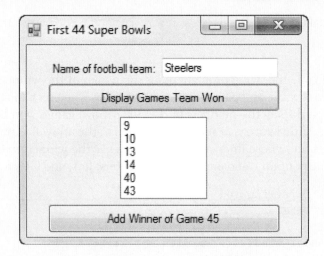

▉ Flag Variables

The Boolean variable *noWins* in the btnDisplay_Click procedure of Example 5 keeps track of whether a certain situation has occurred. Such a variable is called a **flag**. Flags are used within loops to provide information that will be utilized after the loop terminates. Flags also provide an alternative method of terminating a loop.

▉ For Each Loops

Consider Example 3. The entire sequence of ages can be displayed in the list box with the following statements:

```
For i As Integer = 0 To 43
  lstValues.Items.Add(ages(i))
Next
```

The first line of the For ... Next loop also could have been written as

```
For i As Integer = 0 To ages.Count — 1
```

In the two For statements, the lower bound and upper bound are given. Another type of loop, called a **For Each loop**, cycles through all the elements of the array in order with no mention whatsoever of the two bounds. The following block of code has the same output as the For ... Next loop above.

```
For Each age As Integer In ages
  lstValues.Items.Add(age)
Next
```

In general, a block of the form

```
For Each variableName As DataType In arrayName
  statement(s)
Next
```

where *DataType* is the data type of the array, declares the looping variable *variableName* to be of that type, and executes the statement(s) once for each element of the array. That is, at each iteration of the loop, Visual Basic sets the variable to an element in the array and executes the statement(s). When all the elements in the array have been assigned to the variable, the For Each loop terminates and the statement following the Next statement is executed. **Note:** When you use local type inference (allowed when Option Infer is set to On), you can omit the *As DataType* clause.

Although For Each loops are less complicated to write than For . . . Next loops, they have a major limitation. They cannot alter the values of elements of the array.

▓ Passing an Array to a Procedure

An array declared in a procedure is local to that procedure and unknown to all other procedures. However, a local array can be passed to another procedure. The argument in the calling statement consists of the name of the array. The corresponding parameter in the header for the procedure must consist of an array name followed by an empty set of parentheses. Like all other parameters, array parameters are preceded with ByVal or ByRef and are followed with "As DataType" clauses. However, any changes to elements of an array passed by value persist after the procedure terminates.

Example 6   The following variation of Example 4 calculates the maximum value with a Function procedure. Notice that the parameter in the function header is written `ByVal ages()` `As Integer`, not `ByVal ages As Integer`, and the function call is written `Maximum(ages)`, not `Maximum(ages())`.

```
Private Sub btnCalculate_Click(...) Handles btnCalculate.Click
  'Calculate the greatest age at inauguration for the last 9 presidents
  Dim ages() As Integer = {55, 56, 61, 52, 69, 64, 46, 54, 47}
  txtOutput.Text = "The greatest age is " & Maximum(ages) & "."
End Sub

Function Maximum(ByVal ages() As Integer) As Integer
  Dim max As Integer = ages(0)
  For i As Integer = 1 To ages.Count − 1
    If ages(i) > max Then
      max = ages(i)
    End If
  Next
  Return max
End Function
```

[Run, and click on the button. The following is displayed in the text box.]

The maximum age is 69.

▓ User-Defined Array-Valued Functions

A Function procedure with a header of the form

```
Function FunctionName(ByVal var1 As Type1,
                      ByVal var2 As Type2, ...) As DataType()
```

returns an array of type *DataType* as its value. The empty set of parentheses following *DataType* tells us that the Function procedure will return an array instead of just a single value.

 Example 7 The following program calculates the average of several grades. The number of grades and the grades themselves are input by the user via input dialog boxes. The Function procedure GetGrades returns an array containing the grades.

```
Private Sub btnGet_Click(...) Handles btnGet.Click
  Dim numGrades As Integer = CInt(InputBox("Number of grades: ", "Grades"))
  txtAverage.Text = CStr(GetGrades(numGrades).Average)
End Sub

Function GetGrades(ByVal numGrades As Integer) As Double()
  Dim grades(numGrades − 1) As Double
  For i As Integer = 1 To numGrades
    grades(i − 1) = CDbl(InputBox("Grade #" & i & ": ", "Get Grade"))
  Next
  Return grades
End Function
```

[Run, enter 3 as the number of grades, and then enter the grades 80, 85, and 90.]

■ Searching for an Element in an Array

In Example 5, a loop is used to find the indices of the elements having a value specified by the user. Visual Basic has a method for locating elements that is especially efficient with large arrays. Let *numVar* be an integer variable and *value* be a literal or expression of the same type as the elements of *arrayName*. Then a statement of the form

numVar = `Array.IndexOf(`*arrayName, value*`)`

assigns to *numVar* the index of the first occurrence of the requested value in *arrayName*. If the value is not found, then −1 is assigned to *numVar*.

 Example 8 The file States.txt contains the 50 U.S. states in the order in which they joined the union. The first four lines of the file are as follows:

```
Delaware
Pennsylvania
New Jersey
Georgia
```

The following program requests the name of a state and then tells the order in which it joined the union:

```
Dim states() As String = IO.File.ReadAllLines("States.txt")
```

```
Private Sub btnDetermine_Click(...) Handles btnDetermine.Click
  Dim n As Integer, state As String
  state = txtState.Text
  n = Array.IndexOf(states, state)
  If n <> -1 Then
    txtOutput.Text = state & " was state number " & n + 1 & "."
  Else
    MessageBox.Show("Re-enter a state name.", "Error")
    txtState.Clear()
    txtState.Focus()
  End If
End Sub
```

[Run, type a state into the top text box, and click on the button.]

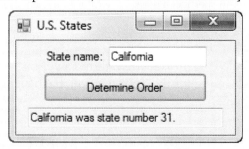

If a value might occur more than once in an array, an extension of the method above will locate subsequent occurrences. A statement of the form

numVar = Array.IndexOf(*arrayName*, *value*, *startIndex*)

where *startIndex* is an integer literal or expression, looks only at elements having index *startIndex* or greater, and assigns to *numVar* the index of the first occurrence of the requested value. If the value is not found, then –1 is assigned to *numVar*.

■ Copying an Array

If *arrayOne* and *arrayTwo* have been declared with the same data type, then the statement

```
arrayTwo = arrayOne
```

makes *arrayTwo* reference the same array as *arrayOne*. It will have the same size and contain the same data. This statement must be used with care, however, since after it is executed, *arrayOne* and *arrayTwo* will share the same portion of memory. Therefore, a change in the value of an element in one of the arrays will affect the other array.

One way to make a copy of an array that does not share the same memory location is illustrated by the following code:

```
'Assume arrayOne and arrayTwo have the same data type and size
For i As Integer = 0 To arrayOne.Count - 1
  arrayTwo(i) = arrayOne(i)
Next
```

■ Split Method and Join Function

The **Split method** provides another way to assign values to an array. The following code creates the array of Example 1:

```
Dim teamNames() As String
Dim line As String = "Packers,Packers,Jets,Chiefs"
teamNames = line.Split(","c)
```

In general, if *strArray* is a string array and the string variable *strVar* has been assigned a string of the form

"value0,value1,value2, . . . ,valueN"

then a statement of the form

```
strArray = strVar.Split(",")
```

resizes *strArray* to an array with upper bound *N* having *strArray*(0) = *value0*, *strArray*(1) = *value1*, . . . , *strArray*(*N*) = *valueN*. That is, the first element of the array contains the text preceding the first comma, the second element the text between the first and second commas, . . . , and the last element the text following the last comma. The comma character is called the **delimiter** for the statement above, and the letter *c* specifies that the comma should have data type Character instead of String. Any character can be used as a delimiter. (The two most common delimiters are the comma character and the space character.) The Split method will play a vital role in Section 7.3.

 Example 9   The following program determines a person's first and last names. The space character is used as the delimiter for the Split method. Each element of the array contains one part of the person's full name.

OBJECT	PROPERTY	SETTING
frmName	Text	Parse a Name
lblFull	Text	Full name:
txtFull		
btnExtract	Text	Extract First and Last Names
lblFirst	Text	First name:
txtFirst	ReadOnly	True
lblLast	Text	Last name:
txtLast	ReadOnly	True

```
Private Sub btnExtract_Click(...) Handles btnExtract.Click
  Dim fullName As String = txtFull.Text
  Dim parsedName() As String = fullName.Split(" "c)
  txtFirst.Text = parsedName.First
  txtLast.Text = parsedName.Last
End Sub
```

[Run, enter a full name, and click on the button.]

The reverse of the Split method is the **Join function**, which returns a string value consisting of the elements of an array concatenated together and separated by a specified delimiter. For instance, the code

```
Dim greatLakes() As String =
            {"Huron", "Ontario", "Michigan", "Erie", "Superior"}
Dim lakes As String
lakes = Join(greatLakes, ","c)
txtOutput.Text = lakes
```

produces the output

```
Huron,Ontario,Michigan,Erie,Superior
```

■ Comments

1. Using a subscript greater than the upper bound of an array is not allowed. For instance, at run time the two lines of code in Fig. 7.3 produce an exception dialog box.

FIGURE 7.3   **Exception dialog box.**

2. The statements **Continue For** and **Exit For** can be used in For Each loops in much the same way they are used in For . . . Next loops. Also, a variable declared inside a For Each loop has block-level scope; that is, the variable cannot be referred to by code outside the loop.

3. After you double-click on the name of a text file and place it into the text editor, you can alter the file's contents and save the altered file. To save the altered file, right-click on the file name in the text editor's tab and click on "Save bin\Debug*fileName*."

Practice Problems 7.1

1. Give four ways to fill an array with the names of the three musketeers—Athos, Porthos, and Aramis.

2. Write two lines of code that add the name of the fourth musketeer, D'Artagnan, to the array filled in Problem 1.

3. Determine the output displayed when the button is clicked.

```
Private Sub btnDisplay_Click(...) Handles btnDisplay.Click
  Dim numWords As Integer
  Dim line As String = "This sentence contains five words."
  Dim words() As String = line.Split(" "c)
  numWords = words.Count
  txtOutput.Text = CStr(numWords)
End Sub
```

EXERCISES 7.1

1. What is the size of an array whose upper bound is 100?
2. What is the upper bound of an array whose size is 100?

In Exercises 3 through 26, determine the output displayed when the button is clicked.

3.
```
Private Sub btnDisplay_Click(...) Handles btnDisplay.Click
  Dim n As Integer = 2
  Dim spoons(n) As String
  spoons(0) = "soup"
  spoons(1) = "dessert"
  spoons(2) = "coffee"
  txtOutput.Text = "Have a " & spoons(n − 2) & " spoon."
End Sub
```

4.
```
Private Sub btnDisplay_Click(...) Handles btnDisplay.Click
  'I'm looking over a four leaf clover.
  Dim leaves(3) As String
  leaves(0) = "sunshine"
  leaves(1) = "rain"
  leaves(2) = "the roses that bloom in the lane"
  leaves(3) = "somebody I adore"
  For i As Integer = 0 To 3
    lstOutput.Items.Add("Leaf " & (i + 1) & ": " & leaves(i))
  Next
End Sub
```

5.
```
Private Sub btnDisplay_Click(...) Handles btnDisplay.Click
  Dim colors(120) As String
  colors(5) = "Blueberry"
  colors(90) = "Bluebell"
  If colors(5).IndexOf(colors(90)) = −1 Then
    txtOutput.Text = "No"
  Else
    txtOutput.Text = "Yes"
  End If
End Sub
```

6.
```
Private Sub btnDisplay_Click(...) Handles btnDisplay.Click
  Dim years(1) As Integer
  years(0) = 1776
  years(1) = Now.Year    'current year as Integer
```

```
    txtOutput.Text = "Age of United States: " & (years(1) - years(0))
End Sub
```

7.
```
Private Sub btnDisplay_Click(...) Handles btnDisplay.Click
    Dim primes() As Integer = {2, 3, 5, 7, 11}
    lstOutput.Items.Add(primes(2) + primes(3))
End Sub
```

8.
```
Private Sub btnDisplay_Click(...) Handles btnDisplay.Click
    Dim pres() As String = {"Grant", "Lincoln", "Adams", "Kennedy"}
    txtOutput.Text = pres(2).Substring(1, 3)
End Sub
```

9.
```
Dim bands() As String = {"soloist", "duet", "trio", "quartet"}

Private Sub btnDisplay_Click(...) Handles btnDisplay.Click
    Dim num As Integer
    ReDim Preserve bands(9)
    bands(4) = "quintet"
    bands(5) = "sextet"
    bands(6) = InputBox("What do you call a group of 7 musicians?")
    num = CInt(InputBox("How many musicians are in your group?"))
    txtOutput.Text = "You have a " & bands(num - 1) & "."
End Sub
```

(Assume the first response is *septet* and the second response is *3*.)

10.
```
Private Sub btnDisplay_Click(...) Handles btnDisplay.Click
    'Compare the values of two chess pieces
    Dim chess() As String = {"king", "queen", ""}
    chess(2) = "rook"
    ReDim Preserve chess(6)
    chess(3) = "bishop"
    txtOutput.Text = "A " & chess(2) & " is worth more than a " & chess(3)
End Sub
```

11.
```
Dim grades(3) As Double

Private Sub frmGrades_Load(...) Handles MyBase.Load
    grades(0) = 80
    grades(1) = 90
End Sub

Private Sub btnDisplay_Click(...) Handles btnDisplay.Click
    Dim average As Double
    grades(2) = 70
    grades(3) = 80
    average = (grades(0) + grades(1) + grades(2) + grades(3)) / 4
    txtOutput.Text = "Your average is " & average
End Sub
```

12.
```
Dim names(3) As String

Private Sub frmNames_Load(...) Handles MyBase.Load
```

```
        names(0) = "Al"
        names(1) = "Gore"
        names(2) = "Vidal"
        names(3) = "Sassoon"
    End Sub


    Private Sub btnDisplay_Click(...) Handles btnDisplay.Click
      For i As Integer = 0 To 2
        lstOutput.Items.Add(names(i) & " " & names(i + 1))
      Next
    End Sub
```

13.
```
    Private Sub btnDisplay_Click(...) Handles btnDisplay.Click
      Dim line As String = "2009,Millionaire,Slumdog"
      Dim films() As String = line.Split(","c)
      txtOutput.Text = films(2) & " " & films(1) & " won in " & films(0)
    End Sub
```

14.
```
    Private Sub btnDisplay_Click(...) Handles btnDisplay.Click
      Dim line As String = "2,7,11,13,3"
      Dim nums() As String = line.Split(","c)
      txtOutput.Text = CStr(CInt(nums(4)) * CInt(nums(2)))
    End Sub
```

15.
```
    Private Sub btnDisplay_Click(...) Handles btnDisplay.Click
      Dim words() As String = {"one", "two", "three"}
      txtOutput.Text = Join(words, ","c)
    End Sub
```

16.
```
    Private Sub btnDisplay_Click(...) Handles btnDisplay.Click
      Dim nums() As Integer = {1, 2, 3}
      Dim temp(2) As String
      For i As Integer = 0 To 2
        temp(i) = CStr(nums(i))
      Next
      txtOutput.Text = Join(temp, ","c)
    End Sub
```

17.
```
    Private Sub btnDisplay_Click(...) Handles btnDisplay.Click
      Dim nums() As Integer = {3, 5, 8, 10, 21}
      Dim total As Integer = 0
      For Each num As Integer In nums
        If (num Mod 2 = 1) Then    '(num Mod 2) = 1 when num is odd
          total += 1
        End If
      Next
      txtOutput.Text = total & " odd numbers"
    End Sub
```

18.
```
    Private Sub btnDisplay_Click(...) Handles btnDisplay.Click
      Dim words() As String = {"When", "in", "the", "course",
                               "of", "human", "events"}
      Dim flag As Boolean = False
      For Each word As String In words
```

```
      If (word.Length = 5) Then
        flag = True
      End If
    Next
    If flag Then
      txtOutput.Text = "at least one five-letter word"
    Else
      txtOutput.Text = "no five-letter word"
    End If
  End Sub
```

In Exercises 19 through 22, assume the five lines of the file Dates.txt contain the numbers 1492, 1776, 1812, 1929, and 1941 and the file is in the program's *bin\Debug* folder.

19.
```
Private Sub btnDisplay_Click(...) Handles btnDisplay.Click
    Dim dates() As String = IO.File.ReadAllLines("Dates.txt")
    txtOutput.Text = "Pearl Harbor: " & dates(4)
  End Sub
```

20.
```
Private Sub btnDisplay_Click(...) Handles btnDisplay.Click
    Dim dates() As String = IO.File.ReadAllLines("Dates.txt")
    txtOutput.Text = "Bicentennial Year: " & (CInt(dates(1)) + 200)
  End Sub
```

21.
```
Private Sub btnDisplay_Click(...) Handles btnDisplay.Click
    Dim dates() As String = IO.File.ReadAllLines("Dates.txt")
    Dim flag As Boolean = False
    For Each yr As String In dates
      If (CInt(yr) >= 1800) And (CInt(yr) <= 1899) Then
        flag = True
      End If
    Next
    If flag Then
      txtOutput.Text = "contains a 19th-century date"
    Else
      txtOutput.Text = "does not contain a 19th-century date"
    End If
  End Sub
```

22.
```
Private Sub btnDisplay_Click(...) Handles btnDisplay.Click
    Dim dates() As String = IO.File.ReadAllLines("Dates.txt")
    Dim total As Integer = 0
    For Each yr As String In dates
      If (CInt(yr) >= 1900) Then
        total += 1
      End If
    Next
    txtOutput.Text = total & " 20th-century dates"
  End Sub
```

23.
```
Private Sub btnDisplay_Click(...) Handles btnDisplay.Click
    Dim words() As String = {"We", "the", "People", "of", "the",
              "United", "States", "in", "Order", "to", "form",
              "a", "more", "perfect", "Union"}
    txtOutput.Text = BeginWithVowel(words) & " words begin with a vowel"
  End Sub
```

```
Function BeginWithVowel(ByVal words() As String) As Integer
  Dim total As Integer = 0
  For Each word As String In words
    word = word.ToUpper
    If word.StartsWith("A") Or word.StartsWith("E") Or
        word.StartsWith("I") Or word.StartsWith("O") Or
        word.StartsWith("U") Then
      total += 1
    End If
  Next
  Return total
End Function
```

24.
```
Private Sub btnDisplay_Click(...) Handles btnDisplay.Click
  Dim grades() As Integer = {85, 95, 90}
  grades = CurveGrades(grades)
  For Each grade As Integer In grades
    lstOutput.Items.Add(grade)
  Next
End Sub

Function CurveGrades(ByVal scores() As Integer) As Integer()
  For i As Integer = 0 To scores.Count - 1
    scores(i) = scores(i) + 7
    If scores(i) > 100 Then
      scores(i) = 100
    End If
  Next
  Return scores
End Function
```

25.
```
Private Sub btnDisplay_Click(...) Handles btnDisplay.Click
  Dim nums() As Integer = {2, 6, 4}
  nums = Reverse(nums)
  For Each num As Integer In nums
    lstOutput.Items.Add(num)
  Next
End Sub

Function Reverse(ByVal nums() As Integer) As Integer()
  Dim n = nums.Count - 1
  Dim temp(n) As Integer
  For i As Integer = 0 To n
    temp(i) = nums(n - i)
  Next
  Return temp
End Function
```

26.
```
Private Sub btnDisplay_Click(...) Handles btnDisplay.Click
  Dim speech() As String = {"Four", "score", "and",
                            "seven", "years", "ago"}
  speech = UpperCase(speech)
  txtOutput.Text = speech(3)
End Sub
```

```
Function UpperCase(ByVal words() As String) As String()
  Dim n As Integer = words.Count — 1
  Dim temp(n) As String
  For i As Integer = 0 To n
    temp(i) = words(i).ToUpper
  Next
  Return temp
End Function
```

27. The array declared with the statement

```
Dim lakes() As String = {"Huron", "Ontario", "Michigan", "Erie",
                         "Superior"}
```

contains the names of the five Great Lakes. Evaluate and interpret each of the following:

   (a) `lakes.Max`   (b) `lakes.Min`
   (c) `lakes.First`   (d) `lakes.Last`
   (e) `lakes.Count`   (f) `lakes(1)`
   (g) `Array.IndexOf(lakes, "Erie")`

28. The array declared with the statement

```
Dim lakeAreas() As Integer = {23000, 8000, 22000, 10000, 32000}
```

contains the surface areas (in square miles) of the five Great Lakes. Evaluate and interpret each of the following:

   (a) `lakeAreas.Max`   (b) `lakeAreas.Min`
   (c) `lakeAreas.First`   (d) `lakeAreas.Last`
   (e) `lakeAreas.Count`   (f) `lakeAreas.Sum`
   (g) `lakeAreas.Average`   (h) `lakeAreas(2)`
   (i) `Array.IndexOf(lakeAreas, 8000)`

29. The array declared with the statement

```
Dim statePops() As Double = {3.5, 6.5, 1.3, 1.1, 0.7, 1.3}
```

contains the populations (in millions) of the six New England states. Evaluate and interpret each of the following:

   (a) `statePops.Max`   (b) `statePops.Min`
   (c) `statePops.First`   (d) `statePops.Last`
   (e) `statePops.Count`   (f) `statePops(3)`
   (g) `Array.IndexOf(statePops, 1.1)`

30. The array declared with the statement

```
Dim statesNE() As String = {"Connecticut", "Massachusetts",
        "New Hampshire", "Rhode Island", "Vermont", "Maine"}
```

contains the names of the six New England states listed in the order in which they became part of the United States. Evaluate and interpret each of the following:

   (a) `statesNE.Max`   (b) `statesNE.Min`
   (c) `statesNE.First`   (d) `statesNE.Last`
   (e) `statesNE.Count`   (f) `statesNE(0)`
   (g) `Array.IndexOf(statesNE, "Maine")`

31. Suppose the array *states* has been filled with the names of the fifty states in the order in which they became part of the United States. Write code to display each of the following states in a list box.

(a) the first state to join the union
(b) the original thirteen states
(c) the most recent state to join
(d) the order number for Ohio
(e) the second state to join the union
(f) the twentieth state to join the union
(g) the last ten states to join the union

32. Suppose the array *pres* has been filled with the names of the 44 U.S. presidents in the order in which they served. Write code to display each of the following in a list box.

(a) the first president
(b) the first six presidents
(c) the most recent president
(d) the number for "James Monroe"
(e) the second president
(f) the tenth president
(g) the last five presidents

Assume the array *nums* contains a list of positive integers. In Exercises 33 through 38, write a Function procedure that calculates the stated value with a For Each loop.

33. the sum of the numbers in the array

34. the average of the numbers in the array

35. the largest odd number in the array (If there are no odd numbers in the array, the Function procedure should return 0.)

36. the smallest number in the array

37. the number of two-digit numbers in the array

38. the number of even numbers in the array

In Exercises 39 through 42, identify the errors.

39. `Dim nums(3) As Integer = {1, 2, 3, 4}`

40. `Dim nums(10) As Integer`
`nums(nums.Count) = 7`

41.
```
Dim nums() As Integer = {1, 2, 3}
'Display 101 + 102 + 103
For Each num As Integer In nums
  num += 100
Next
MessageBox.Show(CStr(nums.Sum))
```

42. `Dim nums() As Integer = IO.File.ReadAllLines("Numbers.txt")`

43. Write a single line of code that displays the number of words in a sentence, where the string variable *line* holds the sentence.

44. Write a single line of code that displays the number of names in the file Names.txt.

45. The file Numbers.txt contains a list of integers. Write a program that displays the number of integers in the file and their sum.

46. The file SomeStates.txt contains a list of some U.S. states. Write a program to determine if the states are in alphabetical order.

47. The file Names2.txt contains a list of names in alphabetical order. Write a program to find and display those entries that are repeated in the file. When a name is found to be repeated, display it only once.

48. Suppose the file Final.txt contains student grades on a final exam. Write a program that displays the average grade on the exam and the percentage of grades that are above average.

49. The file Digits.txt contains a list of digits, all between 0 and 9. Write a program that displays the frequency of each digit.

50. Write a Boolean-valued Function procedure AreSame to compare two integer arrays and determine whether they have the same size and hold identical values—that is, whether $a(i) = b(i)$ for all i.

51. Write a Function procedure to calculate the sum of the entries with even subscripts in an integer array.

52. The file States.txt contains the names of the 50 U.S. states. Write a program that creates an array consisting of the states beginning with "New". The program also should display the names of these states in a list box.

53. Table 7.2 shows the different grades of eggs and the minimum weight required for each classification. Write a program that processes the text file Eggs.txt containing a list of the weights of a sample of eggs. The program should report the number of eggs in each grade and the weight of the lightest and heaviest egg in the sample. Figure 7.4 shows the output of the program. **Note:** Eggs weighing less than 1.5 ounces cannot be sold in supermarkets and therefore will not be counted.

TABLE 7.2   **Grades of eggs.**

Grade	Minimum Weight (in ounces)
Jumbo	2.5
Extra Large	2.25
Large	2
Medium	1.75
Small	1.5

```
57 Jumbo eggs
95 Extra Large eggs
76 Large eggs
96 Medium eggs
77 Small eggs
Lightest egg: 1 ounces
Heaviest egg: 2.69 ounces
```

FIGURE 7.4   Output for Exercise 53.

54. The file USPres.txt contains the names of the 44 U.S. presidents in the order in which they served. Write a program that places the names in an array and displays all presidents for a requested range of numbers. Figure 7.5 on the next page shows one possible outcome. (John Tyler was the tenth president. James Polk was the eleventh president. And so on.)

Exercises 55 through 58 should use the file Colors.txt that contains the names of the colors of Crayola® crayons in alphabetical order.

55. Write a program to read the colors into an array and then display the colors beginning with a specified letter. One possible outcome is shown in Fig. 7.6 on the next page.

56. Write a program that requests a color as input in a text box and then determines whether or not the color is in the text file. The program should use the Boolean-valued Function procedure IsCrayola that returns the value True if the color in the text box is a Crayola color.

57. Redo Exercise 55 with the letter passed to a Function procedure that returns a smaller array containing just the colors beginning with the specified letter.

FIGURE 7.5 Possible outcome of Exercise 54.

FIGURE 7.6 Possible outcome of Exercise 55.

58. Write a program that displays the colors in reverse alphabetical order.

59. The file Sonnet.txt contains Shakespeare's Sonnet 18. Each entry in the file contains a line of the sonnet. Write a program that reports the average number of words in a line and the total number of words in the sonnet.

60. Statisticians use the concepts of range, mean, and standard deviation to describe a collection of numerical data. The **range** is the difference between the largest and smallest numbers in the collection. The **mean** is the average of the numbers, and the **standard deviation** measures the spread or dispersal of the numbers about the mean. Formally, if $x_1, x_2, x_3, \ldots, x_n$ is a collection of numbers, then

$$\text{mean} = \frac{x_1 + x_2 + x_3 + \cdots + x_n}{n} \qquad \text{(denote the mean by } m\text{)}$$

$$\text{standard deviation} = \sqrt{\frac{(x_1 - m)^2 + (x_2 - m)^2 + (x_3 - m)^2 + \cdots + (x_n - m)^2}{n}}$$

Write a program to calculate the range, mean, and standard deviation for the numbers in the file Data.txt.

61. Write a program to display the average grade and the number of above-average grades on an exam. Each time the user clicks a *Record Grade* button, a grade should be read from a text box. The current average grade and the number of above-average grades should be displayed in a list box whenever the user clicks on a *Display Average* button. (Assume that the class has at most 100 students.) Use a Function procedure to count the number of above-average grades. See Fig. 7.7.

FIGURE 7.7 Possible outcome of Exercise 61.

FIGURE 7.8 Outcome of Exercise 62.

62. The file Scores.txt contains scores between 1 and 49. Write a program that uses these scores to create an array *frequencies* as follows:

frequencies(0) = # of scores < 10
frequencies(1) = # of scores with $10 \leq$ score < 20
frequencies(2) = # of scores with $20 \leq$ score < 30
frequencies(3) = # of scores with $30 \leq$ score < 40
frequencies(4) = # of scores with $40 \leq$ score < 50

The program should then display the results in tabular form, as shown in Fig. 7.8.

In Exercises 63 and 64, execute the statement `sentence = sentence.Replace(",", "")` to remove all commas in *sentence*, and then remove other punctuation marks similarly. After that, use the space character as a delimiter for the Split method.

63. A sentence is called a *chain-link* sentence if the last two letters of each word are the same as the first two letters of the next word—for instance, "The head administrator organized education on online networks." Write a program that accepts a sentence as input and determines whether it is a chain-link sentence. Test the program with the sentence "Broadcast station, once certified, educates estimable legions."

64. A *word palindrome* is a sentence that reads the same, word by word, backward and forward (ignoring punctuation and capitalization). An example is "You can cage a swallow, can't you, but you can't swallow a cage, can you?" Write a program that requests a sentence and then determines whether the sentence is a word palindrome. The program should place the words of the sentence in an array and use a Function procedure to determine whether the sentence is a word palindrome. (Test the program with the sentences "Monkey see, monkey do." and "I am; therefore, am I?")

Solutions to Practice Problems 7.1

1. *First:*
```
Dim names(2) As String
     names(0) = "Athos"
     names(1) = "Porthos"
     names(2) = "Aramis"
```

   Second: `Dim names() As String = {"Athos", "Porthos", "Aramis"}`

   Third: `Dim line As String = "Athos,Porthos,Aramis"`
   ```
   Dim names() As String = line.Split(","c)
   ```

   Fourth: Assume the text file Names.txt has the three names in three lines and is located in the *bin\Debug* folder of the program. Then execute the following line of code:
   ```
   Dim names() As String = IO.File.ReadAllLines("Names.txt")
   ```

2. `ReDim Preserve names(3)`   `'resize the array`

   `names(3) = "D'Artagnan"`   `'assign value to last element`

3. 5

7.2   Using LINQ with Arrays

LINQ (Language-INtegrated Query), a recent exciting and powerful innovation in Visual Basic, provides a standardized way to retrieve information from data sources. In this book we use LINQ with arrays, text files, XML documents, and databases. Before LINQ you often had to write complex loops that specified *how* to retrieve information from a data source. With LINQ you simply state *what* you want to achieve and let Visual Basic do the heavy lifting. **Important:** Option Infer must be set to "On" in order to use LINQ. (See Comment 1 at the end of this section.)

■ LINQ Queries

A LINQ *query* for an array is declarative (that is, self-evident) code that describes *what* you want to retrieve from the array. A statement of the form

```
Dim queryName = From var In arrayName Where [condition on var] Select var
```

is called a LINQ query. The variable *var* takes on the values of elements in the array much like the looping variable in a For Each loop. The statement declares a variable *queryName* and assigns it a sequence consisting of the elements of the array that satisfy the condition on *var*. The phrases "**From var In arrayName**", "**Where [condition on var]**", and "**Select var**" are called **query clauses**. The keywords From, Where, and Select are called **query operators,** *var* is called a **range variable,** and *arrayName* is called the **source data**. The entire expression to the right of the equal sign is called a **query expression**.

The LINQ query above is usually written in the style

```
Dim queryName = From var In arrayName
                Where [condition on var]
                Select var
```

As soon as you type the first line, the Code Editor will know that you are declaring a query and will treat each press of the Enter key as signaling a line continuation. However, after you type the last clause of the query, you can press Ctrl + Shift + Enter to tell the Code Editor that the query declaration is complete. (Alternately, you can press the Enter key twice to complete entry of the query.)

Example 1 The file States.txt contains the 50 U.S. states in the order in which they joined the union. The following program first displays the states with five-letter names and then displays the states beginning with "New". Each query expression returns a sequence of states that is displayed with a For Each loop.

```
Private Sub btnDisplay_Click(...) Handles btnDisplay.Click
  Dim states() As String = IO.File.ReadAllLines("States.txt")
  Dim stateQuery1 = From state In states
                    Where state.Length = 5
                    Select state
  For Each state As String In stateQuery1
    lstStates.Items.Add(state)
  Next
  lstStates.Items.Add("")
  Dim stateQuery2 = From state In states
                    Where state.StartsWith("New")
                    Select state
  For Each state As String In stateQuery2
    lstStates.Items.Add(state)
  Next
End Sub
```

[Run, and click on the button.]

The array methods Count, Max, Min, First, and Last apply to all sequences returned by LINQ queries, and the array methods Average and Sum apply to numeric sequences. Also, the successive elements in the sequence can be referred to by indices ranging from 0 to *queryName*.Count − 1. For instance, in Example 1, the values of `stateQuery1(0)`, `stateQuery1(1)`, and `stateQuery1(2)` are Maine, Texas, and Idaho.

Example 2   The following program displays values associated with numeric sequences returned by LINQ queries. *Note:* The integer *n* is even if *n* Mod 2 is 0.

```
Private Sub btnDisplay_Click(...) Handles btnDisplay.Click
  Dim nums() As Integer = {5, 12, 8, 7, 11}
  Dim numQuery1 = From num In nums
                  Where num > 7
                  Select num
  For Each num As Integer In numQuery1
    lstBox.Items.Add(num)
  Next
  lstBox.Items.Add("Largest number: " & numQuery1.Max)
  lstBox.Items.Add("Second number: " & numQuery1(1))
  lstBox.Items.Add("Sum of numbers: " & numQuery1.Sum)
  lstBox.Items.Add("")
  Dim numQuery2 = From num In nums
                  Where num Mod 2 = 0
                  Select num
  lstBox.Items.Add("Number of even numbers: " & numQuery2.Count)
  lstBox.Items.Add("Average of even numbers: " & numQuery2.Average)
  lstBox.Items.Add("Last even number: " & numQuery2.Last)
End Sub
```

[Run, and click on the button.]

The variable in the Select clause can be replaced by an expression involving the variable. For instance, if the clause **Select num** in *numQuery1* of Example 2 were replaced by

```
Select num * num
```

then the first three lines in the list box would be 144, 64, and 121. Also, both Where clauses and Select clauses are optional. When the Where clause is missing, all values in the source data are included. A missing Select clause produces the same effect as the clause **Select var**. In this textbook we always include a Select clause.

▣ The Distinct Operator

The sequence created with a LINQ query might contain duplicate elements. Duplicates can be eliminated by adding the Distinct operator to the query. For instance, using the array *teamNames* from Example 5 of the previous section, the lines of code

```
Dim teamQuery = From team In teamNames
                Select team
                Distinct
For Each team As String In teamQuery
  lstGamesWon.Items.Add(team)
Next
```

display the names of the teams that have won a Super Bowl, with each team listed once.

▣ The ToArray Method

The sequence returned by a LINQ query has many of the features of an array. Its main limitation is that its values cannot be altered with assignment statements. However, the sequence can be converted to an array with the ToArray method. For instance, using the array *teamNames* from Example 5 of the previous section, the lines of code

```
Dim teamQuery = From team In teamNames
                Select team
                Distinct
Dim uniqueWinners() As String = teamQuery.ToArray
```

create the array named *uniqueWinners* containing the names of the teams that have won the Super Bowl, with each team appearing just once as an element of the array.

Use of Function Procedures in Queries

The Where and Select clauses of a LINQ query can use Function procedures, as illustrated in the next example.

 Example 3   The file USPres.txt contains the names of the 44 U.S. presidents. The first two lines of the file are George Washington and John Adams. The following program asks the user to enter a first name and then displays the names of all the presidents having that first name:

```
Dim presidents() As String = IO.File.ReadAllLines("USPres.txt")

Private Sub btnDisplay_Click(...) Handles btnDisplay.Click
  Dim presQuery = From pres In presidents
                  Where FirstName(pres) = txtFirstName.Text
                  Select IncludeTitle(pres)
  lstPres.Items.Clear()
  For Each pres In presQuery
    lstPres.Items.Add(pres)
  Next
End Sub

Function FirstName(ByVal name As String) As String
  'Extract the first name from a full name.
  Dim parsedName() As String = name.Split(" "c)
  Return parsedName.First
End Function

Function IncludeTitle(ByVal pres As String) As String
  Return "President " & pres
End Function
```

[Run, enter a first name, and click on the button.]

The Let Operator

The Let operator, which gives a name to an expression, makes queries easier to read. For instance, the query in Example 3 can be written as

```
Dim presQuery = From pres In presidents
                Where FirstName(pres) = txtFirstName.Text
                Let formalName = IncludeTitle(pres)
                Select formalName
```

Let operators also can significantly improve the readability of queries.

■ The Order By Operator

An array or query result is said to be **ordered** if its values are in either ascending or descending order. With ascending order, the value of each element is less than or equal to the value of the next element. That is,

$$[\text{each element}] \leq [\text{next element}].$$

For string values, the ANSI table is used to evaluate the "less than or equal to" condition.

Putting elements in alphabetical or numeric order (either ascending or descending) is referred to as **sorting**. There are many algorithms for sorting arrays. The most efficient ones use complex nested loops and are tricky to program. However, LINQ provides the Order By query operator that spares us from having to code complicated sorting algorithms. The simplest form of an Order By clause is

```
Order By [expression] Direction
```

where *Direction* is one of the keywords Ascending or Descending, and the expression involves range and/or Let variables.

 Example 4 The following program sorts an array of numbers in ascending order. **Note:** If the word Ascending is replaced by Descending, the array will be sorted in descending order.

```
Private Sub btnSort_Click(...) Handles btnSort.Click
  Dim nums() As Integer = {3, 6, 4, 1}
  Dim numQuery = From num In nums
                 Order By num Ascending
                 Select num
  For Each n As Integer In numQuery
    lstOutput.Items.Add(n)
  Next
End Sub
```

[Run, and click on the button.]

The Order By operator is quite flexible and can order arrays in ways other than just alphabetical or numeric order. Secondary criteria for ordering can be specified by listing two or more criteria separated by commas. In general, an Order By clause of the form

```
Order By expression1 Direction1, expression2 Direction2, ...
```

primarily sorts by expression1 and Direction1, secondarily by expression2 and Direction 2, and so on. For instance, an Order By clause such as

```
Order By lastName Ascending, firstName Ascending
```

can be used to alphabetize a sequence of full names. When two people have the same last name, their first names will be used to determine whose full name comes first.

 Example 5   The following program uses the file States.txt considered in Example 1 and sorts the states by the length of their names in ascending order. States with names of the same length are sorted by their names in reverse alphabetical order.

```
Private Sub btnDisplay_Click(...) Handles btnDisplay.Click
  Dim states() As String = IO.File.ReadAllLines("States.txt")
  Dim stateQuery = From state In states
                   Order By state.Length Ascending, state Descending
                   Select state
  For Each state As String In stateQuery
    lstStates.Items.Add(state)
  Next
End Sub
```

[Run, and click on the button.]

Note: In an Order By clause, the default direction is *Ascending*. For instance, the fourth line of Example 5 could have been written

```
Order By state.Length, state Descending
```

■ The DataSource Property

In Example 5, a For Each loop was used to place the values returned by the query into a list box. The task also can be accomplished with a DataSource property. To use the DataSource property, replace the For Each loop with the following pair of statements. **Note:** The second statement is optional. It prevents having the first item in the list box selected at startup.

```
lstStates.DataSource = stateQuery.ToList
lstStates.SelectedItem = Nothing
```

The DataSource property also can be used to display the contents of an array directly into a list box with a statement of the form

```
lstBox.DataSource = arrayName
```

Note: If a SelectedIndexChanged event procedure has been defined for a list box, then execution of the DataSource property will raise the SelectedIndexChanged event.

■ Binary Search

A large array in ascending order is most efficiently searched with a **binary search**. The Binary-Search method looks for a value in the array by first determining in which half of the array it lies. The other half is then ignored, and the search is narrowed to the retained half. The process is repeated until the item is found or the entire list has been considered. A statement of the form

```
numVar = Array.BinarySearch(arrayName, value)
```

assigns to *numVar* the index of an occurrence of the requested value in *arrayName*. If the value is not found, then a negative number is assigned to *numVar*.

■ Comments

1. The Option Infer setting can be made the default setting for all of your Visual Basic programs or can be made the setting for a single program.

   (a) If a value for Option Infer is set in the Option default project setting window shown in Fig. 3.1 of Section 3.2, then that setting will be the default setting for all new programs.

   (b) To override the default setting for an individual program, enter the statement **Option Infer On** or **Option Infer Off** at the top of the Code Window. Alternately, right-click on the program name at the top of Solution Explorer, click on Properties, click on the Compile tab, and change the value for "Option infer".

2. LINQ Where operators are said to *filter* data, and Select operators are said to *project* data.

3. Visual Basic has a built-in routine for sorting arrays. A statement of the form

   ```
   Array.Sort(arrayName)
   ```

   sorts the array in ascending order. This method is useful for simple sorting where the more advanced capabilities of LINQ are not needed.

Practice Problems 7.2

1. Write a program that uses a LINQ query to calculate the sum of the numbers in the file Numbers.txt.

2. The file USPres.txt contains the full names of the 44 U.S. presidents. The following program finds the full name of the president whose last name is "Eisenhower." Since there is only one such president, a text box (rather than a list box) is sufficient to display the output.

```
Private Sub btnFind_Click(...) Handles btnFind.Click
  Dim presidents() As String = IO.File.ReadAllLines("USPres.txt")
  Dim query = From pres In presidents
              Where pres.EndsWith("Eisenhower")
              Select pres
  txtFullName.Text = query.First
End Sub
```

(a) Since the value of query consists of just one name, why can't the sixth line be replaced with `txtFullName.Text = query`?

(b) What expressions, other than `query.First`, can be used for the right side of the sixth line that would yield the same result?

In Exercises 1 through 26, determine the output displayed when the button is clicked.

1.
```
Private Sub btnDisplay_Click(...) Handles btnDisplay.Click
    Dim nums() As Integer = {5, 7, 2, 3}
    Dim numQuery = From num In nums Where num < 4 Select num
                   Where num > 4
                   Select num
    For Each num As Integer In numQuery
       lstOutput.Items.Add(num)
    Next
End Sub
```

2.
```
Private Sub btnDisplay_Click(...) Handles btnDisplay.Click
    Dim words() As String = {"Houston", "we", "have", "a", "problem"}
    Dim wordQuery = From word In words
                    Where word.ToUpper.StartsWith("H")
                    Select word
    For Each word As String In wordQuery
       lstOutput.Items.Add(word)
    Next
End Sub
```

3.
```
Private Sub btnDisplay_Click(...) Handles btnDisplay.Click
    Dim line As String = "I'm going to make him an offer he can't refuse"
    Dim words() As String = line.Split(" "c)
    Dim wordQuery = From word In words
                    Where word.Length = 5
                    Select word
    lstOutput.DataSource = wordQuery.ToList
    lstOutput.SelectedItem = Nothing
End Sub
```

4.
```
Private Sub btnDisplay_Click(...) Handles btnDisplay.Click
    Dim line As String = "1492,1776,1812,1929,1941"
    Dim dates() As String = line.Split(","c)
    Dim dateQuery = From yr In dates
                    Where CInt(yr) < 1800
                    Select yr
    lstOutput.DataSource = dateQuery.ToList
    lstOutput.SelectedItem = Nothing
End Sub
```

5.
```
Private Sub btnDisplay_Click(...) Handles btnDisplay.Click
    Dim line As String = "If,you,fail,to,plan,then,you,plan,to,fail"
    Dim words() As String = line.Split(","c)
```

```vb
        Dim wordQuery = From word In words
                        Select word
                        Distinct
        txtOutput.Text = CStr(wordQuery.Count)
    End Sub
```

6.
```vb
    Private Sub btnDisplay_Click(...) Handles btnDisplay.Click
        Dim nums() As Integer = {2, 3, 4, 3, 2, 1}
        Dim numQuery = From num In nums
                       Select num
                       Distinct
        txtOutput.Text = CStr(numQuery.Sum)
    End Sub
```

7.
```vb
    Private Sub btnDisplay_Click(...) Handles btnDisplay.Click
        Dim nums() As Integer = {2, 3, 4, 3, 2}
        Dim numQuery = From num In nums
                       Select num + 100
                       Distinct
        txtOutput.Text = CStr(numQuery.Average)
    End Sub
```

8.
```vb
    Private Sub btnDisplay_Click(...) Handles btnDisplay.Click
        Dim words() As String = {"racecar", "motor", "kayak", "civics"}
        Dim wordQuery = From word In words
                        Where IsPalindrome(word)
                        Select word.ToUpper
        For Each word As String In wordQuery
          lstOutput.Items.Add(word)
        Next
    End Sub

    Function IsPalindrome(ByVal word As String) As Boolean
      'A palindrome is a word that reads the same forwards and backwards.
      Dim n As Integer = word.Length
      For i As Integer = 0 To (n − 1) \ 2
        If word.Substring(i, 1) <> word.Substring(n − i − 1, 1) Then
          Return False
        End If
      Next
      Return True
    End Function
```

9.
```vb
    Private Sub btnDisplay_Click(...) Handles btnDisplay.Click
        'The first four lines of Numbers.txt contain the numbers 2, 6, 7, and 8.
        Dim numbers() as String = IO.File.ReadAllLines("Numbers.txt")
        Dim query = From num In numbers
                    Select CInt(num)
        lstOutput.Items.Add(query(0) + query(1))
    End Sub
```

10.
```vb
    Private Sub btnDisplay_Click(...) Handles btnDisplay.Click
        'The first four lines of Words.txt contain scale, top, up, and low.
        Dim words() As String = IO.File.ReadAllLines("Words.txt")
```

```
        Dim query = From word In words
                    Select word
      txtOutput.Text = query(2) & query(0)
    End Sub
```

11.
```
    Private Sub btnDisplay_Click(...) Handles btnDisplay.Click
      Dim grades() As Integer = {66, 68, 72, 76, 90, 92, 93, 94, 95}
      Dim query = From grade In grades
                  Let newGrade = CurveGrade(grade)
                  Where newGrade = 100
                  Select newGrade
      txtOutput.Text = query.Count & " students have a grade of 100"
    End Sub


    Function CurveGrade(ByVal grade As Integer) As Integer
      grade += 7
      If grade > 100 Then
        grade = 100
      End If
      Return grade
    End Function
```

12.
```
    Private Sub btnDisplay_Click(...) Handles btnDisplay.Click
      Dim words() As String = {"rated", "savory", "able", "just"}
      Dim query = From word In words
                  Let opposite = ("un" & word).ToUpper
                  Select opposite
      txtOutput.Text = query.Max
    End Sub
```

13.
```
    Private Sub btnDisplay_Click(...) Handles btnDisplay.Click
      Dim nums() As Integer = {12, 5, 7, 10, 3, 15, 4}
      Dim query = From num In nums
                  Where num < 10
                  Order By num Descending
                  Select num
      lstOutput.DataSource = query.ToList
      lstOutput.SelectedItem = Nothing
    End Sub
```

14.
```
    Private Sub btnDisplay_Click(...) Handles btnDisplay.Click
      Dim words() As String = {"When", "in", "the", "course",
                               "of", "human", "events"}
      Dim query = From word In words
                  Order By word.Length
                  Select word.Length
      Dim greatestLength As Integer = query.Last
      Dim query2 = From word In words
                   Where word.Length = greatestLength
                   Order By word Descending
                   Select word
      lstOutput.DataSource = query2.ToList
      lstOutput.SelectedItem = Nothing
    End Sub
```

15.
```
Private Sub btnDisplay_Click(...) Handles btnDisplay.Click
    Dim grades() As Integer = {60, 70, 90, 80}
    Dim query = From grade In grades
                Order By grade Descending
                Select grade
    grades = query.ToArray
    ReDim Preserve grades(grades.Count — 2)    'drop lowest grade
    Dim str As String = "The average after dropping the lowest grade is "
    txtOutput.Text = str & grades.Average
End Sub
```

16.
```
Private Sub btnDisplay_Click(...) Handles btnDisplay.Click
    Dim golfers(2) As String  'top 3 golfers in tournament
    golfers(0) = "Funk,65,69,69,75"    'total = 278
    golfers(1) = "Ramaro,67,69,65,73"    'total = 274
    golfers(2) = "McNulty,68,70,73,68"    'total = 279
    Dim query = From golfer In golfers
                Let data = golfer.Split(","c)
                Let name = data(0)
                Let score = CInt(data(1)) + CInt(data(2)) +
                            CInt(data(3)) + CInt(data(4))
                Let result = score & "   " & name
                Order By score Ascending
                Select result
    For Each result As String In query
      lstOutput.Items.Add(result)
    Next
End Sub
```

17.
```
Private Sub btnDisplay_Click(...) Handles btnDisplay.Click
    Dim smallPrimes() As Integer = {2, 3, 5, 7, 11, 13, 17, 19, 23,
                                    29, 31, 37, 41, 43, 47, 53, 59,
                                    61, 67, 71, 73, 79, 83, 89, 97}
    Dim n As Integer = CInt(InputBox("Enter a number less than 100:"))
    If Array.BinarySearch(smallPrimes, n) < 0 Then
      txtOutput.Text = n & " is not a prime number"
    Else
      txtOutput.Text = n & " is a prime number"
    End If
End Sub
```
(Assume the response is *37*.)

18.
```
Private Sub btnDisplay_Click(...) Handles btnDisplay.Click
    Dim statesNE() As String = {"Connecticut", "Maine", "Massachusetts",
                                "New Hampshire", "Rhode Island", "Vermont"}
    Dim state As String = InputBox("Enter a state:")
    If Array.BinarySearch(statesNE, state) < 0 Then
      txtOutput.Text = state & " is not in New England."
    Else
      txtOutput.Text = state & " is in New England."
    End If
End Sub
```
(Assume the response is *New York*.)

Use LINQ to carry out the primary tasks of the programs in the remaining exercises of this section. In Exercises 19 through 24, redo the exercises from Section 7.1 using LINQ queries.

19. Exercise 17 of Section 7.1

20. Exercise 18 of Section 7.1

21. Exercise 21 of Section 7.1

22. Exercise 22 of Section 7.1

23. Exercise 25 of Section 7.1

24. Exercise 26 of Section 7.1

In Exercises 25 through 28, use the file SBWinners.txt that lists the winners of the first 44 Super Bowls.

25. Write a program that displays the teams (in alphabetical order) who have won a Super Bowl. Each team should appear only once.

26. Write a program that displays the teams who have won a Super Bowl and whose name begins with the letter entered by the user. Each team should appear only once.

27. Write a program that displays in a text box the number of games won by the team specified. See Fig. 7.9.

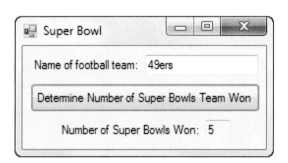

FIGURE 7.9 **Possible outcome of Exercise 27.**   FIGURE 7.10 **Outcome of Exercise 28.**

28. Write a program that displays a list of Super Bowl winners ordered by the number of games won. See Fig. 7.10.

29. The file Final.txt contains student grades on a final exam. Write a program using LINQ that displays the average grade on the exam and the percentage of grades that are above average.

30. Write a program that requests five grades as input and then calculates the average after dropping the two lowest grades.

31. The file States.txt contains the 50 U.S. states in the order in which they joined the union. Write a program to display the original 13 states in alphabetical order.

32. An *anagram* of a word or phrase is another word or phrase that uses the same letters with the same frequency. Punctuation marks, case, and spaces are ignored. Write a program that requests two words (no punctuation) as input and determines if they are anagrams of each other. (Test the program with the words *Elvis* and *lives*.)

33. The file USPres.txt contains the names of the 44 presidents in the order in which they served. The first two lines contain the names George Washington and John Adams. Write a program that displays the presidents ordered by their last name.

34. The file Words.txt contains a list of words. Write a program that displays the words in a list box sorted by the number of different vowels (A, E, I, O and U) in the word. When two words have the same number of different vowels, they should be ordered first by their length (descending) and then alphabetically. The display should show both the word and the number of different vowels in the word. See Fig. 7.11.

FIGURE 7.11   **Output of Exercise 34.**   FIGURE 7.12   **Output of Exercise 35.**

VideoNote

Presidents
(Homework)

35. The file Nations.txt contains the names of the 192 member nations of the United Nations. Write a program that initially displays all the nations in a list box. Each time a letter is typed into a text box, the program should reduce the displayed nations to those beginning with the letters in the text box. Figure 7.12 shows the status after the letters "Ma" are typed into the text box. At any time, the user should be able to click on the name of a nation to have it appear in the text box.

36. The **median** of an ordered set of measurements is a number separating the lower half from the upper half. If the number of measurements is odd, the median is the middle measurement. If the number of measurements is even, the median is the average of the two middle measurements. Write a program that requests a number n and a set of n measurements as input and then displays the median of the measurements.

Solutions to Practice Problems 7.2

1.
```
Private Sub btnDisplay_Click(...) Handles btnDisplay.Click
    Dim numbers() As String = IO.File.ReadAllLines("Numbers.txt")
    Dim query = From num In numbers
                Select CDbl(num)
    MessageBox.Show(CStr(query.Sum), "Total")
End Sub
```

2. **(a)** A text box can be filled only with a string. The value returned by a query is a *sequence* type that contains one string element. Only that element, not the sequence itself can be assigned to the text property of the text box.

   (b) `query(0)`, `query.Last`, `query.Max`, `query.Min`

7.3   Arrays of Structures

Often we work with several pieces of related data. For instance, four related pieces of data about a country are *name*, *continent*, *population*, and *area*. Suppose we are considering this information for the 192 countries in the United Nations. In the early days of programming, the way to work with such information was to put it into four parallel arrays—one array of type String for names, a second array of type String for continents, a third array of type Double for populations, and a fourth array of type Double for areas. The modern way of dealing with such information is to place it into a single array of a composite data type that you define called a **structure** or a **user-defined data type**.

■ Structures

A structure contains variables of (possibly) different types, which are known as **members**. A structure is defined in the Declarations section of the Code Editor by a block of the form

```
Structure StructureName
  Dim memberName1 As MemberType1
  Dim memberName2 As MemberType2
  .
  .
  .
End Structure
```

where *StructureName* is the name of the user-defined data type, *memberName1* and *memberName2* are the names of the members of the user-defined type, and *MemberType1* and *MemberType2* are the corresponding member data types.

Some examples of structures are

```
Structure Nation
  Dim name As String
  Dim continent As String
  Dim population As Double   'in millions
  Dim area As Double         'in square miles
End Structure

Structure Employee
  Dim name As String
  Dim dateHired As Date
  Dim hourlyWage As Double
End Structure

Structure College
  Dim name As String
  Dim state As String        'state abbreviation
  Dim yearFounded As Integer
End Structure
```

Variables having a user-defined data type are declared with Dim statements just like ordinary variables. For instance, the statement

```
Dim country As Nation
```

declares a variable of data type Nation.

Dot notation is used to refer to an individual member of a user-defined variable. For instance, the set of statements

```
country.name = "China"
country.continent = "Asia"
country.population = 1332.5
country.area = 3696100
```

assigns values to the members of the variable *country* declared above. After these assignment statements are executed, the statement

```
txtOutput.Text = country.continent
```

will display the string "Asia" in a text box, and the statement

```
txtOutput.Text = CStr(1000000 * country.population / country.area)
```

will display the population density of China in a text box.

Although structures are always defined in the Declarations section of the Code Editor, variables of user-defined type can be declared anywhere in a program. Just like ordinary variables, they have class-level, local, or block-level scope depending on where they are declared.

✓ **Example 1**   The following program uses the Split method to assign values to the members of a variable having a user-defined type. This technique will play a vital role when values are assigned from text files to an array of structures. **Note:** Since the population member of the structure Nation is given in terms of millions, the value has to be multiplied by one million when used in a calculation.

```
Structure Nation
  Dim name As String
  Dim continent As String
  Dim population As Double    'in millions
  Dim area As Double          'in square miles
End Structure

Dim country As Nation         'class-level variable

Private Sub frmCountry_Load(...) Handles MyBase.Load
  'Assign values to country's member variables
  Dim line As String = "China,Asia,1332.5,3696100"
  Dim data() As String = line.Split(","c)
  country.name = data(0)
  country.continent = data(1)
  country.population = CDbl(data(2))
  country.area = CDbl(data(3))
End Sub

Private Sub btnDisplay_Click(...) Handles btnDisplay.Click
  'Display data in text boxes
  txtName.Text = country.name
  txtContinent.Text = country.continent
  txtPop.Text = FormatNumber(1000000 * country.population, 0)
  txtArea.Text = FormatNumber(country.area, 0) & " square miles"
  txtDensity.Text = FormatNumber(1000000 * country.population / country.area) &
                    " people per square mile"
End Sub
```

[Run, and click on the button.]

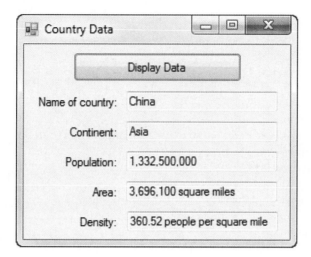

Arrays of Structures

Since a structure is a data type, an array can be declared with a structure as its data type. For instance, the statement

```
Dim nations(191) As Nation
```

declares *nations* to be an array of 192 elements, where each element has data type Nation. For each index *i*, *nations(i)* will be a variable of type Nation, and the values of its members will be *nations(i).name*, *nations(i).continent*, *nations(i).population*, and *nations(i).area*. Filling this 192-element array requires $4 \times 192 = 768$ pieces of data. This amount of data is best supplied by a text file. The optimum design for this text file is to have 192 lines of text, each consisting of 4 pieces of data delimited by commas. The next example uses the file UN.txt that gives data about the 192 members of the United Nations with the countries listed in alphabetical order. Some lines of the file are

```
Canada,North America,32.9,3855000
France,Europe,63.5,211209
New Zealand,Australia/Oceania,4.18,103738
Nigeria,Africa,146.5,356669
Pakistan,Asia,164,310403
Peru,South America,27.9,496226
```

Each line of this text file is called a **record** and each record is said to contain four **fields**—a name field, a continent field, a population field, and an area field. The text file is said to use a **CSV format**. (CSV stands for "Comma Separated Values.")

 Example 2   The following program uses the text file UN.txt to fill an array of structures and then uses the array to display the names of the countries in the continent selected by the user. The program uses two list boxes. Assume the String Collection Editor for lstContinents has been filled at design time with the names of the seven continents. The countries in the selected continent are displayed in lstCountries.

```
Structure Nation
  Dim name As String
  Dim continent As String
```

```
    Dim population As Double    'in millions
    Dim area As Double          'in square miles
End Structure

Dim nations(191) As Nation

Private Sub frmCountry_Load(...) Handles MyBase.Load
    'Place the contents of UN.txt into the array nations.
    Dim line As String
    Dim data() As String
    Dim countries() As String = IO.File.ReadAllLines("UN.txt")
    For i As Integer = 0 To 191
        line = countries(i)
        data = line.Split(","c)
        nations(i).name = data(0)
        nations(i).continent = data(1)
        nations(i).population = CDbl(data(2))
        nations(i).area = CDbl(data(3))
    Next
End Sub


Private Sub lstContinents_SelectedIndexChanged(...) Handles _
                        lstContinents.SelectedIndexChanged
    Dim selectedContinent As String = lstContinents.Text
    lstCountries.Items.Clear()
    If selectedContinent = "Antarctica" Then
        MessageBox.Show("There are no countries in Antarctica.")
    Else
        For i As Integer = 0 To 191
            If nations(i).continent = selectedContinent Then
                lstCountries.Items.Add(nations(i).name)
            End If
        Next
    End If
End Sub
```

[Run, and click on the name of a continent.]

Queries can be used with arrays of structures in much the same way they are used with ordinary arrays.

Example 3   In the following variation of Example 2, the countries are displayed in descending order by their areas. LINQ is used both to filter the countries and to sort them by area. The query returns a sequence of names of countries.

```
Structure Nation
  Dim name As String
  Dim continent As String
  Dim population As Double   'in millions
  Dim area As Double         'in square miles
End Structure

Dim nations(191) As Nation

Private Sub frmCountry_Load(...) Handles MyBase.Load
  Dim line As String
  Dim data() As String
  Dim countries() As String = IO.File.ReadAllLines("UN.txt")
  For i As Integer = 0 To 191
    line = countries(i)
    data = line.Split(","c)
    nations(i).name = data(0)
    nations(i).continent = data(1)
    nations(i).population = CDbl(data(2))
    nations(i).area = CDbl(data(3))
  Next
End Sub

Private Sub lstContinents_SelectedIndexChanged(...) Handles _
                        lstContinents.SelectedIndexChanged
  Dim selectedContinent As String = lstContinents.Text
  Dim query = From country In nations
              Where country.continent = selectedContinent
              Order By country.area Descending
              Select country.name
  lstCountries.Items.Clear()
  If selectedContinent = "Antarctica" Then
    MessageBox.Show("There are no countries in Antarctica.")
  Else
    For Each countryName In query
      lstCountries.Items.Add(countryName)
    Next
  End If
End Sub
```

[Run, and click on the name of a continent.]

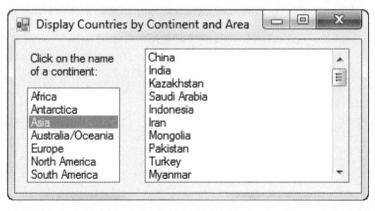

So far, LINQ Select clauses have contained a single item. However, Select clauses can contain multiple items. In that case the query returns a sequence of structures.

The next example uses the file Colleges.txt that contains data (name, state, and year founded) about colleges founded before 1800. The first four lines of the file are

```
Harvard U.,MA,1636
William and Mary,VA,1693
Yale U.,CT,1701
U. of Pennsylvania,PA,1740
```

Example 4   The following program displays colleges alphabetically ordered (along with their year founded) that are in the state specified in a masked text box. In this program we do not assume that the number of colleges in the text file is known in advance. Also, the Select clause returns a sequence of values whose data type is a structure having two members—a name member and a yearFounded member.

```
Structure College
  Dim name As String
  Dim state As String          'state abbreviation
  Dim yearFounded As Integer
End Structure

Dim colleges() As College

Private Sub frmColleges_Load(...) Handles MyBase.Load
  'Place the data for each college into the array schools.
  Dim schools() = IO.File.ReadAllLines("Colleges.txt")
  Dim n As Integer = schools.Count − 1
  ReDim colleges(n)
  Dim line As String    'holds data for a single college
  Dim data() As String
  For i As Integer = 0 To n
    line = schools(i)
    data = line.Split(","c)
    colleges(i).name = data(0)
    colleges(i).state = data(1)
    colleges(i).yearFounded = CInt(data(2))
  Next
End Sub

Private Sub btnDisplay_Click(...) Handles btnDisplay.Click
  Dim query = From col In colleges
              Where col.state = mtbState.Text.ToUpper
              Order By col.name Ascending
              Select col.name, col.yearFounded
  lstColleges.Items.Clear()
  For Each institution In query
    lstColleges.Items.Add(institution.name & " " & institution.yearFounded)
  Next
End Sub
```

[Run, type a state abbreviation into the masked text box, and click on the button.]

In the program above, the query returned a sequence of values whose data type is a structure having two members. (The number of members was determined by the number of items in the Select clause.) The new structure type has no declared name, and thus it is said to have an **anonymous type**. Local type inference (provided by having Option Infer set to On) spares us from having to know the names of anonymous data types.

The DataGridView Control

In Section 7.2, the DataSource property was used to display (as a list) the values returned by a query having a single item in its Select clause. The DataSource property also can be used to display (as a table) the structure values returned by a query having two or more expressions in its Select clause. Instead of a list box, the values are displayed in a DataGridView control. (The DataGridView control is found in the Toolbox's *All Windows Forms* and *Data* groups. The standard prefix for the name of a DataGridView control is *dgv*.)

If the Select clause of a query contains two or more items, then a pair of statements of the form

```
dgvOutput.DataSource = queryName.ToList
dgvOutput.CurrentCell = Nothing
```

displays the values returned by the query in the DataGridView control dgvOutput. (**Note:** The second statement is optional. It prevents having a shaded cell in the table.) For instance, consider the program in the previous example. If the list box is replaced by the DataGridView control dgvColleges, the statement `lstColleges.Items.Clear()` is deleted, and the For Each loop is replaced by the statements

```
dgvColleges.DataSource = query.ToList
dgvColleges.CurrentCell = Nothing
```

then the outcome will be as shown in Fig. 7.13 on the next page.

The blank column at the left side of the DataGridView control can be removed by setting the RowHeadersVisible property of the DataGridView control to False at design time. By default, the column headers contain the member names from the query's Select clause. The column header can be customized with the HeaderText property. Figure 7.14 results when the

FIGURE 7.13   Use of a DataGridView in Example 4.

FIGURE 7.14   Customizing the headers in Example 4.

RowHeadersVisible property is set to False and the following two lines of code are added to the btnDisplay_Click event procedure:

```
dgvColleges.Columns("name").HeaderText = "College"
dgvColleges.Columns("yearFounded").HeaderText = "Year Founded"
```

Note: The DataGridView controls appearing in this textbook have been carefully sized to exactly fit the data. Comment 3 explains how this was accomplished. There is no need for you to strive for such precision when working the exercises.

■ Searching an Array of Structures

Often one member (or pair of members) serves to uniquely identify each element in an array of structures. Such a member (or pair of members) is called a **key**. In Example 4, the *name* member is a key for the array of College structures. Often an array of structures is searched with a LINQ query for the sole element having a specific key value. If so, the query returns a sequence consisting of a single item, and a method such as the First method is used to display the value in a text box.

Example 5 The following program provides information about a college selected from a list box by the user. (**Note:** In this program, the method First can be replaced by other methods, such as Last, Max, or Min.)

```
Structure College
  Dim name As String
  Dim state As String
  Dim yearFounded As Integer
End Structure

Dim colleges() As College

Private Sub frmColleges_Load(...) Handles MyBase.Load
  Dim schools() = IO.File.ReadAllLines("Colleges.txt")
  Dim n = schools.Count − 1
  ReDim colleges(n)
  Dim line As String      'holds data for a single college
  Dim data() As String
  For i As Integer = 0 To n
    line = schools(i)
    data = line.Split(","c)
    colleges(i).name = data(0)
    colleges(i).state = data(1)
    colleges(i).yearFounded = CInt(data(2))
  Next
  Dim query = From institution In colleges
              Order By institution.name
              Select institution
  For Each institution In query
    lstColleges.Items.Add(institution.name)
  Next
End Sub

Private Sub lstColleges_SelectedIndexChanged(...) Handles _
              lstColleges.SelectedIndexChanged
  Dim query = From institution In colleges
              Where institution.name = lstColleges.Text
              Select institution
  txtState.Text = query.First.state
  txtYear.Text = CStr(query.First.yearFounded)
End Sub
```

[Run, and click on a college.]

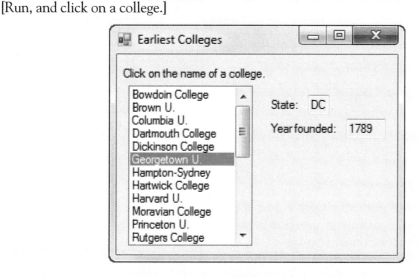

Using General Procedures with Structures

Variables whose type is a structure can be passed to Sub procedures and returned by Function procedures in the same way as variables of other data types.

Example 6 The following program uses general procedures to input grades and to curve the grades.

```
Structure Grades
  Dim exam1 As Double
  Dim exam2 As Double
  Dim final As Double
End Structure

Private Sub btnCalculate_Click(...) Handles btnCalculate.Click
  Dim scores As Grades
  Dim semesterAverage As Double
  GetGrades(scores)
  scores = CurveGrades(scores)
  semesterAverage = (scores.exam1 + scores.exam2 + 2 * scores.final) / 4
  txtOutput.Text = "Semester Average: " & FormatNumber(semesterAverage, 2)
End Sub

Sub GetGrades(ByRef scores As Grades)
  scores.exam1 = 80
  scores.exam2 = 90
  scores.final = 95
End Sub

Function CurveGrades(ByVal scores As Grades) As Grades
  scores.exam1 += 3
  scores.exam2 += 4
  scores.final += 2
  Return scores
End Function
```

[Run, and click on the button.]

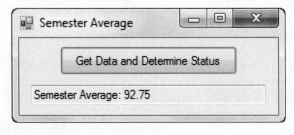

Displaying and Comparing Structure Values

Statements of the form

```
lstBox.Items.Add(structureVar)
```

where *structureVar* is a structure variable, do not perform as intended. Each member of a structure should appear separately in a lstBox.Items.Add statement. Also, comparisons involving structures using the relational operators <, >, =, <>, <=, and >= are valid only with individual members of the structures, not with the structures themselves.

Complex Structures (Optional)

So far, the members of structures have had elementary types; such as String or Integer. However, the type for a member can be another structure or an array. When a member is given an array type, the defining Dim statement must not specify the upper bound; this task must be left to a ReDim statement. Example 7 demonstrates the use of both of these nonelementary types of members.

 Example 7   The following program totals a person's college credits and determines whether that person has enough credits for graduation. **Notes:** The structure variable *person* is local to the btnGet_Click event procedure. In the fifth line of the procedure, **person.name.firstName** should be thought of as **(person.name).firstName**.

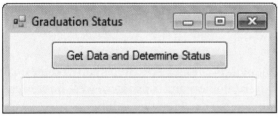

OBJECT	PROPERTY	SETTING
frmStatus	Text	Graduation Status
btnGet	Text	Get Data and Determine Status
txtResult	ReadOnly	True

```
Structure FullName
  Dim firstName As String
  Dim lastName As String
End Structure

Structure Student
  Dim name As FullName
  Dim credits() As Integer
End Structure

Private Sub btnGet_Click(...) Handles btnGet.Click
  Dim numYears As Integer
  Dim person As Student
  txtResult.Clear()
  person.name.firstName = InputBox("First Name:")
  person.name.lastName = InputBox("Last Name:")
  numYears = CInt(InputBox("Number of years completed:"))
  ReDim person.credits(numYears - 1)
  For i As Integer = 0 To numYears - 1
    person.credits(i) = CInt(InputBox("Credits in year " & i + 1))
  Next
  DetermineStatus(person)
End Sub

Sub DetermineStatus(ByVal person As Student)
  Dim query = From num In person.credits
              Select num
  Dim total As Integer = query.Sum
  If (total >= 120) Then
    txtResult.Text = person.name.firstName & " " &
          person.name.lastName & " has enough credits to graduate."
```

```
    Else
      txtResult.Text = person.name.firstName & " " &
                       person.name.lastName & " needs " &
                       (120 - total) & " more credits to graduate."
    End If
End Sub
```

[Run, click on the button, and respond to requests for input with *Miranda, Smith, 3, 34, 33, 34*.]

■ Comments

1. When a Select clause contains two or more items, none of the items can involve computed values. For instance, consider the query in Example 3 and suppose we were interested in the age of each college in 2010. The following query would not be valid:

   ```
   Dim collegeQuery = From col In colleges
                      Where col.state = mtbState.Text.ToUpper
                      Order By col.name Ascending
                      Select col.name, 2010 — col.yearFounded
   ```

   Instead, the query must be written

   ```
   Dim collegeQuery = From col In colleges
                      Where col.state = mtbState.Text.ToUpper
                      Order By col.name Ascending
                      Let age = 2010 — col.yearFounded
                      Select col.name, age
   ```

2. If a column header cell in a DataGridView control is too narrow to accommodate its text, the text is displayed in two or more lines. However, if an ordinary cell is too narrow to accommodate its text, part of the text will be cut off. If you suspect that some cells will be too narrow, set the AutoSizeColumn property to *AllCells*. Then, each column's width will automatically adjust to accommodate the longest entries in the column.

3. When the AutoSizeColumn property of a DataGridView control is left at its default setting of *None*, the control's size is specified by its Size property. The setting for the Size property has the form *w, h*, where *w* is the width of the grid in pixels and *h* is its height in pixels. After the RowHeadersVisible property has been set to False, good values for the Size property are $w = 100 \cdot$ [number of columns] $+ 3$, and $h = 22 \cdot$ [number of rows] $+ 1$. **Note:** If there will be a scroll bar on the right side of the grid, add 17 to *w*. If any column header will occupy more than one line, add 13 to *h* for each additional line.

Practice Problems 7.3

1. Find the errors in the following event procedure.

   ```
   Sub btnDisplay_Click(...) Handles btnDisplay.Click
     Structure Team
   ```

```
      Dim school As String
      Dim mascot As String
    End Structure
    Team.school = "Rice"
    Team.mascot = "Owls"
    txtOutput.Text = Team.school & " " & Team.mascot
  End Sub
```

2. Correct the code in Practice Problem 1.

EXERCISES 7.3

In Exercises 1 through 8, determine the output displayed when the button is clicked.

1.
```
Structure Rectangle
    Dim length As Integer
    Dim width As Integer
End Structure

Private Sub btnDisplay_Click(...) Handles btnDisplay.Click
  Dim soccerField As Rectangle
  soccerField.length = 100    'yards
  soccerField.width = 60      'yards
  Dim area As Integer = soccerField.length * soccerField.width
  txtOutput.Text = "The area of a soccer field is " & area &
                   " square yards."
End Sub
```

2.
```
Structure College
    Dim name As String
    Dim state As String
    Dim yearFounded As Integer
End Structure

Private Sub btnDisplay_Click(...) Handles btnDisplay.Click
  Dim school As College
  school.name = "USC"
  school.state = "CA"
  school.yearFounded = 1880
  'Now.Year is the current year
  Dim age As Integer = Now.Year — school.yearFounded
  txtOutput.Text = school.name & " is " & age & " years old."
End Sub
```

3.
```
Structure College
    Dim name As String
    Dim state As String
    Dim yearFounded As Integer
End Structure

Private Sub btnDisplay_Click(...) Handles btnDisplay.Click
  Dim school As College
```

```vb
        Dim line As String = "Duke,NC,1838"
        Dim data() As String = line.Split(","c)
        school.name = data(0)
        school.state = data(1)
        school.yearFounded = CInt(data(2))
        txtOutput.Text = school.name & " was founded in " & school.state &
                         " in " & school.yearFounded & "."
    End Sub
```

4.
```vb
   Structure College
      Dim name As String
      Dim state As String
      Dim yearFounded As Integer
   End Structure

   Private Sub btnDisplay_Click(...) Handles btnDisplay.Click
      Dim school As College
      Dim data() As String = {"Stanford", "CA", "1885"}
      school.name = data(0)
      school.state = data(1)
      school.yearFounded = CInt(data(2))
      txtOutput.Text = school.name & " was founded in " & school.state &
                       " in " & school.yearFounded & "."
   End Sub
```

5.
```vb
   Structure Appearance
      Dim height As Double
      Dim weight As Double
   End Structure

   Private Sub btnDisplay_Click(...) Handles btnDisplay.Click
      Dim person1, person2 As Appearance
      person1.height = 72
      person1.weight = 170
      person2.height = 12 * 6
      If person1.height = person2.height Then
        lstOutput.Items.Add("heights are same")
      End If
      person2 = person1
      lstOutput.Items.Add(person2.weight)
   End Sub
```

6.
```vb
   Structure Employee
      Dim name As String
      Dim hoursWorked As Double
      Dim hourlyWage As Double
      Dim eligibleForBonus As Boolean
   End Structure

   Dim worker As Employee

   Private Sub frmWages_Load(...) Handles Me.Load
      worker.name = "John Q. Public"
```

```
      worker.hoursWorked = 40
      worker.hourlyWage = 25
      worker.eligibleForBonus = True
   End Sub

   Private Sub btnDetermine_Click(...) Handles btnDetermine.Click
      Dim wage As Double wage = worker.hoursWorked * worker.hourlyWage
      If worker.eligibleForBonus Then
         wage = wage + 0.15 * wage
      End If
      MessageBox.Show("Wage for " & worker.name & ": " & FormatCurrency(wage))
   End Sub
```

7.
```
   Structure TestData
      Dim name As String
      Dim score As Double
   End Structure


   Dim students() As String = IO.File.ReadAllLines("Scores.txt")


   Private Sub btnDisplay_Click() Handles btnDisplay.Click
      Dim student As TestData
      For i As Integer = 0 To students.Count - 1
         student = GetScore(i)
         DisplayScore(student)
      Next
   End Sub


   Function GetScore(ByVal i As Integer) As TestData
      Dim student As TestData
      Dim line As String = students(i)
      Dim data() As String = line.Split(","c)
      student.name = data(0)
      student.score = CDbl(data(1))
      Return student
   End Function


   Sub DisplayScore(ByVal student As TestData)
      lstOutput.Items.Add(student.name & ": " & student.score)
   End Sub
```

(Assume that the three lines of the file Scores.txt contain the following data: Joe,88; Moe,90; Roe,95.)

8.
```
   Structure Employee
      Dim name As String
      Dim dateHired As Date
      Dim hasDependents As Boolean
   End Structure


   Private Sub btnDisplay_Click(...) Handles btnDisplay.Click
      Dim worker As Employee
```

```
        worker.name = "John Jones"
        worker.dateHired = #9/20/2010#
        worker.hasDependents = True
        If DateDiff(DateInterval.Day, worker.dateHired, Today) < 180 Then
          MessageBox.Show("Not eligible to participate in the health plan.")
        Else
          MessageBox.Show("The monthly cost of your health plan is " &
                        HealthPlanCost(worker.hasDependents) & ".")
        End If
    End Sub


    Function HealthPlanCost(ByVal hasDependents As Boolean) As String
        If hasDependents Then
          Return FormatCurrency(75)
        Else
          Return FormatCurrency(50)
        End If
    End Function
```

(Assume that today is 1/1/2011.)

9.
```
    Structure Address
        Dim street As String
        Dim city As String
        Dim state As String
    End Structure


    Structure Citizen
        Dim name As String
        Dim dayOfBirth As Date
        Dim residence As Address
    End Structure


    Private Sub btnDisplay_Click(...) Handles btnDisplay.Click
        Dim person As Citizen
        person.name = "Mr. President"
        person.dayOfBirth = #8/4/1961#
        person.residence.street = "1600 Pennsylvania Avenue"
        person.residence.city = "Washington"
        person.residence.state = "DC"
        txtOutput.Text = person.name & " lives in " &
              person.residence.city & ", " & person.residence.state
    End Sub
```

10.
```
    Structure TaxData
        Dim socSecNum As String
        Dim numWithAllow As Integer   'number of withholding allowances
        Dim maritalStatus As String
        Dim hourlyWage As Double
    End Structure


    Structure Employee
        Dim name As String
        Dim hrsWorked As Double
```

```
    Dim taxInfo As TaxData
  End Structure

  Private Sub btnDisplay_Click(...) Handles btnDisplay.Click
    Dim worker As Employee
    worker.name = "Robert Jones"
    worker.hrsWorked = 40
    worker.taxInfo.hourlyWage = 25
    txtOutput.Text = worker.name & " earned " &
        FormatCurrency(worker.hrsWorked * worker.taxInfo.hourlyWage)
  End Sub
```

In Exercises 11 through 13, determine the errors.

11.
```
Structure Nobel
    Dim peace As String
    Dim yr As Integer
End Structure

  Private Sub btnDisplay_Click(...) Handles btnDisplay.Click
    Dim prize As Nobel
    peace = "Martti Ahtisaari"
    yr = 2008
    txtOutput.Text = peace & " won the " & yr & " Nobel Peace Prize."
  End Sub
```

12.
```
Structure Vitamins
    Dim a As Double
    Dim c As Double
End Structure

  Private Sub btnDisplay_Click(...) Handles btnDisplay.Click
    Dim minimum As Vitamins
    minimum.c = 60
    minimum.a = 5000
    lstOutput.Items.Add(minimum)
  End Sub
```

13.
```
Structure BallGame
    Dim hits As Integer
    Dim runs As Integer
    Dim errors as Integer
End Structure

  Private Sub btnDisplay_Click(...) Handles btnDisplay.Click
    Dim game1, game2 As BallGame
    game1.hits = 18
    game1.runs = 8
    game1.errors = 4
    game2.hits = 14
    game2.runs = 6
    game2.errors = 3
    If game1 > game2 Then
      txtOutput.Text = "The first game was better."
    Else
```

```
      txtOutput.Text = "The second game was at least as good."
   End If
End Sub
```

14. Write lines of code as instructed in Steps (a) through (e) to fill in the missing lines in the following program.

```
Structure Appearance
   Dim height As Double    'inches
   Dim weight As Double    'pounds
End Structure

Structure Person
   Dim name As String
   Dim stats As Appearance
End Structure

Private Sub btnDisplay_Click(...) Handles btnDisplay.Click
   Dim person1, person2 As Person
   (missing lines)
End Sub
```

(a) Give *person1* the name Michael.
(b) Set Michael's height and weight to 71 and 190, respectively.
(c) Give *person2* the name Jacob.
(d) Set Jacob's height and weight to 70 and 175, respectively.
(e) If one person is both taller and heavier than the other, display a sentence of the form "[name of bigger person] is bigger than [name of smaller person]."

In Exercises 15 through 18 describe the output that results from clicking on the button. The programs use the file Cities.txt that contains information about the 25 largest cities in the United States. Each record of the file has four fields—*name, state, population in 2000* (in 100,000s), and *population in 2010* (in 100,000s). The first four lines in the file are as follows:

```
New York,NY,80.1,82.7
Los Angeles,CA,36.9,38.84
Chicago,IL,29.0,28.7
Houston,TX,19.5,22.4
```

Assume that each program contains the following code:

```
Structure City
   Dim name As String
   Dim state As String
   Dim pop2000 As Double
   Dim pop2010 As Double
End Structure

Dim cities() As City

Private Sub frmCities_Load(...) Handles Me.Load
   'Place the data for each city into the array cities.
   Dim cityRecords() = IO.File.ReadAllLines("Cities.txt")
   'Use the array cityRecords to populate the array cities.
   Dim n = cityRecords.Count - 1
```

```
    ReDim cities(n)
    Dim line As String    'holds data for a single city
    Dim data() As String
    For i As Integer = 0 To n
      line = cityRecords(i)
      data = line.Split(","c)
      cities(i).name = data(0)
      cities(i).state = data(1)
      cities(i).pop2000 = CDbl(data(2))
      cities(i).pop2010 = CDbl(data(3))
    Next
  End Sub
```

15.
```
  Private Sub btnDisplay_Click(...) Handles btnDisplay.Click
    Dim query = From cty In cities
                Where cty.state = "TX"
                Order By cty.pop2010 Descending
                Select cty.name, cty.pop2010
    For Each cty In query
      lstOutput.Items.Add(cty.name & "   " &
                        FormatNumber(100000 * cty.pop2010, 0))
    Next
  End Sub
```

16.
```
  Private Sub btnDisplay_Click(...) Handles btnDisplay.Click
    Dim query = From cty In cities
                Where cty.state = "TX"
                Let growth = (cty.pop2010 — cty.pop2000) / cty.pop2000
                Order By growth Descending
                Select cty.name, cty.state, growth
    For Each cty In query
      lstOutput.Items.Add(cty.name & ",  " & cty.state)
    Next
    lstOutput.Items.Add("Greatest growth: " &
                        FormatPercent(query.First.growth))
  End Sub
```

17.
```
  Private Sub btnDisplay_Click(...) Handles btnDisplay.Click
    Dim query = From cty In cities
                Let increase = cty.pop2010 — cty.pop2000
                Where cty.name = "Phoenix"
                Select increase
    txtOutput.Text = FormatNumber(100000 * query.First, 0)
  End Sub
```

18.
```
  Private Sub btnDisplay_Click(...) Handles btnDisplay.Click
    Dim query = From cty In cities
                Order By cty.pop2010 Descending
                Select cty.pop2010
    Dim pops() As Double = query.ToArray
    ReDim Preserve pops(9)
    txtOutput.Text = FormatNumber(100000 * pops.Sum, 0)
  End Sub
```

In Exercises 19 through 22 use the file **USStates.txt** that consists of 50 records and four fields. Each field gives a piece of information about a state—*name, abbreviation, land area* (in square miles), *population in the year 2000.* The records are ordered by the states' date of entry into the union. The first four lines of the file are

```
Delaware,DE,1954,759000
Pennsylvania,PA,44817,12296000
New Jersey,NJ,7417,8135000
Georgia,GA,57906,7637000
```

19. Write a program that accepts a state's abbreviation as input and displays the state's name and its area. See Fig. 7.15.

FIGURE 7.15   Possible outcome of Exercise 19.

FIGURE 7.16   Outcome of Exercise 20.

20. Write a program that displays the names of the states whose abbreviations are different than the first two letters of their name. Both the abbreviations and the states should be displayed. See Fig. 7.16.

21. Write a program that displays the names of the states sorted by their population densities in descending order. Next to each name should be the state's population density. See Fig. 7.17.

FIGURE 7.17   Outcome of Exercise 21.

FIGURE 7.18   Outcome of Exercise 22.

22. Write a program that displays the names of the states ordered by land area. Next to each name should be the percentage of the total U.S. land area in that state. See Fig. 7.18.

In Exercises 23 through 26 use the file Baseball.txt that contains data about the performance of major league baseball players during the 2009 regular season. Each record of the file contains four fields—*name, team, atBats,* and *hits.* Some lines of the file are as follows:

```
Aaron Hill,Blue Jays,682,195
Ichiro Suzuki,Mariners,639,225
Derek Jeter,Yankees,634,212
```

23. Write a program using the file Baseball.txt that requests a team as input from a list and displays the players from that team. The players should be sorted in decreasing order by the number of hits they had during the season. The output should display each player's full name and number of hits. See Fig. 7.19.

FIGURE 7.19 Outcome of Exercise 23.

24. Write a program that requests a team as input and displays the players from that team. The players should be sorted alphabetically by their last names. Players having the same last name should be ordered secondarily by their first names. (**Note:** The Split method can be used to extract first and last names from a person's full name. For instance, the value of `"Babe Ruth".Split(" "c).Last` is `Ruth`.) The output should display each player's full name and batting average. See Fig. 7.20.

FIGURE 7.20 Outcome of Exercise 24.

25. Write a program that displays the highest batting average and the player (or players) having the highest batting average. The output also should display each player's team. See Fig. 7.21.

FIGURE 7.21   Outcome of Exercise 25.   FIGURE 7.22   Outcome of Exercise 26.

26. Write a program using the file Baseball.txt that displays the names of the teams sorted alphabetically. See Fig. 7.22.

In Exercises 27 through 30 use the file Justices.txt that contains data about the Supreme Court justices, past and present. Each record of the file contains six fields—*first name, last name, appointing president, the state from which they were appointed, year appointed,* and *the year they left the court.* (For sitting judges, the last field is set to 0.) The first five lines of the file are as follows:

```
Samuel,Alito,George W. Bush,NJ,2006,0
Henry,Baldwin,Andrew Jackson,PA,1830,1844
Philip,Barbour,Andrew Jackson,VA,1836,1841
Hugo,Black,Franklin Roosevelt,AL,1937,1971
Harry,Blackman,Richard Nixon,MN,1970,1994
```

27. Write a program that displays the sitting justices ordered by the year they joined the Supreme Court.

28. Write a program that requests the name of a president as input from a list and then displays the justices appointed by that president. The justices should be ordered by the length of time they served on the court in descending order. (**Note:** For sitting justices, use **Now.Year - yrAppointed** as their time of service. Otherwise, use **yrLeft - yrAppointed.**) Use the file USPres.txt to fill the presidents list box. That file contains the names of the presidents in the order they served. See Fig. 7.23.

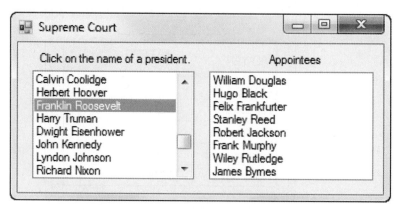

FIGURE 7.23   Possible outcome of Exercise 28.

29. Write a program that requests a state abbreviation as input and displays the justices appointed from that state. The justices should be ordered by their year appointed. The output should also display the last name of the appointing president and the length of time served. (**Note:** For sitting justices, use `Now.Year - yrAppointed` as their time of service. Otherwise, use `yrLeft - yrAppointed`.) Also, the program should inform the user if no justices have been appointed from the requested state. See Fig. 7.24.

FIGURE 7.24   **Possible outcome of Exercise 29.**

FIGURE 7.25   **Outcome of Exercise 30.**

30. Write a program that displays the makeup of the Supreme Court at the beginning of 1980. The justices should be ordered by the year they were appointed, and the names of the appointing presidents should be displayed. See Fig. 7.25.

31. *The Twelve Days of Christmas.* Each year, PNC Advisors of Pittsburgh publishes a Christmas price index. See Table 7.3. Write a program that requests an integer from 1 through 12 and then lists the gifts for that day along with that day's cost. On the nth day, the n gifts are 1 partridge in a pear tree, 2 turtle doves, ..., n of the nth gift. The program also should give the total cost up to and including that day. As an example, Fig. 7.26 shows the output in the list box when the user enters 3. The contents of Table 7.3, along with the day corresponding to each gift, are contained in the file Gifts.txt. The first three lines of the file are as follows:

```
1,partridge in a pear tree,159.99
2,turtle doves,27.99
3,French hens,15
```

TABLE 7.3   **Christmas price index for 2009.**

Item	Cost	Item	Cost
partridge in a pear tree	159.99	swan-a-swimming	750.00
turtle dove	27.99	maid-a-milking	7.25
French hen	15.00	lady dancing	608.11
calling bird	149.99	lord-a-leaping	441.36
gold ring	99.99	piper piping	207.70
goose-a-laying	25.00	drummer drumming	206.26

```
The gifts for day 3 are
1 partridge in a pear tree
2 turtle doves
3 French hens

Cost for day 3: $260.97
Total cost for the first 3 days: $636.93
```

FIGURE 7.26 Sample output for Exercise 31.

The file Famous.txt contains the names of some famous Americans and their birthdays. Use this file in Exercises 32 through 35. The first three lines of the file are

```
Paul Allen,1/21/1953
Lance Armstrong,9/18/1971
Neil Armstrong,8/5/1930
```

32. *Tuesday's child is full of grace.* Display a list of the people in the file Famous.txt born on a Tuesday. (**Hint:** Use the FormatDateTime function.) See Fig. 7.27.

FIGURE 7.27 Output of Exercise 32. FIGURE 7.28 Output of Exercise 33.

33. Display a list of the people in the file Famous.txt born during the 1970s. See Fig. 7.28.

34. Display a table showing all the people in the file Famous.txt along with their ages. The people should be ordered by their ages in descending order.

35. Display a table showing all the people in the file Famous.txt who are in their forties along with their ages in days and the days of the week they were born.

A campus club has 10 members. The following program stores information about the students into an array of structures. Each structure contains the student's name and a list of the courses he or she is currently taking. Exercises 36 through 39 request that an additional event procedure be written for this program.

```
Structure Student
  Dim name As String
  Dim courses() As String
End Structure

Dim club(9) As Student    'Holds all students in the club

Private Sub frmStudents_Load(...) Handles MyBase.Load
  Dim pupil As Student
  pupil.name = "Juan Santana"
  ReDim pupil.courses(2)
  pupil.courses(0) = "CMSC 100"
```

```
pupil.courses(1) = "PHIL 200"
pupil.courses(2) = "ENGL 120"
club(0) = pupil
'Enter data for second student
pupil.name = "Mary Carlson"
ReDim pupil.courses(3)
pupil.courses(0) = "BIOL 110"
pupil.courses(1) = "PHIL 200"
pupil.courses(2) = "CMSC 100"
pupil.courses(3) = "MATH 220"
club(1) = pupil
pupil.name = "George Hu"
ReDim pupil.courses(2)
pupil.courses(0) = "MATH 220"
pupil.courses(1) = "PSYC 100"
pupil.courses(2) = "ENGL 200"
club(2) = pupil
'Enter names and courses for remaining 7 people in the club
End Sub
```

36. Write the code for a btnDisplay_Click event procedure that displays the names of all the students in the club in a list box.

37. Write the code for a btnDisplay_Click event procedure that displays the names of all the students in the club who are registered for three courses.

38. Write the code for a btnDisplay_Click event procedure that displays the names of all the students in the club who are enrolled in CMSC 100.

39. Write the code for a btnDisplay_Click event procedure that displays the names of all the students in the club who are *not* enrolled in CMSC 100.

Solutions to Practice Problems 7.3

1. The event procedure contains two errors. First, the definition of a structure cannot be inside a procedure; it must be typed into the Declarations section of the Code Editor. Second, the statements **Team.school = "Rice"** and **Team.mascot = "Owls"** are not valid. "Team" should be replaced by a variable of type Team that has previously been declared.

2.
```
Structure Team
    Dim school As String
    Dim mascot As String
End Structure

Private Sub btnDisplay_Click(...) Handles btnDisplay.Click
    Dim squad As Team
    squad.school = "Rice"
    squad.mascot = "Owls"
    txtOutput.Text = squad.school & " " & squad.mascot
End Sub
```

7.4   Two-Dimensional Arrays

Each array discussed so far held a single list of items. Such array variables are called **one-dimensional** or **single-subscripted variables**. An array can also hold the contents of a table with several rows and columns. Such array variables are called **two-dimensional** or **double-subscripted variables**. Two tables follow. Table 7.4 on the next page gives the road mileage between certain cities. It has four rows and four columns. Table 7.5 shows the leading universities in three graduate-school programs. It has three rows and five columns.

TABLE 7.4	Road mileage between selected U.S. cities.			
	Chicago	Los Angeles	New York	Philadelphia
Chicago	0	2054	802	738
Los Angeles	2054	0	2786	2706
New York	802	2786	0	100
Philadelphia	738	2706	100	0

TABLE 7.5	Rankings of U.S. university graduate-school programs.				
	1	2	3	4	5
Education	Stanford	Vanderbilt	UCLA	Columbia	U of OR
Engineering	MIT	Stanford	UC Berk	GA Tech	U of IL
Law	Yale	Harvard	Stanford	Columbia	NYU

Source: U.S. News and World Report, 2009.

Two-dimensional array variables store the contents of tables. They have the same types of names as other array variables. The only difference is that they have two subscripts, each with its own upper bound. The first upper bound is determined by the number of rows in the table, and the second upper bound is determined by the number of columns.

VideoNote
Two-dimensional
arrays

■ Declaring a Two-Dimensional Array Variable

The statement

```
Dim arrayName(m, n) As DataType
```

declares an array of type *DataType* corresponding to a table with rows labeled from 0 to m and columns labeled from 0 to n. The entry in the jth row, kth column is *arrayName(j, k)*. For instance, the data in Table 7.4 can be stored in an array named *rm*. The statement

```
Dim rm(3, 3) As Double
```

will declare the array. Each element of the array has the form *rm*(row, column). The values of the elements of the array are

$$rm(0, 0) = 0 \qquad rm(0, 1) = 2054 \qquad rm(0, 2) = 802 \qquad rm(0, 3) = 738$$
$$rm(1, 0) = 2054 \qquad rm(1, 1) = 0 \qquad rm(1, 2) = 2786 \qquad rm(1, 3) = 2706$$
$$rm(2, 0) = 802 \qquad rm(2, 1) = 2786 \qquad rm(2, 2) = 0 \qquad rm(2, 3) = 100$$
$$rm(3, 0) = 738 \qquad rm(3, 1) = 2706 \qquad rm(3, 2) = 100 \qquad rm(3, 3) = 0$$

The data in Table 7.5 can be stored in a two-dimensional string array named *univ*. The appropriate array is declared with the statement

```
Dim univ(2, 4) As String
```

Some of the entries of the array are

$$univ(0, 0) = \text{“Stanford”}$$
$$univ(1, 2) = \text{“UC Berk”}$$
$$univ(2, 3) = \text{“Columbia”}$$

■ Implicit Array Sizing and Initialization

A two-dimensional array can be declared and initialized at the same time with a statement of the form

```
Dim arrayName(,) As DataType = {{ROW0}, {ROW1}, ..., {ROWm}}
```

where ROW0 consists of the entries in the top row of the corresponding table delimited by commas, ROW1 consists of the entries in the next row of the corresponding table delimited by commas, and so on.

 Example 1   The following program stores and accesses the data from Table 7.4.

OBJECT	PROPERTY	SETTING
frmDistances	Text	Intercity Distances
lblCh	Text	1. Chicago
lblLA	Text	2. Los Angeles
lblNY	Text	3. New York
lblPh	Text	4. Philadelphia
lblOrig	Text	Origin:
mtbOrig	Mask	0
lblDest	Text	Destination:
mtbDest	Mask	0
btnShow	Text	Show Mileage Between Origin and Destination
lblMiles	Text	Mileage:
txtMiles	ReadOnly	True

```
Dim rm(,) As Double = {{0, 2054, 802, 738},
                       {2054, 0, 2786, 2706},
                       {802, 2786, 0, 100},
                       {738, 2706, 100, 0}}

Private Sub btnShow_Click(...) Handles btnShow.Click
  'Determine road mileage between cities
  Dim row, col As Integer
  row = CInt(mtbOrig.Text)
  col = CInt(mtbDest.Text)
  If (row >= 1 And row <= 4) And (col >= 1 And col <= 4) Then
    txtMiles.Text = CStr(rm(row − 1, col − 1))
  Else
    MessageBox.Show("Origin and Destination must be numbers from 1 to 4",
                    "Error")
  End If
End Sub
```

[Run, type 3 into the Origin box, type 1 into the Destination box, and click on the button.]

■ The ReDim Statement

A previously declared array can be resized with

```
ReDim arrayName(r, c)
```

which loses the current contents, or with

```
ReDim Preserve arrayName(r, c)
```

which keeps the current values. However, when the keyword Preserve is used, only the second dimension can be resized. The upper bound of the first dimension of the array is given by `arrayName.GetUpperBound(0)`, and the upper bound of the second dimension is given by `arrayName.GetUpperBound(1)`.

So far, two-dimensional arrays have been used only to store data for convenient lookup. In the next example, an array is used to make a valuable computation.

Example 2   The Center for Science in the Public Interest publishes *The Nutrition Scorebook*, a highly respected rating of foods. The top two foods in each of five categories are shown in Table 7.6 along with some information on their composition. The following program computes the nutritional content of a meal. The table is read into three arrays—a one-dimensional array *foods* for the names of the ten foods, a one-dimensional array *nutrients* for the names of the five nutrients, and a two-dimensional array *nutTable* to hold the numbers from the table. (The value of *nutTable*(k, i) is the amount of the ith nutrient in the kth food.) The arrays *foods* and *nutrients* are filled from the files Foods.txt and Nutrients.txt, whose first three lines are as follows:

Foods.txt	Nutrients.txt
cups of spinach	calories
medium sweet potatoes	protein (grams)
8 oz servings of yogurt	fat (grams)

TABLE 7.6   Composition of 10 top-rated foods.

	Calories	Protein (grams)	Fat (grams)	Vit A (IU)	Calcium (mg)
Spinach (1 cup)	23	3	0.3	8100	93
Sweet potato (1 med.)	160	2	1	9230	46
Yogurt (8 oz.)	230	10	3	120	343
Skim milk (1 cup)	85	8	0	500	302
Whole wheat bread (1 slice)	65	3	1	0	24
Brown rice (1 cup)	178	3.8	0.9	0	18
Watermelon (1 wedge)	110	2	1	2510	30
Papaya (1 lg.)	156	2.4	0.4	7000	80
Tuna in water (1 lb)	575	126.8	3.6	0	73
Lobster (1 med.)	405	28.8	26.6	984	190

The array *nutTable* is filled with elements hard-coded into the program.

The program uses an array of structures named *nutFacts* of type NutFact and having five elements (one for each nutrient). The structure NutFact has two members; the first member holding the name of a nutrient and the second holding the total amount of that nutrient in the meal.

The program is written in the input-processing-output format. The input Sub procedure GetAmounts loops through 10 input dialog boxes that request the quantities of each food and places them into a one-dimensional array named *servings*. The processing Function procedure ProcessData uses the array *servings*, along with the arrays *nutrients* and *nutTable*, to fill the array of structures *nutFacts*. Finally, the output Sub procedure ShowData uses the array *nutFacts* to display the nutritional content of the meal into a DataGridView control.

```
Structure NutFact
  Dim nutrient As String    'name of one of the five nutrients
  Dim amount As Double      'amount of the nutrient in the meal
End Structure

Private Sub btnDetermine_Click(...) Handles btnDetermine.Click
  Dim servings(9) As Double
  Dim nutFacts(4) As NutFact        'This array of structures has an
  '                                  element for each nutrient.
  GetAmounts(servings)              'input
  nutFacts = ProcessData(servings)  'processing
  ShowData(nutFacts)                'output
End Sub

Sub GetAmounts(ByRef servings() As Double)
  Dim foods() As String = IO.File.ReadAllLines("Foods.txt")
  'Get the number of servings of each food.
  For i As Integer = 0 To 9
    servings(i) = CDbl(InputBox("How many servings of " & foods(i)))
  Next
End Sub

Function ProcessData(ByVal servings() As Double) As NutFact()
  Dim nutrients() As String = IO.File.ReadAllLines("Nutrients.txt")
  Dim nutTable(,) As Double = {{23, 3, 0.3, 8100, 93},
                               {160, 2, 1, 9230, 46},
                               {230, 10, 3, 120, 343},
                               {85, 8, 0, 500, 302},
                               {65, 3, 1, 0, 24},
                               {178, 3.8, 0.9, 0, 18},
                               {110, 2, 1, 2510, 30},
                               {156, 2.4, 0.4, 7000, 80},
                               {575, 126.8, 3.6, 0, 73},
                               {405, 28.8, 26.6, 984, 190}}
  Dim nutritionFacts(4) As NutFact  'This array of structures has an
  '                                  element for each nutrient.
  For i As Integer = 0 To 4
    nutritionFacts(i).nutrient = nutrients(i)  'Place the name of a nutrient
    '                                           into an array element.
    'The next five lines calculate the total amount of the nutrient
    'in the meal and place it into the array element.
    Dim sum As Double = 0
    For k As Integer = 0 To 9
      sum += servings(k) * nutTable(k, i)
    Next
    nutritionFacts(i).amount = sum   'Place the amount of the nutrient into
    '                                 the array element.
  Next
```

```
        Return nutritionFacts
End Function

Sub ShowData(ByVal nutFacts() As NutFact)
  'Create a query and use it to place the data from the array
  'of structures into a DataGridView control.
  Dim query = From element In nutFacts
              Let Nutrient = element.nutrient
              Let Amount = FormatNumber(element.amount)
              Select Nutrient, Amount
  dgvOutput.DataSource = query.ToList
  dgvOutput.CurrentCell = Nothing
End Sub
```

[Run, click on the button, and enter the following menu: .5 cups of spinach, 1 medium sweet potato, 2 slices of whole wheat bread, .25 of a large papaya, and 1 medium lobster.]

Filling a Two-Dimensional Array with a Text File

Text files used to fill two-dimensional arrays are similar to those used to fill arrays of structures. Each line of the text file corresponds to a row of the table, with the entries for each row separated by commas. For instance, the array *mileage* discussed earlier can be filled with the text file Distances.txt consisting of the following four lines:

```
0,2054,802,738
2054,0,2786,2706
802,2786,0,100
738,2706,100,0
```

The following code creates and fills the array *mileage*.

```
Dim mileage(3, 3) As Double
Dim rowOfNums() As String = IO.File.ReadAllLines("Distances.txt")
Dim line As String
Dim data() As String
For i As Integer = 0 To mileage.GetUpperBound(0)
  line = rowOfNums(i)
  data = line.Split(","c)
  For j As Integer = 0 To mileage.GetUpperBound(1)
    mileage(i, j) = CDbl(data(j))
  Next
Next
```

Note: These eleven lines of code, with slight modifications, are needed in many of the exercises. You can store this block of code (or any frequently used fragment of code) for later use by highlighting it and dragging it from the Code Editor into the Toolbox. To reuse the code, just drag it back from the Toolbox to the Code Editor. A copy of the code will remain in the Toolbox for further use. Alternately, you can click on the location in the Code Editor where you want the code to be inserted, and then double-click on the code in the Toolbox.

We recommend that you place these lines of code in a program, highlight them, and drag them into the Toolbox. Then you can drag them out whenever you need them.

■ Using LINQ with Two-Dimensional Arrays

Although LINQ is not as useful with two-dimensional as it is with one-dimensional arrays, it is sometimes helpful. However, LINQ needs a Cast method to convert the two-dimensional array to a source data consisting of a one-dimensional array. Suppose *nums* is a two-dimensional array of type Double and having m rows and n columns. Then the code

```
Dim query = From num In nums.Cast(Of Double)()
            Select num
```

produces a sequence consisting of the $m \cdot n$ numbers in the array. The methods Count, Max, Min, First, Last, Average, and Sum apply to the query. Also, the sequence of numbers can be displayed in a list box with the DataSource property.

■ Comments

1. We can define three- (or higher-) dimensional arrays much as we do two-dimensional arrays. A three-dimensional array uses three subscripts, and the assignment of values requires a triple-nested loop. As an example, a meteorologist might use a three-dimensional array to record temperatures for various dates, times, and elevations. The array might be declared with the statement

   ```
   Dim temps(30, 23, 14) As Double
   ```

2. A ReDim statement cannot change the number of dimensions of an array. For instance, it cannot change a one-dimensional into a two-dimensional array.

Practice Problems 7.4

1. Consider the road-mileage program in Example 1. How can it be modified so the actual names of the cities can be supplied by the user?

2. In what types of problems are two-dimensional arrays superior to arrays of structures?

EXERCISES 7.4

In Exercises 1 through 16, assume the array *nums* is of type Double and has been filled with the contents of Table 7.7.

TABLE 7.7			
7	3	1	0
2	5	9	8
0	6	4	10

In Exercises 1 through 12, determine or describe the output of the code.

1. ```
lstOutput.Items.Add(nums(0, 2))
```

2. ```
lstOutput.Items.Add(nums(3, 1))
```

3. ```
lstOutput.Items.Add(nums.GetUpperBound(1))
```

4. ```
lstOutput.Items.Add(nums.GetUpperBound(0))
```

5. ```
Dim total As Double = 0
For Each num In nums
   total += num
Next
lstOutput.Items.Add(total)
```

6. ```
Dim total As Double = 0
For c As Integer = 0 To nums.GetUpperBound(1)
   total += nums(3, c)
Next
lstOutput.Items.Add(total)
```

7. ```
Dim total As Double = 0
For r As Integer = 0 To nums.GetUpperBound(0)
   total += nums(r, 2)
Next
lstOutput.Items.Add(total)
```

8. ```
Dim total As Double = 0
For r As Integer = 0 To nums.GetUpperBound(0)
  For c As Integer = 0 To nums.GetUpperBound(1)
     total += nums(r, c)
  Next
Next
lstOutput.Items.Add(total)
```

9. ```
Dim query = From num In nums.Cast(Of Double)()
            Where (num > 8)
            Select num
lstOutput.Items.Add(query.Count)
```

10. ```
Dim query = From num In nums.Cast(Of Double)()
            Select num
lstOutput.Items.Add(query.Max)
```

11. ```
Dim query = From num In nums.Cast(Of Double)()
            Select num
lstOutput.Items.Add(query.Sum)
```

12. ```
Dim query = From num In nums.Cast(Of Double)()
            Where (num Mod 2 = 0)
            Order By num
            Select num / 2
            Distinct
For Each n As Double In query
   lstOutput.Items.Add(n)
Next
```

13. Write code that creates a new array whose entries are twice the entries of *nums*.

14. Write code that uses a For Each loop to find the average of the numbers in *nums*.

15. Write code that finds the sum of the even numbers in *nums* two ways: first with a For Each loop and then with a LINQ query.

16. Write code that finds the average of the odd numbers in *nums* two ways: first with a For Each loop and then with LINQ.

In Exercises 17 and 18, determine the output of the code.

17.
```
Dim nums(1, 2) As Double
Dim rowOfNums() As String = IO.File.ReadAllLines("Digits.txt")
Dim line As String
Dim data() As String
For i As Integer = 0 To nums.GetUpperBound(0)
  line = rowOfNums(i)
  data = line.Split(","c)
  For j As Integer = 0 To nums.GetUpperBound(1)
    nums(i, j) = CDbl(data(j))
  Next
Next
lstOutput.Items.Add(nums(0, 1) + nums(1, 0))
```

(Assume the two lines of the file Digits.txt are `9,7,6` and `5,4,3.`)

18.
```
Dim names(2, 1) As String
Dim rowOfNames() As String = IO.File.ReadAllLines("People.txt")
Dim line As String
Dim data() As String
For i As Integer = 0 To names.GetUpperBound(0)
  line = rowOfNames(i)
  data = line.Split(","c)
  For j As Integer = 0 To names.GetUpperBound(1)
    names(i, j) = data(j)
  Next
Next
lstOutput.Items.Add(names(2, 1) & " " & names(1, 1))
```

(Assume the three lines of the file People.txt are `Felix,Ungar;` `Oscar,Madison;` and `Henry,James.`)

In Exercises 19 through 29, write a program to perform the stated task.

19. A company has two stores (1 and 2), and each store sells three items (1, 2, and 3). The following tables give the inventory at the beginning of the day and the amount of each item sold during that day.

		Beginning Inventory ITEM					Sales for Day ITEM		
		1	2	3			1	2	3
Store	1	25	64	23	Store	1	7	45	11
	2	30	82	19		2	4	24	8

(a) Record the values of each table in an array.
(b) Adjust the values in the first array to hold the inventories at the end of the day and display these new inventories.
(c) Calculate and display the number of items in each store at the end of the day.

20. Table 7.8 gives the results of a survey on the uses of computers in the workplace. Each entry shows the percentage of respondents from the age category that use the computer for the indicated purpose.

(a) Place the data from the table in an array. (Use Workers.txt.)
(b) Determine the average of the percentages in the Calendar/Schedule column.

TABLE 7.8　Workers using computers on the job.

Age	Word Processing	Spreadsheets	Internet/ e-mail	Calendar/ Schedule	Programming
18–24	57.9	56.0	62.1	48.9	12.4
25–29	67.8	66.2	75.6	58.3	18.8
30–39	69.8	68.0	78.3	61.8	18.0
40–49	69.7	66.9	77.1	59.0	17.7
50–59	68.1	62.5	76.5	54.6	15.1
60 and older	63.7	53.8	71.2	46.1	10.6

Source: U.S. Center of Educational Statistics, Digest of Educational Statistics, 2003.

21. A university offers 10 courses at each of three campuses. The number of students enrolled in each course is presented in Table 7.9.

(a) Display the total number of course enrollments on each campus.
(b) Display the total number of students taking each course.

TABLE 7.9　Number of students enrolled in courses.

		Course									
		1	2	3	4	5	6	7	8	9	10
	1	5	15	22	21	12	25	16	11	17	23
Campus	2	11	23	51	25	32	35	32	52	25	21
	3	2	12	32	32	25	26	29	12	15	11

22. Table 7.10 gives the 2007 and 2008 U.S. sales for the top five restaurant chains.

(a) Place the data into a two-dimensional array. (Use Restaurants.txt.)
(b) Display the number that gives the total change in sales for these five restaurant chains.

TABLE 7.10　Top restaurant chains.

	2007 Sales $Bil	2008 Sales $Bil
1. McDonald's	28.7	30.0
2. Subway	8.2	9.6
3. Burger King	8.7	9.3
4. Starbucks	6.6	8.8
5. Wendy's	8.0	8.0

Source: QSR Magazine, October 2009.

23. The scores for the top four golfers at the 2009 U.S. Women's Open are shown in Table 7.11.

(a) Place the data into an array. (Use Golf.txt.)
(b) Display the total score for each player.
(c) Display the average score for each round.

TABLE 7.11   **2009 U.S. Women's Open.**

Round	1	2	3	4
Eun Hee Ji	71	72	70	71
Candie Kung	71	77	68	69
In-Kyung Kim	72	72	72	70
Cristie Kerr	69	70	72	75

24. Table 7.12 contains part of the pay schedule for federal employees in Washington, D.C. Table 7.13 gives the number of employees in each classification in a certain division. Place the data from the two tables into arrays and compute the amount of money this division pays for salaries during the year. (Use GS-Pay.txt and GS-Employees.txt.)

TABLE 7.12   **2009 pay schedule for federal white-collar workers.**

Step	1	2	3	4
GS-1	17,540	18,126	18,709	19,290
GS-2	19,721	20,190	20,842	21,396
GS-3	21,517	22,234	22,951	23,668
GS-4	24,156	24,961	25,766	26,571
GS-5	27,026	27,927	28,828	29,729
GS-6	30,125	31,129	32,133	33,137
GS-7	33,477	34,593	35,709	36,825

TABLE 7.13   **Number of employees in each category.**

	1	2	3	4
GS-1	0	0	2	1
GS-2	2	3	0	1
GS-3	4	2	5	7
GS-4	12	13	8	3
GS-5	4	5	0	1
GS-6	6	2	4	3
GS-7	8	1	9	2

25. Consider Table 7.5, the rankings of three graduate-school programs. Write a program that places the data into an array, allows the name of a university to be input, and displays the categories in which it appears. Of course, a university might appear more than once or not at all. (Use Ranking.txt.)

26. Table 7.14 gives the monthly precipitation for a typical Nebraska city during a five-year period. Write a program that reads the table from a text file into an array and then displays the output shown in Fig. 7.29. (Use Rain.txt.)

TABLE 7.14 **Monthly precipitation (in inches) for a typical Nebraska city.**

	Jan.	Feb.	Mar.	Apr.	May	June	July	Aug.	Sept.	Oct.	Nov.	Dec.
1986	0.88	1.11	2.01	3.64	6.44	5.58	4.23	4.34	4.00	2.05	1.48	0.77
1987	0.76	0.94	2.09	3.29	4.68	3.52	3.52	4.82	3.72	2.21	1.24	0.80
1988	0.67	0.80	1.75	2.70	4.01	3.88	3.72	3.78	3.55	1.88	1.21	0.61
1989	0.82	0.80	1.99	3.05	4.19	4.44	3.98	4.57	3.43	2.32	1.61	0.75
1990	0.72	0.90	1.71	2.02	2.33	2.98	2.65	2.99	2.55	1.99	1.05	0.92

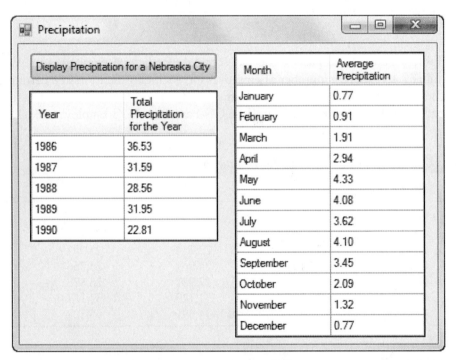

FIGURE 7.29 **Outcome of Exercise 26.**

27. Suppose that a course has up to 15 students enrolled and that five exams are given during the semester. Write a program that accepts each student's name and grades as input, places the names in a one-dimensional array, and places the grades in a two-dimensional array. The program should then display each student's name and semester average. Also, the program should display the median for each exam. (For an odd number of grades, the median is the middle grade after the grades have been ordered. For an even number of grades, it is the average of the two middle grades.)

28. A square array of numbers is called a *magic square* if the sums of each row, each column, and each diagonal are equal. Figure 7.30 shows an example of a magic square. Write a program to determine if an array input by the user is a magic square. **Hint:** If at any time one of the sums is not equal to the sum of the numbers in the first row, then the search is complete.

$$\begin{pmatrix} 4 & 9 & 2 \\ 3 & 5 & 7 \\ 8 & 1 & 6 \end{pmatrix}$$

FIGURE 7.30 **A magic square.**

29. A company has three stores (1, 2, and 3), and each store sells five items (1, 2, 3, 4, and 5). The following tables give the number of items sold by each store and category on a particular day, and the cost of each item.

(a) Place the data from the left-hand table in a two-dimensional array and the data from the right-hand table in a one-dimensional array.

(b) Compute and display the total dollar amount of sales for each store and for the entire company.

Number of Items Sold During Day

		ITEM						ITEM	COST PER ITEM
		1	2	3	4	5		1	$12.00
	1	25	64	23	45	14		2	$17.95
Store	2	12	82	19	34	63		3	$95.00
	3	54	22	17	43	35		4	$86.50
								5	$78.00

Solutions to Practice Problems 7.4

1. Replace the masked text boxes with ordinary text boxes to hold city names. The function FindCityNum can be used to determine the subscript associated with each city. This function and the modified event procedure btnShow_Click are as follows:

```
Function FindCityNum(ByVal city As String) As Integer
  Select Case city.ToUpper
    Case "CHICAGO"
      Return 1
    Case "LOS ANGELES"
      Return 2
    Case "NEW YORK"
      Return 3
    Case "PHILADELPHIA"
      Return 4
    Case Else
      Return 0
  End Select
End Function

Private Sub btnShow_Click(...) Handles btnShow.Click
  Dim orig, dest As String
  Dim row, col As Integer 'Determine road mileage between cities
  orig = txtOrig.Text
  dest = txtDest.Text
  row = FindCityNum(orig)
  col = FindCityNum(dest)
  If (row <> 0) And (col <> 0) Then
    txtMiles.Text = CStr(rm(row - 1, col - 1))
  Else
    MessageBox.Show("Incorrect Origin and/or Destination", "Error")
  End If
End Sub
```

2. Both arrays of structures and two-dimensional arrays are used to hold related data. If some of the data are numeric and some are string, then structures must be used, because all entries of a two-dimensional array must be of the same type. Arrays of structures should also be used if the data will be sorted. Two-dimensional arrays are best suited to tabular data.

7.5 A Case Study: Analyze a Loan

This case study develops a program to analyze a loan. Assume the loan is to be repaid in equal monthly payments and interest is compounded monthly. The program should request the amount (principal) of the loan, the annual rate of interest, and the number of years over which the loan is to be repaid. The five options to be provided by buttons are as follows:

1. Calculate the monthly payment. The formula is

$$[\text{monthly payment}] = \frac{p \cdot r}{1 - (1 + r)^{-n}}$$

where p is the principal of the loan, r is the monthly interest rate (annual rate divided by 12) given as a number between 0 (for 0 percent) and 1 (for 100 percent), and n is the number of months over which the loan is to be repaid. When a payment computed in this manner results in fractions of a cent, the value should be rounded up to the next nearest cent. This corrected payment can be achieved using the formula

[corrected payment] = `Math.Round(originalPayment + 0.005, 2)`

2. Display an amortization schedule—that is, a table showing for each month the amount of interest paid, the amount of principal repaid, and the balance on the loan at the end of the month. At any time, the balance of the loan is the amount of money that must be paid in order to retire the loan. The monthly payment consists of two parts—interest on the balance and repayment of part of the principal. Each month

[interest payment] = r * [balance at beginning of month]

[amount of principal repaid] = [monthly payment] − [interest payment]

[new balance] = [balance at beginning of month] − [amount of principal repaid]

3. Calculate the interest paid during a calendar year. (This amount is deductible when itemizing deductions on a Federal income tax return.) The user should specify the number of the payment made in January of that year. For instance, if the first payment was made in September 2009, then the payment made in January 2010 would be payment number 5.

4. Show the effect of changes in the interest rate. Display a table giving the monthly payment for each interest rate from 1% below to 1% above the specified annual rate in steps of one-eighth of 1%.

5. Quit.

■ The User Interface

Figure 7.31 shows a possible form design and Table 7.15 gives the initial settings for the form and its controls. Figures 7.32, 7.33, 7.34, and 7.35 show possible outputs of the program for each task available through the buttons.

■ Designing the Analyze-a-Loan Program

Every routine uses data from the three text boxes. Therefore, we create a Sub procedure to read the contents of the text boxes and convert the contents into a usable form. Two of the routines

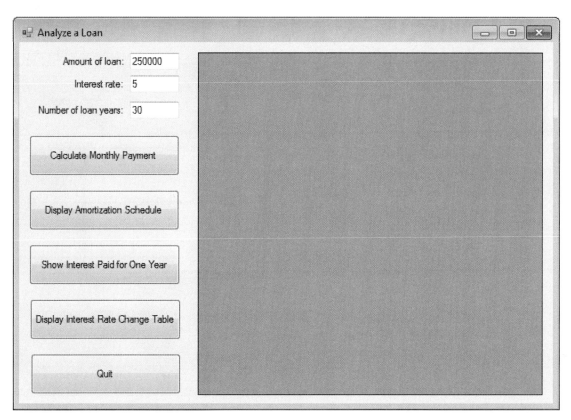

FIGURE 7.31 Template for the Analyze-a-Loan program.

TABLE 7.15 Objects and initial properties for the Analyze-a-Loan program.

Object	Property	Setting
frmLoan	Text	Analysis of a Loan
lblPrincipal	Text	Amount of loan:
txtPrincipal		
lblYearlyRate	Text	Interest rate:
txtYearlyRate		
lblNumYears	Text	Number of loan years:
txtNumYears		
btnPayment	Text	Calculate Monthly Payment
btnAmort	Text	Display Amortization Schedule
btnShow	Text	Show Interest Paid for One Year
btnRateTable	Text	Display Interest Rate Change Table
btnQuit	Text	Quit
dgvOutput	RowHeaderVisible	False

display extensive tables in a DataGridView control. The simplest way to fill a table is to use an array of structures and a LINQ query. We will need two types of structures—one (named Month) to hold the amortization data for a month and the other (named EffectOfRate) to hold monthly payments for different interest rates. Since the array of Month structures is needed by two routines, we use a Function procedure to fill it so we won't have to duplicate the lengthy code. Since the value of the monthly payment is needed several times, we include a Function procedure called Payment.

FIGURE 7.32   Monthly payment for a loan.

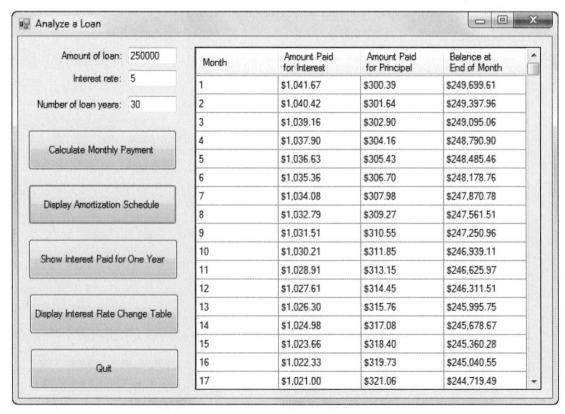

FIGURE 7.33   Amortization schedule for a loan.

FIGURE 7.34 Interest paid during one year.

Interest Rate	Monthly Payment
4.000%	$1,193.54
4.125%	$1,211.63
4.250%	$1,229.85
4.375%	$1,248.22
4.500%	$1,266.72
4.625%	$1,285.35
4.750%	$1,304.12
4.875%	$1,323.03
5.000%	$1,342.06
5.125%	$1,361.22
5.250%	$1,380.51
5.375%	$1,399.93
5.500%	$1,419.48
5.625%	$1,439.15
5.750%	$1,458.94
5.875%	$1,478.85
6.000%	$1,498.88

FIGURE 7.35 Consequences of interest rate change.

The program is divided into the following tasks:

1. Calculate and display the monthly payment.
2. Calculate and display a complete amortization schedule.
3. Calculate and display the interest paid during a specified one-year period.
4. Calculate and display a table showing the effect of different interest rates on the monthly payment.
5. Quit.

Let's consider these tasks one at a time.

1. **Calculate and display the monthly payment.**
   1.1 Input the principal, interest rate, and duration of the loan.
   1.2 Apply the function Payment and display its value.
2. **Display a complete amortization schedule.**
   2.1 Input the principal, interest rate, and duration of the loan.
   2.2 Assign values to each element of the array of elements with type Month.
      2.2.1 Determine the monthly payment.
      2.2.2 For each month, determine the apportionment of the payment into interest payment and amount of principal repaid, and then determine the balance at the end of the month. The balance at the beginning of each month is the same as the balance at the end of the previous month, except for the first month where the beginning balance is the principal. These values are calculated with the three formulas presented earlier, with the exception of the last month. Due to rounding, the last monthly payment will be slightly less than the previous payments. The interest for the last month is calculated the same way as for the previous months. However, the amount of principal repaid will equal the balance at the beginning of the month. That way, the balance at the end of the last month will be 0.
   2.3 Declare a LINQ query to hold the values in the array of Month elements.
   2.4 Use the query to fill the DataGridView control.
   2.5 Specify headers for the table.
3. **Calculate and display the interest paid during a specified one-year period.**
   3.1 Input the principal, interest rate, and duration of the loan.
   3.2 Assign values to each element of the array of elements with type Month. (See the details in 2.2 above.)
   3.3 Request the number of the beginning month.
   3.4 Declare a LINQ query to limit consideration to the interest payments for the twelve months beginning with the requested month.
   3.5 Use the query's Sum method to compute the total of the interest payments for the year.
4. **Calculate and display a table showing the effect of different interest rates on the monthly payment.** First, the interest rate is reduced by one percentage point and the new monthly payment is computed. Then the interest rate is increased by regular increments until it reaches one percentage point above the original rate, with new monthly payment amounts computed for each intermediate interest rate. The subtasks for this task are then as follows:
   4.1 Input the principal, interest rate, and duration of the loan.

4.2 Assign values to each element of the array of elements with type EffectOfRate.

    4.2.1 Reduce the interest rate from the text box by 1%.

    4.2.2 Calculate the new monthly payment and place the interest rate and payment into an element of the array of type EffectOfRate.

    4.2.3 Increase the interest rate by 1/8 of 1%.

    4.2.4 Repeat until the interest rate is 1% percent above the interest rate in the text box.

4.3 Declare a LINQ query to hold the values in the array of EffectOfRate elements.

4.4 Use the query to fill the DataGridView control.

4.5 Specify headers for the table.

5. **Quit.** End the program.

The hierarchy chart in Figure 7.36 shows the stepwise refinement for second, third, and fourth tasks.

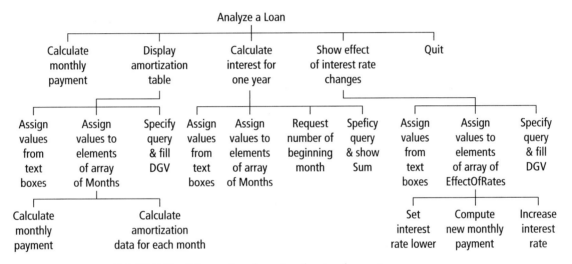

FIGURE 7.36   Hierarchy chart for the Analyze-a-Loan program.

▨ Pseudocode for the Analyze-a-Loan Program

Calculate Monthly Payment button:

    INPUT LOAN DATA (Sub procedure InputData)

    COMPUTE MONTHLY PAYMENT (Function Payment)

    DISPLAY MONTHLY PAYMENT

Display Amortization Schedule button:

    INPUT LOAN DATA (Sub procedure InputData)

    ASSIGN VALUES TO EACH MONTH IN ARRAY OF MONTHS (Sub procedure GenerateMonthsArray)

    DEFINE QUERY TO HOLD DATA FROM ARRAY OF MONTHS

    DISPLAY AMORTIZATION SCHEDULE

Show Interest Paid in One Year button:

    INPUT THE NUMBER OF THE BEGINNING MONTH

    INPUT LOAN DATA (Sub procedure InputData)

ASSIGN VALUES TO EACH MONTH IN ARRAY OF MONTHS (Sub procedure GenerateMonthsArray)

DEFINE QUERY TO HOLD RELEVANT DATA FROM ARRAY OF MONTHS

EVALUATE SUM OF QUERY AND DISPLAY

Display Interest Rate Change Table button:

INPUT LOAN DATA (Sub procedure InputData)

ASSIGN VALUES TO EACH INTEREST RATE IN ARRAY OF EffectOfRates

DEFINE QUERY TO HOLD RELEVANT DATA FROM ARRAY OF EffectOfRates

DISPLAY INTEREST RATE CHANGE TABLE

▩ The Analyze-a-Loan Program

```
Structure Month
  Dim number As Integer
  Dim interestPaid As Double
  Dim principalPaid As Double
  Dim endBalance As Double
End Structure

Structure EffectOfRate
  Dim interestRate As Double
  Dim monthlyPayment As Double
End Structure

Private Sub btnPayment_Click(...) Handles btnPayment.Click
  Dim principal As Double   'Amount of the loan
  Dim yearlyRate As Double 'Annual rate of interest
  Dim numMonths As Integer 'Number of months to repay loan
  InputData(principal, yearlyRate, numMonths)
  Dim monthlyRate As Double = yearlyRate / 12
  Dim monthlyPayment As Double
  'Calculate monthly payment
  monthlyPayment = Payment(principal, monthlyRate, numMonths)
  'Display results
  MessageBox.Show("Monthly payment: " & FormatCurrency(monthlyPayment, 2),
              "Payment")
End Sub

Private Sub btnAmort_Click(...) Handles btnAmort.Click
  Dim principal As Double    'Amount of the loan
  Dim yearlyRate As Double   'Annual rate of interest
  Dim numMonths As Integer   'Number of months to repay loan
  InputData(principal, yearlyRate, numMonths)
  Dim months(numMonths — 1) As Month
  Dim monthlyRate As Double = yearlyRate / 12
  Dim monthlyPayment As Double = Payment(principal, monthlyRate, numMonths)
  months = GenerateMonthsArray(principal, monthlyRate, numMonths)
  Dim query = From mnth In months
          Let num = mnth.number
          Let interest = FormatCurrency(mnth.interestPaid)
          Let prin = FormatCurrency(mnth.principalPaid)
          Let bal = FormatCurrency(mnth.endBalance)
          Select num, interest, prin, bal
```

```vbnet
    dgvResults.DataSource = query.ToList
    dgvResults.CurrentCell = Nothing
    dgvResults.Columns("num").HeaderText = "Month"
    dgvResults.Columns("interest").HeaderText = "Amount Paid for Interest"
    dgvResults.Columns("prin").HeaderText = "Amount Paid for Principal"
    dgvResults.Columns("bal").HeaderText = "Balance at End of Month"
End Sub

Private Sub btnShow_Click(...) Handles btnShow.Click
  Dim principal As Double  'Amount of loan
  Dim yearlyRate As Double 'Annual rate of interest
  Dim numMonths As Integer 'Number of months to repay loan
  InputData(principal, yearlyRate, numMonths)
  Dim months(numMonths − 1) As Month
  Dim monthlyRate As Double = yearlyRate / 12
  Dim monthlyPayment As Double = Payment(principal, monthlyRate, numMonths)
  months = GenerateMonthsArray(principal, monthlyRate, numMonths)
  Dim beginningMonth As Integer = CInt(InputBox("Enter beginning month: "))
  Dim query = From month In months
              Where (month.number >= beginningMonth) And
                    (month.number < beginningMonth + 12)
              Select month.interestPaid
  MessageBox.Show("Interest paid for year beginning with month " &
                  beginningMonth & ": " & FormatCurrency(query.Sum),
                  "Interest For Year")
End Sub

Private Sub btnRateTable_Click(...) Handles btnRateTable.Click
  Dim principal As Double  'Amount of loan
  Dim yearlyRate As Double 'Annual rate of interest
  Dim numMonths As Integer 'Number of months to repay loan
  InputData(principal, yearlyRate, numMonths)
  Dim rates(16) As EffectOfRate
  Dim monthlyRate As Double = yearlyRate / 12
  'Dim monthlyPayment As Double = Payment(principal, monthlyRate, numMonths)
  'Fill rates array
  For i As Integer = 0 To 16
    rates(i).interestRate = (yearlyRate − 0.01) + i * 0.00125
    rates(i).monthlyPayment = Payment(principal,
                              rates(i).interestRate / 12, numMonths)
  Next
  Dim query = From rate In rates
              Let annualRate = FormatPercent(rate.interestRate, 3)
              Let monthlyPayment = FormatCurrency(rate.monthlyPayment)
              Select annualRate, monthlyPayment
  dgvResults.DataSource = query.ToList
  dgvResults.CurrentCell = Nothing
  dgvResults.Columns("annualRate").HeaderText = "Interest Rate"
  dgvResults.Columns("monthlyPayment").HeaderText = "Monthly Payment"
End Sub

Private Sub btnQuit_Click(...) Handles btnQuit.Click
  Me.Close()
End Sub
```

```
Sub InputData(ByRef principal As Double,
              ByRef yearlyRate As Double, ByRef numMonths As Integer)
  'Input loan amount, yearly rate of interest, and duration
  Dim percentageRate As Double, numYears As Integer
  principal = CDbl(txtPrincipal.Text)
  percentageRate = CDbl(txtYearlyRate.Text)
  yearlyRate = percentageRate / 100    'Convert interest rate to decimal form
  numYears = CInt(txtNumYears.Text)
  numMonths = numYears * 12            'Duration of loan in months
End Sub


Function Payment(ByVal principal As Double, ByVal monthlyRate As Double,
                 ByVal numMonths As Double) As Double
  Dim estimate As Double            'Estimate of monthly payment
  estimate = principal * monthlyRate / (1 - (1 + monthlyRate) ^ (-numMonths))
  'Round the payment up if there are fractions of a cent
  If estimate = Math.Round(estimate, 2) Then
    Return estimate
  Else
    Return Math.Round(estimate + 0.005, 2)
  End If
End Function


Function GenerateMonthsArray(ByVal principal As Double,
                            ByVal monthlyRate As Double,
                            ByVal numMonths As Integer) As Month()
  Dim months(numMonths - 1) As Month
  'Fill the months array
  Dim monthlyPayment As Double = Payment(principal, monthlyRate, numMonths)
  'Assign values for first month
  months(0).number = 1
  months(0).interestPaid = monthlyRate * principal
  months(0).principalPaid = monthlyPayment - months(0).interestPaid
  months(0).endBalance = principal - months(0).principalPaid
  'Assign values for interior months
  For i As Integer = 1 To numMonths - 2
    months(i).number = i + 1
    months(i).interestPaid = monthlyRate * months(i - 1).endBalance
    months(i).principalPaid = monthlyPayment - months(i).interestPaid
    months(i).endBalance = months(i - 1).endBalance - months(i).principalPaid
  Next
  'Assign values for last month
  months(numMonths - 1).number = numMonths
  months(numMonths - 1).interestPaid = monthlyRate *
                                   months(numMonths - 2).endBalance
  months(numMonths - 1).principalPaid = months(numMonths - 2).endBalance
  months(numMonths - 1).endBalance = 0
  Return months
End Function
```

CHAPTER 7   SUMMARY

1. For programming purposes, lists of data are most efficiently processed if stored in an *array*. An array is declared with a *Dim* statement, which also can specify its *size* and initial values. The size of an already declared array can be specified or changed with a *ReDim* or *ReDim*

Preserve statement. The methods *Count, First, Last, Max,* and *Min* return the size of the array, first element, last element, largest element, and smallest element, respectively. For numeric arrays, the methods *Average* and *Sum* return the average and total of the numbers in the array.

2. The *IO.File.ReadAllLines* method returns a string array containing the contents of a file.

3. The *Split* method converts a line consisting of strings separated by a delimiter (usually a comma or a blank space) to a string array. The *Join* function is its inverse.

4. A *For Each loop* repeats a group of statements for each element in an array.

5. *LINQ* is a powerful Microsoft technology that provides a standardized way to set criteria for information retrieval from data sources, including arrays. Operators such as *From, Where, Distinct, Order By, Let,* and *Select* are used to create a *query expression* that can retrieve a list of information from the data source. When each element of the list is a single value, the *ToArray* method converts the list to an array. LINQ provides an easy way to sort the contents of an array.

6. The DataSource property can be used to display the sequence returned by a query. If the Select clause contains a single expression, a statement of the form

```
lstOutput.DataSource = query.ToList
```

displays the sequence in a list box. If the select clause contains two or more expressions, a statement of the form

```
dgvOutput.DataSource = query.ToList
```

displays the information returned by the query as a table in a DataGridView control.

7. The *binary search* method provides an efficient way to look for an element of an ordered array.

8. A *structure* is a composite programmer-designed data type with a fixed number of members, each of which can be of any data type. LINQ can be used to sort and search structures and to create new structures of *anonymous* data types.

9. A table can be effectively stored and accessed in a *two-dimensional array*.

CHAPTER 7 PROGRAMMING PROJECTS

1. Table 7.16 contains some lengths in terms of feet. Write a program that displays the nine different units of measure; requests the unit to convert from, the unit to convert to, and the quantity to be converted; and then displays the converted quantity. A typical outcome is shown in Fig. 7.37 on the next page.

TABLE 7.16	Equivalent lengths.
1 inch = .0833 foot	1 rod = 16.5 feet
1 yard = 3 feet	1 furlong = 660 feet
1 meter = 3.28155 feet	1 kilometer = 3281.5 feet
1 fathom = 6 feet	1 mile = 5280 feet
1 nautical mile = 6076.1 feet	

FIGURE 7.37 Possible outcome of Programming Project 1.

2. Statisticians use the concepts of **mean** and **standard deviation** to describe a collection of data. The mean is the average value of the items, and the standard deviation measures the spread or dispersal of the numbers about the mean. Formally, if $x_1, x_2, x_3, \ldots, x_n$, is a collection of data, then

$$\text{mean} = m = \frac{x_1 + x_2 + x_3 + \cdots + x_n}{n}$$

and standard deviation =

$$s = \sqrt{\frac{(x_1 - m)^2 + (x_2 - m)^2 + (x_3 - m)^2 + \cdots + (x_n - m)^2}{n}}$$

The file Scores.txt contains exam scores. The first four lines of the file hold the numbers 59, 60, 65, and 75. Write a program to calculate the mean and standard deviation of the exam scores, assign letter grades to each exam score, ES, as follows, and then display a list of the exam scores along with their corresponding grades, as shown in Fig. 7.38.

$ES \geq m + 1.5s$	A
$m + .5s \leq ES < m + 1.5s$	B
$m - .5s \leq ES < m + .5s$	C
$m - 1.5s \leq ES < m - .5s$	D
$ES < m - 1.5s$	F

For instance, if m were 70 and s were 12, then grades of 88 or above would receive A's, grades between 76 and 87 would receive B's, and so on. A process of this type is referred to as *curving grades*.

3. *Rudimentary Translator.* Table 7.17 gives English words and their French and German equivalents. These words have been placed into the file Dictionary.txt. The first two lines of the file are

`YES,OUI,JA`
`TABLE,TABLE,TISCH`

Write a program that requests an English sentence as input and translates it into French and German. Assume that the only punctuation in the English sentence is a period at the end of the sentence. (**Note:** If a word in the sentence is not in the dictionary, it should appear as itself in the French and German translations. This will allow proper nouns to be translated correctly.) See Fig. 7.39.

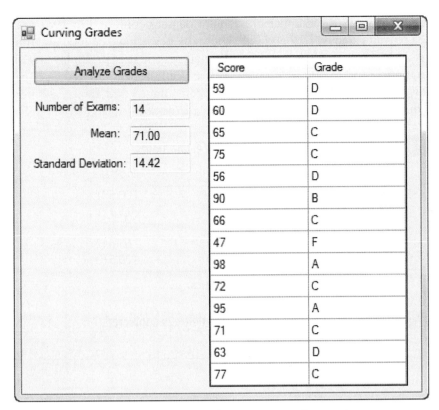

FIGURE 7.38   Output of Programming Project 2.

TABLE 7.17	English words and their French and German equivalents.					
English	French	German	English	French	German
YES	OUI	JA	LARGE	GROS	GROSS
TABLE	TABLE	TISCH	NO	NON	NEIN
THE	LA	DEM	HAT	CHAPEAU	HUT
IS	EST	IST	PENCIL	CRAYON	BLEISTIFT
YELLOW	JAUNE	GELB	RED	ROUGE	ROT
FRIEND	AMI	FREUND	ON	SUR	AUF
SICK	MALADE	KRANK	AUTO	AUTO	AUTO
MY	MON	MEIN	OFTEN	SOUVENT	OFT

FIGURE 7.39   Possible outcome of Programming Project 3.

4. Table 7.18 shows the number of bachelor degrees conferred in 1981 and 2006 in certain fields of study. Tables 7.19 and 7.20 show the percentage change and a histogram of 2006 levels, respectively. Write a program that allows the user to display any one of these tables as an option and to quit as a fourth option. Table 7.18 is ordered alphabetically by field of study, Table 7.19 is ordered by decreasing percentages, and Table 7.20 is ordered by increasing number of degrees. **Note:** Chr(149) is a large dot.

TABLE 7.18   Bachelor degrees conferred in certain fields.

Field of Study	1981	2006
Business	200,521	318,042
Computer and info. science	15,121	47,480
Education	108,074	107,238
Engineering	63,642	67,045
Social sciences and history	100,513	161,485

Source: U.S. National Center of Education Statistics.

TABLE 7.19   Percentage change in bachelor degrees conferred.

Field of Study	% Change (1981–2006)
Computer and info. science	214.0 %
Social sciences and history	60.7 %
Business	58.6 %
Engineering	5.3 %
Education	−0.8 %

TABLE 7.20   Bachelor degrees conferred in 2006 in certain fields.

Field of Study	
Computer and info. science	••••• 47,480
Engineering	••••••• 67,045
Education	••••••••••• 107,238
Social sciences and history	••••••••••••••••• 161,485
Business	•••••••••••••••••••••••••••••••• 318,042

5. Each team in a six-team soccer league played each other team once. Table 7.21 shows the winners. Write a program to

(a) Place the team names in an array of structures that also holds the number of wins.

(b) Place the data from Table 7.21 in a two-dimensional array.

TABLE 7.21   Soccer league winners.

	Jazz	Jets	Owls	Rams	Cubs	Zips
Jazz	—	Jazz	Jazz	Rams	Cubs	Jazz
Jets	Jazz	—	Jets	Jets	Cubs	Zips
Owls	Jazz	Jets	—	Rams	Owls	Owls
Rams	Rams	Jets	Rams	—	Rams	Rams
Cubs	Cubs	Cubs	Owls	Rams	—	Cubs
Zips	Jazz	Zips	Owls	Rams	Cubs	—

(c) Place the number of games won by each team in the array of structures.

(d) Display a listing of the teams giving each team's name and number of games won. The list should be in decreasing order by the number of wins.

6. A poker hand can be stored in a two-dimensional array. The statement

```
Dim hand(3, 12) As Integer
```

declares an array with 52 elements, where the first subscript ranges over the four suits and the second subscript ranges over the thirteen denominations. A poker hand is specified by placing 1's in the elements corresponding to the cards in the hand. See Figure 7.40.

	A	2	3	4	5	6	7	8	9	10	J	Q	K
Club ♣	0	0	0	0	0	0	0	0	1	0	0	0	0
Diamond ♦	1	0	0	0	0	0	0	0	0	0	0	0	0
Heart ♥	1	0	0	0	0	0	0	0	0	0	0	1	0
Spade ♠	0	0	0	0	1	0	0	0	0	0	0	0	0

FIGURE 7.40   **Array for the poker hand A ♥ A ♦ 5 ♠ 9 ♣ Q ♥.**

Write a program that requests the five cards as input from the user, creates the related array, and passes the array to procedures to determine the type of the hand: flush (all cards have the same suit), straight (cards have consecutive denominations—ace can come either before 2 or after King), straight flush, four-of-a-kind, full house (three cards of one denomination, two cards of another denomination), three-of-a-kind, two pairs, one pair, or none of the above.

7. *Airline Reservations*. Write a reservation system for an airline flight. Assume the airplane has 12 rows with 4 seats in each row. Use a two-dimensional array of strings to maintain a seating chart. In addition, create an array to be used as a waiting list in case the plane is full. The waiting list should be "first come, first served"; that is, people who are added early to the list get priority over those added later. Allow the user the following three options:

(a) Add a passenger to the flight or waiting list.

   1. Request the passenger's name.

   2. Display a chart of the seats in the airplane in tabular form.

   3. If seats are available, let the passenger choose a seat. Add the passenger to the seating chart.

   4. If no seats are available, place the passenger on the waiting list.

(b) Remove a passenger from the flight.

   1. Request the passenger's name.

   2. Search the seating chart for the passenger's name and delete it.

   3. If the waiting list is empty, update the array so the seat is available.

   4. If the waiting list is not empty, remove the first person from the list, and give him or her the newly vacated seat.

(c) Quit.

8. The Game of Life was invented by John H. Conway to model some natural laws for birth, death, and survival. Consider a checkerboard consisting of an *n*-by-*n* array of squares. Each square can contain one individual (denoted by 1) or be empty (denoted by −). Figure 7.41(a) shows a 6-by-6 board with four of the squares occupied. The future of each individual depends on the number of his neighbors. After each period of time, called a *generation*, certain individuals will survive, others will die due to either loneliness or over-crowding, and new individuals will be born. Each nonborder square has eight neighboring squares. After each generation, the status of the squares changes as follows:

   (a) An individual *survives* if there are two or three individuals in neighboring squares.

   (b) An individual *dies* if he has more than three individuals or less than two in neighboring squares.

   (c) A new individual *is born* into each empty square that has exactly three individuals as neighbors.

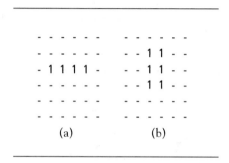

FIGURE 7.41   Two generations.

Figure 7.41(b) shows the status after one generation. Write a program to do the following:

1. Declare a two-dimensional array of size *n* by *n*, where *n* is input by the user, to hold the status of each square in the current generation. To specify the initial configuration, have the user input each row as a string of length *n*, and break the row into 1's or dashes with the Substring method.

2. Declare a two-dimensional array of size *n* by *n* to hold the status of each square in the next generation. Compute the status for each square and produce the display in Figure 7.41(b). **Note:** The generation changes all at once. Only current cells are used to determine which cells will contain individuals in the next generation.

3. Assign the next-generation values to the current generation and repeat as often as desired.

4. Display the individuals in each generation. (**Hint:** The hardest part of the program is determining the number of neighbors a cell has. In general, you must check a 3-by-3 square around the cell in question. Exceptions must be made when the cell is on the edge of the array. Don't forget that a cell is not a neighbor of itself.)

(Test the program with the initial configuration shown in Figure 7.42. It is known as the figure-eight configuration and repeats after eight generations.)

9. Every book is identified by a ten-character International Standard Book Number (ISBN), which is usually printed on the back cover of the book. The first nine characters are digits and the last character is either a digit or the letter X (which stands for ten). Three examples of ISBNs are 0-13-030657-6, 0-32-108599-X, and 0-471-58719-2. The hyphens separate the characters into four blocks. The first block usually consists of a single digit and identifies the language (0 for English, 2 for French, 3 for German, etc.). The second block

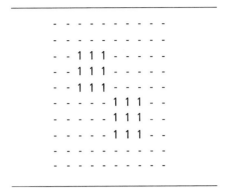

FIGURE 7.42   **The figure eight.**

identifies the publisher (for example, 13 for Prentice Hall, 32 for Addison-Wesley-Longman, and 471 for Wiley). The third block is the number the publisher has chosen for the book. The fourth block, which always consists of a single character called the *check digit*, is used to test for errors. Let's refer to the ten characters of the ISBN as $d_1, d_2, d_3, d_4, d_5, d_6, d_7, d_8, d_9$, and d_{10}. The check digit is chosen so that the sum

$$10 \cdot d_1 + 9 \cdot d_2 + 8 \cdot d_3 + 7 \cdot d_4 + 6 \cdot d_5 + 5 \cdot d_6 + 4 \cdot d_7 + 3 \cdot d_8 + 2 \cdot d_9 + 1 \cdot d_{10} \qquad (*)$$

is a multiple of 11. (**Note:** A number is a multiple of 11 if it is exactly divisible by 11.) If the last character of the ISBN is an X, then in the sum $(*)$, d_{10} is replaced with 10. For example, with the ISBN 0-32-108599-X, the sum would be

$$10 \cdot 0 + 9 \cdot 3 + 8 \cdot 2 + 7 \cdot 1 + 6 \cdot 0 + 5 \cdot 8 + 4 \cdot 5$$
$$+ 3 \cdot 9 + 2 \cdot 9 + 1 \cdot 10 = 165$$

Since 165/11 is 15, the sum is a multiple of 11. This checking scheme will detect every single-digit and transposition-of-adjacent-digits error. That is, if while copying an IBSN number you miscopy a single character or transpose two adjacent characters, then the sum $(*)$ will no longer be a multiple of 11.

(a) Write a program to accept an ISBN type number (including the hyphens) as input, calculate the sum $(*)$, and tell if it is a valid ISBN. (**Hint:** The number n is divisible by 11 if n Mod 11 is 0.) Before calculating the sum, the program should check that each of the first nine characters is a digit and that the last character is either a digit or an X.

(b) Write a program that begins with a valid ISBN (such as 0-13-030657-6) and then confirms that the checking scheme described above detects every single-digit and transposition-of-adjacent-digits error by testing every possible error. [**Hint:** If d is a digit to be replaced, then the nine possibilities for the replacements are $(d + 1)$ Mod 10, $(d + 2)$ Mod 10, $(d + 3)$ Mod 10, ..., $(d + 9)$ Mod 10.]

10. *User-Operated Directory Assistance.* Have you ever tried to call someone at a place of business and been told to type in some letters of their name on your telephone's keypad in order to obtain their extension? Write a program to simulate this type of directory assistance. Suppose the names and telephone extensions of all the employees of a company are contained in the text file Employees.txt. Each set of three lines of the file has three pieces of information: last name, first and middle name(s), and telephone extension. (We have filled the file with the names of the U.S. presidents so that the names will be familiar.) The user should be asked to press buttons for the first three letters of the person's last name followed by the first letter of the first name. For instance, if the person's name were Gary Land, the

user would type in 5264. The number 5264 is referred to as the "push-button encoding" of the name. **Note:** People with different names can have the same push-button encoding—for instance, Herb James and Gary Land. After the user presses four keys on the keypad, the program should display the first names, middle initials, last names and extensions of all the employees having the specified push-button encoding. See Fig. 7.43.

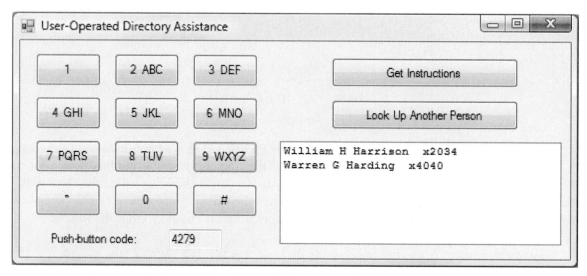

FIGURE 7.43 **Sample run of Programming Project 10.**

11. A fuel-economy study was carried out for five models of cars. Each car was driven 100 miles, and then the model of the car and the number of gallons used were placed in a line of the file Mileage.txt. Table 7.22 shows the data for the entries of the file. Write a program to display the models and their average miles per gallon in decreasing order with respect to mileage. The program should utilize an array of structures with upper bound 4, where each structure has three members. The first member should record the name of each model of car. The second member should record the number of test vehicles for each model. The third member should record the total number of gallons used by that model. [**Hint:** Two Function procedures that are helpful have the headers **Function NumCars(ByVal make As String) As Integer** and **Function NumGals(ByVal make As String) As Double**. *NumCars* calculates the number of cars of the specified model in the table, and *NumGals* calculates the number of gallons used by the model. Both Function procedures are easily coded with LINQ queries.]

TABLE 7.22 **Gallons of gasoline used in 100 miles of driving.**

Model	Gal	Model	Gal	Model	Gal
Prius	2.1	Accord	4.1	Accord	4.3
Camry	4.1	Camry	3.8	Prius	2.3
Sebring	4.2	Camry	3.9	Camry	4.2
Mustang	5.3	Mustang	5.2	Accord	4.4

8

Text Files

8.1 Managing Text Files

This section presents efficient ways to sort, search, reorganize, combine, and retrieve information from text files. The section begins with some preliminaries. You can skip them if you have read Section 7.3.

▓ Preliminaries

The text files considered in Sections 7.1 and 7.2 have a single piece of data per line. For instance, each line of the file States.txt contains the name of a state, and each line of the file USPres.txt contains the name of a president. Another type of text file, called a CSV formatted file, has several items of data on each line with the items separated by commas. (CSV stands for *Comma Separated Values*.) An example is the file USStates.txt, where each line contains four items for each state—*name*, *abbreviation*, *land area* (in square miles), and *population in the year 2000*. The first four lines of the file are

```
Delaware,DE,1954,759000
Pennsylvania,PA,44817,12296000
New Jersey,NJ,7417,8135000
Georgia,GA,57906,7637000
```

Each line of the file is called a **record**, and each of the four categories of data is a **field.** That is, each record consists of four fields—a name field, an abbreviation field, an area field, and a population field.

The Split method is used to access the fields of CSV formatted files. For instance, if the string variable *line* holds the first record of the file USStates.txt, then the value of `line.Split(","c)(0)` is Delaware, the value of `line.Split(","c)(1)` is DE, the value of `CInt(line.Split(","c)(2))` is the number 1954, and the value of `CInt(line.Split(","c)(3))` is the number 759000.

The following code can be used to create a LINQ query holding the contents of the file USStates.txt:

```
Dim states() As String = IO.File.ReadAllLines("USStates.txt")
Dim query = From line In states
            Let data = line.Split(","c)
            Let name = data(0)
            Let abbr = data(1)
            Let area = CInt(data(2))
            Let pop = CInt(data(3))
            Select name, abbr, area, pop
```

After this code is executed, *query* will be a sequence of elements, each element consisting of four components. If the variable *state* is assigned one of the elements, then the four components associated with *state* are denoted *state.name*, *state.abbr*, *state.area*, and *state.pop*. For instance, the following code fills a list box with the names of the states.

```
For Each state In query
  lstBox.Items.Add(state.name)
Next
```

The Select clause in the query above contains four items. A Select clause can contain any number of items. When a Select clause contains just one item, the sequence returned by the query can be displayed in a list box. If a Select clause of a query contains two or more items, all the values returned by the query can be displayed in a table by using a DataGridView control. (The DataGridView control is found in the Toolbox's *All Windows Forms* and *Data* groups.)

The standard prefix for the name of a DataGridView control is *dgv*. With the query above, the statements

```
dgvStates.DataSource = query.ToList
dgvStates.CurrentCell = Nothing
```

display the values returned by the query in the grid shown in Fig. 8.1. (**Note:** The second statement is optional. It prevents having a shaded cell in the grid.) Visual Basic automatically generates the column headings.

FIGURE 8.1   Displaying a table in a DataGridView control.

The blank column at the left side of the DataGridView control can be removed by setting the RowHeadersVisible property of the control to False. The column headers in the DataGridView control can be customized with code that sets the HeaderText property. Figure 8.2 results when the RowHeadersVisible property is set to False at design time and the following four lines of code are added to the two lines of code above:

```
dgvStates.Columns("name").HeaderText = "State"
dgvStates.Columns("abbr").HeaderText = "State Abbreviation"
dgvStates.Columns("area").HeaderText = "Land Area"
dgvStates.Columns("pop").HeaderText = "Population"
```

FIGURE 8.2   States table with modified headers.

Note: The DataGridView controls appearing in this textbook have been carefully sized to exactly fit the data. Comments 2 and 3 of Section 7.3 explain how this was accomplished. There is no need for you to strive for such precision when working the exercises.

VideoNote

Managing text files

■ WriteAllLines Method

In Chapter 7 we copied the contents of files into arrays with the ReadAllLines method. We can reverse the process with the WriteAllLines method. The following line of code creates a new text file and copies the contents of a string array (or a LINQ query that returns string values) into the file, placing one element on each line.

```
IO.File.WriteAllLines("fileName.txt", strArrayOrQueryName)
```

A simple numeric array can be copied into a text file by first converting the array to a string array and then copying the string array into a file using either of the following two sets of code:

```
Dim upperBound As Integer = numArray.Count — 1
Dim strArray(upperBound) As String
For i As Integer = 0 To upperBound
  strArray(i) = CStr(numArray(i))
Next
IO.File.WriteAllLines("fileName.txt", strArray)

Dim query = From num In numArray
            Select CStr(num)
IO.File.WriteAllLines("fileName.txt", query)
```

Note: If the WriteAllLines method references an existing file, the file will be overwritten.

■ Sorting a Text File

Any text file can easily be sorted with a LINQ query.

 Example 1   The first four lines of the file AgeAtInaug.txt are

```
George Washington,57
John Adams,61
Thomas Jefferson,57
James Madison,57
```

Each of the 44 lines in the file contains a president's name and his age at inauguration. The following program orders the data in the file by the age at inauguration and creates a new sorted file.

```
Private Sub btnSort_Click(...) Handles btnSort.Click
  'Sort the file AgeAtInaug.txt by ages
  Dim agesAtInaug() As String = IO.File.ReadAllLines("AgeAtInaug.txt")
  Dim query = From line In agesAtInaug
              Let age = CInt(line.Split(","c)(1))
              Order By age
              Select line
  IO.File.WriteAllLines("Sorted.txt", query)
End Sub
```

[Run, click on the button, and terminate the program. Then click on the *Refresh* button in the Solution Explorer window, click on the *View All Files* button, and double-click on the new text file Sorted.txt in the *bin\Debug* subfolder. The first four lines of the file are as follows.]

```
Theodore Roosevelt,42
John Kennedy,43
Ulysses Grant,46
Bill Clinton,46
```

 Example 2   The following variation of Example 1 displays the data in the file AgeAtInaug.txt in a table ordered by the ages at inauguration.

```
Private Sub btnSort_Click(...) Handles btnSort.Click
  'Sort the file AgeAtInaug.txt by ages
  Dim agesAtInaug() As String = IO.File.ReadAllLines("AgeAtInaug.txt")
  Dim query = From line In agesAtInaug
              Let name = line.Split(","c)(0)
              Let age = CInt(line.Split(","c)(1))
              Order By age
              Select name, age
  dgvOutput.DataSource = query.ToList
  dgvOutput.CurrentCell = Nothing
End Sub
```

[Run, and click on the button.]

Reorganizing the Data in a CSV Text File

LINQ can retrieve specific data from a file and use it to create a new file containing that data.

 Example 3   The first four lines of the file Justices.txt are

```
Samuel,Alito,George W. Bush,NJ,2006,0
Henry,Baldwin,Andrew Jackson,PA,1830,1844
Philip,Barbour,Andrew Jackson,VA,1836,1841
Hugo,Black,Franklin Roosevelt,AL,1937,1971
```

Each line of the file contains the following information about a Supreme Court justice: first name, last name, appointing president, state from which they were appointed, year appointed, and year they left the court. (For sitting justices, the last field is set to 0.) The following program creates a new file, where each line is the full name of a justice and the year they were appointed. The justices are sorted by the year appointed in ascending order. Justices appointed during the same year are sorted by their first name in ascending order.

```
Private Sub btnReorganize_Click(...) Handles btnReorganize.Click
    'Take data from a file. Sort and restructure the data,
    'and write it to a new file.
    Dim justices() As String = IO.File.ReadAllLines("Justices.txt")
    Dim query = From line In justices
                Let data = line.Split(","c)
                Let firstName = data(0)
                Let lastName = data(1)
                Let yrAppointed = CInt(data(4))
                Order By yrAppointed, firstName
                Let newLine = firstName & " " & lastName & "," & yrAppointed
                Select newLine
    IO.File.WriteAllLines("NewFile.txt", query)
End Sub
```

[Run, click on the button, and terminate the program. Then click on the *Refresh* button in the Solution Explorer window, click on the *View All Files* button, and double-click the new text file in the *bin\Debug* subfolder. The first four lines of the file are as follows.]

```
James Wilson,1789
John Blair,1789
John Jay,1789
John Rutledge,1789
```

 Example 4   The following variation of Example 3 displays the requested information in a table.

```
Private Sub btnReorganize_Click(...) Handles btnReorganize.Click
    'Take data from a text file. Sort and restructure the data,
    'and display it in a table.
    Dim justices() As String = IO.File.ReadAllLines("Justices.txt")
    Dim query = From line In justices
                Let data = line.Split(","c)
                Let firstName = data(0)
                Let lastName = data(1)
                Let yrAppointed = CInt(data(4))
                Let fullName = firstName & " " & lastName
                Order By yrAppointed, firstName
                Select fullName, yrAppointed
    dgvOutput.DataSource = query.ToList
    dgvOutput.CurrentCell = Nothing
End Sub
```

[Run, and click on the button.]

Set Operations

Often we want to create a new text file from two existing text files. For instance, we might want to merge the two files (with or without duplications). Or, we might want to update one file by deleting the items that also appear in the other file. Or, we might want the new file to contain the items that appear in both of the existing files. The steps we will use to carry out such operations are as follows:

1. Use the ReadAllLines method to fill two arrays with the contents of the two existing text files.
2. Apply a set operation such as Concat, Union, Intersect, or Except to the arrays or to LINQ queries derived from the arrays.
3. Use the WriteAllLines method to write the resulting array into a new text file.

If *array1* and *array2* are string arrays, then

array1.Concat(array2).ToArray is an array containing the elements of *array1* with *array2* appended, possibly with duplications.

array1.Union(array2).ToArray is an array containing the elements of *array1* with *array2* appended, without duplications.

array1.Intersect(array2).ToArray is an array containing the elements that are in both *array1* and *array2*.

array1.Except(array2).ToArray is an array containing the elements of *array1* with the elements of *array2* removed.

Note: When one of the four operations above is used as the second parameter of a WriteAllLines method, the ToArray method can be omitted.

These four set operations are demonstrated with two simple files in Example 5 and then with more complex files in Example 6.

 Example 5 The contents of two files are as follows:

File1.txt	File2.txt
Alpha	Bravo
Bravo	Delta
Charlie	

The following program combines these two files in four ways. Figure 8.3 shows the form for the program.

FIGURE 8.3 **Form for Example 5.**

```
Dim firstSet() As String = IO.File.ReadAllLines("File1.txt")
Dim secondSet() As String = IO.File.ReadAllLines("File2.txt")

Private Sub btnConcat_Click(...) Handles btnConcat.Click
  IO.File.WriteAllLines("Concat.txt", firstSet.Concat(secondSet))
End Sub

Private Sub btnUnion_Click(...) Handles btnUnion.Click
  IO.File.WriteAllLines("Union.txt", firstSet.Union(secondSet))
End Sub

Private Sub btnIntersect_Click(...) Handles btnIntersect.Click
  IO.File.WriteAllLines("Intersect.txt", firstSet.Intersect(secondSet))
End Sub

Private Sub btnExcept_Click(...) Handles btnExcept.Click
  IO.File.WriteAllLines("Except.txt", firstSet.Except(secondSet))
End Sub
```

[Run, click on each button, and terminate the program. Then click on the *Refresh* button in the Solution Explorer window, click on the *View All Files* button, and look at the new text files in the *bin\Debug* subfolder.]

The file Concat.txt contains the five words Alpha, Bravo, Charlie, Bravo, and Delta.
The file Union.txt contains the four words Alpha, Bravo, Charlie, and Delta.
The file Intersect.txt contains the single word Bravo.
The file Except.txt contains the two words Alpha and Charlie.

In the four set operations, one or both of the arrays can be replaced with LINQ queries. This allows the programmer to order, filter, and project the data before combining files.

 Example 6 The following program demonstrates the set operations with the two files Justices.txt and USPres.txt. The file USPres.txt is a single-field text file containing the names of the 44 presidents. The first four lines of USPres.txt contain the names George Washington,

John Adams, Thomas Jefferson, and James Madison. **Note:** The file Justices.txt shows all Supreme Court appointments as of January 1, 2010.

OBJECT	PROPERTY	SETTING
frmPnJ	Text	Presidents & Justices
btnBoth	Text	Both Justices And Presidents
btnNo	Text	Presidents with No Appointments
btnOr	Text	Presidents Or Justices

```
Dim justices() As String = IO.File.ReadAllLines("Justices.txt")
Dim presidents() As String = IO.File.ReadAllLines("USPres.txt")

Private Sub btnBoth_Click(...) Handles btnBoth.Click
  'Display justices who were also presidents
  Dim queryJustices = From line In justices
                      Let firstName = line.Split(","c)(0)
                      Let lastName = line.Split(","c)(1)
                      Let fullName = firstName & " " & lastName
                      Select fullName
  IO.File.WriteAllLines("Both.txt", queryJustices.Intersect(presidents))
End Sub

Private Sub btnNoAppointments_Click(...) Handles btnNoAppointments.Click
  'Display presidents who made no Supreme Court appointments
  Dim queryAppointers = From line In justices
                        Let president = line.Split(","c)(2)
                        Select president
  Dim queryNoAppoint = From pres In presidents.Except(queryAppointers)
                       Order By pres
                       Select pres
  IO.File.WriteAllLines("NoAppointments.txt", queryNoAppoint)
End Sub

Private Sub btnOr_Click(...) Handles btnOr.Click
  'Display a combined list of presidents and justices
  Dim queryJustices = From line In justices
                      Let firstName = line.Split(","c)(0)
                      Let lastName = line.Split(","c)(1)
                      Let fullName = firstName & " " & lastName
                      Select fullName
  Dim queryEither = From person In presidents.Union(queryJustices)
                    Order By person
                    Select person
  IO.File.WriteAllLines("PresOrJustice.txt", queryEither)
End Sub
```

[Run, click on each button, and terminate the program. Then click on the *Refresh* button in the Solution Explorer window, click on the *View All Files* button, and look at the new text files in the *bin\Debug* subfolder.]

The file Both.txt contains the single name "William Taft".
The file NoAppointments.txt contains the names of four presidents.
The file PresOrJustice.txt contains 154 names.

■ Searching a CSV Text File

In Section 7.3 we searched files having several fields by loading the data into arrays of structures and searching the arrays. The next example provides a more direct way of searching for data—no user-defined structure is used.

 Example 7 Each record of the file USStates.txt contains a name field, an abbreviation field, an area field, and a population field. The first two records of the file are

```
Delaware,DE,1954,759000
Pennsylvania,PA,44817,12296000
```

The following program looks up the name of the state whose abbreviation is given. **Note:** The method First is required in the line **txtName.Text = query.First** because query is a sequence—namely, a sequence of one item.

```
Dim states() As String = IO.File.ReadAllLines("USStates.txt")

Private Sub btnFind_Click(...) Handles btnFind.Click
  'Note: mtbAbbr has the mask LL
  Dim query = From line In states
              Let name = line.Split(","c)(0)
              Let abbreviation = line.Split(","c)(1)
              Where abbreviation = mtbAbbr.Text.ToUpper
              Select name
  If query.Count = 1 Then
    txtName.Text = query.First
  Else
    Dim str As String = " is not a valid state abbreviation."
    MessageBox.Show(mtbAbbr.Text.ToUpper & str, "Error")
    mtbAbbr.Clear()
    mtbAbbr.Focus()
  End If
End Sub
```

[Run, enter a state abbreviation into the masked text box, and click on the button.]

Example 8 The following program searches the file USStates.txt for the states having population density less than 9.5 people per square mile and displays the names of the states and their population densities ordered by their population densities (in ascending order) in a table.

```
Private Sub btnSearch_Click(...) Handles btnSearch.Click
  Dim states() As String = IO.File.ReadAllLines("USStates.txt")
  Dim query = From line In states
              Let data = line.Split(","c)
              Let name = data(0)
              Let popDensity = CDbl(data(3)) / CDbl(data(2))
              Let formattedDensity = FormatNumber(popDensity)
              Where popDensity < 9.5
              Order By popDensity Ascending
              Select name, formattedDensity
  dgvOutput.DataSource = query.ToList
  dgvOutput.CurrentCell = Nothing
  dgvOutput.Columns("name").HeaderText = "State"
  dgvOutput.Columns("formattedDensity").HeaderText = "Population Density"
End Sub
```

[Run, and click on the button.]

The OpenFileDialog Control

Windows applications, such as Word, Excel, and Notepad, all provide the same standard Open dialog box to help you specify the file you want to open. Figure 8.4 shows an Open dialog box that could be used with Notepad to open a text file. The same Open dialog box, with all its functionality, is available to Visual Basic programs courtesy of the OpenFileDialog control.

The OpenFileDialog control is in the *Dialogs* section of the Toolbox. When you double-click on the icon in the Toolbox, the control will appear in the component tray below the Form Designer with the default name OpenFileDialog1. (We will not change the name, since the default name completely describes the control's function.) The only property we will set for the control is the Filter property, which determines the text that appears in the combo box above

FIGURE 8.4 **An Open dialog box.**

the *Open* button and the types of files that will be displayed in the dialog box. The simplest setting has the form

*text for combo box| * .ext*

where *ext* is a two- or three-letter extension describing the types of files to display. For our purposes, the most used setting for the Filter property will be

```
Text Documents (*.txt)|*.txt
```

The statement

```
OpenFileDialog1.ShowDialog()
```

displays the Open dialog box. After a file has been selected and the *Open* button pressed, the value of

```
OpenFileDialog1.FileName
```

will be the file's filespec—including drive, path, filename, and extension.

 Example 9 The following program displays the contents of a text file selected by the user with an Open dialog box.

OBJECT	PROPERTY	SETTING
frmDisplayFile	Text	Display a File
btnSelect	Text	Select a Text File
lstOutput		
OpenFileDialog1	Filter	Text Documents (*.txt)|*.txt

```
Private Sub btnSelect_Click(...) Handles btnSelect.Click
  Dim textFile As String
  OpenFileDialog1.ShowDialog()  'Open dialog box appears and program
  '                              pauses until a selection is made
  textFile = OpenFileDialog1.FileName
  lstOutput.DataSource = IO.File.ReadAllLines(textFile)
  lstOutput.SelectedItem = Nothing
End Sub
```

[Run, and click on the button. (Assume that the user makes choices leading to the situation in Fig. 8.4.) Select the file USPres.txt, and click on the *Open* button in the dialog box.]

Comments 8.1

1. In Example 7, the array *states* could have been omitted and the first line of the query changed to

   ```
   Dim query = From line In IO.File.ReadAllLines("USStates.txt")
   ```

   However, with this change the text file would be read each time the user requested the name of a state. Ideally, a file should be read only once from a disk each time the program is run.

Practice Problems 8.1

1. Consider Example 7. Suppose the last line of the query were changed to

   ```
   Select name, abbr
   ```

   What change would have to be made to the following line?

   ```
   txtName.Text = query.First
   ```

2. The second clause of the query in Example 1 is

   ```
   Let age = CInt(line.Split(","c)(1))
   ```

   The program would produce the correct result even if the CInt function were omitted. Why is that so, and why should CInt be used in general?

3. Does the array `array1.Concat(array2).ToArray` contain the same set of values (disregarding order) as the array `array2.Concat(array1).ToArray`? Is the same true for Union, Intersect, and Except?

Exercises 1 through 10 refer to the file Justices.txt that contains data about the Supreme Court justices, past and present. Each record contains six fields—first name, last name, appointing president, home state, year appointed, and year they left the court. (For sitting judges, the last field is set to 0.) The first two lines of the file are as follows:

```
Samuel,Alito,George W. Bush,NJ,2006,0
Henry,Baldwin,Andrew Jackson,PA,1830,1844
```

In Exercises 1 through 6, determine the first two lines of the new file created by the code.

1.
```
Dim query = From line In IO.File.ReadAllLines("Justices.txt")
            Let data = line.Split(","c)
            Let firstName = data(0)
            Let lastName = data(1)
            Let fullName = lastName & "," & firstName
            Let state = data(3)
            Select fullName & "," & state
IO.File.WriteAllLines("NewFile.txt", query)
```

2.
```
Dim query = From line In IO.File.ReadAllLines("Justices.txt")
            Let data = line.Split(","c)
            Let firstName = data(0)
            Let lastName = data(1)
            Let fullName = (firstName & " " & lastName).ToUpper
            Let yrAppointed = CInt(data(4))
            Select fullName & " was appointed in " & yrAppointed & "."
IO.File.WriteAllLines("NewFile.txt", query)
```

3.
```
Dim query = From line In IO.File.ReadAllLines("Justices.txt")
            Let lastName = line.Split(","c)(1)
            Let pres = line.Split(","c)(2)
            Let presLastName = pres.Split(" "c).Last
            Let phrase = lastName & " was appointed by " & presLastName &
                         " and is still serving."
            Where yearLeft = 0
            Select phrase
IO.File.WriteAllLines("NewFile.txt", query)
```

4.
```
'Note: Today.Year is the current year
Dim query = From line In IO.File.ReadAllLines("Justices.txt")
            Let lastName = line.Split(","c)(1)
            Let yrAppointed = CInt(line.Split(","c)(4))
            Let years = Today.Year - yrAppointed
            Let phrase = lastName & " appointed " & years & " years ago"
            Select phrase
IO.File.WriteAllLines("NewFile.txt", query)
```

5.
```
Dim query = From line In IO.File.ReadAllLines("Justices.txt")
            Let data = line.Split(","c)
            Let firstName = data(0)
            Let lastName = data(1)
            Let yrAppointed = CInt(data(4))
```

```
                    Let newLine = lastName & "," & firstName & "," & yrAppointed
                    Select newLine
        IO.File.WriteAllLines("NewFile.txt", query)
```

6.
```
   Dim query = From line In IO.File.ReadAllLines("Justices.txt")
                    Let data = line.Split(","c)
                    Let lastName = data(1)
                    Let pres = data(2)
                    Let state = data(3)
                    Let presLastName = pres.Split(" "c).Last
                    Let newLine = presLastName & "," & lastName & "," & state
                    Select newLine
        IO.File.WriteAllLines("NewFile.txt", query)
```

In Exercises 7 through 10, describe the new file created by the code.

7.
```
   Dim query = From line In IO.File.ReadAllLines("Justices.txt")
                    Let data = line.Split(","c)
                    Let firstName = data(0)
                    Let lastName = data(1)
                    Let yrAppointed = CInt(data(4))
                    Let fullName = firstName & " " & lastName
                    Let newLine = fullName & "," & yrAppointed
                    Where yrAppointed.StartsWith("19") Order By yrAppointed
                    Select newLine
        IO.File.WriteAllLines("NewFile.txt", query)
```

8.
```
   Dim query = From line In IO.File.ReadAllLines("Justices.txt")
                    Let data = line.Split(","c)
                    Let firstName = data(0)
                    Let lastName = data(1)
                    Let state = data(3)
                    Let yrAppointed = CInt(data(4))
                    Let fullName = firstName & " " & lastName
                    Let newLine = state & "," & fullName
                    Where (yrAppointed >= 1800) And (yrAppointed < 1900)
                    Order By state
                    Select newLine
        IO.File.WriteAllLines("NewFile.txt", query)
```

9.
```
   Dim query = From line In IO.File.ReadAllLines("Justices.txt")
                    Let data = line.Split(","c)
                    Let firstName = data(0)
                    Let lastName = data(1)
                    Let pres = data(2)
                    Let newLine = firstName & "," & lastName & "," & pres
                    Select newLine
        IO.File.WriteAllLines("NewFile.txt", query)
```

10.
```
    Dim query = From line In IO.File.ReadAllLines("Justices.txt")
                    Let data = line.Split(","c)
                    Let firstName = data(0)
                    Let lastName = data(1)
                    Let yrAppointed = CInt(data(4))
```

```
            Let yrLeft = CInt(data(5))
            Let fullName = firstName & " " & lastName
            Let newLine = fullName & "," & yrAppointed
            Where yrLeft = 0
            Order By yrAppointed
            Select newLine
    IO.File.WriteAllLines("NewFile.txt", query)
```

In Exercises 11 through 14, describe the new file created by the code. Assume the file
NYTimes.txt contains the names of the subscribers to the *New York Times* and the file
WSJ.txt contains the names of the subscribers to the *Wall Street Journal.*

11. ```
Dim times() As String = IO.File.ReadAllLines("NYTimes.txt")
Dim wsj() As String = IO.File.ReadAllLines("WSJ.txt")
IO.File.WriteAllLines("NewFile.txt", times.Union(wsj))
```

12. ```
Dim times() As String = IO.File.ReadAllLines("NYTimes.txt")
Dim wsj() As String = IO.File.ReadAllLines("WSJ.txt")
IO.File.WriteAllLines("NewFile.txt", times.Intersect(wsj))
```

13. ```
Dim times() As String = IO.File.ReadAllLines("NYTimes.txt")
Dim wsj() As String = IO.File.ReadAllLines("WSJ.txt")
IO.File.WriteAllLines("NewFile.txt", times.Except(wsj))
```

14. ```
Dim times() As String = IO.File.ReadAllLines("NYTimes.txt")
Dim wsj() As String = IO.File.ReadAllLines("WSJ.txt")
Dim unionArray() As String = times.Union(wsj).ToArray
Dim intersectArray() As String = times.Intersect(wsj).ToArray
IO.File.WriteAllLines("NewFile.txt", unionArray.Except(intersectArray))
```

In Exercises 15 through 18, use the file USPres.txt that contains the names of all the presidents
of the United States and the file VPres.txt that contains the names of all the vice-presidents.

15. Write a program that creates a file containing the names of every president who also
served as vice-president. The program also should display the number of those presidents
in a message box.

16. Write a program that creates a file containing the names of every person who served as
either vice-president or president. The program also should display the number of those
names in a message box.

17. Write a program that creates a file containing the names of every person who served as
either vice-president or president, but not both. The program also should display the number of those names in a message box.

18. Write a program that creates a file containing the names of every president who did not
also serve as vice-president. The program also should display the number of those presidents in a message box.

In Exercises 19 through 26, write a program for the stated example or exercise from Section 7.3
without using a structure.

19. Section 7.3, Example 2   20. Section 7.3, Example 4
21. Section 7.3, Exercise 18   22. Section 7.3, Exercise 19
23. Section 7.3, Exercise 20   24. Section 7.3, Exercise 21
25. Section 7.3, Exercise 22   26. Section 7.3, Exercise 24

27. At the beginning of 1990, a complete box of Crayola[1] crayons had 72 colors (in the file Pre1990.txt). During the 1990s, 8 colors were retired (in the file Retired.txt) and 56 new colors were added (in the file Added.txt). Write a program that creates a text file listing the post-1990s set of 120 colors in alphabetical order.

Exercises 28 through 34 should use the file Justices.txt discussed at the beginning of this exercise set.

28. Write a program to create a file in which each record consists of two fields—the full name of a Supreme Court justice, and the justice's state.

29. Write a program to create a file similar to Justices.txt, but with the state field deleted.

30. Write a program that displays the entire contents of the file Justices.txt in a DataGridView control.

31. The file USStates.txt contains information about each of the 50 states. Each record contains four fields—name, abbreviation, land area (in square miles), population in the year 2000. The records are ordered by the states' date of entry into the union. The first four lines of the file are

```
Delaware,DE,1954,759000
Pennsylvania,PA,44817,12296000
New Jersey,NJ,7417,8135000
Georgia,GA,57906,7637000
```

Write a program that creates a file consisting of the states that have not produced any Supreme Court justices.

32. The first Supreme Court justice was appointed in 1789. Write a program to create a file that lists the years from 1789 through 2009 in which no Supreme Court justices were appointed. The first four lines of the file will be **1792, 1794, 1795,** and **1797.**

33. Write a program to create a file that lists the states that have produced Supreme Court justices, along with the number of justices produced. The states should be in alphabetical order by their abbreviations. The first four lines of the file will be **AL,3; AZ,2; CA,5; CO,1.**

34. Write a program to create a file that lists the presidents who have appointed Supreme Court justices, along with the number of justices appointed. The presidents should be in alphabetical order by their full names. The first two lines of the file will be **Abraham Lincoln,5; Andrew Jackson,5.**

35. Consider the file USStates.txt described in Exercise 31. Write a program to display the entire contents of the file in a DataGridView control with the states in alphabetical order.

Solutions to Practice Problems 8.1

1. The line would have to be changed to

   `txtName.Text = query.First.name`

2. The ages of the presidents are all two-digit numbers and therefore will be ordered correctly when sorted as strings. In general, however, with arbitary ages, the query would not produce a correct result. For instance, a nine-year-old would be considered to be older than an eighty-year-old, and a centenarian would be considered to be younger than a nine-year-old.

3. The answer to the first question is "Yes." The same is true for Union and Intersect. However, the two arrays are different when Except is used. For instance, if the two arrays were reversed in the last event procedure of Example 5, then the contents of the file Except.txt would be the single word Delta.

---

[1] Crayola is a registered trademark of Binney & Smith.

8.2 StreamReaders, StreamWriters, and Structured Exception Handling

So far we have accessed the data in a text file by filling an array with the lines of the file and then accessing the array. However, sometimes we want to read or write a text file directly one line at a time without using arrays as intermediaries.

VideoNote

StreamReaders and StreamWriters

▥ Reading a Text File with a StreamReader

Lines of a text file can be read in order and assigned to variables with the following steps:

1. Execute a statement of the form

```
Dim srVar As IO.StreamReader
```

A StreamReader is a class from the Input/Output namespace that can read a stream of characters coming from a disk. The Dim statement declares the variable *srVar* to be of type StreamReader.

2. Execute a statement of the form

```
srVar = IO.File.OpenText(filespec)
```

where *filespec* identifies the text file to be read. If *filespec* consists only of a filename (that is, if no path is given), Visual Basic will look for the file in the program's *bin\Debug* folder. This statement, which establishes a communications link between the computer and the disk drive for reading data from the disk, is said to **open a file for input**. Data then can be input from the specified file and assigned to variables in the program.

Just as with other variables, the declaration and assignment statements in Steps 1 and 2 can be combined into the single statement

```
Dim srVar As IO.StreamReader = IO.File.OpenText(filespec)
```

3. Read lines in order, one at a time, from the file with the ReadLine method. Each line is retrieved as a string. A statement of the form

```
strVar = srVar.ReadLine
```

causes the program to look in the file for the next unread line of data and assign it to the variable *strVar*.

The OpenText method sets a pointer to the first line in the specified file. Each time a ReadLine method is executed, the line pointed to is read, and the pointer is then moved to the next line. After all lines have been read from the file, the value of

```
srVar.EndOfStream
```

will be True. The EndOfStream property can be used in the condition of a Do loop to cycle through every line of a text file. Such a loop might begin with the statement `Do Until srVar.EndOfStream`.

4. After the desired lines have been read from the file, terminate the communications link set in Step 2 with the statement

```
srVar.Close()
```

Example 1 The following program uses a StreamReader to carry out the same task as the program in Example 7 of the previous section. That is, it finds the name of the state whose abbreviation is given in a masked text box.

```
Private Sub btnFind_Click(...) Handles btnFind.Click
  Dim sr As IO.StreamReader = IO.File.OpenText("USStates.txt")
  Dim abbr As String = mtbAbbr.Text.ToUpper    'mask is LL
  Dim line As String
  Dim foundFlag As Boolean = False
  Do Until foundFlag Or sr.EndOfStream
    line = sr.ReadLine
    If line.Split(","c)(1) = abbr Then
      txtName.Text = line.Split(","c)(0)
      foundFlag = True
    End If
  Loop
  If Not foundFlag Then
    Dim str As String = " is not a valid state abbreviation."
    MessageBox.Show(mtbAbbr.Text.ToUpper & str, "Error")
    mtbAbbr.Clear()
    mtbAbbr.Focus()
  End If
End Sub
```

[Run, enter a state abbreviation into the masked text box, and click on the button.]

Creating a Text File with a StreamWriter

In Section 8.1 we created text files by copying the contents of an array into the files with the WriteAllLines method. However, sometimes we want to write to a text file directly one line at a time without using an array. The following steps create a new text file and write data to it.

1. Choose a *filespec*.

2. Execute a statement of the form

```
Dim swVar As IO.StreamWriter = IO.File.CreateText(filespec)
```

where *swVar* is a variable name. This process is said to **open a file for output**. It establishes a communications link between the program and the disk drive for storing data onto the disk. It allows data to be output from the program and recorded in the specified file. If *filespec* consists only of a filename (that is, if no path is given), Visual Basic will place the file in the program's *bin\Debug* folder. **Caution:** If an existing file is opened for output, Visual Basic will replace the file with a new empty file.

3. Place data into the file with the WriteLine method. If *info* is a literal, variable, or expression of any data type, then the statement

> *swVar*.**WriteLine(*info*)**

writes the information into a new line of the file.

4. After all the data have been recorded in the file, execute

> *swVar*.**Close()**

This statement is very important because the WriteLine method actually places data into a temporary buffer, and the Close method transfers the data to the disk. Therefore, if you omit the statement *swVar*.**Close(),** some data might be lost. The statement also breaks the communications link with the file. Therefore its omission might prevent other procedures from accessing the file.

 Example 2 The following program creates a text file consisting of several last names of computer pioneers and then displays the entire contents of the file in a list box.

```
Private Sub btnCreateFile_Click(...) Handles btnCreateFile.Click
    'Create the file Pioneers.txt
    Dim sw As IO.StreamWriter = IO.File.CreateText("Pioneers.txt")
    sw.WriteLine("Atanasoff")
    sw.WriteLine("Babbage")
    sw.WriteLine("Codd")
    sw.WriteLine("Dijkstra")
    sw.WriteLine("Eckert")
    sw.WriteLine("Faggin")
    sw.WriteLine("Gates")
    sw.WriteLine("Hollerith")
    sw.Close()    'If this line is omitted, the file will be empty.
    MessageBox.Show("Names recorded in file", "File Status")
End Sub

Private Sub btnDisplayFile_Click(...) Handles btnDisplayFile.Click
    'Display the contents of the file Pioneers.txt in a list box
    Dim sr As IO.StreamReader = IO.File.OpenText("Pioneers.txt")
    lstNames.Items.Clear()
    Do Until sr.EndOfStream
        lstNames.Items.Add(sr.ReadLine)
    Loop
End Sub
```

[Run, click on the first button, and then click on the second button.]

▓ Adding Items to a Text File

Data can be added to the end of an existing text file with the following steps.

1. Execute the statement

```
Dim swVar As IO.StreamWriter = IO.File.AppendText(filespec)
```

where *swVar* is a variable name and *filespec* identifies the file. This process is said to **open a file for append**. It allows data to be output and recorded at the end of the specified file. If *filespec* consists only of a filename (that is, if no path is given), Visual Basic will look for the file in the program's *bin\Debug* folder.

2. Place data into the file with the WriteLine method.

3. After all the data have been recorded into the file, close the file with the statement

```
swVar.Close()
```

The IO.File.AppendText option is used to add data to an existing file. However, it also can be used to create a new file. If the file does not exist, then the IO.File.AppendText option creates the file.

The three states "open for input," "open for output," and "open for append" are referred to as **modes**. A file should not be open in two modes at the same time. For instance, after a file has been opened for output and data have been written to it, the file should be closed before being opened for input. Had the statement `swVar.Close()` in Example 2 been omitted, then the program would have crashed when the second button was clicked on.

An attempt to open a nonexistent file for input terminates the program with a FileNotFoundException message box, stating that the file could not be found. There is a method that tells us whether a certain file already exists. If the value of

```
IO.File.Exists(filespec)
```

is True, then the specified file exists. Therefore, prudence dictates that files be opened for input with code such as

```
Dim sr As IO.StreamReader
If IO.File.Exists(filespec) Then
  sr = IO.File.OpenText(filespec)
Else
  message = "Either no file has yet been created or the file "
  message &= filespec & " is not where expected."
  MessageBox.Show(message, "File Not Found")
End If
```

There is one file-management operation that we have yet to discuss: changing or deleting an item of information from a text file. An individual item of a file cannot be changed or deleted directly. A new file must be created by reading each item from the original file and recording it, with the single item changed or deleted, into the new file. The old file is then erased, and the new file is renamed with the name of the original file. Regarding these last two tasks, the Visual Basic statement

```
IO.File.Delete(filespec)
```

removes the specified file from the disk, and the statement

```
IO.File.Move(oldfilespec, newfilespec)
```

changes the filespec of a file. **Note 1:** The IO.File.Delete and IO.File.Move methods cannot be used with open files; doing so generates an exception. **Note 2:** Nothing happens if the file referenced in an IO.File.Delete method doesn't exist. However, a nonexistent *oldfilespec* in an IO.File.Move method generates an exception.

■ System.IO Namespace

Creating a program that has extensive file handling can be simplified by placing the statement

```
Imports System.IO
```

at the top of the Code Editor, before the **Class** *frmName* statement. Then there is no need to insert the prefix "IO." before the words StreamReader, StreamWriter, and File.

 Example 3 The following program manages Names.txt, a file of names. The Boolean function IsInFile returns the value True if the file Names.txt exists and the name entered in the text box is in the file.

OBJECT	PROPERTY	SETTING
frmNames	Text	Manage File
lblName	Text	Name
txtName		
btnAdd	Text	Add Person to File
btnDetermine	Text	Determine if Person is in File
btnDelete	Text	Delete Person from File

```
Imports System.IO      'Appears at top of Code Editor

Private Sub btnAdd_Click(...) Handles btnAdd.Click
  'Add a person's name to the file
  Dim person As String = txtName.Text
  If person <> "" Then
    If IsInFile(person) Then
      MessageBox.Show(person & " is already in the file.", "Alert")
    Else
      Dim sw As StreamWriter = File.AppendText("Names.txt")
      sw.WriteLine(person)
      sw.Close()
      MessageBox.Show(person & " added to file.", "Name Added")
      txtName.Clear()
      txtName.Focus()
    End If
  Else
    MessageBox.Show("You must enter a name.", "Information Incomplete")
  End If
End Sub

Private Sub btnDetermine_Click(...) Handles btnDetermine.Click
  'Determine if a person is in the file
  Dim person As String = txtName.Text
```

```vbnet
    If person <> "" Then
      If IsInFile(person) Then
        MessageBox.Show(person & " is in the file.", "Yes")
      Else
        MessageBox.Show(person & " is not in the file.", "No")
      End If
    Else
      MessageBox.Show("You must enter a name.", "Information Incomplete")
    End If
    txtName.Clear()
    txtName.Focus()
End Sub

Private Sub btnDelete_Click(...) Handles btnDelete.Click
  'Remove the person in text box from the file
  Dim person As String = txtName.Text
  If person <> "" Then
    If IsInFile(person) Then
      'code to remove person
      Dim sr As StreamReader = File.OpenText("Names.txt")
      Dim sw As StreamWriter = File.CreateText("Temp.txt")
      Dim individual As String
      Do Until sr.EndOfStream
        individual = sr.ReadLine
        If individual <> person Then
          sw.WriteLine(individual)
        End If
      Loop
      sr.Close()
      sw.Close()
      File.Delete("Names.txt")
      File.Move("Temp.txt", "Names.txt")
      MessageBox.Show(person & " removed from file.", "Name Removed")
    Else
      MessageBox.Show(person & " is not in the file.", "Name Not Found")
    End If
  Else
    MessageBox.Show("You must enter a name.", "Information Incomplete")
  End If
  txtName.Clear()
  txtName.Focus()
End Sub

Function IsInFile(ByVal person As String) As Boolean
  'Determine if person is currently in a file named Names.txt
  If File.Exists("Names.txt") Then
    Dim sr As StreamReader = File.OpenText("Names.txt")
    Dim individual As String
    Do Until sr.EndOfStream
      individual = sr.ReadLine
      If individual = person Then
        sr.Close()
        Return True
      End If
    Loop
```

```
      sr.Close()
   End If
   Return False
End Function
```

[Run, add, delete some names, or search for some names. After terminating the program, click on the *Refresh* button in the Solution Explorer window, click on the *View All Files* button, and look at Names.txt in the *bin\Debug* subfolder.]

■ Structured Exception Handling

There are two categories of problems that a software program might encounter when it executes. The first is a *logic error*, which is caused by code that does not perform as intended. Common examples of logic errors are typos, using the wrong formula, and accessing the wrong property value. The second category is an *exception*, which typically occurs due to circumstances beyond the program's control. Two situations where exceptions occur are when invalid data are input and when a file cannot be accessed. (In Chapter 4, we showed another way to prevent invalid-data exceptions from occurring.) For example, if a user enters a word when the program prompts for a number, an exception is generated and the program terminates abruptly. In this situation, the programmer did not employ faulty logic or mistype. If the user had followed the directions, no problem would have occurred. Even though the user is at fault, however, it is still the programmer's responsibility to anticipate exceptions and to include code to work around their occurrence.

The Visual Studio environment contains powerful tools that programmers can use to find and correct bugs. These debugging tools are discussed extensively in Appendix D. This section describes techniques used to anticipate and deal with exceptions (in programming terms, this is called "handling exceptions").

An unexpected problem causes Visual Basic to raise an exception. If the programmer does not explicitly include exception-handling code in the program, then Visual Basic handles an exception with a default handler. This handler terminates execution, displays the exception's message in a window and highlights the line of code where the exception occurred. Consider a program that contains the following code:

```
Dim taxCredit As Double

Private Sub btnCompute_Click(...) Handles btnCompute.Click
   Dim numDependents As Integer
   numDependents = CInt(InputBox("How many dependents?"))
   taxCredit = 1000 * numDependents
End Sub
```

A user with no dependents might just leave the input dialog box blank and click on the *OK* button. If so, Visual Basic terminates the program and displays the box shown in Fig. 8.5. (The problem was caused by the fact that the default value in an input dialog box, the empty string, cannot be converted to an integer. Text boxes also have the empty string as their default value.) It also highlights the fourth line of code, since the exception was thrown while executing the CInt function. The program also would have crashed had the user typed in an answer like "TWO".

A more robust program explicitly handles the previous exception by protecting the code in a Try-Catch-Finally block. This allows the program to continue regardless of whether or not an exception was thrown. The computer tries to execute the code in the Try block. As soon as an exception occurs, execution jumps to the code in the Catch block. Regardless of whether

FIGURE 8.5   Exception handled by Visual Basic.

an exception occurred, the code in the Finally block is then executed. The following code is illustrative:

```
Dim taxCredit As Double

Private Sub btnCompute_Click(...) Handles btnCompute.Click
  Dim numDependents As Integer, message As String
  Try
    numDependents = CInt(InputBox("How many dependents?"))
  Catch
    message = "You did not answer the question with an " &
              "integer value. We will assume your answer is zero."
    MessageBox.Show(message, "Improper Response")
    numDependents = 0
  Finally
    taxCredit = 1000 * numDependents
  End Try
End Sub
```

This type of exception handling is known as **data validation**. It catches situations where invalid data cannot be converted to a particular type. An exception is thrown if the user enters data that cannot be converted to an integer using the CInt function. Table 8.1 on the next page lists several exceptions and descriptions of why they are thrown.

The Catch block above will be executed when *any* exception occurs. Visual Basic also allows Try-Catch-Finally blocks to have one or more specialized Catch clauses that handle only a specific type of exception. The general form of a specialized Catch clause is

```
Catch exc As ExceptionType
```

where the variable *exc* will be assigned the name of the exception. The code in this block will be executed only when the specified exception occurs.

The general form of a Try-Catch-Finally block is

```
Try
  normal code
Catch exc1 As FirstException
  exception-handling code for FirstException
```

TABLE 8.1	Some common exceptions.

Exception Name	Description and Example
ArgumentOutOfRangeException	An argument to a method is out of range. `str = "Goodbye".Substring(12,3)`

IndexOutOfRangeException	An array's subscript is out of range.
	
	`Dim arr(3) As Integer`
	`arr(5) = 2`

InvalidCastException	A value cannot be converted to another type. `Dim num As Integer = CInt("one")`

NullReferenceException	A method is called on a variable that is set to Nothing.
	
	`Dim str As String, len As Integer`
	`len = str.Length`

OverflowException	A number too big for the data type is assigned.
	
	`Dim num As Integer = 2000000000`
	`num = 2 * num`

IO.DirectoryNotFoundException	A file within a missing folder is accessed.
	
	`Dim sr As IO.StreamReader =`
	`   IO.File.OpenText("C:\BadDir\File.txt")`

IO.FileNotFoundException	A missing file is accessed.
	
	`Dim sr As IO.StreamReader =`
	`   IO.File.OpenText("Missing.txt")`

IO.IOException	Any file-handling exception, including those mentioned above. For instance, an attempt is made to delete or rename an open file, to change the name of a closed file to an already used name, or when a disk drive specified contains no disk. **Note:** If a series of IO exceptions is being tested with Catch clauses, this exception should be the last one tested. `IO.File.Move(filespec, AlreadyExistingName)`

```
Catch exc2 As SecondException
  exception-handling code for SecondException
.
.
.
Catch
  exception-handling code for any remaining exceptions
Finally
  clean-up code
End Try
```

The *normal code* is the code that you want to monitor for exceptions. If an exception occurs during execution of any of the statements in this section, Visual Basic transfers control to the code in one of the Catch blocks. As with a Select Case block, the Catch clauses are considered one at a time until the first matching exception is located. The last Catch clause in the preceding code functions like the Case Else clause. The *clean-up code* in the Finally block always executes last regardless of whether any *exception-handling code* has executed. In most situations, this code *cleans up* any resources such as files that were opened during the *normal code*. If clean-up is not necessary, then the Finally block can be omitted. However, to complete a Try block, a Catch block or a Finally block must appear.

In addition to data validation, a popular use of exception handling is to account for errors when accessing files. Visual Basic has the capability to access files stored on remote servers via the Internet. An exception is thrown if a desired file is missing (IO.FileNotFoundException) or if the file cannot be read because the Internet connection between the computer and the server is broken (IO.IOException).

 Example 4 The following program reads the first line from a file on a CD. The program expects the file to reside in the folder DataFiles of the CD. Note that the clean-up code, **sr.Close()**, in the Finally block is enclosed in a Try-Catch block of its own. This protects the Close method from any exceptions that might occur.

```
Private Sub btnDisplay_Click(...) Handles btnDisplay.Click
  Dim sr As IO.StreamReader
  Dim message As String
  Try
    sr = IO.File.OpenText("E:\DataFiles\USPres.txt")
    message = "The first President was " & sr.ReadLine & "."
    MessageBox.Show(message, "President")
  Catch exp As IO.DirectoryNotFoundException
    message = "The requested folder is not on the CD."
    MessageBox.Show(message, "Error")
  Catch exp As IO.FileNotFoundException
    message = "The file is not in the specified folder of the CD."
    MessageBox.Show(message, "Error")
  Catch exp As IO.IOException
    message = "Check to see if there is a CD in drive E:."
    MessageBox.Show(message, "Error")
  Finally
    Try
      sr.Close()
    Catch
      'Disregard any exceptions during the Close() method
    End Try
  End Try
End Sub
```

[Remove the CD from the E: drive, run the program, and then click on the button.]

[Insert the CD containing the file USPres.txt (in the folder DataFiles) into the E: drive and then click on the button.]

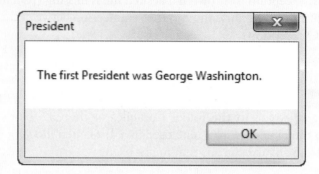

■ **Comments**

1. Any variable declared within a Try-Catch-Finally block has block-level scope. That is, it will not be available after the block terminates.

2. Text files are also called *sequential files* because a SteamReader reads the records one at a time in sequence.

Practice Problems 8.2

1. Give three different ways to display the last record of the file USStates.txt in a message box.

2. Consider the following event procedure.

```
Private Sub btnCreate_Click(...) Handles btnCreate.Click
    Dim sw As IO.StreamWriter = IO.File.CreateText("ABC.txt")
    sw.WriteLine("abc")
End Sub
```

Describe the file ABC.txt after the button is pressed.

EXERCISES 8.2

In Exercises 1 through 10, determine the output displayed in the text box when the button is clicked.

```
1. Private Sub btnDisplay_Click(...) Handles btnDisplay.Click
    Dim salutation As String
    Dim sw As IO.StreamWriter = IO.File.CreateText("Greetings.txt")
    sw.WriteLine("Hello")
    sw.WriteLine("Aloha")
    sw.Close()
    Dim sr As IO.StreamReader = IO.File.OpenText("Greetings.txt")
    salutation = sr.ReadLine
    txtOutput.Text = salutation
    sr.Close()
End Sub
```

2. ```
Private Sub btnDisplay_Click(...) Handles btnDisplay.Click
    Dim salutation, welcome As String
    Dim sw As IO.StreamWriter = IO.File.CreateText("Greetings.txt")
    sw.WriteLine("Hello")
    sw.WriteLine("Aloha")
    sw.Close()
    Dim sr As IO.StreamReader = IO.File.OpenText("Greetings.txt")
    salutation = sr.ReadLine
    welcome = sr.ReadLine
    txtOutput.Text = welcome
    sr.Close()
End Sub
```

3. ```
Private Sub btnDisplay_Click(...) Handles btnDisplay.Click
    Dim salutation As String
    Dim sw As IO.StreamWriter = IO.File.CreateText("Greetings.txt")
    sw.WriteLine("Hello")
    sw.WriteLine("Bon Jour")
    sw.WriteLine("Aloha")
    sw.Close()
    Dim sr As IO.StreamReader = IO.File.OpenText("Greetings.txt")
    Do Until sr.EndOfStream
      salutation = sr.ReadLine
      txtOutput.Text = salutation
    Loop
    sr.Close()
End Sub
```

4. Assume that the contents of the file Greetings.txt are as shown in Figure 8.6.

```
Hello
Aloha
Bon Jour
```

FIGURE 8.6   Contents of the file Greetings.txt.

```
Private Sub btnDisplay_Click(...) Handles btnDisplay.Click
    Dim file, welcome As String
    file = "Greetings.txt"
    Dim sw As IO.StreamWriter = IO.File.AppendText(file)
    sw.WriteLine("Buenos Dias")
    sw.Close()
    Dim sr As IO.StreamReader = IO.File.OpenText(file)
    For i As Integer = 1 To 4
      welcome = sr.ReadLine
      txtOutput.Text = welcome
    Next
    sr.Close()
End Sub
```

5. ```
Private Sub btnDisplay_Click(...) Handles btnDisplay.Click
    Dim num As Integer
    'Assume that txtBox is empty
```
```

```vb
        Try
          num = CInt(txtBox.Text)
          txtOutput.Text = "Your number is " & num
        Catch
          txtOutput.Text = "You must enter a number."
        End Try
      End Sub
```

6.
```vb
   Private Sub btnDisplay_Click(...) Handles btnDisplay.Click
     Dim nafta() As String = {"Canada", "United States", "Mexico"}
     Try
       txtOutput.Text = "The third member of NAFTA is " & nafta(3)
     Catch exc As IndexOutOfRangeException
       txtOutput.Text = "Error occurred."
     End Try
   End Sub
```

7.
```vb
   Private Sub btnDisplay_Click(...) Handles btnDisplay.Click
     Try
       Dim usPop As Integer = 304000000    'Approx population of U.S.
       Dim worldPop As Integer
       worldPop = 21 * usPop
       txtOutput.Text = CStr(worldPop)
     Catch exc As ArgumentOutOfRangeException
       txtOutput.Text = "Oops"
     Catch exc As OverflowException
       txtOutput.Text = "Error occurred."
     End Try
   End Sub
```

8.
```vb
   Private Sub btnDisplay_Click(...) Handles btnDisplay.Click
     Dim flower As String = "Bougainvillaea", lastLetter As String
     Try
       lastLetter = flower.Substring(14, 1)
       txtOutput.Text = lastLetter
     Catch exc As InvalidCastException
       txtOutput.Text = "Oops"
     Catch exc As ArgumentOutOfRangeException
       txtOutput.Text = "Error occurred."
     End Try
   End Sub
```

9. Assume that the file Ages.txt is located in the *Debug* subfolder of the folder *bin* and the first line of the file is "Twenty-one".

```vb
   Private Sub btnDisplay_Click(...) Handles btnDisplay.Click
     Dim sr As IO.StreamReader
     Dim age As Integer
     Try
       sr = IO.File.OpenText("Ages.txt")    'FileNotFound if fails
       age = CInt(sr.ReadLine)              'InvalidCast if fails
       txtOutput.Text = "Age is " & age
     Catch exc As IO.FileNotFoundException
       txtOutput.Text = "File Ages.txt not found"
```

```
   Catch exc As InvalidCastException
      txtOutput.Text = "File Ages.txt contains an invalid age."
   Finally
      Try
         sr.Close() 'This code executes no matter what happens above
      Catch
         'Disregard any exceptions thrown during the Close() method
      End Try
   End Try
End Sub
```

10. Redo Exercise 9 with the assumption that the file Ages.txt is not located in the *Debug* sub-folder of the folder *bin*.

11. Assume that the contents of the file Greetings.txt are as shown in Figure 8.3 (on page 380). What is the effect of the following program?

```
Private Sub btnDisplay_Click(...) Handles btnDisplay.Click
   Dim g As String
   Dim sr As IO.StreamReader = IO.File.OpenText("Greetings.txt")
   Dim sw As IO.StreamWriter = IO.File.CreateText("Welcome.txt")
   Do Until sr.EndOfStream
      g = sr.ReadLine
      If (g <> "Hello") Then
         sw.WriteLine(g)
      End If
   Loop
   sr.Close()
   sw.Close()
End Sub
```

12. Assume that the file Names.txt contains a list of names in alphabetical order. What is the effect of the Mystery function?

```
Private Sub btnFind_Click(...) Handles btnFind.Click
   MessageBox.Show(CStr(Mystery("Laura")))
End Sub

Function Mystery(ByVal name As String) As Boolean
   Dim sr As IO.StreamReader = IO.File.OpenText("Names.txt")
   Dim inputName As String
   Dim missingFlag As Boolean = False
   Do Until sr.EndOfStream
      inputName = sr.ReadLine
      If inputName = name Then
         Return True
      ElseIf inputName > name Then
         Return False
      End If
   Loop
   Return False
End Function
```

In Exercises 13 through 18, identify any errors. Assume that the contents of the file Greetings.txt is as shown in Fig. 8.6.

13.
```
Private Sub btnDisplay_Click(...) Handles btnDisplay.Click
    Dim sw As IO.StreamWriter = IO.File.AppendText(Greetings.txt)
    sw.WriteLine("Guten Tag")
    sw.Close()
End Sub
```

14.
```
Private Sub btnDisplay_Click(...) Handles btnDisplay.Click
    Dim term As String
    Dim sw As IO.StreamWriter = IO.File.CreateText("Greetings.txt")
    term = sw.Readline
    txtOutput.Text = term
    sw.Close()
End Sub
```

15.
```
Private Sub btnDisplay_Click(...) Handles btnDisplay.Click
    'Copy the contents of the file Greetings.txt into the file NewGreet.txt
    Dim name, greeting As String
    Dim sr As IO.StreamReader = IO.File.OpenText("Greetings.txt")
    name = "NewGreet.txt"
    Dim sw As IO.StreamWriter = IO.File.CreateText("name")
    Do Until sr.EndOfStream
      greeting = sr.ReadLine
      sw.WriteLine(greeting)
    Loop
    sr.Close()
    sw.Close()
End Sub
```

16.
```
Private Sub btnDisplay_Click(...) Handles btnDisplay.Click
    Dim sw As IO.StreamReader = IO.File.CreateText("Greetings.txt")
    "Greetings.txt".Close()
End Sub
```

17.
```
Private Sub btnDisplay_Click(...) Handles btnDisplay.Click
    Try
      Dim age As Integer
      age = CInt(InputBox("Enter your age."))
    Catch
      MessageBox.Show("Invalid age.")
    End Try
    MessageBox.Show("You are " & age & " years old")
End Sub
```

18.
```
Private Sub btnDisplay_Click(...) Handles btnDisplay.Click
    Dim sw As IO.StreamWriter
    Try
      sw = IO.File.CreateFile("E:\Lakes.txt")
    Catch IO.IOException
      MessageBox.Show("Is there a CD in the E: drive?")
    End Try
```

```
    sw.Close()
End Sub
```

Exercises 19 through 24 are related and use the data in Table 8.2. The file created in Exercise 19 should be used in Exercises 20 through 24.

19. Write a program to create the text file Cowboy.txt containing the information in Table 8.2.

TABLE 8.2 Prices paid by cowboys for certain items in mid-1800s.	
Colt Peacemaker	12.20
Holster	2.00
Levi Strauss jeans	1.35
Saddle	40.00
Stetson	10.00

20. Suppose the price of saddles is reduced by 30%. Use the file Cowboy.txt to create a file, Cowboy3.txt, containing the new price list.

21. Write a program to add the data Winchester Rifle, 20.50 to the end of the file Cowboy.txt.

22. Suppose an order is placed for 3 Colt Peacemakers, 2 Holsters, 10 pairs of Levi Strauss jeans, 1 Saddle, and 4 Stetsons. Write a program to perform the following tasks:

(a) Create the file Order.txt to hold the numbers 3, 2, 10, 1, and 4.
(b) Use the files Cowboy.txt and Order.txt to display a sales receipt with three columns giving the quantity, name, and cost for each item ordered.
(c) Compute the total cost of the items and display it at the end of the sales receipt.

23. Write a program to request an additional item and price from the user. Then create a file called Cowboy2.txt containing all the information in the file Cowboy.txt with the additional item (and price) inserted in its proper alphabetical sequence. Run the program for both of the following data items: Boots, 20.00 and Horse, 35.00.

24. Write a program to allow additional items and prices to be input by the user and added to the end of the file Cowboy.txt. Include a method to terminate the process.

25. Write a program using a StreamReader that displays the contents of the file Cowboy.txt in a DataGridView control.

26. Visual Basic cannot delete a file that is open. Attempting to do so generates an exception. Write a short program that uses structured exception handling to handle such an exception.

In Exercises 27 through 32, write a program to carry out the task without using arrays or LINQ. Assume that the file Numbers.txt contains a list of integers.

27. Display the number of numbers in the file Numbers.txt.

28. Display the largest number in the file Numbers.txt.

29. Display the smallest number in the file Numbers.txt.

30. Display the sum of the numbers in the file Numbers.txt.

31. Display the average of the numbers in the file Numbers.txt.

32. Display the last number in the file Numbers.txt.

Solutions to Practice Problems 8.2

1. *First:*
```
Dim sr As IO.StreamReader = IO.File.OpenText("USStates.txt")
Dim temp As String = ""
```

```
         Do Until sr.EndOfStream
           temp = sr.ReadLine
         Loop
         MessageBox.Show(temp)
         sr.Close()
```

Second: `Dim states() As String = IO.File.ReadAllLines("USStates.txt")`
`MessageBox.Show(states.Last)`

Third: `Dim states() As String = IO.File.ReadAllLines("USStates.txt")`
`MessageBox.Show(states(states.Count − 1))`

2. The file ABC.txt will be present in the program's *bin\Debug* folder. However, the file will be empty. In order for the string *abc* to be placed in the file, the statement **sw.Close()** must be executed.

8.3   XML

As we have seen, CSV files are quite useful. However, the expansion of the Internet mandated a standard text file format for transmitting data. The World Wide Web Consortium recommends a format called XML (eXtensible Markup Language) to be that standard.

Consider the CSV file USStates.txt. Let's look at a text file consisting of the first two lines of USStates.txt. That is, the two lines of the new file are

```
Delaware,DE,1954,759000
Pennsylvania,PA,44817,12296000
```

We are familiar with these records and know what each field represents. However, if we showed this file to someone else, they might not know how to interpret the information. One way to present it in great detail and in an organized format would be as follows:

```
U.S. States
  state
    name: Delaware
    abbreviation: DE
    area: 1954
    population: 749000
  state
    name: Pennsylvania
    abbreviation: PA
    area: 44817
    population: 1229600
```

■ Format of XML Files

VideoNote
XML

The XML format for the state data, which has the look and feel of the presentation above, is as follows:

```
<?xml version='1.0'?>
<!-- This file contains data on two of the 50 U.S. states.-->
<us_states>
  <state>
    <name>Delaware</name>
    <abbreviation>DE</abbreviation>
    <area>1954</area>
    <population>749000</population>
  </state>
```

```
<state>
  <name>Pennsylvania</name>
  <abbreviation>PA</abbreviation>
  <area>44817</area>
  <population>1229600</population>
</state>
</us_states>
```

Comments on XML format

1. Don't be concerned about the colorization. If the file is created in the Visual Basic IDE and given the extension ".xml", Visual Basic will automatically color it.

2. The first line identifies the format of the file.

3. The second line is a comment and is treated like any Visual Basic comment. It may appear anywhere in the file, is colored green, and will be totally ignored by any program accessing the file. Comments start with `<!--` and end with `-->`.

4. A line such as `<area>1954</area>` is called an **element** and the bracketed entities are called **tags**. Specifically, `<area>` is the **start tag** for the element and `</area>` is the **end tag**. The two tags are identical except for the presence of a forward slash (/) following the less-than sign in the end tag. The word inside the brackets, in this case *area*, is called the **name of the element**. The text surrounded by the two tags, in this case 1954, is called the **content** of the element.

5. Element names are case sensitive. For instance, the tag `<Area>` is different than the tag `<area>`. Also, start and end tags must have the same case.

6. Element names should convey the meaning of the content of the element. Element names cannot start with a number or punctuation character and can contain numbers and characters. However, they cannot contain spaces and cannot start with the letters *xml*.

7. In the XML file above, the content of the elements *name*, *abbreviation*, *area*, and *population* is text. However, the content of an element can be other elements. For instance, in the XML file above,

```
<state>
  <name>Delaware</name>
  <abbreviation>DE</abbreviation>
  <area>1954</area>
  <population>749000</population>
</state>
```

is such an element. Its start tag is `<state>` and its end tag is `</state>`. The elements that constitute its content are said to be its **children**. For instance, we say that *name* is a child of *state*. We also say that *state* is a **parent** of *name*, and that *name* and *abbreviation* are **siblings**.

8. The element *us_states* is called the **root element** of the file. An XML file can have only one root element.

LINQ to XML

LINQ can be used with XML files in much the same way as with CSV files—with three differences:

1. Instead of being loaded into an array, the file is loaded into an XElement object with a statement of the form

```
Dim xmlElementName As XElement = XElement.Load(filespec)
```

2. The From clause references the elements to be considered—namely, the children of each child of the root element.

3. Instead of using the Split method to extract the value of a field, queries use an expression of the form `<childName>.Value`.

 Example 1   The file USStates.xml extends the records shown above to all 50 states. The following program uses the file to display the population densities of the states that begin with the word *North*. The states are displayed in decreasing order of their densities.

```
Private Sub btnDisplay_Click(...) Handles btnDisplay.Click
  Dim stateData As XElement= XElement.Load("USStates.xml")
  Dim query = From st In stateData.Descendants("state")
              Let name = st.<name>.Value
              Let pop = CInt(st.<population>.Value)
              Let area = CInt(st.<area>.Value)
              Let density = pop / area
              Let formattedDensity = FormatNumber(density)
              Order By density Descending
              Where name.StartsWith("North")
              Select name, formattedDensity
  dgvStates.DataSource = query.ToList
  dgvStates.CurrentCell = Nothing
  dgvStates.Columns("name").HeaderText = "State"
  dgvStates.Columns("formattedDensity").HeaderText = "Density"
End Sub
```

[Run, and click on the button.]

 Example 2   The following rewrite of Example 7 in Section 8.1 uses an XML file rather than a CSV file. The variable *stateData* is given class-level scope so that the XML file will not be reread from disk each time a new state abbreviation is entered.

```
Dim stateData As XElement = XElement.Load("USStates.xml")

Private Sub btnFind_Click(...) Handles btnFind.Click
  Dim query = From st In stateData.Descendants("state")
              Let name = st.<name>.Value
              Let abbr = st.<abbreviation>.Value
              Where abbr = mtbAbbr.Text.ToUpper
              Select name
```

```
   If query.Count = 1 Then
     txtName.Text = query.First
   Else
     Dim str As String = " is not a valid state abbreviation."
     MessageBox.Show(mtbAbbr.Text.ToUpper & str, "Error")
     mtbAbbr.Clear()
     mtbAbbr.Focus()
   End If
End Sub
```

[Run, enter a state abbreviation into the masked text box, and click on the button.]

Comments

1. The content of an element can contain any characters except for "<" and "&". These characters must be replaced with "<" and "&", respectively. For instance, the following two lines might appear in XML files:

```
<college>William &amp; Mary</college>
<inequality> x &lt; 7</inequality>
```

Practice Problems 8.3

1. Suppose the query in Example 1 is replaced by

```
Dim query = From st In stateData.Descendants("state")
            Let name = st.<name>.Value
            Let pop = st.<population>.Value
            Order By pop Descending
            Select name, pop
```

Explain why this query will not display the states in descending order of their population.

2. Consider Example 2. Suppose the last line of the query is changed to

```
Select name, abbr
```

What change would have to be made to the following line?

```
txtName.Text = query.First
```

EXERCISES 8.3

In Exercises 1 through 6, determine if the name is a proper name for an element of an XML file.

1. 7up   2. vicePresident   3. _77   4. Fred   5. xmlTitle   6. ?mark

In Exercises 7 through 10, determine if the expression is a proper element.

7. <begin>Hello</end>   8. <team>Oakland Raiders</team>

9. <city>New York<City>   10. <first name>John</first name>

11. The first two lines of the file AgeAtInaug.txt are

    ```
    George Washington,57
    John Adams,61
    ```

    where each record has two fields—name of president and his age when inaugurated. Create an XML file containing these two records.

12. The first two lines of the file Justices.txt are

    ```
    Samuel,Alito,George W. Bush,NJ,2006,0
    Henry,Baldwin,Andrew Jackson,PA,1830,1844
    ```

    where each record has six fields—first name, last name, appointing president, the state from which the justice was appointed, year appointed, and year they left the court. (For sitting judges, the last field is set to 0.) Create an XML file containing these two records.

In Exercises 13 through 20, write a program to extract and display the requested information from the file USStates.xml.

13. The total population of the United States in the year 2000.

14. The total area of the United States.

15. The population density of the United States.

16. The state (or states) with the longest name.

17. The states with area greater than 100,000 square miles. Display both the name and area of each state, with the states in decreasing order by area.

18. The states with population less than one million. Display both the name and population of each state, with the states in increasing order by population.

19. The state (or states) whose name contains the most different vowels.

20. The states whose abbreviation is different than the first two letters of their names. Display both the name and abbreviation of each state in alphabetical order by the abbreviation.

The file Colleges.xml contains data on the colleges founded before 1800. The first thirteen lines of the file are shown in Fig. 8.7. Use this file in Exercises 21 through 24.

```
<?xml version='1.0'?>
<!-- This file contains data on the earliest U.S. colleges -->
<colleges>
  <college>
    <name>Harvard U.</name>
    <state>MA</state>
    <yearFounded>1636</yearFounded>
  </college>
  <college>
    <name>William &amp; Mary</name>
    <state>VA</state>
    <yearFounded>1693</yearFounded>
  </college>
```

FIGURE 8.7   Beginning of the file Colleges.xml.

21. Write a program that displays the colleges alphabetically ordered (along with their year founded) that are in the state specified in a masked text box. See Fig. 8.8.

FIGURE 8.8 Possible outcome of Exercise 21.

FIGURE 8.9 Possible outcome of Exercise 22.

22. Write a program that provides information about a college selected from a list box by the user. The colleges should be displayed in alphabetical order. See Fig. 8.9.

23. Write a program that fills a list box with the years before 1800 in which colleges were founded. When the user selects a year, the colleges founded that year should be displayed in another list box. See Fig. 8.10.

FIGURE 8.10 Possible outcome of Exercise 23.

FIGURE 8.11 Outcome of Exercise 24.

24. Write a program that displays the colleges and their states in a DataGridView control where the colleges are ordered alphabetically by their state abbreviations and secondarily by the year they were founded. See Fig. 8.11.

25. The CSV file Senate111.txt contains a record for each member of the 111th U.S. Senate. (The 111th U.S. Senate was installed in 2009.) Each record contains three fields—name, state, and party affiliation. Some records in the files are

```
John McCain,Arizona,R
Joseph Lieberman,Connecticut,I
Kirsten Gillibrand,New York,D
```

(a) Write a program that uses the file Senate111.txt and creates an XML file containing the same information.

(b) Write a program that uses the XML file from part (a) to display the names, states, and party affiliation of all the senators in a DataGridView ordered by their state. The two senators from each state should be ordered by their first names.

26. The file Top25HR.xml contains statistics for the top 25 home-run hitters of all time in major league baseball. The first nine lines of the file are shown in Fig. 8.12.

    (a) Write a program that displays the contents of this file in a DataGridView control in descending order by the number of home runs hit.

    (b) Write a program that uses the file Top25HR.xml and creates a CSV file containing the same information.

```
<?xml version='1.0'?>
<!-- This file contains data on the all-time top 25 home -->
<!-- run hitters in major league baseball prior to 2010. -->
<home_run_hitters>
  <player>
    <name>Babe Ruth</name>
    <atBats>8399</atBats>
    <homeRuns>714</homeRuns>
  </player>
```

FIGURE 8.12   Beginning of the file Top25HR.xml.

Solutions to Practice Problems 8.3

1. The problem is with the clause

```
Let pop = st.<population>.Value
```

Since there are no arithmetic operators or numeric conversion functions in the clause, local type inference will interpret *pop* to be a string variable. When the program is run, the first state listed will be Rhode Island, whose population is 998,000. The program will run as intended only if the clause is

```
Let pop = CDbl(st.<population>.Value)
```

2. The line would have to be changed to

```
txtName.Text = query.First.name
```

8.4   A Case Study: Recording Checks and Deposits

The purpose of this section is to take you through the design and implementation of a quality program for personal checkbook management. That a user-friendly checkbook management program can be written in less than four pages of code clearly shows Visual Basic's ability to improve the productivity of programmers. It is easy to imagine an entire finance program, similar to programs that have generated millions of dollars of sales, being written in only a few weeks by using Visual Basic!

■ Design of the Program

Though many commercial programs are available for personal financial management, they include so many bells and whistles that their original purposes—keeping track of transactions and reporting balances—have become obscured. The program in this section was designed specifically as a checkbook program. It keeps track of expenditures and deposits and produces a report. The program showcases many of the techniques and tools available in Visual Basic.

The general design goals for the program include the following abilities:

- Automatically enter the user's name on each check and deposit slip.
- Automatically provide the next consecutive check or deposit slip number. (The user can override this feature if necessary.)
- Automatically provide the date. (Again, this feature can be overridden.)
- For each check, record the payee, the amount, and optionally a memo.
- For each deposit slip, record the source, the amount, and optionally a memo.
- Display the current balance at all times.
- Produce a report detailing all transactions.

▦ User Interface

With Visual Basic, we can place a replica of a check or deposit slip on the screen and let the user supply the information as if actually filling out a check or deposit slip. Figure 8.13 shows the form in its check mode. The DataGridView control at the bottom of the form will be used to display a report detailing all the transactions. The purposes of the four buttons and the text box above the DataGridView control are obvious.

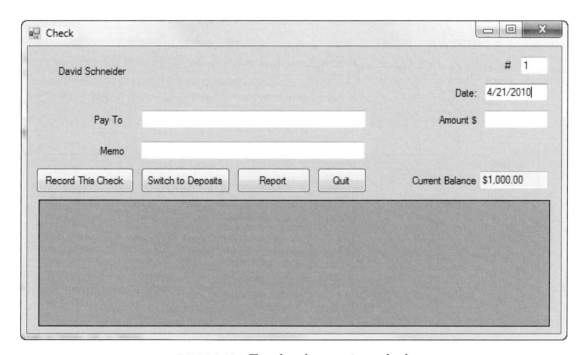

FIGURE 8.13   Template for entering a check.

The first time the program is run, the user is asked for his or her name, the starting balance, and the numbers of the first check and deposit slip. Suppose the user's name is David Schneider, the starting balance is $1000, and both the first check number and deposit slip number are 1. Figure 8.13 shows the form after the four pieces of information are entered. The upper part of the form looks like a check. The form has a color of light blue when in check mode. The Date box is automatically set to today's date but can be altered by the user. The user fills in the payee, amount, and optionally a memo. When the user clicks on the *Record This Check* button, the information is written to a text file, the balance is updated, and check number 2 appears.

To record a deposit, the user clicks on the *Switch to Deposits* button. The form then appears as in Fig. 8.14. The form's title bar now reads Deposit Slip, the words Pay To change to Source,

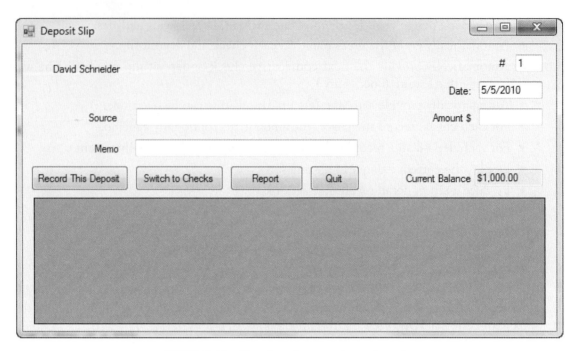

FIGURE 8.14 **Template for entering a deposit.**

and the color of the form changes to light yellow. Also, in the buttons at the bottom of the slip, the words *Check* and *Deposit* are interchanged. A deposit is recorded in much the same way as a check. When the *Report* button is clicked on, a report similar to the one in Fig. 8.15 is displayed in the DataGridView control.

Transaction Date	Description	Recipient or Source	Memo	Amount	Balance
4/21/2010	Check #1	Land's End	shirts	$75.95	$924.05
4/29/2010	Check #2	Whole Foods	groceries	$125.00	$799.05
5/5/2010	Deposit #1	Pearson	production costs	$245.00	$1,044.05
5/6/2010	Check #3	Borders	books	$79.05	$965.00
5/10/2010	Deposit #2	Staples	refund	$25.00	$990.00

FIGURE 8.15 **Sample transaction report.**

The common design for the check and deposit slip allows one set of controls to be used for both items. The text of the label lblName is set to the user's name, while the text of the label lblToFrom will change back and forth between Pay To and Source.

Table 8.3 lists the objects and their initial property settings. Because the program will always begin by displaying the next check, all the text for the labels and the BackColor property of the form could have been set at design time. We chose instead to leave these assignments to the SetupCheck method, which normally is used to switch from deposit entry to check entry but also can be called by the form's Load event procedure to prepare the initial mode (check or deposit) for the form.

The program uses CSV formatted text files named InitialInfo.txt and Transactions.txt. The file InitialInfo.txt consists of a single line containing four comma-delimited pieces of

TABLE 8.3   **Objects and initial property settings for the checkbook management program.**

Object	Property	Setting
frmAccount		
lblName		
lblNum	Text	#
txtNum		
lblDate	Text	Date:
txtDate		
lblToFrom		
txtToFrom		
lblAmount	Text	Amount $
txtAmount		
lblMemo	Text	Memo
txtMemo		
btnRecord	Text	&Record This Check
btnMode	Text	&Switch to Deposits
btnReport	Text	Re&port
btnQuit	Text	&Quit
lblCurBal	Text	Current Balance
txtBalance	ReadOnly	True
dgvTransactions	RowHeaderVisible	False

information: the name to appear on the check and deposit slips, the starting balance, the number of the first check, and the number of the first deposit slip. The file Transactions.txt contains a line for each transaction—that is, writing a check or making a deposit. Each transaction is recorded as a sequence of eight comma-delimited items: the type of transaction, the contents of txtToFrom, the current balance, the number of the last check, the number of the last deposit slip, the amount of money, the memo, and the date.

■ Coding the Program

The second row of the hierarchy chart in Fig. 8.16 identifies the different events to which the program must respond. Table 8.4 lists the corresponding event procedures and the general procedures they call.

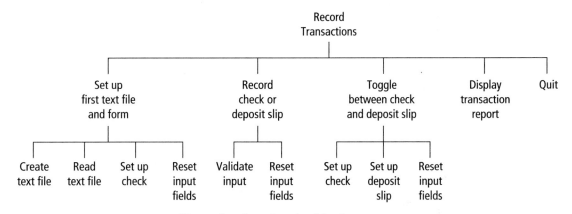

FIGURE 8.16   **Hierarchy chart for checkbook management program.**

TABLE 8.4	**Tasks and their procedures.**

Task	Procedure
1. Set up first text file and form	frmAccount_Load
1.1 Create first text file	InitializeData
1.2 Read text files	InitializeData
1.3 Set up check	SetupCheck
1.4 Reset input fields	ResetInput
2. Record check or deposit slip	btnRecord_Click
2.1 Validate input	DataValid
2.2 Reset input fields	ResetInput
3. Toggle between check & deposit slip	btnMode_Click
3.1 Set up check	SetupCheck
3.2 Set up deposit slip	SetupDeposit
3.3 Reset input fields	ResetInput
4. Display transaction report	btnReport_Click
5. Quit	btnQuit_Click

Let's examine each event procedure:

1. **frmAccount_Load** first calls the InitializeData Sub procedure to process the text file. This procedure first looks to see if the file InitialInfo.txt exists. If it does exist, the procedure uses it (along with possibly the last entry of Transactions.txt) to determine all information needed to proceed. If InitialInfo.txt does not exist, the Sub procedure prompts the user for the name to appear on the checks and deposit slips, the starting balance, and the numbers of the first check and deposit slip and then writes these items to the text file. The event procedure calls the SetupCheck Sub procedure next to set the transaction type to Check and sets the appropriate text and background color for a check. The event procedure then calls ResetInput, which initializes all the text boxes. The InitializeData Sub procedure employs structured exception handling to protect the code from invalid user input.

2. **btnRecord_Click** first confirms that the required fields contain valid entries. This is accomplished by calling the function DataValid. If the value returned is True, then btnRecord_Click updates the current balance, opens the text file in append mode, writes eight pieces of data to the file, and then closes the file. When DataValid returns False, the function itself pops up a message box to tell the user where information is needed or invalid. The user must type in the information and then click on the *Record* button again. The DataValid function uses structured exception handling to ensure that the user's input is valid. If either the amount or number field is not a number, the InvalidCastException is thrown. The Catch block handles this exception by displaying an appropriate message asking the user to reenter the information.

3. **btnMode_Click** toggles back and forth from a check to a deposit slip. It calls SetupCheck, or its analog SetupDeposit, and then calls ResetInput.

4. **btnReport_Click** displays a complete history of all transactions, as shown in Fig. 8.15.

5. **btnQuit_Click** ends the program.

```
'class-level named constants and variables
Const INIT_FILE As String = "InitialInfo.txt"
Const TRANS_FILE As String = "Transactions.txt"
'variables used for each entry
Dim isCheck As Boolean
Dim nameOnChk As String    'name to appear on checks and deposit slips
```

```
Dim lastCkNum As Integer   'number of last check written
Dim lastDpNum As Integer   'number of last deposit slip written
Dim curBal As Double       'current balance in account

Private Sub frmAccount_Load(...) Handles MyBase.Load
  'Set the class-level variables.
  InitializeData()
  'Set the name and balance labels.
  lblName.Text = nameOnChk
  txtBalance.Text = FormatCurrency(curBal)
  'Set the date field to the current date.
  txtDate.Text = CStr(Today)
  SetupCheck()
  ResetInput()
End Sub


Private Sub InitializeData()
  If IO.File.Exists(INIT_FILE) Then
    Dim data() As String   'holds the data from a line of a file
    Dim initFileContents() As String = IO.File.ReadAllLines(INIT_FILE)
    'Split the single line of INIT_FILE using the delimiter.
    data = initFileContents.First.Split(","c)
    'Load the name to appear on checks, current balance, number of
    'last check written, and number of last deposit slip processed.
    nameOnChk = data(0)
    curBal = CDbl(data(1))
    lastCkNum = CInt(data(2))
    lastDpNum = CInt(data(3))
    'Possibly update numeric values by looking at last record of TRANS_FILE
    If IO.File.Exists(TRANS_FILE) Then
      Dim transFileContents() As String = IO.File.ReadAllLines(TRANS_FILE)
      data = transFileContents.Last.Split(","c)
      curBal = CDbl(data(2))
      lastCkNum = CInt(data(3))
      lastDpNum = CInt(data(4))
    End If
  Else
    'INIT_FILE does not exist, so get initial data from user
    Dim sw As IO.StreamWriter
    nameOnChk = InputBox("Name to appear on checks and deposit slips:")
    Try
      curBal = CDbl(InputBox("Starting Balance:"))
      'get numbers of last check and deposit slip
      lastCkNum = CInt(InputBox("Number of first check:")) - 1
      lastDpNum = CInt(InputBox("Number of first deposit slip:")) - 1
      'The single record in the text file records the name to
      'appear on checks plus the initial data for the account.
      Dim outputLine As String = nameOnChk & "," & curBal & "," &
                                 lastCkNum & "," & lastDpNum
      sw = IO.File.CreateText(INIT_FILE)
      sw.WriteLine(outputLine)
    Catch
      'If a number cannot be converted, then display message and quit.
      MessageBox.Show("Invalid number. Program terminating.", "Error")
      Me.Close()
```

```vb
      Finally
        'Close the writer no matter what happens above.
        sw.Close()
      End Try
    End If
End Sub


Private Sub btnRecord_Click(...) Handles btnRecord.Click
  'Store the input into the transactions file.
  Dim amt As Double
  Dim transType As String
  'store only if all required fields are filled and valid
  If DataValid() Then
    amt = CDbl(txtAmount.Text)
    'adjust balance by amount depending on check or deposit slip mode
    If isCheck Then
      curBal = curBal — amt
      lastCkNum = CInt(txtNum.Text)
      transType = "Check"
    Else
      curBal += amt
      lastDpNum = CInt(txtNum.Text)
      transType = "Deposit"
    End If
    txtBalance.Text = FormatCurrency(curBal)
    'string array contains information to be stored
    Dim transOutput() As String = {transType, txtToFrom.Text,
      CStr(curBal), CStr(lastCkNum), CStr(lastDpNum), CStr(amt),
      txtMemo.Text, txtDate.Text}
    Dim sw As IO.StreamWriter = IO.File.AppendText(TRANS_FILE)
    'append the info to the text file, separated by the delimiter
    sw.WriteLine(Join(transOutput, ","c))
    sw.Close()
    'reset input text boxes to blank for next entry
    ResetInput()
  End If
End Sub


Function DataValid() As Boolean
  'return True if all data are valid, or display a message if not
  Dim errorMessage As String = ""
  'If one of the two essential pieces of information
  'is missing, assign its name to errorMessage.
  If txtToFrom.Text.Trim = "" Then
    If isCheck Then
      errorMessage = "Pay To"
    Else
      errorMessage = "Source"
    End If
    txtToFrom.Focus()
  ElseIf txtAmount.Text.Trim = "" Then
    errorMessage = "Amount"
    txtAmount.Focus()
  End If
  'if no errors yet, then check syntax of the two numerical fields
```

```vb
  If errorMessage = "" Then
    'check syntax of the amount field (Double)
    Try
      If CDbl(txtAmount.Text) <= 0 Then
        errorMessage = "The amount must be greater than zero."
        txtAmount.Focus()
      End If
    Catch exc As InvalidCastException
      errorMessage = "The amount " & txtAmount.Text & " is invalid."
      txtAmount.Focus()
    End Try
  Else
    errorMessage = "The '" & errorMessage & "' field must be filled."
  End If
  'display error message if available
  If errorMessage = "" Then
    'all required data fields have been filled; recording can proceed
    Return True
  Else
    'advise user of invalid data
    MessageBox.Show(errorMessage & " Please try again.")
    Return False
  End If
End Function

Private Sub btnMode_Click(...) Handles btnMode.Click
  'toggle mode between Check and Deposit Slip
  If isCheck Then
    SetupDeposit()
  Else
    SetupCheck()
  End If
  'set fields for next entry
  ResetInput()
End Sub


Sub SetupCheck()
  'prepare form for the entry of a check
  isCheck = True
  Me.Text = "Check"   'set the title bar of the form
  lblToFrom.Text = "Pay To"
  btnRecord.Text = "&Record This Check"
  btnMode.Text = "&Switch to Deposits"
  Me.BackColor = Color.LightBlue
End Sub


Sub SetupDeposit()
  'prepare form for the entry of a deposit
  isCheck = False
  Me.Text = "Deposit Slip"    'sets the title bar of the form
  lblToFrom.Text = "Source"
  btnRecord.Text = "&Record This Deposit"
  btnMode.Text = "&Switch to Checks"
  Me.BackColor = Color.LightYellow
End Sub
```

```vb
Sub ResetInput()
  'reset all text entry fields except date
  txtToFrom.Clear()
  txtAmount.Clear()
  txtMemo.Clear()
  If isCheck Then
    'make txtNum text box reflect next check number
    txtNum.Text = CStr(lastCkNum + 1)
  Else
    'make txtNum text box reflect next deposit slip number
    txtNum.Text = CStr(lastDpNum + 1)
  End If
  'set focus on To/From text box for the next entry
  txtToFrom.Focus()
End Sub

Private Sub btnReport_Click(...) Handles btnReport.Click
  If IO.File.Exists(TRANS_FILE) Then
    Dim transFileContents() As String = IO.File.ReadAllLines(TRANS_FILE)
    Dim query = From trans In transFileContents
                Let data = trans.Split(","c)
                Let transDate = CDate(data(7))
                Let number = FormNumber(data(0), data(3), data(4))
                Let toFrom = data(1)
                Let Memo = data(6)
                Let Amount = FormatCurrency(data(5))
                Let Balance = FormatCurrency(data(2))
                Select transDate, number, toFrom, Memo, Amount, Balance
    dgvTransactions.DataSource = query.ToList
    dgvTransactions.CurrentCell = Nothing
    dgvTransactions.Columns("transDate").HeaderText = "Transaction Date"
    dgvTransactions.Columns("number").HeaderText = "Description"
    dgvTransactions.Columns("toFrom").HeaderText = "Recipient or Source"
  Else
    MessageBox.Show("There are no transactions to report.")
  End If
End Sub

Function FormNumber(ByVal type As String, ByVal checkNumber As String,
                    ByVal depositNumber As String) As String
  If type = "Check" Then
    Return "Check #" & checkNumber
  Else
    Return "Deposit #" & depositNumber
  End If
End Function

Private Sub btnQuit_Click(...) Handles btnQuit.Click
  Me.Close()     'exit the program
End Sub
```

CHAPTER 8   SUMMARY

1. The *IO.File.WriteAllLines* method copies an array to a text file.

2. When data are stored in text files with the fields of each record separated by commas, LINQ can be used to sort, search, and reorganize the data with a little help from the Split method.

3. Arrays and queries can be combined with the set methods *Concat*, *Union*, *Intersect*, and *Except*.

4. When text files are opened, the program must specify whether they will be read using a *StreamReader* or written using a *StreamWriter*. Files used for input are specified with the IO.File.ReadText method. Output files can be created (IO.File.CreateText) or just added to (IO.File.AppendText). A line of data is written to a file with the WriteLine method and read from a file with the ReadLine method.

5. *Structured exception handling* can reduce the likelihood that a program will crash. If an exception occurs while the code in the Try block is executing, execution branches to the code in a Catch block that alerts the user of an error and provides a workaround. The Finally block contains code that executes regardless of whether an exception occurs.

6. *XML files* are text files of a special format that is popular for data transmitted over the Internet.

CHAPTER 8   PROGRAMMING PROJECTS

1. Data for the 2009 American League season is contained in the files ALE.txt (East division), ALC.txt (Central division), and ALW.txt (West division). Each file contains the city, number of wins, number of losses, home wins-losses, and road wins-losses. Table 8.5 shows the American League East data.

   Write a program that allows the user to select the division and the manner in which to sort the data (by percentage of games won, home record, or road record.

TABLE 8.5	American League East games won and lost in 2009.			
Team	Wins	Losses	Home Record	Road Record
Baltimore	64	98	39-42	25-56
Boston	95	67	56-25	39-42
New York	103	59	57-24	46-35
Tampa Bay	84	78	52-29	32-49
Toronto	75	87	44-37	31-50

2. The file Senate110.txt contains the members of the 110th U.S. Senate—that is, the Senate prior to the 2008 election. Each record of the file consists of three fields—name, state, and party affiliation.[2] Some records in the file are as follows:

```
Richard Selby,Alabama,R
Joseph Lieberman,Connecticut,I
Barack Obama,Illinois,D
```

---

[2] We refer to anyone who is neither a Republican nor a Democrat as Independent.

The file RetiredSen.txt contains the records from the file Senate110.txt for senators who left the Senate after the 2008 election due to retirement, defeat, death, or resignation. Some records in the file are as follows:

```
Barack Obama,Illinois,D
Hillary Clinton,New York,D
Elizabeth Dole,North Carolina,R
```

The file NewSen.txt contains records for the senators who were newly elected in 2008 or who were appointed to fill the seats of senators who left after the 2008 election. Some records in the file are as follows:

```
Mike Johanns,Nebraska,R
Kirsten Gillibrand,New York,D
Mark Warner,Virginia,D
```

(a) Write a program that uses the three files above to create the file Senate111.txt that contains records (each consisting of three fields) for the members of the 111th Senate. Use this file in parts (b), (c), and (d).

(b) Write a program that determines the number of senators of each party affiliation.

(c) Write a program that determines the number of states whose two senators have the same party affiliation. **Hint:** Use a procedure with the heading `Function SameParty(ByVal state As String) As Boolean`.

(d) Write a program that asks the user to select a state from a list box, and then displays the two senators from that state. See Fig. 8.17.

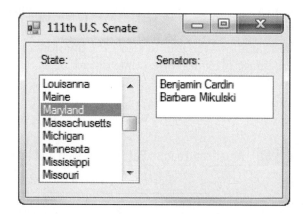

FIGURE 8.17 **Possible outcome of Programming Project 2.**

3. The file Names.txt contains a list of names in alphabetical order. Write two programs that request a name from the user and insert the name into the list in its proper location. If it is already in the list, the name should not be inserted.

(a) Write the first program without using any arrays or LINQ; that is, use only a Stream-Reader and a StreamWriter.

(b) Write the second program using arrays and LINQ.

4. *Create and Maintain Telephone Directories.* Write a program to create and maintain telephone directories. Each telephone directory should be contained in a separate text file. In addition, a file named Directories.txt should hold the names of the telephone directories. At any time, names of all the telephone directories should be displayed in a list box. After a telephone directory is selected, it becomes the *current phone directory*. The following buttons should be available.

(a) Create a new telephone directory. (The filename should be provided by an input dialog box.)

(b) Add a listing (as given in text boxes) to the end of the current phone directory.

(c) Delete a name (as given in a text box) from the current phone directory.

(d) Display the names and phone numbers in the current phone directory. See Fig. 8.18

FIGURE 8.18   Sample output of Programming Project 4.

5. Each item in a supermarket is identified by its Universal Product Code (UPC), which consists of a sequence of 12 digits appearing below a rectangle of bars. See Fig. 8.19. The bars have these digits encoded in them so that the UPC can be read by an optical scanner. Let's refer to the UPC as d_1-d_2 d_3 d_4 d_5 d_6-d_7 d_8 d_9 d_{10} d_{11}-d_{12}. The single digit on the left, d_1, identifies the type of product (for instance, 0 for general groceries, 2 for meat and produce, 3 for drug and health products, and 5 for coupons). The first set of five digits, d_2 d_3 d_4 d_5 d_6, identifies the manufacturer, and the second set of five digits, $d_6$$d_7$ d_8 d_9 d_{10} d_{11}, identifies the product. The twelfth digit on the right, d_{12}, is a check digit. It is chosen so that

$$3 \cdot d_1 + d_2 + 3 \cdot d_3 + d_4 + 3 \cdot d_5 + d_6 + 3 \cdot d_7 + d_8$$
$$+ 3 \cdot d_9 + d_{10} + 3 \cdot d_{11} + d_{12}. \tag{*}$$

is a multiple of 10. For instance, for the UPC in Figure 8.19,

$$3 \cdot 0 + 7 + 3 \cdot 0 + 7 + 3 \cdot 3 + 4 + 3 \cdot 0 + 0 + 3 \cdot 9 + 0 \cdot 0 + 3 \cdot 3 + 4 = 40.$$

VideoNote

DNA sequence data (Homework)

0   70734 00003   4

FIGURE 8.19   A Universal Product Code.

Since $40 = 4*10$, 40 is a multiple of 10. In the event that the cashier has to enter the UPC manually and mistypes a digit, the above sum will usually not add up to a multiple of 10.

Write a program to simulate an automated check-out at a supermarket. A master file, called UPC.txt, should have a record for each item in the supermarket consisting of fields for the UPC, the name of the item, and the price of the item. For instance, the file might contain the following records:

```
037000004301,Jif Peanut Butter - 22 oz,2.29
070734000034,Celestial Seasonings Sleepytime Tea,2.59
099482403645,365 Soda Root Beer,.55
```

The program should allow the cashier to enter UPCs one at a time and should place the UPCs in a separate text file. Each UPC should be validated with the sum (*) as soon as it is entered and should be reentered if the sum is not a multiple of 10. After all items have been processed, the program should calculate the subtotal, apply a tax of 7%, and then calculate the grand total. Use the two text files to display (in a list box) a receipt similar to the one in Fig. 8.20.

```
Jif Peanut Butter - 22 oz                  2.29
Celestial Seasons Sleepytime Tea           2.59
SubTotal =============================>   $4.88
Tax                                        $0.34
Total ===============================>    $5.22
```

FIGURE 8.20   Sample output of Programming Project 5.

6. The file Baseball.xml contains data about the performance of major league players in the 2009 regular season. (Only players with at least 350 at bats are included in the file.) Figure 8.21 shows the beginning of the file. Write a program using the file Baseball.xml that requests a team as input from a list and displays the players from that team whose batting average was above the average of his teammates' batting averages that are listed in the file. The players should be sorted in decreasing order by their batting averages. The output should display each player's full name and batting average. See Fig. 8.22.

```xml
<?xml version='1.0'?>
<!-- This file contains data on major league baseball players.-->
<major_league_baseball>
  <player>
    <name>Aaron Hill</name>
    <team>Blue Jays</team>
    <atBats>682</atBats>
    <hits>195</hits>
  </player>
```

FIGURE 8.21   XML file for Programming Project 6.

FIGURE 8.22   Possible outcome of Programming Project 6.

9

Additional Controls

and Objects

9.1 List Boxes and Combo Boxes

The **list box** and **combo box** controls allow the user to make selections by clicking on an item. Certain styles of combo boxes also allow for input by assisted typing.

▇ A Review of List Box Features

A list box can be populated at design time with the String Collection Editor. Items are typed directly into the editor or copied (with Ctrl + C) from another application like Excel, Word, or Notepad and pasted (with Ctrl + V) into the editor. A list box can be populated at run time with the Items.Add method or by setting its DataSource property to an array or a query (converted to a list).

The items in a list box are indexed with zero-based numbering. That is, the items in a list box are identified as lstBox.Items(0), lstBox.Items(1), and so on. Table 9.1 summarizes the properties, methods, and events for list boxes that were presented in earlier chapters.

TABLE 9.1 Previously discussed properties, methods, and events.

lstBox.Items.Add(*value*)	Method: Insert the value into the list box.
lstBox.Items.Clear()	Method: Remove all items from the list box.
lstBox.Text	Property: The selected item as a string.
lstBox.Items.Count	Property: The number of items in the list box.
lstBox.Sorted	Property: If set to True, items will be displayed in ascending ANSI order.
lstBox.SelectedIndex	Property: The index of the selected item. If no item is selected, the value is −1.
lstBox.SelectedItem	Property: The currently selected item. It must be converted to a string before being displayed in a text or message box.
lstBox.Items(*n*)	Property: The item having index *n*. It must be converted to a string before being displayed in a text or message box.
lstBox.DataSource	Property: The source of data to populate the list box.
lstBox.SelectedIndexChanged	Event: Occurs when the value of the SelectedIndex property changes. It is the default event procedure.
lstBox.Click	Event: Occurs when the user clicks on the list box.
lstBox.DoubleClick	Event: Occurs when the user double-clicks on the list box.

Note: You can programmatically change the selected (that is highlighted) item by changing the SelectedIndex value in code: the corresponding item in the list box will appear highlighted.

Example 1   The following program shows two ways to copy the contents of a list box into a text file. When the top button is clicked, the items in the list box populate an array that is then used to create a text file. When the bottom button is clicked, a StreamWriter is used to copy the contents of the list box directly into a text file. Notice that the StreamWriter does not have to convert the items in the list box to strings before copying them into the file.

OBJECT	PROPERTY	SETTING
frmGreetings	Text	Greetings
lstBox	Items	(shown in screen capture)
btnArray	Text	Save Contents of List Box Using an Array
btnSW	Text	Save Contents of List Box Using a StreamWriter

```
Private Sub btnArray_Click(...) Handles btnArray.Click
  Dim ub As Integer = lstBox.Items.Count - 1    'upper bound of array
  Dim a(ub) As String
  For i As Integer = 0 To ub
    a(i) = CStr(lstBox.Items(i))
  Next
  IO.File.WriteAllLines("Greetings1.txt", a)
End Sub

Private Sub btnSW_Click(...) Handles btnSW.Click
  Dim sw As IO.StreamWriter = IO.File.CreateText("Greetings2.txt")
  For i As Integer = 0 To lstBox.Items.Count - 1
    sw.WriteLine(lstBox.Items(i))
  Next
  sw.Close()
End Sub
```

[Run, and click on each of the two buttons. Then end the program, click on the *Refresh* button in the Solution Explorer window, click on the *View All Files* button, and look at the new text files in the *bin\Debug* subfolder. Each text file will contain the contents of the list box.]

■ Some Additional Features of List Boxes

Table 9.2 shows some additional useful methods for list boxes.

TABLE 9.2   Some additional list box methods.

lstBox.Items.IndexOf(*value*)	Method: Index of the first item to have the value.
lstBox.Items.RemoveAt(*n*)	Method: Delete item having index *n*.
lstBox.Items.Remove(*strValue*)	Method: Delete first occurrence of the string value.
lstBox.Items.Insert(*n, value*)	Method: Insert the value as the item of index *n*.

Example 2   The following program removes all duplicates from a list box. The program looks at the first item in the list box and removes every matching item that follows it. The program then repeats the process with the next item remaining in the list box, and so on.

OBJECT	PROPERTY	SETTING
frmDOW	Text	DOW
btnRemove	Text	Remove Duplicates
lstDOW	Items	(shown in screen capture)

```
Private Sub btnRemove_Click(...) Handles btnRemove.Click
  Dim i As Integer = 0, j As Integer = 0
  Do While i < (lstDOW.Items.Count — 1)
    j = i + 1
    Do While j < lstDOW.Items.Count
      If CStr(lstDOW.Items(j)) = CStr(lstDOW.Items(i)) Then
        lstDOW.Items.RemoveAt(j)
      Else
        j += 1
      End If
    Loop
    i += 1
  Loop
End Sub
```

[Run, and then click on the button.]

VideoNote

List boxes and combo boxes

■ The Combo Box Control

A combo box control can be thought of as a text box with a list box attached to it. Combo boxes have all the properties, methods, and events that list boxes have, plus a few more. The three different styles of combo box are shown in Fig. 9.1. (Each combo box's String Collection Editor was used to populate the combo box with the names of the seven continents.) The style of a combo box control is specified by setting its DropDownStyle property to Simple, Drop-Down, or DropDownList. In a Simple style combo box the list box is always visible. With the other two styles, the list box appears only at run time when the user clicks on the down-arrow button. See Fig. 9.2. The standard prefix for the name of a combo box is *cbo*.

FIGURE 9.1 The three settings for the DropDownStyle property.

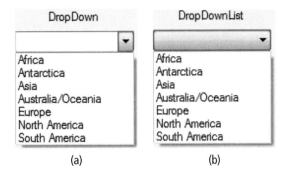

FIGURE 9.2 Combo boxes at run time after their down-arrows are clicked.

With a Simple or DropDown combo box, the user can fill the text box either by typing directly into it or by selecting an item from the list. With a DropDownList style combo box, the user can fill the text box only by selecting an item from the list. (DropDown is the default setting of a combo box's DropDownStyle property.) A list that has dropped down disappears when the user clicks on an item or presses the Enter key. With any of the three styles, the value of

`cboBox.Text`

is the contents of the text box at the top of the combo box. Just like list boxes, combo boxes can be populated with their String Collection Editor, the Items.Add method, and the DataSource property.

 Example 3 The following program uses a Simple combo box to obtain a person's title for the first line of the address of a letter.

OBJECT	PROPERTY	SETTING
frmAddress	Text	Letter Address
lblTitle	Text	Title
cboTitle	Items	(shown in screen capture)
	DropDownStyle	Simple
lblName	Text	Name:
txtName		
btnDisplay	Text	Display Full Name
txtDisplay	ReadOnly	True

```
Private Sub btnDisplay_Click(...) Handles btnDisplay.Click
  txtDisplay.Text = cboTitle.Text & " " & txtName.Text
End Sub
```

[Run, select an item from the combo box, type a name into the Name text box, and click on the button.]

The same program with a DropDown style combo box produces the form shown in Fig. 9.3. The form will look about the same when a DropDownList style combo box is used.

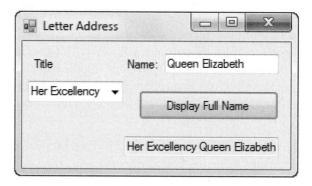

FIGURE 9.3   **Example 3 with a DropDown style combo box.**

✓ **Example 4**   The following variation of Example 3 uses the same form design and settings as Example 3 except that the combo box is not filled at design time.

```
Private Sub frmAddress_Load(...) Handles MyBase.Load
  Dim titles() As String = {"Mr.", "Ms.", "Dr.",
                            "The Honorable", "Her Excellency"}
  'Fill combo box with elements from array
  cboTitle.DataSource = titles
End Sub


Private Sub btnDisplay_Click(...) Handles btnDisplay.Click
  txtDisplay.Text = cboTitle.Text & " " & txtName.Text
End Sub
```

▨ A Helpful Feature of Combo Boxes

The file Nations.txt contains the names of the 192 members of the United Nations. Suppose a Simple style combo box has been filled with the nations in alphabetical order. Figure 9.4(a) shows the combo box when the program starts. Each time a letter is typed into the text box at the top of the combo box the list scrolls in a helpful way. For instance, after the letter *N* is typed, the combo box appears as shown in Fig. 9.4(b). The combo box has scrolled down so that the first nation beginning with the letter *N* is at the top of the list. Similarly, typing additional letters causes the list to scroll down so that the first nation beginning with the typed letters is at the top of the list. See Figs. 9.4(c) and 9.4(d). (**Notes:** When the scroll box reaches the bottom of the scroll bar, no further scrolling will take place. Also, if the typed letters do not correspond to any nation, the list will return to the state in Fig. 9.4(a). Analogous results apply to DropDown style combo boxes.)

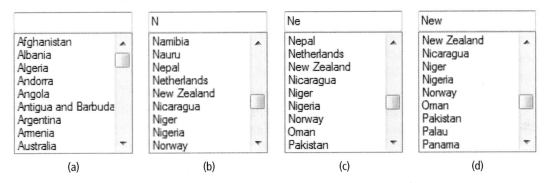

FIGURE 9.4   Successive combo box displays.

Practice Problems 9.1

1. Will the following two statements always have the same effect?

```
lstOxys.Items.RemoveAt(lstOxys.SelectedIndex)
lstOxys.Items.Remove(lstOxys.Text)
```

EXERCISES 9.1

In Exercises 1 through 8, determine the effect of the code on the list box lstBox shown below. (Assume that the Sorted property is set to True.)

1. `lstBox.Items.Remove("Bach")`

2. `lstBox.Items.RemoveAt(0)`

3. `lstBox.Items.RemoveAt(lstBox.SelectedIndex)`

4. `lstBox.Items.RemoveAt(lstBox.Items.Count − 1)`

5. `lstBox.Items.Add("Hayden")`

6.
```
Dim total As Integer = 0
For i As Integer = 0 To lstBox.Items.Count 1
  If CStr(lstBox.Items(i)).Length > 6 Then
    total += 1
  End If
Next
txtOutput.Text = CStr(total)
```

7.
```
Dim highestIndex As Integer = lstBox.Items.Count — 1
Dim composers(highestIndex) As String
For i As Integer = 0 To highestIndex
  composers(i) = CStr(lstBox.Items(i))
Next
lstBox.Items.Clear()
lstBox.Sorted = False
For i As Integer = highestIndex To 0 Step —1
  lstBox.Items.Add(composers(i))
Next
```

8.
```
Dim highestIndex As Integer = lstBox.Items.Count — 1
Dim composers(highestIndex) As String
For i As Integer = 0 To highestIndex
  composers(i) = CStr(lstBox.Items(highestIndex — i))
Next
lstBox.Sorted = False
lstBox.DataSource = composers
```

In Exercises 9 through 16, assume that cboBox has style Simple and appears as shown below, and that its Sorted property is set to True. Give a statement or statements that will carry out the stated task. (The statements should do the job even if additional items have been added to the list.)

9. Highlight the name Moliere.
10. Highlight the third item of the list.
11. Delete the name Shakespeare.
12. Delete the name Goethe.
13. Delete the last name in the list.
14. Display every other item of the list in another list box.
15. Delete every item beginning with the letter M.
16. Determine if Cervantes is in the list.
17. The file PopularNames.txt contains the 20 most popular names given to newborns in a recent year. Write a program that uses a list box to sort the names into alphabetical order and then places the alphabetized list into a new ordered text file.
18. Rework the program in Example 2 using LINQ.

19. Suppose all the items in lstBox are numbers. Write a program to display them in lstBox in increasing numerical order. *Note:* Setting `lstBox.Sorted = True` will not do the job.

20. Suppose all the items in lstBox are words. Write a program to display them in lstBox in decreasing alphabetical order.

21. Write a program that contains a list box (with Sorted = False), a label, and two buttons captioned *Add an Item* and *Delete an Item*. When the *Add an Item* button is clicked, the program should request an item with an input dialog box and then insert the item above the currently highlighted item. When the *Delete an Item* button is clicked, the program should remove the highlighted item from the list. At all times, the label should display the number of items in the list.

22. Consider the Length Converter in Fig. 9.5. Write a program to carry out the conversion. (See the first programming project in Chapter 7 for a table of equivalent lengths.)

FIGURE 9.5   **Possible output for Exercise 22.**

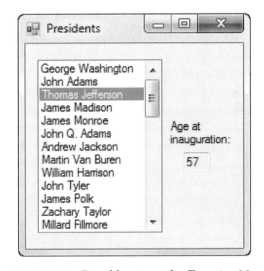

FIGURE 9.6   **Possible output for Exercise 23.**

23. The file AgesAtInauguaral.txt gives the ages at inauguration of the first 44 U.S. presidents. The first four lines of the file contain the data 57, 61, 57, 57; the ages of Washington, Adams, Jefferson, and Madison at their inaugurations. The file USPres.txt contains the names of the first 44 United States presidents in the order they were inaugurated. Write a program that places the names of the presidents into an unsorted list box and the ages at inauguration into an array. When the user clicks on the name of a president, his age at inauguration should be displayed in a text box. (**Hint:** A president's index number in the list box will be the same as the index number of his age at inauguration in the array.) See Fig. 9.6.

24. Write a program to ask a person which Monopoly® space he or she has landed on and then display the result in a text box. The response should be obtained with a combo box listing the squares most commonly landed on: Park Place, Illinois Avenue, Go, B&O Railroad, and Free Parking. (One possible outcome to be displayed in the text box is "You have landed on Park Place.")

25. Write a program to question a person about his or her computer and then display a descriptive sentence in a text box. The form should contain combo boxes for brand, amount of memory, and screen size. The lists should contain the most common responses for each category. Some common computers are Compaq, Dell, Hewlett Packard, Lenovo, and Apple. The most common amounts of memory are 1 GB, 2 GB, and 4 GB. The most common

screen sizes are 17, 19, 20, and 24 inches. (One possible outcome to be displayed in the text box is "You have a Dell computer with 2 GB of memory and a 17-inch monitor.")

Solutions to Practice Problems 9.1

1. Yes, if all the items in the list box are distinct. However, if an item is repeated and the second occurrence is selected, then the first statement will delete that item, whereas the second statement will delete the earlier occurrence of the item.

9.2 Eight Additional Controls and Objects

VideoNote

Additional controls

The Timer Control

The **timer** control, which is not visible on the form during run time, raises an event after a specified amount of time has passed. (The timer control is found only in the *All Windows Forms* group of the Toolbox. When you double-click on the timer control in the Toolbox, it appears in the **component tray**, at the bottom of the Form Designer.) The length of time, measured in milliseconds, is set with the Interval property to be any integer from 1 to 2,147,483,647 (about 596 hours). The event raised each time Timer1.Interval milliseconds elapses is called Timer1.Tick. In order to begin timing, a timer must first be turned on by setting its Enabled property to True. A timer is turned off by setting its Enabled property to False. The standard prefix for the name of a timer control is *tmr*.

 Example 1 The following program creates a stopwatch that updates the time every tenth of a second.

OBJECT	PROPERTY	SETTING
frmStopwatch	Text	Stopwatch
btnStart	Text	Start
lblSeconds	Text	Seconds:
txtSeconds	ReadOnly	True
btnStop	Text	Stop
tmrWatch	Interval	100

```
Private Sub btnStart_Click(...) Handles btnStart.Click
  txtSeconds.Text = "0"        'Reset watch
  tmrWatch.Enabled = True
End Sub

Private Sub btnStop_Click(...) Handles btnStop.Click
  tmrWatch.Enabled = False
End Sub

Private Sub tmrWatch_Tick(...) Handles tmrWatch.Tick
  'Next line displays the time rounded to one decimal place
  txtSeconds.Text = CStr((CDbl(txtSeconds.Text) + 0.1))
End Sub
```

[Run, click on the Start button, wait 10.5 seconds, and click on the Stop button.]

■ The Random Class

Visual Basic has a useful object called a random number generator that is declared with a statement of the form

```
Dim randomNum As New Random
```

If *m* and *n* are whole numbers, with *m* < *n*, then the value of

```
randomNum.Next(m, n)
```

is a randomly selected whole number from *m* through *n*, including *m* but excluding *n*. The Next method of this built-in object allows us to produce some interesting applications.

 Example 2   A lottery number is obtained by selecting a Ping-Pong ball from each of three separate bowls. Each ball is numbered with an integer from 1 through 9. The following program produces a lottery number. Such a program is said to **simulate** the selection of Ping-Pong balls.

```
Private Sub btnSelect_Click(...) Handles btnSelect.Click
  'Display the winning lottery number
  Dim randomNum As New Random
  Dim num1, num2, num3 As Integer
  num1 = randomNum.Next(1, 10)
  num2 = randomNum.Next(1, 10)
  num3 = randomNum.Next(1, 10)
  txtNumbers.Text = num1 & "   " & num2 & "   " & num3
End Sub
```

[Run, and then click on the button.]

■ The ToolTip Control

The Visual Basic IDE uses tooltips to identify buttons on the Toolbar and icons in the Toolbox. When we hover the mouse over one of these items, a small rectangular box appears after $\frac{1}{2}$ second and remains visible for 5 seconds. The ToolTip control allows us to create tooltips for the controls in our programs.

A *ToolTip Walkthrough*

1. Start a new program. (There is no need to give a name to the program.)
2. Double-click on the ToolTip control in the Toolbox. (The control will appear with the default name ToolTip1 in the component tray at the bottom of the Form Designer.)
3. Place controls on the form and enter code as shown in Example 3. (The setting for the "ToolTip on ToolTip1" property of txtRate holds the information that will appear when the mouse hovers over the text box.)

 Example 3   In the following program, suppose the sales tax rate is 5%. The user might not know whether to enter 5 or .05 into the text box. A tooltip comes to the rescue.

OBJECT	PROPERTY	SETTING
frmName	Text	Sales Tax
lblRate	Text	Sales tax rate:
txtRate	ToolTip on Tooltip1	Such as 5, 5.25, 5.5 ….
lblPrice	Text	Price:
txtPrice		
btnCalculate	Text	Calculate Total Cost
lblTotalCost	Text	Total cost:
txtTotalCost	ReadOnly	True

```
Private Sub btnCalculate_Click(...) Handles btnCalculate.Click
  Dim taxRate As Double = CDbl(txtRate.Text) / 100
  Dim price As Double = CDbl(txtPrice.Text)
  Dim totalCost As Double = price + taxRate * price
  txtTotalCost.Text = FormatCurrency(totalCost)
End Sub
```

[Run, and hover the mouse over the first text box.]

Normally, a control placed on a form does not have a "ToolTip on ToolTip1" property. That property appears in the Properties window only after a ToolTip control has been added to the component tray.

In the example above, we created a tooltip for only one of the text boxes. However, we could have specified a tooltip for the other controls.

By default, a tooltip appears $\frac{1}{2}$ second after the cursor hovers over a control and lasts for 5 seconds. These two durations can be altered with the Tooltip control's AutomaticDelay and AutoPopDelay properties. The numeric settings for these two properties are in milliseconds. Specifically, the AutomaticDelay setting determines the length of time required for a tooltip to appear, and the AutoPopDelay setting determines the length of time the tooltip remains visible while the cursor is stationary inside a control.

The Clipboard

The **Clipboard** object is used to copy or move information from one location to another. It is maintained by Windows and therefore even can be used to transfer information from one Windows application to another. It is actually a portion of memory that holds information and has no properties or events.

If *str* is a string, then the statement

```
Clipboard.SetText(str)
```

replaces any text currently in the Clipboard with the value of *str*. The statement

```
str = Clipboard.GetText
```

assigns the text in the Clipboard to the string variable *str*. The statement

```
Clipboard.SetText("")
```

deletes the contents of the Clipboard.

A portion of the text in a text box or combo box can be **selected** by dragging the mouse across it or by moving the cursor across it while holding down the Shift key. After you select text, you can place it into the Clipboard by pressing Ctrl + C. Also, if the cursor is in a text box and you press Ctrl + V, the contents of the Clipboard will be pasted at the cursor position. These tasks also can be carried out in code. The SelectedText property of a text box holds the selected string from the text box, and a statement such as

```
Clipboard.SetText(txtBox.SelectedText)
```

copies this selected string into the Clipboard. The statement

```
txtBox.SelectedText = Clipboard.GetText
```

replaces the selected portion of txtBox with the contents of the Clipboard. If nothing has been selected, the statement inserts the contents of the Clipboard into txtBox at the cursor position.

The Picture Box Control

The **picture box** control is designed to hold drawings created with graphics commands or pictures stored in graphics files such as bmp files created with Windows Paint, ico files of icons that come with Windows, or gif and jpeg images used on the World Wide Web. By convention, names of picture box controls have the prefix *pic*.

A statement of the form

```
picBox.CreateGraphics.DrawRectangle(Pens.Blue, x, y, w, h)
```

where x, y, w, h are of type Integer, draws a blue rectangle of width w pixels and height h pixels in the picture box. The upper-left corner of the rectangle will be x pixels from the left side and y pixels from the top side of the picture box. (See Fig. 9.7.) To get a feel for how big a pixel is, the initial size of the form when you create a new project is 300 pixels by 300 pixels.

FIGURE 9.7 **Rectangle arguments.**

FIGURE 9.8 **Ellipse arguments.**

The color Blue can be replaced by other colors. If DrawRectangle is replaced with DrawEllipse, the statement above will draw the ellipse that would be inscribed in the rectangle just described. See Fig. 9.8. Also, if w and h have the same value, the ellipse will be a circle with a diameter of that value. In Fig. 9.9, the picture box has a size of 140 by 140 pixels, a white background, and a FixedSingle border style. The circle is drawn with the statement

```
picBox.CreateGraphics.DrawEllipse(Pens.Red, 35, 35, 70, 70)
```

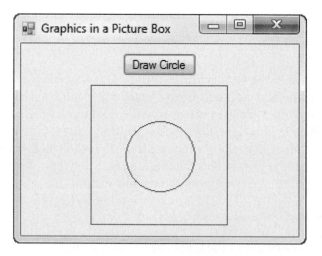

FIGURE 9.9 **Picture box containing red circle.**

A picture can be placed in a picture box control with the Image property. If you double-click on the Image property during design time, an Open dialog box appears and assists you in selecting an appropriate file. However, prior to setting the Image property, you should set the SizeMode property. If the SizeMode property is set to AutoSize, the picture box control will be resized to fit the picture. If the SizeMode property is set to StretchImage, the picture will be resized to fit the picture box control. Therefore, with the StretchImage setting, pictures can be reduced (by placing them into a small picture box control) or enlarged (by placing them into a picture box control bigger than the picture). Figure 9.10 shows a picture created with Paint and reduced by StretchImage to fit the picture box.

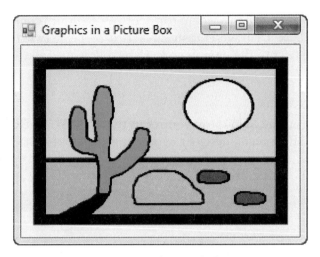

FIGURE 9.10   **Picture box with desert scene.**

A picture also can be assigned to a picture box control at run time. However, a statement such as

```
picBox.Image = filespec
```

will not do the job. Instead, we must create an Image object with a statement such as

```
picBox.Image = Image.FromFile(filespec)
```

The SizeMode property can be altered at run time with a statement such as

```
picBox.SizeMode = PictureBoxSizeMode.AutoSize
```

■ The MenuStrip Control

Visual Basic forms can have menu bars similar to those in most Windows applications. Figure 9.11 shows a typical menu bar, with the *Order* menu revealed. Here, the menu bar contains two menu items (*Order* and *Color*), referred to as **top-level** menu items. When the *Order* menu item is clicked, a drop-down list containing two second-level menu items (*Ascending* and *Descending*) appears. Although not visible here, the drop-down list under *Color* contains the two second-level menu items *Foreground* and *Background*. Each menu item is treated as a distinct control that responds to a Click event. The Click event is raised not only by the click of the mouse button, but also for top-level items by pressing Alt + *accessKey* and for second-level items by just pressing the access key. The event procedure for the *Ascending* or *Descending* menu item also can be raised by pressing the shortcut key combination Ctrl + A or Ctrl + D.

FIGURE 9.11   **A simple menu.**

Menus are created with the MenuStrip control—the third control in the *Menus & Toolbars* group of the Toolbox. Each menu item has a Text property (what the user sees) and a Name property (used to refer to the item in code.) The following walkthrough creates the menu bar in Fig. 9.11:

1. Start a new program.

2. Double-click on the MenuStrip control in the Toolbox. The control appears in the component tray, and a menu designer appears just below the title bar in the Form Designer. See Fig. 9.12.

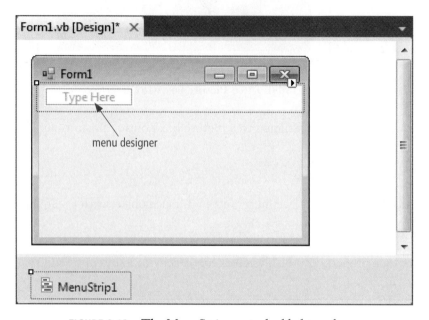

FIGURE 9.12 **The MenuStrip control added to a form.**

3. Click on the rectangle that says "Type Here", type in "&Order", and press the Enter key. (The ampersand specifies O as an access key for the menu item.) "Type Here" rectangles appear below and to the right of the *Order* menu item. The rectangle below the *Order* menu item is used to create a second-level item for the *Order* menu. The rectangle on the right is used to create a new first-level menu item.

4. Type "&Ascending" into the rectangle below the *Order* rectangle, and press the Enter key.

5. Click on the *Ascending* menu item to display its Property window. In the Property window, change the Name property of the menu item from AscendingToolStripMenuItem to mnuOrderAsc. Also, click on the down-arrow at the right of the ShortcutKeys Settings box, click on the *Ctrl* check box under Modifiers, click on the down-arrow button of the Key combo box, click on A in the drop-down list, and press the Enter key. ("Ctrl + A" will appear to the right of the word *Ascending*.)

6. Type "&Descending" into the rectangle below the *Ascending* rectangle, set the Name property of the *Descending* menu item to mnuOrderDesc, and set the ShortcutKeys Property to Ctrl + D.

7. Click on the rectangle to the right of the *Order* rectangle and enter the text "&Color".

8. Type "&Foreground" into the rectangle below the *Color* rectangle, and set its Name property to mnuColorFore.

9. Type "&Background" into the rectangle below the *Foreground* rectangle, and set its Name property to mnuColorBack.

10. Click on the *Foreground* rectangle, and type "&Red" into the rectangle on its right. (We have just created a third-level menu item.) Set its Name property to mnuColorForeRed.

11. Type "&Blue" into the rectangle below the *Red* rectangle, and set its Name property to mnuColorForeBlue.

12. Click on the *Background* rectangle, type "&Yellow" into the rectangle on its right, and set its Name property to mnuColorBackYellow.

13. Type "&White" into the rectangle below the *Yellow* rectangle, and set its Name property to mnuColorBackWhite. Then set its Checked property to True. A check mark will appear to the left of the word "White".

14. Run the program; click on *Order* to see its menu items; click on *Color* and hover over the word *Foreground* to see its menu items. The menu items are useful only after we write code for their Click event procedures.

Example 4   The following program uses the menu just created to alter the color of the text in a list box and the order of its items. The form has the text "Demonstrate Menus" in its title bar.

```
Private Sub frmDemo_Load(...) Handles MyBase.Load
  lstOutput.Items.Add("makes")
  lstOutput.Items.Add("haste")
  lstOutput.Items.Add("waste")
End Sub

Private Sub mnuOrderAsc_Click(...) Handles mnuOrderAsc.Click
  lstOutput.Sorted = True
End Sub

Private Sub mnuOrderDesc_Click(...) Handles mnuOrderDesc.Click
  'This code uses the fact that if a list is in ascending order,
  'then displaying it backwards gives a descending list
  Dim temp(2) As String     'Hold ascending array of items
  lstOutput.Sorted = True   'Sort the items alphabetically
  For i As Integer = 0 To 2 'Place sorted items into the array
    temp(i) = CStr(lstOutput.Items(i))
  Next
  lstOutput.Sorted = False 'Turn off the Sorted property
  lstOutput.Items.Clear()
  For i As Integer = 2 To 0 Step -1
    lstOutput.Items.Add(temp(i))
  Next
End Sub

Private Sub mnuColorForeRed_Click(...) Handles mnuColorForeRed.Click
  lstOutput.ForeColor = Color.Red
End Sub

Private Sub mnuColorForeBlue_Click(...) Handles mnuColorForeBlue.Click
  lstOutput.ForeColor = Color.Blue
End Sub

Private Sub mnuColorBackYellow_Click(...) Handles _
          mnuColorBackYellow.Click
  'Make Yellow the background color of the list box, guarantee that a
```

```
      'check mark appears in front of the menu item Yellow and not in front
      'of the White menu item
    lstOutput.BackColor = Color.Yellow
    mnuColorBackYellow.Checked = True
    mnuColorBackWhite.Checked = False
End Sub


Private Sub mnuColorBackWhite_Click(...) Handles mnuColorBackWhite.Click
    lstOutput.BackColor = Color.White
    mnuColorBackYellow.Checked = False
    mnuColorBackWhite.Checked = True
End Sub
```

[Run, click on *Ascending* in the *Order* menu, click on the *Color* menu, hover over *Foreground*, and click on *Red.*]

▦ The Horizontal and Vertical Scroll Bar Controls

Figure 9.13 shows the two types of **scroll bars**. When the user clicks on one of the arrow buttons, the scroll box moves a small distance toward that arrow. When the user clicks between the scroll box and one of the arrow buttons, the scroll box moves a large distance toward that

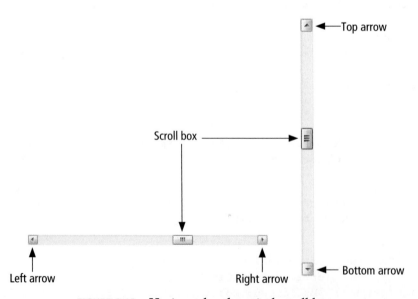

FIGURE 9.13 **Horizontal and vertical scroll bars.**

arrow. The user can also move the scroll box by dragging it. The main properties of a scroll bar control are Minimum, Maximum, Value, SmallChange, and LargeChange, which are set to integers. The standard prefix for the name of a scroll bar is *hsb* or *vsb*. At any time, hsbBar.Value is a number between hsbBar.Minimum and hsbBar.Maximum determined by the position of the left side of the scroll box. If the left side of the scroll box is halfway between the two arrows, then hsbBar.Value is a number halfway between hsbBar.Minimum and hsbBar.Maximum. If the scroll box is near the left arrow button, then hsbBar.Value is an appropriately proportioned value near hsbBar.Minimum. When the user clicks on an arrow button, hsbBar.Value changes by hsbBar.SmallChange and the scroll box moves accordingly. When the bar between the scroll box and one of the arrows is clicked, hsbBar.Value changes by hsbBar.LargeChange and the scroll box moves accordingly. When the scroll box is dragged, hsbBar.Value changes accordingly. The default values of Minimum, Maximum, Value, SmallChange, and LargeChange are 0, 100, 0, 1, and 10, respectively. However, these values are usually changed at design time. The width of the scroll box is equal to the value of LargeChange. Since hsbBar.Value is determined by the left side of the scroll box, the greatest value it can assume is (hsbBar.Maximum − hsbBar.LargeChange + 1). Vertical scroll bars behave similarly.

Note: The setting for the Minimum property must be less than the setting for the Maximum property. The Minimum property determines the values for the left and top arrows. The Maximum property determines the values for the right and bottom arrows.

The two controls are referred to as HScrollBar and VScrollBar in the Toolbox. Their default event, Scroll, is raised whenever the user clicks on any part of the scroll bar.

 Example 5   The following program uses scroll bars to move a smiling face around the form. The face is a large Wingdings character J inside a label. The values lblFace.Left and lblFace.Top are the distances in pixels of the label from the left side and top of the form.

OBJECT	PROPERTY	SETTING
frmFace	Text	Smiling Face
hsbXPos	Minimum	0
	Maximum	300
	SmallChange	10
	LargeChange	50
	Value	0
vsbYPos	Minimum	30
	Maximum	300
	SmallChange	10
	LargeChange	50
	Value	30
lblFace	Text	J
	Font	Wingdings, 24pt

```
Private Sub hsbXpos_Scroll(...) Handles hsbXpos.Scroll
    lblFace.Left = hsbXpos.Value
End Sub

Private Sub vsbYpos_Scroll(...) Handles vsbYpos.Scroll
    lblFace.Top = vsbYpos.Value
End Sub
```

[Run, and move the scroll boxes on the scroll bars.]

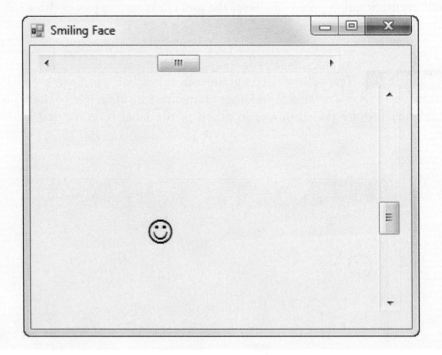

Practice Problems 9.2

1. What is the effect of the following event procedure?

```
Private Sub btnDisplay_Click(...) Handles btnDisplay.Click
    Dim randomNum As New Random
    Dim contestant() As String = {"Mary", "Pat", "Linda",
                                  "Barbara", "Maria"}
```

```
      Dim number As Integer, temp As String
      For i As Integer = 0 To 3
        number = randomNum.Next(i, 5)
        temp = contestant(i)
        contestant(i) = contestant(number)
        contestant(number) = temp
      Next
      lstOutput.Items.Clear()
      For i As Integer = 0 To 4
        lstOutput.Items.Add(contestant(i))
      Next
  End Sub
```

EXERCISES 9.2

In Exercises 1 through 6, determine the effect of setting the property to the value shown.

1. Timer1.Interval = 5000
2. Timer1.Enabled = False
3. ToolTip1.AutomaticDelay = 1000
4. ToolTip1.AutoPopDelay = 4000
5. mnuOrderAsc.Checked = True
6. mnuOrderAsc.Checked = False

In Exercises 7 through 25, describe the effect of executing the statement(s).

7. ```
Timer1.Interval = CInt(intVar * 1000)
```

8. ```
Dim randomNum As New Random
txtBox.Text = CStr(randomNum.Next(1, 100))
```

9. ```
Dim randomNum As New Random
Dim number As Integer
'Assume the array pres() contains the names of the 44 U.S. presidents
number = randomNum.Next(0, 44)
txtBox.Text = pres(number)
```

10. ```
Dim randomNum As New Random
'95 characters can be produced by the computer keyboard
txtBox.Text = Chr(randomNum.Next(32, 127))
```

11. ```
Dim randomNum As New Random
Dim number As Integer, temp As String
'Suppose the array states() contains the names of the 50 states
number = randomNum.Next(0, 50)
lstBox.Items.Add(states(number))
temp = states(number)
states(number) = states(49)
states(49) = temp
lstBox.Items.Add(states(randomNum.Next(0, 49)))
```
```

12.
```
Dim randomNum As New Random
Dim suit() As String = {"Hearts", "Clubs", "Diamonds", "Spades"}
Dim denomination() As String = {"2", "3", "4", "5", "6",
        "7", "8", "9", "10", "Jack", "Queen", "King", "Ace"}
txtBox.Text = denomination(randomNum.Next(0, 13)) & " of " &
                suit(randomNum.Next(0, 4))
```

13.
```
Clipboard.SetText("")
```

14.
```
Clipboard.SetText("Hello")
```

15.
```
Clipboard.SetText(txtBox.Text)
```

16.
```
txtBox.SelectedText = Clipboard.GetText()
```

17.
```
txtBox.Text = Clipboard.GetText
```

18.
```
Dim strVar As String = "Happy"
Clipboard.SetText(strVar)
```

19.
```
Dim strVar As String
strVar = Clipboard.GetText
```

20.
```
PictureBox1.SizeMode = PictureBoxSizeMode.StretchImage
```

21.
```
PictureBox1.CreateGraphics.DrawEllipse(Pens.Blue, 20, 30, 100, 100)
```

22.
```
PictureBox1.CreateGraphics.DrawRectangle(Pens.Green, 25, 50, 200, 100)
```

23.
```
PictureBox1.Image = Image.FromFile("Airplane.bmp")
```

24.
```
HScrollBar2.Value = CInt((HScrollBar2.Maximum + HScrollBar2.Minimum) / 2)
```

25.
```
VScrollBar2.SmallChange = VScrollBar2.LargeChange
```

In Exercises 26 through 44, write one or more lines of code to carry out the task.

26. Specify that Timer1 raise an event every half second.

27. Specify that Timer1 cease to raise the Tick event.

28. The array *names* contain thirty names. Display a randomly selected name in txtBox.

29. Display in txtBox a randomly selected number from 1 to 12.

30. Display in txtBox a letter randomly selected from the alphabet.

31. The file Towns.txt contains the names of twenty-five cities. Display a randomly selected city in txtBox.

32. Display in txtBox the sum of the faces after tossing a pair of dice.

33. Suppose the array *rivers* contains the names of rivers. Randomly select two different rivers from the array and display them in lstBox.

34. Replace the selected portion of txtBox with the contents of the Clipboard.

35. Clear the contents of the Clipboard.

36. Place the word "Hyacinth" into the Clipboard.

37. Copy the selected text in txtBox into the Clipboard.

38. Delete the selected portion of txtBox.

39. Assign the contents of the Clipboard to the integer variable *amount*.

40. Draw a yellow circle of diameter 100 pixels in PictureBox1.

41. Remove the check mark in front of the menu item named mnuOrderDesc.

42. Change the text for mnuOrderDesc to "Sort in Decreasing Order".

43. Move the scroll box of VScrollBar2 as high as possible.

44. Move the scroll box of HScrollBar2 one-third of the way from the left arrow to the right arrow.

Exercises 45 and 46 refer to Example 4.

45. Make a conjecture on the effect of the following statement and test your conjecture.

```
mnuOrderAsc.Enabled = False
```

46. Make a conjecture on the effect of the following statement and test your conjecture.

```
mnuOrderAsc.Visible = False
```

47. Write a program to create a decorative digital clock. The clock in the Digital Clock form in Fig. 9.14 is inserted in a picture box control containing the Trees.bmp picture. The values for hour, minute, and second can be obtained as Hour(Now), Minute(Now), and Second(Now).

FIGURE 9.14   Sample run of Exercise 47.

FIGURE 9.15   Sample run of Exercise 48.

48. Write a program using the form in Fig. 9.15. Each time the button is pressed, a Random object is used to simulate a coin toss and the values are updated. The figure shows the status after the button has been pressed 607 times. **Note:** You can produce tosses quickly by just holding down the Enter key. Although the percentage of heads initially will fluctuate considerably, it should stay close to 50% after many (say, 1000) tosses.

49. The file Members.txt contains the names of the members of a large club. Write a program to randomly select people to serve as President, Treasurer, and Secretary. **Note:** A person cannot hold more than one office.

50. Place the names of the 52 playing cards into the array *deckOfCards*. Then display the names of five randomly chosen cards in lstPokerHand.

51. Write a program that repeatedly rolls a pair of dice and tallies the number of rolls and the number of those rolls that total seven. The program should stop when 1000 sevens have been rolled, and then report the approximate odds of rolling a seven. (The approximate odds will be "1 in " followed by the result of dividing the number of rolls by the number of rolls that came up seven.)

52. Write a program to randomly select 40 different people from a group of 100 people whose names are contained in the text file Names.txt.

53. *The Birthday Problem.* Given a random group of 23 people, how likely is it that two people have the same birthday? To answer this question, write a program that creates an array of 23 elements, randomly assigns to each subscripted variable one of the integers from 1 through 365, and checks to see if any of the subscripted variables have the same value. (Make the simplifying assumption that no birthdays occur on February 29.) Now expand the program to repeat the process 1000 times and determine the percentage of the time that there is a match.

54. Consider a carnival game in which two cards are drawn at random from a deck of 52 cards. If either one or both of the cards is a diamond, you win one dollar. If neither card is a diamond, you lose one dollar. Simulate playing the game 1000 times and determine how much money you win or lose.

55. Write a program containing text boxes named txtName and txtAge. The tooltip "Enter your full name." or "Enter your age." should appear when the mouse hovers over the corresponding text box.

56. Write a program containing a list box. The tooltip "Double-click on an item to delete it from the list." should appear when the mouse hovers over the list box.

57. Write a program to display a picture (contained in a .bmp file on the hard drive) in a picture box. The .bmp file should be selected with an OpenFileDialog control.

58. Write a program with a single text box and a menu having the single top-level item *Edit* and the three second-level items *Copy*, *Paste*, and *Cut*. *Copy* should place a copy of the selected portion of the text box into the Clipboard, *Paste* should duplicate the contents of the Clipboard at the cursor position, and *Cut* should delete a selected portion of the text box and place it in the Clipboard.

59. The Ch09\Pictures folder contains files named Moon1.bmp, Moon2.bmp, ..., Moon8.bmp, which show eight phases of the moon. Create a form consisting of a picture box control and a timer control. Every two seconds assign another file to the Image property of the picture box control to see the moon cycle through its phases every 16 seconds. One phase is shown in Fig. 9.16.

FIGURE 9.16   Sample run of Exercise 59.

FIGURE 9.17   Sample run of Exercise 60.

60. Write a program to synchronize the two thermometers shown in the Temperatures form in Fig. 9.17. When the scroll box of either thermometer is moved, the other thermometer should move to the corresponding temperature, and the two temperatures displayed above the thermometers should be updated. **Note**: F = (9/5)C + 32.

61. *Simulation of the Times Square Ball.* Create a form with a vertical scroll bar and a timer control. When the program is run, the scroll box should be at the top of the scroll bar. Each second the scroll box should descend one-tenth of the way down. When the scroll box reaches the bottom after 10 seconds, a message box displaying HAPPY NEW YEAR should appear.

Solution to Practice Problem 9.2

1. The event procedure places the names of the contestants in a list box in a random order.

9.3   Multiple-Form Programs

A Visual Basic program can contain more than one form. Additional forms are added from the menu bar's *Project* menu by clicking on *Add Windows Form*, which brings up an Add New Item dialog box with "Windows Form" highlighted. To add the new form, optionally type in a name and press the *Add* button. The new form has a default name such as Form1 or Form2. The name of each form in the program appears in the Solution Explorer window. See Fig. 9.18. When you double-click on the name of a form, its Form Designer appears in the Document window. In practice, forms are given descriptive names. However, we will initially use the default names.

VideoNote

Multiple-form programs

FIGURE 9.18   **Solution Explorer window after a second form is added.**

The most common use of an additional form is as a customized input dialog box (Fig. 9.19) or a customized message dialog box (Fig. 9.20). The form in Fig. 9.19 could appear to limit access to the rest of the program only to a user who enters a registered user name and password. In Fig. 9.20 the output of the Weekly Payroll case study from Chapter 5 is displayed in a second form instead of in a list box.

FIGURE 9.19   **Customized input dialog box.**   **FIGURE 9.20**   **Customized message dialog box.**

■ Startup Form

When a program starts running, only one form (called the **startup form**) will be loaded. By default, the first form created is the startup form. The following steps change the startup form.

1. Right-click on the name of the program at the top of the Solution Explorer window and click on *Properties* in the drop-down context menu. The program's Project Designer will appear.

2. Click the Application tab.

3. Select a form from the *Startup form* drop-down list.

4. Close the Project Designer by clicking the ✕ symbol on its tab.

▩ Scope of Variables, Constants, and Procedures

We have considered block-level, procedure-level (or local-level), and class-level (or module-level) scope. A variable or constant declared inside a block (such as a Do loop or If block) can no longer be referred to when execution passes out of the block. If you declare a variable or constant inside a procedure but outside any block within that procedure, you can think of the variable as having block-level scope, where the block is the entire procedure. You declare a class-level variable or constant for a form by placing its Dim or Const statement outside of any procedure. Class-level variables or constants can be referred to anywhere in the form's code.

If a program has more than one form, then you can extend the scope of a class-level variable to all the forms in the program by using the keyword Public in place of the keyword Dim in its declaration statement. The variable is then said to have **namespace-level scope**. Let's refer to the form in which the variable is declared as its *declaration form*. When such a variable is referred to in the code of another form, the declaration form's name (followed by a period) must precede the name of the variable. For instance, the variable *total* declared as a class- level variable in Form1 with the statement

```
Public total as Double
```

must be referred to as *Form1 .total* when used in Form2.

The scope of a class-level constant is converted to namespace-level by preceding the keyword Const with the keyword Public. A general procedure and a Structure declaration have namespace-level scope by default. Preceding their header with the keyword Private will limit their access to their declaration form. Controls always have namespace-level scope. Just as with variables, the names of namespace-level constants, general procedures, and controls must be preceded by their declaration form's name (followed by a period) when referred to in another form's code.

▩ Modality

A form can invoke another form as a modal or modeless form. A **modal** form must be closed before the user can continue working with the rest of the program. (Ordinary input and message dialog boxes are examples of modal forms.) With a **modeless** (or **nonmodal**) form, the user can shift the focus between the form and another form without having to first close the initial form. (Visual Basic's *Find* dialog box is an example of a modeless form.) In this book, new forms will always be invoked as modal forms.

▩ Close and ShowDialog Methods

The statement `Me.Close()` closes the form whose code contains it. The Close method actually can be used to close any form in the program. The statement

```
frmOther.Close()
```

where *frmOther* is a form other than the form containing the statement, closes frmOther.

The statement

```
frmOther.ShowDialog()
```

displays the other form as a modal form and gives it the focus. (The statement `frmOther.Show()` displays the other form as a modeless form.)

The FormClosing Event Procedure

The Load event procedure occurs before a form is displayed for the first time or before it is displayed after having been closed. Analogous to the Load event is the FormClosing event that occurs before the form is closed. (A form is closed by the execution of a Close method, by the user's clicking on the form's Close button in the title bar, or by the user's pressing Alt + F4.)

Importing an Existing Form

You can add a form created in another program to the current program with the following steps:

1. Click on *Add Existing Item* in the menu bar's *Project* menu.
2. Navigate to the program containing the form. The program will contain a file named *formName*.vb.
3. Double-click on *formName*.vb. That file will be copied into your program's Solution Explorer and you will have added its form to your program. **Note:** If the added form refers to a text file, the text file will have to be copied separately into your program's *bin\Debug* folder.

Deleting a Form from a Program

To remove a form from a program, right-click on its name in the Solution Explorer, and click on *Delete* in the drop-down context menu. (An input dialog box will ask you to confirm the deletion.) If the deleted form was the startup form, you will have to select a new startup form.

 Example 1 The following program uses a second form as a dialog box to obtain and total the different sources of income. Initially, only frmIncome is visible. The user types in his or her name and then can either type in the total income or click on the button for assistance in totaling the different sources of income. Clicking on the button from frmIncome causes frmSources to appear and be active. The user fills in the three text boxes and then clicks on the button to have the amounts totaled and displayed in the "Total income" text box of frmIncome.

OBJECT	PROPERTY	SETTING
frmIncome	Text	Income
lblName	Text	Name:
txtName		
lblTotIncome	Text	Total income:
txtTotIncome		
btnDetermine	Text	Determine Total Income

OBJECT	PROPERTY	SETTING
frmSources	Text	Sources of Income
lblName	Text	Name:
txtName	ReadOnly	True
lblWages	Text	Wages:
txtWages		
lblIntIncome	Text	Interest income:
txtIntIncome		
lblDivIncome	Text	Dividend income:
txtDivIncome		
btnCompute	Text	Compute Total Income

```
'frmIncome's code     (startup form)

Private Sub btnDetermine_Click(...) Handles btnDetermine.Click
  frmSources.txtName.Text = txtName.Text
  frmSources.ShowDialog()       'Show the second form and wait until it closes.
  '                              Then execute the rest of the code in this procedure.
  txtTotIncome.Text = FormatCurrency(frmSources.sum)
End Sub


'frmSources's code

Public sum As Double      'holds the sum of the text boxes' values

Private Sub frmSources_Load(...) Handles MyBase.Load
  txtWages.Clear()
  txtIntIncome.Clear()
  txtDivIncome.Clear()
End Sub


Private Sub btnCompute_Click(...) Handles btnCompute.Click
  'Store the total into the namespace-level variable sum.
  sum = CDbl(txtWages.Text) + CDbl(txtIntIncome.Text) +
        CDbl(txtDivIncome.Text)
  Me.Close()    'Close the form since it is not needed any more
End Sub
```

[Run, enter a name, click on the button, and fill in the sources of income.] **Note:** After the *Compute Total Income* button is pressed, frmSources will disappear and the sum of the three numbers will be displayed in the Total Income text box of frmIncome.

 Example 2   The following program uses two forms. The startup form, frmOrder, processes an order after first requesting a user name and password with frmLogin. Even though frmOrder is the startup form, frmLogin is actually the first form seen by the user. It is invoked by frmOrder's Load event procedure.

The form frmLogin uses the text file MasterFile.txt to check for a registered user name and password. Each line of the text file consists of a user name concatenated with an underscore character and a password. The first three lines of the file contain the data dcook_idol08,

JQPublic_vbguy21, and shawnj_dance09. After checking that the text boxes have been filled in, the program uses a query to determine if the user name and password combination is in the text file. The user gets three chances to enter an acceptable response. Code in a FormClosing event procedure prevents the user from closing the login form without first giving a satisfactory user name and password.

OBJECT	PROPERTY	SETTING
frmLogin	Text	Login Form
lblUserName	Text	User name:
txtUserName		
lblPassword	Text	Password:
txtPassword		
btnContinue	Text	Continue

OBJECT	PROPERTY	SETTING
frmOrder	Text	Order Form
lblUserName	Text	User name:
txtUserName	ReadOnly	True
lblNumItems	Text	Number of items ordered:
txtNumItems		
btnProcess	Text	Process Order
lblTotalCost	Text	Total cost:
txtTotalCost	ReadOnly	True
btnLogOut	Text	Log Out

```
'frmOrder's code    (startup form)

Private Sub frmOrder_Load(...) Handles MyBase.Load
  frmLogin.ShowDialog()
  txtUserName.Text = frmLogin.userName
End Sub


Private Sub btnProcess_Click(...) Handles btnProcess.Click
  Dim numItems As Integer
  Dim totalCost As Double
  numItems = CInt(txtNumItems.Text)
  'cost per item: $20; shipping cost: $8
  totalCost = (numItems * 20) + 8
  txtTotalCost.Text = FormatCurrency(totalCost)
End Sub


Private Sub btnLogOut_Click(...) Handles btnLogOut.Click
  Me.Close()
End Sub

'frmLogin's code

Public userName As String
Dim numTries As Integer = 0
Dim idVerified As Boolean = False
```

```
Private Sub btnContinue_Click(...) Handles btnContinue.Click
  If (txtUserName.Text = "") Or (txtPassword.Text = "") Then
    MessageBox.Show("You must enter both a user name and a password.")
  Else
    If Confirm(txtUserName.Text, txtPassword.Text) Then
      idVerified = True
      userName = txtUserName.Text
      Me.Close()
    Else
      MessageBox.Show("Improper user name or password.")
      txtUserName.Clear()
      txtPassword.Clear()
    End If
  End If
  numTries += 1
  If (numTries = 3) And (Not idVerified) Then
    MessageBox.Show("This program is being terminated.")
    frmOrder.Close()
    Me.Close()
  End If
End Sub


Function Confirm(ByVal userName As String,
                ByVal password As String) As Boolean
  Dim query = From line In IO.File.ReadAllLines("MasterFile.txt")
              Where line = userName & "_" & password
              Select line
  If query.Count = 1 Then
    Return True
  Else
    Return False
  End If
End Function


Private Sub frmLogin_FormClosing(...) Handles Me.FormClosing
  If Not idVerified Then
    MessageBox.Show("This program is being terminated.")
    frmOrder.Close()
  End If
End Sub
```

[Run, enter a user name and password into the form.]

[Click on the button in the Login form. Then enter a quantity into the text box of the Order form below and click on the *Process Order* button.]

 Example 3   We can easily modify the Weekly Payroll case study from Chapter 5 so that instead of the output being displayed in a list box, it is displayed in the form shown in Fig. 9.20. The steps are as follows:

1. Start a new program with the name 9-3-3.

2. Delete Form1.vb from the Solution Explorer.

3. Add the existing form frmPayroll from the program 5-5 (Weekly Payroll) to the new program.

4. Change the startup form to frmPayroll.

5. Add a new form to the program and name it frmReceipt.

6. Design the form for frmReceipt as shown in Fig. 9.20 on page 449 with the settings in Fig. 9.21.

OBJECT	PROPERTY	SETTING
frmReceipt	Text	Payroll Receipt
lblGrossPay	Text	Gross pay this period:
txtGrossPay		
lblTotalPay	Text	Year-to-date-earnings:
txtTotalPay		
lblFicaTax	Text	FICA tax this period:
txtFicaTax		
lblFedTax	Text	Income tax withheld:
txtFedTax		
lblCheck	Text	Net pay (check amount):
txtCheck		
btnPrint	Text	Print
btnReturn	Text	Return to Data-Entry Form

FIGURE 9.21   Controls and settings for frmReceipt.

7. Double-click on the PrintForm control in the *Visual Basic PowerPacks* group of the Toolbox. The control will appear with the default name PrintForm1 in the component tray.

8. Add the code shown in Fig. 9.22 to frmReceipt. **Note:** The code inside the btnPrint event procedure prints the contents of the form on the printer.

```
Sub SetPayrollInfo(ByVal empName As String, ByVal pay As Double,
                   ByVal totalPay As Double, ByVal ficaTax As Double,
                   ByVal fedTax As Double, ByVal check As Double)
  txtName.Text = empName
  txtGrossPay.Text = FormatCurrency(pay)
  txtTotalPay.Text = FormatCurrency(totalPay)
  txtFicaTax.Text = FormatCurrency(ficaTax)
  txtFedTax.Text = FormatCurrency(fedTax)
  txtCheck.Text = FormatCurrency(check)
End Sub


Private Sub btnPrint_Click(...) Handles btnPrint.Click
  PrintForm1.PrintAction = Printing.PrintAction.PrintToPrinter
  PrintForm1.Print()
End Sub


Private Sub btnReturn_Click(...) Handles btnReturn.Click
  Me.Close()
End Sub
```

FIGURE 9.22   Code for frmReceipt.

9. In the btnDisplay_Click procedure of frmPayroll, replace the line

```
ShowPayroll(empName, pay, totalPay, ficaTax, fedTax, check) 'Task 6
```

with

```
frmReceipt.SetPayrollInfo(empName, pay, totalPay, ficaTax,
                          fedTax, check)              'Task 6
frmReceipt.ShowDialog()
```

Practice Problems 9.3

1. Rewrite the program in Example 2 without using the namespace-level variable *userName*.

EXERCISES 9.3

In Exercises 1 through 4, determine the output displayed when the button is clicked.

1.
```
'Form1's code     (startup form)
Private Sub btnDisplay_Click(...) Handles btnDisplay.Click
  Form2.ShowDialog()
  txtOutput.Text = FormatCurrency(Form2.totalCost)
End Sub


Function GetTotalCost(ByVal price As Double) As Double
  Return price + (Form2.SALES_TAX_RATE * price)
End Function
```

```
'Form2's code
Public Const SALES_TAX_RATE As Double = 0.06
Public totalCost As Double

Private Sub Form2_Load(...) Handles Me.Load
  Dim price = InputBox("What is the price?")
  totalCost = Form1.GetTotalCost(CDbl(price))
  Me.Close()
End Sub
```

(Assume that the response is 100.)

2. ```
'Form1's code   (startup form)
Private Sub Form1_Load(...) Handles MyBase.Load
  Form2.ShowDialog()
  Dim name As String = Form2.txtName.Text
  Dim dob As Date = CDate(Form2.txtDateOfBirth.Text)
  Dim parsedName() As String = name.Split(" "c)
  Dim firstName = parsedName.First
  Dim message As String
  If dob.AddYears(21) <= Today Then
    message = ", you are at least 21 years old."
  Else
    message = ", you are not yet 21 years old."
  End If
  txtOutput.Text = firstName & message
End Sub
```

```
'Form2's code
Private Sub Form2_Load(...) Handles MyBase.Load
  txtName.Text = "John Doe"
  txtDateOfBirth.Text = "2/3/1989"
End Sub

Private Sub btnRecord_Click(...) Handles btnRecord.Click
  Me.Close()
End Sub
```

3. ```
'Form1's code   (startup form)
Private Sub Form1_Load(...) Handles MyBase.Load
  Form2.ShowDialog()
  Dim name As String = Form2.fullName
  Dim lastName As String = Form2.GetLastName(name)
  txtOutput.Text = "Your last name begins with " &
                   lastName.Substring(0, 1) & "."
End Sub
```

```
'Form2's code
Public fullName As String

Private Sub btnDetermine_Click(...) Handles btnDetermine.Click
  fullName = "John Fitzgerald Kennedy"
```

```
    Me.Close()
  End Sub


  Function GetLastName(ByVal nom As String) As String
    Dim parsedName() As String = nom.Split(" "c)
    Return parsedName.First
  End Function
```

4. ```
   'Form1's code     (startup form)
   Public average As Double


   Private Sub Form1_Load(...) Handles MyBase.Load
     Form2.ShowDialog()
   End Sub


   Private Sub btnComputeAverage_Click(...) Handles btnComputeAverage.Click
     Dim num As Double = 0
     Dim count As Integer = 0
     Dim sum As Double = 0
     num = CDbl(InputBox("Enter a number"))
     Do While num <> −1
       count += 1
       sum += num
       num = CDbl(InputBox("Enter a number"))
     Loop
     average = sum / count
     Form3.ShowDialog()
     Me.Close()
   End Sub


   'Form2's code
   Private Sub Form2_Load(...) Handles MyBase.Load
     Dim message As String = "The purpose of this program is to" &
         " calculate the average of a set of nonnegative numbers" &
         " input by the user. Enter the numbers one at a time" &
         " and enter −1 to signal the end of data entry."
     MessageBox.Show(message, "Instructions")
     Me.Close()
   End Sub


   'Form3's code
   Private Sub Form3_Load(...) Handles MyBase.Load
     txtAverage.Text = "The average is " & Form1.average & "."
   End Sub
   ```

   (Assume the responses are 80, 100, and −1.)

5. Consider Example 2 of Section 6.1. Alter the program so that a second form appears (instead of a message box) when the button is pressed. The second form should allow the user to make a selection by clicking on one of three radio buttons with the captions *Movie 1*, *Movie 2*, and *Movie 3*.
   ```

6. Consider the program in Example 9 from Section 7.1 that determines a person's first and last names. Alter the program so that the person's full name is typed into the startup form and a second form is used to display their first and last names.

7. Consider Example 4 of Section 6.1. Alter the program so that a second form showing the balance after each year appears when the button is clicked on. See Fig. 9.23.

FIGURE 9.23 **Possible outcome of Exercise 7.**

8. Consider the Analyze-a-Loan case study from Chapter 7. Alter the program so that the amortization table and the interest-rate-change table are each displayed in a separate form when requested. The program should have three forms, and the startup form should not contain a DataGridView control.

9. Consider the Recording Checks and Deposits case study from Chapter 8. Alter the program so that the list of transactions is displayed in a second form when requested.

10. Write a program that allows student grades on three exams to be entered one student at a time in frmStudent and then displays each student's average and the class average in frmGrades. Initially, frmGrades (the startup form) should look like Fig. 9.24 with the text box and DataGridView controls empty. The form frmStudent should initially look like Fig. 9.25 with the four text boxes empty. The Load event procedure of frmGrades should invoke frmStudent.

Each time a student's name and grades are recorded, the number in the title bar of frmStudent should increase by 1. The *Terminate* button should be clicked on after all students have been recorded. The data for the students should be stored in an array of structures with the structure having four members.

FIGURE 9.24 **frmGrades**

FIGURE 9.25 **frmStudent**

11. Write a program consisting of three forms that gathers customer billing information. The first form (the startup form) should initially look like Fig. 9.26, but with the text box and list box blank and no radio button selected. (The second and third forms should initially look like Figs. 9.27 and 9.29 with all text boxes blank.) After the user provides a name, selects a billing method, and clicks on the button in frmCustomer, either frmCustInfo or frmCardInfo should appear to obtain the necessary information.

FIGURE 9.26   **frmCustomer**

FIGURE 9.27   **frmCustInfo**

Let's first consider frmCustInfo, that appears when the *Bill Customer* radio button is selected. The Name read-only text box should be filled automatically with the name that was entered in frmCustomer. The user enters information into the other text boxes, selects a state from the sorted drop-down-list combo box, and clicks on the button to display the mailing address in the list box of frmCustomer as shown in Fig. 9.26. **Note:** The names of the states can be obtained from the file States.txt.

The form frmCardInfo, which appears when the *Bill Credit Card* radio button in frm-Customer has been selected, contains two text boxes, one simple combo box (for type of credit card) and two DropDownList style combo boxes. The Name text box is initially automatically filled with the name that was entered in frmCustomer. However, the name can be

FIGURE 9.28   **frmCustomer**

FIGURE 9.29   **frmCardInfo**

altered, if necessary, to look exactly like the name printed on the credit card. The list for the Year combo box should be filled by the Load event procedure and should contain the current year followed by the next five years. (**Note:** The current year is given by Today.Year.) After the user provides the requested data, the information is displayed in the list box of frm-Customer as shown in Fig. 9.28.

12. Write a program containing the two forms shown in Fig. 9.30. Initially, the Number to Dial form appears. When the *Show Push Buttons* button is clicked, the Push Buttons form appears. The user enters a number by clicking on successive push buttons and then clicking on *Enter* to have the number transferred to the read-only text box at the bottom of the first form.

FIGURE 9.30 **Sample run of Exercise 12.**

Solutions to Practice Problems 9.3

1. In frmLogin's code, delete the two lines

```
Public userName As String
```
and
```
userName = txtUserName.Text
```
In frmOrder's code, change the line
```
txtUserName.Text = frmLogin.userName
```
to
```
txtUserName.Text = frmLogin.txtUserName.Text
```

9.4 Graphics

In this section, we draw bar charts and pie charts in a picture box, and illustrate one method for creating animation on a form.

Caution: Since the programs in this section mix text and graphics, what you see on the monitor will vary with the monitor's DPI setting. To guarantee the intended outcomes, you should check that your monitor is set to display 96 DPI (Dots Per Inch). For details, see the first item under "Configuring the Windows Environment" in Appendix B.

VideoNote

Graphics

■ Graphics Objects

A statement of the form

```
Dim gr As Graphics = picBox.CreateGraphics
```

declares *gr* to be a Graphics object for the picture box picBox.

The unit of measurement used in graphics methods is the **pixel**. To get a feel for how big a pixel is, the title bar of a form is 30 pixels high, and the border of a form is four pixels thick. The setting for the Size property of a picture box is two numbers separated by a comma. The two numbers give the width and height of the picture box in pixels. You can alter these numbers to specify a precise size. Each point of a picture box is identified by a pair of coordinates

`(x, y)`

where x (between 0 and picBox.Width) is its distance in pixels from the left side of the picture box, and y (between 0 and picBox.Height) is its distance in pixels from the top of the picture box.

Text is placed in a picture box with a statement of the form

`gr.DrawString(string, Me.Font, Brushes.Color, x, y)`

where *string* is either a string variable or literal, Me.Font specifies that the Form's font be used to display the text, and the upper-left corner of the first character of the text has coordinates (x, y). The color of the text is determined by *Color*. IntelliSense will provide a list of about 140 possible colors after `"Brushes."` is typed. As an example, the statements

```
Dim gr As Graphics = picBox.CreateGraphics
Dim strVar As String = "Hello"
gr.DrawString(strVar, Me.Font, Brushes.Blue, 4, 30)
gr.DrawString("World", Me.Font, Brushes.Red, 35, 50)
```

produce the output shown in Fig. 9.31.

FIGURE 9.31   **DrawString method.**

◼ Lines, Rectangles, Circles, and Sectors

Let *gr* be a Graphics object for picBox. Then the statement

`gr.DrawLine(Pens.Color, x1, y1, x2, y2)`

draws a straight line segment from the point with coordinates $(x1, y1)$ to the point with coordinates $(x2, y2)$. The color of the line is determined by *Color*. IntelliSense will provide an extensive list of possible colors after `"Pens."` is typed. For instance, the statement

`gr.DrawLine(Pens.Blue, 50, 20, 120, 75)`

draws a blue line from the point with the coordinates (50, 20) to the point with the coordinates (120, 75). See Fig. 9.32.

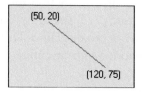

FIGURE 9.32   **DrawLine method.**

The statement

`gr.FillRectangle(Brushes.Color, x, y, w, h)`

draws a solid rectangle of width w and height h in the color specified and having the point with coordinates (x, y) as its upper-left vertex. The left side of the rectangle will be x pixels from the left side of the picture box and the top side of the rectangle will be y pixels from the top of the picture box. For instance, the statement

```
gr.FillRectangle(Brushes.Blue, 50, 20, 70, 55)
```

draws the rectangle shown in Fig. 9.33.

FIGURE 9.33   FillRectangle method.

The FillEllipse method draws a solid ellipse of a specified color, given the specifications of a circumscribed rectangle. The rectangle is specified by the coordinates of its upper-left point, its width, and its height. This method produces a circle when the width and height of the rectangle are the same. In particular, the statement

```
gr.FillEllipse(Brushes.Color, a − r, b − r, 2 * r, 2 * r)
```

draws a solid circle of the specified color with center (a, b) and radius r. For instance, the statement

```
gr.FillEllipse(Brushes.Blue, 80 − 40, 50 − 40, 2 * 40, 2 * 40)
```

draws a solid blue circle with center $(80, 50)$ and radius 40. **Note:** If a rectangle were circumscribed about the circle, the rectangle would be a square with its upper-left vertex at $(40, 10)$ and each side of length 80.

The FillPie method draws a solid sector of an ellipse in a color. The ellipse is specified by giving the coordinates, width, and height for the circumscribing rectangle, as in the FillEllipse method. The sector is determined by a radius line and the angle swept out by the radius line. We are interested solely in the case where the ellipse is a circle. The shaded region in Fig. 9.34 is a typical sector (or pie-shaped region) of a circle. The sector is determined by the two angles θ_1 and θ_2. The start angle, θ_1, is the angle through which the horizontal radius line must be rotated clockwise to reach the starting radius line of the sector. Angle θ_2 is the number of degrees through which the starting radius line must sweep (clockwise) to reach the ending radius line of the sector. The angles θ_1 and θ_2 are referred to as the **start angle** and the **sweep angle**, respectively. Figure 9.35 on the next page shows the start and sweep angles for three sectors of a circle.

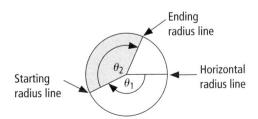

FIGURE 9.34   A typical sector of a circle.

FIGURE 9.35 **FillPie method.**

In general, a statement of the form

```
gr.FillPie(Brushes.Color, a - r, b - r, 2 * r, 2 * r,
           startAngle, sweepAngle)
```

draws a sector of a circle of the specified color with center (a, b), radius r, and the given start and sweep angles. For instance, the middle image of Fig. 9.35 can be drawn with a statement such as

```
gr.FillPie(Brushes.Blue, 80 - 40, 80 - 40, 2 * 40, 2 * 40, 45, 180)
```

The Brushes, Pens, and Fonts appearing in the drawing statements so far are literals of objects. Variables also can be used to provide these values. For instance, the statement gr.Fill-Rectangle(Brushes.Blue, 50, 20, 70, 55) can be replaced by the pair of statements

```
Dim br As Brush = Brushes.Blue
gr.FillRectangle(br, 50, 20, 70, 55)
```

The first statement declares br to be a variable of type Brush and assigns it the value Brushes.Blue.

Numeric variables used in the Draw and Fill statements discussed in this section must be of type Integer or Single. The **Single data type** is similar to the Double data type but has a smaller range. A variable of type Single can hold whole numbers, fractions, or mixed numbers between about $-3.4 \cdot 10^{38}$ and $3.4 \cdot 10^{38}$. The **CSng** function converts other data types to the Single data type.

◼ Pie Charts

Consider the three pieces of data in Table 9.3. A pie chart can be used to graphically display the relative sizes of these numbers. The first step in creating a pie chart is to convert the numbers to percents. Since the total expenditures are \$419 billion, the federal outlay is $33/419 \approx .08$ or 8%. Similarly, the state and local expenditures are 49% and 43%. See Table 9.4. Our goal is to write a program to display the information in the pie chart of Fig. 9.36.

TABLE 9.3	Financing for public schools (in billions).
Federal	\$33
State	\$206
Local	\$180

TABLE 9.4	Financing for public schools.
Federal	.08 or 8%
State	.49 or 49%
Local	.43 or 43%

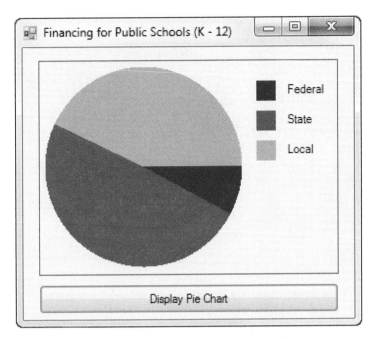

FIGURE 9.36   **Pie chart for Example 1.**

The blue sector in Fig. 9.36 has start angle 0 degrees and sweep angle .08 * 360 degrees . The red sector has start angle .08 * 360 and sweep angle .49 * 360. The tan sector has start angle .08 * 360 + .49 * 360 [or (.08 + .49) * 360 degrees] and sweep angle .43 * 360° degrees. Notice that each start angle is (sum of previous percentages) * 360. The sweep angle for each sector is the corresponding percentage times 360.

Example 1   The following program creates the pie chart (see Fig. 9.36) for the financing of public schools. The program is written so that it can be easily converted to handle a pie chart with up to six sectors. All that is required is to change the first two Dim statements and the Me.Text statement. The "Dim br() As Brush" line, which creates an array of brushes, has six brushes in order to accommodate additional sectors.

```
Private Sub btnDisplay_Click(...) Handles btnDisplay.Click
  Dim legend() As String = {"Federal", "State", "Local"}
  Dim quantity() As Single = {33, 206, 180}
  Dim percent(quantity.Count - 1) As Single
  Dim sumOfQuantities As Single = 0
  Dim sumOfSweepAngles As Single = 0
  Dim br() As Brush = {Brushes.Blue, Brushes.Red, Brushes.Tan,
          Brushes.Green, Brushes.Orange, Brushes.Gray}
  Dim gr As Graphics = picOutput.CreateGraphics
  'The picture box has width 312 and height 215
  Dim r As Integer = 100    'Radius of circle
  Dim c As Integer = 105    'Center of circle has coordinates (c, c)
  Me.Text = "Financing for Public Schools (K - 12)"
  'Sum the numbers for the quantities
  For i As Integer = 0 To quantity.Count - 1
    sumOfQuantities += quantity(i)
  Next
```

```
'Convert the quantities to percents
For i As Integer = 0 To quantity.Count - 1
  percent(i) = quantity(i) / sumOfQuantities
Next
'Display the pie chart and the legends
For i As Integer = 0 To quantity.Count - 1
  gr.FillPie(br(i), c - r, c - r, 2 * r, 2 * r,
          sumOfSweepAngles, percent(i) * 360)
  sumOfSweepAngles += percent(i) * 360
  'Display small colored square and legend
  gr.FillRectangle(br(i), 220, 20 + 30 * i, 20, 20)
  gr.DrawString(legend(i), Me.Font, Brushes.Black, 250, 22 + 30 * i)
Next
End Sub
```

■ Bar Charts

Our goal here is to produce the bar chart of Fig. 9.37. The picture box for the chart has a width of 210 and height of 150 pixels. (Here, the BorderStyle property is set to FixedSingle for instructional reasons. In general, the bar chart will look better with the BorderStyle property of the picture box left at its default setting: None.)

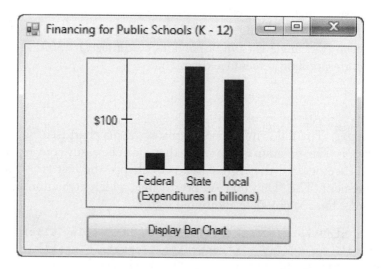

FIGURE 9.37   **Bar chart for Example 2.**

The three magnitudes for the graph are 33, 206, and 180. If we let a pixel correspond to one unit, then the largest rectangle will be 206 pixels high—a bit too large. With a pixel corresponding to 2 units, the largest rectangle will be 206/2 or 103 pixels high—a reasonable size. By setting the x-axis 110 pixels from the top of the picture box, the largest rectangle is accommodated comfortably. The top of the largest rectangle is $110 - 103$ [that is, $110 - (206/2)$] pixels from the top of the picture box. In general, a rectangle corresponding to the quantity q will be $110 - (q/2)$ pixels from the top of the picture box, and the height will be $q/2$ pixels.

Example 2   The following program produces the bar chart of Fig. 9.37. Each rectangle is 20 pixels wide, and there are 20 pixels between rectangles.

```
Private Sub btnDisplay_Click(...) Handles btnDisplay.Click
  Dim quantity() As Single = {33, 206, 180}
  Dim gr As Graphics = picOutput.CreateGraphics
  'The picture box has width 210 and height 150
  gr.DrawLine(Pens.Black, 40, 110, 210, 110) 'x-axis
  gr.DrawLine(Pens.Black, 40, 110, 40, 0)    'y-axis
  gr.DrawLine(Pens.Black, 35, 60, 45, 60)       'tick mark; 60 = 110 - (100/2)
  gr.DrawString("$100", Me.Font, Brushes.Black, 5, 55)
  Me.Text = "Financing for Public Schools (K - 12)"
  For i As Integer = 0 To quantity.Count - 1
    gr.FillRectangle(Brushes.Blue, 60 + i * 40,
                  (110 - quantity(i) / 2), 20, quantity(i) / 2)
  Next
  gr.DrawString("Federal  State     Local", Me.Font,
            Brushes.Black, 50, 115)
  gr.DrawString("(Expenditures in billions)", Me.Font,
            Brushes.Black, 50, 130)
End Sub
```

■ **Animation**

One way to produce animation on a form is to place an image into a picture box and then move the picture by steadily changing the location of the picture box. Figure 9.38 shows a ball placed inside a small picture box.

 Example 3   In the following program, the ball in Fig. 9.38 will initially move diagonally in a southeast direction and then bounce off any side of the form it hits. The **client area** of a form is the gray area within the title bar and borders of the form. The values of Me.ClientSize.Height and Me.ClientSize.Width are the height and width of the white area. The values of picBox.Top and picBox.Left are the distances of the picture box from the top and left sides of the client area.

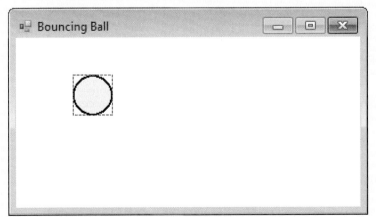

OBJECT	PROPERTY	SETTING
frmBall	Text	Bouncing Ball
	BackColor	White
picBall	Image	Moon5.bmp
Timer1	Interval	10

FIGURE 9.38   The form for Example 3.

The speed at which the ball moves is determined by the setting for the Interval property of Timer1. At each tick, the ball will move x pixels horizontally, where $x = 1$ or -1. When $x = 1$ the ball moves to the right, and when $x = -1$ the ball moves to the left. The value of x reverses when the ball strikes the right or left side of the form. The value of y determines the vertical motion of the ball in a similar manner,

```
Dim x As Integer = 1
Dim y As Integer = 1

Private Sub frmBall_Load(...) Handles MyBase.Load
  Timer1.Enabled = True
End Sub

Private Sub Timer1_Tick(...) Handles Timer1.Tick
  If picBall.Left <= 0 Or
      picBall.Left >= (Me.ClientSize.Width - picBall.Width) Then
    x = -x
  End If
  picBall.Left += x
  If picBall.Top <= 0 Or
      picBall.Top >= (Me.ClientSize.Height - picBall.Height) Then
    y = -y
  End If
  picBall.Top += y
End Sub
```

■ Printing Graphics

Graphics can be printed with a PrintDocument control in the same way that text was printed in Section 3.3.

 Example 4   The following program produces the same output as Example 2. However, the output is printed instead of being displayed in a picture box. The changes from Example 2 are as follows:

1. The code was moved from the btnDisplay_Click event procedure to the procedure Print-Document1_PrintPage.

2. The source of the graphics object *gr* was changed from picOutput.CreateGraphics to e.Graphics.

3. The Me.Text statement was replaced with a DrawString statement.

4. The values of the *x*-coordinates were increased by 300 to approximately center the graph horizontally, and the values of the *y*-coordinates were increased by 200 to lower the graph from the top edge of the page.

OBJECT	PROPERTY	SETTING
frmBarChart	Text	Bar Chart
btnPrint	Text	Print Bar Chart
btnPreview	Text	Preview Bar Chart
PrintDocument1		
PrintPreviewDialog1		

PrintDocument1   PrintPreviewDialog1

```
Private Sub btnPrint_Click(...) Handles btnPrint.Click
  PrintDocument1.Print()
End Sub

Private Sub PrintDocument1_PrintPage(...) Handles PrintDocument1.PrintPage
  Dim quantity() As Single = {33, 207, 180}
  Dim gr As Graphics = e.Graphics
  gr.DrawLine(Pens.Black, 340, 310, 510, 310)     'x-axis
  gr.DrawLine(Pens.Black, 340, 310, 340, 200)     'y-axis
  gr.DrawLine(Pens.Black, 335, 260, 345, 260)     'tick mark
  gr.DrawString("$100", Me.Font, Brushes.Black, 305, 255)
  gr.DrawString("Financing for Public Schools (K — 12)", Me.Font,
                Brushes.Black, 300, 175)
  For i As Integer = 0 To quantity.Count — 1
    gr.FillRectangle(Brushes.Blue, 360 + i * 40,
                    (310 — quantity(i) / 2), 20, quantity(i) / 2)
  Next
  gr.DrawString("Federal    State    Local", Me.Font,
                Brushes.Black, 350, 315)
  gr.DrawString("(Expenditures in billions)", Me.Font,
                Brushes.Black, 350, 330)
End Sub

Private Sub btnPreview_Click(...) Handles btnPreview.Click
  PrintPreviewDialog1.Document = PrintDocument1
  PrintPreviewDialog1.ShowDialog()
End Sub
```

■ Comments

1. A statement of the form

   ```
   Dim pn As Pen = Pens.Color
   ```

   declares *pn* to be a variable of type Pen and assigns it the value Pens.*Color*.

2. A statement of the form

   ```
   Dim fnt As Font = New Font(fontName, size)
   ```

   declares *fnt* to be a variable of type Font and assigns it the specified font and size. For instance, the statements

```
Dim gr As Graphics = picBox.CreateGraphics
Dim fnt As Font = New Font("Courier New", 10)
gr.DrawString("Hello", fnt, Brushes.Blue, 4, 30)
```

display the word Hello in 10-point Courier New font.

3. The statement

```
picBox.Refresh()
```

clears all graphics and text from the picture box.

Practice Problems 9.4

1. (True or False) The Draw and Fill methods discussed in this section use colored Brushes.

2. Write lines of code that place a smiling face in the upper left corner of the form. **Note:** The letter *J* corresponds to a smiling face in the Wingdings font.

EXERCISES 9.4

In Exercises 1 through 4, write a program to draw the given figures in a picture box.

1. Draw a circle whose center is located at the center of a picture box.
2. Draw a circle whose rightmost point is at the center of a picture box.
3. Use the FillEllipse method to create an unfilled red circle of radius 20.
4. Draw a triangle with two sides of the same length.

In Exercises 5 through 18 display the graphics in a picture box.

In Exercises 5 through 8, write a program to create the flag of the designated country. Refer to Fig. 9.39. Note: The Swiss flag is square. For the other three flags, the width is 1.5 times the height.

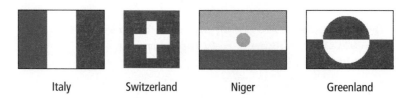

Italy   Switzerland   Niger   Greenland

FIGURE 9.39 **Flags of four countries.**

5. Italy   6. Switzerland   7. Niger   8. Greenland

9. Write a program to draw displays such as the one in Fig. 9.40. Let the user specify the maximum number (in this display, 8).

FIGURE 9.40 **Drawing for Exercise 9.**

10. Write a program to draw displays such as the one in Fig. 9.41. Let the user specify the number of lines (in this display, 3).

———————— Line 1

———————— Line 2

———————— Line 3

FIGURE 9.41   **Drawing for Exercise 10.**

11. Use the data in Table 9.5 to create a pie chart.

TABLE 9.5	United States recreational beverage consumption.	
	Soft Drinks	52.9%
	Beer	14.7%
	Bottled Water	11.1%
	Other	21.3%

12. Use the data in Table 9.6 to create a bar chart.

TABLE 9.6	United States minimum wage.	
	1959	1.00
	1968	1.15
	1978	2.65
	1988	3.35
	1998	5.15
	2009	7.25

13. Write a program to create the line chart in Fig. 9.42. Use the data in Table 9.7.

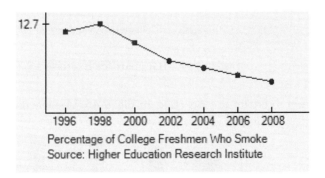

FIGURE 9.42   **Line chart for Exercise 13.**

TABLE 9.7	Percentage of College Freshmen Who Smoke.						
	1996	1998	2000	2002	2004	2006	2008
Percent	11.6	12.7	10.0	7.4	6.4	5.3	4.4

Source: Higher Education Research Institute.

14. Write a program to create the line chart in Fig. 9.43. Use the data in Table 9.8

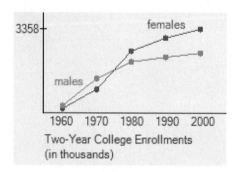

FIGURE 9.43   **Line chart for Exercise 14.**

TABLE 9.8	Two-year college enrollments (in thousands).				
	1960	1970	1980	1990	2000
Male	283	1375	2047	2233	2398
Female	170	945	2479	3007	3358

15. Write a program to create the bar chart in Fig. 9.44.

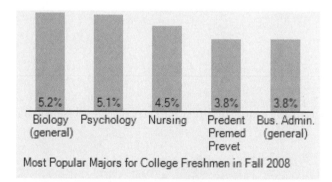

FIGURE 9.44   **Bar chart for Exercise 15.**

16. Write a program to create the bar chart in Fig. 9.45. Use the data in Table 9.9.

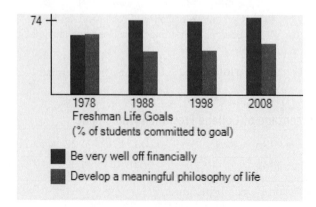

FIGURE 9.45   **Bar chart for Exercise 16.**

TABLE 9.9 Freshman Life Goals (% of students committed to goal).

	1978	1988	1998	2008
Be very well off financially	59	74	73	77
Develop a meaningful philosophy of life	60	43	44	51

Source: Higher Education Research Institute.

17. Write a program to create the bar chart in Figure 9.46. Use the data in Table 9.10. **Note:** Mandarin and Wu are spoken primarily in China.

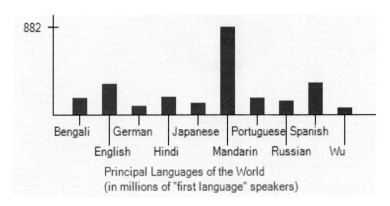

FIGURE 9.46 Bar chart for Exercise 17.

TABLE 9.10 Principal languages of the world.

Bengali	173
English	311
German	96
Hindi	182
Japanese	128
Mandarin	882
Portuguese	179
Russian	146
Spanish	326
Wu	78

18. Write a program that allows the user to display a budget as a pie chart. See Fig. 9.47. After the user enters numbers into the six text boxes and click on the button, the pie chart should be displayed.

19. Write a program in which an airplane flies horizontally to the right across a form. After it flies off the form, the airplane should reappear on the left and fly horizontally across the screen again. **Note:** Use the image Airplane.bmp found in the folder Ch09\Pictures.

20. Rewrite the program in Example 1 so that the pie chart is printed instead of being displayed in a picture box. **Note:** You will most likely want to replace the variable c with the pair of variables cx and cy. Then the center of the circle will have coordinates (cx, cy).

21. Refer to Exercise 5. Write a program to print the flag of Italy.

22. Refer to Exercise 7. Write a program to print the flag of Niger.

FIGURE 9.47   **Form for Exercise 18.**

Solutions to Practice Problems 9.4

1. False. Only the Fill methods and the DrawString method use colored Brushes. The DrawLine method uses colored Pens.

2.
```
Dim gr As Graphics = Me.CreateGraphics
Dim fnt As Font = New Font("Wingdings", 20)
gr.DrawString("J", fnt, Brushes.Red, 0, 0)
```

CHAPTER 9   SUMMARY

1. *List boxes* provide easy access to lists of data. Items() holds the items stored in the list box. Each item is identified by an index number. The lists can be automatically sorted (Sorted property = True) and altered (Items.AddItem, Items.RemoveAt, and Items.Remove methods), the currently highlighted item identified (Text property), and the number of items determined (Items.Count property).

2. Simple and DropDown style *combo boxes* are enhanced text boxes. They allow the user to fill the text box by selecting an item from a list or by typing the item directly into the text box. The contents of the text box are assigned to the combo box's Text property. A DropDownList style combo box is essentially a list box that drops down instead of being permanently displayed.

3. The *timer control* raises an event repeatedly after a specified time interval.

4. An object of type *Random* can generate a randomly selected integer from a specified range.

5. The *ToolTip control* allows the program to display guidance when the mouse hovers over a control.

6. The *Clipboard* is filled with the SetText method or by pressing Ctrl + C, and its contents are copied with the GetText method or by pressing Ctrl + V.

7. The *picture box control*, which displays pictures or geometric shapes, can expand to accommodate the size of a picture or have a picture alter its size to fit the control.

8. Menus, similar to the menus of the Visual Basic IDE itself, can be created with the *MenuStrip control*.

9. *Horizontal* and *vertical scroll bar controls* permit the user to select from among a range of integers by clicking or dragging with the mouse. The range is determined by the Minimum and Maximum properties. The Scroll event is raised by clicking on the scroll bar.

10. Additional forms can be added to a program to serve as customized dialog boxes. They are revealed with the *ShowDialog* method and removed with the *Close* method.

11. After a graphics object is produced with a *CreateGraphics* method, the *DrawString, DrawLine, FillRectangle, FillEllipse*, and *FillPie* methods can be used to display strings, lines, solid rectangles, solid ellipses, and solid sectors with colors supplied by Pen and Brush objects.

12. *Animation* can be produced by steadily moving a picture box containing an image.

CHAPTER 9   PROGRAMMING PROJECTS

1. *Membership List.* Write a menu-driven program to manage a membership list. See Fig. 9.48. Assume that the names and phone numbers of all members are stored in alphabetical order (by last name, then by first name) in the text file MemberPhones.txt. Each record consists of two fields—a name field and a phone number field. The names should appear in a list box when the form is loaded. When a name is highlighted, both the name and phone number of the person should appear in the text boxes at the bottom of the form. To delete a person, highlight his or her name and click on the *Delete* menu item. To change either a person's name or phone number, make the corrections in the text boxes and click on the menu item *Modify*. To add a new member, type his or her name and phone number into the text boxes and click on the menu item *Add*. When the *Exit* menu item is clicked, the new membership list should be written to the file and the program should terminate.

FIGURE 9.48   **Form for Programming Project 1.**

2. *Inventory Control.* Write a menu-driven multiform inventory program for a bookstore with data saved in a text file. Each record of the text file should consist of five fields—*title, author, category, wholesale price*, and *number in stock*. (The two categories are *fiction* and

nonfiction.) At any time, the program should display the titles of the books in stock in a list box. The user should have the option of displaying either all titles or just those in one of the two categories. The user should be able to add a new book, delete a book, or alter any of the fields of a book in stock. The adding and editing processes use the second form, frmDetails. See Fig. 9.49. At any time, the user should be able to calculate the total value of all books, or the total value of the books in either category. The menu item *File* contains the two second-level menu items *Save* and *Exit*. The menu items *Display* and *Values* each contain the three second-level menu items *All*, *Fiction*, and *Nonfiction*. (**Hint:** Store the data about the books in an array of structures.)

FIGURE 9.49   The two forms for Programming Project 2.

3. *Voting Machine.* The members of a club bring a computer to their annual meeting to use in the election of a new president. Write a program to handle the election. The program should add each candidate to a list box as he or she is nominated. After the nomination process is complete, club members should be able to approach the computer one at a time and double-click on the candidate of their choice to place their vote. When a *Tally Votes* button is clicked on, a second list box, showing the number of votes received by each candidate, should appear alongside the first list box. Also, the name(s) of the candidate(s) with the highest number of votes should be displayed in the list box, showing the percentage by which the candidate(s) won.

4. *Airplane Seating Chart.* An airplane has 15 rows (numbered 1 through 15), with six seats (labeled A, B, C, D, E, and F) in each row. Write a multiform program that keeps track of the seats that have been reserved and the type of meal requested by each passenger. The seating chart should be displayed in a list box with a line for each row. See Fig. 9.50(a). When the ticket agent clicks on the desired row in the list box, the row number and the status of the seats in the row should be displayed in seven read-only text boxes at the bottom of the form. When the agent clicks on one of the text boxes, a second form containing four option buttons labeled *Unoccupied*, *Regular*, *Low Calorie*, and *Vegetarian* should appear. See Fig. 9.50(b). Clicking on a radio button should close the second form and update both the text box and the row for that seat in the list box. Unoccupied seats are denoted with a period, and occupied seats are denoted with the first letter of their meal type. At any time, the agent should be able to request the number of seats filled, the number of window seats vacant, the number of aisle seats vacant, and the numbers of each type of meal ordered.

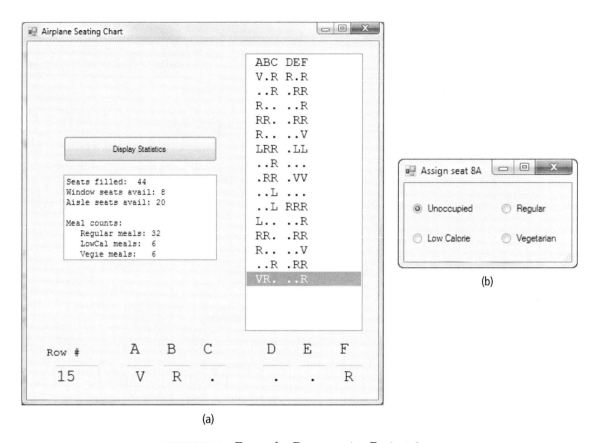

FIGURE 9.50 **Forms for Programming Project 4.**

5. *The Underdog and the World Series.* What is the probability that the underdog will win the World Series of Baseball? What is the average number of games for a World Series? Write an animated program to answer these questions. For instance, suppose that the underdog is expected to win 40% of the time. We say that the probability of the underdog's winning a game is 40%. (In order for a team to be the underdog, the probability that the team wins a game must be less than 50%.) Figure 9.51 shows that the probability of a 40% underdog's winning the World Series is about 29%, and that such a series would last an average of about 5.67 games. The program should simulate the playing of 10,000 World Series where the underdog has the probability of winning that was entered into the first text box. The values of the horizontal scroll bars should extend from 0 to 10,000 and should be calculated after each series so that the scroll boxes steadily move across the bars. **Note:** In order to spare Visual Basic from being overwhelmed with changing the values in the twelve text boxes to the right of the scroll bars too often, just change the values after every ten series. Also, every time the values are changed, execute a Refresh method for each of these text boxes.

6. *Spread of an Epidemic.* A community of 10,000 individuals is exposed to a flu epidemic in which infected individuals are sick for two days and then are immune from the illness. When we first start to observe the epidemic (that is, on day 0), 200 people have had the illness for one day, and 100 people have had the illness for two days. At any time, the rate at which the epidemic is spreading is proportional to the product of the number currently ill and the number susceptible. Specifically, each day

[# of individuals in the first day of the illness] =
      CInt(0.0001735 * [# sick the previous day] * [# susceptible the previous day])

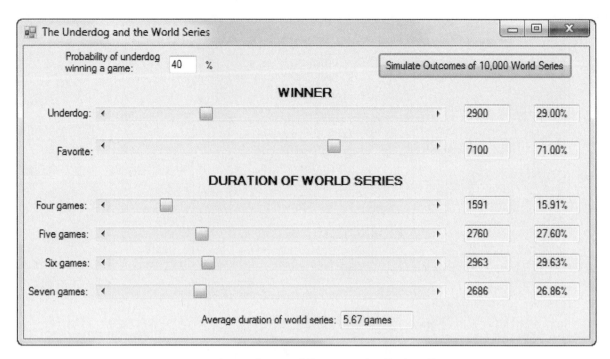

FIGURE 9.51 **A sample run of Programming Project 5.**

Write a program that displays successive bar graphs illustrating the progress of the epidemic. When the *Show Day 0* button is clicked on, the bar graph should show the distribution for day 0. See Fig. 9.52. Each time the *Advance One Day* button is clicked on, a bar graph showing the distribution for the next day should appear. Figure 9.53 shows the bar graph after this button has been clicked on three times.

FIGURE 9.52 **Initial distribution of epidemic.**

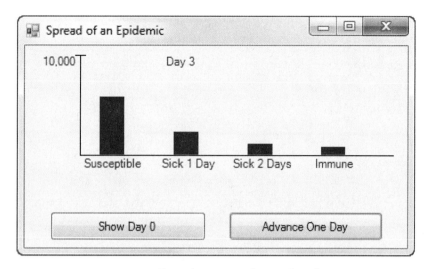

FIGURE 9.53   Distribution on day 3 of epidemic.

10

Databases

10.1 An Introduction to Databases

VideoNote

Introduction to
databases

The management of databases is one of the most important uses of computers today. Airlines use databases to handle nearly 1.5 billion passenger reservations per year. The 7,500 hospitals in the United States utilize databases to document the care of over 30 million patients per year. Banks in the United States employ databases to monitor 1.6 billion credit cards. Although databases vary considerably in size and complexity, most of them adhere to the fundamental principles of design discussed in this chapter. That is, they are composed of a collection of interrelated tables.

A **table** is a rectangular array of data. Table 10.1 provides information about large cities. Each column of the table is called a **field**. (The third column gives the 2010 population in millions and the fourth column the projected 2015 population in millions.) The names of the fields are *name*, *country*, *pop2010*, and *pop2015*. Each row, called a **record**, contains the same type of information as every other row. Also, the pieces of information in each row are related because they all apply to a specific city. Table 10.2, Countries, has three fields and ten records.

TABLE 10.1   Cities.

name	country	pop2010	pop2015
Bombay	India	20.1	22.0
Buenos Aires	Argentina	13.1	13.4
Calcutta	India	15.6	17.0
Delhi	India	17.0	18.7
Dhaka	Bangladesh	14.8	17.0
Mexico City	Mexico	19.5	20.2
New York	USA	19.4	20.0
Sao Paulo	Brazil	19.6	20.1
Shanghai	China	15.8	17.2
Tokyo	Japan	36.1	36.4

Note: The population figures are for "urban agglomerations"—that is, contiguous densely populated urban areas.

TABLE 10.2   Countries.

name	pop2010	monetaryUnit
Argentina	41.9	peso
Bangladesh	152.6	raka
Brazil	195.2	real
China	1379.7	yuan
India	1196.8	rupee
Indonesia	258.5	rupiah
Japan	129.0	yen
Mexico	117.4	peso
Pakistan	184.2	rupee
USA	310.1	dollar

A **relational database** contains a collection of one or more (usually related) tables that has been created with **database-management** software. Microsoft Access is one of the best known database-management products. Some other prominent ones are Oracle, SQL Server, and MySQL. VB 2010 can interact with a database that has been created with any of these products.

The databases needed for the exercises in this textbook are contained in the materials downloaded from the companion website. They are in the folder Programs\Ch10\Databases. The database files were created with Microsoft Access 2007 and have the extension *accdb* (an abbreviation for *ACCess DataBase*). For instance, Megacities.accdb is the database file containing the two tables presented above. When the tables were created, each field was given a name and a data type. In the Cities table, the fields *pop2010* and *pop2015* were given data type Double and the other fields a data type compatible with the String data type.

Accessing a Database Table

Before a program can access a table from a database, a connection must be established. The following steps provide one way to connect to the Megacities database and bind to the Cities table.

1. Start a new program.

2. Add a BindingSource control to the Form Designer. (The BindingSource control can be found in the *All Windows Forms* or *Data* groups of the Toolbox.) After you double-click on the control in the Toolbox, a control named BindingSource1 appears in the component tray at the bottom of the Form Designer.

3. Go to the Properties window for BindingSource1 and click on the down-arrow at the right side of the DataSource property's Settings box. The panel in Fig. 10.1 appears.

FIGURE 10.1   Panel produced by Step 3.

4. Click on *Add Project Data Source*. The Data Source Configuration Wizard in Fig. 10.2 on the next page appears and asks you to "Choose a Data Source Type".

5. Select the Database icon in the Data Source Configuration Wizard and click on the *Next* button. The Wizard now asks you to "Choose a Database Model".

6. Select the Dataset icon and click on the *Next* button. The Wizard now asks you to "Choose Your Data Connection".

7. Click on the *New Connection* button. An Add Connection window similar to the one in Fig. 10.3 appears.

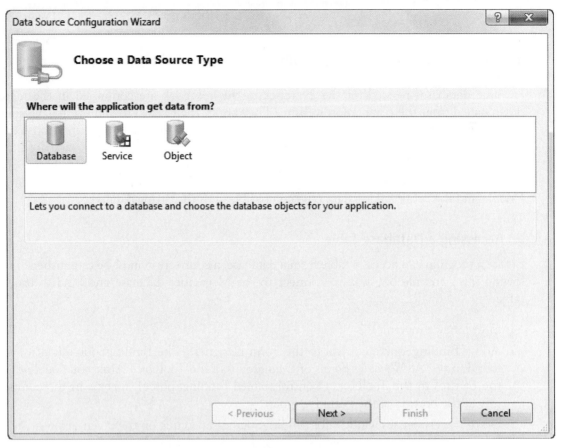

FIGURE 10.2 Window produced by Step 4.

FIGURE 10.3 Window produced by Step 7.

8. If the "Data source:" text box does not say "Microsoft Access Database File (OLE DB)", click on the *Change* button. A Change Data Source window will appear. Select *Microsoft Access Database File* from the window's list box and click on the *OK* button. You will be returned to the Add Connection window shown in Fig. 10.3.

9. Click on the *Browse* button, navigate to and open the Databases folder (a subfolder of Programs\Ch10), double-click on Megacities.accdb, and click on the *OK* button. The Data Source Configuration Wizard that appeared in Step 6 reappears with the text box now containing Megacities.accdb.

10. Click on the *Next* button. The window in Fig. 10.4 appears, asking whether you would like to place a copy of the file Megacities.accdb into the program.

FIGURE 10.4   **Window produced by Step 10.**

11. Click on the *Yes* button. The Data Source Configuration Wizard will appear and ask whether you would like to Save the Connection String to the Application Configuration File. See Fig. 10.5 on the next page.

12. Make sure that the Yes check box is checked and then click on the *Next* button. The Data Source Configuration Wizard in Fig. 10.6 will appear.

13. Check the *Tables* check box and then click on the *Finish* button. The DataSource property of BindingSource1 is now set to MegacitiesDataSet, and a MegacitiesDataSet icon has appeared in the component tray.

14. In the BindingSource1 Properties window, click on the down-arrow at the right side of the DataMember property's Settings box. A drop-down list containing the tables in the Megacities database will appear.

15. Click on *Cities* in the drop-down list. A CitiesTableAdapter icon will appear in the component tray. Also, a Load event procedure containing one line of executable code is generated in the Code Editor. See Fig. 10.7 on page 487.

The Cities table can now be accessed by the program. You can easily view a list of the fields for both of the tables in the Megacities database. Just bring up the Solution Explorer window and double-click on the file MegacitiesDataSet.xsd to display the page in Fig. 10.8. (**Note:** To close the page, click on the × symbol on its tab.)

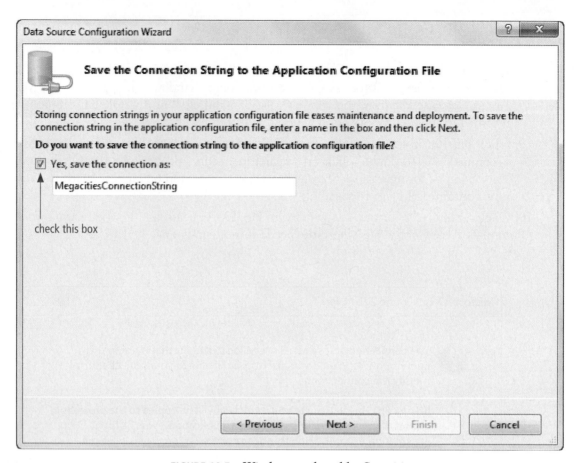

FIGURE 10.5   Window produced by Step 11.

FIGURE 10.6   Window produced by Step 12.

```
Private Sub Form1_Load(...) Handles MyBase.Load
  'TODO: This line of code loads data into the 'MegacitiesDataSet.Cities'
  'table. You can move, or remove it, as needed.
  Me.CitiesTableAdapter.Fill(Me.MegacitiesDataSet.Cities)
End Sub
```

FIGURE 10.7   Code generated by Step 15.

FIGURE 10.8   Tables and fields in the Megacities database.

■ Binding to Additional Tables

A program can access many tables through one database connection. The following steps bind the Countries table to the program created in the walkthrough above.

1. Add another BindingSource control to the Form Designer.

2. Set its DataSource property to MegacitiesDataSet. (After you click on the down-arrow, click on the right-pointing triangle (or plus box) to the left of Other Data Sources, click on the right-pointing triangle (or plus box) to the left of Project Data Sources, and then click on MegacitiesDataSet.)

3. Set the DataMember property of the new BindingSource control to Countries. A CountriesTableAdapter icon will appear in the component tray, and another line of code will be added to the Load event procedure.

■ Browsing a Connected Database

After a database has been connected to a program, any table from the database can easily be displayed. The following steps display a table from the Megacities database.

1. Right-click on the name of the database (Megacities.accdb) in the Solution Explorer and click on *Open* in the context menu. With Visual Basic Express the Database Explorer window in Fig. 10.9

FIGURE 10.9   Database Explorer window.

will appear in the location occupied by the Toolbox. (With Visual Studio, the Server Explorer window will appear.)

2. Click on the right-pointing triangle (or plus box) to the left of the Tables folder. The folder will open and reveal the names of the two tables.

3. Right-click on Cities, and click on *Retrieve Data* (with VB Express) or *Preview Data* (with Visual Studio) in the context menu. The contents of the Cities table will be displayed in the tabbed page shown in Fig. 10.10.

4. Click on the × symbol on the page's tab to close the page.

	name	country	pop2010	pop2015
▶	Bombay	India	20.1	22
	Buenos Aires	Argentina	13.1	13.4
	Calcutta	India	15.6	17
	Delhi	India	17	18.7
	Dhaka	Bangladesh	14.8	17
	Mexico City	Mexico	19.5	20.2
	New York	USA	19.4	20
	Sao Paulo	Brazil	19.6	20.1
	Shanghai	China	15.8	17.2
	Tokyo	Japan	36.1	36.4
*	*NULL*	*NULL*	*NULL*	*NULL*

Cities: Query(C:\U...1\Megacities.accdb) × | Form1.vb [Design]*

◀ | 1 of 10 | ▶ ▶| ▶※ (■)

FIGURE 10.10 **Contents of the Cities table.**

VideoNote

Querying tables

▨ Querying a Table with LINQ

Databases are usually quite large and so we rarely want to display an entire table. LINQ can be used to extract information from a data table using similar syntax as used to extract information from an array of records, a CSV text file, or an XML file.

A database table can be thought of a sequence of rows with each row containing several fields. If *line* is a row of a data table, then the elements of the row are indentified by the names `line.fieldName1`, `line.fieldName2`, and so on. For instance, if *city* is the first row of the Cities table above, then the value of `city.name` is Bombay, the value of `city.country` is India, the value of `city.pop2010` is 20.1, and the value of `city.pop2015` is 22.0.

✔ | **Example 1** The following program uses the Cities table of the Megacities database and displays the names of the cities that are located in India. The cities are sorted by their 2010 population in decreasing order. The program also displays the total population of those cities in a text box. MegacitiesDataSet.Cities serves as the data source for the LINQ query. **Note:** In the

Order By clause of query1, there was no need to use the CDbl function. The data type Double was given to the *pop2010* field when the database was created, and therefore LINQ knows that `city.pop2010` has type Double.

OBJECT	PROPERTY	SETTING
frmCities	Text	Megacities
btnDisplay	Text	Display Cities in India
lstOutput		
lblTotalPop	Text	Total population:
txtTotalPop	ReadOnly	True

```
Private Sub frmCities_Load(...) Handles MyBase.Load
   'code generated automatically when DataMember was set to Cities
   Me.CitiesTableAdapter.Fill(Me.MegacitiesDataSet.Cities)
End Sub


Private Sub btnDisplay_Click(...) Handles btnDisplay.Click
   Dim query1 = From city In MegacitiesDataSet.Cities
                Where city.country = "India"
                Order By city.pop2010 Descending
                Select city.name
   lstOutput.DataSource = query1.ToList
   lstOutput.SelectedItem = Nothing
   Dim query2 = From city In MegacitiesDataSet.Cities
                Where city.country = "India"
                Select city.pop2010
   txtTotalPop.Text = CStr(query2.Sum)
End Sub
```

[Run, and click on the button.]

Example 2 The following program searches the Countries table for a country requested by the user. Notice that the DataSource method displays "name", "pop2010", and "monetaryUnit" in the headers of the table, not "country.name", "country.pop2010", and "country.monetaryUnit". The variable *country* plays a supporting role similar to that of a looping variable in a For Each loop.

```
Private Sub frmCountries_Load(...) Handles MyBase.Load
  'code generated automatically when DataMember was set to Cities
  Me.CountriesTableAdapter.Fill(Me.MegacitiesDataSet.Countries)
End Sub

Private Sub btnDisplay_Click(...) Handles btnDisplay.Click
  Dim query = From country In MegacitiesDataSet.Countries
              Where country.name = txtName.Text
              Select country.name, country.pop2010, country.monetaryUnit
  If query.Count = 1 Then
    dgvOutput.DataSource = query.ToList
    dgvOutput.CurrentCell = Nothing
  Else
    MessageBox.Show("Country is not in the table.", "Not Found")
  End If
End Sub
```

[Run, enter a country into the text box, and click on the button.]

 Example 3 The following program uses the Cities table of the Megacities database and displays the cities whose populations are predicted to increase by more than 1 million people from 2010 to 2015. The cities are ordered by their projected population increase, and both the city names and population increases (in millions) are displayed.

```
Private Sub frmCities_Load(...) Handles MyBase.Load
  Me.CitiesTableAdapter.Fill(Me.MegacitiesDataSet.Cities)
End Sub

Private Sub btnDisplay_Click(...) Handles btnDisplay.Click
  Dim query = From city In MegacitiesDataSet.Cities
              Let popIncrease = city.pop2015 — city.pop2010
              Let formattedIncr = FormatNumber(popIncrease, 1)
              Where popIncrease > 1
              Order By popIncrease Descending
              Select city.name, formattedIncr
```

```
   dgvOutput.DataSource = query.ToList
   dgvOutput.CurrentCell = Nothing
   dgvOutput.Columns("name").HeaderText = "City"
   dgvOutput.Columns("formattedIncr").HeaderText = "Population Increase"
End Sub
```

[Run, and click on the button.]

Example 4   The following program displays the cities from the Cities table in a list box sorted by their population in 2010. When the user clicks on one of the cities, its country, population in 2010, and population in 2015 are displayed in text boxes. In the second event procedure, a query is used to search for the desired record of the table. In this case, the query returns a sequence of one value. Since a sequence cannot be assigned to a text box, the First method is used to obtain the desired value. *Note:* Notice that the statement `lstCities.DataSource = query.ToList` in the Load event procedure is not followed by the statement `lstCities.SelectedItem = Nothing`. Had the SelectedItem statement been added, the initial display would show the data about Tokyo without revealing the city that the data referred to.

```
Private Sub frmCities_Load() Handles MyBase.Load
  Me.CitiesTableAdapter.Fill(Me.MegacitiesDataSet.Cities)
  Dim query = From city In MegacitiesDataSet.Cities
              Order By city.pop2010 Descending
              Select city.name
  lstCities.DataSource = query.ToList
End Sub


Private Sub lstCities_SelectedIndexChanged(...) Handles _
            lstCities.SelectedIndexChanged
  Dim query = From city In MegacitiesDataSet.Cities
              Where city.name = lstCities.Text
              Select city.country, city.pop2010, city.pop2015
  txtCountry.Text = query.First.country
  txtPop2010.Text = FormatNumber(query.First.pop2010, 1)
  txtPop2015.Text = FormatNumber(query.First.pop2015, 1)
End Sub
```

[Run, and click on one of the cities in the list box.]

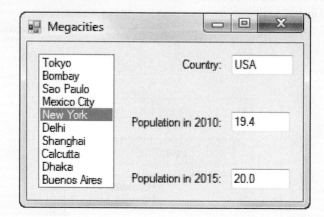

Primary and Foreign Keys

A well-designed table should have a field (or set of fields) that can be used to uniquely identify each record. Such a field (or set of fields) is called a **primary key**. For instance, in the Cities and Countries tables, each *name* field is a primary key. Databases of student enrollments in a college usually use a field of student ID numbers as the primary key. Student names would not be a good choice, because there could easily be two students having the same name.

When a table is created, a field can be specified as a primary key. If so, Visual Basic will insist that every record has an entry in the primary key and that the same entry does not appear in two different records. If the user tries to add a record with no data in the primary key, the error message "Index or primary key cannot contain a Null Value." will be generated. If the user tries to add a record with the same primary key data as another record, an error message will be displayed: "The changes you requested to the table were not successful because they would create duplicate values in the index, primary key, or relationship. Change the data in the field or fields that contain duplicate data, remove the index, or redefine the index to permit duplicate entries and try again."

When a database contains two or more tables, they are usually related. For instance, the two tables Cities and Countries are related by their fields that hold names of countries. Let's refer to these two fields as *Cities.country* and *Countries.name*. Notice that every entry in *Cities.country* appears uniquely in *Countries.name* and that *Countries.name* is a primary key of the Countries table. We say that *Cities.country* can serve as a **foreign key** of *Countries.name*. Foreign keys are usually specified when a database is first created. If so, Visual Basic will enforce the **Rule of Referential Integrity**—namely, that each value in the foreign key must also appear as a value in the primary-key field of the other table.

In the Megacities database, *Cities.name* and *Countries.name* have been specified as primary keys for their respective tables, and *Cities.country* has been specified as a foreign key of *Countries.name*. If the user tries to add to the Cities table a city whose country does not appear in the Countries table, an error message will be displayed: "You cannot add or change a record because a related record is required in table 'Countries'." The message will also be generated if the user tries to delete a country from the *Countries.name* field that appears in the *Cities.country* field.

The Join of Two Tables

A foreign key allows Visual Basic to link (or **join**) two tables from a relational database in a meaningful way. For instance, when the two tables Cities and Countries from the Megacities database are joined based on the foreign key *Cities.country*, the result is Table 10.3. The record for each city is expanded to show its country's 2010 population and its monetary unit. This joined table is very handy if, say, we want to display a city's currency.

TABLE 10.3   A join of two tables.

Cities.name	Cities. country	Cities. pop2010	Cities. pop2015	Countries. name	Countries. pop2010	Countries. monetaryUnit
Bombay	India	20.1	22.0	India	1196.8	rupee
Buenos Aires	Argentina	13.1	13.4	Argentina	41.9	peso
Calcutta	India	15.6	17.0	India	1196.8	rupee
Delhi	India	17.0	18.7	India	1196.8	rupee
Dhaka	Bangladesh	14.8	17.0	Bangladesh	152.6	rupee
Mexico City	Mexico	19.5	20.2	Mexico	117.4	peso
New York	USA	19.4	20.0	USA	310.1	dollar
Sao Paulo	Brazil	19.6	20.1	Brazil	195.2	real
Shanghai	China	15.8	17.2	China	1379.7	yuan
Tokyo	Japan	36.1	36.4	Japan	129.0	yen

The query that creates the join above begins as follows:

```
Dim query = From city In MegacitiesDataSet.Cities
            Join country In MegacitiesDataSet.Countries
            On city.country Equals country.name
```

The From clause is standard. The Join clause says that the Countries table should be joined with the Cities table. The On clause indentifies the two fields whose values are matched in order to join the tables. The variables *city* and *country* in the first two clauses are looping variables and can have any names we choose. For instance, the query above could have been written

```
Dim query = From town In MegacitiesDataSet.Cities
            Join nation In MegacitiesDataSet.Countries
            On town.country Equals nation.name
```

Example 5   The following program displays Table 10.3, the join of the two tables from the Megacities database.

```
Private Sub frmCities_Load(...) Handles MyBase.Load
  Me.CountriesTableAdapter.Fill(Me.MegacitiesDataSet.Countries)
  Me.CitiesTableAdapter.Fill(Me.MegacitiesDataSet.Cities)
End Sub


Private Sub btnDisplay_Click(...) Handles btnDisplay.Click
  Dim query = From city In MegacitiesDataSet.Cities
              Join country In MegacitiesDataSet.Countries
              On city.country Equals country.name
              Let cityName = city.name
              Let cityPop2010 = FormatNumber(city.pop2010, 1)
              Let cityPop2015 = FormatNumber(city.pop2015, 1)
              Let countryName = country.name
              Let countryPop2010 = FormatNumber(country.pop2010, 1)
              Select cityName, city.country, cityPop2010, cityPop2015,
                  countryName, countryPop2010, country.monetaryUnit
```

```
      dgvOutput.DataSource = query.ToList
      dgvOutput.CurrentCell = Nothing
End Sub
```

[Run, and click on the button.]

cityName	country	cityPop2010	cityPop2015	countryName	countryPop2010	monetaryUnit
Bombay	India	20.1	22.0	India	1,196.8	rupee
Buenos Aires	Argentina	13.1	13.4	Argentina	41.9	peso
Calcutta	India	15.6	17.0	India	1,196.8	rupee
Delhi	India	17.0	18.7	India	1,196.8	rupee
Dhaka	Bangladesh	14.8	17.0	Bangladesh	152.6	raka
Mexico City	Mexico	19.5	20.2	Mexico	117.4	peso
New York	USA	19.4	20.0	USA	310.1	dollar
Sao Paulo	Brazil	19.6	20.1	Brazil	195.2	real
Shanghai	China	15.8	17.2	China	1,379.7	yuan
Tokyo	Japan	36.1	36.4	Japan	129.0	yen

 Example 6   The following program uses the join of the two tables in the Megacities database. When the form is loaded, the Currencies list box is filled with the monetary units from the Countries table in alphabetical order. When the user selects a currency, the cities that use that currency are displayed in the Cities list box in alphabetical order. **Note:** The Cities list box was filled with the Add method rather than the DataSource method, so that the word NONE could be displayed when no cities use the selected currency.

OBJECT	PROPERTY	SETTING
frmCities	Text	Megacities
lblCurrencies	Text	Currencies
lstCurrencies		
lblCities	Text	Cities
lstCities		

```
Private Sub frmCities_Load(...) Handles MyBase.Load
    Me.CountriesTableAdapter.Fill(Me.MegacitiesDataSet.Countries)
    Me.CitiesTableAdapter.Fill(Me.MegacitiesDataSet.Cities)
    Dim query = From country In MegacitiesDataSet.Countries
                Order By country.monetaryUnit Ascending
                Select country.monetaryUnit
                Distinct
    lstCurrencies.DataSource = query.ToList
End Sub
```

```
Private Sub lstCurrencies_SelectedIndexChanged(...) Handles _
                     lstCurrencies.SelectedIndexChanged
  Dim query = From city In MegacitiesDataSet.Cities
              Join country In MegacitiesDataSet.Countries
              On city.country Equals country.name
              Where country.monetaryUnit = lstCurrencies.Text
              Order By city.name Ascending
              Select city.name
  lstCities.Items.Clear()
  If query.Count > 0 Then
    For Each city As String In query
      lstCities.Items.Add(city)
    Next
  Else
    lstCities.Items.Add("NONE")
  End If
End Sub
```

[Run, and click on a currency in the Currencies list box.]

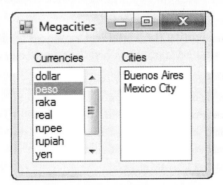

Comments

1. A database resides on a disk, and a DataSet resides in memory. A table adapter serves as a conduit to allow bidirectional data transfer between the two. A binding source is used to simplify attaching form controls to data sources.

2. The requirement that no record may have a null entry in a primary key and that entries for primary keys be unique is called the **Rule of Entity Integrity**.

3. The Join of two tables is a virtual construct. It exists only in memory.

Practice Problems 10.1

1. Consider the query in the Load event procedure of Example 6. What would happen if the LINQ operator Distinct were omitted?

2. Consider the query in Example 5. Why can't the Select clause be written as follows?

```
Select city.name, city.country, cityPop2010, cityPop2015,
       country.name, countryPop2010, country.monetaryUnit
```

EXERCISES 10.1

Figure 10.11 contains the outputs produced by the event procedures in Exercises 1 through 6.

cityName	monetaryUnit
Dhaka	raka
Buenos Aires	peso

(a)

cityName	country
Shanghai	China
Calcutta	India

(b)

name	country
Calcutta	India
Dhaka	Bangladesh

(c)

name	monetaryUnit
Indonesia	rupiah
USA	dollar

(d)

name	country
Dhaka	Bangladesh
Sao Paulo	Brazil

(e)

name	monetaryUnit
Japan	yen
China	yuan

(f)

FIGURE 10.11   Outputs for Exercises 1 through 6.

In Exercises 1 through 6, identify the DataGridView in Fig. 10.11 that is the output of the event procedure. Assume that each program has the same Load event procedure as Example 5.

1.
```
Private Sub btnDisplay_Click(...) Handles btnDisplay.Click
    Dim query = From country In MegacitiesDataSet.Countries
                Where country.monetaryUnit.StartsWith("y")
                Select country.name,country.monetaryUnit
    dgvOutput.DataSource = query.ToList
    dgvOutput.CurrentCell = Nothing
End Sub
```

2.
```
Private Sub btnDisplay_Click(...) Handles btnDisplay.Click
    Dim query = From city In MegacitiesDataSet.Cities
                Where city.pop2015 = 17.0
                Select city.name, city.country
    dgvOutput.DataSource = query.ToList
    dgvOutput.CurrentCell = Nothing
End Sub
```

3.
```
Private Sub btnDisplay_Click(...) Handles btnDisplay.Click
    Dim query = From country In MegacitiesDataSet.Countries
                Where (country.pop2010 > 250) And (country.pop2010 < 350)
                Select country.name, country.monetaryUnit
    dgvOutput.DataSource = query.ToList
    dgvOutput.CurrentCell = Nothing
Sub
```

4.
```
Private Sub btnDisplay_Click(...) Handles btnDisplay.Click
    Dim query = From city In MegacitiesDataSet.Cities
                Where city.name.EndsWith("a")
                Select city.name, city.country
    dgvOutput.DataSource = query.ToList
    dgvOutput.CurrentCell = Nothing
End Sub
```

5.
```
Private Sub btnDisplay_Click(...) Handles btnDisplay.Click
   Dim query = From city In MegacitiesDataSet.Cities
               Join country In MegacitiesDataSet.Countries
               On city.country Equals country.name
               Let cityName = city.name
               Where country.pop2010 > (75 * city.pop2010)
               Order By city.country Ascending
               Select cityName, city.country
   dgvOutput.DataSource = query.ToList
   dgvOutput.CurrentCell = Nothing
End Sub
```

6.
```
Private Sub btnDisplay_Click(...) Handles btnDisplay.Click
   Dim query = From country In MegacitiesDataSet.Countries
               Where country.name.Length = 5
               Order By country.name Descending
               Select country.name, country.monetaryUnit
   dgvOutput.DataSource = query.ToList
   dgvOutput.CurrentCell = Nothing
End Sub
```

Exercises 7 through 16 require the Megacities database.

7. Write a program that displays (in a DataGridView control) the names of all the cities, their countries, and the projected percentage growth of their populations from 2010 to 2015. Records should be sorted in descending order by their projected population growth. See Fig. 10.12.

City	Country	Projected Population Growth
Dhaka	Bangladesh	14.86%
Delhi	India	10.00%
Bombay	India	9.45%
Calcutta	India	8.97%
Shanghai	China	8.86%
Mexico City	Mexico	3.59%
New York	USA	3.09%
Sao Paulo	Brazil	2.55%
Buenos Aires	Argentina	2.29%
Tokyo	Japan	0.83%

FIGURE 10.12   **Output of Exercise 7.**

8. Write a program that shows (in a list box) the names of all the countries from the Cities table. When the user clicks on one of the countries, the program should display (in a text box) the name of its most populous city in 2010.

9. Write a program that displays (in a list box) the names of the cities in the Cities table whose populations are projected to exceed 20 million by the year 2015. The cities should be ordered by their projected population in descending order.

10. Write a program that displays (in a DataGridView control) the names of the cities in the Cities table whose 2010 populations are between 13 and 19 million. The countries and their 2010 populations also should be displayed, and the records should be ordered alphabetically by the names of the countries.

11. Write a program to find and display (in a DataGridView control) the entire record for the city in the Cities table that will experience the greatest percentage growth from 2010 to 2015. **Note:** The percentage growth is (pop2015 – pop2010) / pop2010.

12. Write a program that displays (in a DataGridView control) the names of all the cities, their countries, and for each city the percentage of its country's population that lived in that city in 2010. Records should be sorted in descending order by the percentages.

13. Write a program that displays the cities in a list box. When the user clicks on one of the cities, the program should display (in a text box) the percentage of its country's population that lived in that city in 2010.

14. Write a program that displays the cities in a list box. When the user clicks on one of the cities, the program should display (in a text box) the city's currency.

15. Write a program that creates a CSV text file containing the contents of the Cities table. Run the program, and compare the size of the text file with the size of the file Megacities.accdb.

16. Write a program that creates an XML file containing the contents of the Cities table.

The database UN.accbd has the single table Nations that contains data for the 192 member countries of the United Nations. The fields for the table are *name, continent, population,* and *area*. (Population is given in millions and area in square miles.) Use the United Nations database in Exercises 17 through 19. Some records in the table are

Canada	North America	32.9	3855000
France	Europe	63.5	211209
New Zealand	Australia/Oceania	4.18	103738
Nigeria	Africa	146.5	356669
Pakistan	Asia	164	310403
Peru	South America	27.9	496226

17. Write a program that displays the names of the continents from the Nations table in a list box. When the user clicks on a continent's name, the countries in that continent should be displayed in two other list boxes. One list box should display the countries in descending order by their population, and the other should display the countries in descending order by their area. See Fig. 10.13.

18. Write a program that displays the names of the continents from the Nations table in a list box. When the user clicks on a continent's name, the countries in that continent should be displayed (in a DataGridView) along with their population densities. The records should be in ascending order by their population densities.

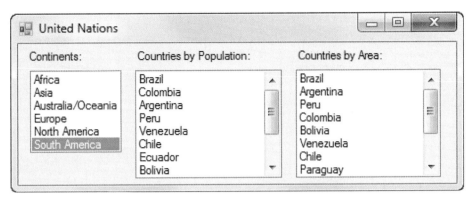

FIGURE 10.13 Sample output of Exercise 17.

19. Write a program to find and display (in a DataGridView control) two entire records, where the first record gives the data for the country with the largest population, and the second the data for the country with the smallest population.

The database Exchrate.accdb has the single table Rates that gives the exchange rates (in terms of American dollars) for 45 currencies of major countries in December, 2009. Figure 10.14 shows the first eight records in the database in a DataGridView control. The dollarRate column gives the number of units of the currency that can be purchased for one American dollar. For instance, one American dollar purchases 1.05875 Canadian dollars. Use the Exchrate database in Exercises 20 through 22.

country	monetaryUnit	dollarRate
America	Dollar	1
Argentina	Peso	3.81072
Australia	Dollar	1.10248
Brazil	Real	1.76002
Canada	Dollar	1.05875
Chile	Peso	499.978
China	Yuan	6.83236
Colombia	Peso	1994.5

FIGURE 10.14 Exchange rates.

20. Write a program that shows the names of the countries in a list box. When the user clicks on one of the names, the monetary unit and the exchange rate should be displayed.

21. Write a program that displays the names of the countries in a list box in ascending order determined by the number of units that can be purchased by one American dollar. When the user clicks on one of the names, the monetary unit and exchange rate should be displayed.

22. Write a program containing two list boxes as shown in Fig. 10.15 on the next page. When the user selects two countries, enters an amount of money, and clicks on the button, the program should convert the amount from one currency to the other.

FIGURE 10.15   A possible output for Exercise 22.

The database Baseball.accdb has the two tables Players and Teams. The fields for the Players table are *name, team, atBats,* and *hits*. The fields for the Teams table are *name, location, league, stadium, atBats,* and *hits*. The database has been filled with information from the 2009 baseball season for the major league. The Players table lists all major-league players with at least 350 at bats during the season. The Teams table lists all major-league teams. Use the Baseball database in Exercises 23 through 38. Here are three sample records from each table:

Players

Aaron Hill	Blue Jays	682	195
Ichiro Suzuki	Mariners	639	225
Derek Jeter	Yankees	634	212

Teams

Cubs	Chicago	National	Wrigley Field	5486	1398
Nationals	Washington D.C.	National	National Park	5493	1432
Red Sox	Boston	American	Fenway Park	5543	1495

23. Write a program that shows all the teams from the Teams table in a list box. When the user clicks on one of the teams, the program should display the team's home stadium in a text box.

24. Write a program to display in a list box the player (or players) in the Players table with the highest batting average.

25. Write a program to display in a list box the player (or players) in the Players table with the most hits.

26. Write a program to display in a DataGridView control the names of all the teams, their home stadiums, and the teams' batting averages. Records should be sorted in ascending order by the batting averages.

27. Write a program that shows all the teams from the Teams table in a list box. When the user clicks on one of the teams, the program should display in a DataGridView control the names of all the players in the Players table from that team, along with their batting averages. The players should be listed in descending order of their batting averages. See Fig. 10.16.

28. Write a program that shows all the players' batting averages above .300 in a list box. When the user clicks on one of the batting averages, the program should display in a DataGrid-View control the names of all the players in the Players table with that batting average,

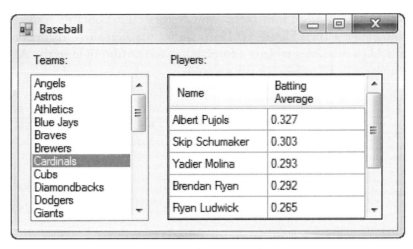

FIGURE 10.16   Sample output of Exercise 27.

along with their teams. The players should be listed in alphabetical order of their last names.

29. Write a program that contains two radio buttons captioned *American League* and *National League*. When the user clicks on one of them, the program should display in a DataGridView control the names of all the teams in the Teams table from that league, along with their team batting averages. The teams should be listed in descending order of their batting averages.

30. Write a program that uses the Teams table to calculate the total number of hits by teams in the National League.

31. Write a program that uses the Teams table to calculate the overall batting average for players in the American League.

32. Write a program to count the number of players in the Players table who play for a New York team.

33. Write a program to count the number of players in the Players table who play for a National League team.

34. Write a program that contains two radio buttons captioned *American League* and *National League*. When the user clicks on one of the radio buttons, the program should display (in a DataGridView control) the names of all the players from the league who had more than 150 hits, along with their batting averages and home stadiums. The players should be listed in descending order of their batting averages.

35. Write a program that shows all the teams from the Teams table in a list box. When the user clicks on one of the teams, the program should display (in another list box) the names of all the players in the Players table from that team, whose batting average was greater than their team's batting average. The players should be listed in descending order of their batting averages.

36. Write a program to display (in a list box) the player (or players) in the American League with the most hits.

37. Write a program to display the player (or players) in the National League with the highest batting average.

38. Write a program that requests a batting average and a league (American or National) and then displays (in a list box) the names of all the players in the league whose batting average is greater than the given batting average. The players should be listed in descending order by the number of hits they had during the season. The program should not allow the given batting average to be greater than 1 or less than 0.

The database Movies.accdb has two tables named Lines and Actors. The Lines table contains famous lines from films that were spoken by the leading male actor. The first field of the table gives the famous line and the second field gives the film. Figure 10.17(a) shows the

first three records of the Lines table. The Actors table contains some names of films and their leading male actors. Figure 10.17(b) shows the first three records of the Actors table. The *film* field in the Lines table is a foreign key to the *film* field in the Actors table. Use the Movies database in Exercises 39 through 44.

famousLine	film	film	maleLead
Rosebud.	Citizen Kane	On the Waterfront	Marlon Brando
We'll always have Paris.	Casablanca	Sudden Impact	Clint Eastwood
I coulda been a contender.	On the Waterfront	Taxi Driver	Robert DeNiro

      (a) **Lines**   (b) **Actors**

FIGURE 10.17   Some records from the tables in the Movies database.

39. What is the primary key in the Actors table?

40. What is the primary key in the Lines table?

41. Write a program that fills a list box with the names of the films in the Lines table. When the user clicks on the name of a film, the lead male actor in that film should be displayed in a text box. See Fig. 10.18.

FIGURE 10.18   Sample outcome of Exercise 41.

42. Write a program that displays a DataGridView control containing all the famous lines from the Lines table along with the actors who spoke them and the films. See Fig. 10.19. **Note:** Set the AutoSizeColumnMode property of the DataGridView control to AllCells.

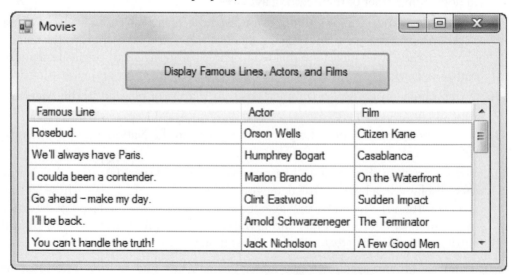

FIGURE 10.19   Outcome of Exercise 42.

43. Write a program that displays the names of the actors from the Actors table in a list box. When the user clicks on an actor's name, the famous lines from the Lines table that he spoke should be displayed in a second list box.

44. Write a program that displays the names of the films from the Actors table in a list box. When the user clicks on a film's name, the famous lines from the Lines table that were spoken in that film should be displayed in a second list box.

Solutions to Practice Problems 10.1

1. In the absence of the Distinct operator, both "peso" and "rupee" would appear twice in the list box.

2. The problem here is that the Select clause contains both *city.name* and *country.name*. The query would try to create two fields named *name*.

10.2   Editing and Designing Databases

In Section 10.1, we showed how to connect to a database and how to use LINQ queries to manipulate information retrieved from the database. In this section we learn how to alter records, delete records, and add new records to a database table. We end the section with a discussion of good database design.

▓ A Program to Edit the Cities Table

VideoNote
Editing
databases

We begin by examining a program that edits the Cities table of the Megacities database; then we show how to create the program. The program, named 10-2-1, is in the folder Programs\Ch10 that you downloaded from the companion website for this book.

Figure 10.20 shows the form for the program. All of the controls on the form are familiar except for the navigation toolbar docked at the top of the form. Figure 10.21 shows the toolbar and identifies its components.

FIGURE 10.20   Form for the editing program.

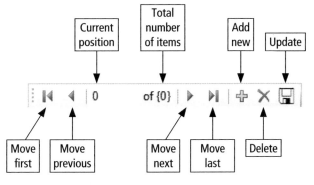

FIGURE 10.21   Navigation toolbar.

Figure 10.22 shows the form just after the program is run. The contents of the first record are shown in the four text boxes arranged vertically on the left side of the form. The *Move first* and *Move previous* buttons are disabled, since there are no records preceding the first record. When you click on the *Move next* button, the second record appears. In general, the four *Move* buttons allow you to navigate to any record of the Cities table. The first record of the table is said to have position 1, the second record position 2, and so on. If you place a number from 1 through 10 in the navigation toolbar's "Current position" box and then press the Enter key, the record having that position number will be displayed. For instance, if you enter 7 into the "Current position" box, the information for New York will be displayed. Another way to obtain a specific record is to type the name of a city into the text box labeled "City to find:" and then click on the *Search for City* button.

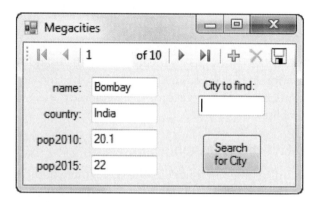

FIGURE 10.22   Table-editing program at startup.

To alter the data in the currently displayed record, just replace the value in one or more of the text boxes and then click on one of the *Move* buttons.

To add a new record to the Cities table, click on the *Add new* button (✚). The text boxes for the four fields will become blank. After you type in the data for the new record, and click on one of the *Move* buttons, the new record will be added and the number in the "Total number of items" box will change from 10 to 11.

To remove the currently displayed record from the Cities table, click on the *Delete* button (✗). The record will be deleted and the number in the "Total number of items" box will decrease by 1.

Each time the Cities table is altered in any way, only the copy of the table in memory is actually altered. To alter the database file on the disk, you must click on the *Update* button (🖫). **Note 1:** The Solution Explorer actually contains two copies of the file Megacities.accdb. One copy is always displayed near the bottom of the Solution Explorer. A second copy is located in the *bin\Debug* folder. It is this second copy that can be updated by the program. **Note 2:** If the changes you made violate the Rule of Referential Integrity (every value in the foreign key must also appear in the primary key of the other table), the program will crash when the database file is updated. **Note 3:** Changes that violate the Rule of Entity Integrity (no record may have a null entry in its primary key and entries for primary keys must be unique) cause the program to crash as soon as a *Move* button is pressed. Exercises 10 through 12 discuss techniques for addressing the issues in Notes 2 and 3.

The following walkthrough will better acquaint you with the operation of the program.

1. Open and run the program named 10-2-1.

2. Press the *Move next* button in the navigation toolbar twice to reveal the third record, the one for Calcutta.

3. Type "New York" into the "City to find:" text box and then click on the *Search for City* button to display the record for New York.

4. Click on the *Add new* button in the navigation toolbar and then enter the following data into the vertical set of four empty text boxes for the fields: Los Angeles, USA, 12.8, 13.2.

5. Click on one of the *Move* buttons in the navigation toolbar. Notice that the "Total number of items" box now shows that there are 11 records.

6. Terminate and then rerun the program. Notice that the "Total number of items" box shows that there are 10 records. The Megacities database file in the *bin\Debug* folder was not updated because we did not click on the *Update* button before terminating the program.

7. Redo steps 4 and 5, and then click on the *Update* button.

8. Terminate and then rerun the program. Notice that the "Total number of items" box shows that there are 11 records. The Megacities database file in the *bin\Debug* folder was updated.

9. Experiment further with the program to test its other features.

■ Designing the Form for the Table-Editing Program

The following steps create the navigation toolbar for program 10-2-1, create the four sets of labels and text boxes on the left side of the form, bind the text boxes to the navigation toolbar, and implement the search capability.

1. Start a new program and bind the Cities table as was done in Section 10.1.

2. Add a BindingNavigator control to the form designer. (This control can be found in the *All Windows Forms* or *Data* groups of the Toolbox.) After you double-click on the control in the Toolbox, a control named BindingNavigator1 appears in the component tray at the bottom of the Form Designer. Also, a navigation toolbar will appear anchored to the top of the form.

3. Go to the Properties window for BindingNavigator1, click on the down-arrow at the right side of the BindingSource property's Settings box, and set the BindingSource property to BindingSource1.

4. Notice that the toolbar is missing the *Update* button. The rightmost item on the toolbar (see Fig. 10.23) is used to add an update button to the navigation toolbar. Click on the small down-arrow on the right side of the rightmost item and then click on *Button* in the drop-down list that appears. A button showing a mountain (🖼) appears.

FIGURE 10.23   Original navigation toolbar.

5. Open the Properties window for the mountain button, change its name from ToolStripButton1 to btnUpdate, and set its Text property to Update.

6. Click on the ellipses at the right side of the Image property's Settings box, and then click on the *Import* button in the Select Resource dialogue box that appears. (An Open dialog box appears.)

7. Browse to locate the folder Programs\Ch10, and double-click on the file Disk.bmp to place its picture in the Select Resource window.

8. Click on the *OK* button to change the image on btnUpdate to a diskette (💾).

9. Click on the *Data* menu in the Visual Basic Toolbar, and then click on *Show Data Sources*. A Data Sources window showing the names of the tables in the database will appear in the location occupied by the Solution Explorer window.

10. Double-click on *Cities* in the Data Sources window to obtain the display in Fig. 10.24.

FIGURE 10.24   Data Sources window.

11. Click on *name* and drag it onto the form. Both a label and text box for the field *name* appear on the form. The label will be named NameLabel and the text box will be named NameTextBox.

12. Repeat Step 11 for each of the other three fields. The left side of the form has now been created and the four text boxes have been bound to the navigation toolbar.

13. Create the remaining controls in Fig 10.20 in the usual way.

■ Writing the Table-Editing Program

We have seen that each record of the Cities table is given a position number from 1 through 10 by the navigation toolbar. For programming purposes, each record has an **index number** that ranges from 0 through 9. That is, the record for Bombay has index number 0, the record for Buenos Aires has index number 1, and so on. BindingSource controls have a Position property and a Find method that return index numbers.

Assume the program is running. Let's refer to the record whose fields are displayed as the **current record**. At any time, the value of

```
BindingSource1.Position
```

is the index of the current record. Pay particular attention to the fact that the Position property gives the index, not the position!

If *n* is a nonnegative integer, then the statement

```
BindingSource1.Position = n
```

makes the record of index *n* the current record.

If *strVar* is a string variable whose value is a city in the Cities table, then the value of

```
BindingSource1.Find("name", strVar)
```

is the index of the record for that city. If the value of *strVar* is not a city in the table, then the Find method returns the value 0. **Note:** The Find method returns the same value, 0, both for Bombay and for a city not present in the Cities table.

 Example 1   The following program edits the Cities table. Assume that the Cities table has been bound, and the navigation toolbar, text boxes, and *Search for City* button have been created as described above. The second statement inside the Load event procedure is optional. It prevents the city Bombay from being highlighted when the program is first run. In the btnSearch_Click event procedure, the two statements that refer to *currentCity* are optional. If they are omitted, the program will display the record for the first city (in this case Bombay) after an unsuccessful search. The remaining statements are self-explanatory.

OBJECT	PROPERTY	SETTING
frmCities	Text	Megacities
NameLabel	Text	name:
NameTextBox		
CountryLabel	Text	country:
CountryTextBox		
Pop2010Label	Text	pop2010:
Pop2010TextBox		
Pop2015Label	Text	pop2015:
Pop2015TextBox		
lblCity	Text	City to find:
txtCity		
btnSearch	Text	Search for City

```
Private Sub frmCities_Load(...) Handles MyBase.Load
  Me.CitiesTableAdapter.Fill(Me.MegacitiesDataSet.Cities)
End Sub


Private Sub btnUpdate_Click(...) Handles btnUpdate.Click
  'These two lines update the database file in the bin\Debug folder.
  BindingSource1.EndEdit()
  CitiesTableAdapter.Update(MegacitiesDataSet.Cities)
End Sub


Private Sub btnSearch_Click(...) Handles btnSearch.Click
  Dim currentCity As String = NameTextBox.Text
  If txtCity.Text <> "" Then
    BindingSource1.Position = BindingSource1.Find("name", txtCity.Text)
    If NameTextBox.Text <> txtCity.Text Then
      MessageBox.Show("City not found.")
      BindingSource1.Position = BindingSource1.Find("name", currentCity)
    End If
  Else
    MessageBox.Show("You must enter the name of a city.")
  End If
End Sub
```

■ Principles of Database Design

Good relational database design is more of an art than a science. However, the designer should keep in mind certain fundamental guidelines.

- *Data should often be stored in their smallest parts.*

   For instance, city, state, and zip code are usually best stored in three fields. So doing will allow you to easily sort a mailing by zip code or target a mailing to the residents of a specific city.

- *Avoid redundancy.*

   The process of avoiding redundancy by splitting a table into two or more related tables is called **data normalization**. For instance, the excessive duplication in Table 10.4 can be avoided by replacing the table with the two related tables 10.5(a) and 10.5(b).

TABLE 10.4 **A table with redundant data.**

Course	Section	Name	Time	Credits	Prerequisites
CS102	1001	Intro to Databases	MWF 8-9	3	CS101
CS102	1002	Intro to Databases	MWF 1-2	3	CS101
CS102	1003	Intro to Databases	MWF 2-3	3	CS101
CS102	1004	Intro to Databases	MWF 3-4	3	CS101
CS105	1001	Visual Basic	MWF 1-2	4	CS200

TABLE 10.5(a)

Course	Section	Time
CS102	1001	MWF 8-9
CS102	1002	MWF 1-2
CS102	1003	MWF 2-3
CS102	1004	MWF 3-4
CS105	1001	MWF 1-2

TABLE 10.5(b)

Course	Name	Credits	Prerequisites
CS102	Intro to Databases	3	CS101
CS105	Visual Basic	4	CS200

- *Avoid tables with intentionally blank entries.*

  Tables with entries that are intentionally left blank use space inefficiently. Table 10.6, which serves as a directory of faculty and students, has an excessive number of blank entries. The table should be split into two tables, each dealing with just one of the groups.

TABLE 10.6 **A table with an excessive number of blank entries.**

Name	ssn	Classification	Date Hired	Dept	Office Number	gpa	Credits Earned
Sarah Brown	816-34-9012	student				3.7	78
Pat Riley	409-22-1234	faculty	9/1/02	biology	Y-3014		
Joe Russo	690-32-1108	faculty	9/1/05	math	T-2008		
Juan Lopez	509-43-4110	student				3.2	42

- *Strive for table cohesion.*

  Each table should have a basic topic to which all the data in the table are connected.

- *Avoid fields whose values can be calculated from existing fields.*

  For instance, if a table has fields for both the population and area of countries, then there is no need to include a field for the population density.

■ Comments

1. Since the *name* field of the Cities table is the primary key, each record of the table must have a value assigned to its *name* field. However, the database does not require that values be assigned to the other three fields.

2. In Example 1, the four pairs of labels and text boxes on the left side of the form have the names given to them by Visual Basic when the fields were dragged from the Data Sources window to the Form Designer. You can change these names if you like. For instance, CountryTextBox can be changed to txtCountry. Also, the names of the controls BindingSource1 and BindingNavigator1 can be changed to more meaningful ones, such as CitiesBindingSource and CitiesBindingNavigator.

Practice Problems 10.2

1. Can a record for any city be added to the Cities table?
2. Can a record for any country be added to the Countries table?
3. Can any record in the Cities table be deleted?
4. Can any record in the Countries table be deleted?

EXERCISES 10.2

In Exercises 1 through 8, carry out the following tasks on the Cities table with the program from Example 1.

1. Change the name of the city Bombay to Mumbai.
2. Add the following record: Karachi, Pakistan, 13.1, 14.9.
3. Use the *Search for City* button to find the record for Calcutta.
4. Find the record for the city in position 8.
5. Delete the record for Dhaka.
6. Add a record that will raise an exception when you try to Update the database file.
7. Add a record that will raise an exception as soon as you move to another record.
8. Add a record with some empty fields.
9. Consider Example 1. Let *strVar* be a string variable. Give a condition that will be True if the value of *strVar* is not the name of a city in the Cities table.
10. Consider Example 1. If you violate the Rule of Referential Integrity, an exception is generated when you click on the *Update* button. Revise the btnUpdate_Click event procedure so that the program will not crash when the principle is violated. **Note:** The name of the exception is OleDB.OleDbException.
11. Modify Example 1 so that a Rule of Referential Integrity violation is caught as soon as an improper country is entered into the country text box.
12. Modify Example 1 so that a Rule of Entity Integrity violation is caught as soon as the user leaves an empty NameTextBox or a NameTextBox whose entry duplicates a city from another record.

Exercises 13 through 18 refer to the database Movies.accdb discussed in the exercises for Section 10.1.

13. Write a program that can be used to make changes to the Lines table. (There is no need to include a Search capability.)
14. Write a program that can be used to make changes to the Actors table. (There is no need to include a Search capability.)
15. Use the program created in Exercise 13 to change the famous line "Here's looking at you kid." to the line "Play it Sam." Both lines are from the same film.
16. Use the program created in Exercise 14 to add the following record to the Actors table: Patton, George Scott.
17. Why can't the following record be added to the Lines table: "Houston, we have a problem.", Apollo 13?
18. Why can't the following record be deleted from the Actors table: Casablanca, Humphrey Bogart?

19. Eliminate the redundancy in Table 10.7.

TABLE 10.7	A table with redundancies.			
name	address	city	state	stateCapital
R. Myers	3 Maple St.	Seattle	Washington	Olympia
T. Murphy	25 Main St.	Seattle	Washington	Olympia
L. Scott	14 Park Ave.	Baltimore	Maryland	Annapolis
B. Jones	106 5th St.	Seattle	Washington	Olympia
W. Smith	29 7th Ave.	Baltimore	Maryland	Annapolis
V. Miller	4 Flower Ave.	Chicago	Illinois	Springfield

20. Eliminate the redundancy in Table 10.8, a table of members of the U.S. House of Representatives. (**Note:** The value of *numColleges* is the number of colleges in the representative's state.)

TABLE 10.8	A table with redundancies.			
name	state	party	statePop	numColleges
J. Dingell	Michigan.	Democratic	10.2	97
E. Cantor	Virginia	Republican	7.8	83
J. Moran	Virginia	Democratic	7.8	83
J. Sarbanes	Maryland	Democratic	5.8	97
S. Hoyer	Maryland	Democratic	5.8	97
F. Wolf	Virginia	Republican	7.8	83

21. The database Justices.accdb in the Programs\Ch10\Databases folder was current as of January 1, 2010. If some justices have retired and new justices have been appointed since then, update the database.

Solutions to Practice Problems 10.2

1. No. The city must be from a country appearing in the Countries table.

2. Yes.

3. Yes.

4. No. Only the records for Pakistan and Indonesia can be deleted.

CHAPTER 10 **SUMMARY**

1. A *table* is a group of data items arranged in a rectangular array, with each row containing the same categories of information. Each row is called a *record*. Each category (column) is called a *field*. A *database* is a collection of one or more tables that are usually related.

2. A *BindingSource control* can be used to bind a table of a database to a program.

3. *Database Explorer* in VB Express and *Server Explorer* in Visual Studio can be used to view the table from a database that has been connected to a program.

4. *LINQ* can be used to set criteria for information retrieval from a table.

5. A sequence of records resulting from the execution of a LINQ query can be displayed in a *DataGridView control*.

6. A *primary key* is a field or set of fields that uniquely identifies each record of a table. The *Rule of Entity Integrity* states that no record can have a null entry in a primary key and that entries for primary keys must be unique. A *foreign key* is a field or set of fields in one table that refers to a primary key in another table. The *Rule of Referential Integrity* states that each value in the foreign key must also appear in the primary key in the related table.

7. The *Join operator* links two tables based on matching field values.

8. A *navigation toolbar*, which has icons on its buttons similar to those on a DVD player, can be used to view records, alter records, delete records, and add new records to a database table. A *BindingNavigator control* binds the navigation toolbar to the table via a Binding-Source control. Searching for records in the table can be facilitated with the *Position property* and the *Find methods* of the BindingSource control.

9. Some fundamental design principles help database designers create efficient databases.

CHAPTER 10 PROGRAMMING PROJECTS

VideoNote
Richard's catering (Homework)

1. The database Microland.accdb is maintained by the Microland Computer Warehouse, a mail-order computer-supply company. Tables 10.9 through 10.11 show parts of three tables in the database. The table Customers identifies each customer by an ID number and gives, in addition to the name and address, the total amount of purchases during the current year prior to today. The table Inventory identifies each product in stock by an ID number and gives, in addition to its description and price (per unit), the quantity in stock at the beginning of the day. The table Orders gives the orders received today. Suppose that it is now the end of the day. Write a program that uses the three tables to do the following two tasks.

TABLE 10.9 First three records of the Customers table.

CustID	Name	Street	City	AmtPurchases
1	Michael Smith	2 Park St	Dallas, TX 75201	234.50
2	Brittany Jones	5 2nd Ave.	Tampa, FL 33602	121.90
3	Warren Pease	7 Maple St.	Boston, MA 02101	387.20

TABLE 10.10 First three records of the Inventory table.

itemID	description	price	quantity
PL208	Visual Basic	89.50	12
SW109	MS Office Upgrade	195.95	2
HW913	Scanner	49.95	8

TABLE 10.11 First four records of the Orders table.

custID	itemID	quantity
3	SW109	1
1	PL208	3
1	HW913	2
2	PL208	1

(a) Display in a list box the items that are out of stock and those that must be reordered to satisfy today's orders. Show the ID, quantity on backorder, description, and cost to acquire. See Fig. 10.25(a).

(b) Display in a list box bills for all customers who ordered during the day. Each bill should show the customer's name, address, items ordered (with costs), and total cost of the order. See Fig. 10.25(b).

(a)

(b)

FIGURE 10.25 **Output of Programming Project 1.**

2. *Grade Book.* A teacher maintains a database containing two tables—Students and Grades. The Students table has three fields: *studentID*, *lastName*, and *firstName*. The Grades table has four fields: *studentID*, *firstExam*, *secondExam*, and *finalExam*. At the beginning of the semester, the Students table is filled in completely with a record for each student in a class, and the Grades table has a record for each student that contains only the student's ID number. (**Note:** The database is contained in the file Gradebook.accdb from the folder Ch10\Databases.) Write a program that allows the instructor to record and process the grades for the semester. The program should do the following:

(a) Use a navigation toolbar to fill the Grades table.

(b) After all grades have been entered, display a DataGridView control showing the name of each student and his or her semester average. The semester average should be calculated as (firstExam + secondExam + 2·finalExam)/4. See Fig. 10.26.

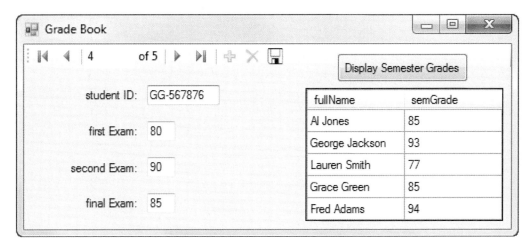

FIGURE 10.26   Possible outcome of Programming Project 2.

11

Object-Oriented Programming

11.1 Classes and Objects

noun A word used to denote or name a person, place, thing, quality, or act.

verb That part of speech that expresses existence, action, or occurrence.

adjective Any of a class of words used to modify a noun or other substantive by limiting, qualifying, or specifying.

The American Heritage Dictionary of the English Language

"A good rule of thumb for object-oriented programming is that classes are the nouns in your analysis of the problem. The methods in your object correspond to verbs that the noun does. The properties are the adjectives that describe the noun."

Gary Cornell & David Jezak

Practical experience in the financial, scientific, engineering, and software design industries has revealed some difficulties with traditional program design methodologies. As programs grow in size and become more complex, and as the number of programmers working on the same project increases, the number of dependencies and interrelationships throughout the code increases exponentially. A small change made by one programmer in one place may have many effects, both intended and unintended, in many other places. The effects of this change may ripple throughout the entire program, requiring the rewriting of a great deal of code along the way.

A partial solution to this problem is "data hiding" where, within a unit, as much implementation detail as possible is hidden. Data hiding is an important principle underlying object-oriented programming. An object is an encapsulation of data and procedures that act on the data. A programmer using an object is concerned only with the tasks that the object can perform and the parameters used by these tasks. The details of the data structures and procedures are hidden within the object.

VideoNote

Classes and objects

Two types of objects will be of concern to us: **control objects** and **code objects**. Examples of control objects are text boxes, list boxes, buttons, and all the other controls that can be created from the Toolbox. So far, most of our programs have contained a single class block beginning with a line such as "Public Class frmName" and ending with the line "End Class." A code object is a specific instance of a user-defined type, called a **class**, which is defined similarly to a structure, but in a separate class block of the form

```
Class ClassName
    statements
End Class
```

Each class block is delineated in the Code Editor by an elongated left bracket appearing to the left of the block. Both control objects and class objects have properties, methods, and events. The main differences are that control objects are predefined and have physical manifestations, whereas the programmer must create the class blocks for code objects. In this section, when we use the word "object" without a qualifier, we mean "code object."

Whenever you double-click on the TextBox icon in the Toolbox, a new text box is created. Although each text box is a separate entity, they all have the same properties, methods, and events. Each text box is said to be an **instance** of the class TextBox. In some sense, the TextBox icon in the Toolbox is a template or blueprint for creating text boxes. When you look at the Properties window for a text box, the drop-down list box at the top of the window reads something like "TextBox1 System.Windows.Forms.TextBox." TextBox1 is the name of the control object and it is said to be an instance of the class "TextBox." You can't set properties or invoke methods of the TextBox class; you can only set properties or invoke methods of the specific text boxes that are instances of the class. The analogy is often made between a class and a cookie cutter. The cookie cutter is used to create cookies that you can eat, but you can't eat the cookie cutter.

Object-oriented programs are populated with objects that hold data, have properties, respond to methods, and raise events. (The generation of events will be discussed in the next section.) Six examples of objects are as follows:

1. In a professor's program to assign and display semester grades, a student object might hold a single student's name, social security number, midterm grade, and final exam grade. A CalcSemGrade method might calculate the student's semester grade. Events might be raised when improper data are passed to the object.

2. In a payroll program, an employee object might hold an employee's name, hourly wage, and hours worked. A CalculatePay method would tell the object to calculate the wages for the current pay period.

3. In a checking account program, a check register object might have methods that record and total the checks written during a certain month, a deposit slip object might record and total the deposits made during a certain month, and an account object might keep a running total of the balance in the account. The account object would raise an event to alert the bank when the balance got too low.

4. In a bookstore inventory program, a textbook object might hold the name, author, quantity in stock, and wholesale price of an individual textbook. A CalculateRetailPrice method might instruct the textbook object to calculate the selling price of the textbook. An event could be raised when the book went out of stock.

5. In a game program, an airplane object might hold the location of an airplane. At any time, the program could tell the object to display the airplane at its current location or to drop a bomb. An event could be raised each time a bomb was released so that the program could determine if anything was hit.

6. In a card game program, a card object might hold the denomination and suit of a specific card. An IdentifyCard method might return a string such as "Ace of Spades." A deck-of-cards object might consist of an array of card objects and a ShuffleDeck method that thoroughly shuffled the deck. A Shuffling event might indicate the progress of the shuffle.

An important object-oriented term is **class**. A class is a template from which objects are created. The class specifies the properties and methods that will be common to all objects that are instances of that class. Classes are formulated in class blocks. An object, which is an instance of a class, can be created in a program with a pair of statements of the form

```
Dim objectName As ClassName
objectName = New ClassName(arg1, arg2, ...)
```

The first of these two lines of code declares what type of object the variable will refer to. The actual object does not exist until it is created with the New keyword, as done in the second line. This is known as creating an **instance** of an object and is where an object is actually created from its class. After this second line of code executes, the object is then ready for use. The first line can appear either in the Declarations section of a program (to declare a class-level variable) or inside a procedure (to declare a local variable). The instantiation line can appear only in a procedure; however, any object variable can be instantiated when declared (as either class level or local) by using the single line

```
Dim objectName As New ClassName(arg1, arg2, ...)
```

In a program, properties, methods, and events of the object are accessed with statements of the form shown in the following table:

TASK	STATEMENT
Assign a value to a property	`objectName.propertyName = value`
Assign the value of a property to a variable	`varName = objectName.propertyName`
Carry out a method	`objectName.methodName(arg1, ...)`
Raise an event	`RaiseEvent eventName`

The program in Example 1 uses a class named Student to calculate and display a student's semester grade. The information stored by an object of the type Student consists of a student's name, social security number, and grades on two exams (midterm and final). This data is stored in variables declared with the statements

```
Private m_name As String        'Name
Private m_ssn As String         'Social security number
Private m_midterm As Double     'Numerical grade on midterm exam
Private m_final As Double       'Numerical grade on final exam
```

The word Private guarantees that the variables cannot be accessed directly from outside the object. In object-oriented programming terminology, these variables are called **member variables** (or **instance variables**). We will follow the common convention of beginning the name of each member variable with the prefix "m_". Each of these variables is used to hold the value of a property. However, instead of being accessed directly, each member variable is accessed indirectly with a **property block**. For instance, the following property block consists of a Get property procedure to retrieve (or *read*) the value of the Name property and a Set property procedure to assign (or *write*) the value of the Name property:

```
Public Property Name() As String
  Get
    Return m_name
  End Get
  Set(ByVal value As String)
    m_name = value
  End Set
End Property
```

In a property block, additional code can be added after the Get and Set statements to validate the data before they are returned or stored. The word Public allows the property to be accessed from outside the code for the Student class block. For instance, the Name property can be accessed by code in the form's class block. On the other hand, since the member variables were declared as Private, they cannot be accessed directly from code in the form's block. They can be accessed only through Property procedures that allow values to be checked and perhaps modified. Also, a Property procedure is able to take other steps necessitated by a change in the value of a member variable.

A property block needn't contain both Get and Set property procedures. For instance, the block

```
Public WriteOnly Property Midterm() As Double
  Set(ByVal value As double)
    m_midterm = value
  End Set
End Property
```

specifies the Midterm property as "write only." This property could be specified to be "read only" with the block

```
Public ReadOnly Property Midterm() As Double
  Get
    Return m_midterm
  End Get
End Property
```

Methods are constructed with Sub or Function procedures. A Function procedure is used when the method returns a value; otherwise a Sub procedure will suffice. For instance, the method CalcSemGrade, which is used to calculate a student's semester grade, is created as follows:

```
Function CalcSemGrade() As String
  Dim grade As Double
  grade = (m_midterm + m_final) / 2
  grade = Math.Round(grade) 'Round the grade.
  Select Case grade
    Case Is >= 90
      Return "A"
    Case Is >= 80
      Return "B"
    Case Is >= 70
      Return "C"
    Case Is >= 60
      Return "D"
    Case Else
      Return "F"
  End Select
End Function
```

An object of the type Student is declared in the form's code with a pair of statements such as

```
Dim pupil As Student      'Declare pupil as an object of type Student
pupil = New Student()     'Create an instance of type Student
```

After these two statements are executed, properties and methods can be utilized with statements such as

```
pupil.Name = "Adams, Al"               'Assign a value to m_name
txtBox.text = pupil.Name               'Display the student's name
lstBox.Items.Add(pupil.CalcSemGrade)   'Display semester grade
```

The first statement calls the Set property procedure for the Name property, the second statement calls the Get property procedure for the Name property, and the third statement calls the method CalcSemGrade.

Example 1 The following program uses the class Student to calculate and display a student's semester grade. The structure Person in frmGrades is used by the btnDisplay_Click procedure to place information into the DataGridView control.

OBJECT	PROPERTY	SETTING
frmGrades	Text	Semester Grade
lblName	Text	Name:
txtName		
lblSSN	Text	SSN:
mtbSSN	Mask	000-00-0000
lblMidterm	Text	Midterm:
txtMidterm		
lblFinal	Text	Final:
txtFinal		
btnEnter	Text	&Enter Information
btnDisplay	Text	&Display Grade
btnQuit	Text	&Quit
dgvGrades	RowHeadersVisible	False

```
Public Class frmGrades
   Dim pupil As Student   'pupil is an object of class Student

   Structure Person   'for use in btnDisplay_Click
      Dim name As String
      Dim socSecNum As String
      Dim semGrade As String
   End Structure

   Private Sub btnEnter_Click(...) Handles btnEnter.Click
      pupil = New Student()     'Create an instance of Student.
      'Read the values stored in the text boxes.
      pupil.Name = txtName.Text
      pupil.SocSecNum = mtbSSN.Text
      pupil.Midterm = CDbl(txtMidterm.Text)
      pupil.Final = CDbl(txtFinal.Text)
      'Clear text boxes and list box
      txtName.Clear()
      mtbSSN.Clear()
      txtMidterm.Clear()
      txtFinal.Clear()
      'Notify user that grades for the student have been recorded.
      MessageBox.Show("Student Recorded.")
   End Sub

   Private Sub btnDisplay_Click(...) Handles btnDisplay.Click
      Dim persons(0) As Person
      persons(0).name = pupil.Name
      persons(0).socSecNum = pupil.SocSecNum
      persons(0).semGrade = pupil.CalcSemGrade
      Dim query = From someone In persons
                  Select someone.name, someone.socSecNum, someone.semGrade
      dgvGrades.DataSource = query.ToList
      dgvGrades.CurrentCell = Nothing
      dgvGrades.Columns("name").HeaderText = "Student Name"
      dgvGrades.Columns("socSecNum").HeaderText = "SSN"
      dgvGrades.Columns("semGrade").HeaderText = "Grade"
   End Sub
```

```
      Private Sub btnQuit_Click(...) Handles btnQuit.Click
        Me.Close()
      End Sub
    End Class        'frmGrades

    Class Student
      Private m_name As String          'Name
      Private m_ssn As String           'Social security number
      Private m_midterm As Double       'Numerical grade on midterm exam
      Private m_final As Double          'Numerical grade on final exam

      Public Property Name() As String
        Get
          Return m_name
        End Get
        Set(ByVal value As String)
          m_name = value
        End Set
      End Property

      Public Property SocSecNum() As String
        Get
          Return m_ssn
        End Get
        Set(ByVal value As String)
          m_ssn = value
        End Set
      End Property

      Public WriteOnly Property Midterm() As Double
        Set(ByVal value As Double)
          m_midterm = value
        End Set
      End Property

      Public WriteOnly Property Final() As Double
        Set(ByVal value As Double)
          m_final = value
        End Set
      End Property

      Function CalcSemGrade() As String
        Dim grade As Double
        grade = (m_midterm + m_final) / 2
        grade = Math.Round(grade)  'Round the grade.
        Select Case grade
          Case Is >= 90
            Return "A"
          Case Is >= 80
            Return "B"
          Case Is >= 70
            Return "C"
          Case Is >= 60
            Return "D"
```

```
        Case Else
            Return "F"
    End Select
  End Function
End Class        'Student
```

[Run, enter the data for a student (such as "Adams, Al", "123-45-6789", "82", "87"), click on the *Enter Information* button to send the data to the object, and click on the *Display Grade* button to display the student's name, social security number, and semester grade.]

In summary, the following six steps are used to create a class:

1. Identify a *thing* in your program that is to become an object.
2. Determine the properties and methods that you would like the object to have. (As a rule of thumb, properties should access data, and methods should perform operations.)
3. A class will serve as a template for the object. The code for the class is placed in a class block of the form

```
Class ClassName
  statements
End Class
```

4. For each of the properties in Step 2, declare a private member variable with a statement of the form

```
Private variableName As DataType
```

Member variables can be preceded with the keyword Public, which allows direct access to the member variables from the code in the form. However, this is considered poor programming practice. By using Set property procedures to update the data, we can enforce constraints and carry out validation.

5. For each of the member variables in Step 4, create a Property block with Get and/or Set procedures to retrieve and assign values of the variable. The general forms of the procedures are

```
Public Property PropertyName() As DataType
  Get
    (Possibly additional code)
    Return variableName
  End Get
  Set(ByVal value As DataType)
    (Possibly additional code)
```

```
    variableName = value
  End Set
End Property
```

In the Get or Set code, additional code can be added to prevent the object from storing or returning invalid or corrupted data. For example, an If block could be added to only allow valid social security numbers, alerting the user in the event of an invalid number.

6. For each method in Step 2, create a Sub procedure or Function procedure to carry out the task.

Example 2   The following modification of the program in Example 1 calculates semester grades for students who have registered on a "Pass/Fail" basis. We create a new class, named PFStudent, with the same member variables and property procedures as the class Student. The only change needed in the class block occurs in the CalcSemGrade method. The new code for this method is

```
Function CalcSemGrade() As String
  Dim grade As Double
  grade = (m_midterm + m_final) / 2
  grade = Math.Round(grade)   'Round the grade.
  If grade >= 60 Then
    Return "Pass"
  Else
    Return "Fail"
  End If
End Function
```

The only change needed in the form's code is to replace the two occurrences of *Student* with *PFStudent*. When the program is run with the same input as in Example 1, the output will be

```
Adams, Al    123-45-6789  Pass
```

▣ Object Constructors

Each class has a special method called a **constructor** that is always invoked when an object is instantiated. The constructor takes zero or more arguments, and the code inside the procedure block performs any tasks needed for initializing an object. It is often used to set default values for member variables and to create other objects associated with this object. The first line of the constructor for a class has the form

```
Public Sub New(ByVal par1 As DataType1, ByVal par2 As DataType2, ...)
```

The graphical program in Example 3 illustrates the use of a constructor to specify the size and initial placement of a circle. This task involves pixels. To get a feel for how big a pixel is, the initial size of the form when you create a new project is 300 pixels by 300 pixels. Section 9.4 explains how graphics are created inside a picture box with the Graphics object gr = picBox.CreateGraphics. In Example 3, the statement

```
gr.DrawEllipse(Pens.Black, Xcoord, Ycoord, Diameter, Diameter)
```

draws a circle inside a picture box, where Xcoord and Ycoord are the distances (in pixels) of the circle from the left side and top of the picture box.

Example 3   The following program contains a Circle object. The object keeps track of the location and diameter of the circle. (The location is specified by two numbers, called the coordinates, giving the distance from the left side and top of the picture box. Distances and the diameter are measured in pixels.) A Show method displays the circle, and a Move method adds 20 pixels to each coordinate of the circle. Initially, the (unseen) circle is located at the upper-left corner of the picture box and has a diameter of 40. The form has a button captioned *Move and Show Circle* that invokes both methods. Notice that the Xcoord, Ycoord, and Diameter properties, rather than the member variables, appear in the methods.

OBJECT	PROPERTY	SETTING
frmCircle	Text	Moving Circle
btnMove	Text	Move and Show Circle
btnQuit	Text	Quit
picCircle		

```
Public Class frmCircle
  Dim round As New Circle()

  Private Sub btnMove_Click(...) Handles btnMove.Click
    round.Move(20)
    round.Show(picCircle.CreateGraphics)
  End Sub

  Private Sub btnQuit_Click(...) Handles btnQuit.Click
    Me.Close()
  End Sub
End Class        'frmCircle

Class Circle
  Private m_x As Integer   'Dist from left side of picture box to circle
  Private m_y As Integer   'Distance from top of picture box to the circle
  Private m_d As Integer   'Diameter of circle

  Public Sub New()
    'Set the initial location of the circle to the upper-left
    'corner of the picture box, and set its diameter to 40.
    Xcoord = 0
    Ycoord = 0
    Diameter = 40
  End Sub
```

```
Public Property Xcoord() As Integer
  Get
    Return m_x
  End Get
  Set(ByVal value As Integer)
    m_x = value
  End Set
End Property

Public Property Ycoord() As Integer
  Get
    Return m_y
  End Get
  Set(ByVal value As Integer)
    m_y = value
  End Set
End Property

Public Property Diameter() As Integer
  Get
    Return m_d
  End Get
  Set(ByVal value As Integer)
    m_d = value
  End Set
End Property

Sub Show(ByVal gr As Graphics)
  'Draw a circle with the given graphics context.
  gr.DrawEllipse(Pens.Black, Xcoord, Ycoord, Diameter, Diameter)
End Sub

Sub Move(ByVal distance As Integer)
  Xcoord += distance
  Ycoord += distance
End Sub
End Class      'Circle
```

[Run, and click on the *Move* button ten times.]

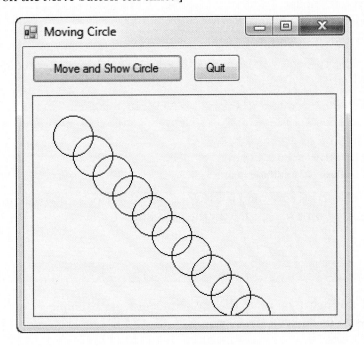

When the line that instantiates an object contains arguments, the values of these arguments are passed to the object's New procedure. For instance, in Example 3, the first line typed in the form's code can be changed to

```
Dim round As New Circle(0, 0, 40)
```

and the New procedure for the Circle class can be changed to

```
Public Sub New(ByVal x As Integer, ByVal y As Integer,
               ByVal d As Integer)
  'Set the initial location of the circle to x pixels from
  'the left side and y pixels from the top of the picture box.
  'Set the diameter to d pixels.
  Xcoord = x
  Ycoord = y
  Diameter = d
End Sub
```

■ Auto-Implemented Properties

Some property blocks are very clear-cut in that they do not contain ReadOnly or WriteOnly keywords and have no additional code in their Get or Set blocks. Such property blocks can use the new-to-VB2010 **auto-implemented properties** feature. This feature allows you to reduce a clear-cut property block to just its header, and to omit declaring a member variable for the property. Visual Basic automatically creates hidden Get and Set procedures and a hidden member variable. The name of the member variable is the property name preceded by an underscore character. For example, if you declare an auto-implemented property named SocSecNum, the member variable will be named _SocSecNum. We will use auto-implemented properties in the remainder of this chapter.

Practice Problems 11.1

1. Which of the following analogies is out of place?

    (a) class : object
    (b) sewing pattern : garment
    (c) blueprint : house
    (d) programmer : program
    (e) cookie cutter : cookie

2. In Example 1, suppose that the first five lines of the event procedure btnEnter_Click are replaced with

    ```
    Private Sub btnEnter_Click(...) Handles btnEnter.Click
      Dim ssn As String = "123-45-6789"    'Social security Number
      'Create an instance of Student.
      pupil = New Student(ssn)
      pupil.Name = txtName.Text
    ```

    Create a New procedure and revise the SocSecNum property block for the Student class to be consistent with the last line in the preceding code.

EXERCISES 11.1

Exercises 1 through 14 refer to the class Student from Example 1. When applicable, assume that *pupil* is an instance of the class.

1. What will be the effect if the *Midterm* property block is changed to the following?

```
Public WriteOnly Property Midterm() As Double
  Set(ByVal value As Double)
    Select Case value
      Case Is < 0
        m_midterm = 0
      Case Is > 100
        m_midterm = 100
      Case Else
        m_midterm = value
    End Select
  End Set
End Property
```

2. What will be the effect if the *Midterm* property block is changed to the following?

```
Public WriteOnly Property Midterm() As Double
  Set(ByVal value As Double)
    m_midterm = value + 5
  End Set
End Property
```

3. Modify the class block for *Student* so that the following statement will display the student's midterm grade:

```
MessageBox.Show(CStr(pupil.Midterm))
```

4. Modify the class block for *Student* so that the student's semester average can be displayed with a statement of the form

```
MessageBox.Show(CStr(pupil.Average))
```

5. In the class block for Student, why can't the third line of the CalcSemGrade method be written as follows?

```
grade = (Midterm + Final) / 2
```

6. Write code for the class block that sets the two grades to 15 whenever an instance of the class is created.

7. What is the effect of adding the following code to the class block?

```
Public Sub New()
  SocSecNum = "999-99-9999"
End Sub
```

In Exercises 8 through 14, determine the errors in the given form code.

8.
```
Dim scholar As Student

Private Sub btnGo_Click(...) Handles btnGo.Click
  Dim firstName as String
  scholar.Name = "Warren"
  firstName = scholar.Name
End Sub
```

9.
```
Dim scholar As Student

Private Sub btnGo_Click(...) Handles btnGo.Click
  Dim nom as String
  scholar = Student()
```

```
        scholar.Name = "Peace, Warren"
        nom = scholar.Name
    End Sub
```

10. ```
    Dim scholar As Student

    Private Sub btnGo_Click(...) Handles btnGo.Click
      Dim nom as String
      scholar = New Student()
      m_name = "Peace, Warren"
      nom = scholar.Name
    End Sub
    ```

11. ```
    Dim scholar As Student

    Private Sub btnGo_Click(...) Handles btnGo.Click
      Dim nom As String
      scholar = New Student()
      scholar.Name = "Peace, Warren"
      nom = m_name
    End Sub
    ```

12. ```
    Dim scholar As Student

    Private Sub btnGo_Click(...) Handles btnGo.Click
      Dim grade As String
      scholar = New Student()
      scholar.CalcSemGrade = "A"
      grade = scholar.CalcSemGrade()
    End Sub
    ```

13. ```
    Dim pupil, scholar As Student

    Private Sub btnGo_Click(...) Handles btnGo.Click
      scholar = New Student()
      pupil = New Student()
      scholar.Midterm = 89
      pupil.Midterm = scholar.Midterm
      lstGrades.Items.Add(pupil.Midterm)
    End Sub
    ```

14. ```
    Dim scholar As Student
    scholar = New Student()

    Private Sub btnGo_Click(...) Handles btnGo.Click
      scholar.Name = "Transmission, Manuel"
    End Sub
    ```

15. In the following program, determine the output displayed in the list box when the button is clicked on:

    ```
    Public Class frmCountry
      Dim nation As New Country("Canada", "Ottawa")

      Private Sub btnDisplay_Click(...) Handles btnDisplay.Click
        nation.Population = 31
        lstBox.Items.Add("Country: " & nation.Name)
        lstBox.Items.Add("Capital: " & nation.Capital)
    ```
    ```

```
          lstBox.Items.Add("Pop: " & nation.Population & " million")
      End Sub
  End Class        'frmCountry

  Class Country
    Private m_name As String
    Private m_capital As String
    Private m_population As Double

    Sub New(ByVal name As String, ByVal capital As String)
      m_name = name
      m_capital = capital
    End Sub

    Public ReadOnly Property Name() As String
      Get
        Return m_name
      End Get
    End Property

    Public ReadOnly Property Capital() As String
      Get
        Return m_capital
      End Get
    End Property

    Public Property Population() As Double
      Get
        Return m_population
      End Get
      Set(ByVal value As Double)
        m_population = value
      End Set
    End Property
  End Class         'Country
```

Exercises 16 through 18 refer to the class *Circle*.

16. Enhance the program in Example 3 so that the Get and Set property procedures of the Xcoord and Ycoord properties are used by the form code.

17. Modify Example 3 so that the circle originally has its location at the lower-right corner of the picture box and moves diagonally upward each time *btnMove* is clicked on.

18. Modify the form code of Example 3 so that each time *btnMove* is clicked on, the distance moved (in pixels) is a randomly selected number from 0 to 25.

19. Write the code for a class called Square. The class should have three properties—Length, Perimeter, and Area—with their obvious meanings. When a value is assigned to one of the properties, the values of the other two should be recalculated automatically. When the following form code is executed, the numbers 5 and 20 should be displayed in the text boxes:

```
Dim poly As Square

Private Sub btnGo_Click(...) Handles btnGo.Click
  poly = New Square()
  poly.Area = 25
```

```
txtLength.Text = CStr(poly.Length)
txtPerimeter.Text = CStr(poly.Perimeter)
End Sub
```

20. Modify the class Square in the previous exercise so that all squares will have lengths between 1 and 10. For instance, the statement `poly.Area = 0.5` should result in a square of length 1, and the statement `poly.Area = 200` should result in a square with each side having length 10.

21. Write the code for a class called PairOfDice. A Random object should be used to obtain the value for each die. When the following form code is executed, three numbers (such as 3, 4, and 7) should be displayed in the text boxes.

```
Dim cubes As PairOfDice

Private Sub btnGo_Click(...) Handles btnGo.Click
  cubes = New PairOfDice()
  cubes.Roll()
  txtOne.Text = CStr(cubes.Die1)
  txtTwo.Text = CStr(cubes.Die2)
  txtSum.Text = CStr(cubes.SumOfFaces)
End Sub
```

22. Write a program to roll a pair of dice 1000 times, and display the number of times that the sum of the two faces is 7. The program should use an instance of the class PairOfDice discussed in the previous exercise.

23. Write the code for a class called College. The class should have properties Name, NumStudents, and NumFaculty. The method SFRatio should compute the student–faculty ratio. When the following form code is executed, the number 12.4 should be displayed in the text box:

```
Dim school As College

Private Sub btnGo_Click(...) Handles btnGo.Click
  school = New College()
  school.Name = "University of Maryland, College Park"
  school.NumStudents = 36041
  school.NumFaculty = 2896
  txtBox.Text = FormatNumber(school.SFRatio, 1)
End Sub
```

24. Write a program that calculates an employee's pay for a week based on the hourly wage and the number of hours worked. All computations should be performed by an instance of the class Wages.

25. Write a program to implement the cash register in Fig. 11.1. The program should have a class called CashRegister that keeps track of the balance and allows deposits and withdrawals. The class should not permit a negative balance.

FIGURE 11.1   Form for Exercise 25.

FIGURE 11.2   Form for Exercise 26.

26. Write a program that calculates the average of up to 50 numbers input by the user and stored in an array. See Fig. 11.2. The program should use a class named Statistics and have an AddNumber method that stores numbers into an array one at a time. The class should have a Count property that keeps track of the number of numbers stored and a method called Average that returns the average of the numbers.

27. Write a program that calculates an employee's FICA tax, with all computations performed by an instance of a class FICA. The FICA tax has two components: the social security benefits tax, which in 2009 is 6.2% of the first $106,800 of earnings for the year, and the Medicare tax, which is 1.45% of earnings.

28. Write a program that adds two fractions and displays their sum in reduced form. The program should use a Fraction class that stores the numerator and denominator of a fraction and has a Reduce method that divides each of the numerator and denominator by their greatest common divisor. Exercise 29 of Section 6.1 contains an algorithm for calculating the greatest common divisor of two numbers.

Solutions to Practice Problems 11.1

1. (d) A programmer is not a template for creating a program.

2.
```
Public Sub New(ByVal ssn As String)
   'Assign the value of ssn to the member variable m_ssn.
  m_ssn = ssn
End Sub

Public ReadOnly Property SocSecNum() As String
  Get
    Return m_ssn
  End Get
End Property
```

Note: Since a student's social security number never changes, there is no need to have a Set property procedure for SocSecNum.

11.2 Working with Objects

"An object without an event is like a telephone without a ringer."

Anonymous

Arrays of Objects

The elements of an array can have any data type—including a class. The program in Example 1 uses an array of type Student.

VideoNote

Arrays of objects

✓ **Example 1**   In the following program, which uses the same form design as Example 1 of the previous section, the user enters four pieces of data about a student into text boxes. When the *Enter Information* button is clicked on, the data are used to create and initialize an appropriate object and the object is added to an array. When the *Display Grades* button is clicked on, the name, social security number, and semester grade for each student in the array are displayed in the grid.

```
Public Class frmGrades
  Dim students(50) As Student
  Dim lastStudentAdded As Integer = -1    'Position in array of student
  '                                        most recently added
```

```vb
Private Sub btnEnter_Click(...) Handles btnEnter.Click
  lastStudentAdded += 1
  students(lastStudentAdded) = New Student
  students(lastStudentAdded).Name = txtName.Text
  students(lastStudentAdded).SocSecNum = mtbSSN.Text
  students(lastStudentAdded).Midterm = CDbl(txtMidterm.Text)
  students(lastStudentAdded).Final = CDbl(txtFinal.Text)
  'Clear text boxes
  txtName.Clear()
  mtbSSN.Clear()
  txtMidterm.Clear()
  txtFinal.Clear()
  txtName.Focus()
  MessageBox.Show("Student Recorded.")
End Sub


Private Sub btnDisplay_Click(...) Handles btnDisplay.Click
  ReDim Preserve students(lastStudentAdded)
  Dim query = From pupil In students
              Select pupil.Name, pupil.SocSecNum, pupil.CalcSemGrade
  dgvGrades.DataSource = query.ToList
  dgvGrades.CurrentCell = Nothing
  dgvGrades.Columns("Name").HeaderText = "Student Name"
  dgvGrades.Columns("SocSecNum").HeaderText = "SSN"
  dgvGrades.Columns("CalcSemGrade").HeaderText = "Grade"
  ReDim Preserve students(50)
  txtName.Focus()
End Sub


Private Sub btnQuit_Click(...) Handles btnQuit.Click
  Me.Close()
End Sub
End Class        'frmGrades


Class Student
  Private m_midterm As Double
  Private m_final As Double


  Public Property Name() As String


  Public Property SocSecNum() As String


  Public WriteOnly Property Midterm() As Double
    Set(ByVal value As Double)
      m_midterm = value
    End Set
  End Property


  Public WriteOnly Property Final() As Double
    Set(ByVal value As Double)
      m_final = value
    End Set
  End Property
```

```
Function CalcSemGrade() As String
  Dim grade As Double
  grade = (m_midterm + m_final) / 2
  grade = Math.Round(grade)   'Round the grade.
  Select Case grade
    Case Is >= 90
      Return "A"
    Case Is >= 80
      Return "B"
    Case Is >= 70
      Return "C"
    Case Is >= 60
      Return "D"
    Case Else
      Return "F"
  End Select
End Function
End Class       'Student
```

[Run, type in data for Al Adams, click on the *Enter Information* button, repeat the process for Brittany Brown and Carol Cole, click on the *Display Grades* button, and then enter data for Daniel Doyle.]

▓ Events

In the previous section, we drew a parallel between classes and controls and showed how to define properties and methods for classes. Events can be defined by the programmer to communicate changes of properties, errors, and the progress of lengthy operations. Such events are called **user-defined events**. The statement for raising an event is located in the class block, and the event is dealt with in the form's code. Suppose that the event is named UserDefinedEvent and has the parameters *par1*, *par2*, and so on. In the class block, the statement

```
Public Event UserDefinedEvent(ByVal par1 As DataType1,
                            ByVal par2 As DataType2, ...)
```

should be placed in the Declarations section, and the statement

```
RaiseEvent UserDefinedEvent(arg1, arg2, ...)
```

should be placed at the locations in the class block code at which the event should be raised. In the form's code, an instance of the class, call it *object1*, must be declared with a statement of the type

```
Dim WithEvents object1 As ClassName
```

or the type

```
Dim WithEvents object1 As New ClassName
```

in order to be able to respond to the event. That is, the keyword WithEvents must be inserted into the declaration statement. The header of an event procedure for *object1* will be

```
Private Sub object1_UserDefinedEvent(ByVal par1 As DataType1,
                                     ByVal par2 As DataType2,...) _
                                     Handles object1.UserDefinedEvent
```

 Example 2   Consider the Circle class defined in Example 3 of Section 11.1. In the following program, we add an event that is raised whenever the location of a circle changes. The event has parameters to pass the location and diameter of the circle. The form's code uses the event to determine if part (or all) of the drawn circle will fall outside the picture box. If so, the event procedure displays the message "Circle Off Screen" in a text box. Let's call the event PositionChanged.

OBJECT	PROPERTY	SETTING
frmCircle	Text	Moving Circle
btnMove	Text	Move and Show Circle
btnQuit	Text	Quit
txtCaution	ReadOnly	True
picCircle		

```
Public Class frmCircle
  Dim WithEvents round As New Circle()

  Private Sub btnMove_Click(...) Handles btnMove.Click
    round.Move(20)
    round.Show(picCircle.CreateGraphics)
  End Sub

  Private Sub btnQuit_Click(...) Handles btnQuit.Click
    Me.Close()
  End Sub

  Private Sub round_PositionChanged(ByVal x As Integer,
    ByVal y As Integer, ByVal d As Integer) Handles round.PositionChanged
    'This event is raised when the location of the circle changes.
    'The code determines if part of the circle is off the screen.
    If (x + d > picCircle.Width) Or
       (y + d > picCircle.Height) Then
      txtCaution.Text = "Circle Off Screen"
    End If
  End Sub
End Class        'frmCircle

Class Circle
  Public Event PositionChanged(ByVal x As Integer,
                                ByVal y As Integer, ByVal d As Integer)
  'Event is raised when the circle moves.

  Public Sub New()
    'Set the initial location of the circle to the upper-left
    'corner of the picture box, and set its diameter to 40.
    Xcoord = 0
    Ycoord = 0
    Diameter = 40
  End Sub

  Public Property Xcoord() As Integer

  Public Property Ycoord() As Integer

  Public Property Diameter() As Integer

  Sub Show(ByVal gr As Graphics)
    'Draw a circle with the given graphics context.
    gr.DrawEllipse(Pens.Black, Xcoord, Ycoord, Diameter, Diameter)
  End Sub

  Sub Move(ByVal distance As Integer)
    Xcoord += distance
    Ycoord += distance
    RaiseEvent PositionChanged(Xcoord, Ycoord, Diameter)
  End Sub
End Class        'Circle
```

[Run, and click on the *Move and Show Circle* button eleven times.]

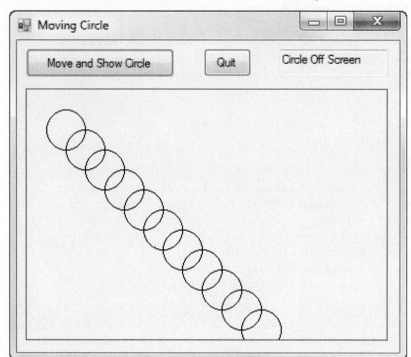

Note: As the last circle appears, the words "Circle Off Screen" are displayed in the text box.

■ Containment

We say that class A **contains** class B when a member variable of class A makes use of an object of type class B. In Example 3, the class DeckOfCards contains the class Card.

 Example 3 The following program deals a five-card poker hand. The program has a DeckOfCards object containing an array of 52 Card objects. The Card object has two properties, Denomination and Suit, and one method, IdentifyCard. The IdentifyCard method returns a string such as "Ace of Spades". In the DeckOfCards object, the New event procedure assigns denominations and suits to the 52 cards. The method ReadCard(n) returns the string identifying the *n*th card of the deck. The method ShuffleDeck uses the Random class to mix up the cards while making 2000 passes through the deck. The event

```
Shuffling(n As Integer, nMax As Integer)
```

is raised during each shuffling pass through the deck, and its parameters communicate the number of the pass and the total number of passes, so that the program that uses it can keep track of the progress.

OBJECT	PROPERTY	SETTING
frmPoker	Text	Poker Hand
lstHand		
btnShuffle	Text	&Shuffle
btnDeal	Text	&Deal
btnQuit	Text	&Quit

```
Public Class frmPoker
  Dim WithEvents cards As New DeckOfCards()

  Private Sub btnShuffle_Click(...) Handles btnShuffle.Click
    cards.ShuffleDeck
  End Sub

  Private Sub btnDeal_Click(...) Handles btnDeal.Click
    Dim str As String
    lstHand.Items.Clear()
    For i As Integer = 0 To 4
      str = cards.ReadCard(i)
      lstHand.Items.Add(str)
    Next
  End Sub

  Private Sub btnQuit_Click(...) Handles btnQuit.Click
    Me.Close()
  End Sub

  Private Sub cards_Shuffling(ByVal n As Integer,
                      ByVal nMax As Integer) Handles cards.Shuffling
    'n is the number of the specific pass through the deck (1, 2, 3...).
    'nMax is the total number of passes when the deck is shuffled.
    lstHand.Items.Clear()
    lstHand.Items.Add("Shuffling Pass: " & n & " out of " & nMax)
    For i As Integer = 1 To 1000000      'Slow down the shuffle.
    Next
    lstHand.Update()   'Refresh contents of list box
  End Sub
End Class        'frmPoker

Class Card
  Private m_denomination As Integer   'A number from 0 through 12
  Private m_suit As String            'Hearts, Clubs, Diamonds, Spades

  Public Property Denomination() As Integer
    Get
      Return m_denomination
    End Get
    Set(ByVal value As Integer)
      'Only store valid values.
      If (value >= 0) And (value <= 12) Then
        m_denomination = value
      End If
    End Set
  End Property

  Public Property Suit() As String
    Get
      Return m_suit
    End Get
    Set(ByVal value As String)
      'Only store valid values.
      If (value = "Hearts") Or (value = "Clubs") Or
         (value = "Diamonds") Or (value = "Spades") Then
```

```
          m_suit = value
        End If
      End Set
    End Property

    Function IdentifyCard() As String
      Dim denom As String = ""
      Select Case Denomination + 1
        Case 1
          denom = "Ace"
        Case Is <= 10
          denom = CStr(Denomination + 1)
        Case 11
          denom = "Jack"
        Case 12
          denom = "Queen"
        Case 13
          denom = "King"
      End Select
      Return denom & " of " & m_suit
    End Function
End Class          'Card


Class DeckOfCards
    Private m_deck(51) As Card 'Class DeckOfCards contains class Card
    Public Event Shuffling(ByVal n As Integer, ByVal nMax As Integer)

    Public Sub New()
      'Make the first thirteen cards hearts, the
      'next thirteen cards diamonds, and so on.
      Dim suits() As String = {"Hearts", "Clubs", "Diamonds", "Spades"}
      For i As Integer = 0 To 3
        'Each pass corresponds to one of the four suits.
        For j As Integer = 0 To 12
          'Assign numbers from 0 through 12 to the
          'cards of each suit.
          m_deck(i * 13 + j) = New Card()
          m_deck(i * 13 + j).Suit = suits(i)
          m_deck(i * 13 + j).Denomination = j
        Next
      Next
    End Sub

    Function ReadCard(ByVal cardNum As Integer) As String
      Return m_deck(cardNum).IdentifyCard()
    End Function

    Sub Swap(ByVal i As Integer, ByVal j As Integer)
      'Swap the ith and jth cards in the deck.
      Dim tempCard As Card
      tempCard = m_deck(i)
      m_deck(i) = m_deck(j)
      m_deck(j) = tempCard
    End Sub
```

```
  Sub ShuffleDeck()
    'Do 2000 passes through the deck.  On each pass,
    'swap each card with a randomly selected card.
    Dim index As Integer
    Dim randomNum As New Random()
    For i As Integer = 1 To 2000
      For k As Integer = 0 To 51
        index = randomNum.Next(0, 52)   'Randomly select a number
        'from 0 through 51 inclusive.
        Swap(k, index)
      Next
      RaiseEvent Shuffling(i, 2000)
    Next
  End Sub
End Class       'DeckOfCards
```

[Run, click on the *Shuffle* button, and click on the *Deal* button after the shuffling is complete.]

Practice Problems 11.2

Consider the program in Example 1 of Section 11.1, and suppose that mtbSSN is an ordinary (rather than a masked) text box.

1. Alter the Set SocSecNum property procedure to raise the event ImproperSSN when the social security number does not have 11 characters. The event should pass the length of the social security number and the student's name to the form's code.
2. What statement must be placed in the Declarations section of the Student class?
3. Write an event procedure to handle the event ImproperSSN.
4. What statement in the form's code must be altered?

EXERCISES 11.2

1. In Example 1 of this section, modify the event procedure btnDisplay_Click so that only the students who receive a grade of A are displayed.

   The file UnitedStates.txt provides data on the 50 states. (This file is used in Exercises 2 through 5.) Each record contains five pieces of information about a single state: name, abbreviation, date it entered the union, land area (in square miles), and population in the year 2000. The records are ordered by the date of entry into the union. The first three lines of the file are

```
Delaware,DE,12/7/1787,1954,759000
Pennsylvania,PA,12/12/1787,44817,12296000
New Jersey,NJ,12/18/1787,7417,8135000
```

2. Create a class State with five properties to hold the information about a single state and a method that calculates the density (people per square mile) of the state.

3. Write a program that requests a state's name in an input dialog box and displays the state's name, density, and date of entrance into the union. The program should use an array of State objects.

4. Write a program that displays the names of the states and their densities in a DataGridView ordered by density. The program should use an array of State objects.

5. Write a program that reads the data from the file one line at a time into an array of State objects and raises an event whenever the population of a state exceeds ten million. States with a large population should have their names and populations displayed in a list box by the corresponding event procedure. (**Hint**: Create a class called UnitedStates that contains the array and defines a method Add that adds a new state to the array. The Add method should raise the event.)

6. Consider the class Square from Exercise 19 of Section 11.1. Add the event IllegalNumber that is raised when any of the properties is set to a negative number. Show the new class block and write an event procedure for the event that displays an error message.

7. Consider the CashRegister class in Exercise 25 of Section 11.1. Add the event AttemptToOverdraw that is raised when the user tries to subtract more money than is in the cash register.

8. Consider the class PairOfDice discussed in Exercise 21 of Section 11.1. Add the event SnakeEyes that is raised whenever two ones appear during a roll of the dice. Write a program that uses this event.

9. Consider the Fraction class in Exercise 29 of Section 11.1. Add the event ZeroDenominator that is raised whenever a denominator is set to 0. Write a program that uses the event.

10. Write a program for the fraction calculator shown in Fig. 11.3. After the numerators and denominators of the two fractions to the left of the equals sign are placed in the four text boxes, one of four operations buttons should be clicked on. The result appears to the right of the equals sign. The program should use a Calculator class, which contains three members of the type Fraction discussed in Exercise 28 of Section 11.1. **Note:** In Fig. 11.3, the fraction bars are very short list boxes.

FIGURE 11.3   Sample Output for Exercise 10.   FIGURE 11.4   Sample Output for Exercise 11.

11. Write a program for a simple game in which each of two players rolls a pair of dice. The person with the highest tally wins. See Fig. 11.4. The program should use a class called HighRoller having two member variables of the type PairOfDice discussed in Exercise 21 of Section 11.1.

12. Write a program that takes orders at a fast food restaurant. See Fig. 11.5. The restaurant has two menus—a regular menu and a kids menu. An item is ordered by highlighting it in one of the list boxes and then clicking on the >> or << button to place it in the order list box in the center of the form. As each item is ordered, a running total is displayed in the text box at the lower right part of the form. The program should use a Choices class, which contains a Food class. (The contents of each of the three list boxes should be treated as Choices objects.) Each Food object should hold the name and price of a single food item. The Choices class should have a ChoiceChanged event that can be used by the form code to update the cost of the order.

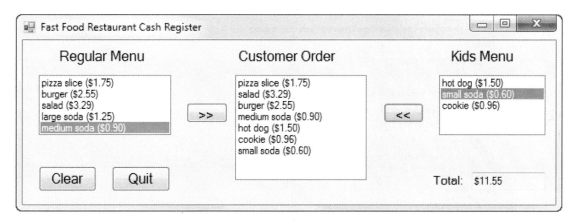

FIGURE 11.5 Sample output for Exercise 12.

13. Write a program to produce an employee's weekly paycheck receipt. The receipt should contain the employee's name, amount earned for the week, total amount earned for the year, FICA tax deduction, withholding tax deduction, and take-home amount. The program should use an Employee class and a Tax class. The Tax class must have properties for the amount earned for the week, the prior total amount earned for the year, the number of withholding allowances, and marital status. It should have methods for computing FICA and withholding taxes. The Employee class should store the employee's name, number of withholding allowances, marital status, hours worked this week, hourly salary, and previous amount earned for the year. The Employee class should use the Tax class to calculate the taxes to be deducted. The formula for calculating the FICA tax is given in Exercise 27 of Section 11.1. To compute the withholding tax, multiply the number of withholding allowances by $70.19, subtract the product from the amount earned, and use Table 11.1 or Table 11.2.

TABLE 11.1   **2009 Federal income tax withheld for a single person paid weekly.**

Adjusted Weekly Income	Income Tax Withheld
$0 to $138	$0
Over $138 to $200	10% of amount over $138
Over $200 to $696	$6.20 + 15% of amount over $200
Over $696 to $1,279	$80.60 + 25% of amount over $696
Over $1,279 to $3,338	$226.35 + 28% of amount over $1,279
Over $3,338 to $7,212	$802.87 + 33% of amount over $3,338
Over $7,212	$2,081.29 + 35% of amount over $7,212

TABLE 11.2	2009 Federal income tax withheld for a married person paid weekly.	
	Adjusted Weekly Income	Income Tax Withheld
	$0 to $303	$0
	Over $303 to $ 470	10% of amount over $303
	Over $470 to $1,455	$16.70 + 15% of amount over $470
	Over $1,455 to $2,272	$164.45 + 25% of amount over $1,455
	Over $2,272 to $4,165	$368.70 + 28% of amount over $2,272
	Over $4,165 to $7,321	$898.74 + 33% of amount over $4,165
	Over $7,321	$1,940.22 + 35% of amount over $7,321

Solutions to Practice Problems 11.2

1.
```
Public Property SocSecNum() As String
  Get
    Return m_ssn
  End Get
  Set(ByVal value As String)
    If value.Length = 11 Then
      m_ssn = value
    Else
      RaiseEvent ImproperSSN(value.Length, m_name)
    End If
  End Set
End Property
```

2.
```
Public Event ImproperSSN(ByVal length As Integer,
                         ByVal studentName As String)
```

3.
```
Private Sub pupil_ImproperSSN(ByVal length As Integer,
            ByVal studentName As string) Handles pupil.ImproperSSN
  MessageBox.Show("The social security number entered for " &
       studentName & " consisted of " & length &
       " characters. Reenter the data for " & studentName & ".")
End Sub
```

4. The statement

```
Dim pupil As Student
```

must be changed to

```
Dim WithEvents pupil As Student
```

VideoNote
Inheritance

11.3 Inheritance

The three relationships between classes are "use," "containment," and "inheritance." One class **uses** another class if it manipulates objects of that class. We say that class A **contains** class B when a member variable of class A makes use of an object of type class B. Section 11.2 presents examples of use and containment.

    Inheritance is a process by which one class (the **child** or **derived** class) inherits the properties, methods, and events of another class (the **parent** or **base** class). The child has access to all of its parent's properties, methods and events as well as to all of its own. If the parent is itself a child, then it and its children have access to all of its parent's properties, methods and events. Consider the classes shown in Fig. 11.6. All three children inherit Property A and Sub B from their parent. Child2 and Child3 have an additional event and a property, respectively. GrandChild1 has access to Property A, Sub B, and Event C from its parent and adds Function E and Sub F. The collection of a parent class along with its descendants is called a **hierarchy**.

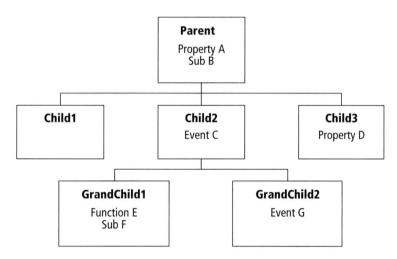

FIGURE 11.6   **Example of inheritance hierarchy.**

There are two main benefits gained by using inheritance: First, it allows two or more classes to share some common features yet differentiate themselves on others. Second, it supports code reusability by avoiding the extra effort required to maintain duplicate code in multiple classes. For these reasons, inheritance is one of the most powerful tools of object-oriented programming. Considerable work goes into planning and defining the member variables and methods of the parent class. The child classes are beneficiaries of this effort.

Just as structured programming requires the ability to break complex problems into simpler subproblems, object-oriented programming requires the skill to identify useful hierarchies of classes and derived classes. Software engineers are still working on the guidelines for when and how to establish hierarchies. One useful criterion is the **ISA test**: If one class *is a* more specific case of another class, the first class should be derived from the second class.

The Visual Basic keyword Inherits identifies the parent of a class. The code used to define the class Parent and its child class Child2 as illustrated in Fig. 11.6 is

```
Class Parent
  Public Property A
    'Property Get and Set blocks
  End Property

  Sub B()
    'Code for Sub procedure B
  End Sub
End Class


Class Child2
  Inherits Parent
  Event C()
End Class
```

As Child2 is itself a parent, its child GrandChild1 can be declared using a similar statement:

```
Class GrandChild1
  Inherits Child2

  Function E()
    'Code for function E
  End Function

  Sub F()
    'Code for Sub procedure F
  End Sub
End Class
```

 Example 1 In the following program, the user is presented with a basic adding machine. The Calculator class implements the Multiply and Divide methods and inherits the FirstNumber and SecondNumber properties and the Add and Subtract methods from its AddingMachine parent. When the *Adding Machine* radio button is selected, the user may add or subtract two numbers using an AddingMachine object. When the *Calculator* radio button is selected, the user may add, subtract, multiply, or divide two numbers using a Calculator object. Notice that the multiply and divide buttons are hidden when the Adding Machine is selected, and how the Click event procedures for the *btnAdd* and *btnSubtract* buttons examine the state of the radio button to determine which machine to use.

OBJECT	PROPERTY	SETTING
frmCalculate	Text	Calculations
lblNumber1	Text	First Number:
txtNumber1		
lblNumber2	Text	Second Number:
txtNumber2		
lblResult	Text	Result:
txtResult	ReadOnly	True
grpMachine	Text	Machine
radAddingMachine	Text	Adding Machine
	Checked	True
radCalculator	Text	Calculator
btnAdd	Text	+
btnSubtract	Text	−
btnMultiply	Text	×
btnDivide	Font	Symbol
	Text	¸ (Cedilla)

```
Public Class frmCalculate
  'Create both machines.
  Dim adder As New AddingMachine()
  Dim calc As New Calculator()

  Private Sub radAddingMachine_CheckedChanged(...) Handles _
                  radAddingMachine.CheckedChanged
    'Hide the multiply and divide functionality.
    btnMultiply.Visible = False
    btnDivide.Visible = False
  End Sub
```

```
    Private Sub radCalculator_CheckedChanged(...) Handles
                            radCalculator.CheckedChanged
      'Show the multiply and divide functionality.
      btnMultiply.Visible = True
      btnDivide.Visible = True
    End Sub


    Private Sub btnAdd_Click(...) Handles btnAdd.Click
      'Add two numbers.
      If radAddingMachine.Checked Then
        'If adding machine selected, use it to get the result.
        adder.FirstNumber = CDbl(txtNumber1.Text)
        adder.SecondNumber = CDbl(txtNumber2.Text)
        txtResult.Text = CStr(adder.Add)
      Else
        'If calculator selected, use it to get the result.
        calc.FirstNumber = CDbl(txtNumber1.Text)
        calc.SecondNumber = CDbl(txtNumber2.Text)
        txtResult.Text = CStr(calc.Add)
      End If
    End Sub


    Private Sub btnSubtract_Click(...) Handles btnSubtract.Click
      'Subtract two numbers.
      If radAddingMachine.Checked Then
        'If adding machine selected, use it to get the result.
        adder.FirstNumber = CDbl(txtNumber1.Text)
        adder.SecondNumber = CDbl(txtNumber2.Text)
        txtResult.Text = CStr(adder.Subtract)
      Else
        'If calculator selected, use it to get the result.
        calc.FirstNumber = CDbl(txtNumber1.Text)
        calc.SecondNumber = CDbl(txtNumber2.Text)
        txtResult.Text = CStr(calc.Subtract)
      End If
    End Sub


    Private Sub btnMultiply_Click(...) Handles btnMultiply.Click
      'Multiply two numbers.
      calc.FirstNumber = CDbl(txtNumber1.Text)
      calc.SecondNumber = CDbl(txtNumber2.Text)
      txtResult.Text = CStr(calc.Multiply)
    End Sub


    Private Sub btnDivide_Click(...) Handles btnDivide.Click
      'Divide two numbers.
      calc.FirstNumber = CDbl(txtNumber1.Text)
      calc.SecondNumber = CDbl(txtNumber2.Text)
      txtResult.Text = CStr(calc.Divide)
    End Sub
End Class       'frmCalculate


Class AddingMachine

  Public Property FirstNumber() As Double
```

```
  Public Property SecondNumber() As Double

  Function Add() As Double
    Return FirstNumber + SecondNumber
  End Function

  Function Subtract() As Double
    Return FirstNumber - SecondNumber
  End Function
End Class        'AddingMachine

Class Calculator
  Inherits AddingMachine
  'Calculator inherits properties FirstNumber and SecondNumber
  'and functions Add() and Subtract().

  Function Multiply() As Double
    Return FirstNumber * SecondNumber
  End Function

  Function Divide() As Double
    Return FirstNumber / SecondNumber
  End Function
End Class        'Calculator
```

[Run, type in 12 and 3, and click on the + and − buttons. Click on the *Calculator* radio button, and click on the +, −, ×, and ÷ buttons.]

■ Polymorphism and Overriding

The set of properties, methods, and events for a class is called the class **interface**. In essence, the interface of a class defines how it should behave. The interfaces of the classes AddingMachine and Calculator used in Example 1 are shown in Table 11.3.

Consider the classes used in Examples 1 and 2 of Section 11.1. Both Student and PFStudent have the same interface, even though they carry out the task of computing a semester grade differently. See Table 11.4.

TABLE 11.3	Interfaces used in Example 1.	
	AddingMachine	**Calculator**
Properties	FirstNumber	FirstNumber
	SecondNumber	SecondNumber
Methods	Add	Add
	Subtract	Subtract
		Multiply
		Divide
Events	(none)	(none)

TABLE 11.4	Interfaces used in Examples 1 and 2 in Section 11.1.	
	Student	**PFStudent**
Properties	Name	Name
	SocSecNum	SocSecNum
	Midterm	Midterm
	Final	Final
Methods	CalcSemGrade	CalcSemGrade
Events	(none)	(none)

If a programmer wants to write a program that manipulates objects from these two classes, he or she need only know how to use the interface. The programmer need not be concerned with what specific implementation of that interface is being used. The object will then behave according to its specific implementation.

The programmer need only be aware of the CalcSemGrade method and needn't be concerned about its implementation. The feature that two classes can have methods that are named the same and have essentially the same purpose, but different implementations, is called **polymorphism**.

A programmer may employ polymorphism in three easy steps. First, the properties, methods, and events that make up an interface are defined. Second, a parent class is created that performs the functionality dictated by the interface. Finally, a child class inherits the parent and overrides the methods that require different implementation than the parent. The keyword **Overridable** is used to designate the parent's methods that can be overridden, and the keyword **Overrides** is used to designate the child's methods that are doing the overriding.

There are situations where a child class needs to access the parent class's implementation of a method that the child is overriding. Visual Basic provides the keyword **MyBase** to support this functionality.

Consider the code from Example 1 of Section 11.1. To employ polymorphism, the keyword Overridable is inserted into the header of the CalcSemGrade method in the Student class:

```
Overridable Function CalcSemGrade() As String
```

The PFStudent class inherits all of the properties and methods from its parent, overriding the CalcSemGrade method as follows:

```
Class PFStudent
  Inherits Student
```

```
Overrides Function CalcSemGrade() As String
  'The student's grade for the semester
  If MyBase.CalcSemGrade = "F" Then
    Return "Fail"
  Else
    Return "Pass"
  End If
End Function
End Class          'PFStudent
```

 Example 2 In the following program, the user can enter student information and display the semester grades for the class. The PFStudent class inherits all of the properties from its parent Student, but overrides the CalcSemGrade method with its own implementation. The btnEnter_Click event procedure stores an element created by either class into the *students* array. However, the btnDisplay_Click event procedure does not need to know which elements are from which class, thus demonstrating polymorphism. **Note:** In the sixth line of the btn_Enter event procedure, the statement **pupil = New PFStudent()** is valid, since, due to inheritance, every PFStudent *is a* Student.

OBJECT	PROPERTY	SETTING
frmGrades	Text	Semester Grade
lblName	Text	Name:
txtName		
lblSSN	Text	SSN:
mtbSSN	Mask	000-00-0000
lblMidterm	Text	Midterm:
txtMidterm		
lblFinal	Text	Final:
txtFinal		
grpGradingOption	Text	Grading Option
radLetterGrade	Text	Letter Grade
	Checked	True
radPassFail	Text	Pass/Fail
btnEnter	Text	&Enter Information
btnDisplay	Text	&Display Grades
btnQuit	Text	&Quit
dgvGrades		

```
Public Class frmGrades
  Dim students(50) As Student              'Stores the class
  Dim lastStudentAdded As Integer = -1   'Last student added to students()

  Private Sub btnEnter_Click(...) Handles btnEnter.Click
    'Stores a student into the array.
    Dim pupil As Student
    'Create the appropriate object depending upon the radio button.
    If radPassFail.Checked Then
      pupil = New PFStudent()
    Else
      pupil = New Student()
    End If
    'Store the values in the text boxes into the object.
    pupil.Name = txtName.Text
```

```vb
      pupil.SocSecNum = mtbSSN.Text
      pupil.Midterm = CDbl(txtMidterm.Text)
      pupil.Final = CDbl(txtFinal.Text)
      'Add the student to the array.
      lastStudentAdded += 1
      students(lastStudentAdded) = pupil
      'Clear text boxes and list box.
      txtName.Clear()
      mtbSSN.Clear()
      txtMidterm.Clear()
      txtFinal.Clear()
      MessageBox.Show("Student #" & lastStudentAdded + 1 &
                      " recorded.")
      txtName.Focus()
    End Sub

    Private Sub btnDisplay_Click(...) Handles btnDisplay.Click
      ReDim Preserve students(lastStudentAdded)
      Dim query = From pupil In students
                  Select pupil.Name, pupil.SocSecNum, pupil.CalcSemGrade
      dgvGrades.DataSource = query.ToList
      dgvGrades.CurrentCell = Nothing
      dgvGrades.Columns("Name").HeaderText = "Student Name"
      dgvGrades.Columns("SocSecNum").HeaderText = "SSN"
      dgvGrades.Columns("CalcSemGrade").HeaderText = "Grade"
      ReDim Preserve students(50)
      txtName.focus()
    End Sub

    Private Sub btnQuit_Click(...) Handles btnQuit.Click
      'Quit the program
      Me.Close()
    End Sub
End Class       'frmGrades

Class Student
  'Member variables to hold the property values
  Private m_midterm As Double
  Private m_final As Double

  Public Property Name() As String

  Public Property SocSecNum() As String

  Public WriteOnly Property Midterm() As Double
    'The student's score on the midterm exam
    Set(ByVal value As Double)
      m_midterm = value
    End Set
  End Property

  Public WriteOnly Property Final() As Double
    'The student's score on the final exam
    Set(ByVal value As Double)
      m_final = value
    End Set
  End Property
```

```
Overridable Function CalcSemGrade() As String
  'The student's grade for the semester
  Dim grade As Double
  'The grade is based upon average of the midterm and final exams.
  grade = (m_midterm + m_final) / 2
  grade = Math.Round(grade)   'Round the grade.
  Select Case grade
    Case Is >= 90
      Return "A"
    Case Is >= 80
      Return "B"
    Case Is >= 70
      Return "C"
    Case Is >= 60
      Return "D"
    Case Else
      Return "F"
  End Select
End Function
End Class       'Student

Class PFStudent
  Inherits Student

  Overrides Function CalcSemGrade() As String
    'The student's grade for the semester
    If MyBase.CalcSemGrade = "F" Then
      Return "Fail"
    Else
      Return "Pass"
    End If
  End Function
End Class        'PFStudent
```

[Enter the data and click on the *Enter Information* button for three students. Then click on the *Display Grades* button, and finally enter the data for another student.]

Example 2 employs inheritance and overriding to provide functionality to one child class. If a program contains two or more children of a class, however, the technique of overriding can lead to confusing programs. Visual Basic provides a cleaner design through the use of abstract classes.

■ Abstract Properties, Methods, and Classes

Sometimes you want to insist that each child of a class have a certain property or method that it must implement for its own use. Such a property or method is said to be **abstract** and is declared with the keyword **MustOverride**. An **abstract** property or method consists of just a header with no code following it. It has no corresponding `End Property`, `End Sub`, or `End Function` statement. Its class is called an **abstract base class** and must be declared with the keyword **MustInherit**. Abstract classes cannot be instantiated; only their children can be instantiated.

 Example 3   The following program calculates the area of several regular two-dimensional shapes, given the length of one side. (A regular shape is a shape whose sides have identical length and whose interior angles are identical.) The abstract parent class Shape implements the Length property and declares the Name and Area functions as MustOverride. Notice that methods declared with MustOverride do not have any implementation code. Each child class inherits the property from the parent and implements the two functions. The btnDisplay_Click event procedure uses polymorphism to set the shapes' length and display the shapes' names and areas.

OBJECT	PROPERTY	SETTING
frmShapes	Text	Two-Dimensional Shapes
lblLength	Text	Length of a side:
txtLength		
btnDisplay	Text	Display
lstOutput		

```
Public Class frmShapes
  'Declare shape array.
  Dim shape(3) As Shape

  Private Sub frmShapes_Load(...) Handles MyBase.Load
    'Populate the array with shapes.
    shape(0) = New EquilateralTriangle()
    shape(1) = New Square()
    shape(2) = New Pentagon()
    shape(3) = New Hexagon()
  End Sub

  Private Sub btnDisplay_Click(...) Handles btnDisplay.Click
    Dim length As Double
    'Set lengths of all shapes.
    length = CDbl(txtLength.Text)
    For i As Integer = 0 To 3
      shape(i).Length = length
    Next
```

```vbnet
      'Display results.
      lstOutput.Items.Clear()
      For i As Integer = 0 To 3
        lstOutput.Items.Add("The " & shape(i).Name & " has area " &
                        FormatNumber(shape(i).Area)) & "."

      Next
    End Sub
  End Class          'frmShapes

MustInherit Class Shape
  Public Property Length() As Double

  MustOverride Function Name() As String
  'Returns the name of the shape.

  MustOverride Function Area() As Double
  'Returns the area of the shape.
End Class          'Shape

Class EquilateralTriangle
  Inherits Shape

  Overrides Function Name() As String
    'The name of this shape
    Return "Equilateral Triangle"
  End Function

  Overrides Function Area() As Double
    'Formula for the area of an equilateral triangle
    Return Length * Length * Math.Sqrt(3) / 4
  End Function
End Class          'EquilateralTriangle

Class Square
  Inherits Shape

  Overrides Function Name() As String
    'The name of this shape
    Return "Square"
  End Function

  Overrides Function Area() As Double
    'Formula for the area of a square
    Return Length * Length
  End Function
End Class          'Square

Class Pentagon
  Inherits Shape

  Overrides Function Name() As String
    'The name of this shape
    Return "Pentagon"
  End Function
```

```
   Overrides Function Area() As Double
     'Formula for the area of a pentagon
     Return Length * Length * Math.Sqrt(25 + (10 * Math.Sqrt(5))) / 4
   End Function
End Class      'Pentagon

Class Hexagon
  Inherits Shape

  Overrides Function Name() As String
    'The name of this shape
    Return "Hexagon"
  End Function

  Overrides Function Area() As Double
    'Formula for the area of a hexagon
    Return Length * Length * 3 * Math.Sqrt(3) / 2
  End Function
End Class      'Hexagon
```

[Run the program, enter 5, and click on the *Display* button.]

■ Comments

1. Visual Basic uses inheritance in every Windows application that is written. Examination of any program's code reveals that the form's class inherits from the .NET framework class System.Windows.Forms.Form.

2. In Example 2, the btnDisplay_Click event procedure does not need to know which elements of the Student array are instances of the Student class and which are instances of the PFStudent class. In some situations, however, the program may want to know this. Visual Basic provides the expression **TypeOf...Is** to test if an instance was created from a particular class (or from the class' parents, grandparents, etc.) For example, the following procedure counts the number of pass/fail students in the *students* array:

```
Sub CountPassFail()
   Dim query = From student In students
               Where TypeOf (student) Is PFStudent
               Select student
   Dim numPF = query.Count
   MessageBox.Show("There are " & numPF & " pass/fail students out of " &
                   lastStudentAdded + 1 & " students in the class.")
End Sub
```

3. Child classes do not have access to the parent's Private member variables.

1. In the class AddingMachine of Example 1, the Add function could have been defined with

```
Function Add() As Double
   Return _FirstNumber + _SecondNumber
End Function
```

Explain why the Multiply function of the class Calculator cannot be defined with

```
Function Multiply() As Double
   Return _FirstNumber * _SecondNumber
End Function
```

2. Consider the hierarchy of classes shown below. What value is assigned to the variable *phrase* by the following two lines of code?

```
Dim mammal As New Mammals()
Dim phrase As String = mammal.Msg
Class Animals
  Overridable Function Msg() As String
    Return "Can move"
  End Function
End Class

Class Vertebrates
  Inherits Animals
  Overrides Function Msg() As String
    Return MyBase.Msg & " " & "Has a backbone"
  End Function
End Class

Class Mammals
  Inherits Vertebrates
  Overrides Function Msg() As String
    Return MyBase.Msg & " " & "Nurtures young with mother's milk"
  End Function
End Class

Class Arthropods
  Inherits Animals
  Overrides Function Msg() As String
    Return MyBase.Msg & " " & "Has jointed limbs and no backbone"
  End Function
End Class
```

In Exercises 1 through 4, identify the output of the code that uses the following two classes:

```
Class Square
  Overridable Function Result(ByVal num As Double) As Double
    Return num * num
  End Function
End Class
```

```
Class Cube Inherits Square
  Overrides Function Result(ByVal num As Double) As Double
    Return num * num * num
  End Function
End Class
```

1. ```
   Dim sq As Square = New Square()
   txtOutput.Text = CStr(sq.Result(2))
   ```

2. ```
   Dim cb As Cube = New Cube()
   txtOutput.Text = CStr(cb.Result(3))
   ```

3. ```
   Dim m As Square = New Square()
   Dim n As Cube = New Cube()
   txtOutput.Text = CStr(m.Result(n.Result(2)))
   ```

4. ```
   Dim m As Square = New Cube()
   txtOutput.Text = CStr(m.Result(2))
   ```

5. Consider the class hierarchy in the second practice problem. What value is assigned to the variable *phrase* by the following two lines of code?

   ```
   Dim anthropod As New Arthropods()
   Dim phrase As String = arthropod.Msg
   ```

6. Consider the class hierarchy in the second practice problem. What value is assigned to the variable *phrase* by the following two lines of code?

   ```
   Dim vertebrate As New Vertebrates()
   Dim phrase As String = vertebrate.Msg
   ```

In Exercises 7 through 16, identify the errors in the code.

7. ```
   Class Hello
     Function Hi() As String
       Return "hi!"
     End Function
   End Class

   Class Greetings
     Overrides Hello
     Function GoodBye() As String
       Return "goodbye"
     End Function
   End Class
   ```

8. ```
   Class Hello
     Function Hi() As String
       Return "hi!"
     End Function
   End Class
   ```

```
Class Greetings
  Inherits Hi()

  Function GoodBye() As String
    Return "goodbye"
  End Function
End Class
```

9.
```
Class Hello
  Function Hi() As String
    Return "hi!"
  End Function
End Class

Class Aussie
  Inherits Hello

  Function Hi() As String
    Return "G'day mate!"
  End Function
End Class
```

10.
```
Class Hello
  Function Hi() As String
    Return "hi!"
  End Function
End Class

Class WithIt
  Inherits Hello

  Overrides Function Hi() As String
    Return "Hey"
  End Function
End Class
```

11.
```
Class Hello
  Overrides Function Hi() As String
    Return "hi!"
  End Function
End Class

Class Cowboy Inherits Hello
  Overridable Function Hi() As String
    Return "howdy!"
  End Function
End Class
```

12.
```
Class Hello
  MustOverride Function Hi() As String
    Return "hi!"
  End Function
End Class
```

```
        Class DragRacer
          Inherits Hello

          Overrides Function Hi() As String
            Return "Start your engines!"
          End Function
        End Class
```

13.
```
    Class Hello
        MustInherit Function Hi() As String
    End Class

    Class Gentleman
      Inherits Hello

      Overrides Function Hi() As String
        Return "Good day"
      End Function
    End Class
```

14.
```
    Class Hello
        MustOverride Function Hi() As String
    End Class

    Class Euro
      Inherits Hello

      Overrides Function Hi() As String
        Return "Caio"
      End Function
    End Class
```

15.
```
    MustOverride Class Hello
        MustOverride Function Hi() As String
    End Class

    Class Southerner
      Inherits Hello

      Overrides Function Hi() As String
        Return "Hi y'all"
      End Function
    End Class
```

16.
```
    MustInherit Class Hello
        MustOverride Function Hi() As String
    End Class

    Class NorthEasterner
      Inherits Hello

      Overrides Function Hi(ByVal name As String) As String
        Return "How ya doin', " & name
      End Function
    End Class
```

17. Expand Example 1 to use a class ScientificCalculator that is derived from the class Calculator and has an exponentiation button in addition to the four arithmetic buttons.

18. Rewrite Example 2 so that the class Student has an abstract method CalcSemGrade and two derived classes called LGStudent (LG stands for "Letter Grade") and PFStudent.

19. Consider the class CashRegister from Exercise 25 of Section 11.1. Create a derived class called FastTrackRegister that could be used at a toll booth to collect money from vehicles and keep track of the number of vehicles processed. Write a program using the class and having the form in Fig. 11.7. One dollar should be collected from each car and two dollars from each truck.

FIGURE 11.7 **Form for Exercise 19.**

FIGURE 11.8 **Sample output for Exercise 20.**

VideoNote

Student registration (Homework)

20. Consider the class Statistics from Exercise 26 of Section 11.1. Create a derived class called CompleteStats that also provides a Spread function and an event called NewSpread. This event should be raised whenever the spread changes. (The *spread* is the difference between the highest and the lowest grades.) Write a program that uses the classes to analyze up to 50 exam grades input by the user. The program should display the number of grades and the current spread at all times. When the *Calculate Average* button is clicked on, the program should display the average of the grades. A sample output is shown in Fig. 11.8.

21. Write a program that keeps track of a bookstore's inventory. The store orders both trade books and textbooks from publishers. The program should define an abstract class Book that contains the MustOverride property Price, and the ordinary properties Quantity, Name, and Cost. The Textbook and Tradebook classes should be derived from the class Book and should override property Price by adding a markup. (Assume that the markup is 40% for a trade book and 20% for a textbook.) The program should accept input from the user on book orders and display the following statistics: total number of books, number of textbooks, total cost of the orders, and total value of the inventory. (The value of the inventory is the amount of money that the bookstore can make if it sells all of the books in stock.) A sample output is shown in Fig. 11.9.

22. Write a program that records the weekly payroll of a department that hires both salaried and hourly employees. The program should accept user input and display the number of employees, the number of salaried employees, the total payroll, and the average number of hours worked. The abstract class Employee should contain Name and Rate properties. (The Rate text box should be filled in with the weekly salary for salaried workers and the hourly wage for hourly workers.) The Salaried and Hourly classes should inherit the Employee

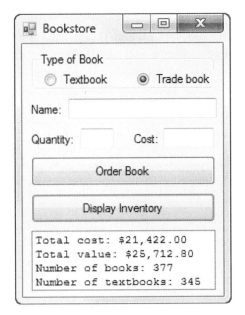

FIGURE 11.9 Sample output for Exercise 21.

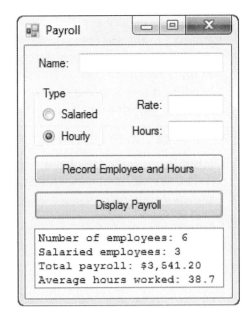

FIGURE 11.10 Sample output for Exercise 22.

class and override the method GrossPay that accepts the number of hours worked as a parameter. A sample output is shown in Fig. 11.10. (**Hint:** Use an array of a structure that holds the employee object and the number of hours worked during the week.)

Solutions to Practice Problems 11.3

1. While the derived class Calculator has access to the Properties and Methods of the base class AddingMachine, it does not have access to its Private member variables.

2. The string "Can move Has a backbone Nurtures young with mother's milk"

CHAPTER 11 **SUMMARY**

1. An *object* is an entity that stores data, has methods that manipulate the data, and can raise events. A *class* is a template from which objects are created. A *method* specifies the way in which an object's data are manipulated. An *event* is a message sent by an object to signal the occurrence of a condition.

2. Each class is defined in a separate block of code starting with Class *ClassName* and ending with End Class. Data are stored in member variables and accessed by procedures called properties.

3. A property routine contains a Get block to retrieve the value of a member variable or a Set block to assign a value to a member variable. These procedures can also be used to enforce constraints and carry out validation.

4. Visual Basic automatically invokes a New procedure when an object is created.

5. An object variable is declared with a statement of the form `Dim objectName As ClassName`, and the object is created with a statement of the form `objectName = New ClassName(arg1, arg2, ...)`. These two statements are often combined into the single statement `Dim objectName As New ClassName(arg1, arg2, ...)`.

6. *Auto-implemented properties* enable you to quickly specify a property of a class without having to write code to Get and Set the property.

7. Events are declared in the Declarations section of a class with a statement of the form `Public Event UserDefinedEvent(arg1, arg2, ...)` and raised with a `RaiseEvent` statement. The declaration statement for the object must include the keyword `WithEvents` in order for the events coming from the object to be processed. The header of an event-handling procedure has the form `Private Sub procedureName(par1, par2, ...) Handles objectName.UserDefinedEvent`.

8. The properties, methods, and events of a class are referred to as its *interface*.

9. *Inheritance*, which is implemented with the keyword Inherits, allows a new class (called the *derived* or *child* class) to be created from an existing class (called the *base* or *parent* class) and to gain its interface.

10. *Polymorphism* is the feature that two classes can have methods that are named the same and have essentially the same purpose, but different implementations.

11. The keywords *Overridable*, *Overrides*, *MustInherit*, and *MustOverride* allow derived classes to customize inherited properties and methods.

CHAPTER 11 PROGRAMMING PROJECTS

1. *Bank Account*. Write a program to maintain a person's Savings and Checking accounts. The program should keep track of and display the balances in both accounts, and maintain a list of transactions (deposits, withdrawals, fund transfers, and check clearings) separately for each account. The two lists of transactions should be stored in text files.

   Consider the form in Fig. 11.11. The two drop-down combo boxes should each contain the items Checking and Savings. Each of the four group boxes corresponds to a type of transaction. (When Savings is selected in the Account combo box, the Check group box should disappear.) The user makes a transaction by typing data into the text boxes of a group box and pressing the associated button. The items appearing in the DataGridView

FIGURE 11.11 Bank accounts.

control should correspond to the type of account that has been selected. The caption of the second label in the Transfer group box should toggle between "to Checking" and "to Savings" depending on the item selected in the "Transfer from" combo box. If a transaction cannot be carried out, a message (such as "Insufficient funds") should be displayed. Two text files should be maintained (one for each type of account) and should be updated each time a transaction is carried out.

The program should use two classes, Transaction and Account. The class Transaction should have properties for transaction name, amount, date, and whether it is a credit (deposit) or debit (withdrawal/check).

The class Account, which will have both a checking account and a savings account as instances, should use an array of Transaction objects. In addition, it should have properties for name (Checking or Savings) and balance. It should have methods to carry out a transaction (if possible) and to load the set of transactions from a text file. The events InsufficientFunds and TransactionCommitted should be raised at appropriate times.

2. Write a program for the game BlackJack. See Fig. 11.12. The program should use a DeckOfCards class similar to the one presented in Example 3 of Section 11.2. Include an option to display game statistics, including the total games, total wins, and the percentage of wins.

FIGURE 11.12 Sample output for Programming Project 2.

12

Web Applications

12.1   Programming for the Web, Part I

In earlier chapters all of our programs ran directly under Windows. Now we'll create programs that run in a Web browser (such as Internet Explorer, Firefox, Chrome, or Safari). The programs in this chapter cannot be created with Visual Basic 2010 Express; we'll need to use Visual Web Developer 2010 Express (provided on the DVD accompanying this book) or a full version of Visual Studio 2010. Our discussion will refer to Visual Web Developer 2010 Express (abbreviated as VWD), but it can easily be modified to apply to Visual Studio.

When you use a Web browser, your computer (referred to as a **client**) is making requests to another computer (referred to as a **server**). Some requests ask the server to send a particular Web page. Others require the server to perform an operation using input provided by the client and then to return a new version of a page. Visual Web Developer uses a Microsoft technology called ASP.NET to respond to requests. (ASP stands for **Active Server Pages.**)

Although the client and server are normally separate computers, VWD allows Web programs to be developed on a single computer. When VWD runs a Web program, it launches a Web server and then opens a Web browser that connects to the server. After the programs are developed, they can be transferred to a dedicated server and can then be accessed by any computer's Web browser. A dedicated server running programs created with VWD requires special Web server software called IIS (Internet Information Services).

VideoNote

Programming
for the Web

■ Creating a Web Program with Visual Web Developer

As we will soon see, a Web program is created in much the same way as a Visual Basic Windows program. We break up the creation of a Web program here into three walkthroughs to be performed in succession. After each walkthrough we present a table showing how the steps of the Web program walkthrough differ from their Visual Basic counterparts.

First walkthrough: Starting a new Web program

1. Click on the Windows *Start* button, click on *All Programs*, and click on *Microsoft Visual Web Developer 2010 Express* in the list of programs. (A Start page very similar to the Visual Basic Start page will appear.)

2. Click on *Options* in the *Tools* menu, select *General* from the left side of the Options dialog box, and click on the *Design View* radio button in the *Start Pages in* section. (This step will not have to be done for subsequent programs.) Optionally, set the value for the "Tab and indent size" to 2. Click on the *OK* button to close the Options window.

3. Click on *New Web Site* in the *File* menu. (A New Web Site dialog box will appear. *Visual Basic* should be selected as the Installed Template and *File System* as the "Web location." If not, change these items.)

4. The wide combo box at the center-bottom of the dialog box gives the location and name of the program. (The default name will be WebSite1.) We recommend changing the name to something like MyWebProgram. Also, you might want to change the path.

5. Double-click on *ASP.NET Web Site*. The IDE for VWD appears in design mode. See Fig. 12.1. The text and controls will be entered inside the red rectangle with tab "Main-Content (Custom)". We will refer to this region as the **Main Content region**.

Table 12.1 shows three ways in which starting a program in VWD differs from starting a program in Visual Basic.

Second walkthrough: Designing the Web page

Note 1: This walkthrough is a continuation of the first walkthrough.

Note 2: In VWD, text can be typed into a page and formatted in somewhat the same way as in a word processor.

FIGURE 12.1 The VWD integrated development environment in design mode.

TABLE 12.1	**Web program counterparts to starting a Visual Basic program.**
Visual Basic Windows Program	VWD Program
1. Program can be created with Visual Basic Express.	Program must be created with Visual Web Developer Express or Visual Studio.
2. You launch a program by clicking on *New Project* from the *File* menu and then double-clicking on *Windows Forms Application*.	You launch a program by clicking on *New Web Site* from the *File* menu and then double-clicking *ASP.NET Web Site*.
3. The name given to a program when it is launched is temporary. The actual name is specified with the *Save All* command.	The name given to a program when it is launched is permanent. It is *not* specified after you click on the *Save All* button.

1. Select the text in the Main Content region and then press the DEL key to delete the text in the region.

2. Type the words "Tip Calculator" into the Main Content window, drag the cursor across the two words and click on the *Bold* button (**B**) on the Toolbar. (The words now appear in boldface. Other buttons on the Toolbar can be used to change the font name, the font size, and the foreground and background colors of the words.)

3. Press the Enter key and type the words "Cost of meal:". (Notice that a faint blue rectangle with the tag labeled *p* appears. Think of *p* as standing for "paragraph". As with a word processor, the pressing of the Enter key creates a new paragraph.)

4. Press the space bar twice and then double-click on the TextBox control in the *Standard* group of the Toolbox. Notice that a text box appears at the insertion point (that is, at the cursor location).

5. Make sure that the text box is selected. In the Properties window, click on the *Alphabetize* button, locate the ID property near the top of the Properties window, and set the value of the ID property to txtCost. (VWD's ID property is the counterpart to Visual Basic's Name property. Notice that the tab above the text box reads "asp:TextBox#txtCost".)

6. Position the cursor to the right of the text box, press the Enter key, type "Percent tip (such as, 15, 18.5, or 20):", press the space bar twice, and double-click on the TextBox control in the Toolbar. (Another text box appears.)

7. Set the text box's ID property to txtPercent.

8. Position the cursor to the right of the text box, press the Enter key, double-click on the Button control in the Toolbox (a button appears at the insertion point), set the button's ID property to btnCalculate, and set its Text property to "Calculate Tip".

9. Position the cursor to the right of the button, press the Enter key, type "Amount of tip:", press the space bar twice, double-click on the TextBox control in the Toolbox (a text box appears at the insertion point), set the text box's ID property to txtTip, set its ReadOnly property to *True*, and position the cursor to the right of the text box. The screen now appears as in Fig. 12.2.

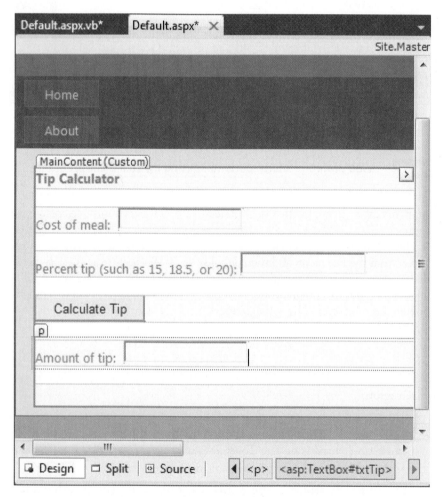

FIGURE 12.2 **The Designer for our program.**

The counterpart in VWD of a Visual Basic Windows form is referred to as a **Web page**. Table 12.2 shows seven ways in which designing a Web page differs from designing a Visual Basic form.

TABLE 12.2   **Web page counterparts to designing a Visual Basic Windows form.**

Visual Basic Windows Form	VWD Web Page
1. There is no cursor on the form designer.	The page designer has a cursor (also referred to as the *insertion point*).
2. Text to appear permanently on a form is usually placed in a label and formatted with settings from the Properties window.	Permanent text (called *static text*) can be typed directly into the page at the insertion point and formatted from the Toolbar in the same way as text typed into a word processor.
3. The most frequently used controls (such as Button, ListBox, and TextBox) are found in the *Common Controls* group of the Toolbox.	The most frequently used controls (such as Button, ListBox, and TextBox) are found in the *Standard* group of the Toolbox.
4. When you double-click on a control in the Toolbox, the control appears either in the upper-left corner of the form or just below the most recently created control.	When you double-click on a control in the Toolbox, the control appears at the insertion point.
5. The name of a control is specified by setting its Name property.	The name of a control is specified by setting its ID property.
6. In design mode, controls are placed anywhere on a form and aligned with the *Format* menu.	In design mode, text and controls are placed in a top-to-bottom fashion, each entered at the insertion point.
7. The tab for the Designer reads "*frmName*.vb [Design]".	The tab for the Designer reads "Default.aspx".

Third walkthrough: Coding and executing a Web program

Note: This walkthrough is a continuation of the second walkthrough.

1. Double-click on the *Calculate* button. (The Code Editor will appear with a template for the button's default event procedure, btnCalculate_Click. In VWD, the code in the Code Editor is called the **code-behind**.)

2. Type the following three lines of code into the btnCalculate_Click event procedure:

```
Dim cost As Double = CDbl(txtCost.Text)
Dim percent As Double = CDbl(txtPercent.Text) / 100
txtTip.Text = FormatCurrency(percent * cost)
```

3. Press Ctrl + F5 to run the program without debugging. (Your Web browser will open after a few seconds. Figure 12.3 shows the upper-left corner of the Web page in the browser.)

4. Type *20* into txtCost, type *15* into txtPercent, and click on the button. The value $3.00 will appear in txtTip.

5. Click on the browser's *Close* button to terminate the program and return to the Code Editor. Notice that the tab for the Code Editor reads *Default.aspx.vb*. (An Output window appears below the Code Editor. You can remove the Output window by clicking on its *Close* button.)

6. At this point you can alter the code in the Code Editor if desired or click on the *Default.aspx* tab or return to the Designer and make further changes to the form.

FIGURE 12.3   Contents of the Web browser after the program is run.

7. Click on the *Save All* button to save the program and then click on *Close Project* in the *File* menu to close the program. (**Note:** If you are using Visual Studio instead of VWD, click on *Close Solution* in the *File* menu to close the program.)

Table 12.3 shows four ways in which coding and executing a Web program differs from coding and executing a Visual Basic form.

TABLE 12.3	Web program counterparts to coding and executing a Visual Basic program.
Visual Basic Program	**Web Program**
1. The tab for the Code Editor reads "frmName.vb".	The tab for the Code Editor reads "Default.aspx.vb".
2. We usually run a program by pressing F5 or clicking on the *Start Debugging* button on the Toolbar.	We will usually run a program by pressing Ctrl + F5 to start *without* debugging.
3. Programs are run as a Windows application.	Programs are run in a Web browser interacting with a Web server.
4. Programs are terminated by clicking on the form's *Close* button or pressing Alt + F4.	Programs are terminated by closing the browser.

▥ Using a Table to Lay Out a Web Page's Content

The layout of the page created in the second walkthrough is not as nice looking as those we have been creating with Visual Basic. In our Visual Basic design, the three text boxes would be left-aligned and the button would be centered horizontally in the form. A table control can be used with VWD to improve the appearance of the Web page.

A table control is a rectangular array of cells, where text and/or controls can be placed into each cell. The columns of the table are used to align text and controls. The following walkthrough uses a table to create an improved version of the previous program.

A table walkthrough: Using a table to improve the design of a Web program

Note: This walkthrough is a not a continuation of the previous walkthroughs. It produces the same program, but with a more attractive page design.

1. Start a new Web program with the name TipCalculator, and clear the contents of the Main Content region as before.

2. Click on *Insert Table* from the *Table* menu to produce the Insert Table dialog box shown in Fig. 12.4.

FIGURE 12.4 **The Insert Table dialog box.**

3. Set the number of rows to 5 and the number of columns to 2. (The labels for the text boxes will be placed right-justified into the first column and the text boxes will be placed left-justified into the second column.)

4. Click on the first *In pixels* radio button and change the number in the accompanying text box from 100 to 500. (The table will be 500 pixels wide.)

5. Click on the *OK* button to generate the faint 5-by-2 grid shown in Fig. 12.5. (We will use the grid at design time to align text and controls. The grid will not be visible at run time.)

FIGURE 12.5 A table with five rows and two columns.

6. Hover the mouse over the top of the first column until a down-arrow (↓) appears; then click on the left mouse button. (The first column has now been selected.) In the Properties window, set the Align property to *right*. This will cause the entries in that column to be right-justified. **Note:** There is no need to set the Align property for the right column, since its default alignment is *left*.

7. Type "Cost of meal:" into the first column of the second row. Move the cursor to the second column of the second row and double-click on the TextBox control in the Toolbox. (A text box appears at the insertion point.) Give the text box the name txtCost by setting its ID property to txtCost.

8. Use a process similar to Step 7 to place "Percent tip (such as 15, 18.5, or 20):" into the left column of the third row and a text box named txtPercent into the right column.

9. Use a process similar to Step 7 to place "Amount of tip:" into the left column of the fifth row and a read-only text box named txtTip into the right column.

10. Drag the mouse over the cells in the first row to select the row. Then hover over *Modify* in the *Table* menu and click on *Merge Cells*. (The first row will now be reduced from two cells to one cell.)

11. With the first row still highlighted, set its Align property to *center*, type the words "Tip Calculator" into the row, and make the words boldface.

12. In a manner similar to Steps 10 and 11, place a button named btnCalculate and text "Calculate Tip" in the center of the fourth row.

13. Resize the text boxes, columns, rows, and table to remove extraneous space. The best way to resize a text box is to change the value of its Width property. To resize a column, hover the mouse over the double bar on the right side of the column until a horizontal double-arrow (⟺) appears; then drag the arrow. To resize a row, hover the mouse over the double bar at the bottom side of the row until a vertical double-arrow (↕) appears; then drag the arrow. To resize the table, hover the mouse over the upper-left corner of the table until an arrow cross (✥) appears; then click the left mouse button. The table will now be selected, and it can be resized by dragging its sizing handles. The Main Content region of the Web page should look like Fig. 12.6.

14. Double-click on the button and enter the following code into the btnCalculate event procedure:

```
Dim cost As Double = CDbl(txtCost.Text)
Dim percent As Double = CDbl(txtPercent.Text) / 100
txtTip.Text = FormatCurrency(percent * cost)
```

FIGURE 12.6   Web page in design mode.   FIGURE 12.7   Web page in run time.

15. Press Ctrl + F5 to run the program, enter values into the first two text boxes, and click on the button. Figure 12.7 shows a possible output.

Some additional features of tables are as follows:

1. In the walkthrough we used a down-arrow to select an entire column. To select an entire row in an analogous way, hover the mouse over the left side of the row until a right-arrow (➡) appears; then click the left mouse button.

2. To add a new row to a table, click on a row of the table, click on *Insert* in the *Table* menu, and click on *Row Above* or *Row Below*. A similar process can be used to add a new column.

3. To delete a row or column from a table, hover over *Delete* in the *Table* menu, and then click on *Delete Rows* or *Delete Columns*.

4. To delete a table, hover the mouse over the upper-left corner of the table until an arrow cross appears, press the left mouse button to select the entire table, and then click on the DEL key.

5. Both rows and cells have an Align property.

6. The Align property specifies horizontal alignment. The valign property specifies vertical alignment.

▦ Accessing a Text File in a Web Program

With Visual Basic, we placed text files in the program's *bin\Debug* folder and accessed the file with a statement of the form

```
Dim strArrayName() As String = IO.File.ReadAllLines(filespec)
```

VWD does not have a *bin\Debug* folder. With VWD, text files are usually placed in the App_Data folder of the Solution Explorer window and accessed with a statement of the form

```
Dim strArrayName() As String =
              IO.File.ReadAllLines(MapPath("App_Data\" & filename))
```

We can then use LINQ with such an array, as we did earlier with Visual Basic programs.

■ Binding a Control to a LINQ Query

The following pair of statements display the results of a LINQ query in a list box:

```
lstBox.DataSource = query
lstBox.DataBind()
```

In VWD, the counterpart of the DataGridView control is the GridView control. The following pair of statements bind a GridView control to a query:

```
grvGrid.DataSource = query
grvGrid.DataBind()
```

There is no need to set a GridView's CurrentCell property to Nothing, or to specify its size. (VWD will automatically size the control.) By default a GridView control does not use row headers, therefore there is no RowHeadersVisible property that needs to be set to False. Also, there is no need to set the SelectedItem property of a list box to Nothing. Column headers can be specified with statements such as

```
grvGrid.HeaderRow.Cells(0).Text = header for first column
grvGrid.HeaderRow.Cells(1).Text = header for second column
```

■ Opening an Existing Web Program

The following steps open the program MyWebProgram that was created in the first three walk-throughs:

1. Click on *Open Web Site* in the *File* menu.
2. Navigate to the folder named *MyWebProgram* that was created in the walkthrough.
3. Click on the *Open* button. (If a program is currently loaded, you may be prompted to save it.)
4. If the Designer or Code Editor is not visible, right-click on the file Default.aspx in the Solution Explorer window and click on *View Designer* or *View Code*.

■ Building on an Existing Web Program

Some exercises in this text require you to create a new program that extends an already created program. The following steps save you from having to design the page and enter the code a second time:

1. Start the new program, note the path to its folder, and close the new program.
2. Launch Windows Explorer.
3. Open the folder containing the old program, press Ctrl + A to select its contents, and press Ctrl + C to copy the contents of the folder into the Clipboard.
4. Open the folder containing the new program, press Ctrl + A to select its contents, press the DEL key to delete the contents, and press Ctrl + V to paste the contents of the old folder into the new folder.
5. In VWD, click on *Recent Projects and Solutions* in the *File* menu, and click on the first line of the drop-down list that appears.

You have created a new program that is a copy of the old program. You can now proceed to make modifications.

■ Comments

1. Important reminders: When starting a new Web program, click on *New Web Site*, not *New Project*, from the *File* menu. When opening an existing Web program, click on *Open Web*

Site, not *Open Project*, from the *File* menu. However, when closing a Web program, click on *Close Project*.

2. We have been running Web programs by pressing Ctrl + F5 to run *without* debugging. However, if you prefer, you can click on the *Start Debugging* button in the Toolbar instead. If so, you might have to click on an *OK* button in a dialog box to proceed. Also, the program might still be running after you exit the browser. If so, you will have to click on *Stop Debugging* in the *Debug* menu to terminate the program.

3. Renaming a Web program is much easier than renaming a Windows program. Just close the program and use Windows Explorer to rename the program's folder.

4. In design mode, the bottom of the Designer contains three buttons labeled *Design*, *Split*, and *Source*. If you click on the *Source* button, you will see ASP.NET code corresponding to the design of the page. This code can be altered directly to change the page design. If you press the *Split* button, you will see a split screen showing both the page and its ASP.NET code.

EXERCISES 12.1

In Exercises 1 through 4, write a Web program corresponding to the outcome shown.

1.

First number:	22
Second number:	45
Third number:	33

Find Largest Number

| Largest number: | 45 |

2. **Determine Final Cost**

| Price of item: | 100 |
| Percent sales tax: | 6 |

Calculate Cost of Item

| Cost: | $106.00 |

3.

Enter an integer: 4

Display Poem

```
1 potato
2 potato
3 potato
4
```

4.

Enter an integer: 5

Display Triangle

```
*
**
***
****
*****
```

5. If a bond is purchased for *n* dollars and sold one year later for *m* dollars, then the *discount rate* is $\frac{m - n}{m}$ and the *interest rate* is $\frac{m - n}{n}$, where each is expressed as a percent. Write a Web program to calculate the discount rate and interest rate for a bond. See Fig. 12.8.

Bond Rates

| Purchase price: | 950 |
| Redemption value 1 yr. later: | 1000 |

Calculate Rates

| Discount rate: | 5.00% |
| Interest rate: | 5.26% |

Current Dividend Yield

| Most recent full-year dividend: | 1.96 |
| Current share price: | 62.89 |

Calculate CDY

| Current dividend yield: | 3.12% |

FIGURE 12.8 **An outcome of Exercise 5.**   FIGURE 12.9 **An outcome of Exercise 6.**

6. The *current dividend yield* for common stock is calculated with the formula

$$\text{current dividend yield} = \frac{\text{most recent full-year dividend}}{\text{current share price}}.$$

Write a Web program to calculate the current dividend yield for a stock. See Fig. 12.9.

In Exercises 7 through 16, rework the example or exercise as a Web program.

7. Example 9 of Section 4.2
8. Example 3 of Section 5.1
9. Exercise 35 of Section 5.2
10. Exercise 36 of Section 5.2
11. Example 3 of Section 5.3
12. Exercise 11 of Section 5.3
13. Example 3 of Section 6.2
14. Exercise 30 of Section 6.1
15. Exercise 48 of Section 7.1
16. Example 9 of Section 7.1

The file States.txt contains the 50 U.S. states in the order in which they joined the union. Use this text file in Exercises 17 through 20.

17. Write a program whose page contains a button and a list box. When the user clicks on the button, the names of the states that end with "ia" should be displayed in the list box.

18. Write a program whose page contains a button and a list box. When the user clicks on the button, the program should determine the greatest length of the names of the states and then display (in the list box) all states having names of that length.

19. Write a program whose page contains a text box, a button, and a list box. When the user enters a letter into the text box and clicks on the button, the states beginning with that letter should be displayed in the list box.

20. Write a program whose page contains two buttons, a text box, and a list box. See Fig. 12.10. The user should be able to display a list of all states beginning with a vowel or all states beginning with a consonant (in alphabetical order) and determine the number of such states. **Note:** List boxes in VWD do not have a Sorted property.

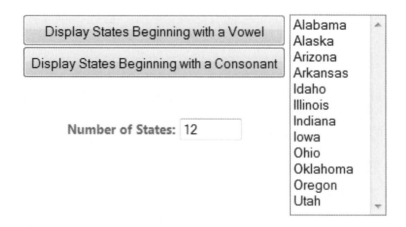

FIGURE 12.10 An outcome of Exercise 20.

12.2 Programming for the Web, Part II

In this section we explore some controls that are unique to VWD and some special features of Visual Web Developer.

Multiple Web Pages

VideoNote
Multiple
Web pages

Web applications commonly use several Web pages. The pages contain links (called **hyperlinks**) that allow the user to navigate between pages. A hyperlink usually appears on a page as underlined text. Additional Web pages and hyperlinks can be easily added to Web programs.

The following steps add a new Web page to a program.

1. Click on the current Web page to ensure that it has the focus.
2. Click on *Add New Item* in the *Website* menu. (An Add New Item dialog box will appear.)
3. Click on *Web Form* in the center pane, type a name into the *Name* box, and click on the *Add* button. (The Designer for the new Web page will appear and the name of the page in the Solution Explorer will have the extension *aspx*.)

To switch from one Web page to another in Design mode, right-click on the name of the Web page in the Solution Explorer window, and click on either *View Designer* or *View Code* in the context menu that appears.

There are several ways to navigate from one page to another at run time. The most common way is to use a hyperlink control (found in the *General* group of the Toolbox). The following walkthrough adds an additional Web page to the tip-calculator program from Section 12.1.

Hyperlink walkthrough

1. Follow the steps in the "Building on an Existing Web Program" discussion at the end of Section 12.1 to create a program named TipWithHelp that builds on the program Tip-Calculator.
2. Add a new page (that is, Web Form) named Help.aspx to the program via the *Add New Item* entry in the *Website* menu. (The Designer for the new page will appear.)
3. Add text to the new Web page as shown in the first four lines of Fig. 12.11.

Tip Guideline

The standard restaurant tip is 15% to 20% of your pretax bill.

If you are dissatisfied with your service, leave 15% anyway

and tell the manager why you weren't happy.

Return to Tip Calculator

FIGURE 12.11   **The Help.aspx page.**

4. Press the Enter key and then double-click on the HyperLink control in the *Standard* group of the Toolbox to place a hyperlink control below the text.
5. Set the ID property of the hyperlink control to *lnkReturn* and set the Text property to *Return to Tip Calculator*. See Fig. 12.11.
6. Click on the ellipsis button in the hyperlink's NavigateUrl property Settings box. (A Select URL dialog box will appear.)
7. Double-click on *Default.aspx* in the right pane of the Select URL dialog box to set the hyperlink's NavigateUrl property to ~/Default.aspx.

8. Right-click on *Default.aspx* in the Solution Explorer window and then click on *View Designer* in the context menu to display the Designer for the original Web page.

9. Place the cursor on the line of the table containing the *Calculate Tip* button, hover the mouse over *Insert* in the *Table* menu, and click on *Row Below*. (A blank row will be created in the table with the insertion point in that row.)

10. Double-click on the HyperLink control in the Toolbox to place a hyperlink control in the new row.

11. Set the ID property to *lnkHelp*, set the Text property to *Tipping Help*, and set the NavigateUrl property to ~/*Help.aspx*. (To specify the setting for the NavigateUrl property, click on the ellipsis in the Settings box and then click on *Help.aspx* in the right pane of the Select URL dialog box that appears.)

12. Set the Align property of the row containing the hyperlink control to *Center*. Figure 12.12 shows the Designer.

FIGURE 12.12   **The Default.aspx page.**

13. Run the program and click on the hyperlink. (The Help page appears.)

14. After you read the advice, click on the *Return to Tip Calculator* hyperlink to go back to the Tip Calculator Web page. (You can now calculate the amount of a tip.)

■ Validation Controls

The *Validation* group in the Toolbox contains five controls that can be used to check user input. In this section we use the RequiredFieldValidator control and the RangeValidator control to authenticate user input.

The RequiredFieldValidator control is used with text boxes to ensure that they contain data and is used with list boxes to check that an item has been selected. The two key properties of the RequiredFieldValidator control are ControlToVerify and ErrorMessage. Suppose you are adding validation for a page containing an input text box control named txtBox and a list box control named lstBox. Two RequiredFieldValidator controls will be needed; let's call the controls rfvText and rfvList. The setting for ControlToVerify in rfvText will be txtBox and in rfvList will be lstBox. If a button on the page is clicked on before data has been entered into the text box, or before an item in the list box has been selected, then the button's Click event will not be executed. In both of these situations, the setting for the ErrorMessage property will be displayed in the RequiredFieldValidator control.

The RangeValidator control checks that an entry in a text box falls within a set range of values. The five key properties of the RangeValidator control are ControlToVerify, ErrorMessage, Type, MinimumValue, and MaximumValue. The possible settings for the Type property are *String*, *Integer*, *Double*, *Date*, and *Currency*. The settings for the Minimum and Maximum properties should be suitable for the specified type, and the setting for the Minimum property should be less than or equal to the setting for the Maximum property. Suppose that the setting for the ControlToVerify property is a text box and that data outside of the specified range is typed into the text box. Then the error message will be displayed in the RangeValidator control as soon as the text box loses focus.

Example 1   The following program is an extension of the tip-calculator program from Section 12.1. The RequiredFieldValidator control is located to the right of the cost text box and the RangeValidator control is located to the right of the percent tip text box. When the user clicks on the button, the program checks to see that a cost has been entered and that the percentage for the tip is reasonable. (The assumption is made that a tip should never exceed 100%.) To be completely protected, an additional RequiredFieldValidator control for the *Percent* tip text box could have been added. Figure 12.13 shows the contents of the Designer and Fig. 12.14 shows the settings for the controls. The two red sentences will not appear initially in the Web browser when the program is run.

Tip Calculator

Cost of meal: [ ]   **You must enter the cost!**

Percent tip (such as 15, 18.5, 20): [ ]   **Not a valid percentage!**

[Calculate Tip]

Amount of tip: [ ]

FIGURE 12.13   **Design for Example 1.**

OBJECT	PROPERTY	SETTING
txtCost		
CostRequiredFieldValidator	ControlToValidate	txtCost
	ErrorMessage	You must enter the cost!
	Font/Bold	True
	ForeColor	Red
txtPercent		
PercentRangeValidator	ControlToValidate	txtPercent
	ErrorMessage	Not a valid percentage!
	Type	Double
	MaximumValue	100
	MinimumValue	0
	Font/Bold	True
	ForeColor	Red
btnCalculate	Text	Calculate Tip
txtTip	ReadOnly	True

FIGURE 12.14   **Property settings for Example 1.**

```
Protected Sub btnCalculate_Click(...) Handles btnCalculate.Click
  Dim cost As Double = CDbl(txtCost.Text)
  Dim percent As Double = CDbl(txtPercent.Text) / 100
  txtTip.Text = FormatCurrency(percent * cost)
End Sub
```

[Run, enter 15 for the tip percent, neglect to enter a cost, and click on the *Calculate Tip* button.]

Tip Calculator

Cost of meal: [____] **You must enter the cost!**

Percent tip (such as 15, 18.5, 20): [15____]

[Calculate Tip]

Amount of tip: [____]

■ Postback

Consider the tip-calculator program. When the user enters two proper values into the text boxes and presses the *Calculate* button, the values in the text boxes are sent back to the server, the tip calculation is made, and then an updated page is generated and sent to the Web browser. The page is said to be *posted back* to the server for processing, and a **postback** is said to have occurred.

When a validation control is triggered, the matter is handled entirely by the browser—no postback occurs. Also, no postback occurs when the browser requests a new page from the server.

■ The Page Load Event

The **page load event** is the Web analog of the form load event in a Windows program. They differ chiefly in that the form load event occurs only once, whereas the page load event occurs when a Web program is first run and also every time there is a postback to a page. The reason is that after a Web page is sent to a browser, the program is terminated until another postback occurs. At that point, for all practical purposes the program is being run for the first time. Therefore, the page load event occurs again.

There is a way for you to guarantee that the code inside the page load event procedure is executed only once while working with a single page. Place the code inside an If . . . Then block whose condition uses the IsPostBack property. The general form of the event procedure is as follows:

```
Protected Sub Page_Load(...) Handles Me.Load
  If Not Page.IsPostBack Then
    (code to execute just once)
  End If
End Sub
```

■ Class-Level Variables

Local variables act the same in Web programs as they do in Windows programs. They do not exist until a procedure is called, and they cease to exist after the procedure terminates. Class-level variables in a Web program, on the other hand, cease to exist whenever a page is sent to the Web browser. Therefore, whatever values were assigned to them will be gone when the next postback occurs.

There are ways to have a value persist between postbacks. For instance, a value can be placed in a HiddenField control. Some more advanced methods for retaining values involve the use of session variables and cookies.

▦ The RadioButtonList Control

Figure 12.15 shows the form used in Example 3 of Section 4.4. The four radio buttons are inside a group box control with the caption *Age*.

FIGURE 12.15   Example 3 from Section 4.4.

Visual Web Developer does not have a group box control capable of holding a list of radio buttons. The counterpart is the radio-button list control. The following VWD walkthrough creates an enhanced Web form of the program in Fig. 12.15. The Web program has the additional feature that a warning message is displayed if a radio button has not been selected when the *Determine Fee* button is clicked on.

A RadioButtonList Walkthrough

1. Start a VWD program with the name AdmissionFee and delete the text in the Main Content region.
2. Place a table having 3 rows, 2 columns, and width 275px onto the page.
3. Use the Table menu to merge the three cells in the left column of the table.
4. Type two spaces followed by the word *Age* into the left column.
5. Double-click on the word *Age* and make it boldface by clicking on the *Bold* button on the Toolbar.
6. Position the cursor to the right of the word *Age* and press the Enter key.
7. Double-click on *RadioButtonList* in the *Standard* Group of the Toolbox to place a radio-button list control on the page.
8. Set the control's ID property to *rblAges*.
9. Click on the control's *Tasks* button and then click on *Edit Items*. (The ListItem Collection Editor in Fig. 12.16 on the next page appears.)
10. Click on the *Add* button and then type "child (< 6)" into the setting for the Text property, as shown in Fig. 12.17.
11. Click on the *Add* button and type in "minor (6-17)" for the Text property.
12. Repeat Step 11 for "adult (18-64)" and for "senior (65+)".
13. Click on the OK button to indicate that all of the radio buttons have been added to the list.
14. Place a button with the name btnDetermine and Text setting "Determine Fee" into the first row of the right column.
15. Type the word "Fee:" into the second row of the right column, and then to the right of the word add a text box. Set its ID property to *txtFee* and its ReadOnly property to *True*.
16. Place a RequiredFieldValidator (with name rfvAge) in the third row of the right column.

FIGURE 12.16 **ListItem Collection Editor.**

FIGURE 12.17 **ListItem Collection Editor for a RadioButtonList control.**

17. Set the ControlToValidate property of rfvAge to *rblAges*, set the ErrorMessage property to "You must select an age!", set the ForeColor to *Red*, and set the Font Bold property to *True*. (See Fig. 12.18.)

FIGURE 12.18 **Designer from walkthrough.**

18. The radio-button list control is similar to the Visual Basic list box control in that the value of its Text property is the selected item represented as a string. Double-click on the button and enter the following code:

```
Protected Sub btnDetermine_Click(...) Handles btnDetermine.Click
  Select Case rblAges.Text
    Case "child (<6)"
      txtFee.Text = FormatCurrency(0)
    Case "minor (6-17)"
      txtFee.Text = FormatCurrency(5)
    Case "adult (18-64)"
      txtFee.Text = FormatCurrency(10)
    Case "senior (65+)"
      txtFee.Text = FormatCurrency(7.5)
  End Select
End Sub
```

■ The Check Box Control

Figure 12.19 shows the forms from Examples 4 and 5 in Section 4.4. In Example 4 the user first selects check boxes and then clicks on the *Determine* button to obtain the total cost. Nothing happens until the button is clicked on. In Example 5, an event procedure is declared that is

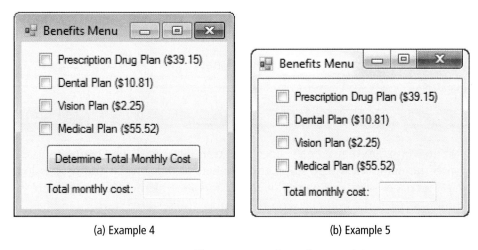

(a) Example 4   (b) Example 5

FIGURE 12.19 **Two programs from Section 4.4.**

raised whenever one of the check boxes is clicked on. That event procedure updates the total cost. The difference between the two examples is that in Example 5 a computation is made every time the user clicks on a check box, whereas in Example 4 clicking on a check box does not cause a computation.

Both examples can be converted to Web programs with the same controls, settings, and code as in Section 4.4. The Web version of Example 4 will work just fine, but Example 5 will not work as expected. This happens because computations can be made only if there is a post-back to the server. Clicking on a button triggers a postback, but clicking on a check box does not. The situation in the Web version of Example 5 is easily remedied. The check box control has an AutoPostBack property that is set to *False* by default. However, if it is changed to *True*, then clicking on the check box will trigger a postback and thus will allow a computation to be made. Therefore, all that is required to make the Web version of Example 5 work as intended is to change the AutoPostBack setting for each of the four check boxes.

By default, clicking on a button causes VWD to check for validation. Such is not the case with a check box. However, if you change a check box's CausesValidation property to True, clicking on it will invoke a validation check.

■ Comments

1. As an alternative to using a hyperlink control, a line of code of the form

```
Response.Redirect("WebPageName.aspx")
```

can be used to navigate to another Web page.

2. In Windows programs, a list box's String Collection Editor can be used to fill the contents of the list box at design time. In Web programs this task is accomplished with a ListItem Collection Editor that is identical to the one for the radio-button list control.

Practice Problems 12.2

A statement such as

```
Dim states() As String = IO.File.ReadAllLines(MapPath("App_Data/States.txt"))
```

cannot be placed in the Declarations section of a Web program as is commonly done in Windows programs.

1. Why did we often avoid placing ReadAllLines statements inside event procedures in Windows programs?

2. Why is the answer to Practice Problem 1 not relevant to Web programs?

EXERCISES 12.2

1. Write a program that uses the page design in Fig. 12.20. The list box should be populated with the names of the 50 states in alphabetical order when the page is loaded. (The file States.txt contains the names of the U.S. states in the order in which they joined the union.) When the user clicks on the button, the selected state should be deleted from the list box. A validation control should be used to assure that a state has been selected before the button is clicked on. At all times the read-only text box should display the number of states remaining in the list.

FIGURE 12.20 Web page design for Exercise 1.

2. Rework Exercise 20 from Section 4.4 (Presidential Eligibility) as a Web program. Add two validation controls for the "Date of birth" text box. One validation control should check that the date entered is 1/21/1978 or earlier (to guarantee that the person will be 35 by inauguration day in 2013) and the other should require that a date has been entered. The code for the button's Click event procedure can be shortened, since the date would have already been validated.

3. Rework Exercise 17 of Section 4.4 (Cost of a Computer) as a Web program. Use a RequiredFieldValidator control to assure that one of the radio buttons is selected. **Note 1:** If you set the radio-button list's RepeatDirection property to *Horizontal*, then the radio buttons will be displayed in a row. **Note 2:** You must set each check box's CausesValidation property to *True*.

4. Rework Exercise 25 of Section 4.4 (Health Club Fees) as a Web program. Use a RequiredFieldValidator control to assure that one of the radio buttons is selected before the fee is calculated.

5. Rework Example 1 of Section 5.1 (Convert Fahrenheit to Celsius) as a Web program. Require that the input text box contain a value when the button is clicked on and that the value is in the range from −459.67 °F (absolute zero) to 11,000 °F (approximate temperature of the surface of the sun).

6. Consider the program in the hyperlink walkthrough. Replace the hyperlink control in the Help page with a button having the caption "Return to Tip Calculator".

7. Rework Exercise 35 of Section 5.2 (Highest Two Grades) as a Web program. Require that data be entered into each input text box before the button's Click event is processed and validate that each grade is between 0 and 100. See Fig. 12.21.

Grades

First grade:

Second grade:

Third grade:

Determine Highest Two Grades

First grade missing!   Second grade missing!   Third grade missing!

First grade invalid!   Second grade invalid!   Third grade invalid!

FIGURE 12.21 Page design for Exercise 7.

8. Rework Example 3 of Section 5.1 (Weekly Pay) as a Web program. Require that data be entered into each input text box before the button's Click event is processed and validate that the number of hours worked is at most 168 (the number of hours in a week).

9. Rework Exercise 37 of Section 5.2 (Alphabetize Two Words) as a Web program with the additional provision that both words must begin with lower-case letters. Use a Required-FieldValidator and a RangeValidator control with each text box.

10. Rework Example 3 of Section 7.3 (Display Countries by Continent and Area) as a Web program without using a structure.

11. Rework Exercise 29 of Section 7.3 (Display Justices from a Specified State) as a Web program without using a structure.

12. Rework Example 1 of Section 7.4 (Intercity Distances) as a Web program. Use a Required-FieldValidator and a RangeValidator control with each input text box.

Solutions to Practice Problems 12.2

1. This was done to avoid reading a text file from a disk into an array more than once.

2. With a Web program, any array loses its values between postbacks.

12.3   Using Databases in Web Programs

Databases play a prominent role in Web applications. In this section we show how to use LINQ to manipulate information retrieved from databases. The information will be displayed both in bar charts and in grids. Our bar charts will be generated by the Chart control, which is new to Visual Web Developer 2010.

This section uses the same types of databases as Chapter 10. However, we will use them in a different format called a Microsoft SQL Server format. (SQL is pronounced *sequel.*) The databases will have the extension *mdf.* In order to open these databases when using VWD Express, you must have Microsoft SQL Server installed on your computer. (Microsoft SQL Server Express is contained on the DVD accompanying this book and is usually installed when you install Visual Basic Express or Visual Web Developer Express.)

■ Creating a Bar Chart from a Database

The following walkthrough uses the Megacities database discussed in Section 10.2 and displays a bar chart showing the cities and their 2010 populations. The cities will be displayed in descending order of their 2010 populations. **Note:** VWD refers to a *bar chart* as a *column chart*.

The walkthrough proceeds in four stages.

Stage 1: Design the Web page.

Stage 2: Add a database connection.

Stage 3: Create an *object model* for the database. (The object model is used to enable LINQ queries to be performed on data retrieved from relational databases.)

Stage 4: Use a LinqDataSource control to display data in a Chart control.

Stage 1: Design the web page

1. Start a VWD program with the name PopBarChart and delete the text in the Main Content region.

2. Place a button control on the form, set its ID property to btnDisplay, set its Width property to 300px, and set its Text property to "Display City Populations in Descending Order".

3. Place the cursor to the right of the button control, press the Enter key twice, and then double-click on the Chart control (in the *Data* group of the Toolbox) to place a chart control on the page. The chart control will display a generic bar chart as a placeholder. (See Fig. 12.22.)

4. Set the ID property of the chart control to *chtMegacities*.

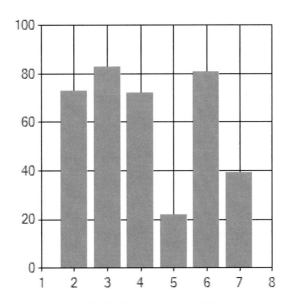

FIGURE 12.22   **Default.aspx page in Design view.**

Stage 2: Add a database connection

1. Open the Database Explorer window by clicking on its tab. Alternatively, select *Other Windows* from the *View* menu and click on *Database Explorer*. **Note:** In Visual Studio, *Database Explorer* is called *Server Explorer*.

2. Right-click on *Data Connections* in the Database Explorer window and then click on *Add Connection*. (The Add Connection dialog box in Fig. 12.23 on the next page will appear.)

3. If the Data source is not set to "Microsoft SQL Server Database File (SqlClient)", click on the *Change* button and select that data source.

4. Click on the *Browse* button, navigate to the folder Programs\Ch12\Databases in the materials you downloaded from the Pearson Web site for this book, and double-click on the file Megacities.mdf.

5. Click on the *Test Connection* button to verify that you are connected to the database.

6. Click on the *OK* button.

Stage 3: Create an object model for the database

1. Click on the Web page and then click on *Add New Item* in the *Website* menu. (An Add New Item dialog box will appear.)

2. Select *LINQ to SQL Classes*, change the name from the default name *DataClasses.dbml* to *Megacities.dbml*, and click on the *Add* button. (The window in Fig. 12.24 will appear.)

3. Click on the *Yes* button. (An Object Relational Designer consisting of two panes separated by a vertical scroll bar will fill the Document window.)

FIGURE 12.23 The Add Connection dialog box.

FIGURE 12.24 Placement dialog box.

4. Open Database Explorer and click on the right-pointing triangle (or plus box) to the left of Megacities.mdf to display a list of folders.

5. Click on the right-pointing triangle (or plus box) to the left of the *Tables* folder to display a list of the two tables in the database.

6. Drag each table onto the left pane of the Object Relational Designer. (The screen should look something like Fig. 12.25. Also, the dialog box in Fig. 12.26 will appear after the first table is dragged. Click on the *Yes* button in the dialog box.)

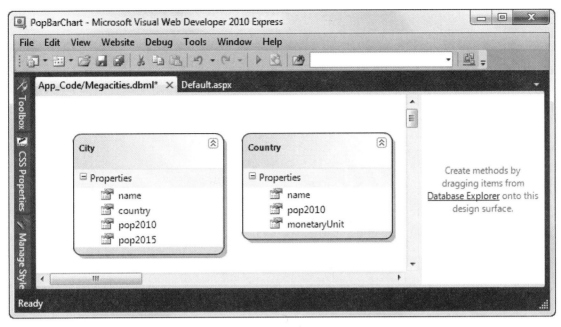

FIGURE 12.25   Object Relational Designer.

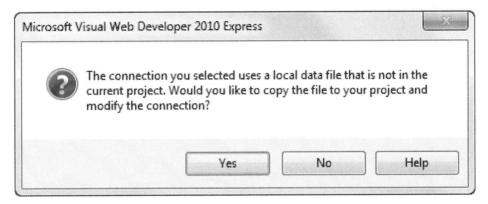

FIGURE 12.26   Copy File to Project dialog box.

7. Click on the *Save All* button in the Toolbar.

Stage 4: Use a LinqDataSource control to display data in a chart control

1. Click on the Default.aspx tab to return to the Designer and place a LinqDataSource control (from the Toolbox's *Data* group) at the bottom of the page. **Note:** This control will not be visible at run time.

2. Click on the LinqDataSource control's *Tasks* button and click on *Configure Data Source* to bring up the Configure Data Source dialog box.

3. Select MegacitiesDataContext in the "Choose your context object" combo box and click on the *Next* button. (You will now be asked to configure the data selection.)

4. The default selections made in the Configure Data Source dialog box are fine as is. Click on the *Finish* button.

5. Double-click on the *Display* button to bring up the code-behind editor, and then enter the following code:

```
Protected Sub btnDisplay_Click(...) Handles btnDisplay.Click
   Dim mcDC As New MegacitiesDataContext
   Dim query = From city In mcDC.Cities
               Order By city.pop2010 Descending
               Select city.name, city.pop2010
   chtMegacities.DataBindTable(query, "name")
   chtMegacities.ChartAreas(0).AxisX.Interval = 1
   chtMegacities.ChartAreas(0).AxisX.Title = "City"
   chtMegacities.ChartAreas(0).AxisY.Title = "2010 Population in Millions"
End Sub
```

Note: The line following the query statement binds the chart to the query and uses the *name* field to populate the *x*-values. The next line guarantees that all *x*-values will be displayed.

6. Run the program and click on the *Display* button. Figure 12.27 shows the output.

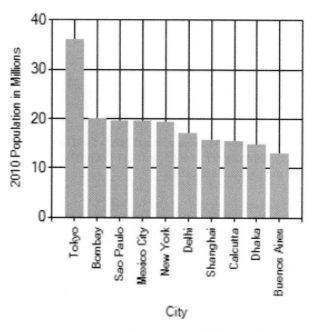

FIGURE 12.27   Output of walkthrough.

▦ Displaying Database Information in a Grid

VideoNote

Displaying information in a grid

A slight variation of the program developed in the walkthrough above will fill a GridView control with the same information. The changes required are as follows:

1. In stage 1 place a GridView control on the page instead of a chart control. Name the control grvMegacities.

2. In the fifth step of stage 4, replace the chtMegacities statements with the four statements

```
grvMegacities.DataSource = query
grvMegacities.DataBind()
grvMegacities.HeaderRow.Cells(0).Text = "City"
grvMegacities.HeaderRow.Cells(1).Text = "2010 Population in Millions"
```

3. Figure 12.28 shows the output when the program is run and the button is clicked on.

City	2010 Population in Millions
Tokyo	36.1
Bombay	20.1
Sao Paulo	19.6
Mexico City	19.5
New York	19.4
Delhi	17
Shanghai	15.8
Calcutta	15.6
Dhaka	14.8
Buenos Aires	13.1

Display City Populations in Descending Order

FIGURE 12.28   Output of GridView program.

■ Comments

1. The chart control can produce clustered bar charts. For instance, if the LINQ clause

   ```
   Select city.name, city.pop2010
   ```

   from the program PopBarChart is changed to

   ```
   Select city.name, city.pop2010, city.pop2015
   ```

   and the string "2010 Population in Millions" is changed to "2010 & 2015 Population in Millions", then the clustered bar chart in Fig. 12.29 will be produced.

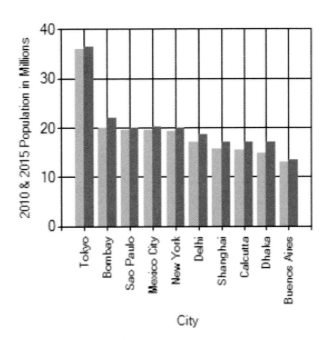

FIGURE 12.29   Clustered bar chart.

2. When LINQ is used to produce a bar chart, one of the items in the Select clause must have type String and the remaining items must have a numeric type. However, when a LINQ query is used to produce a grid, the items in the Select clause can have any data types.

Practice Problem 12.3

1. Write a VWD program that uses the database Megacities.mdf to generate a bar chart displaying the 2010 populations of the countries whose currency is the peso.

EXERCISES 12.3

In Exercises 1 through 10, write a Web program that uses the database **Megacities.mdf** to generate the bar chart.

1.

2.

3.

4.

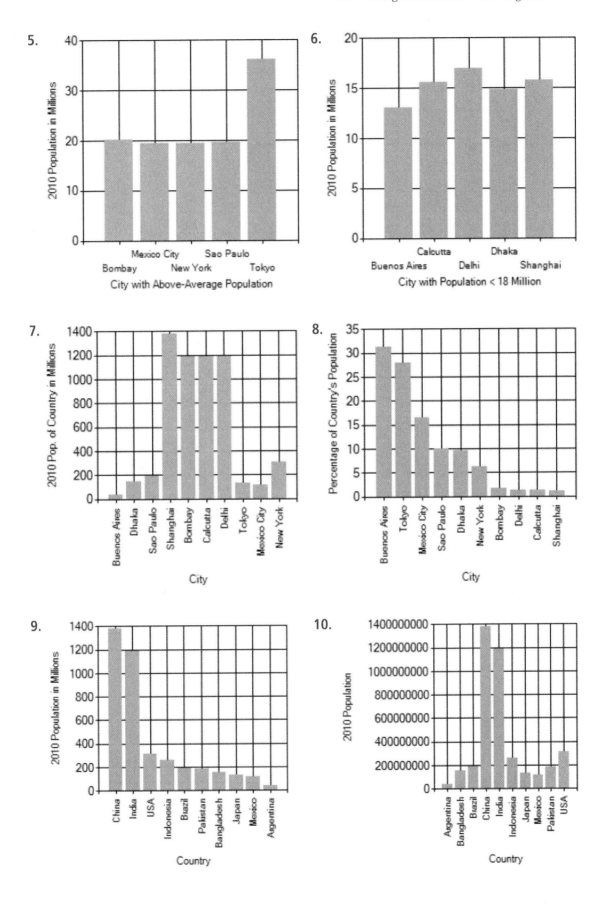

In Exercises 11 through 16, write a Web program that uses the database Megacities.mdf to generate the grid.

11.

City	Population Increase
Dhaka	14.86%
Delhi	10.00%
Bombay	9.45%
Calcutta	8.97%
Shanghai	8.86%
Mexico City	3.59%
New York	3.09%
Sao Paulo	2.55%
Buenos Aires	2.29%
Tokyo	0.83%

12.

City	Population Increase
Dhaka	2,200,000
Bombay	1,900,000
Delhi	1,700,000
Calcutta	1,400,000
Shanghai	1,400,000
Mexico City	700,000
New York	600,000
Sao Paulo	500,000
Buenos Aires	300,000
Tokyo	300,000

13.

Country	Population in 2010
China	1,379,700,000
India	1,186,800,000
USA	310,100,000
Indonesia	258,500,000
Brazil	195,200,000
Pakistan	184,200,000
Bangladesh	152,600,000
Japan	129,000,000
Mexico	117,400,000
Argentina	41,900,000

14.

City	2010 Pop.	2015 Pop.
Bombay	20,100,000	22,000,000
Buenos Aires	13,100,000	13,400,000
Calcutta	15,600,000	17,000,000
Delhi	17,000,000	18,700,000
Dhaka	14,800,000	17,000,000
Mexico City	19,500,000	20,200,000
New York	19,400,000	20,000,000
Sao Paulo	19,600,000	20,100,000
Shanghai	15,800,000	17,200,000
Tokyo	36,100,000	36,400,000

15.

City	Country	Currency
Bombay	India	rupee
Buenos Aires	Argentina	peso
Calcutta	India	rupee
Delhi	India	rupee
Dhaka	Bangladesh	raka
Mexico City	Mexico	peso
New York	USA	dollar
Sao Paulo	Brazil	real
Shanghai	China	yuan
Tokyo	Japan	yen

16.

City	Country	% of Country's Pop.
Buenos Aires	Argentina	31.3%
Tokyo	Japan	28.0%
Mexico City	Mexico	16.6%
Sao Paulo	Brazil	10.0%
Dhaka	Bangladesh	9.7%
New York	USA	6.3%
Bombay	India	1.7%
Delhi	India	1.4%
Calcutta	India	1.3%
Shanghai	China	1.1%

The database Pizza.mdf has a single table *Pizzerias* that contains data for the eight leading pizza chains. The fields for the table are *name, sales2007, sales2008, numStores2007,* and *numStores2008.* (Sales are given in thousands of dollars.) Two records in the table are

Pizza Hut	5100000	5300000	7466	7564
Domino's Pizza	3194485	3037703	5136	5047

In Exercises 17 through 22, write a Web program that uses the database Pizza.mdf to generate the bar chart.

17.

18.

19.

20.

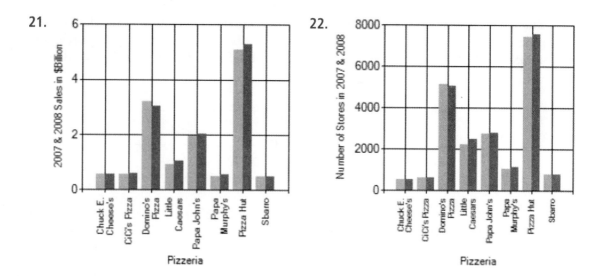

In Exercises 23 and 24, write a Web program that uses the database Pizza.mdf to generate the grid.

23.

Pizzeria	2007 Sales	2008 Sales	Change
Pizza Hut	$5,100,000,000	$5,300,000,000	3.92%
Domino's Pizza	$3,194,485,000	$3,037,703,000	-4.91%
Papa John's	$1,969,258,000	$2,033,255,000	3.25%
Little Caesars	$930,000,000	$1,055,000,000	13.44%
CiCi's Pizza	$570,000,000	$585,000,000	2.63%
Chuck E. Cheese's	$575,000,000	$569,500,000	-0.96%
Papa Murphy's	$504,000,000	$544,000,000	7.94%
Sbarro	$503,500,000	$500,000,000	-0.70%

24.

Pizzeria	# Stores in 2007	# Stores in 2008	Change
Pizza Hut	7,466	7,564	0.19%
Domino's Pizza	5,136	5,047	-0.28%
Papa John's	2,760	2,792	0.16%
Little Caesars	2,241	2,500	2.78%
Papa Murphy's	1,057	1,118	1.21%
Sbarro	795	775	-0.40%
CiCi's Pizza	619	634	0.26%
Chuck E. Cheese's	509	515	0.10%

In Exercises 25 through 28 write a program that uses the database Pizza.mdf and displays the stated information for the year 2008 in a read-only text box or in a list box.

25. The total number of stores for the top eight pizza chains.

26. The names of the top three pizza chains in sales.

27. The name of the pizza chain having the least number of stores of any of the top eight.

28. The name of the pizza chain having the greatest increase in sales of any of the top eight.

Solution to Practice Problems 12.3

1. There is no need to carry out the four stages from the walkthrough, since we have already created an object model and LinqDataSource control for this database. The following steps create the new program, and Fig. 12.30 shows the bar chart that is produced:

   (a) Start a new Web program with the name PracticeProb and then close the program.
   (b) Use the process for building on an existing Web program discussed at the end of Section 12.1 to make PracticeProb a clone of the program created in the walkthrough.

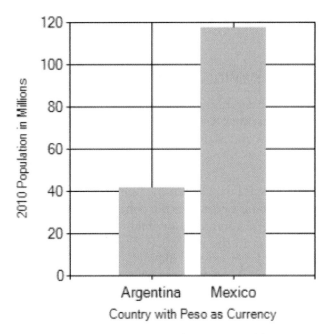

FIGURE 12.30   Output of Practice Problem.

   (c) Open PracticeProb in VWD and change the query to the following:

```
Dim query = From country In mcDC.Countries
            Where country.monetaryUnit = "peso"
            Select country.name, country.pop2010
```

   (d) Change the string in the next to last line of the code from "City" to "Country with Peso as Currency".

CHAPTER 12 SUMMARY

1. *Visual Web Developer* (VWD) is used to create programs that reside on a server and run in the Web browser of a client computer.

2. There are many similarities between creating a Web program with VWD and creating a Visual Basic Windows program. However, there are some important differences. For one thing, text can be typed and formatted directly into Web pages. Also, not as many controls are available in VWD as in Visual Basic, and controls that are common to both have fewer properties and events in VWD than in Visual Basic.

3. The *table control* is helpful for aligning text and controls in VWD.

4. *Validation controls* allow the browser to check input before it is sent to the server.

5. The *hyperlink control* is used to request different pages from the server.

6. A *postback* occurs when the browser sends a request containing data back to the server for processing.

7. The *page load event* is raised each time the server receives a page request.

8. *Radio-button list* and *check box* controls have the same functionality as their counterparts in Visual Basic. A required field validation control is often used to verify that a radio button has been selected.

9. The *chart control*, along with LINQ to SQL, enhances the programmer's ability to graphically display data retrieved from a database.

CHAPTER 12 PROGRAMMING PROJECTS

1. Write a program that determines whether or not a person is from New England. People who do not know their state's abbreviation should be able to get help in the form of a list box showing the states and their abbreviations. Figure 12.31 shows the initial Web page at design time. In addition to two text boxes and a button, the page contains a hyperlink control that navigates to the help page in Fig. 12.32 and a required field validation control that verifies the top text box. (When the help page is loaded, the file USStates.txt should be used to populate the list box. This file contains information about each of the 50 states. Each record of the file contains four fields—name, abbreviation, land area (in square miles), and population in the year 2000. The records are ordered by the states' dates of entry into the union.) After a state abbreviation is typed into the input text box and the button is clicked on, the word YES or NO should be displayed in the *Answer* text box.

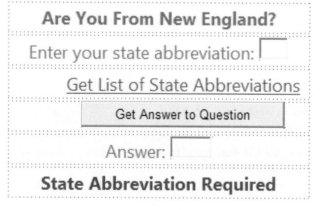

FIGURE 12.31 **Initial page in design mode.**

FIGURE 12.32 **Help page during run time.**

VideoNote

Web based
Richard's catering
(Homework)

2. Write a Web program that uses the Megacities.mdf database and displays the interface shown in Fig. 12.33. After the user makes a selection from each list of radio buttons and clicks on the *Display Bar Chart* button, the requested bar chart should be displayed. Use two RequiredFieldValidator controls to ensure that selections are made from both lists.

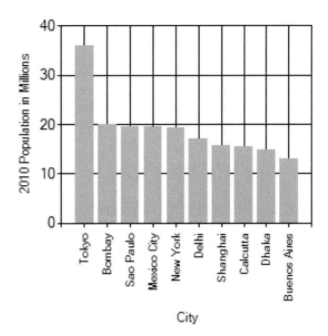

FIGURE 12.33   Possible outcome of Programming Project 2.

Appendix A

ANSI Values

ANSI Value	Character	ANSI Value	Character	ANSI Value	Character
000	(null)	046	.	092	\
001	□	047	/	093	]
002	□	048	0	094	∧
003	□	049	1	095	_
004	□	050	2	096	`
005	□	051	3	097	a
006	□	052	4	098	b
007	□	053	5	099	c
008	□	054	6	100	d
009	(tab)	055	7	101	e
010	(line feed)	056	8	102	f
011	□	057	9	103	g
012	□	058	:	104	h
013	(carriage return)	059	;	105	i
014	□	060	<	106	j
015	□	061	=	107	k
016	□	062	>	108	l
017	□	063	?	109	m
018	□	064	@	110	n
019	□	065	A	111	o
020	□	066	B	112	p
021	□	067	C	113	q
022	□	068	D	114	r
023	□	069	E	115	s
024	□	070	F	116	t
025	□	071	G	117	u
026	□	072	H	118	v
027	□	073	I	119	w
028	□	074	J	120	x
029	□	075	K	121	y
030	□	076	L	122	z
031	□	077	M	123	{
032	(space)	078	N	124		
033	!	079	O	125	}
034	"	080	P	126	~
035	#	081	Q	127	□
036	$	082	R	128	□
037	%	083	S	129	□
038	&	084	T	130	,
039	'	085	U	131	*f*
040	(	086	V	132	"
041	)	087	W	133	…
042	*	088	X	134	†
043	+	089	Y	135	‡
044	,	090	Z	136	^
045	–	091	[	137	‰

ANSI Value	Character	ANSI Value	Character	ANSI Value	Character
138	Š	190	3/4	242	ò
139	‹	191	¿	243	ó
140	Œ	192	À	244	ô
141	□	193	Á	245	õ
142	Ž	194	Â	246	ö
143	□	195	Ã	247	÷
144	□	196	Ä	248	ø
145	'	197	Å	249	ù
146	'	198	Æ	250	ú
147	"	199	Ç	251	û
148	"	200	È	252	ü
149	•	201	É	253	‡
150	–	202	Ê	254	þ
151	—	203	Ë	255	ÿ
152	~	204	Ì		
153	™	205	Í		
154	š	206	Î		
155	›	207	Ï		
156	œ	208	Ð		
157	□	209	Ñ		
158	ž	210	Ò		
159	Ÿ	211	Ó		
160	(no-break space)	212	Ô		
161	¡	213	Õ		
162	¢	214	Ö		
163	£	215	×		
164	¤	216	Ø		
165	¥	217	Ù		
166	¦	218	Ú		
167	§	219	Û		
168	¨	220	Ü		
169	©	221	ý		
170	ª	222	þ		
171	«	223	ß		
172	¬	224	à		
173		225	á		
174	®	226	â		
175	‾	227	ã		
176	°	228	ä		
177	±	229	å		
178	^{2}	230	æ		
179	^{3}	231	ç		
180	´	232	è		
181	µ	233	é		
182	¶	234	ê		
183	·	235	ë		
184	¸	236	ì		
185	^{1}	237	í		
186	º	238	î		
187	»	239	ï		
188	1/4	240	ð		
189	1/2	241	ñ		

APPENDIX B

HOW TO

Note: These How To's apply to Visual Basic. Many, however, are also relevant to Visual Web Developer.

Launch and Exit Visual Basic

Note: Visual Basic is part of a suite of programs called Visual Studio, which also contains the C# (pronounced "C-sharp") programming language.

A. Invoke Visual Basic Express Edition

    1. Click the *Start* button.
    2. Hover over *All Programs*.
    3. Click on Microsoft Visual Basic 2010 Express Edition.

B. Exit Visual Basic

    1. Click on *Exit* in the *File* menu, or click on the red *Close* button located at the upper-right corner of the window. **Note:** If the current program has not been saved, Visual Basic will prompt you about saving it.

Manage Visual Basic Programs

A. Create a new program.

    1. Click on *New Project* in the *File* menu, or click on the *New Project* button (▣) on the Toolbar, or press Ctrl + N. **Note:** If the current program has not been saved, Visual Basic will prompt you about saving it.
    2. Check that Windows Forms Application is highlighted.
    3. Optionally, type a name for the program into the *Name* box.
    4. Click on the *OK* button.

B. Run the current program.

    1. Click on the *Start Debugging* button (▶) in the Toolbar, or press F5, or click on *Start Debugging* in the *Debug* menu.

C. Save the current program.

    1. Click the *Save All* button (▤) on the Toolbar, or click on *Save All* in the *File* menu.
    2. If the program has not been saved previously, give it a name and then click on the *Save* button. **Important:** If the "Create directory for solution" check box is checked, then click on the check box to uncheck it. (You

only have to uncheck this check box once; it will stay unchecked for all future programs.)

D. Close the current program.

  1. Click on *Close Project* in the *File* menu. **Note:** If the current program has not been saved, Visual Basic will prompt you about saving it.

E. Open a recently saved program.

  1. Hover the mouse over *Recent Projects and Solutions* in the *File* menu. (A numbered list of recent programs will appear on the right.)

  2. Click on a recent program, or press the corresponding number.

F. Open a program stored on a disk.

  1. Click on *Open Project* in the *File* menu, or press Ctrl + O. **Note:** If the current program has not been saved, Visual Basic will prompt you about saving it.

  2. Navigate to the program's folder.

  3. Double-click on the folder, or highlight the folder and click on *Open*. (Several subfolders and files will be displayed.)

  4. Double-click on the file with extension *sln*.

  5. If neither the Form Designer nor the Code Editor for the program appears, double-click on *formName*.vb in the Solution Explorer window.

G. Change the name of a program.

  1. Open the program if it is not already open.

  2. Right-click on the name of the program at the top of the Solution Explorer, click on *Rename* in the drop-down context menu, and provide a new name for the program.

  3. Right-click on the new name of the program at the top of the Solution Explorer, click on *Properties* in the drop-down context menu, select *Application* on the large tab at the left side of the window that opens, and change the contents of the "Assembly name:" text box to the new name.

  4. Save and close the program.

  5. In Windows Explorer, navigate to the program's folder, change the name of the folder to the new name, open the folder, and change the base name of the file with extension *sln* to the new name.

H. Use the Solution Explorer window to view the Code Editor or the Form Designer.

Note: If the Solution Explorer window is not visible, click on *Solution Explorer* in the *View* menu.

  1. In the Solution Explorer window, right-click on *fileName*.vb.

  2. Click on either *View Code* or *View Designer*.

Text Manipulation

A. Select (or highlight) a block of text.

  1. Move the cursor to the beginning or end of the text.

  2. Hold down a Shift key, use the direction keys to highlight a block of text, and release the Shift key.

or

1. Move the mouse to the beginning or end of the text.
2. Hold down the left mouse button, move the mouse to the other end of the text, and release the left mouse button.

Note 1: To deselect text, press the Esc key or click outside the text.

Note 2: To select a word, double-click on it. To select a line, move the mouse pointer just far enough into the left margin so that the pointer changes to an arrow, and then single-click there.

B. Move text.

1. Select the text as a block, and drag it to the new location with the mouse.

C. Use the Clipboard to move or duplicate text.

1. Select the text as a block.
2. Press Ctrl + X to delete the block and place it into the Clipboard, or press Ctrl + C to place a copy of the block into the Clipboard.
3. Move the cursor to the location where you desire to place the block.
4. Press Ctrl + V to place a copy of the text from the Clipboard at the cursor position.

D. Undo a change.

1. Click on *Undo* in the *Edit* menu or press Ctrl + Z to undo the last change made.

Note: An undone change can be redone by pressing Shift + Alt + Backspace.

E. Increase or decrease size of text.

1. Hold down the Ctrl key and move the mouse scroll wheel forward to increase the size of the text and backward to decrease the size.

Manage Visual Basic Controls

A. Resize a control.

1. Select the control and drag one of its sizing handles. Or, select the control, hold down the Ctrl key, and press the arrow keys. Or, change the setting of the control's Size property. Or, use the *Make Same Size* option in the *Format* menu to give the control the same width and/or length as another control.

B. Move a control.

1. Select the control and drag it to a new location. Or, select the control, hold down the Shift key, and press the arrow keys. Or, use the *Align* option in the *Format* menu to line up the control with another control.

C. Center a control in a form.

1. Select the control.
2. Use the *Center in Form* option of the *Format* menu.

D. Select multiple controls.

1. Click on a control.
2. Hold down the Ctrl key while clicking on additional controls.

or

1. Click on a place in the Form Designer outside of the controls and start dragging. (A dotted rectangle will appear.)
2. Drag the rectangle around a group of controls.
3. Release the mouse button.

Note: Multiple selected controls can be moved and resized as a group with the arrow keys as in parts A and B. Also, any property that is common to all of the controls in the group can be set simultaneously.

E. Create uniform spacing in a group of controls.

1. Select *Make Equal* from the *Horizontal Spacing* or *Vertical Spacing* options of the *Format* menu.

Note: After uniform spacing has been achieved, you can click on *Increase* or *Decrease* from the *Horizontal Spacing* or *Vertical Spacing* options of the *Format* menu to widen or narrow the spacing.

F. Let a label caption use more than one line.

1. Change the label's AutoSize property setting to False and increase its height. (If the label is not wide enough to accommodate the entire caption on one line, part of the caption will wrap to additional lines. If the label height is too small, then part or all of these additional lines will not be visible.)

G. Let a text box display more than one line.

1. Set the text box's MultiLine property to True. (If the text box is not wide enough to accommodate the text entered by the user, the text will wrap down to new lines. If the text box is not tall enough, lines will scroll out of view but can be displayed with the cursor up or down keys.)

H. Allow a particular button control to be activated by a press of the Enter key.

1. Set the form's AcceptButton property to the particular button control.

I. Allow the pressing of Esc to activate a particular button control.

1. Set the form's CancelButton property to the particular button control.

J. Have the form appear in the center of the screen when the program executes.

1. Set the form's StartPosition property to CenterScreen.

K. Change the Name property of Form1 to frmElse.

1. In the Solution Explorer window, right-click on the file Form1.vb.
2. Click on *Rename* in the context menu that appears.
3. Change the name of the file Form1.vb to frmElse.vb. (**Caution:** Don't forget to retain the extension *vb*.)

L. Specify a custom background or foreground color for a control.

1. In the Properties window, select the BackColor or ForeColor property.
2. Click on the down arrow in the right part of the Settings box.
3. Click on the Custom tab to display a grid of colors.
4. Right-click on one of the sixteen white boxes at the bottom of the grid to display the Define Color dialog box. (The dialog box theoretically allows you to create over 16 million custom colors. The large variegated square is called the *color field* and the narrow rectangle the *color slider*.)
5. To select a custom color, click on any point in the color field and then use the arrow head to move along the color slider. (At any time, the rectangle labeled "Color|Solid" displays the current color.)
6. Click on the *Add Color* button.

M. Remove the blank column on the left side of a DataGridView control.

1. Set the control's RowHeadersVisible property to False.

N. Optimal sizing of a DataGridView control.

1. If you suspect that some cells will be too narrow to accommodate their contents, set the control's AutoSizeColumn property to *AllCells*.

Otherwise,

1. Set the first parameter of the control's Size property to 100·[number of columns] + 3. If there will be a scroll bar on the right side of the grid, add 17 to the setting of the parameter.
2. Set the second parameter of the control's Size property to 22·[number of rows] + 1. If any column header will occupy more than one line, add 13 to the parameter for each additional line.

O. Obtain a description of a property of a control.

1. If the Description pane is not visible, right-click on the Properties window and then click on *Description* in the drop-down context menu.
2. Highlight the property in the Properties window. Its purpose will appear in the Description pane below.

P. Specify the control that will have the focus when the program executes.

1. Set the control's TabIndex property to 0.

Q. Make the Properties window easier to use.

1. Double-click on the Properties window's title bar. (The Properties window will become undocked, and it will be larger and easier to use.)
2. After you have finished using the window, right-click on its title bar and click on *Dock*.

Working with Code

A. Rename all instances of a variable, control, Sub procedure, or Function.

1. Select the name.
2. Right-click on the name and click on *Rename* in the drop-down context menu. (A Rename dialog box will appear.)

3. Type the new name into the "New Name" text box.
4. Click on the *OK* button to carry out the changes.

Note: This process is known as *symbolic rename*. If the name of a local (or block-level) variable is changed, the change will be limited to the procedure (or block) containing the variable.

B. Hide a long procedure.

1. Scroll to the top of the procedure.
2. Click on the box with a minus sign in it that is to the left of the header of the procedure. (Notice that the box now contains a plus sign and that the entire procedure is hidden on the one line. Click on the box again to show the procedure.)

C. Add a collapsible region.

1. Type #Region *"regionName"* on the line before the code to be included in the region.
2. Type #End Region on the line after the last line of code in the region.
3. The region of code can then be collapsed by clicking on the minus box and restored by clicking on the plus box.

Note: A region cannot be defined within an event, Function, or Sub procedure.

Setting Options

A. Turn off IntelliSense.

1. Click on *Options* in the *Tools* menu.
2. If the check box to the left of "Show all settings" is unchecked, check it.
3. In the left pane, expand "Text Editor".
4. Expand the subheading "Basic".
5. Click on the subtopic "General".
6. Ensure that all the check boxes under the "Statement completion" heading are unchecked, then click on *OK*.

B. Wrap words to the next line in the Code Editor rather than having a horizontal scrollbar.

1. Follow steps 1 through 5 of part A above.
2. In the right pane, place a check mark in the check box labeled "Word wrap".

C. Instruct the Code Editor to indent by two spaces.

1. Follow steps 1 through 4 of part A.
2. Click on the subtopic "Tabs".
3. In the right pane, change the number in the "Indent size:" text box to 2.

Manage Text Files

Note: If the Solution Explorer window is not visible, click on *Solution Explorer* in the *View* menu. If the *bin* folder does not show in the Solution Explorer window, click on the *Show All Files* button in the Solution Explorer toolbar.

A. Display a text file associated with an open program.

1. In the Solution Explorer window, open the *bin* folder by double-clicking on it.
2. Open the *Debug* subfolder of the *bin* folder by double-clicking on it. (The text file should appear in a list of several files. If the file is not listed in the *Debug* subfolder, click the *Refresh* button in the Solution Explorer.)
3. Double-click on the text file to open it. (The contents of the file will be displayed in a tabbed Text Editor in the Documents window, and the filename will appear in the tab.)

B. Save the file that is displayed in the Text Editor.

1. Right-click on the tab and then click on *Save filename* in the drop-down context menu. Or, press Ctrl + S. Or, click on *Save filename* in the *File* menu.

C. Close an open Text Editor.

1. Click on the close button (☒) on the tab. Or, right-click on the tab containing the filename at the top of the Document window and click on *Close* in the drop-down context menu. **Note:** If the text file has not been saved, Visual Basic will prompt you about saving it.

D. Import an existing text file into an open program.

Note: This task is especially useful when importing a file from a "Text_Files_for_Exercises" folder.

1. Use Windows Explorer to locate the file.
2. Right-click on the file, and click on *Copy* in the drop-down context menu. Or, click on the file and press Ctrl + C.
3. In the Solution Explorer window, right-click on the *Debug* subfolder of the *bin* folder and click on *Paste* in the drop-down context menu. Or, click on the *Debug* subfolder and press Ctrl + V.

E. Create a new text file in an open program.

1. Click on the name of the program at the top of the Solution Explorer window.
2. Click on *Add New Item* in the *Project* menu. (An "Add New Item" input dialog box will appear.) Alternately, click on the *Add New Item* button in the Toolbar.
3. Select the Text File icon in the input dialog box, and enter a base name for the file in the "Name" text box. (Visual Basic will automatically add the extension ".txt" to the name.)
4. Click on the *Add* button. (A tabbed Text Editor will appear in the Document window.)
5. Type the contents of the file into the Text Editor.
6. Right-click on the tab and click on *Save filename* in the drop-down context menu.
7. Right-click on the tab and click on *Close* in the drop-down context menu.
8. Locate the text file at the bottom of the Solution Explorer window.
9. Move the text file to the *Debug* subfolder of *bin*. (The move can be accomplished either by drag-and-drop or by Cut and Paste.)

F. Modify the contents of an existing text file in an open program.

1. In the Solution Explorer window, locate the text file in the *bin\Debug* subfolder.
2. Double-click on the filename to display the contents of the file in a tabbed Text Editor.
3. Alter the contents of the file using the Text Editor.
4. Save the file and close the Text Editor.

G. Delete an existing text file from an open program.

1. In the Solution Explorer window, locate the text file in the *bin\Debug* subfolder.
2. Right-click on the filename and click on *Delete* in the drop-down context menu.
3. Click on the *OK* button in the message box that appears.

Configuring the Windows Environment

A. Determine and/or change the DPI setting for the monitor.

<u>Windows XP</u>

1. Right-click on the Windows desktop to display a context menu.
2. Click *Properties* in the context menu to bring up the "Display Properties" dialog box.
3. Click the Settings tab on the "Display Properties" dialog box.
4. Click the *Advanced* button to display the monitor properties dialog box. The current DPI setting will be shown in the "DPI setting" box.
5. If you would like to change the setting, select a different DPI setting in the "DPI setting" drop-down box. [**Note:** The screen captures in this book were done with a DPI setting of "Normal Size (96 DPI)." With that setting, the forms you see on your screen will appear like those in the book.]
6. If you changed the DPI setting, click on "Restart the computer before applying the new display settings."
7. Click the *OK* button. (If you did not change the DPI setting, nothing will happen. You will be returned to the "Display Properties" dialog box, and you can press the *OK* button to return to the desktop.)
8. If you changed the DPI setting, a message box will be displayed. Click the *OK* button twice, answer "Yes" to the question posed, click the *Close* button at the bottom of the "Display Properties" dialog box, and click on the *Yes* button to restart your computer and allow the changes to take effect.

<u>Windows Vista</u>

1. Right-click on the Windows desktop to display a context menu.
2. Click *Personalize* on the context menu to display the "Personalize appearance and sounds" window.
3. In the left pane, click "Adjust font size (DPI)". (If you are prompted for an administrator password or confirmation, type the password or provide confirmation by pressing the *Continue* button.) The current DPI setting will be indicated.
4. If you would like to select the other DPI setting, click on it. [**Note:** The screen captures in this book were done with a DPI setting of "Default scale

(96 DPI)". With that setting, the forms you see on your screen will look like those in the book.]

5. Click on the *OK* button. (If you did not change the DPI setting, nothing will happen. You will be returned to the Personalize window, and you can close the window to return to the desktop.)

6. If you changed the DPI setting, restart your computer to allow the changes to take effect.

<u>Windows 7</u>

1. Right-click on the Windows desktop to display a context menu.
2. Click *Personalize* on the context menu to display the Personalization window.
3. Click on *Display* near the bottom of the left pane. Three radio buttons (labeled Smaller − 100%, Medium − 125%, and Larger − 150%) will appear with the current setting selected. **Note:** The screen captures in this book were made with a setting of "Smaller − 100%". With that setting, the forms you see on your screen will look like those in the book.
4. If you do not want to change the setting, close the window.
5. Otherwise, select a different setting and click on the *Apply* button. (You will be instructed to log off your computer in order to allow the change to take effect. **Note:** You will not have to restart your computer.)

B. Configure Windows to display filename extensions.

<u>Windows XP</u>

1. Click on *Folder Options* in the *Tools* menu. (A Folders Options dialog box will appear.)
2. Click on the *View* tab in the dialog box.
3. If there is a check mark in the box next to "Hide extensions for known file types", click on the box to remove the check mark.
4. Click on the *OK* button to close the Folders Options dialog box.

<u>Windows Vista and Windows 7</u>

1. Click on the *Start* button.
2. **Windows Vista** Type "Folder Options" into the "Start Search" box and press the Enter key. (A Folders Options dialog box will appear.)
   Windows 7 Type "Folder Options" into the "Search programs and files" box. (A Control Panel box will appear.) Click on *Folder Options*. (A Folders Options dialog box will appear.)
3. Click on the View tab in the Folder Options dialog box.
4. If there is a check mark in the box next to "Hide extensions for known file types", click on the box to remove the check mark.
5. Click on the *OK* button to close the Folders Options dialog box.

Use a Printer

A. Obtain a printout of a program.

1. Invoke the Code Editor.
2. Click on *Print* in the *File* menu. Or, press Ctrl + P.
3. Click on the *OK* button.

B. Print the current form.

    1. Double-click on the PrintForm control in the *Visual Basic PowerPacks* group of the Toolbox. (The control will appear with the default name PrintForm1 in the component tray at the bottom part of the Form Designer.)

    2. Execute the following code:

```
PrintForm1.PrintAction = Printing.PrintAction.PrintToPrinter
PrintForm1.Print()
```

C. Print the contents of a DataGridView control.

    1. After a PrintDocument control has been added to the form, the following code prints the DataGridView control named dgvColleges when btnPrint is clicked:

```
Private Sub btnPrint_Click(...) Handles btnPrint.Click
  PrintDocument1.Print()
End Sub

Private Sub PrintDocument1_PrintPage(...) Handles _
                                    PrintDocument1.PrintPage
  Dim bm As Bitmap = New Bitmap(dgvColleges.Width,
                               dgvColleges.Height)
  dgvColleges.DrawToBitmap(bm, dgvColleges.DisplayRectangle)
  e.Graphics.DrawImageUnscaled(bm, New Point(75, 100))
End Sub
```

The argument **New Point(75, 100)** causes the table to be printed one inch from the left side and one inch from the top of the page. In general, **New Point(x, y)** causes the table to be printed about $(1/4 + x/100)$ inches from the left side and $y/100$ inches from the top of the page.

D. Print the contents of a list box.

    1. The code in part C above also can be used to print the contents of a list box. Just replace the name of the DataGridView control with the name of the list box.

Miscellaneous

A. Enlarge the Document window to fill the entire screen.

    1. Click on *Full Screen* in the *View* menu. (To return to the regular screen, click on the newly created *Full Screen* button at the right side of the menu bar.)

B. Return the IDE to its original layout.

    1. Click on *Reset Window Layout* in the *Window* menu.

C. Store frequently used code for easy inclusion into other programs.

    1. Select the code as a block.

    2. Drag the block of code into the Toolbox. (You will now have the code in both the Code Editor and the Toolbox.)

Note: The block of code will be visible in the Toolbox whenever the Code Editor is open. At any time you can drag a copy of the code into the Code Editor.

D. Open Windows Explorer.

    1. Right-click on the *Start* button and click on *Explore* (XP or Vista) or *Open Windows Explorer* (Windows 7) in the context menu.

E. Display all the characters in a font.

    1. Click on the Windows *Start* button.
    2. Hover over *All Programs*.
    3. Click on *Accessories*.
    4. Click on *System Tools*.
    5. Click on *Character Map*.
    6. Click on the down-arrow at the right end of the Font box.
    7. Select the desired font.

Appendix C

Files and Folders

We use the word **disk** to refer to either the hard disk, a diskette, a USB flash drive, a CD, or a DVD. Each drive is identified by a letter. Normally, the hard drive is identified by C, the diskette drive by A, and the CD (or DVD) drive by D or E. Disk management is handled by Windows.

Disks hold not only programs, but also collections of data stored in files. The term **file** refers to either a program file, a text file, or some other kind of data file. Each file has a name consisting of a base name followed by an optional extension consisting of a period and one or more characters. The term **filename** refers to the combination of the base name, the period, and the extension. A filename can contain up to 215 characters, typically consisting of letters, digits, spaces, periods, and other assorted characters. (The only characters that cannot be used in filenames are \, /, :, *, ?, <, >, ", and |.) Extensions are normally used to identify the type of file. For example, spreadsheets created with Excel have the extension *xlsx* or *xls* (eXceL Spreadsheet), documents created with Word have the extension *docx* or *doc* (DOCument), and files created with Notepad have the extension *txt* (TeXT document). Some examples of filenames are "Annual Sales.xls*x*", "Letter to Mom.doc*x*", and "Phone.txt".

Because a disk is capable of holding thousands of files, locating a specific file can be quite time consuming. Therefore, related files are grouped into collections called **folders**. For instance, one folder might hold all your Visual Basic programs, and another the documents created with your word processor.

Think of a disk as a large folder, called the **root folder**, that contains several smaller folders, each with its own name. (The naming of folders follows the same rules as the naming of files.) Each of these smaller folders can contain yet other named folders. Any folder contained inside another folder is said to be a **subfolder** of that folder. Each folder is identified by listing its name preceded by the names of the successively larger folders that contain it, with each folder name preceded by a backslash. Such a sequence is called a **path**. For instance, the path \Sales\NY08\July identifies the folder July, contained in the folder NY08, which in turn is contained in the folder Sales. Think of a file, along with its name, as written on a slip of paper that can be placed into either the root folder or one of the smaller folders. The combination of a drive letter followed by a colon, a path, and a filename is called a **filespec**, an abbreviation of "file specification." Some examples of filespecs are C:\VB01\VB.exe and E:\Personal\Income09.txt.

Neither Windows nor Visual Basic distinguishes between uppercase and lowercase letters in folder names and filenames. For instance, the names COSTS02.TXT, Costs02.Txt, and costs02.txt are equivalent.

In many cases folders are referred to as **directories**. Many Visual Basic objects and commands still refer to folders as directories. The terms "root folder" and "path" are a reference to the "tree" metaphor commonly used to describe the organization of files. In this metaphor, the large folder at the lowest level of the disk is the root folder. The smaller folders contained in the root folder can be thought of as branches that emanate from the root. Each branch may have smaller branches, which in turn may have their own smaller branches, and so on. Finally, a file in one of these folders can be thought of as a leaf on a branch. The leaf is reached by starting at the root and following a path through the branches.

APPENDIX D
VISUAL BASIC DEBUGGING TOOLS

Errors in programs are called **bugs**, and the process of finding and correcting them is called **debugging**. Since Visual Basic does not discover errors due to faulty logic, these errors present the most difficulties in debugging. One method of discovering a logic error is by **desk checking**—that is, tracing the values of variables on paper by writing down their expected value after "mentally executing" each line in the program. Desk checking is rudimentary and highly impractical except for small programs.

Another method of debugging involves placing MessageBox.Show statements at strategic points in the program and displaying the values of selected variables or expressions until the error is detected. After correcting the error, you can remove the MessageBox.Show statements. For older programming environments, desk checking and MessageBox.Show statements were the only debugging methods available to the programmer.

The Visual Basic debugger offers an alternative to desk checking and to inserting MessageBox.Show statements. It allows you to pause during the execution of your program in order to view and alter values of variables. These values can be accessed through the Immediate, Watch, and Locals windows, known as debugging windows.

The Three Program Modes

At any time, a program is in one of three modes—**design mode**, **run mode**, or **debug mode**. (Debug mode is also known as **break mode**.) When the current mode is "run"

Title bar, Menu bar, and Toolbar during design mode.

Title bar, Menu bar, and Toolbar during run mode.

Title bar, Menu bar, and Toolbar during debug mode.

or "debug," the words "Running" or "Debugging" are displayed (in parentheses) in the Visual Basic title bar. The absence of these words indicates that the current mode is "design."

With the program in design mode, you place controls on a form, set their initial properties, and write code. Run mode is initiated by pressing F5 or the *Start Debugging* button. Debug mode is invoked automatically when a run-time error occurs. You can use Debug options to break the program at specified places. While the program is in debug mode, you can hover the cursor over any variable to obtain its current value. Also, you can use the debugging windows, such as the Immediate, Watch, and Locals windows, to examine values of expressions. When you enter debug mode, the Toolbar contains a *Continue* button. You can click on it to continue with the execution of the program.

Stepping through a Program

The program can be executed one statement at a time, with each press of an appropriate function key executing a statement. This process is called **stepping**. After each step, values of variables, expressions, and conditions can be displayed in the debugging windows, and the values of variables can be changed.

When a procedure is called, the lines of the procedure can be executed one at a time, referred to as **stepping into** the procedure, or the entire procedure can be executed at once, referred to as **stepping over** a procedure. A step over a procedure is called a **procedure step**. In addition, you can execute the remainder of the current procedure at once, referred to as **stepping out** of the procedure. The three toolbar buttons shown in Figure D.1 can be used for stepping.

FIGURE D.1   The Toolbar buttons used to Step Into, Step Over, and Step Out.

As another debugging tool, Visual Basic allows the programmer to specify certain lines as **breakpoints**. Then, when the program is run, execution will stop at the first breakpoint reached. The programmer can then either step through the program or continue execution to the next breakpoint. Also, the programmer can place the cursor on any line in the program and have execution stop at that line with a "Run to Cursor" command. Program execution normally proceeds in order through the statements in a procedure. However, at any time the programmer can specify the next statement to be executed.

The tasks discussed previously are summarized next, along with a means to carry out each task. The tasks invoked with function keys also can be produced from the menu bar, the context menu (produced by clicking the right mouse button), or the Toolbar.

Run to cursor	Press Ctrl + F8
Step Into	Press F8
Step Over	Press Shift + F8
Step Out	Press Ctrl + Shift + F8
Set a breakpoint	Move cursor to line, press F9
Remove a breakpoint	Move cursor to line containing breakpoint, press F9
Clear all breakpoints	Press Ctrl + Shift + F9
Continue execution of the program	Press F5
Stop debugging	Ctrl + Alt + Break

The Immediate Window

While in break mode, you can set the focus to the **Immediate window** by clicking on it (if visible), by pressing Ctrl + Alt + I, or by hovering the cursor over *Windows* in the *Debug* menu and clicking on *Immediate*. When you type a statement into the Immediate window and press the Enter key, the statement is executed at once. A statement of the form

`? expression`

displays the value of the expression on the next line of the Immediate window. (The question mark is shorthand for Debug.Print.) A statement of the form

`var = value`

assigns a value to a variable. In Figure D.2, the variable *numVar* had the value 10 when the program was interrupted.

FIGURE D.2   Three statements executed in the Immediate window.

The Watch Window

The **Watch window**, which can be viewed only in break mode, permits you to view the values of variables and expressions. The Watch window in Figure D.3 shows the values of one variable and two expressions. If you don't see a Watch window when you enter break mode, hover the cursor over *Windows* in the *Debug* menu, and then click on *Watch*.

Name	Value	Type
num	100	Integer
5 * num	500	Integer
num>90	True	Boolean

FIGURE D.3   A typical Watch window.

Although you can type directly into the Watch window, the easiest way to add an expression to the window is to right-click on a variable in the Code Editor and then click on *Add Watch* in the context menu. You can then alter the expression in the Name column of the Watch window. To delete an expression from the Watch window, right-click on the expression and then click on *Delete Watch*. Also, you can directly change the value of any variable in the Watch window and have the values of the other expressions change accordingly.

The Locals Window

While in break mode, you can open the Locals window from the *Debug* menu by positioning the cursor over *Windows* and then clicking on *Locals*. This window automatically displays the names, values, and types of all variables in scope. See Figure D.4. You can use the window to alter the values of variables at any time.

Name	Value	Type
⊞ ◆ Me	{WindowsApplication1.Form1, Text: Form1 🔍 ▾	WindowsApplication1.Form
⊞ ◆ e	{X = 17 Y = 21 Button = Left {1048576}}	System.EventArgs
◆ num1	3	Integer
◆ num2	4	Integer
◆ phrase	"Hello world." 🔍 ▾	String
⊞ ◆ sender	{Text = "Button1"}	Object

FIGURE D.4   **A typical Locals window.**

Six Walkthroughs

The following walkthroughs use the debugging tools with the programming structures covered in Chapters 3, 4, 5, and 6.

Stepping through an Elementary Program: Chapter 3

The following walkthrough demonstrates several capabilities of the debugger:

1. Create a form with a button (btnPush) and a text box (txtBox).

2. Double-click on the button and enter the following event procedure:

```
Private Sub btnPush_Click(...) Handles btnPush.Click
  Dim num As Integer
  num = CInt(InputBox("Enter a number:"))
  num += 1
  num += 2
  txtBox.Text = CStr(num)
End Sub
```

3. Place the cursor on the line beginning Private Sub, press the right mouse button, and click on *Run to Cursor*. The program will execute, and the form will appear.

4. Click on the button. The Code Editor appears and a yellow arrow points to the Private Sub statement.

5. Press F8. The yellow arrow now points to the statement containing InputBox to indicate that it is to be executed next. (Pressing F8 is referred to as *stepping into*. You can also step to the next statement of a program with the *Step Into* option from the *Debug* menu or with the *Step Into* icon in the Toolbar.)

6. Press F8. The statement containing InputBox is executed, and an input dialog box requesting a number appears. Respond to the request by typing 5 and clicking the *OK* button.

7. Press F8 again to execute the statement **num += 1**.

8. Let the mouse hover over any occurrence of the variable *num* for a second or so. The current value of the variable will be displayed in a small box. See Figure D.5.

FIGURE D.5   Obtaining the value of a variable.

9. Press the *Stop Debugging* button on the Toolbar. (You also can stop debugging by clicking on *Stop Debugging* in the *Debug* menu.)

10. Move the cursor to the line

    ```
    num += 2
    ```

    and then press F9. A red dot appears on the gray border to the left of the line. This indicates that the line is a breakpoint. Pressing F9 is referred to as *toggling a breakpoint*.

11. Press F5 and click on the button. Respond to the request by entering 5 and clicking on *OK*. The program executes the first three lines inside the procedure and stops at the breakpoint. At this point, the breakpoint line has not yet executed.

12. Open the Immediate window by pressing Ctrl + Alt + I. If necessary, clear the contents of the window by pressing the right mouse button and selecting "Clear All". Type the statement

    ```
    ? num
    ```

    into the Immediate window, and then press Enter to execute the statement. The appearance of "6" on the next line of the Immediate window confirms that the breakpoint line was not executed.

13. Click on the Code Editor.

14. Move the cursor to the line `num += 1`, click the right mouse button, and then click on "Set next Statement".

15. Press F8 to execute the selected line.

16. Return to the Immediate window by clicking on it. Type the statement "? num" and press Enter to confirm that the value of *num* is now 7. Then return to the Code Editor.

17. Move the cursor to the breakpoint line and press F9 to deselect the line as a breakpoint.

18. Press F5 to execute the remaining lines of the program. Observe that the value displayed in the text box is 9.

Stepping through Programs Containing Selection Structures: Chapter 4

If Blocks

The following walkthrough demonstrates how the condition of an If statement is evaluated to determine whether to take an action:

1. Create a form with a button (btnPush), a text box (txtBox), and the following code:

```
Private Sub btnPush_Click(...) Handles btnPush.Click
  Dim wage As Double
  wage = CDbl(InputBox("Wage:"))
  If wage < 7.25 Then
    txtBox.Text = "Below minimum wage."
  Else
    txtBox.Text = "Wage Ok."
  End If
End Sub
```

2. Place the cursor on the line beginning "Private Sub", press the right mouse button, and click on "Run to Cursor". The program will execute and the form will appear.

3. Click on the button, and then press F8. The yellow arrow points to the statement containing InputBox.

4. Press F8 once to execute the statement containing InputBox. Type a wage of 6.25, and press the Enter key. The If statement is highlighted but has not been executed.

5. Press F8 once, and notice that the yellow arrow has jumped to the statement **txtBox.Text = "Below minimum wage."** Because the condition "wage < 7.25" is true, the action associated with Then was chosen.

6. Press F8 to execute the txtBox.Text statement. Notice that Else is skipped and the yellow arrow points to End If.

7. Press F8 again. We are through with the If block, and the statement following the If block, End Sub, is highlighted.

8. Press Ctrl + Alt + Break to terminate debugging.

9. If desired, try stepping through the program again with 7.75 entered as the wage. Since the condition "wage < 7.25" will be false, the Else action will be executed instead of the Then action.

Select Case Blocks

The following walkthrough illustrates how a Select Case block uses the selector to choose from among several actions.

1. Create a form with a button (btnPush) and a text box (txtBox). Double-click on the button and enter the following procedure:

```
Private Sub btnPush_Click(...) Handles btnPush.Click
  Dim age, price As Double
  age = CDbl(InputBox("Age:"))
  Select Case age
    Case Is < 12
      price = 0
    Case Is < 18
      price = 3.5
    Case Is >= 65
      price = 4
    Case Else
      price = 5.5
  End Select
  txtBox.Text = "Your ticket price is " & FormatCurrency(price)
End Sub
```

2. Place the cursor on the line beginning "age =", press the right mouse button, and click on "Run to Cursor". The program will execute, and the form will appear.

3. Click on the button. The arrow will point to the statement beginning "age =".

4. Press F8 once to execute the statement beginning "age =". Type an age of 8, and press the Enter key. The arrow points to the Select Case statement, but the statement has not been executed.

5. Press F8 twice, and observe that the arrow points to the action associated with "Case Is < 12".

6. Press F8 once to execute the assignment statement. Notice that the arrow now points to End Select. This demonstrates that when more than one Case clause is true, only the first is acted upon.

7. Press Ctrl + Alt + Break to terminate debugging.

8. If desired, step through the program again, entering a different age and predicting which Case clause will be acted upon. (Some possible ages to try are 12, 14, 18, 33, and 67.)

Stepping through a Program Containing a General Procedure: Chapter 5

The following walkthrough uses the single-stepping feature of the debugger to trace the flow through a Sub procedure.

1. Create a form with a button (btnPush) and a text box (txtBox). Then enter the following two procedures:

```
Private Sub btnPush_Click(...) Handles btnPush.Click
  Dim p, b As Double
  p = 1000          'Principal
  UpdateBalance(p, b)
  txtBox.Text = "The balance is " & FormatCurrency(b)
End Sub


Sub UpdateBalance(ByVal prin As Double, ByRef bal As Double)
  'Calculate the balance at 5% interest rate
  Dim interest As Double
```

```
      interest = 0.05 * prin
      bal = prin + interest
   End Sub
```

2. Place the cursor on the line beginning "Private Sub", press the right mouse button, and click on "Run to Cursor". The program will execute, and the form will appear.

3. Click on the button. In the Code Editor, a yellow arrow points to the Private Sub statement.

4. Press F8 once, and observe that the yellow arrow now points to the statement **p** = **1000**. This statement will be executed when F8 is next pressed.

5. Press F8 again. The statement **p** = **1000** was executed, and the yellow arrow now points to the statement calling the Sub procedure GetBalance.

6. Press F8, and observe that the yellow arrow is now pointing to the header of the Sub procedure.

7. Press F8 three times to execute the assignment statements. The yellow arrow now points to the End Sub statement. (Notice that the Dim and comment statements were skipped.)

8. Press F8, and notice that the yellow arrow has moved back to the btnPush_Click event procedure and is pointing to the calling statement. By hovering the cursor over the variable *b*, you can verify that the Sub procedure was executed.

9. Press the *Stop Debugging* button to terminate debugging.

10. Repeat Steps 2 through 5, and then press Shift + F8 to *step over* the Sub procedure GetBalance. The Sub procedure has been executed in its entirety.

11. Press Ctrl + Alt + Break to terminate debugging.

Communicating between Arguments and Parameters: Chapter 5

The following walkthrough uses the Locals window to monitor the values of arguments and parameters during the execution of a program.

1. If you have not already done so, type the preceding program into the Code Editor.

2. Place the cursor on the line beginning "Private Sub", press the right mouse button, and click on "Run to Cursor". The program will execute, and the form will appear.

3. Click on the button.

4. Click on the *Debug* menu, hover the cursor over *Windows*, and then click on *Locals*. Notice that the variables *b* and *p* from the btnPush_Click event procedure appear in the Locals window. The other variables in the list (Me, sender, and e) needn't concern us.

5. Press F8 twice to point to the calling statement. Notice that the value of the variable *p* has changed.

6. Press F8 to call the Sub procedure. Notice that the variables displayed in the Locals window are now those of the procedure GetBalance.

7. Press F8 three times to execute the procedure.

8. Press F8 to return to the btnPush_Click event procedure. Notice that the value of the variable *b* has inherited the value of the variable *bal*.

9. Press Ctrl + Alt + Break to terminate debugging.

Stepping through a Program Containing a Do Loop: Chapter 6

The following walkthrough demonstrates the use of the Watch window to monitor the value of a condition in a Do loop that searches for a name:

1. Create a form with a list box (lstNames), a button (btnPush), and a text box (txtBox). Then double-click on the button and enter the following event procedure:

```
Private Sub btnPush_Click(...) Handles btnPush.Click
  'Look for a specific name
  Dim searchName As String, name = ""
  Dim i As Integer = 0
  Dim numNames As Integer = lstNames.Items.Count
  searchName = InputBox("Name:")  'Name to search for in list
  Do While (name <> searchName) And (i < numNames)
    name = CStr(lstNames.Items(i))
    i += 1
  Loop
  If name = searchName Then
    txtBox.Text = name
  Else
    txtBox.Text = "Name not found"
  End If
End Sub
```

2. Fill the list box's String Collection Editor with four lines containing the names Bert, Ernie, Grover, and Oscar.

3. Place the cursor on the line beginning "Private Sub", press the right mouse button, and click on "Run to Cursor". The program will execute, and the form will appear.

4. Click on the button. The yellow arrow points to the header of the event procedure.

5. Right-click on the variable *searchName*, and click on "Add Watch". The variable *searchName* has been added to a window titled Watch.

6. Repeat Step 5 for the variable *name*.

7. Drag the mouse across the words `name <> searchName` to highlight them. Then click the right mouse button, and click on "Add Watch". The Boolean expression has been added to the Watch window.

8. Press F8 five times to execute the statement containing InputBox. Enter the name "Ernie" in the input dialog box, and then click OK.

9. Press F8 repeatedly until the entire event procedure has been executed. Pause after each keypress, and notice how the values of the expressions in the Watch window change.

10. Press the *Close* button on the form to terminate debugging.

ANSWERS
To Selected Odd-Numbered Exercises

CHAPTER 2

EXERCISES **2.2**

1. After a button is clicked, it has a blue border.

3. Click on the form to make it the selected object.
   Click on the Properties window or Press F4 to activate the Properties window.
   Select the Text property.
   Type "CHECKING ACCOUNT".

5. Double-click the TextBox icon in the Toolbox.
   Activate the Properties window.
   Select the BackColor property.
   Click on the down-arrow to the right of the Settings box.
   Click on the Custom tab, and then click on the desired yellow in the palette.
   Click on the form to see the empty yellow text box.

7. Double-click on the Label icon in the Toolbox.
   Activate the Properties window, and select the AutoSize property.
   Set the AutoSize property to False.
   Select the Text property and type the requested sentence.
   Select the TextAlign property.
   Click on the down-arrow button to the right of the Settings box, and click on one of the center rectangles.
   Resize the label so that the sentence occupies three lines.

9. Double-click on the TextBox icon in the Toolbox.
   Activate the Properties window.
   Set the Name property to txtLanguage.
   Select the Text property and type "Visual Basic 2010".
   Select the Font property and click on the ellipsis to the right of the Settings box.
   Scroll up the Font list box, and click on Courier New in the Font box.
   Click OK.
   Widen the text box to accommodate its text.

11. Double-click on the Button icon in the Toolbox.
    Activate the Properties window, and select the BackColor property.
    Click on the down-arrow button to the right of the Settings box.
    Click on the Custom tab, and then click on the white square in upper-left corner of the palette.
    Select the Text property and type "PUSH".
    Select the Font property, and click on the ellipsis.
    Click on *Italic* (with XP or Vista) or *Oblique* (with Windows 7) in the "Font style" list.
    Click on 24 in the Size box and click OK.
    Resize the button.

13. Double-click on the Button icon in the Toolbox.
Activate the Properties window.
Select the Text property and type "PUS&H".
Click on the form to see the resulting button.

15. Double-click on the Label icon in the Toolbox.
Activate the Properties window.
Select the Name property and type "lblAKA".
Select the Text property and type "ALIAS".
Select the AutoSize property and set it to False.
Select the Font property and click on the ellipsis.
Click on *Italic* (with XP or Vista) or *Oblique* (with Windows 7) in the "Font style" list.
Click OK.
Select the TextAlign property, click on the down-arrow box to the right of the Settings box, and click on one of the center rectangles.

17. Double-click on the Label icon in the Toolbox.
Activate the Properties window, and select the TextAlign property.
Click on the down-arrow box to the right of the Settings box, and click on one of the rectangles on the right.
Select the AutoSize property and set it to False.
Select the Text property, type "VISUAL BASIC", and press Enter.
If the words "VISUAL BASIC" are on one line, resize the label until the words occupy two lines.

19. Double-click on the Label icon in the Toolbox.
Activate the Properties window, and select the Font property.
Click on the ellipsis to the right of the Settings box.
Click on Wingdings in the Font box.
Click on the largest size available (72) in the Size box.
Click OK.
Select the Text property and change the setting to a less than sign (<).
Click on the label.

(**Note:** If you didn't know that the less than symbol corresponded to a diskette in the Wingdings font, you could double-click on the diskette character in the Character Map, click the *Copy* button, select the Text property, and press Ctrl+V. The less than character will appear in the Text settings box.)

21. Double-click on the ListBox icon in the Toolbox.
Activate the Properties window, and select the BackColor property.
Click on the down-arrow button to the right of the Settings box.
Click on the Custom tab and click on the desired yellow square in the palette.
Click on the form to see the yellow list box.

23. In the Solution Explorer window, right click on "Form1.vb" and select *Rename* from the context menu.
Type "frmYellow.vb".
Right-click on the form in the Form Designer, and select Properties from the context menu.
Click on BackColor property in the Properties window.
Click on the down-arrow button in the right part of the Settings box, click on the Custom tab, and click on a yellow square.

25. Begin a new project.
Change the text in the form's title bar to "Dynamic Duo".

Place two buttons on the form and position and resize as shown.
Enter "Batman" as the text of the first button, and enter "Robin" as the text of the second button.
Increase the font size for both buttons to 14.

27. Begin a new project.
Change the text in the form's title bar to "Fill the Blank".
Place a label, a text box, and another label on the form at appropriate locations.
Change the Text setting of the first label to "I'm the king of the" and the Text setting of the second label to "A Quote by Leonardo DiCaprio".

29. Begin a new project.
Change the text in the form's title bar to "Uncle's Advice".
Place five labels and three buttons on the form.
Change the Text setting of each label as indicated.
Change the settings of the buttons' Text properties to "1", "2", and "3".
Resize and position the labels and buttons.

33. 1   35. Each arrow key moves the text box in the indicated direction.

37. Pressing the right and left arrow keys widens and narrows the text boxes, buttons, and list boxes in the group of selected controls. The up and down arrow keys shorten and lengthen the buttons and list boxes in the group. The arrow keys have no effect on the labels, and only the left and right arrow keys affect the text boxes.

39. Drag a label and a list box onto the form.
Click on the label.
Hold down the Ctrl key and click on the list box. (You have now selected a group of two controls.)
In the Properties window, click on the plus sign (in XP) or the right-pointing triangle (Vista or Windows 7) to the left of the Font property.
Click on the Size property, change the setting to 12, and press the Enter key.

(**Alternative:** Replace the last three lines with the following steps.)

In the Properties window, select the Font property.
Click on the ellipsis button to the right of the Settings box.
Click on 12 in the Size list and click OK.

41. The label is positioned just to the left of the text box, and the middles of the two controls are aligned.

43. *Center* refers to the midpoint horizontally, whereas *middle* refers to the midpoint vertically.

45. First blue snap line: tops of the two controls are aligned
Purple snap line: middles of the two controls are aligned
Second blue snap line: bottoms of the two controls are aligned

47. The setting is cycling through the different available colors.

EXERCISES 2.3

1. The word "Hello"   3. The word "Hello" on an orange-colored background

5. The text box vanishes.   7. The word "Hello" in green letters

9. The word "Hello" on a gold background.   11. Form1.Text should be Me.Text.

13. Blue should be replaced with Color.Blue.

15. Font.Size is a read-only property. The statement `txtOutput.Text = txtBox.Font.Size` is valid since it is reading the value of txtBox.Font.Size. However, `txtBox.Font.Size = 20` is not valid since it is setting the value of txtBox.Font.Size.

17. `lblTwo.Text = "E.T. phone home."`

19. `txtBox.ForeColor = Color.Red`
    `txtBox.Text = "The stuff that dreams are made of."`

21. `txtBox.Enabled = False`   23. `lblTwo.Visible = False`

25. `btnOutcome.Enabled = True`   27. `txtBoxTwo.Focus()`

29. The Enter event occurs when a control gets the focus.

31. ```
    Private Sub Label1_Click(...) Handles Label1.Click
        lstOutput.Items.Add("Click")
    End Sub

    Private Sub Label1_DoubleClick(...) Handles Label1.DoubleClick
        lstOutput.Items.Add("Double Click")
    End Sub
    ```

    Whenever the DoubleClick event is raised, the Click event is also raised.

33. ```
    Private Sub btnLeft_Click(...) Handles btnLeft.Click
        txtBox.Text = "Left Justify"
        txtBox.TextAlign = HorizontalAlignment.Left
    End Sub

    Private Sub btnCenter_Click(...) Handles btnCenter.Click
        txtBox.Text = "Center"
        txtBox.TextAlign = HorizontalAlignment.Center
    End Sub

    Private Sub btnRight_Click(...) Handles btnRight.Click
        txtBox.Text = "Right Justify"
        txtBox.TextAlign = HorizontalAlignment.Right
    End Sub
    ```

35. ```
    Private Sub btnRed_Click(...) Handles btnRed.Click
        txtBox.BackColor = Color.Red
    End Sub

    Private Sub btnBlue_Click(...) Handles btnBlue.Click
        txtBox.BackColor = Color.Blue
    End Sub

    Private Sub btnWhite_Click(...) Handles btnWhite.Click
        txtBox.ForeColor = Color.White
    End Sub

    Private Sub btnYellow_Click(...) Handles btnYellow.Click
        txtBox.ForeColor = Color.Yellow
    End Sub
    ```

37. ```
    Private Sub txtLife_Enter(...) Handles txtLife.Enter
        txtQuote.Text = "I like life, it's something to do."
    End Sub

    Private Sub txtFuture_Enter(...) Handles txtFuture.Enter
        txtQuote.Text = "The future isn't what it used to be."
    End Sub

    Private Sub txtTruth_Enter(...) Handles txtTruth.Enter
        txtQuote.Text = "Tell the truth and run."
    End Sub
    ```

39.
```
Private Sub btnOne_Click(...) Handles btnOne.Click
  btnOne.Visible = False
  btnTwo.Visible = True
  btnThree.Visible = True
  btnFour.Visible = True
End Sub

Private Sub btnTwo_Click(...) Handles btnTwo.Click
  btnOne.Visible = True
  btnTwo.Visible = False
  btnThree.Visible = True
  btnFour.Visible = True
End Sub

Private Sub btnThree_Click(...) Handles btnThree.Click
  btnOne.Visible = True
  btnTwo.Visible = True
  btnThree.Visible = False
  btnFour.Visible = True
End Sub

Private Sub btnFour_Click(...) Handles btnFour.Click
  btnOne.Visible = True
  btnTwo.Visible = True
  btnThree.Visible = True
  btnFour.Visible = False
End Sub
```

41.
```
Private Sub btnVanish_Click(...) Handles btnVanish.Click
  lblFace.Visible = False
End Sub

Private Sub btnReappear_Click(...) Handles btnReappear.Click
  lblFace.Visible = True
End Sub
```

43.
```
Private Sub btnAny_Click(...) Handles btnOne.Click, btnTwo.Click
  txtOutput.Text = "You just clicked on a button."
End Sub
```

CHAPTER 3

EXERCISES 3.1

1. 12   3. .125   5. 8   7. 2   9. 1   11. Not valid

13. Valid   15. Not valid   17. 10   19. 16   21. 9

23.
```
Private Sub btnCompute_Click(...) Handles btnCompute.Click
  lstOutput.Items.Add((7 * 8) + 5)
End Sub
```

25.
```
Private Sub btnCompute_Click(...) Handles btnCompute.Click
  lstOutput.Items.Add(0.055 * 20)
End Sub
```

27.
```
Private Sub btnCompute_Click(...) Handles btnCompute.Click
  lstOutput.Items.Add(17 * (3 + 162))
End Sub
```

29.

	x	y
`Private Sub btnEvaluate_Click(...) Handles btnEvaluate.Click`		
`Dim x, y As Double`	0	0
`x = 2`	2	0
`y = 3 * x`	2	6
`x = y + 5`	11	6
`lstResults.Items.Clear()`	11	6
`lstResults.Items.Add(x + 4)`	11	6
`y = y + 1`	11	7
`End Sub`		

31. 6   **33.** 1   **35.** 1   **37.** 2
               9   64   15
              18

39. The third line should read `c = a + b`

41. The first assignment statement should not contain a comma. The second assignment statement should not contain a dollar sign.

43. 6X is not a valid variable name; in the second line, there must be an * after the 2.

45. `Dim quantity As Integer = 12`

47. 10   **49.** 6   **51.** 3.128   **53.** −3   **55.** 0   **57.** 6

59.
```
Private Sub btnCompute_Click(...) Handles btnCompute.Click
    Dim revenue, costs, profit As Double
    revenue = 98456
    costs = 45000
    profit = revenue — costs
    lstOutput.Items.Add(profit)
End Sub
```

61.
```
Private Sub btnCompute_Click(...) Handles btnCompute.Click
    Dim price, discountPercent, markdown As Double
    price = 19.95
    discountPercent = 30
    markdown = (discountPercent / 100) * price
    price = price — markdown
    lstOutput.Items.Add(Math.Round(price, 2))
End Sub
```

63.
```
Private Sub btnCompute_Click(...) Handles btnCompute.Click
    Dim balance As Double
    balance = 100
    balance += 0.05 * balance
    balance += 0.05 * balance
    balance += 0.05 * balance
    lstOutput.Items.Add(Math.Round(balance, 2))
End Sub
```

65.
```
Private Sub btnCompute_Click(...) Handles btnCompute.Click
    Dim balance As Double
    balance = 100
    balance = balance * (1.05 ^ 10)
    lstOutput.Items.Add(Math.Round(balance, 2))
End Sub
```

67.
```
Private Sub btnCompute_Click(...) Handles btnCompute.Click
    Dim acres, yieldPerAcre, corn As Double
    acres = 30
    yieldPerAcre = 18
    corn = yieldPerAcre * acres
    lstOutput.Items.Add(corn)
End Sub
```

69.
```
Private Sub btnCompute_Click(...) Handles btnCompute.Click
    Dim distance, elapsedTime, averageSpeed As Double
    distance = 233
    elapsedTime = 7 - 2
    averageSpeed = distance / elapsedTime
    lstOutput.Items.Add(averageSpeed)
End Sub
```

71.
```
Private Sub btnCompute_Click(...) Handles btnCompute.Click
    Dim waterPerPersonPerDay, people, days, waterUsed As Double
    waterPerPersonPerDay = 1600
    people = 315000000
    days = 365
    waterUsed = waterPerPersonPerDay * people * days
    lstOutput.Items.Add(waterUsed)
End Sub
```

EXERCISES 3.2

1. Visual Basic   3. Ernie   5. flute   7. 123   9. Your age is 21.

11. A ROSE IS A ROSE IS A ROSE   13. 5.5   15. goodbye   17. WALLAWALLABINGBANG

19. ABC
2
4
55 mph
STU

21. 12
MUNICIPALITY
city
6

23. 8 (0 through 7)   25. True

27. The variable *phoneNumber* should be declared as type String, not Double.

29. *End* is a keyword and cannot be used as a variable name.

31. IndexOf cannot be applied to a numeric variable; it is a **string** method.

33.
```
Private Sub btnDisplay_Click(...) Handles btnDisplay.Click
    Dim firstName, middleName, lastName As String
    Dim yearOfBirth As Integer
    firstName = "Thomas"
    middleName = "Alva"
    lastName = "Edison"
    yearOfBirth = 1847
    txtOutput.Text = firstName & " " & middleName & " " & lastName &
                ", " & yearOfBirth
End Sub
```

35.
```
Private Sub btnDisplay_Click(...) Handles btnDisplay.Click
    Dim publisher As String
    publisher = "Prentice Hall, Inc."
    txtOutput.Text = "(c) " & publisher
End Sub
```

```
37. Dim str As String   'Place in the Declarations section of the program
```

```
39. Private Sub btnCompute_Click(...) Handles btnCompute.Click
        Dim distance As Double
        distance = CDbl(txtNumSec.Text) / 5
        distance = Math.Round(distance, 2)
        txtOutput.Text = "The distance of the storm is " & distance & " miles."
    End Sub
```

```
41. Private Sub btnCompute_Click(...) Handles btnCompute.Click
        Dim cycling, running, swimming, pounds As Double
        cycling = CDbl(txtCycle.Text)
        running = CDbl(txtRun.Text)
        swimming = CDbl(txtSwim.Text)
        pounds = (200 * cycling + 475 * running + 275 * swimming) / 3500
        pounds = Math.Round(pounds, 1)
        txtWtLoss.Text = pounds & " pounds were lost."
    End Sub
```

```
43. Private Sub btnCompute_Click(...) Handles btnCompute.Click
        Dim revenue, expenses, income As Double
        revenue = CDbl(txtRevenue.Text)
        expenses = CDbl(txtExpenses.Text)
        income = revenue — expenses
        txtNetIncome.Text = CStr(income)
    End Sub
```

```
45. Private Sub btnCompute_Click(...) Handles btnCompute.Click
        Dim amount, percentage, tip As Double
        amount = CDbl(txtAmount.Text)
        percentage = CDbl(txtPercentage.Text)
        tip = amount * (percentage / 100)
        txtTip.Text = CStr(Math.Round(tip, 2))
    End Sub
```

```
47. Dim number As Integer = 100   'in Declarations section
    'Note: the Text property of txtOutput was set to 100 at design time

    Private Sub btnPressMe_Click(...) Handles btnPressMe.Click
      number = number — 1  'decrease number by 1
      txtOutput.Text = CStr(number)
    End Sub
```

49.
```
Private Sub btnModifySentence_Click(...) Handles btnModifySentence.Click
    Dim sentence, oldWord, newWord As String
    Dim position As Integer
    sentence = txtSentence.Text
    oldWord = txtOriginalWord.Text
    newWord = txtReplacementWord.Text
    position = sentence.IndexOf(oldWord)
    txtOutput.Text = sentence.Substring(0, position) & newWord &
                     sentence.Substring(position + oldWord.Length)
End Sub
```

51.
```
Private Sub btnDisplay_Click(...) Handles btnDisplay.Click
    Dim speed, distance As Double
    distance = CDbl(txtDistanceSkidded.Text)
    speed = Math.Sqrt(24 * distance)
    speed = Math.Round(speed, 2)
    txtEstimatedSpeed.Text = speed & " mph"
End Sub
```

53.
```
Dim sum As Double    'sum of the scores entered
Dim num As Integer   'number of scores entered
```

```
Private Sub btnRecord_Click(...) Handles btnRecord.Click
  num += 1
  sum += CDbl(txtScore.Text)
  txtScore.Clear()
  txtScore.Focus()
End Sub


Private Sub btnCalculate_Click(...) Handles btnCalculate.Click
  txtAverage.Text = CStr(sum / num)
End Sub
```

55. ```
Private Sub btnCompute_Click(...) Handles btnCompute.Click
  Dim num1, num2, sum As Double
  num1 = CDbl(txtFirstNum.Text)
  num2 = CDbl(txtSecondNum.Text)
  sum = num1 + num2
  txtSum.Text = CStr(sum)
End Sub

Private Sub txtEitherNum_TextChanged(...) Handles _
                txtFirstNum.TextChanged, txtSecondNum.TextChanged
  txtSum.Clear()
End Sub
```

## EXERCISES 3.3

1. `1,235`   3. `1,234.0`   5. `0.0`   7. `-0.67`   9. `12,346.000`   11. `12`

13. `$23,457`   15. `($0.23)`   17. `$0.80`   19. `7.50%`   21. `100.00%`

23. `66.67%`   25. `Pay to France $27,267,622.00`

27. `25.6% of the U.S. population 25+ years old are college graduates.`

29. `The likelihood of Heads is 50%`   31. `10/23/2010`

33. `Thursday, November 25, 2010`   35. `10/2/2011`   37. `4/5/2013`   39. `29`

41. `You might win 360 dollars.`   43. `Hello John Jones`   45. `$106.00`

47. Prints the words Hello World using a 10-point bold Courier New font in blue letters 2 inches from the left side of the page and 2 inches from the top of the page.

49. The second line is an error. You cannot change the value of a constant. The multiplication should be done in the 3rd line.

51. The second line should use CDbl to convert the right-hand side to type Double.

53. FormatNumber(123456) is a string and therefore cannot be assigned to a numeric variable.

55. You must insert `.Show`, after the word `MessageBox`.

57. `000`   59. `LLL000`   61. `0-00-000000-&`

63. `MessageBox.Show("First check the weather.  Then decide whether to wear shorts and sandals.", "Good advice")`

65. ```
Private Sub btnDisplay_Click(...) Handles btnDisplay.Click
  Dim begOfYearCost, endOfYearCost As Double
  Dim percentIncrease As Double
  begOfYearCost = 200
  endOfYearCost = CDbl(InputBox("Enter cost at the end of the year:"))
  percentIncrease = (endOfYearCost - begOfYearCost) / begOfYearCost
  txtOutput.Text = "The increase in cost for the year is " &
                FormatPercent(percentIncrease) & "."
End Sub
```

67.
```
Private Sub btnDisplay_Click(...) Handles btnDisplay.Click
    Dim firstDayOfYr, firstDayOfNextYr As Date
    Dim numDays As Double
    firstDayOfYr = CDate("1/1/" & mtbYear.Text)
    firstDayOfNextYr = firstDayOfYr.AddYears(1)
    numDays = DateDiff(DateInterval.Day, firstDayOfYr, firstDayOfNextYr)
    txtNumDays.Text = CStr(numDays)
End Sub
```

69.
```
Private Sub Determine_Click(...) Handles btnDetermine.Click
    Dim dt As Date = CDate(mtbDate.Text)
    Dim fullDate As String = FormatDateTime(dt, DateFormat.LongDate)
    Dim position As Integer = fullDate.IndexOf(",")
    Dim dayOfWeek As String = fullDate.Substring(0, position)
    txtDayOfWeek.Text = dayOfWeek
End Sub
```

71.
```
Private Sub Determine_Click(...) Handles btnDetermine.Click
    Dim month, yr As Integer    'month given as 1 through 12
    Dim dt, dt2 As Date
    Dim numDays As Double
    month = CInt(txtMonth.Text)
    yr = CInt(mtbYear.Text)
    dt = CDate(month & "/1/" & yr)
    dt2 = dt.AddMonths(1)
    numDays = DateDiff(DateInterval.Day, dt, dt2)
    txtNumDays.Text = CStr(numDays)
End Sub
```

73.
```
Private Sub txtPhoneNumber_Enter(...) Handles txtPhoneNumber.Enter
    MessageBox.Show("Be sure to include the area code!", "Reminder")
End Sub
```

75.
```
Private Sub btnCompute_Click(...) Handles btnCompute.Click
    Dim principal, intRate, yrs, amt As Double
```

```
    lstOutput.Items.Clear()
    principal = CDbl(txtPrincipal.Text)
    intRate = CDbl(txtIntRate.Text)
    yrs = 10
    amt = principal * (1 + intRate) ^ yrs
    lstOutput.Items.Add("When " & FormatCurrency(principal) & " is")
    lstOutput.Items.Add("invested at " & FormatPercent(intRate))
    lstOutput.Items.Add("for " & yrs & " years, the ")
    lstOutput.Items.Add("balance is " & FormatCurrency(amt) & ".")
End Sub
```

77.
```
Const ONE_INCH As Integer = 100      'number of points in an inch
Const LINE_HEIGHT As Integer = 20    'one-quarter of an inch

Private Sub btnPrint_Click(...) Handles btnPrint.Click
  PrintDocument1.Print()
End Sub

Private Sub PrintDocument1_PrintPage(...) Handles PrintDocument1.PrintPage
  Dim gr As Graphics = e.Graphics
  Dim x1 As Integer = ONE_INCH             'use one inch beyond left margin
  Dim x2 As Integer = CInt(1.5 * ONE_INCH)     'offset for second column
  Dim x3 As Integer = CInt(2.25 * ONE_INCH)    'offset for third column
  Dim y As Integer = ONE_INCH              'use one inch top margin
  Dim font1 As New Font("Courier New", 10, FontStyle.Underline)
  Dim font2 As New Font("Courier New", 10, FontStyle.Regular)
  gr.DrawString("% of", font2, Brushes.Black, x3, y)
  y += LINE_HEIGHT
  gr.DrawString("Rank", font1, Brushes.Black, x1, y)
  gr.DrawString("Country", font1, Brushes.Black, x2, y)
  gr.DrawString("WW Users", font1, Brushes.Black, x3, y)
  y += LINE_HEIGHT
  gr.DrawString("1", font2, Brushes.Black, x1, y)
  gr.DrawString("USA", font2, Brushes.Black, x2, y)
  gr.DrawString(FormatPercent(0.16, 1), font2, Brushes.Black, x3, y)
  y += LINE_HEIGHT
  gr.DrawString("2", font2, Brushes.Black, x1, y)
  gr.DrawString("China", font2, Brushes.Black, x2, y)
  gr.DrawString(FormatPercent(0.119, 1), font2, Brushes.Black, x3, y)
  y += LINE_HEIGHT
  gr.DrawString("3", font2, Brushes.Black, x1, y)
  gr.DrawString("Japan", font2, Brushes.Black, x2, y)
  gr.DrawString(FormatPercent(0.065, 1), font2, Brushes.Black, x3, y)
End Sub

Private Sub btnPreview_Click(...) Handles btnPreview.Click
  PrintPreviewDialog1.Document = PrintDocument1
  PrintPreviewDialog1.ShowDialog()
End Sub
```

CHAPTER 4

EXERCISES 4.1

1. `hi`   3. `The letter after G is H`

5. `"We're all in this alone." - Lily Tomlin`

7. True   9. True   11. True   13. True   15. False   17. False   19. True   21. True

23. False   25. False   27. False   29. True   31. Equivalent   33. Not Equivalent

35. Equivalent   37. Not Equivalent   39. Equivalent   41. `a >= b`

43. `(a >= b) Or (c = d)`   45. `(a = "") Or (a >= b) Or (a.Length >= 5)`

[In Exercises 46 through 49, execute a statement of the form `txtOutput.Text = Boolean expression`.]

47. True   49. False   51. False   53. False   55. True   57. False   59. True

EXERCISES 4.2

1. `Less than ten.`   3. `Remember, tomorrow is another day.`   5. `10`

7. `To be, or not to be.`   9. `No output`   11. `You are old enough to vote in 7 days.`

13. Syntax error. Third line should be `If ((1 < num) And (num < 3)) Then`

15. Syntax error. Fourth line should be `If ((major = "Business") Or (major = "Computer Science")) Then`

17. `a = 5`

19.
```
message = "Is Alaska bigger than Texas and California combined?"
answer = InputBox(message)
If (answer.Substring(0, 1).ToUpper = "Y") Then
  txtOutput.Text = "Correct"
Else
  txtOutput.Text = "Wrong"
End If
```

21.
```
Private Sub btnCompute_Click(...) Handles btnCompute.Click
  Dim cost, tip As Double
  cost = CDbl(InputBox("Enter cost of meal:"))
  tip = cost * 0.15
  If tip < 1 Then
    tip = 1
  End If
  txtOutput.Text = "Leave " & FormatCurrency(tip) & " for the tip."
End Sub
```

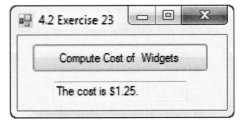

23.
```
Private Sub btnCompute_Click(...) Handles btnCompute.Click
    Dim num, cost As Double
    num = CDbl(InputBox("Number of widgets:"))
    If num < 100 Then
      cost = 0.25 * num   '25 cents each
    Else
      cost = 0.2 * num    '20 cents each
    End If
    txtOutput.Text = "The cost is " & FormatCurrency(cost) & "."
End Sub
```

25.
```
Private Sub btnAskQuestion_Click(...) Handles btnAskQuestion.Click
    Dim name As String
    name = (InputBox("Who was the first Ronald McDonald?")).ToUpper
    If name = "WILLARD SCOTT" Then
      txtOutput.Text = "Correct."
    Else
      txtOutput.Text = "Nice try."
    End If
End Sub
```

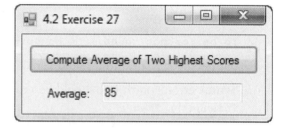

27.
```
Private Sub btnCompute_Click(...) Handles btnCompute.Click
    Dim s1, s2, s3 As Double  '3 scores
    Dim avg As Double          'average of the two highest scores
    s1 = CDbl(InputBox("Enter the first of the three scores."))
    s2 = CDbl(InputBox("Enter the second of the three scores."))
    s3 = CDbl(InputBox("Enter the third of the three scores."))
    If (s1 <= s2) And (s1 <= s3) Then      's1 is smallest number
      avg = (s2 + s3) / 2
    ElseIf (s2 <= s1) And (s2 <= s3) Then  's2 is smallest number
      avg = (s1 + s3) / 2
    Else                                   's3 is smallest number
      avg = (s1 + s2) / 2
    End If
    txtAverage.Text = CStr(avg)
End Sub
```

29.
```
Private Sub btnCompute_Click(...) Handles btnCompute.Click
    Dim weight, cost, amount, change As Double
    weight = CDbl(txtWeight.Text)
    amount = CDbl(txtAmount.Text)
    cost = weight * 1.7
    If (amount >= cost) Then
      change = amount − cost
      txtOutput.Text = "Your change is " & FormatCurrency(change) & "."
    Else
      txtOutput.Text = "I need " & FormatCurrency(cost − amount) & " more."
    End If
End Sub
```

31.
```vb
Private Sub btnCompute_Click(...) Handles btnCompute.Click
    Dim wage, hours, grossPay As Double
    wage = CDbl(txtHourlyWage.Text)     'Hourly pay
    hours = CDbl(txtHoursWorked.Text)   'Hours worked
    If hours <= 40 Then
      grossPay = wage * hours
    Else
      grossPay = (wage * 40) + (1.5 * wage * (hours − 40))
    End If
    txtGrossPay.Text = FormatCurrency(grossPay)
End Sub
```

33.
```vb
Dim numLines As Integer = 0  'In Declarations section of Code Editor
'numLines tells the number of lines that have been displayed.

Private Sub btnBogart_Click(...) Handles btnBogart.Click
  If numLines = 0 Then
    lstOutput.Items.Add("I came to Casablanca for the waters.")
    numLines += 1
  ElseIf numLines = 2 Then
    lstOutput.Items.Add("I was misinformed.")
    numLines += 1
  End If
End Sub

Private Sub btnRaines_Click(...) Handles btnRaines.Click
  If numLines = 1 Then
    lstOutput.Items.Add("But we're in the middle of the desert.")
    numLines += 1
  End If
End Sub
```

35.
```
Dim numGuesses As Integer = 0

Private Sub btnEvaluate_Click(...) Handles btnEvaluate.Click
  'Assume that the Text property of txtNumberOfGuesses
  'was set to 0 in the Form Designer
  numGuesses += 1
  txtNumberOfGuesses.Text = CStr(numGuesses)
  Dim msg As String
  If txtAnswer.Text.ToUpper.IndexOf("COOLIDGE") <> -1 Then
    MessageBox.Show("Calvin Coolidge was born on July 4, 1872.",
                    "Correct")
    Me.Close()
  ElseIf CInt(numGuesses) = 10 Then
    msg = "Calvin Coolidge was born on July 4, 1872."
    MessageBox.Show(msg, "You've Run Out of Guesses")
    Me.Close()
  Else
    If CInt(numGuesses) = 3 Then
      msg = "He once said, 'If you don't say anything," &
      " you won't be called upon to repeat it.'"
    ElseIf CInt(numGuesses) = 7 Then
      msg = "His nickname was 'Silent Cal.'"
    Else
      msg = "Sorry!"
    End If
    MessageBox.Show(msg, "Incorrect")
  End If
  txtAnswer.Clear()
  txtAnswer.Focus()
End Sub
```

37.
```
Private Sub btnDisplay_Click(...) Handles btnDisplay.Click
  If lblLanguage.Visible Then
    lblLanguage.Visible = False
    btnDisplay.Text = "Show Name of Language"
  Else
    lblLanguage.Visible = True
    btnDisplay.Text = "Hide Name of Language"
  End If
End Sub
```

39.
```
Private Sub btnCompute_Click(...) Handles lblDetermine.Click
  Dim day As String
  Dim day1, day2 As Date
  Dim numDays As Double
  day = "1/1/" & txtYear.Text
  day1 = CDate(day)
  day2 = day1.AddYears(1)
  numDays = DateDiff(DateInterval.Day, day1, day2)
```

```
      If numDays = 366 Then
        txtLeapYear.Text = "YES"
      Else
        txtLeapYear.Text = "NO"
      End If
  End Sub
```

41.
```
Private Sub Determine_Click(...) Handles btnDetermine.Click
    Dim dt, dt2 As Date
    Dim approximateAge As Double
    dt = CDate(mtbDate.Text)
    approximateAge = DateDiff(DateInterval.Year, dt, Today)
    dt2 = dt.AddYears(CInt(approximateAge))
    If Today < dt2 Then
      txtAge.Text = CStr(approximateAge − 1)
    Else
      txtAge.Text = CStr(approximateAge)
    End If
  End Sub
```

43.
```
Private Sub btnDetermine_Click(...) Handles btnDetermine.Click
    Dim gpa As Double = CDbl(txtGPA.Text)
    Dim honors As String = ""
    If gpa >= 3.9 Then
      honors = " summa cum laude."
    End If
    If (3.6 <= gpa) And (gpa < 3.9) Then
      honors = " magna cum laude."
    End If
    If (3.3 <= gpa) And (gpa < 3.6) Then
      honors = " cum laude."
    End If
    If (2 <= gpa) And (gpa < 3.3) Then
      honors = "."
    End If
    txtOutput.Text = "You graduated" & honors
  End Sub
```

EXERCISES 4.3

1.
```
The price is $6.75
The price is $8.00
```

3.
```
Mesozoic Era
Paleozoic Era
?
```

5.
```
The equation has no real solutions.
The equation has two solutions.
The equation has exactly one solution.
```

7. Should have a Case clause before the 4th line.

9. `Case nom = "Bob"` should be `Case "Bob"`

11. Logic error: `>= "Peach"` should be `>= "PEACH"`.

Syntax error: `"ORANGE TO PEACH"` should be `"ORANGE" To "PEACH"`.

13. Valid   **15.** Invalid   **17.** Valid

19.
```
Select Case a
  Case 1
    txtOutput.Text = "one"
  Case Is > 5
    txtOutput.Text = "two"
End Select
```

21.
```
Select Case a
  Case 2
    txtOutput.Text = "maybe"
  Case 7
    txtOutput.Text = "yes"
  Case Else
    txtOutput.Text = "no"
End Case
```

23.
```
Private Sub btnDescribe_Click(...) Handles btnDescribe.Click
  Dim percent As Double
  percent = CDbl(InputBox("Percentage of cloud cover:"))
  Select Case percent
    Case 0 To 30
      txtOutput.Text = "Clear"
    Case 31 To 70
      txtOutput.Text = "Partly cloudy"
    Case 71 To 99
      txtOutput.Text = "Cloudy"
    Case 100
      txtOutput.Text = "Overcast"
    Case Else
      txtOutput.Text = "Percentage must be between 0 and 100."
  End Select
End Sub
```

25.
```
Private Sub btnCompute_Click(...) Handles btnCompute.Click
  Dim shapeNum As Integer
  Dim radius, length, height, width As Double
  'Input choice of shape and its dimensions
  '1. Circle   2. Parallelogram   3. Kite
  shapeNum = CInt(mtbSelection.Text)     'Mask is 0
  Select Case shapeNum
    Case 1
      radius = CDbl(InputBox("Input the radius of the circle: "))
      txtArea.Text = CStr(3.141593 * radius ^ 2)
```

```
     Case 2
       length = CDbl(InputBox("Input the length of the parallelogram: "))
       height = CDbl(InputBox("Input the height of the parallelogram: "))
       txtArea.Text = CStr(length * height)
     Case 3
       length = CDbl(InputBox("Input the length of the kite: "))
       width = CDbl(InputBox("Input the width of the kite: "))
       txtArea.Text = CStr((length * width) / 2)
     Case Else
       MessageBox.Show("Your choice is not valid.", "Try Again.")
       mtbSelection.Clear()
   End Select
   mtbSelection.Focus()
 End Sub
```

27.
```
Private Sub btnAssign_Click(...) Handles btnAssign.Click
   Dim score As Integer, letterGrade As String
   score = CInt(InputBox("What is the score?"))
   Select Case score
     Case 90 To 100
       letterGrade = "A"
     Case 80 To 89
       letterGrade = "B"
     Case 70 To 79
       letterGrade = "C"
     Case 60 To 69
       letterGrade = "D"
     Case 0 To 59
       letterGrade = "F"
     Case Else
       letterGrade = "Invalid"
   End Select
   txtOutput.Text = "The letter grade is " & letterGrade & "."
 End Sub
```

29.
```
Private Sub btnDescribe_Click(...) Handles btnDetermine.Click
   Dim amountRecovered, payment As Double
   amountRecovered = CDbl(InputBox("How much was recovered?"))
   Select Case amountRecovered
     Case Is <= 75000
       payment = 0.1 * amountRecovered
     Case Is <= 100000
       payment = 7500 + 0.05 * (amountRecovered - 75000)
     Case Is > 100000
       payment = 8750 + 0.01 * (amountRecovered - 100000)
       If payment > 50000 Then
         payment = 50000
       End If
   End Select
```

```
          txtOutput.Text = "The amount given as reward is " &
                              FormatCurrency(payment) & "."
      End Sub
31. Private Sub btnDisplay_Click(...) Handles btnDisplay.Click
      Dim pres, state, trivia, whichBush As String
      pres = txtLastName.Text
      Select Case pres.ToUpper
        Case "CARTER"
          state = "Georgia"
          trivia = "The only soft drink served in the Carter " &
                    "White House was Coca-Cola."
        Case "REAGAN"
          state = "California"
          trivia = "His secret service code name was Rawhide."
        Case "BUSH"
          state = "Texas"
          whichBush = InputBox("Are his middle initials HW or W?")
          Select Case whichBush.ToUpper
            Case "HW"
              trivia = "He celebrated his 85th birthday by parachuting " &
                        "out of an airplane."
            Case "W"
              trivia = "He once owned the Texas Rangers baseball team."
          End Select
        Case "CLINTON"
          state = "Arkansas"
          trivia = "In college he did a good imitation of Elvis Presley."
        Case "OBAMA"
          state = "Illinois"
          trivia = "He was the eighth left-handed president."
        Case Else
          state = ""
          trivia = ""
      End Select
      If state <> "" Then
        lstOutput.Items.Clear()
        lstOutput.Items.Add("President " & pres & "'s" &
                            " home state was " & state & ".")
        lstOutput.Items.Add(trivia)
      End If
    End Sub
```

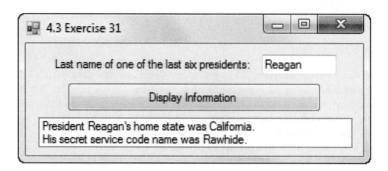

EXERCISES 4.4

1. The word "Income" becomes the caption embedded in the top of GroupBox1.

3. The **CheckBox1** check box becomes (or remains) unchecked.

5. The radio button becomes (or remains) unselected.

7. The radio button's caption becomes "Clear <u>A</u>ll".

9. `RadioButton1.Text = "Yes"`   **11.** `CheckBox1.Checked = True`

13. `RadioButton2` is on and `RadioButton1` is off.   **15.** Yes

17.
```
Private Sub CheckedChanged(...) Handles _
      radDeluxe.CheckedChanged, radSuper.CheckedChanged,
      chkUpgradedVideo.CheckedChanged, chkModem.CheckedChanged,
      chkMemory.CheckedChanged
  If radDeluxe.Checked Or radSuper.Checked Then
    Dim cost As Double = 0
    'Add amounts to the cost based upon selections.
    If radDeluxe.Checked Then
      cost += 1000
    Else   'Super model
      cost += 1500
    End If
    If chkUpgradedVideo.Checked Then
      cost += 200
    End If
    If chkModem.Checked Then
      cost += 30
    End If
    If chkMemory.Checked Then
      cost += 120
    End If
    txtTotalCost.Text = FormatCurrency(cost)
  Else
    MessageBox.Show("You must first select a model!")
  End If
End Sub
```

19.
```
Private Sub btnVote_Click(...) Handles btnVote.Click
  If radCandidate1.Checked Then
    txtVote.Text = "You voted for Kennedy."
  ElseIf radCandidate2.Checked Then
    txtVote.Text = "You voted for Nixon."
  Else
    txtVote.Text = "You voted for neither."
  End If
End Sub

Private Sub btnClear_Click(...) Handles btnClear.Click
  radCandidate1.Checked = False
  radCandidate2.Checked = False
End Sub
```

21.
```
Private Sub btnRecord_Click(...) Handles btnRecord.Click
  Dim majorSelected As Boolean
  Dim yearSelected As Boolean
  If lstMajors.Text = "" Then
    majorSelected = False
  Else
    majorSelected = True
  End If
```

```
      If (radFrosh.Checked Or radSoph.Checked Or radJunior.Checked Or
                        radSenior.Checked) Then
        yearSelected = True
      Else
        yearSelected = False
      End If
      If majorSelected And yearSelected Then
        MessageBox.Show("Information Processed")
      ElseIf Not majorSelected Then
        If Not yearSelected Then
          MessageBox.Show("You must select a Major and a Year.")
        Else
          MessageBox.Show("You must select a Major.")
        End If
      Else
        MessageBox.Show("You must select a Year.")
      End If
    End Sub
```

23.
```
    Private Sub CheckedChanged(...) Handles _
                  chkSenior.CheckedChanged, chkBlind.CheckedChanged,
                  chkSpouse.CheckedChanged, chkSpouseBlind.CheckedChanged
      Dim count As Integer = 0
      If chkSenior.Checked Then
        count += 1
      End If
      If chkBlind.Checked Then
        count += 1
      End If
      If chkSpouse.Checked Then
        count += 1
      End If
      If chkSpouseBlind.Checked Then
        count += 1
      End If
      txtOutput.Text = CStr(count)
    End Sub
```

25.
```
    Private Sub btnCalculate_Click(...) Handles btnCalculate.Click
      Dim fee As Double = 0
      If radAdult.Checked Or radSenior.Checked Then
        Dim numExtras As Integer = 0
        If chkTennis.Checked Then
          numExtras += 1
        End If
        If chkLocker.Checked Then
          numExtras += 1
        End If
        If chkLaundry.Checked Then
          numExtras += 1
        End If
        If radAdult.Checked Then
          fee = 100 + numExtras * 25
        Else
          fee = 75 + numExtras * 25
        End If
        txtFee.Text = FormatCurrency(fee)
      Else
        MessageBox.Show("You must select a membership category.")
      End If
    End Sub
```

CHAPTER 5

EXERCISES 5.1

1. 203   **3.** The population will double in 24 years.

5. 27 is an odd number.   **7.** Your state income tax is 750.

9. age before beauty

11. The function header should end with "As String", not "As Integer".

13.
```
Private Sub btnDetermine_Click(...) Handles btnDetermine.Click
    Dim radius, height As Double
    lstOutput.Items.Clear()
    radius = CDbl(InputBox("Enter radius of can (in centimeters):"))
    height = CDbl(InputBox("Enter height of can (in centimeters):"))
    lstOutput.Items.Add("A can of radius " & radius & " and height " &
                        height)
    lstOutput.Items.Add("requires " & TinArea(radius, height) &
                        " square centimeters")
    lstOutput.Items.Add("of tin.")
End Sub

Function TinArea(ByVal radius As Double, ByVal ht As Double) As Double
    'Calculate surface area of a cylindrical can.
    Return 6.283 * (radius ^ 2 + radius * ht)
End Function
```

15.
```
Private Sub btnCalculate_Click(...) Handles btnCalculate.Click
    Dim weight As Double = CDbl(txtWeight.Text)
    Dim height As Double = CDbl(txtHeight.Text)
    txtBMI.Text = CStr(BMI(weight, height))
End Sub

Function BMI(ByVal w As Double, ByVal h As Double) As Double
    Return Math.Round((703 * w) / (h ^ 2))
End Function
```

17.
```
Private Sub btnDetermine_Click(...) Handles btnDetermine.Click
    Dim popcorn, butter, bucket, price As Double  'amount in dollars
    popcorn = CDbl(InputBox("What is the cost of the popcorn kernels?"))
    butter = CDbl(InputBox("What is the cost of the butter substitute?"))
    bucket = CDbl(InputBox("What is the cost of the bucket?"))
    price = CDbl(InputBox("What is the sale price?"))
    txtProfit.Text = FormatCurrency(Profit(popcorn, butter, bucket, price))
End Sub
```

```
Function Profit(ByVal popcorn As Double, ByVal butter As Double,
               ByVal bucket As Double, ByVal price As Double) As Double
  'Calculate the profit on a bucket of popcorn
  Return price − (popcorn + butter + bucket)
End Function
```

19.
```
Private Sub btnCompute_Click(...) Handles btnCompute.Click
   Dim weight As Double
   weight = CDbl(txtWeight.Text)
   txtOutput.Text = "The cost of mailing the letter was " &
                    FormatCurrency(Cost(weight)) & "."
End Sub

Function Ceil(ByVal x As Double) As Double
  Return −Int(−x)
End Function

Function Cost(ByVal weight As Double) As Double
  Return 0.05 + 0.1 * Ceil(weight − 1)
End Function
```

21.
```
Private Sub btnAddressNGreet_Click(...) Handles btnAddressNGreet.Click
   Dim name As String
   name = InputBox("Enter the senator's name:")
   lstOutput.Items.Add("The Honorable " & name)
   lstOutput.Items.Add("United States Senate")
   lstOutput.Items.Add("Washington, DC 20001")
   lstOutput.Items.Add("")
   lstOutput.Items.Add("Dear Senator " & LastName(name) & ",")
End Sub

Function LastName(ByVal name As String) As String
  Dim spacePos As Integer
  spacePos = name.IndexOf(" ")
  Return name.Substring(spacePos + 1)
End Function
```

```
23. Private Sub btnDetermine_Click(...) Handles btnDetermine.Click
      If IsLeapYear(CInt(mtbYear.Text)) Then    'mask is 0000
        txtOutput.Text = mtbYear.Text & " is a leap year."
      Else
        txtOutput.Text = mtbYear.Text & " is not a leap year."
      End If
    End Sub

    Function IsLeapYear(ByVal yr As Integer) As Boolean
      Dim date1 As Date = CDate("#1/1/" & yr & "#")
      Dim date2 As Date = CDate("#1/1/" & (yr + 1) & "#")
      If DateDiff(DateInterval.Day, date1, date2) = 366 Then
        Return True
      Else
        Return False
      End If
    End Function
```

EXERCISES 5.2

1. 88 keys on a piano

3. You look dashing in blue.

5. 1440 minutes in a day

7. Why do clocks run clockwise?

   Because they were invented in the northern hemisphere where sundials go clockwise.

9. It was the best of times.
   It was the worst of times.

11. divorced
    beheaded
    died
    divorced
    beheaded
    survived

13. 24 blackbirds
    baked in
    a pie.

15. The first 6 letters are Visual.

17. Cost: $550.00
    Shipping cost: $20.00
    Total cost: $570.00

19. You passed with a grade of 92.

21. There is a parameter in the Sub procedure, but no argument in the statement calling the Sub procedure.

23. Since Handles is a keyword, it cannot be used as the name of a Sub procedure.

```
25. Private Sub btnDisplay_Click(...) Handles btnDisplay.Click
      Dim num As Integer = 7
      Lucky(num)
    End Sub

    Sub Lucky(ByVal num As Integer)
      txtOutput.Text = num & " is a lucky number."
    End Sub

27. Private Sub btnDisplay_Click(...) Handles btnDisplay.Click
      Tallest("redwood", 362)
      Tallest("pine", 223)
    End Sub

    Sub Tallest(ByVal tree As String, ByVal ht As Double)
      lstBox.Items.Add("The tallest " & tree &
                    " tree in the U.S. is " & ht & " feet.")
    End Sub
```

29.
```
Private Sub btnDisplay_Click(...) Handles btnDisplay.Click
  DisplaySource()
  Majors(16.7, "business")
  Majors(1.0, "computer science")
End Sub

Sub DisplaySource()
  Dim phrase As String
  phrase = "According to a 2008 survey of college freshmen" &
            " taken by"
  lstOutput.Items.Add(phrase)
  lstOutput.Items.Add("the Higher Education Research Institute:")
End Sub

Sub Majors(ByVal percentOfStudents As Double, ByVal field As String)
    lstOutput.Items.Add(percentOfStudents &
               " percent said they intend to major in " & field & ".")
End Sub
```

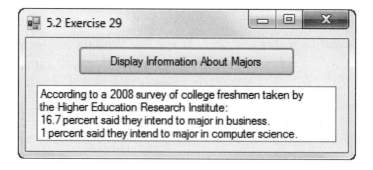

31.
```
Private Sub btnDisplay_Click(...) Handles btnDisplay.Click
  Dim num As Double
  num = CDbl(txtBox.Text)
  Sum(num)
  Product(num)
End Sub

Sub Sum(ByVal num As Double)
  Dim phrase As String
  phrase = "The sum of your favorite number with itself is "
  lstOutput.Items.Add(phrase & (num + num) & ".")
End Sub

Sub Product(ByVal num As Double)
  Dim phrase As String
  phrase = "The product of your favorite number with itself is "
  lstOutput.Items.Add(phrase & (num * num) & ".")
End Sub
```

33.
```
Private Sub btnDisplay_Click(...) Handles btnDisplay.Click
    ShowVerse("lamb", "baa")
    ShowVerse("duck", "quack")
    ShowVerse("firefly", "blink")
End Sub

Sub ShowVerse(ByVal animal As String, ByVal sound As String)
    'Display a verse from Old McDonald Had a Farm
    lstOutput.Items.Add("Old McDonald had a farm. Eyi eyi oh.")
    lstOutput.Items.Add("And on his farm he had a " & animal &
                   ".  Eyi eyi oh.")
    lstOutput.Items.Add("With a " & sound & " " & sound & " here, and a " &
                   sound & " " & sound & " there.")
    lstOutput.Items.Add("Here a " & sound & ", there a " & sound &
                   ", everywhere a " & sound & " " & sound & ".")
    lstOutput.Items.Add("Old McDonald had a farm. Eyi eyi oh.")
    lstOutput.Items.Add("")
End Sub
```

35.
```
Private Sub btnDetermine_Click(...) Handles btnDetermine.Click
    Dim grade1 As Double = CDbl(txtGrade1.Text)
    Dim grade2 As Double = CDbl(txtGrade2.Text)
    Dim grade3 As Double = CDbl(txtGrade3.Text)
    DisplayHighestTwo(grade1, grade2, grade3)
End Sub

Sub DisplayHighestTwo(ByVal grade1 As Double, ByVal grade2 As Double,
                   ByVal grade3 As Double)
    Dim first, second As Double
    first = Max(grade1, grade2)
    If first = grade1 Then
        second = Max(grade2, grade3)
    Else
        second = Max(grade1, grade3)
    End If
```

```
        txtOutput.Text = "The highest two grades are " & first &
                         " and " & second & "."
    End Sub

    Function Max(ByVal num1 As Double, ByVal num2 As Double) As Double
      If num1 <= num2 Then
        Return num2
      Else
        Return num1
      End If
    End Function
```

37.
```
    Private Sub btnAlphabetize_Click(...) Handles btnAlphabetize.Click
      Dim word1 = txtWord1.Text
      Dim word2 = txtWord2.Text
      DisplayWords(word1, word2)
    End Sub

    Sub DisplayWords(ByVal word1 As String, ByVal word2 As String)
      Dim first, second As String
      If word1 <= word2 Then
        first = word1
        second = word2
      Else
        first = word2
        second = word1
      End If
      lstOutput.Items.Add(first)
      lstOutput.Items.Add(second)
    End Sub
```

EXERCISES 5.3

1. `Gabriel was born in the year 1980.`

3. `The state flower of Florida is the Orange Blossom.`

5. `The first 3 letters of EDUCATION are EDU.`

7. `Current inventory: 2` is displayed both times the button is clicked. The second click also produces the message "Insufficient inventory, purchase cancelled.")

9.
```
sum = 4
difference = 2
```

11.
```
    Private Sub btnDisplay_Click(...) Handles btnDisplay.Click
      Dim firstName As String = ""
      Dim lastName As String = ""
      Dim salary, newSalary As Double
      InputData(firstName, lastName, salary)
      newSalary = RaisedSalary(salary)
      DisplayOutput(firstName, lastName, newSalary)
    End Sub

    Sub InputData(ByRef firstName As String, ByRef lastName As String,
                  ByRef salary As Double)
      firstName = txtFirstName.Text
      lastName = txtLastName.Text
      salary = CDbl(txtCurrentSalary.Text)
    End Sub
```

```
Function RaisedSalary(ByVal salary As Double) As Double
  If salary <= 40000 Then
    Return 1.05 * salary
  Else
    Return salary + 2000 + 0.02 * (salary — 40000)
  End If
End Function

Sub DisplayOutput(ByVal firstName As String, ByVal lastName As String,
               ByVal newSalary As Double)
  txtOutput.Text = "New salary for " & firstName & " " & lastName &
               " is " & FormatCurrency(newSalary) & "."
End Sub
```

13.
```
Private Sub btnCalculate_Click(...) Handles btnCalculate.Click
  Dim annualRateOfInterest, monthlyPayment, begBalance As Double
  Dim intForMonth, redOfPrincipal, endBalance As Double
  InputData(annualRateOfInterest, monthlyPayment, begBalance)
  Calculate(annualRateOfInterest, monthlyPayment, begBalance,
        intForMonth, redOfPrincipal, endBalance)
  DisplayData(intForMonth, redOfPrincipal, endBalance)
End Sub

Sub InputData(ByRef annualRateOfInterest As Double,
         ByRef monthlyPayment As Double,
         ByRef begBalance As Double)
  annualRateOfInterest = CDbl(txtAnnualRateOfInterest.Text)
  monthlyPayment = CDbl(txtMonthlyPayment.Text)
  begBalance = CDbl(txtBegBalance.Text)
End Sub

Sub Calculate(ByVal annualRateOfInterest As Double,
         ByVal monthlyPayment As Double,
         ByVal begBalance As Double, ByRef intForMonth As Double,
         ByRef redOfPrincipal As Double, ByRef endBalance As Double)
  Dim monthlyRateOfInterest As Double = annualRateOfInterest / 12
  intForMonth = (monthlyRateOfInterest / 100) * begBalance
  redOfPrincipal = monthlyPayment — intForMonth
  endBalance = begBalance — redOfPrincipal
End Sub

Sub DisplayData(ByVal intForMonth, ByVal redOfPrincipal,
            ByVal endBalance)
  txtIntForMonth.Text = FormatCurrency(intForMonth)
  txtRedOfPrincipal.Text = FormatCurrency(redOfPrincipal)
  txtEndBalance.Text = FormatCurrency(endBalance)
End Sub
```

CHAPTER 6

EXERCISES 6.1

1. 18   3. 15   5. Maximum number: 7

7. It is an infinite loop, and the listbox will have the letter q, not the value of q in it.

9. Do and Loop are interchanged   11. While num >= 7   13. Until response <> "Y"

15. `Until name = ""`   **17.** `Until (a <= 1) Or (a >= 3)`   **19.** `While n = 0`

21.
```
Private Sub Button1_Click(...) Handles btnDisplay.Click
    Dim name As String
    Dim i As Integer
    Do While i < 3
      name = InputBox("Enter a number from 1 to 9:")
      lstOutput.Items.Add(name)
      i = i + 1
    Loop
End Sub
```

23.
```
Private Sub btnDisplay_Click(...) Handles btnDisplay.Click
    Dim celsius As Double = 10
    lstOutput.Items.Add("Celsius    Fahrenheit")
    Do While celsius <= 95
      lstOutput.Items.Add("    " & celsius & "            " &
                          Fahrenheit(celsius))
      celsius += 5
    Loop
End Sub

Function Fahrenheit(ByVal celsius As Double) As Double
    'Convert Celsius to Fahrenheit
    Return (9 / 5) * celsius + 32
End Function
```

25.
```
Private Sub btnLocate_Click(...) Handles btnLocate.Click
    Dim word As String = ""
    Dim rPlace, nPlace As Integer
    Do
      InputWord(word)
      rPlace = word.IndexOf("r")
      nPlace = word.IndexOf("n")
```

```
      If (rPlace = -1) Or (nPlace = -1) Then
        MessageBox.Show("That word does not contain both r and n.", "")
      End If
    Loop Until (rPlace > -1) And (nPlace > -1)
    ShowFirst(rPlace, nPlace)
  End Sub

  Sub InputWord(ByRef word As String)
    Dim prompt As String
    prompt = "Enter a word containing the letters 'r' and 'n'."
    word = InputBox(prompt, "Enter Word")
  End Sub

  Sub ShowFirst(ByVal rPlace As Integer, ByVal nPlace As Integer)
    'Tell which letter, r or n, comes first.
    If nPlace > rPlace Then
      txtOutput.Text = "The letter r is first."
    Else
      txtOutput.Text = "The letter n is first."
    End If
  End Sub
```

27.
```
Private Sub btnCompute_Click(...) Handles btnCompute.Click
    Dim num, max, min As Double
    Dim count As Double = 0
    Dim prompt As String = "Enter a nonnegative number. " &
                           "Enter -1 to terminate entering numbers."
    num = CDbl(InputBox(prompt))
    max = num
    min = num
    Do While num >= 0
      count += 1
      num = CDbl(InputBox(prompt))
      If (num <> -1) Then
        If num < min Then
          min = num
        End If
        If num > max Then
          max = num
        End If
      End If
    Loop
    If count > 0 Then
      txtRange.Text = CStr(max - min)
    Else
      MessageBox.Show("No numbers were entered.")
    End If
  End Sub
```

```
29. Private Sub btnFind_Click(...) Handles btnFind.Click
        Dim m, n, t As Integer
        InputIntegers(m, n)
        Do While n <> 0
          t = n
          n = m Mod n      'Remainder after m is divided by n
          m = t
        Loop
        txtOutput.Text = CStr(m)
    End Sub

    Sub InputIntegers(ByRef m As Integer, ByRef n As Integer)
        m = CInt(txtM.Text)
        n = CInt(txtN.Text)
    End Sub
```

```
31. Private Sub btnCompute_Click(...) Handles btnCompute.Click
        Dim age As Integer = 1
        Do While 1980 + age <> age ^ 2
          age += 1
        Loop
        txtOutput.Text = age & " years old"
    End Sub
```

```
33. Private Sub btnDetermine_Click(...) Handles btnDetermine.Click
        Dim amount As Double = 100
        Dim yrs As Integer = 0
        Do Until amount < 1
          amount = 0.5 * amount
          yrs += 28
        Loop
        txtOutput.Text = yrs & " years"
    End Sub
```

```
35. Private Sub btnDetermine_Click(...) Handles btnDetermine.Click
        Const INTEREST_PER_MONTH As Double = 0.005
        Dim loanAmount As Double = 15000
        Dim months As Integer = 0
        Dim balance As Double = loanAmount
        Do Until balance < loanAmount / 2
          balance = (1 + INTEREST_PER_MONTH) * balance — 290
          months += 1
        Loop
        txtOutput.Text = months & " months"
    End Sub
```

```
37. Private Sub btnDetermine_Click(...) Handles btnDetermine.Click
        Dim months As Integer = 0
        Dim balance As Double = 10000
        Do Until balance < 600
          balance = 1.003 * balance — 600
```

```
        months += 1
    Loop
    txtOutput.Text = months & " months; " & FormatCurrency(balance)
End Sub
```

EXERCISES **6.2**

1. Pass #1
   Pass #2
   Pass #3
   Pass #4

3. 2
   4
   6
   8
   Who do we appreciate?

5. 5
   6
   7

7. 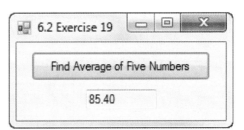•••••••••

9. 4

11. The loop is never executed since 25 is greater than 1 and the step is negative.

13. The For … Next loop will not execute since 20 is greater than 0. You must add **step −1** to the end of the For statement.

15.
```
Private Sub btnDisplay_Click(...) Handles btnDisplay.Click
    For num As Integer = 1 To 9 Step 2
      lstBox.Items.Add(num)
    Next
End Sub
```

17.
```
Private Sub btndisplay_Click(...) Handles btndisplay.Click
    For i As Integer = 2 To 100 Step 2
      lstOutput.Items.Add(i)
    Next
End Sub
```

19.
```
Private Sub btnFind_Click(...) Handles btnFind.Click
    Dim sum As Double = 0, num as Double = 0
    For i As Integer = 1 To 5
      num = CDbl(InputBox("Enter #" & i))
      sum += num
    Next
    txtAverage.Text = FormatNumber(sum / 5, 2)
End Sub
```

21.
```
Private Sub btnCompute_Click(...) Handles btnCompute.Click
    Dim sum As Double = 0
    For denominator As Double = 1 To 100
      sum += 1 / denominator
    Next
    txtOutput.Text = FormatNumber(sum, 5)
End Sub
```

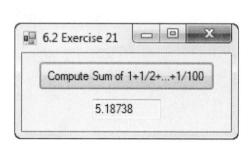

23.
```
Private Sub btnCalculate_Click(...) Handles btnCalculate.Click
    Dim value As Double = 20000
    For i As Integer = 1 To 5
      value = 0.85 * value
      lstOutput.Items.Add(i & ": " & FormatCurrency(value))
    Next
End Sub
```

25.
```
Private Sub btnCompute_Click(...) Handles btnCompute.Click
    Dim PERCENT_RAISE As Double = 0.05
    Dim name As String, age As Integer, salary As Double
    Dim earnings As Double = 0
    name = txtName.Text
    age = CInt(txtAge.Text)
    salary = CDbl(txtSalary.Text)
    For i As Integer = age To 64
      earnings += salary
      salary = salary + (PERCENT_RAISE * salary)
    Next
    txtOutput.Text = name & " will earn about " &
                     FormatCurrency(earnings, 0) & "."
End Sub
```

```
27. Private Sub btnComputeIdealWeights_Click(...) Handles _
                     btnComputeIdealWeights.Click
      Dim lower, upper As Integer
      lstWeightTable.Items.Clear()
      InputBounds(lower, upper)
      ShowWeights(lower, upper)
    End Sub

    Function IdealMan(ByVal height As Integer) As Double
      'Compute the ideal weight of a man given his height
      Return 4 * height - 128
    End Function

    Function IdealWoman(ByVal height As Integer) As Double
      'Compute the ideal weight of a woman given her height
      Return 3.5 * height - 108
    End Function

    Sub InputBounds(ByRef lower As Integer, ByRef upper As Integer)
      lower = CInt(InputBox("Enter lower bound on height in inches:"))
      upper = CInt(InputBox("Enter upper bound on height in inches:"))
    End Sub

    Sub ShowWeights(ByVal lower As Integer, ByVal upper As Integer)
      lstWeightTable.Items.Add("          " & "WEIGHT  " & " " & "WEIGHT")
      lstWeightTable.Items.Add("HEIGHT" & "  " & "WOMEN   " & " " & "MEN")
      For height As Integer = lower To upper
        lstWeightTable.Items.Add(height & "      " &
                 FormatNumber(IdealWoman(height), 1) &
                 "    " & FormatNumber(IdealMan(height), 1))
      Next
    End Sub


29. Private Sub btnDisplay_Click(...) Handles btnDisplay.Click
      Dim balance As Double = 0
      Dim yr As Integer = 2010
      For i As Integer = 1 To 120
        balance = (1.0025) * balance + 100
        If i Mod 12 = 0 Then
          lstOutput.Items.Add(yr & "  " & FormatCurrency(balance))
          yr += 1
        End If
      Next
    End Sub


31. Private Sub btnAnalyze_Click(...) Handles btnAnalyze.Click
      Const DECAY_RATE As Double = 0.12
      Dim grams As Double
      grams = 10
      For yearNum As Integer = 1 To 5
        grams = (1 - DECAY_RATE) * grams
      Next
      lstOutput.Items.Add("Beginning with 10 grams of cobalt 60,")
      lstOutput.Items.Add(FormatNumber(grams) &
                     " grams remain after 5 years.")
    End Sub
```

33.
```
Private Sub btnDisplay_Click(...) Handles btnDisplay.Click
    Dim price, quantity As Double
    lstOutput.Items.Clear()
    quantity = 80   'current crop of soybeans in millions of bushels
    lstOutput.Items.Add("YEAR" & "    " & "QUANTITY" & "    " & "PRICE")
    For yr As Integer = 2010 To 2020
      price = 20 — 0.1 * quantity
      lstOutput.Items.Add(yr & "    " & FormatNumber(quantity) &
                          "       " & FormatCurrency(price))
      quantity = 5 * price — 10
    Next
  End Sub
```

35.
```
Private Sub btnAnalyzeOptions_Click(...) Handles btnAnalyzeOptions.Click
    'Compare salaries
    Dim opt1, opt2 As Double
    opt1 = Option1()
    opt2 = Option2()
    lstOutput.Items.Add("Option 1 = " & FormatCurrency(opt1))
    lstOutput.Items.Add("Option 2 = " & FormatCurrency(opt2))
    If opt1 > opt2 Then
      lstOutput.Items.Add("Option 1 pays better.")
    ElseIf opt1 = opt2 Then
      lstOutput.Items.Add("Options pay the same.")
    Else
      lstOutput.Items.Add("Option 2 pays better.")
    End If
  End Sub

  Function Option1() As Double
    'Compute total salary with a flat salary of $100/day
    Dim sum As Integer = 0
    For i As Integer = 1 To 10
      sum += 100
    Next
    Return sum
  End Function

  Function Option2() As Double
    'Compute total salary starting at $1 and doubling each day
    Dim sum As Integer = 0, daySalary As Integer = 1
    For i As Integer = 1 To 10
      sum += daySalary
      daySalary = 2 * daySalary
    Next
    Return sum
  End Function
```

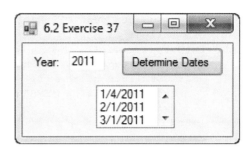

37.
```
Private Sub btnDetermine_Click(...) Handles btnDetermine.Click
    Dim dt As Date = CDate("#1/1/" & mtbYear.Text & "#")
    Dim d As Date
    For i As Integer = 0 To 11
      d = dt.AddMonths(i)
      lstOutput.Items.Add(FirstTuesday(d))
    Next
End Sub

Function FirstTuesday(ByVal d As Date) As Date
    For i As Integer = 0 To 6
      If FormatDateTime(d.AddDays(i),
                        DateFormat.LongDate).StartsWith("Tuesday") Then
        Return d.AddDays(i)
      End If
    Next
End Function
```

EXERCISES 6.3

1. Mozart　　3. Tchaikovsky　　5. 3　　7. 90　　9. 80　　11. 240

13.
```
Private Sub btnCount_Click(...) Handles btnCount.Click
    Dim numWon As Integer = 0
    For i As Integer = 0 To lstBox.Items.Count − 1
      If CStr(lstBox.Items(i)) = "USC" Then
        numWon += 1
      End If
    Next
    txtOutput.Text = CStr(numWon)
End Sub
```

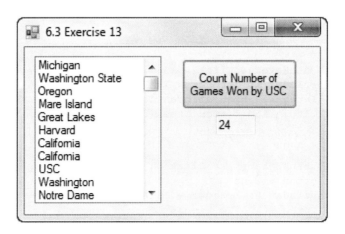

15.
```
Private Sub btnCount_Click(...) Handles btnDetermine.Click
    Dim college As String = txtCollege.Text
    txtOutput.Clear()
    For i As Integer = 0 To lstBox.Items.Count — 1
      If CStr(lstBox.Items(i)) = college Then
        txtOutput.Text = "YES"
        Exit For
      End If
    Next
    If txtOutput.Text = "" Then
      txtOutput.Text = "NO"
    End If
End Sub
```

or

```
Private Sub btnCount_Click(...) Handles btnDetermine.Click
  Dim college As String = txtCollege.Text
  Dim i As Integer = 0
  Dim found As Boolean = False
  Do Until (found = True) Or (i = lstBox.Items.Count)
    If CStr(lstBox.Items(i)) = college Then
      found = True
    End If
    i += 1
  Loop
  If found Then
    txtOutput.Text = "YES"
  Else
    txtOutput.Text = "NO"
  End If
End Sub
```

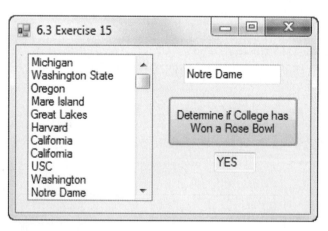

17.
```
Private Sub btnReverse_Click(...) Handles btnReverse.Click
    Dim highestIndex As Integer = lstBox.Items.Count — 1
    For i As Integer = highestIndex To 0 Step —1
      lstBox2.Items.Add(lstBox.Items(i))
    Next
End Sub
```

19.
```
Private Sub btnAlphabetize_Click(...) Handles btnAlphabetize.Click
    lstBox2.Sorted = True
    Dim highestIndex As Integer = lstBox.Items.Count — 1
    For i As Integer = 0 To highestIndex
      lstBox2.Items.Add(lstBox.Items(i))
    Next
End Sub
```

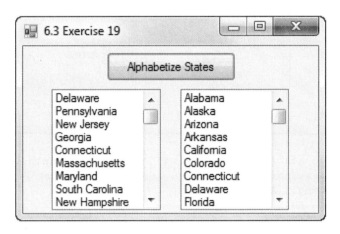

21.
```
Private Sub btnDisplay_Click(...) Handles btnDisplay.Click
    Dim highestIndex As Integer = lstBox.Items.Count − 1
    Dim state As String
    For i As Integer = 0 To highestIndex
      state = CStr(lstBox.Items(i))
      If state.Length = 7 Then
        lstBox2.Items.Add(state)
      End If
    Next
End Sub
```

23.
```
Private Sub btnDetermine_Click(...) Handles btnDetermine.Click
    Dim highestIndex As Integer = lstBox.Items.Count − 1
    Dim state As String
    For i As Integer = 0 To highestIndex
      state = CStr(lstBox.Items(i))
      If state.StartsWith("New") Then
        txtOutput.Text = state
        Exit For
      End If
    Next
  End Sub
```

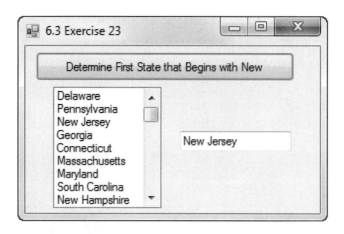

25.
```
Private Sub btnDisplay_Click(...) Handles btnDisplay.Click
    Dim highestIndex As Integer = lstBox.Items.Count − 1
    Dim maxLength As Integer = 0
    Dim state As String
    For i As Integer = 0 To highestIndex
      state = CStr(lstBox.Items(i))
      If state.Length > maxLength Then
        maxLength = state.Length
      End If
    Next
    For i As Integer = 0 To highestIndex
      state = CStr(lstBox.Items(i))
      If state.Length = maxLength Then
        lstBox2.Items.Add(state)
      End If
    Next
  End Sub
```

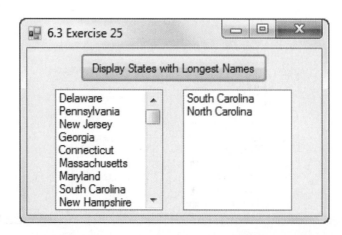

27.
```
Private Sub btnDetermine_Click(...) Handles btnDetermine.Click
    Dim highestIndex As Integer = lstBox.Items.Count - 1
    Dim state As String
    For i As Integer = 0 To highestIndex
      state = CStr(lstBox.Items(i))
      If NumberOfVowels(state) = 4 Then
        lstBox2.Items.Add(state)
      End If
    Next
End Sub

Function NumberOfVowels(ByVal word As String) As Integer
  Dim numVowels As Integer = 0
  word = word.ToUpper
  Dim letter As String
  Dim numLetters As Integer = word.Length
  For i As Integer = 0 To (numLetters - 1)
    letter = word.Substring(i, 1)
    If (letter = "A") Or (letter = "E") Or (letter = "I") Or
      (letter = "O") Or (letter = "U") Then
      numVowels += 1
    End If
  Next
  Return numVowels
End Function
```

29.
```
Private Sub btnDetermine_Click(...) Handles btnDetermine.Click
    Dim highestIndex As Integer = lstBox.Items.Count - 1
    Dim state As String
    Dim maxNumOfVowels = 0
    For i As Integer = 0 To highestIndex
      state = CStr(lstBox.Items(i))
      If NumberOfVowels(state) > maxNumOfVowels Then
        maxNumOfVowels = NumberOfVowels(state)
      End If
    Next
    txtOutput.Text = CStr(maxNumOfVowels)
End Sub

Function NumberOfVowels(ByVal word As String) As Integer
  Dim numVowels As Integer = 0
  word = word.ToUpper
  Dim letter As String
```

```
      Dim numLetters As Integer = word.Length
      For i As Integer = 0 To (numLetters — 1)
        letter = word.Substring(i, 1)
        If (letter = "A") Or (letter = "E") Or (letter = "I") Or
           (letter = "O") Or (letter = "U") Then
          numVowels += 1
        End If
      Next
      Return numVowels
    End Function
```

31.
```
Private Sub btnDisplay_Click(...) Handles btnDisplay.Click
    txtOutput.Text = CStr(lstBox.Items(0))
End Sub
```

33.
```
Private Sub btnDisplay_Click(...) Handles btnDisplay.Click
    txtOutput.Text = CStr(lstBox.Items(4))
End Sub
```

35.
```
Private Sub btnRecord_Click(...) Handles btnRecord.Click
    lstGrades.Items.Add(txtGrade.Text)
    txtGrade.Clear()
    txtGrade.Focus()
End Sub
```

```
    Private Sub btnCalculate_Click(...) Handles btnCalculate.Click
      Dim sum As Double = 0
      Dim minGrade As Double = 100
      If lstGrades.Items.Count > 0 Then
        For i As Integer = 0 To lstGrades.Items.Count − 1
          sum += CDbl(lstGrades.Items(i))
          If CDbl(lstGrades.Items(i)) < minGrade Then
            minGrade = CDbl(lstGrades.Items(i))
          End If
        Next
      Else
        MessageBox.Show("You must first enter some grades.")
      End If
      txtAverage.Text = FormatNumber(sum / lstGrades.Items.Count, 2)
      txtLowest.Text = CStr(minGrade)
    End Sub
```

37.
```
    Private Sub btnRecord_Click(...) Handles btnRecord.Click
      lstGrades.Items.Add(txtGrade.Text)
      txtGrade.Clear()
      txtGrade.Focus()
    End Sub

    Private Sub btnCalculate_Click(...) Handles btnCalculate.Click
      Dim sum As Double = 0
      Dim maxGrade As Double = 0
      Dim minGrade As Double = 100
      If lstGrades.Items.Count > 0 Then
        For i As Integer = 0 To lstGrades.Items.Count − 1
          sum += CDbl(lstGrades.Items(i))
          If CDbl(lstGrades.Items(i)) > maxGrade Then
            maxGrade = CDbl(lstGrades.Items(i))
          End If
          If CDbl(lstGrades.Items(i)) < minGrade Then
            minGrade = CDbl(lstGrades.Items(i))
          End If
        Next
      Else
        MessageBox.Show("You must first enter some grades.")
      End If
      txtAverage.Text = FormatNumber(sum / lstGrades.Items.Count, 2)
      txtRange.Text = CStr(maxGrade − minGrade)
    End Sub
```

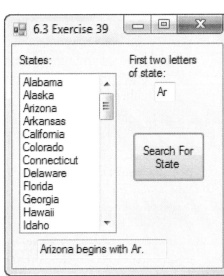

39.
```
Private Sub btnSearch_Click(...) Handles btnSearch.Click
    Dim letters As String = mtbFirstTwoLetters.Text.ToUpper
    Dim i As Integer = 49     'index of the state currently considered
    Do Until (CStr(lstStates.Items(i)).ToUpper <= letters) Or (i = 0)
      i = i - 1
    Loop
    If CStr(lstStates.Items(i + 1)).ToUpper.StartsWith(letters) Then
      txtOutput.Text = CStr(lstStates.Items(i + 1)) & " begins with " &
                    mtbFirstTwoLetters.Text & "."
    ElseIf CStr(lstStates.Items(0)).ToUpper.StartsWith(letters) Then
      txtOutput.Text = CStr(lstStates.Items(0)) & " begins with " &
                    mtbFirstTwoLetters.Text & "."
    Else
      txtOutput.Text = "No state begins with " &
                    mtbFirstTwoLetters.Text & "."
    End If
End Sub
```

CHAPTER 7

EXERCISES 7.1

1. `101`   3. `Have a soup spoon.`   5. `No`   7. `12`

9. `You have a trio.`   11. `Your average is 80`

13. `Slumdog Millionaire won in 2009`   15. `one,two,three`

17. `29`   19. `Pearl Harbor: 1941`

21. `contains a 19th-century date`   23. `6 words begin with a vowel`

25. `4`
    `6`
    `2`

27. a. `Superior` (last name in alphabetical order)
    b. `Erie`   (first name in alphabetical order)
    c. `Huron`   (first name in the array)
    d. `Superior` (last name in the array)
    e. `5`   (number of names in the array)
    f. `Ontario` (second name in the array)
    g. `3`   (first array subscript whose element is Erie)

29. a. `6.5` (greatest population of a New England state)
    b. `0.7` (least population of a New England state)
    c. `3.5` (first population in the array)
    d. `1.3` (last population in the array)
    e. `6`   (number of numbers in the array)
    f. `1.1` (fourth population in the array)
    g. `3`   (first array subscript whose element is 1.1)

31. a. `lstOutput.Items.Add(states.First)`
       or `lstOutput.Items.Add(states(0))`
    b. `For i As Integer = 0 To 12`
          `lstOutput.Items.Add(states(i))`
       `Next`
    c. `lstOutput.Items.Add(states.Last)`
       or `lstOutput.Items.Add(states(49))`

d. `lstOutput.Items.Add(CStr(Array.IndexOf(states, "Ohio") + 1))`

e. `lstOutput.Items.Add(states(1))`

f. `lstOutput.Items.Add(states(19))`

g.
```
For i As Integer = (states.Count - 9) To (states.Count)
    lstOutput.Items.Add(states(i - 1))
Next
```

33.
```
Function Task(ByVal nums() As Integer) As Integer
    Dim sum As Integer = 0
    For Each num As Integer In nums
        sum += num
    Next
    Return sum
End Function
```

35.
```
Private Function LargestOdd(ByVal arrNums() As Integer) As Integer
    Dim i As Integer
    Dim curLargest As Integer = 0
    For i = 0 To arrNums.Length - 1
        If (arrNums(i) Mod 2 = 1) Then
            If arrNums(i) > curLargest Then
                curLargest = arrNums(i)
            End If
        End If
    Next
    Return curLargest
End Function
```

37.
```
Function Task(ByVal nums() As Integer) As Integer
    Dim twoDigits As Integer = 0
    For Each num As Integer In nums
        If (num > 9) And (num < 100) Then
            twoDigits += 1
        End If
    Next
    Return twoDigits
End Function
```

39. `nums(3)` should be changed to `nums()`

41. Logic error. The values of the array elements cannot be altered inside a For Each loop. The output will be 6.

43. `lstBox.Items.Add(line.Split(" "c).Count)`

45.
```
Private Sub btnDisplay_Click(...) Handles btnDisplay.Click
    Dim numStr() As String = IO.File.ReadAllLines("Numbers.txt")
    Dim nums(numStr.Count - 1) As Integer
    For i As Integer = 1 To nums.Count - 1
        nums(i) = CInt(numStr(i))
    Next
    lstOutput.Items.Add("Number of integers in the file: " & nums.Count)
    lstOutput.Items.Add("Sum of integers in the file: " & nums.Sum)
End Sub
```

47.
```
Private Sub btnDetermine_Click(...) Handles btnDetermine.Click
    Dim names() As String = IO.File.ReadAllLines("Names2.txt")
    Dim dups(names.Count - 1) As String
    Dim n As Integer = 0          'index for dups
    For i As Integer = 0 To names.Count - 2
        If (names(i + 1) = names(i)) And
                        (Array.IndexOf(dups, names(i)) = -1) Then
```

```
          dups(n) = names(i)
          n += 1
        End If
      Next
      If n = 0 Then
        lstOutput.Items.Add("No duplicates.")
      Else
        For i As Integer = 0 To n — 1
          lstOutput.Items.Add(dups(i))
        Next
      End If
    End Sub
```

49.
```
Private Sub btnDisplay_Click(...) Handles btnDisplay.Click
    Dim strDigits() As String = IO.File.ReadAllLines("Digits.txt")
    Dim freq(9) As Integer
    For i As Integer = 0 To strDigits.Count — 1
      freq(CInt(strDigits(i))) += 1
    Next
    lstOutput.Items.Add("Digit    Frequency")
    For i As Integer = 0 To 9
      lstOutput.Items.Add("  " & i & "            " & freq(i))
    Next
End Sub
```

51.
```
'Calculate the sum of even indexed entries in an array
Private Function SumAllEvenSubscripts(ByVal arrNums()) As Integer
  Dim sum As Integer = 0
  For i = 2 To arrNums.Length - 1 Step 2
    sum += arrNums(i)
  Next
  Return sum
End Function
```

53.
```
Private Sub btnProcessEggs_Click(...) Handles btnProcessEggs.Click
    Dim heaviest, lightest, ounces As Double
    Dim jumbo, xLarge, large, med, small As Integer
    heaviest = 0      'can be any number lower than lightest egg
    lightest = 100   'can be any number greater than heaviest egg
    Dim strEggs() As String = IO.File.ReadAllLines("Eggs.txt")
    Dim eggs(strEggs.Count — 1) As Double
    For i As Integer = 0 To eggs.Count — 1
      eggs(i) = CDbl(strEggs(i))
    Next
    For i As Integer = 0 To eggs.Count — 1
      ounces = eggs(i)
      If ounces > heaviest Then
        heaviest = ounces
      End if
      If ounces < lightest Then
        lightest = ounces
      End If
      Select Case ounces
        Case Is < 1.5
          'too small & cannot be sold
        Case Is < 1.75
          small += 1
        Case Is < 2
          med += 1
        Case Is < 2.25
          large += 1
        Case Is < 2.5
          xLarge += 1
        Case Else
          jumbo += 1
      End Select
    Next
    lstOutput.Items.Clear()
    lstOutput.Items.Add(jumbo & " Jumbo eggs")
    lstOutput.Items.Add(xLarge & " Extra Large eggs")
    lstOutput.Items.Add(large & " Large eggs")
    lstOutput.Items.Add(med & " Medium eggs")
    lstOutput.Items.Add(small & " Small eggs")
    If lightest <> 100 Then
      lstOutput.Items.Add("Lightest egg: " & lightest & " ounces")
      lstOutput.Items.Add("Heaviest egg: " & heaviest & " ounces")
    Else
      lstOutput.Items.Add("File is empty")
    End If
End Sub
```

55.
```
Dim colors() As String = IO.File.ReadAllLines("Colors.txt")

Private Sub btnDisplay_Click(...) Handles btnDisplay.Click
  Dim letter As String = mtbLetter.Text.ToUpper
  lstColors.Items.Clear()
  For Each hue As String In colors
    If hue.StartsWith(letter) Then
      lstColors.Items.Add(hue)
    End If
  Next
End Sub
```

57.
```
Dim colors() As String = IO.File.ReadAllLines("Colors.txt")

Private Sub btnDisplay_Click(...) Handles btnDisplay.Click
  Dim letter As String = mtbLetter.Text.ToUpper     'mask L
  lstColors.Items.Clear()
  For Each hue As String In SmallerArray(letter)
    lstColors.Items.Add(hue)
  Next
End Sub

Function SmallerArray(ByVal letter As String) As String()
  Dim smArray(colors.Count − 1) As String
  Dim counter As Integer = 0
  For Each hue As String In colors
    If hue.StartsWith(letter) Then
      smArray(counter) = hue
      counter += 1
    End If
  Next
  ReDim Preserve smArray(counter − 1)
  Return smArray
End Function
```

59.
```
Private Sub btnDisplay_Click(...) Handles btnDisplay.Click
  Dim lines() As String = IO.File.ReadAllLines("Sonnet.txt")
  Dim n = lines.Count − 1
  Dim numWords(n) As Integer
  For i As Integer = 0 To n
    numWords(i) = lines(i).Split(" "c).Count
  Next
  lstOutput.Items.Add("Average number of words per line: " &
                      FormatNumber(numWords.Average, 2))
  lstOutput.Items.Add("Total number of words: " & numWords.Sum)
End Sub
```

61.
```
Dim grades(99) As Integer        'stores grades
Dim numGrades As Integer         'number of grades stored

Private Sub btnRecord_Click(...) Handles btnRecord.Click
  'Add a score to the array
  'If no more room, then display error message.
  If numGrades >= 100 Then
    MessageBox.Show("100 scores have been entered.", "No more room.")
  Else
    grades(numGrades) = CInt(txtScore.Text)
    numGrades += 1
    lstOutput.Items.Clear()
    txtScore.Clear()
    txtScore.Focus()
  End If
End Sub


Private Sub btnDisplay_Click(...) Handles btnDisplay.Click
  'Display average of grades and the number of above average grades
  Dim temp() As Integer = grades
  ReDim Preserve temp(numGrades — 1)
  lstOutput.Items.Clear()
  lstOutput.Items.Add("The average grade is " &
                    FormatNumber(temp.Average, 2) & ".")
  lstOutput.Items.Add(NumAboveAverage(temp) &
                    " students scored above the average.")
End Sub


Function NumAboveAverage(ByVal temp() As Integer) As Integer
  'Count the number of scores above the average grade
  Dim avg As Double = temp.Average
  Dim num As Integer = 0
  For Each grade In temp
    If grade > avg Then
      num += 1
    End If
  Next
  Return num
End Function
```

63.
```
Private Sub btnDisplay_Click(...) Handles btnDisplay.Click
  If IsChainLink(txtSentence.Text) Then
    txtOutput.Text = "This sentence is a chain-link sentence."
  Else
    txtOutput.Text = "This sentence is not a chain-link sentence."
  End If
End Sub


Function IsChainLink(ByVal sentence As String) As Boolean
  'Analyze a sentence to see whether it is a chain-link sentence.
  Dim words(), ending As String
  'Split the sentence into words, removing commas first
  words = txtSentence.Text.Replace(",", "").Split(" "c)
  For i As Integer = 0 To words.Count — 2
    If (words(i).Length < 2) Or (words(i + 1).Length < 2) Then
      Return False    'If any word has is less than two letters.
    End If
    ending = words(i).Substring(words(i).Length — 2).ToUpper
```

```
        If ending <> words(i + 1).Substring(0, 2).ToUpper Then
          Return False    'If ending does not match beginning of next word.
        End If
      Next
      Return True  'If all words are ok, then it is a chain-link sentence.
  End Function
```

EXERCISES **7.2**

1. 2
   3

3. going
   offer
   can't

5. 6

7. 103

9. 8

11. 3 students have a grade of 100

13. 7
    5
    4
    3

15. The average after dropping the lowest grade is 80

17. 37 is a prime number

19.
```
Private Sub btnDisplay_Click(...) Handles btnDisplay.Click
    Dim nums() As Integer = {3, 5, 8, 10, 21}
    Dim query = From num In nums
                Where num Mod 2 = 0
                Select num
    txtOutput.Text = query.count & " even numbers"
End Sub
```

21.
```
Private Sub btnDisplay_Click(...) Handles btnDisplay.Click
    Dim dates() As String = IO.File.ReadAllLines("Dates.txt")
    Dim query = From yr In dates
                Where (CInt(yr) >= 1800) And (CInt(yr) <= 1899)
                Select yr
    If query.Count > 0 Then
      txtOutput.Text = "contains a 19th century date."
    Else
      txtOutput.Text = "does not contain a 19th century date."
    End If
End Sub
```

23.
```
Private Sub btnDisplay_Click(...) Handles btnDisplay.Click
    Dim nums() As Integer = {2, 6, 4}
    Dim query = From num In nums
                Order By Array.IndexOf(nums, num) Descending
    For Each num As Integer In query
      lstOutput.Items.Add(num)
    Next
End Sub
```

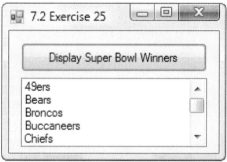

25.
```
Private Sub btnDisplay_Click(...) Handles btnDisplay.Click
    Dim teams() As String = IO.File.ReadAllLines("SBWinners.txt")
    Dim query = From team In teams
                Order By team Ascending
                Distinct
    For Each team As String In query
      lstOutput.Items.Add(team)
    Next
End Sub
```

27.
```
Dim teamNames() As String = IO.File.ReadAllLines("SBWinners.txt")

Private Sub btnDetermine_Click(...) Handles btnDetermine.Click
    'Display the number of Super Bowls won by the team in the text box
    Dim query = From team In teamNames
                Where team.ToUpper = txtName.Text.ToUpper
                Select team
    txtNumWon.Text = CStr(query.Count)
End Sub
```

29.
```
Private Sub btnDisplay_Click(...) Handles btnDisplay.Click
    Dim query1 = From grade In IO.File.ReadAllLines("Final.txt")
                 Select CInt(grade)
    Dim avg As Double = query1.Average
    Dim query2 = From grade In IO.File.ReadAllLines("Final.txt")
                 Where CInt(grade) > avg
                 Select grade
    txtAverage.Text = FormatNumber(avg)
    txtAboveAve.Text = FormatPercent(query2.Count / query1.Count)
End Sub
```

31.
```
Private Sub btnDisplay_Click(...) Handles btnDisplay.Click
    Dim states() As String = IO.File.ReadAllLines("States.txt")
    ReDim Preserve states(12)
    Dim query = From state In states
                Order By state
                Select state
```

```
      For Each state As String In query
        lstOutput.Items.Add(state)
      Next
    End Sub
```

33.
```
Private Sub btnDisplay_Click(...) Handles btnDisplay.Click
    Dim query = From pres In IO.File.ReadAllLines("USPres.txt")
                Let lastName = pres.Split(" "c).Last
                Order By lastName
                Select pres
    For Each pres As String In query
      lstOutput.Items.Add(pres)
    Next
    Distinct
End Sub
```

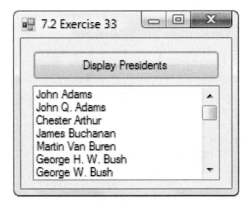

35.
```
Dim nations() As String = IO.File.ReadAllLines("Nations.txt")

Private Sub frmNations_Load(...) Handles MyBase.Load
  lstNations.DataSource = nations
  lstNations.SelectedItem = Nothing
End Sub

Private Sub txtNations_TextChanged(...) Handles txtNation.TextChanged
  Dim query = From nation In nations
              Where nation.StartsWith(txtNation.Text)
              Select nation
  lstNations.DataSource = query.ToList
  lstNations.SelectedItem = Nothing
End Sub
```

```
Private Sub lstNations_Click(...) Handles lstNations.Click
  txtNation.Text = lstNations.Text
End Sub
```

EXERCISES 7.3

1. `The area of a soccer field is 6000 square yards.`

3. `Duke was founded in NC in 1838.`   5. `heights are same`
                                            `170`

7. `Joe: 88`   9. `Mr. President lives in Washington, DC`
   `Moe: 90`
   `Roe: 95`

11. In the event procedure, `peace` should be `prize.peace` and `yr` should be `prize.yr`.

13. The condition `(game1 > game2)` is not valid. Structures can only be compared one field at a time.

15. The cities in Texas, along with their populations. The cities are ordered by the sizes of their populations beginning with the most populous city.

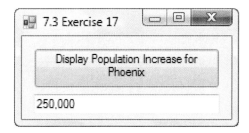

17. The population growth of Phoenix from 2000 to 2010.

19.
```
Structure State
    Dim name As String
    Dim abbreviation As String
    Dim area As Double
    Dim pop As Double
End Structure

Dim states() As State

Private Sub frmStates_Load(...) Handles MyBase.Load
  Dim stateRecords() As String = IO.File.ReadAllLines("USStates.txt")
  Dim n As Integer = stateRecords.Count — 1
  ReDim states(n)
  Dim line As String
  Dim data() As String
  For i As Integer = 0 To n
    line = stateRecords(i)
    data = line.Split(","c)
```

```
                states(i).name = data(0)
                states(i).abbreviation = data(1)
                states(i).area = CDbl(data(2))
                states(i).pop = CDbl(data(3))
            Next
        End Sub


        Private Sub btnFind_Click(...) Handles btnFind.Click
            Dim stateAbbr As String = mtbAbbrev.Text.ToUpper
            Dim query = From state In states
                        Where state.abbreviation = stateAbbr
                        Select state.name, state.area
            txtOutput.Text = "The area of " & query.First.name & " is " &
                                FormatNumber(query.First.area, 0) & " square miles."
        End Sub
```

21. (Begin with the code from Exercise 19 and replace the Click event procedure with the following.)

```
        Private Sub btnDisplay_Click(...) Handles btnDisplay.Click
            Dim query = From state In states
                        Let density = state.pop / state.area
                        Let formattedDensity = FormatNumber(density, 2)
                        Order By density Descending
                        Select state.name, formattedDensity
            dgvOutput.DataSource = query.ToList
            dgvOutput.CurrentCell = Nothing
            dgvOutput.Columns("name").HeaderText = "State"
            dgvOutput.Columns("formattedDensity").HeaderText =
                                "People per Square Mile"
        End Sub
```

23.
```
    Structure Player
        Dim name As String
        Dim team As String
        Dim atBats As Double
        Dim hits As Double
    End Structure

    Dim players() As Player

    Private Sub frmBaseball_Load(...) Handles MyBase.Load
        Dim playerStats() As String = IO.File.ReadAllLines("Baseball.txt")
        Dim n As Integer = playerStats.Count — 1
        ReDim players(n)
        Dim line As String
        Dim data() As String
        For i As Integer = 0 To n
          line = playerStats(i)
          data = line.Split(","c)
          players(i).name = data(0)
          players(i).team = data(1)
          players(i).atBats = CDbl(data(2))
          players(i).hits = CDbl(data(3))
        Next
        Dim query = From person In players
                    Order By person.team Ascending
                    Select person.team
                    Distinct
        lstTeams.DataSource = query.ToList
    End Sub
```

```vb
        Private Sub lstTeams_SelectedIndexChanged(...) Handles _
                          lstTeams.SelectedIndexChanged
          Dim selectedTeam = lstTeams.Text
          Dim query = From person In players
                        Where person.team = selectedTeam
                        Order By person.hits Descending
                        Select person.name, person.hits
          dgvOutput.DataSource = query.ToList
          dgvOutput.CurrentCell = Nothing
          dgvOutput.Columns("name").HeaderText = "Player"
          dgvOutput.Columns("hits").HeaderText = "Hits"
        End Sub
```

25.
```vb
    Structure Player
      Dim name As String
      Dim team As String
      Dim atBats As Double
      Dim hits As Double
    End Structure


    Dim players() As Player


    Private Sub frmBaseball_Load(...) Handles MyBase.Load
      Dim playerStats() As String = IO.File.ReadAllLines("Baseball.txt")
      Dim n As Integer = playerStats.Count − 1
      ReDim players(n)
      Dim line As String
      Dim data() As String
      For i As Integer = 0 To n
        line = playerStats(i)
        data = line.Split(","c)
        players(i).name = data(0)
        players(i).team = data(1)
        players(i).atBats = CDbl(data(2))
        players(i).hits = CDbl(data(3))
      Next
    End Sub


    Private Sub btnDisplay_Click(...) Handles btnDisplay.Click
      Dim query = From person In players
                    Let ave = person.hits / person.atBats
                    Select ave
      Dim best As Double = query.Max
      txtBestAverage.Text = FormatNumber(best, 3)
      Dim query2 = From person In players
                    Where person.hits / person.atBats = best
                    Select person.name, person.team
      dgvOutput.DataSource = query2.ToList
      dgvOutput.CurrentCell = Nothing
      dgvOutput.Columns("name").HeaderText = "Player"
      dgvOutput.Columns("team").HeaderText = "Team"
    End Sub
```

27.
```vb
    Structure Justice
      Dim firstName As String
      Dim lastName As String
      Dim apptPres As String
      Dim state As String      'state abbreviation
      Dim yrAppointed As Double
      Dim yrLeft As Double
    End Structure
```

```
Dim justices() As Justice

Private Sub frmJustices_Load(...) Handles MyBase.Load
  Dim justiceRecords() As String = IO.File.ReadAllLines("Justices.txt")
  Dim n As Integer = justiceRecords.Count — 1
  ReDim justices(n)
  Dim line As String
  Dim data() As String
  For i As Integer = 0 To n
    line = justiceRecords(i)
    data = line.Split(","c)
    justices(i).firstName = data(0)
    justices(i).lastName = data(1)
    justices(i).apptPres = data(2)
    justices(i).state = data(3)
    justices(i).yrAppointed = CDbl(data(4))
    justices(i).yrLeft = CDbl(data(5))
  Next
End Sub

Private Sub btnDisplay_Click(...) Handles btnDisplay.Click
  Dim query = From person In justices
              Where person.yrLeft = 0
              Order By person.yrAppointed
              Select person.firstName & " " & person.lastName
  lstOutput.DataSource = query.ToList
  lstOutput.SelectedItem = Nothing
End Sub
```

29. (Begin with the code from Exercise 27 and replace the Click event procedure with the following.)

```
Private Sub btnDisplay_Click(...) Handles btnDisplay.Click
  Dim query = From person In justices
              Where person.state = mtbState.Text
              Let fullName = person.firstName & " " & person.lastName
              Let yrs = YearsServed(person.yrAppointed, person.yrLeft)
              Let presLastName = person.apptPres.Split(" "c).Last
              Select fullName, presLastName, yrs
  If query.Count = 0 Then
    MessageBox.Show("No justices appointed from that state.", "NONE")
    mtbState.Focus()
```

```
    Else
      dgvOutput.DataSource = query.ToList
      dgvOutput.CurrentCell = Nothing
      dgvOutput.Columns("fullName").HeaderText = "Justice"
      dgvOutput.Columns("presLastName").HeaderText = "Appointing President"
      dgvOutput.Columns("yrs").HeaderText = "Years Served"
    End If
End Sub

Function YearsServed(ByVal enter As Double,
                     ByVal leave As Double) As Double
    If leave = 0 Then
      Return (Now.Year — enter)
    Else
      Return (leave — enter)
    End If
End Function
```

31.
```
Structure Day
    Dim num As Integer
    Dim present As String
    Dim price As Double
End Structure

Dim days() As Day

Private Sub frmXmas_Load(...) Handles MyBase.Load
    Dim gifts() As String = IO.File.ReadAllLines("Gifts.txt")
    Dim n As Integer = gifts.Count — 1
    ReDim days(n)
    Dim data() As String
    For i As Integer = 0 To n
      data = gifts(i).Split(","c)
      days(i).num = CInt(data(0))
      days(i).present = data(1)
      days(i).price = CDbl(data(2))
    Next
End Sub
```

```
Private Sub btnDisplayGifts_Click(...) Handles btnDisplayGifts.Click
  Dim dayNum = CInt(txtDayNum.Text)
  Dim cost As Double = 0
  Dim totalCost As Double = 0
  lstOutput.Items.Clear()
  lstOutput.Items.Add("The gifts for day " & dayNum & " are")
  For i As Integer = 0 To (dayNum — 1)
    lstOutput.Items.Add(days(i).num & " " & days(i).present)
    cost += days(i).num * days(i).price
    totalCost += days(i).num * days(i).price *
                 (dayNum + 1 — days(i).num)
  Next
  lstOutput.Items.Add("")
  lstOutput.Items.Add("Cost for day " & dayNum & ": " &
                      FormatCurrency(cost))
  lstOutput.Items.Add("Total cost for the first " & dayNum &
                      " days: " & FormatCurrency(totalCost))
End Sub
```

33.
```
Structure FamousPerson
  Dim name As String
  Dim dateOfBirth As Date
End Structure

Dim famousPersons() As FamousPerson

Private Sub frmFamous_Load(...) Handles MyBase.Load
  Dim people() As String = IO.File.ReadAllLines("Famous.txt")
  Dim n As Integer = people.Count — 1
  ReDim famousPersons(n)
  Dim line As String
  Dim data() As String
  For i As Integer = 0 To n
    line = people(i)
    data = line.Split(","c)
    famousPersons(i).name = data(0)
    famousPersons(i).dateOfBirth = CDate(data(1))
  Next
End Sub

Private Sub btnDisplay_Click(...) Handles btnDisplay.Click
  Dim query = From person In famousPersons
              Where (person.dateOfBirth >= #1/1/1970#) And
                    (person.dateOfBirth < #1/1/1980#)
              Select person.name
  lstOutput.DataSource = query.ToList
  lstOutput.SelectedItem = Nothing
End Sub
```

35.
```
Dim people() As Person

Private Sub frmFamous_Load(...) Handles MyBase.Load
  'Place the data for each person into the array people.
  Dim group() As String = IO.File.ReadAllLines("Famous.txt")
  Dim n As Integer = group.Count — 1
  ReDim people(n)
  Dim data() As String
```

```
    For i As Integer = 0 To n
      data = group(i).Split(","c)
      people(i).name = data(0)
      people(i).dateOfBirth = CDate(data(1))
    Next
  End Sub

  Private Sub btnDisplay_Click(...) Handles btnDisplay.Click
    Dim query = From individual In people
                Let ageInDays = FormatNumber(DateDiff(DateInterval.Day,
                    individual.dateOfBirth, Today), 0)
                Let dayOfBirth = DayOfWeek(individual.dateOfBirth)
                Where individual.dateOfBirth.AddYears(40) <= Today And
                    individual.dateOfBirth.AddYears(50) > Today
                Select individual.name, ageInDays, dayOfBirth
    dgvOutput.DataSource = query.ToList
    dgvOutput.CurrentCell = Nothing
  End Sub

  Function DayOfWeek(ByVal d As Date) As String
    Dim d1 As String = FormatDateTime(d, DateFormat.LongDate)
    Dim d2() As String = d1.Split(","c)
    Return First
  End Function
```

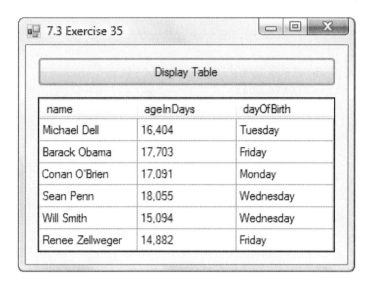

37.
```
  Private Sub btnDisplay_Click(...) Handles btnDisplay.Click
    lstOutput.Items.Clear()
    For i As Integer = 0 To club.Count - 1
      If club(i).courses.Count = 3 Then
        lstOutput.Items.Add(club(i).name)
      End If
    Next
  End Sub
```

39.
```
  Private Sub btnDisplay_Click(...) Handles btnDisplay.Click
    'Displays the students who are not enrolled in CMSC 100
    Dim subject = "CMSC 100"
    Dim ub = club.Count - 1
    Dim checkList(ub) As Boolean
    For i As Integer = 0 To ub
      For j As Integer = 0 To club(i).courses.Count - 1
```

```
          If club(i).courses(j) = subject Then
            checkList(i) = True
          End If
      Next
    Next
    For i As Integer = 0 To ub
      If Not checkList(i) Then
        lstOutput.Items.Add(club(i).name)
      End If
    Next
  End Sub
```

EXERCISES 7.4

1. 1   3. 3   5. 55   7. 14   9. 2   11. 55

13.
```
Dim twice(2, 3) As Double
For r As Integer = 0 To 2
  For c As Integer = 0 To 3
    twice(r, c) = 2 * nums(r, c)
  Next
Next
```

15.
```
'use a For Each loop
Dim total As Double = 0
For Each num As Double In nums
  If num Mod 2 = 0 Then
    total += num
  End If
Next
lstOutput.Items.Add(total)

'use LINQ
Dim query = From num In nums.Cast(Of Double)()
            Where (num Mod 2 = 0)
            Select num
lstOutput.Items.Add(query.Sum)
```

17. 12

19.
```
Private Sub btnDisplay_Click(...) Handles btnDisplay.Click
    'Display a company's inventory from its two stores
    Dim inventory(,) As Integer = {{25, 64, 23}, {30, 82, 19}}
    Dim sales(,) As Integer = {{7, 45, 11}, {4, 24, 8}}
    Dim total(2) As Integer
    'Adjust the inventory values to reflect today's sales
    For store As Integer = 1 To 2
      For item As Integer = 1 To 3
        inventory(store − 1, item − 1) =
```

```
          inventory(store - 1, item - 1) - sales(store - 1, item - 1)
        'Accumulate the total inventory per store
        total(store) += inventory(store - 1, item - 1)
      Next
   Next
   'Display the store's inventory and totals
   lstOutput.Items.Add("   1    2    3    TOTAL")
   For store As Integer = 1 To 2
     lstOutput.Items.Add(store & "    " & inventory(store - 1, 0) &
                  "   " & inventory(store - 1, 1) & "    " &
                  inventory(store - 1, 2) & "    " & total(store))
   Next
End Sub
```

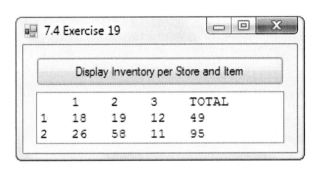

21.
```
Private Sub btnDisplay_Click(...) Handles btnDisplay.Click
    'Display the course and campus enrollments
    'enrollment array named er
    Dim er(,) As Integer = {{5, 15, 22, 21, 12, 25, 16, 11, 17, 23},
                            {11, 23, 51, 25, 32, 35, 32, 52, 25, 21},
                            {2, 12, 32, 32, 25, 26, 29, 12, 15, 11}}
    'Define the arrays to accumulate the information
    Dim campusTotal(2), courseTotal(9) As Integer
    For campus As Integer = 0 To 2
      For course As Integer = 0 To 9
        campusTotal(campus) += er(campus, course)
        courseTotal(course) += er(campus, course)
      Next
    Next
    'Display the campus enrollment
    lstOutput.Items.Add("CAMPUS ENROLLMENT")
    For campus As Integer = 0 To 2
      lstOutput.Items.Add((campus + 1) & ": " & campusTotal(campus))
    Next
    'Display the course enrollment
```

```
    lstOutput.Items.Add("COURSE ENROLLMENT")
    For course As Integer = 0 To 9
      lstOutput.Items.Add((course + 1) & ": " & courseTotal(course))
    Next
  End Sub
```

23.
```
Private Sub btnDisplay_Click(...) Handles btnDisplay.Click
    'Load golf data, cumulate totals, and display results
    Dim scores(3, 3) As Integer
    Dim golfers(3) As String
    Dim table() As String = IO.File.ReadAllLines("Golf.txt")
    Dim data() As String
    Dim golferTotal(3) As Integer, roundTotal(3) As Integer
    For i As Integer = 0 To 3
      data = table(i).Split(","c)
      golfers(i) = data(0)
      For j = 0 To 3
        scores(i, j) = CInt(data(j + 1))
      Next
    Next
    For golfer As Integer = 0 To 3
      For round As Integer = 0 To 3
        golferTotal(golfer) += scores(golfer, round)
        roundTotal(round) += scores(golfer, round)
      Next
    Next
    'Display golfer's totals
    lstOutput.Items.Add("GOLFER TOTALS")
    For golfer As Integer = 0 To 3
      lstOutput.Items.Add(golfers(golfer) & ": " & golferTotal(golfer))
    Next
    lstOutput.Items.Add("")
    'Display average per round
    lstOutput.Items.Add("ROUND AVERAGE")
    For round As Integer = 0 To 3
      lstOutput.Items.Add(round + 1 & ": " &
                      FormatNumber(roundTotal(round) / 4))
    Next
  End Sub
```

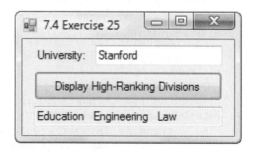

25.
```
Private Sub btnDisplay_Click(...) Handles btnDisplay.Click
    Dim ranking(2, 4) As String
```

```
    Dim disciplines(2) As String
    Dim table() As String = IO.File.ReadAllLines("Ranking.txt")
    Dim data() As String
    For field As Integer = 0 To 2
      data = table(field).Split(","c)
      disciplines(field) = data(0)
      For rank As Integer = 0 To 4
        ranking(field, rank) = data(rank + 1)
      Next
    Next
    Dim result As String = ""
    For category As Integer = 0 To 2
      For rank As Integer = 0 To 4
        If txtName.Text.ToUpper = ranking(category, rank).ToUpper Then
          'Append category name to result
          result &= disciplines(category) & "    "
        End If
      Next
    Next
    If result = "" Then
      txtOutput.Text = "None."
    Else
      txtOutput.Text = result
    End If
  End Sub
```

27.
```
Dim scores(14, 4) As Integer        'Stores students' exam scores
Dim count As Integer                'Current number of students stored
Dim names(14) As String             'Stores students' names

Private Sub btnAdd_Click(...) Handles btnAdd.Click
  If (count = 15) Then
    MessageBox.Show("Fifteen students already stored.", "Warning")
  Else
    count += 1
    names(count - 1) = txtName.Text
    scores(count - 1, 0) = CInt(txtExam1.Text)
    scores(count - 1, 1) = CInt(txtExam2.Text)
    scores(count - 1, 2) = CInt(txtExam3.Text)
    scores(count - 1, 3) = CInt(txtExam4.Text)
    scores(count - 1, 4) = CInt(txtExam5.Text)
    'Reset input
    txtName.Clear()
    txtExam1.Clear()
    txtExam2.Clear()
    txtExam3.Clear()
    txtExam4.Clear()
    txtExam5.Clear()
    txtName.Focus()
  End If
End Sub

Private Sub btnDisplay_Click(...) Handles btnDisplay.Click
  Dim sum As Double, even As Boolean
  lstOutput.Items.Clear()
  lstOutput.Items.Add("Semester Averages")
  For i As Integer = 0 To count - 1
    sum = 0
    For exam As Integer = 0 To 4
      sum += scores(i, exam)
    Next
```

```
          lstOutput.Items.Add(names(i) & ": " & FormatNumber(sum / 5))
        Next
        'Display median on the exams
        lstOutput.Items.Add("Exam Medians")
        even = (Int(count / 2) = count / 2)
        For exam As Integer = 0 To 4
          lstOutput.Items.Add(exam + 1 & ": " &
                        Median(scores, count, exam, even))
        Next
      End Sub
```

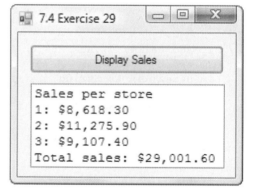

```
29. Private Sub btnDisplay_Click(...) Handles btnDisplay.Click
      'Load data into an array, cumulate totals, and display a report
      Dim totalSales As Double
      Dim sales(,) As Integer = {{25, 64, 23, 45, 14},
                                 {12, 82, 19, 34, 63},
                                 {54, 22, 17, 43, 35}}
      Dim price() As Double = {12, 17.95, 95, 86.5, 78}
      'Cumulate totals
      Dim totals(2) As Double
      For store As Integer = 0 To 2
        For item As Integer = 0 To 4
          totals(store) += sales(store, item) * price(item)
        Next
      Next
      'Display report, storing grand total in totals(0)
      lstOutput.Items.Add("Sales per store")
      For store As Integer = 0 To 2
        lstOutput.Items.Add(store + 1 & ": " & FormatCurrency(totals(store)))
        totalSales += totals(store)
      Next
      lstOutput.Items.Add("Total sales: " & FormatCurrency(totalSales))
    End Sub
```

CHAPTER 8

EXERCISES 8.1

1. `Alito,Samuel- NJ`
   `Baldwin,Henry- PA`

3. `Alito was appointed by Bush and is still serving.`
   `Breyer was appointed by Clinton and is still serving.`

5. `Alito,Samuel,2006`
   `Baldwin,Henry,1830`

7. Each line in the file will contain first name and last name (separated by a space), then a comma, then year appointed. Only records in Justices.txt where the year appointed is in the 1900s will be selected for inclusion in the new file.

9. The new file is the same as the original file except that the last three fields have been deleted from each record.

11. The new file contains the names of the people who subscribe to either the New York Times or the Wall Street Journal, or both.

13. The new file contains the names of the people who subscribe to the New York Times but not the Wall Street Journal.

15.
```
Private Sub btnBoth_Click(...) Handles btnBoth.Click
    'Create a file of presidents who were also vice presidents
    Dim vicePres() As String = IO.File.ReadAllLines("VPres.txt")
    Dim presidents() As String = IO.File.ReadAllLines("USPres.txt")
    Dim both() As String = presidents.Intersect(vicePres).ToArray
    IO.File.WriteAllLines("Both.txt", both)
    MessageBox.Show(both.Count & " presidents", "File Created")
End Sub
```

17.
```
Private Sub btnXor_Click(...) Handles btnXor.Click
    'Create a file of people who were pres or VP but not both
    Dim vicePres() As String = IO.File.ReadAllLines("VPres.txt")
    Dim presidents() As String = IO.File.ReadAllLines("USPres.txt")
    Dim eitherOr() As String = presidents.Union(vicePres).ToArray
    Dim both() As String = presidents.Intersect(vicePres).ToArray
    Dim exclusiveOr() As String = eitherOr.Except(both).ToArray
    IO.File.WriteAllLines("Xor.txt", exclusiveOr)
    MessageBox.Show(exclusiveOr.Count &
        " presidents or vice presidents, but not both", "File Created")
End Sub
```

19.
```
Dim countries() As String = IO.File.ReadAllLines("UN.txt")

'lstContinents was filled at design time
Private Sub lstContinents_SelectedIndexChanged(...) Handles _
                    lstContinents.SelectedIndexChanged
    Dim selectedContinent As String = lstContinents.Text
    If selectedContinent = "Antarctica" Then
```

```
        lstCountries.DataSource = Nothing
        MessageBox.Show("There are no countries in Antarctica.")
      Else
        Dim query = From nation In countries
                    Let data = nation.Split(","c)
                    Let name = data(0)
                    Let continent = data(1)
                    Where continent = selectedContinent
                    Select name
        lstCountries.DataSource = query.ToList
        lstCountries.SelectedItem = Nothing
      End If
    End Sub
```

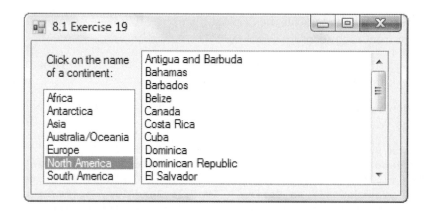

21.
```
Private Sub btnDisplay_Click(...) Handles btnDisplay.Click
    Dim cities() As String = IO.File.ReadAllLines("Cities.txt")
    Dim query = From city In cities
                Let data = city.Split(","c)
                Let pop2010 = CDbl(data(3))
                Order By pop2010 Descending
                Select pop2010
    Dim pops() As Double = query.ToArray
    ReDim Preserve pops(9)
    txtOutput.Text = FormatNumber(100000 * pops.Sum, 0)
  End Sub
```

23.
```
Private Sub btnDisplay_Click(...) Handles btnDisplay.Click
    Dim states() As String = IO.File.ReadAllLines("USStates.txt")
    Dim query = From line In states
                Let name = line.Split(","c)(0).ToUpper
                Let abbrev = line.Split(","c)(1)
                Where Not name.StartsWith(abbrev)
                Order By name Ascending
                Select abbrev, name
```

```
    dgvOutput.DataSource = query.ToList
    dgvOutput.CurrentCell = Nothing
    dgvOutput.Columns("abbrev").HeaderText = "State Abbreviation"
    dgvOutput.Columns("name").HeaderText = "State"
End Sub
```

25.
```
Private Sub btnDisplay_Click(...) Handles btnDisplay.Click
    Dim states() As String = IO.File.ReadAllLines("USStates.txt")
    Dim query1 = From line In states
                 Let area = CInt(line.Split(","c)(2))
                 Select area
    Dim totalArea = query1.Sum
    Dim query2 = From line In states
                 Let name = line.Split(","c)(0)
                 Let area = CInt(line.Split(","c)(2))
                 Let percentArea = FormatPercent(area / totalArea)
                 Order By area Descending
                 Select name, percentArea
    dgvOutput.DataSource = query2.ToList
    dgvOutput.CurrentCell = Nothing
    dgvOutput.Columns("name").HeaderText = "State"
    dgvOutput.Columns("percentArea").HeaderText =
                               "Percentage of Total Area"
End Sub
```

27.
```
Private Sub btnUpdate_Click(...) Handles btnUpdate.Click
    Dim colors() As String = IO.File.ReadAllLines("Pre1990Colors.txt")
    Dim retired() As String = IO.File.ReadAllLines("RetiredColors.txt")
    Dim added() As String = IO.File.ReadAllLines("AddedColors.txt")
    Dim tempArray() As String = colors.Except(retired).ToArray
    Dim query = From color In tempArray.Concat(added)
                Order By color
                Select color
    IO.File.WriteAllLines("NewColors.txt", query)
End Sub
```

29.
```
Private Sub btnCreate_Click(...) Handles btnCreate.Click
    Dim justices() As String = IO.File.ReadAllLines("Justices.txt")
```

```
        Dim query = From justice In justices
                Let data = justice.Split(","c)
                Let firstName = data(0)
                Let secondName = data(1)
                Let pres = data(2)
                Let yrAppt = data(4)
                Let yrLeft = data(5)
                Select firstName & "," & secondName & "," & pres & "," &
                        yrAppt & "," & yrLeft
        IO.File.WriteAllLines("JusticesNoState.txt", query)
      End Sub
```

31.
```
   Private Sub btnCreate_Click(...) Handles btnDisplay.Click
      'query1: all states; query2: states with justices
      Dim states() As String = IO.File.ReadAllLines("USStates.txt")
      Dim justices() As String = IO.File.ReadAllLines("Justices.txt")
      Dim query1 = From state In states
                Let abbrev = state.Split(","c)(1)
                Select abbrev
      Dim query2 = From justice In justices
                Let state = justice.Split(","c)(3)
                Select state
      IO.File.WriteAllLines("NoJustices.txt", query1.Except(query2))
   End Sub
```

33.
```
   Dim justices() As String = IO.File.ReadAllLines("Justices.txt")

   Private Sub Create_Click(...) Handles Create.Click
      Dim query = From line In justices
                Let state = line.Split(","c)(3)
                Order By state Ascending
                Select state & "," & NumberOfJustices(state)
                Distinct
      IO.File.WriteAllLines("NewFile.txt", query)
   End Sub

   Function NumberOfJustices(ByVal state As String) As Integer
      Dim query = From line In justices
                Let place = line.Split(","c)(3)
                Where place = state
                Select place
      Return query.Count
   End Function
```

```
35. Private Sub btnDisplay_Click(...) Handles btnDisplay.Click
        Dim query = From state In IO.File.ReadAllLines("USStates.txt")
                    Let data = state.Split(","c)
                    Let name = data(0)
                    Let abbrev = data(1)
                    Let area = FormatNumber(data(2), 0)
                    Let pop = FormatNumber(data(3), 0)
                    Order By name
                    Select name, abbrev, area, pop
        dgvStates.DataSource = query.ToList
        dgvStates.CurrentCell = Nothing
    End Sub
```

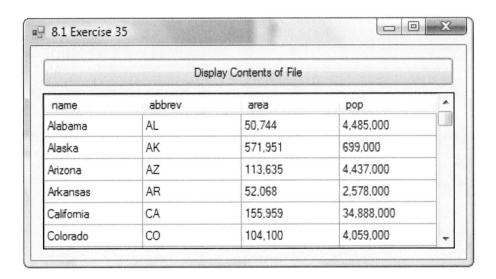

EXERCISES 8.2

1. `Hello`   3. `Aloha`   5. `You must enter a number.`

7. `Error occurred.`   9. `File Ages.txt contains an invalid age.`

11. The Welcome.txt file will have only 2 records, with the values Aloha and Bon Jour.

13. The filespec `Greetings.txt` should be delimited with quotation marks.

15. There should be no quotations around the variable `name` as the argument to the CreateText method.

17. The variable *age* is declared within the Try-Catch-Finally block. Therefore it has block-level scope and is not available below the line `End Try`.

```
19. Private Sub btnCreate_Click(...) Handles btnCreate.Click
        'Create a text file and populate it
        Dim sw As IO.StreamWriter = IO.File.CreateText("Cowboy.txt")
        sw.WriteLine("Colt Peacemaker,12.20")
        sw.WriteLine("Holster,2.00")
        sw.WriteLine("Levi Strauss jeans,1.35")
        sw.WriteLine("Saddle,40.00")
        sw.WriteLine("Stetson,10.00")
        sw.Close()  'Always close the writer when finished.
        MessageBox.Show("The file has been created.", "Done")
    End Sub
```

21. ```
Private Sub btnAdd_Click(...) Handles btnAdd.Click
    'Append item to a text file
    Dim sw As IO.StreamWriter = IO.File.AppendText("Cowboy.txt")
    sw.WriteLine("Winchester Rifle,20.50")
    sw.Close()
    MessageBox.Show("The item has been added to the file.", "DONE")
End Sub
```

23. ```
Private Sub btnAdd_Click(...) Handles btnAdd.Click
    Dim item As String
    Dim price As Double
    Dim sr As IO.StreamReader = IO.File.OpenText("Cowboy.txt")
    Dim sw As IO.StreamWriter = IO.File.CreateText("Cowboy2.txt")
    Dim flag As Boolean = False
    Dim line As String = ""
    Dim data() As String
    Do While (line < txtItem.Text) And (Not sr.EndOfStream)
      line = sr.ReadLine
      data = line.Split(","c)
      item = data(0)
      price = CDbl(data(1))
      If item > txtItem.Text Then
        sw.WriteLine(txtItem.Text & "," & FormatNumber(txtPrice.Text))
        'Set flag to True so we don't add it again at the end
        flag = True
      End If
      sw.WriteLine(line)
    Loop
    Do Until sr.EndOfStream
      line = sr.ReadLine
      sw.WriteLine(line)
    Loop
    If Not flag Then
      sw.WriteLine(txtItem.Text & "," & FormatNumber(txtPrice.Text))
    End If
```

```
        sr.Close()
        sw.Close()
        MessageBox.Show("Item added to Cowboy2.txt")
        txtItem.Clear()
        txtPrice.Clear()
    End Sub
```

25. ```
Private Sub btnDisplay_Click(...) Handles btnDisplay.Click
    Dim sr As IO.StreamReader = IO.File.OpenText("Cowboy.txt")
    Dim lines(4) As String
    For i As Integer = 0 To 4
      lines(i) = sr.ReadLine
    Next
    Dim query = From line In lines
                Let data = line.Split(","c)
                Let item = data(0)
                Let cost = FormatCurrency(data(1))
                Select item, cost
    dgvOutput.DataSource = query.ToList
    dgvOutput.CurrentCell = Nothing
End Sub
```

27. ```
Private Sub btnDetermine_Click(...) Handles btnDetermine.Click
    Dim sr As IO.StreamReader = IO.File.OpenText("Numbers.txt")
    Dim counter As Integer = 0
    Dim num As Double
    Do Until sr.EndOfStream
      num = CDbl(sr.ReadLine)
      counter += 1
    Loop
    txtOutput.Text = CStr(counter)
    sr.Close()
End Sub
```

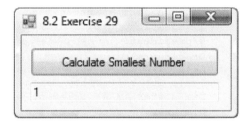

29. ```
Private Sub btnCalculate_Click(...) Handles btnCalculate.Click
    Dim sr As IO.StreamReader = IO.File.OpenText("Numbers.txt")
    Dim num As Double
    Dim min As Double = CDbl(sr.ReadLine)
    Do Until sr.EndOfStream
      num = CDbl(sr.ReadLine)
      If num < min Then
        min = num
      End If
    Loop
    txtOutput.Text = CStr(min)
    sr.Close()
End Sub
```

31. ```
Private Sub btnCalculate_Click(...) Handles btnCalculate.Click
    Dim sr As IO.StreamReader = IO.File.OpenText("Numbers.txt")
```

```
      Dim counter As Integer = 0
      Dim total As Double = 0
      Dim num As Double
      Do Until sr.EndOfStream
        num = CDbl(sr.ReadLine)
        counter += 1
        total += num
      Loop
      txtOutput.Text = FormatNumber(total / counter)
      sr.Close()
   End Sub
```

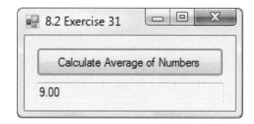

EXERCISES 8.3

1. No   3. No   5. No   7. No   9. Improper

11.
```
<?xml version='1.0'?>
<!-- This file contains the ages of the presidents when inaugurated.-->
<Presidents>
  <president>
    <name>George Washington</name>
    <ageAtInauguation>57</ageAtInauguation>
  </president>
  <president>
    <name>John Adams</name>
    <ageAtInauguation>61</ageAtInauguation>
  </president>
</Presidents>
```

13.
```
Private Sub btnDisplay_Click(...) Handles btnDisplay.Click
   Dim stateData As XElement = XElement.Load("USStates.xml")
   Dim query = From st In stateData.Descendants("state")
               Let pop = CInt(st.<population>.Value)
               Select pop
   txtOutput.Text = FormatNumber(query.Sum, 0)
End Sub
```

15.
```
Private Sub btnDisplay_Click(...) Handles btnDisplay.Click
   Dim stateData As XElement = XElement.Load("USStates.xml")
```

```
    Dim queryPop = From st In stateData.Descendants("state")
                 Let pop = CInt(st.<population>.Value)
                 Select pop
    Dim queryArea = From st In stateData.Descendants("state")
                 Let area = CInt(st.<area>.Value)
                 Select area
    txtOutput.Text = FormatNumber(queryPop.Sum / queryArea.Sum) &
                 " people per square mile"
  End Sub
```

17. ```
Private Sub btnDisplay_Click(...) Handles btnDisplay.Click
    Dim stateData As XElement = XElement.Load("USStates.xml")
    Dim query = From st In stateData.Descendants("state")
              Let name = st.<name>.Value
              Let area = CDbl(st.<area>.Value)
              Let formattedArea = FormatNumber(area, 0)
              Where area > 100000
              Order By area Descending
              Select name, formattedArea
    dgvStates.DataSource = query.ToList
    dgvStates.CurrentCell = Nothing
    dgvStates.Columns("name").HeaderText = "State"
    dgvStates.Columns("formattedArea").HeaderText = "Area"
  End Sub
```

19. ```
Private Sub btnDisplay_Click(...) Handles btnDisplay.Click
    Dim stateData As XElement = XElement.Load("USStates.xml")
    Dim query1 = From st In stateData.Descendants("state")
              Let name = st.<name>.Value
              Let numVowels = NumberOfVowels(name)
              Order By numVowels Descending
              Select numVowels
    Dim maxVowels As Integer = query1.First
    Dim query2 = From st In stateData.Descendants("state")
              Let name = st.<name>.Value
              Where NumberOfVowels(name) = maxVowels
              Select name
    lstOutput.DataSource = query2.ToList
    lstOutput.SelectedItem = Nothing
  End Sub
```

```
Function NumberOfVowels(ByVal word As String) As Integer
  word = word.ToUpper
  Dim num As Integer = 0
  If word.IndexOf("A") <> -1 Then
    num += 1
  End If
  If word.IndexOf("E") <> -1 Then
    num += 1
  End If
  If word.IndexOf("I") <> -1 Then
    num += 1
  End If
  If word.IndexOf("O") <> -1 Then
    num += 1
  End If
  If word.IndexOf("U") <> -1 Then
    num += 1
  End If
  Return num
End Function
```

21.
```
Dim colleges As XElement = XElement.Load("Colleges.xml")

Private Sub btnDisplay_Click(...) Handles btnDisplay.Click
  'Display the colleges in Colleges.xml located in the given state
  Dim chosenState As String = mtbState.Text.ToUpper    'mask LL
  Dim query = From col In colleges.Descendants("college")
              Let name = col.<name>.Value
              Let state = col.<state>.Value
              Let yearFounded = col.<yearFounded>.Value
              Where state = chosenState
              Order By name Ascending
              Select name & " " & yearFounded
  lstColleges.DataSource = query.ToList
  lstColleges.SelectedItem = Nothing
End Sub
```

23.
```
Dim colleges As XElement = XElement.Load("Colleges.xml")

Private Sub frmColleges_Load(...) Handles MyBase.Load
  'Place the years for each college into the left list box
  Dim query = From col In colleges.Descendants("college")
              Let yearFounded = col.<yearFounded>.Value
              Order By yearFounded Ascending
              Select yearFounded
              Distinct
  For Each yr in query
    lstYears.Items.Add(yr)
  Next
End Sub

Private Sub lstYears_SelectedIndexChanged(...) Handles _
              lstYears.SelectedIndexChanged
  Dim chosenYear As String = lstYears.Text
  Dim query = From col In colleges.Descendants("college")
              Let name = col.<name>.Value
              Let yearFounded = col.<yearFounded>.Value
              Where yearFounded = chosenYear
              Select name
  lstColleges.DataSource = query.ToList
  lstColleges.SelectedItem = Nothing
End Sub
```

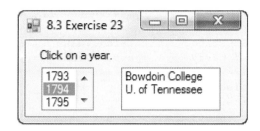

25(a).

```
Private Sub btnSenate_Click(...) Handles btnSenate.Click
  Dim sr As IO.StreamReader = IO.File.OpenText("Senate111.txt")
  Dim sw As IO.StreamWriter = IO.File.CreateText("Senate111.xml")
  sw.WriteLine("<?xml version='1.0'?>")
  sw.WriteLine("<!-- This file contains data on the 111th Senate -->")
  sw.WriteLine("<Senate111>")
  Dim temp As String = ""
  Do Until sr.EndOfStream
    temp = sr.ReadLine
    sw.WriteLine("  <senator>")
    sw.WriteLine("    <name>" & temp.Split(","c)(0) & "</name>")
    sw.WriteLine("    <state>" & temp.Split(","c)(1) & "</state>")
    sw.WriteLine("    <party>" & temp.Split(","c)(2) & "</party>")
    sw.WriteLine("  </senator>")
  Loop
  sw.WriteLine("</Senate111>")
  sr.Close()
  sw.Close()
  MessageBox.Show("File Created")
End Sub
```

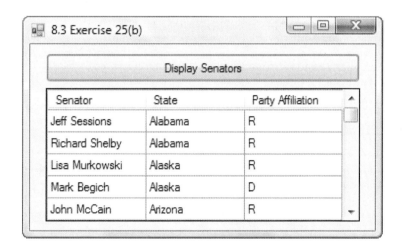

25(b).

```
Private Sub btnDisplay_Click(...) Handles btnDisplay.Click
  Dim senateData As XElement = XElement.Load("Senate111.XML")
```

```
            Dim query = From st In senateData.Descendants("senator")
                        Let name = st.<name>.Value
                        Let state = st.<state>.Value
                        Let party = st.<party>.Value
                        Order By state, name Ascending
                        Select name, state, party
        dgvSenators.DataSource = query.ToList
        dgvSenators.CurrentCell = Nothing
        dgvSenators.Columns("name").HeaderText = "Senator"
        dgvSenators.Columns("state").HeaderText = "State"
        dgvSenators.Columns("party").HeaderText = "Party Affiliation"
    End Sub
```

CHAPTER 9

EXERCISES 9.1

1. The first item in the listbox is removed, and the remaining items move up.

3. The currently selected item in **lstBox,** Mozart, is deleted.

5. The item Haydn is inserted into **lstBox** between Chopin and Mozart.

7. The names in the list box will appear in descending alphabetical order.

9. `cboBox.SelectedIndex = 2`

11. `cboBox.Items.Remove("Shakespeare")`

13. `cboBox.Items.RemoveAt(cboBox.Items.Count − 1)`

15.
```
Dim i As Integer = 0
Do While i < cboBox.Items.Count
  If CStr(cboBox.Items(i)).Substring(0, 1) = "M" Then
    cboBox.Items.RemoveAt(i)
  Else
    i += 1
  End If
Loop
```

17.
```
Private Sub btnSort_Click(...) Handles btnSort.Click
  Dim names() As String = IO.File.ReadAllLines("PopularName.txt")
  lstOutput.Sorted = True
  lstOutput.DataSource = names
  lstOutput.SelectedItem = Nothing
  For i As Integer = 0 To lstOutput.Items.Count − 1
    names(i) = CStr(lstOutput.Items(i))
  Next
  IO.File.WriteAllLines("SortedNames.txt", names)
  MessageBox.Show("The ordered file has been created.", "Done")
End Sub
```

23.
```
Dim ages() As String = IO.File.ReadAllLines("AgesAtInaugural.txt")

Private Sub frmPres_Load(...) Handles MyBase.Load
  Dim pres() As String = IO.File.ReadAllLines("USPres.txt")
  lstPres.DataSource = pres
End Sub
```

```
Private Sub lstPres_SelectedIndexChanged(...) Handles _
                    lstPres.SelectedIndexChanged
  txtAge.Text = ages(lstPres.SelectedIndex)
End Sub
```

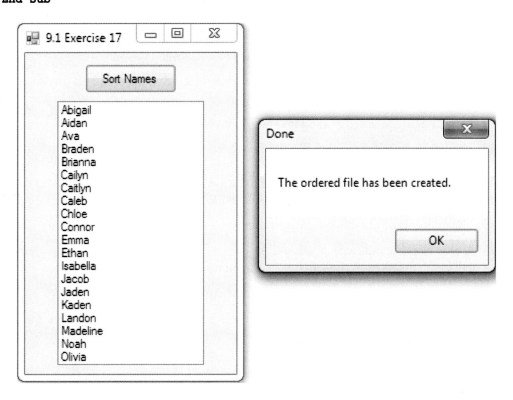

25.
```
'Note: This event procedure handles events from all three combo boxes
Private Sub SelectedIndexChanged(...) Handles _
                    cboBrand.SelectedIndexChanged,
                    cboMemory.SelectedIndexChanged,
                    cboMonitor.SelectedIndexChanged
  'Update output if all choices have been made.
  If (cboBrand.SelectedIndex >= 0) And
     (cboMemory.SelectedIndex >= 0) And
     (cboMonitor.SelectedIndex >= 0) Then
    txtOutput.Text = "You have a " & cboBrand.Text &
              " computer with " & cboMemory.Text &
              " of memory and a " & cboMonitor.Text & " monitor."
  End If
End Sub
```

1. The Tick event will be triggered every 5 seconds (5000 milliseconds).

3. The tooltip will appear one second after the cursor is hovered over a control.

5. A check mark appears in front of the `mnuOrderAsc` menu item.

7. The Tick event will be triggered every *intVar* seconds.

9. The name of one of the 44 U.S. presidents is selected at random and displayed in `txtBox.`

11. Two states are selected at random and displayed in the list box.

13. The contents of the Clipboard are deleted.

15. Copies the entire contents of the textbox to the Windows Clipboard.

17. The contents of the Clipboard are displayed in `txtBox.`

19. The contents of the Clipboard are assigned to the variable *strVar*.

21. A blue circle of radius 50 pixels will be drawn in the picture box. Its upper- leftmost point will be 20 pixels from the left side of the picture box and 30 pixels from the top side.

23. A picture of an airplane will be placed in the picture box.

25. Clicking on the arrow on either end of the scroll bar will move the button the same ("large") distance as clicking on the bar between the scroll box and an arrow.

27. `Timer1.Enabled = False`

29.
```
Dim randomNum As New Random()
txtBox.Text = CStr(randomNum.Next(1, 13))
```

31.
```
Dim sr As IO.StreamReader = IO.Files.ReadText("Towns.txt")
Dim randomNum As New Random()
Dim num As Integer = randomNum.Next(1, 26)
Dim city As String
For i As Integer = 1 To num
  city = sr.ReadLine
Next
txtBox.Text = city
```

33.
```
Dim n As Integer = rivers.Count
If n ≥ 2 Then
  Dim randomNum As New Random()
  Dim firstNumber, secondNumber As Integer
  firstNumber = randomNum.Next(0, n)
  Do
    secondNumber = randomNum.Next(0, n)
  Until secondNumber <> firstNumber
  lstBox.Items.Add(rivers(firstNumber))
  lstBox.Items.Add(rivers(secondNumber))
Else
  MessageBox.Show("The array has fewer than two elements.")
End If
```

35. `Clipboard.SetText("")`

37. `Clipboard.SetText(txtBox.SelectedText)`

39.
```
Dim amount As Integer
amount = CInt(Clipboard.GetText)
```

41. `mnuOrderDesc.Checked = False`

43. `VScrollBar2.Value = VScrollBar2.Minimum`

45. The menu item *mnuOrderAsc* is grayed out and cannot be selected.

49.
```
Private Sub btnSelect_Click(...) Handles btnSelect.Click
    'Assume there are at least three members in the club.
    Dim names() As String = IO.File.ReadAllLines("Members.txt")
    Dim n As Integer = names.Count
    Dim p As Integer
    Dim randomNum As New Random()
    p = randomNum.Next(0, n)
    txtPresident.Text = names(p)
    'Swap President with the person in the last array element.
    names(p) = names(n — 1)
    names(n — 1) = txtPresident.Text
    'Choose a random person from first n—1 for Treasurer.
    p = randomNum.Next(0, n — 1)
    txtTreasurer.Text = names(p)
    'Swap Treasurer with the person in the next to last array element.
    names(p) = names(n — 2)
    names(n — 2) = txtTreasurer.Text
    'Choose a random person from first n—2 for Secretary.
    p = randomNum.Next(0, n — 2)
    txtSecretary.Text = names(p)
End Sub
```

51.
```
Dim randomNum As New Random()

Private Sub btnPlay_Click(...) Handles btnPlay.Click
    'Roll a pair of dice until 7 appears 1000 times.
    Dim die1, die2 As Integer
    Dim numberOfSevens As Integer = 0
    Dim numberOfRolls As Integer = 0
    Do
        'Roll the dice
        die1 = randomNum.Next(1, 7)
        die2 = randomNum.Next(1, 7)
        'If lucky 7, increment the sevens counter.
        If (die1 + die2) = 7 Then
            numberOfSevens += 1
        End If
        numberOfRolls += 1      'Increment the rolls counter.
    Loop Until (numberOfSevens = 1000)
    'Display the result to two decimal places.
    txtOutput.Text = FormatNumber(numberOfRolls / numberOfSevens, 2)
End Sub
```

57.
```
Private Sub btnDisplay_Click(...) Handles btnDisplay.Click
    'Display the open file dialog box to get the file
    Dim fileSpec As String
    OpenFileDialog1.ShowDialog()
    fileSpec = OpenFileDialog1.FileName
    'Display picture contained in the file.
    picBox.Image = Image.FromFile(fileSpec)
End Sub
```

59.
```
Private Sub tmrMoon_Tick(...) Handles tmrMoon.Tick
    'Update the phase and display the image.
    'Timer Interval setting is 2000; Timer Enabled setting is True
    phase += 1
    If phase = 9 Then
      phase = 1
    End If
    picBox.Image = Image.FromFile("Moon" & phase & ".bmp")
End Sub
```

61.
```
Private Sub tmrBall_Tick(...) Handles tmrBall.Tick
    'Update the value of the scroll bar and label.
    'Timer Interval setting is 1000
    'vsbBall.Minimum = 0, vsbBall.Maximum = 10
    count = count − 1
    vsbBall.Value = 10 − count
    lblBall.Text = CStr(count)
    'If at zero, display the message and end program.
    If count = 0 Then
      tmrBall.Enabled = False
      MessageBox.Show("HAPPY NEW YEAR!!!!", "NYE")
      Me.Close()
    End If
End Sub
```

EXERCISES 9.3

1. $106.00 3. The textbox will display "Your first name begins with J."

5. 'Form1's code
```
   Private Sub btnDisplay_Click(...) Handles btnDisplay.Click
     Form2.ShowDialog()
     txtQuotation.Text = Form2.quotation
   End Sub

   'Form2's code
   Public quotation As String

   Private Sub btnProcessSelection_Click(...) Handles _
             btnProcessSelection.Click
     If rad1.Checked Then
       quotation = "Plastics."
     End If
     If rad2.Checked Then
       quotation = "Rosebud."
     End If
     If rad3.Checked Then
       quotation = "That's all folks."
     End If
     Me.Close()
   End Sub
```

7. 'Code for frmMillionaire
```
   Public numberOfYrs As Integer
   Public Const INTEREST_RATE As Double = 0.06

   Private Sub btnCalculate_Click(...) Handles btnCalculate.Click
     Dim balance As Double, numYears As Integer
     balance = CDbl(txtAmount.Text)
     Do While balance < 1000000
       balance += INTEREST_RATE * balance
       numYears += 1
     Loop
     txtWhen.Text = "In " & numYears & _
       " years you will have a million dollars."
     numberOfYrs = numYears
     frmBalance.ShowDialog()
   End Sub

   'Code for frmBalance
   Structure Year
     Dim num As Integer
     Dim amount As Double
   End Structure
```

```
Private Sub frmBalance_Activated(...) Handles Me.Load
  Dim a(frmMillionaire.numberOfYrs) As Year
  a(0).num = 0
  a(0).amount = CDbl(frmMillionaire.txtAmount.Text)
  For i As Integer = 1 To a.Count − 1
    a(i).num = i
    a(i).amount = (1 + frmMillionaire.INTEREST_RATE) * a(i − 1).amount
  Next
  Dim query = From yr In a
              Let Year = yr.num
              Let Amount = FormatCurrency(yr.amount)
              Select Year, Amount
  dgvBalance.DataSource = query.ToList
  dgvBalance.CurrentCell = Nothing
End Sub


Private Sub frmBalance_FormClosing(...) Handles Me.FormClosing
  frmMillionaire.txtAmount.Clear()
  frmMillionaire.txtWhen.Clear()
  frmMillionaire.txtAmount.Focus()
End Sub
```

11. ```
'Form1's code (Customer)
Private Sub btnGet_Click(...) Handles btnGet.Click
  If radBillCust.Checked Then
    Form2.ShowDialog()
  Else
    Form3.ShowDialog()
  End If
End Sub

'Form2's code (Customer Info)
Private Sub Form2_Load(...) Handles MyBase.Load
  txtName.Text = Form1.txtName.Text
End Sub

Private Sub btnRecord_Click(...) Handles btnRecord.Click
  Dim city, state, zip As String
  Form1.lstOutput.Items.Add("Mail bill to:")
  Form1.lstOutput.Items.Add(txtName.Text)
  Form1.lstOutput.Items.Add(txtAddress.Text)
  city = txtCity.Text
  state = cboState.Text
  zip = txtZip.Text
  Form1.lstOutput.Items.Add(city & ", " & state & " " & zip)
  Me.Close()
End Sub

'Form3's code (Credit Card Info)
Private Sub Form3_Load(...) Handles MyBase.Load
  Dim num As Integer = Today.Year
  For i As Integer = num To num + 5
    cboYear.Items.Add(i)
  Next
End Sub

Private Sub btnRecord_Click(...) Handles btnRecord.Click
  Form1.lstOutput.Items.Add("Bill " & cboCard.Text)
  Form1.lstOutput.Items.Add("Name on card: " & txtName.Text)
  Form1.lstOutput.Items.Add("Card number: " & txtCardNumber.Text)
```
```

```
        Form1.lstOutput.Items.Add("Expiration date: " &
            cboMonth.Text & "/" & cboYear.Text)
    Me.Close()
End Sub
```

EXERCISES 9.4

```
1. Private Sub btnDraw_Click(...) Handles btnDraw.Click
    Dim gr As Graphics = picBox.CreateGraphics
    Dim x As Double = picBox.Width / 2
    Dim y As Double = picBox.Height / 2
    Dim r As Double = x / 2
    If r > y / 2 Then
      r = y / 2
    End If
    gr.FillEllipse(Brushes.Black, CSng(x — r), CSng(y — r),
                CSng(2 * r), CSng(2 * r))
End Sub
```

```
3. Private Sub btnDraw_Click(...) Handles btnDraw.Click
    Dim gr As Graphics = picBox.CreateGraphics
    Dim x As Double = picBox.Width / 2
    Dim y As Double = picBox.Height / 2
    Dim r As Double = 20
    gr.FillEllipse(Brushes.Red, CSng(x — r), CSng(y — r),
                        CSng(2 * r), CSng(2 * r))
    r = 19
    gr.FillEllipse(Brushes.White, CSng(x — r), CSng(y — r),
                        CSng(2 * r), CSng(2 * r))
End Sub
```

```
5. Private Sub btnCreate_Click(...) Handles btnCreate.Click
    Dim gr As Graphics = picFlag.CreateGraphics
    Dim br() As Brush = {Brushes.Green, Brushes.White, Brushes.Red}
    'picFlag.Width = 149; picFlag.Height = 99
    For i As Integer = 0 To 2
      gr.FillRectangle(br(i), 0 + i * 50, 0, 50, 99)
    Next
    gr.DrawLine(Pens.Black, 0, 0, 148, 0)      'top border
```

```
      gr.DrawLine(Pens.Black, 0, 0, 0, 98)      'left border
      gr.DrawLine(Pens.Black, 0, 98, 148, 98)   'bottom border
      gr.DrawLine(Pens.Black, 148, 0, 148, 98)  'right border
    End Sub
```

7.
```
    Private Sub btnCreate_Click(...) Handles btnCreate.Click
      Dim gr As Graphics = picFlag.CreateGraphics
      Dim br() As Brush = {Brushes.Orange, Brushes.White, Brushes.Green}
      Dim r As Integer = 12    'radius of circle
      'picFlag.Width = 149; picFlag.Height = 99
      For i As Integer = 0 To 2
        gr.FillRectangle(br(i), 0, 0 + i * 33, 149, 33)
      Next
      gr.FillPie(Brushes.Orange, 75 − r, 49 − r, 2 * r, 2 * r, 0, 360)
      gr.DrawLine(Pens.Black, 0, 0, 148, 0)      'top border
      gr.DrawLine(Pens.Black, 0, 0, 0, 98)       'left border
      gr.DrawLine(Pens.Black, 0, 98, 148, 98)    'bottom border
      gr.DrawLine(Pens.Black, 148, 0, 148, 98)   'right border
    End Sub
```

9.
```
    Private Sub btnDraw_Click(...) Handles btnDraw.Click
      Dim numbers As String = ""
      Dim gr As Graphics = picBox.CreateGraphics
      picBox.Refresh()
      Dim n As Integer = CInt(txtNumber.Text)
      'Font is Microsoft Sans Serif
      For i As Integer = 0 To n
        If i < 9 Then
          numbers &= i & "        "
        Else
          numbers &= i & "       "
        End If
        gr.DrawLine(Pens.Blue, 12 + (24 * i), 5, 12 + (24 * i), 15)
      Next
      gr.DrawLine(Pens.Blue, 0, 10, 24 * (n + 1), 10)
      gr.DrawString(numbers, Me.Font, Brushes.Blue, 8, 20)
    End Sub
```

CHAPTER 10

EXERCISES 10.1

1. Datagridview (f)   3. Datagridview (d)   5. (b)

7.
```
    Private Sub frmCities_Load(...) Handles MyBase.Load
      Me.CitiesTableAdapter.Fill(Me.MegacitiesDataSet.Cities)
    End Sub
```

```
      Private Sub btnDisplay_Click(...) Handles btnDisplay.Click
         Dim query = From city In MegacitiesDataSet.Cities
                     Let popGrowth = (city.pop2015 — city.pop2010) / city.pop2010
                     Let formattedPopGrowth = FormatPercent(popGrowth)
                     Order By popGrowth Descending
                     Select city.name, city.country, formattedPopGrowth
         dgvOutput.DataSource = query.ToList
         dgvOutput.CurrentCell = Nothing
         dgvOutput.Columns("name").HeaderText = "City"
         dgvOutput.Columns("country").HeaderText = "Country"
         dgvOutput.Columns("formattedPopGrowth").HeaderText =
                               "Projected Population Growth"
      End Sub
```

17.
```
    Private Sub frmNations_Load(...) Handles MyBase.Load
       Me.NationsTableAdapter.Fill(Me.UNDataSet.Nations)
       Dim query = From nation In UNDataSet.Nations
                   Order By nation.continent Ascending
                   Select nation.continent
                   Distinct
       lstContinents.DataSource = query.ToList
    End Sub

    Private Sub lstContinents_SelectedIndexChanged(...) Handles _
                     lstContinents.SelectedIndexChanged
       Dim queryPop = From nation In UNDataSet.Nations
                   Where nation.continent = lstContinents.Text
                   Order By nation.population Descending
                   Select nation.name
       lstCountriesPop.DataSource = queryPop.ToList
       lstCountriesPop.SelectedItem = Nothing
       Dim queryArea = From nation In UNDataSet.Nations
                   Where nation.continent = lstContinents.Text
                   Order By nation.area Descending
                   Select nation.name
       lstCountriesArea.DataSource = queryArea.ToList
       lstCountriesArea.SelectedItem = Nothing
    End Sub
```

21.
```
    Private Sub frmCurrencies_Load(...) Handles MyBase.Load
       Me.RatesTableAdapter.Fill(Me.ExchrateDataSet.Rates)
       Dim query = From money In ExchrateDataSet.Rates
                   Order By money.dollarRate Ascending
                   Select money.country
```

```
        lstCountries.DataSource = query.ToList
    End Sub

    Private Sub lstCountries_SelectedIndexChanged(...) Handles _
                lstCountries.SelectedIndexChanged
      Dim query = From money In ExchrateDataSet.Rates
                  Where money.country = lstCountries.Text
                  Select money.monetaryUnit, money.dollarRate
      txtCurrency.Text = query.First.monetaryUnit
      txtRate.Text = CStr(query.First.dollarRate)
    End Sub
```

23.
```
    Private Sub frmBaseball_Load(...) Handles MyBase.Load
      Me.TeamsTableAdapter.Fill(Me.BaseballDataSet.Teams)
      Dim query = From team In BaseballDataSet.Teams
                  Order By team.name
                  Select team.name
        lstTeams.DataSource = query.ToList
      End Sub

    Private Sub lstTeams_SelectedIndexChanged(...) Handles _
                lstTeams.SelectedIndexChanged
      Dim query = From team In BaseballDataSet.Teams
                  Where team.name = lstTeams.Text
                  Select team.stadium
      txtStadium.Text = query.First
    End Sub
```

33.
```
    Private Sub frmBaseball_Load(...) Handles MyBase.Load
      Me.TeamsTableAdapter.Fill(Me.BaseballDataSet.Teams)
      Me.PlayersTableAdapter.Fill(Me.BaseballDataSet.Players)
    End Sub

    Private Sub btnCount_Click(...) Handles btnCount.Click
      Dim query = From player In BaseballDataSet.Players
                  Join team In BaseballDataSet.Teams
                  On player.team Equals team.name
                  Where team.league = "National"
                  Select player.name
      txtNational.Text = FormatNumber(query.Count, 0)
    End Sub
```

39. film

41.
```
    Private Sub frmMovies_Load(...) Handles MyBase.Load
      Me.LinesTableAdapter.Fill(Me.MoviesDataSet.Lines)
      Me.ActorsTableAdapter.Fill(Me.MoviesDataSet.Actors)
      Dim query = From line In MoviesDataSet.Lines
                  Select line.film
                  Distinct
      lstFilms.DataSource = query.ToList
    End Sub
```

```
    Private Sub lstFilms_SelectedIndexChanged(...) Handles _
                    lstFilms.SelectedIndexChanged
      Dim query = From line In MoviesDataSet.Lines
                  Join flick In MoviesDataSet.Actors
                  On line.film Equals flick.film
                  Where line.film = lstFilms.Text
                  Select flick.maleLead
      txtLead.Text = query.First
    End Sub
```

43.
```
    Private Sub frmFilms_Load(...) Handles MyBase.Load
      Me.LinesTableAdapter.Fill(Me.MoviesDataSet.Lines)
      Me.ActorsTableAdapter.Fill(Me.MoviesDataSet.Actors)
      Dim query = From flick In MoviesDataSet.Actors
                  Select flick.maleLead
                  Distinct
      lstActors.DataSource = query.ToList
    End Sub


    Private Sub lstFilms_SelectedIndexChanged(...) Handles _
                    lstActors.SelectedIndexChanged
      Dim query = From line In MoviesDataSet.Lines
                  Join flick In MoviesDataSet.Actors
                  On line.film Equals flick.film
                  Where flick.maleLead = lstActors.Text
                  Select line.famousLine
      lstLines.DataSource = query.ToList
      lstLines.SelectedItem = Nothing
    End Sub
```

EXERCISES **10.2**

7. Add a record to the Cities table whose name field is empty or contains the same name as an already existing record.

9. `(BindingSource1.Find("name", strVar) = 0) And (strVar <> "Bombay")`

11. Create a control named BindingSource2 that has the Countries table as its DataMember.

```
    Private Sub CountryTextBox_Leave(...) Handles _
                    CountryTextBox.Leave, BindingNavigator1.Click
      BindingSource2.Position = BindingSource2.Find("name",
                    CountryTextBox.Text)
      If (CountryTextBox.Text <> "") And
         (BindingSource2.Position = 0) And
         (CountryTextBox.Text <> "Argentina") Then
        MessageBox.Show("Not a valid country.", "ERROR")
        CountryTextBox.Focus()
      End If
    End Sub
```

13.
```
Private Sub frmMovies_Load(...) Handles MyBase.Load
   Me.LinesTableAdapter.Fill(Me.MoviesDataSet.Lines)
End Sub

Private Sub btnUpdate_Click(...) Handles btnUpdate.Click
   'These two lines update the database file on the hard drive.
   BindingSource1.EndEdit()
   LinesTableAdapter.Update(MoviesDataSet.Lines)
End Sub
```

17. Apollo 13 does not appear in the key field of the Actors table. Thus the Rule of Referential Integrity would be violated.

19. Replace the table with two tables. The first table should contain the fields *name*, *address*, and *city*. The second table should contain the fields *city*, *state*, and *stateCapital*.

Chapter 11

EXERCISES 11.1

1. Any negative grade will be recorded as 0 and any grade greater than 100 will be recorded as 100.

3. Remove the keyword `WriteOnly` from the `Midterm` property block and add the following Get property procedure to it:

```
Get
   Return m_midterm
End Get
```

5. The properties `Midterm` and `Final` are write only.

7. The property `SocSecNum` is initialized to the value `999-99-9999`.

9. The keyword `New` is missing from the third line of the event procedure.

11. The statement `nom = m_name` is not valid. *m_name* would need to be Public and referred to by *scholar.m_name*.

13. The statements `pupil.Midterm = scholar.Midterm` and `lstGrades.Items.Add(pupil.Midterm)` are not valid. The Midterm property is write only; it can be set, but cannot return a value.

15.
```
Country: Canada
Capital: Ottawa
Pop: 31 million
```

17. Change 20 to –20 in the btnMove_Click event procedure, and create a **frmCircle_Load** event procedure with the following lines,

```
round.Xcoord = picCircle.Width — 40
round.Ycoord = picCircle.Height — 40
```

21.
```
Class PairOfDice
  Private m_die1, m_die2 As Integer
  Dim randomNum As New Random()

  Public ReadOnly Property Die1() As Integer
    Get
      Return m_die1
    End Get
  End Property

  Public ReadOnly Property Die2() As Integer
    Get
      Return m_die2
    End Get
  End Property

  Public ReadOnly Property SumOfFaces() As Integer
    Get
      Return m_die1 + m_die2
    End Get
  End Property
```

```
       Sub Roll()
         m_die1 = randomNum.Next(1, 7)
         m_die2 = randomNum.Next(1, 7)
       End Sub
     End Class    'PairOfDice
```

25.
```
Public Class frmCashRegister
  Dim register As New CashRegister()

  Private Sub btnAdd_Click(...) Handles btnAdd.Click
    'Add an amount to the balance.
    register.Add(CDbl(txtAmount.Text))
    txtBalance.Text = FormatCurrency(register.Balance)
    txtAmount.Clear()
    txtAmount.Focus()
  End Sub

  Private Sub btnSubtract_Click(...) Handles btnSubtract.Click
    'Subtract an amount from the balance.
    register.Subtract(CDbl(txtAmount.Text))
    txtBalance.Text = FormatCurrency(register.Balance)
    txtAmount.Clear()
    txtAmount.Focus()
  End Sub
End Class    'frmCashRegister

Class CashRegister
  Private m_balance As Double

  Public ReadOnly Property Balance() As Double
    Get
      Return m_balance
    End Get
  End Property

  Sub Add(ByVal amount As Double)
    If (m_balance + amount) >= 0 Then   'Ensure balance stays nonnegative
      m_balance += amount
    End If
  End Sub

  Sub Subtract(ByVal amount As Double)
    If (m_balance − amount) >= 0 Then   'Ensure balance stays nonnegative
      m_balance = m_balance − amount
    End If
  End Sub
End Class       'CashRegister
```

Exercises 11.2

1.
```
Sub btnDisplay_Click(...) Handles btnDisplay.Click
  ReDim Preserve students(lastStudentAdded)
  Dim query = From pupil In students
              Let name = pupil.Name
              Let ssn = pupil.SocSecNum
              Let semGrade = pupil.CalcSemGrade
              Where semGrade = "A"
              Select pupil.Name, pupil.SocSecNum, pupil.CalcSemGrade
```

```
       dgvGrades.DataSource = query.ToList
       dgvGrades.CurrentCell = Nothing
       dgvGrades.Columns("Name").HeaderText = "Student Name"
       dgvGrades.Columns("SocSecNum").HeaderText = "SSN"
       dgvGrades.Columns("CalcSemGrade").HeaderText = "Grade"
     ReDim Preserve students(50)
     txtName.Focus()
   End Sub
```

7.
```
   Public Class frmCashRegister
     Dim WithEvents register As New CashRegister()

     Private Sub btnAdd_Click(...) Handles btnAdd.Click
       'Add an amount to the balance.
       register.Add(CDbl(txtAmount.Text))
       txtBalance.Text = FormatCurrency(register.Balance)
       txtAmount.Clear()
       txtAmount.Focus()
     End Sub

     Private Sub btnSubtract_Click(...) Handles btnSubtract.Click
       'Subtract an amount from the balance.
       register.Subtract(CDbl(txtAmount.Text))
       txtBalance.Text = FormatCurrency(register.Balance)
       txtAmount.Clear()
       txtAmount.Focus()
     End Sub

     Private Sub AttemptToOverdraw(ByVal amt As Double) Handles _
                                        register.AttemptToOverdraw
       MessageBox.Show("You would have been overdrawn by " &
                 FormatCurrency(amt) & ".", "Withdrawal Denied")
     End Sub
   End Class    'frmCashRegister

   Class CashRegister
     Private m_balance As Double

     Public Event AttemptToOverdraw(ByVal amt As Double)

     Public ReadOnly Property Balance() As Double
       Get
         Return m_balance
       End Get
     End Property

     Sub Add(ByVal amount As Double)
       If (m_balance + amount) >= 0 Then  'Ensure balance stays nonnegative
         m_balance += amount
       Else
         RaiseEvent AttemptToOverdraw(amount + m_balance)
       End If
     End Sub

     Sub Subtract(ByVal amount As Double)
       If (m_balance − amount) >= 0 Then  'Ensure balance stays nonnegative
         m_balance = m_balance − amount
       Else
         RaiseEvent AttemptToOverdraw(amount − m_balance)
```

```
        End If
    End Sub
End Class        'CashRegister
```

EXERCISES 11.3

1. 4   3. 64   5. Can move Has jointed limbs and no backbone

7. The keyword Overrides should be Inherits.

9. The Hi function should be declared with the Overridable keyword in class Hello and with the keyword Overrides keyword in class Aussie.

11. The Hi function should be declared with the Overridables keyword in class Hello. The Hi function should be declared with the Overrides keyword in class Cowboy.

13. The Hello class should be declared with the MustInherit keyword, and the function Hi should be declared with the MustOverride keyword.

15. The Hello class should be declared with the MustInherit keyword, not MustOverride.

19.
```
Public Class frmRegister
    Dim tollBooth As New FastTrackRegister()

    Private Sub btnProcess_Click(...) Handles btnProcess.Click
        If radCar.Checked Then
            tollBooth.ProcessCar()
        Else
            tollBooth.ProcessTruck()
        End If
        txtRevenue.Text = FormatCurrency(tollBooth.Balance)
        txtNumVehicles.Text = CStr(tollBooth.Count)
    End Sub
End Class        'frmRegister

Class CashRegister
    Private m_balance As Double

    Sub Deposit(ByVal amount As Double)
        m_balance += amount
    End Sub

    Sub WithDrawal(ByVal amount As Double)
        m_balance = m_balance - amount
    End Sub

    Public ReadOnly Property Balance() As Double
        Get
            Return m_balance
```

```
      End Get
    End Property
End Class      'CashRegister

Class FastTrackRegister
   Inherits CashRegister

   Private m_count As Integer

   Public ReadOnly Property Count() As Integer
     Get
       Return m_count
     End Get
   End Property

   Sub ProcessCar()
     m_count += 1     'Process a car: $1.00
     Deposit(1)
   End Sub

   Sub ProcessTruck()
     m_count += 1     'Process a truck: $2.00
     Deposit(2)
   End Sub
End Class        'FastTrackRegister
```

CHAPTER 12

EXERCISES 12.1

```
1. Protected Sub btnFind_Click(...) Handles btnFind.Click
     Dim max As Double = CDbl(txtFirstNum.Text)
     If CDbl(txtSecondNum.Text) > max Then
       max = CDbl(txtSecondNum.Text)
     End If
     If CDbl(txtThirdNum.Text) > max Then
       max = CDbl(txtThirdNum.Text)
     End If
     txtLargestNum.Text = CStr(max)
   End Sub
```

3. ```
Protected Sub btnDisplay_Click(...) Handles btnDisplay.Click
    Dim num As Integer = CInt(txtNumber.Text)
    For i As Integer = 1 To num — 1
        lstOutput.Items.Add(i & " potato")
    Next
    lstOutput.Items.Add(num)
End Sub
```

5. ```
Protected Sub btnCalculate_Click(...) Handles btnCalculate.Click
    Dim purchPrice As Double = CDbl(txtPurPrice.Text)
    Dim redemValue As Double = CDbl(txtRedValue.Text)
    txtDiscRate.Text = FormatPercent((redemValue — purchPrice) / redemValue)
    txtIntRate.Text = FormatPercent((redemValue — purchPrice) / purchPrice)
End Sub
```

EXERCISES 12.2

1. ```
Protected Sub Page_Load(...) Handles Me.Load
    If Not IsPostBack Then
        Dim states() As String =
                    IO.File.ReadAllLines(MapPath("App_Data\States.txt"))
        Dim query = From state In states
                    Order By state
                    Select state
        lstStates.DataSource = query
        lstStates.DataBind()
        txtNumStates.Text = CStr(lstStates.Items.Count)
    End If
End Sub

Protected Sub btnDelete_Click(...) Handles btnDelete.Click
    lstStates.Items.Remove(lstStates.Text)
    txtNumStates.Text = CStr(lstStates.Items.Count)
End Sub
```

## 12.2 Exercise 3

Model

◉ Deluxe  ◉ Super

☑ Upgraded Video Card

☐ Internal Modem + Wi-Fi

☐ 1 GB additional memory

Total cost: [＿＿＿＿＿＿]

**You must select a model!**

3. ```
'Note: The AutoPostBack and CausesValidation properties were
'set to True for each check box.
Protected Sub rblModel_SelectedIndexChanged(...) Handles _
    rblModel.SelectedIndexChanged, chkUpgradedVideo.CheckedChanged,
    chkModem.CheckedChanged, chkMemory.CheckedChanged
    Dim cost As Double = 0
    'Add amounts to the cost based upon selections.
    If rblModel.Text = "Deluxe" Then
        cost += 1000
```

```
    Else
      cost += 1500
    End If
    If chkUpgradedVideo.Checked Then
      cost += 200
    End If
    If chkModem.Checked Then
      cost += 30
    End If
    If chkMemory.Checked Then
      cost += 120
    End If
    txtOutput.Text = FormatCurrency(cost)
  End Sub
```

9.
```
  'In RangeValidator controls, Minimum is "a" and Maximum is "zzzzzzz".
  Protected Sub btnAlphabetize_Click(...) Handles btnAlphabetize.Click
    Dim word1 = txtWord1.Text
    Dim word2 = txtWord2.Text
    DisplayWords(word1, word2)
  End Sub

  Sub DisplayWords(ByVal word1 As String, ByVal word2 As String)
    lstOutput.Items.Clear()
    If word1 <= word2 Then
      lstOutput.Items.Add(word1)
      lstOutput.Items.Add(word2)
    Else
      lstOutput.Items.Add(word2)
      lstOutput.Items.Add(word1)
    End If
  End Sub
```

12.2 Exercise 9

First word: |

Second word: |

Alphabetize Words

Unbound

First word missing!   Second word missing!
First letter of first word is not lower-case!   First letter of second word is not lower-case!

11.
```
  Protected Sub btnDisplay_Click(...) Handles btnDisplay.Click
    Dim justices() As String =
        IO.File.ReadAllLines(MapPath("App_Data\Justices.txt"))
    Dim stateAbbrev As String = txtState.Text.ToUpper
    Dim query = From justice In justices
              Let data = justice.Split(","c)
              Let name = data(0) & " " & data(1)
              Let pres = data(2)
              Let state = data(3)
              Let yrsServed = YearsServed(data(4), data(5))
              Where state = stateAbbrev
```

```
                    Select name, pres, yrsServed
      grvJustices.DataSource = query
      grvJustices.DataBind()
      grvJustices.HeaderRow.Cells(0).Text = "Justice"
      grvJustices.HeaderRow.Cells(1).Text = "Appointing President"
      grvJustices.HeaderRow.Cells(2).Text = "Years Served"
    End Sub

    Function YearsServed(ByVal enter As Double,
                         ByVal leave As Double) As Double
      If leave = 0 Then
        Return (Now.Year — enter)
      Else
        Return (leave — enter)
      End If
    End Function
```

12.2 Exercise 11

State abbreviation: MD

Display Justices

Justice	Appointing President	Years Served
Samuel Chase	George Washington	15
Gabriel Duval	James Madison	25
Thomas Johnson	George Washington	2
John Roberts	George W. Bush	5
Roger Taney	Andrew Jackson	28

EXERCISES 12.3

7.
```
Protected Sub btnDisplay_Click(...) Handles btnDisplay.Click
  Dim mcDC As New MegacitiesDataContext
  Dim query = From city In mcDC.Cities
              Join country In mcDC.Countries On city.country Equals
              country.name
              Select city.name, country.pop2010
  chtMegacities.DataBindTable(query, "name")
  chtMegacities.ChartAreas(0).AxisX.Interval = 1
  chtMegacities.ChartAreas(0).AxisX.Title = "City"
  chtMegacities.ChartAreas(0).AxisY.Title =
                            "2010 Pop. of Country in Millions"
End Sub
```

17.
```
Protected Sub btnDisplay_Click(...) Handles btnDisplay.Click
  Dim pizzaDC As New PizzaDataContext
  Dim query = From chain In pizzaDC.Pizzerias
              Order By chain.sales2008 Descending
              Let amount = chain.sales2008 / 1000000
              Select chain.name, amount
  chtPizzaChains.DataBindTable(query, "name")
  chtPizzaChains.ChartAreas(0).AxisX.Interval = 1
  chtPizzaChains.ChartAreas(0).AxisX.Title = "Pizzeria"
  chtPizzaChains.ChartAreas(0).AxisY.Title = "2008 Sales in Billions"
End Sub
```

25.
```
Protected Sub btnDisplay_Click(...) Handles btnDisplay.Click
   Dim pizzaDC As New PizzaDataContext
   Dim query = From chain In pizzaDC.Pizzerias
               Select chain.numStores2008
   txtOutput.Text = FormatNumber(query.Sum, 0)
End Sub
```

12.3 Exercise 25

Display Total Number of Stores

Total number of stores: 20,945

INDEX